This book presents the first analytical account in Eng[lish of the devel]opments within Byzantine culture, society and the [ad]ministrative period from *c.* 610 to 717. Since its original publication in 1990, the text has been revised throughout to take account of the latest research.

The seventh century saw the final collapse of ancient urban civilisation and municipal culture, the rise of Islam, the evolution of patterns of thought and social structure which made imperial iconoclasm possible, and the development of state apparatuses – military, civil and fiscal – typical of the middle Byzantine state. Over the same period, orthodox Christianity finally became the unquestioned dominant cultural and religious framework of belief, to the exclusion of alternative systems, which were henceforth marginalised or proscribed.

Conflicting ideas of how these changes and developments are to be understood have proliferated in the past fifty years. This book is the first serious attempt to provide a comprehensive, detailed survey of all the major changes in this period.

BYZANTIUM IN THE SEVENTH CENTURY

BYZANTIUM
IN THE SEVENTH CENTURY

The transformation of a culture

Revised edition

J.F. HALDON

*Professor of Byzantine History
Director of the Centre for Byzantine,
Ottoman and Modern Greek Studies,
University of Birmingham*

CAMBRIDGE UNIVERSITY PRESS

Published by the Press Syndicate of the University of Cambridge
The Pitt Building, Trumpington Street, Cambridge CB2 1RP
40 West 20th Street, New York, NY 10011-4211, USA
10 Stamford Road, Oakleigh, Melbourne 3166, Australia

© Cambridge University Press 1990

First published 1990
Reprinted 1993,1995
First paperback edition published 1997

Printed in Great Britain at the University Press, Cambridge

British Library cataloguing in publication data
Haldon, J.F.
Byzantium in the seventh century: the transformation of a culture
1. Byzantine civilisation, to 717
I. Title
949.5'01

Library of Congress cataloguing in publication data
Haldon, John F.
Byzantium in the seventh century: the transformation of a culture
J. F. Haldon.
p.   cm.
Includes bibliographical references
ISBN 0-521-26492-8
1. Byzantine Empire – Civilisation – 527-1081.   I. Title
II. Title: Byzantium in the 7th century.
DF571.H35   1990
949.5'01 – dc20   89-17309 CIP

ISBN 0 521 26492 8 hardback
ISBN 0 521 31917 X paperback

For V.J.W.

Contents

List of plates		*page* x
List of maps		xii
Preface and acknowledgements		xiii
Preface to the revised edition		xv
List of abbreviations		xvii
The sources		xxi
	Introduction	1
1	The background: state and society before Heraclius	9
2	The East Roman world c. 610–717: the politics of survival	41
3	Social relations and the economy: the cities and the land	92
4	Social relations and the economy: rural society	125
5	The state and its apparatus: fiscal administration	173
6	The state and its apparatus: military administration	208
7	Society, state and law	254
8	The imperial church and the politics of authority	281
9	Religion and belief	324
10	Forms of social and cultural organisation: infrastructures and hierarchies	376
11	Forms of representation: language, literature and the icon	403
	Conclusion The transformation of a culture	436
	Addendum: Further observations on the question of the late ancient city	459
	Bibliography	462
	Index	482

Plates

1.1	Justinian. Copper *follis*	page	19
1.2	Justin II. Gold *solidus*		32
1.3	Tiberius Constantine. Copper *follis*		34
1.4	Maurice. Gold *solidus*		34
1.5	Phocas. Gold *solidus*		37
2.1	Heraclius. Gold *solidus*		42
2.2	Constans II. Gold *solidus*		54
2.3	Constantine IV. Gold *solidus*		64
2.4	Leontius II. Gold *solidus*		70
2.5	Tiberius III Apsimar. Gold *solidus*		75
2.6	Justinian II (second reign). Gold *solidus*		75
2.7	Philippicus Bardanes. Gold *solidus*		79
2.8	Anastasius II. Gold *solidus*		79
2.9	Theodosius III. Gold *solidus*		82
2.10	Leo III. Gold *solidus*		84
9.1	Seventh-century icon (from a triptych) of St Theodore Tiro		357
9.2	Sixth- to seventh-century icon of St Peter		358
9.3	Seventh- to eighth-century icon of St Athanasius and St Basil		359
11.1	The Empress Theodora and attendants, San Vitale, Ravenna		408
11.2(a)	Late sixth- to seventh-century mosaic decoration from St Demetrius, Thessaloniki (water-colour W. S. George)		410
(b)	St Demetrius with patrons and benefactors. Mosaic of post-reconstruction period, second quarter of seventh century		411
11.3	Icon of the Virgin and child (detail) between St Theodore and St George, with flanking angels, monastery of St Catherine, Sinai		413

11.4(a)	*Solidus* of Justinian I (obverse and reverse)	414
(b)	*Solidus* of Constans II with Constantine, his son (obverse and reverse)	414
11.5(a)	*Solidus* of Justin II (obverse and reverse)	416
(b)	*Solidus* of Maurice (obverse)	416
(c)	*Solidus* of Phocas (obverse)	416
(d)	*Solidus* of Heraclius and Heraclius Constantine (obverse)	416
(e)	*Solidus* of Constantine IV (obverse and reverse)	417
(f)	*Solidus* of Justinian II (obverse)	417
(g)	*Solidus* of Anastasius II (obverse)	417
(h)	*Solidus* of Philippicus Bardanes (obverse and reverse)	417

ACKNOWLEDGEMENTS

Reproduction of the plates has been possible through the courtesy of the following:

The Barber Institute of Fine Arts, University of Birmingham (plates 1.1–5, 2.1–10, 11.4(a) and (b) and 11.5(a)–(h))

The Michigan–Princeton–Alexandria Expedition to Mount Sinai (plates 9.1–3 and 11.3)

A. Michalakis, Athens (plates 11.1 and 2(b))

The Courtauld Institute of Art and the British School at Athens (plate 11.2(a))

Maps

I	The empire in A.D. 565: approximate extent	page 18
II	Nominal extent of imperial territory in *c*. A.D. 600	33
III	The empire in *c*. A.D. 650–700: the process of devastation	65
IV	The empire at the accession of Leo III (A.D. 717)	83
V	The Anatolian frontier region in the seventh and early eighth centuries	106
VI	Justinianic prefectures and provinces *c*. A.D. 565	228
VII	The Anatolian *themata* and the late Roman provinces *c*. A.D. 660	230

Preface and acknowledgements

The present work was originally conceived as a general and introductory account of aspects of seventh-century East Roman (Byzantine) state, society and culture. In the event, a simple survey of sources and literature and the presentation of a general synthesis proved less and less worthwhile, or indeed desirable. It became necessary in many places to go into considerably greater detail than planned.

Many technical matters of state and social organisation remained both unclear and insufficiently researched; many questions of crucial importance for the history of social and cultural development in the Byzantine world of that period remained unasked. This book is, consequently, an attempt to provide a coherent general overview by means of the analysis of a series of specific themes and the corresponding problems which accompany them. Inevitably, the themes I have discussed represent a selective choice – I have concentrated on those aspects which I felt to be most in need of attention, most amenable to some form of constructive solution and most relevant to our understanding of how East Roman cultural, social and state forms functioned and evolved as a dynamic whole throughout the seventh century.

In writing this book, I have enjoyed the help and advice, both direct and indirect, of many friends and colleagues. I would like in particular to thank Wolfram Brandes, Marie-Theres Fögen, Rodney Hilton, Alexander Každan, Ralph Lilie, Greg McLennan, Spiros Troianos, Chris Wickham and Friedhelm Winkelmann, all of whom – at various times and in various places over the last few years – have, not always knowingly, contributed in one way or another to the formation of my views. In particular, I should like to thank my friends and colleagues at the Centre for Byzantine, Ottoman and Modern Greek Studies at the University of Birmingham, especially Michael Ursinus. Under its director, Anthony Bryer, the Centre has provided the means for fruitful research and the scholarly atmosphere in which to work. I would also like to thank my friend and colleague at King's College,

London, Averil Cameron, for her constructive criticism and comments on the penultimate version of the typescript, as well as for her interest and encouragement in general; and my friends Leslie Brubaker, for much fruitful discussion on art, representation and perception; Ludwig Burgmann and Bernard Stolte, for their willingness to read through and offer constructive suggestions on problems relating to early Byzantine law and legal texts; and Robin Cormack and Lucy-Anne Hunt for their help and advice with regard to photographs. Nubar Hampartumian patiently guided me through the extensive seventh-century Byzantine coin holdings of the Barber Institute of Fine Arts at Birmingham; and Harry Buglass of the Department of Ancient History and Archaeology at Birmingham is to be congratulated on making sense of my original sketch-maps.

I should also like to thank the British Academy, the Alexander von Humboldt-Stiftung and the Max-Planck-Institut für Europäische Rechtsgeschichte, under its director Dieter Simon, who all provided financial support and an academic refuge at various times towards the completion of the present project.

Last, but, as usual, by no means least, thanks are due to Iris Hunter of Cambridge University Press, whose efficient, rigorous and constructive sub-editing has turned the original sow's ear into something resembling a silk purse.

Preface to the revised edition

It is a great pleasure to be able to introduce this revised edition of *Byzantium in the seventh century*. I have made a number of emendations and additions to the notes and to the bibliography, and also a brief *Addendum* on the current state of the question of the fate of urban centres in the seventh century. But for technical reasons I have not incorporated all the changes I would, predictably, have wished to make, simply because that would have involved the substantial expansion or rewriting of some sections to take into account the work of colleagues and scholars in the various fields upon which this book touches. This was not too difficult, however, since, six years on, I believe that the analysis of the events which so transformed the late Roman world as I have tried to present them here is still a valid interpretation of the material at our disposal. Naturally, there are areas where one would wish to add nuance, or change emphasis, but, on the whole, the broad thrust and the direction of the interpretation remain unchanged, a point reinforced, as far as I am able to judge it, by the work of other scholars in the field in the past few years. The results of a good deal of work on the literary sources – Greek, Syriac and Arabic – have now become available, for example, which adds substantially to our knowledge of both the development of older as well as newer genres. The cross-cultural connections between Greek and Syriac writing, especially in the fields of historiography, hagiography and theology, and the nature and tendency of anti-Jewish polemic, have all been studied in greater depth, and the results of this work further enhance or modify the conclusions reached in those chapters of this book in which these texts are evaluated or used as sources of evidence. Similarly, the results of recent archaeological and field survey work need to be taken into account in evaluating the differential and highly localised pattern of development of urban and fortified centres during the period in question, although the general line of the argument presented in the relevant chapters below is confirmed.

In the process of re-evaluating the views expressed in this book, and reassessing the sources for the analysis of the history of the East Roman empire in the seventh century, I am grateful to many friends and colleagues for stimulating criticism and advice. I should especially like to acknowledge Wolfram Brandes, Paul Speck, Chris Wickham and Averil Cameron: they almost certainly disagree with each other across a whole range of issues, and they may not always agree with my interpretation; but I have benefited enormously from their critical engagement, their scholarly advice and expertise, and their friendship.

Birmingham, February 1997

Abbreviations

AB	*Analecta Bollandiana* (Brussels 1882–)
AHAS	*Acta Historica Academiae Scientiarum Hungaricae* (Budapest 1952–)
AIPHOS	*Annuaire de l'Institut de Philologie et d'Histoire Orientales et Slaves* (Brussels 1932–)
Ἀνάλεκτα	Ἀνάλεκτα Ἱεροσολυμιτικῆς Σταχυλογίας, I–IV, ed. A. Papadopoulos-Kerameus (St Petersburg 1891–9)
AS	*Acta Sanctorum* (Antwerp 1643–)
B	*Byzantion* (Brussels and Paris 1924–)
BAR	British Archaeological Reports
BBA	*Berliner Byzantinistische Arbeiten* (Berlin 1955–)
BCH	*Bulletin de Correspondance Hellénique* (Paris 1877–)
BF	*Byzantinische Forschungen* (Amsterdam 1966–)
BGA	*Bibliotheca Geographorum Araborum*, ed. M.-J. De Goeje (Leiden 1870–). Nunc continuata consultantibus R. Blachère (etc.) (Leiden 1938–)
BHG[3]	F. Halkin, *Bibliotheca Hagiographica Graeca* (Brussels, third edn, 1957)
BHG, Auct.	F. Halkin, *Auctarium Bibliothecae Hagiographicae Graecae* (Brussels 1969)
BMGS	*Byzantine and Modern Greek Studies* (Oxford 1975–83; Birmingham 1984–)
BNJ	*Byzantinisch-Neugriechische Jahrbücher* (Berlin and Athens 1920–)
ByzBulg	*Byzantinobulgarica* (Sofia 1962–)
BS	*Byzantinoslavica* (Prague 1929–)
BZ	*Byzantinische Zeitschrift* (Leipzig and Munich 1892–)
CEHE	*Cambridge Economic History of Europe* (Cambridge 1941–)

CFHB	*Corpus Fontinum Historiae Byzantinae* (Washington 1967– (Series Washingtoniensis); Berlin and New York 1967– (Series Berolinensis); Vienna 1975– (Series Vindobonensis); Rome 1975– (Series Italica); Brussels 1975– (Series Bruxellensis))
CI	*Codex Iustinianus*
CIC	*Corpus Iuris Civilis*
CM	*Classica et Medievalia* (Copenhagen 1938–)
CMH	*Cambridge Medieval History* (Cambridge 1913–)
CPG	*Clavis Patrum Graecorum*, III: *A Cyrillo Alexandrino ad Iohannem Damascenum*, ed. M. Geerard (Turnhout 1979); IV: *Concilia Catenae*, ed. M. Geerard (Turnhout 1980)
CSCO	*Corpus Scriptorum Christianorum Orientalium* (Paris and Louvain 1903–)
CSEL	*Corpus Scriptorum Ecclesiasticorum Latinorum* (Vienna 1866–)
CSHB	*Corpus Scriptorum Historiae Byzantinae* (Bonn 1828–97)
De Cer.	*De Cerimoniis*
ΔΙΕΕ	*Δελτίον τῆς Ἱστορικῆς καὶ Ἐθνολογικῆς Ἑτερείας τῆς Ἑλλάδος* (Athens 1883–)
DOP	*Dumbarton Oaks Papers* (Cambridge, Mass., and Washington 1941–)
ΔΧΑΕ	*Δελτίον τῆς Χριστιανικῆς Ἀρχαιολογικῆς Ἑταιρείας* (Athens 1892–); περίοδος Α', vols. 1–10 (Athens 1892–1911); περίοδος Β', vols. 1–2 (Athens 1924–5); περίοδος Γ', vols. 1–4 (Athens 1933–9); περίοδος Δ', vols. 1ff (Athens 1960–)
ΕΕΒΣ	*Ἐπετερὶς Ἑταιρείας Βυζαντινῶν Σπουδῶν* (Athens 1924–)
EHR	*English Historical Review* (London 1885–)
EI	*Encyclopaedia of Islam*, new edn (Leiden and London 1960–)
EO	*Echos d'Orient*, 1–39 (Paris, Constantinople and Bucharest 1897–1941/2)
ERE	See Bury, *A History of the Eastern Roman Empire*
FHG	*Fragmenta Historicorum Graecorum*, ed. C. and Th. Müller, 5 vols. (Paris 1874–85)
FM	*Fontes Minores* (Frankfurt am Main, 1976–)
GCS	*Die griechischen christlichen Schriftsteller der ersten (drei) Jahrhunderte* (Leipzig and Berlin 1897–)
GRBS	*Greek, Roman and Byzantine Studies* (1: *Greek and Byzantine Studies*) (San Antonio, University of Mississippi, Cambridge, Mass., and Durham 1958–)

HC	*L'Hellénisme Contemporain* (Athens 1947–)
HGM	*Historici Graeci Minores*, 2 vols., ed. L. Dindorf (Leipzig 1870–1)
IGR	*Ius Graecoromanum*
IRAIK	*Izvestija Russkago Arkheologičeskago Instituta v Konstantinopole*, 1–16 (Odessa and Sofia 1896–1912)
JHS	*Journal of Hellenic Studies* (London 1880–)
JIAN	*Journal Internationale d'Archéologie Numismatique* (Athens 1897–1927)
JÖB	*Jahrbuch der österreichischen Byzantinistik* 18– (Vienna, Cologne and Graz 1969–)
JÖBG	*Jahrbuch der österreichischen byzantinischen Gesellschaft* 1–17 (Vienna, Cologne and Graz 1951–68)
JRS	*Journal of Roman Studies* (London 1911–)
Klet. Phil.	*Kletorologion tou Philotheou* (see Bibliography: Primary sources)
LRE	See Jones, *The Later Roman Empire*
MGH(AA)	*Monumenta Germaniae Historica (Auctores Antiquissimi)*, edd. G. Pertz, Th. Mommsen et al. (Berlin 1877–1919)
NPB	*Nova Patrum Bibliotheca*, ed. A. Mai, vols. I–VII (Rome 1852–4); ed. I. Cozza-Luzi, vols. VIII–X (Rome 1871–1905)
OC	*Oriens Christianus* (Leipzig 1901–)
OCP	*Orientalia Christiana Periodica* (Rome 1935–)
PG	*Patrologiae Cursus Completus, series Graeco-Latina*, ed. J.P. Migne (Paris 1857–66; 1880–1903)
PL	*Patrologiae Cursus Completus, series Latina*, ed. J.P. Migne (Paris 1844–1974)
PO	*Patrologia Orientalis*, edd. R. Graffin, F. Nau (Paris 1930–)
PP	*Past and Present* (London 1952–)
RAC	*Reallexikon für Antike und Christentum, Sachwörterbuch zur Auseinandersetzung des Christentums mit der antiken Welt*, ed. Th. Klauser (Stuttgart 1950–)
RB	*Reallexikon der Byzantinistik*, ed. P. Wirth (ser. A, vol. I, fascicles 1–6 only) (Amsterdam 1968–76)
RbK	*Reallexikon zur byzantinischen Kunst*, eds. K. Wessel and M. Restlé, vols. I– (Stuttgart 1963–)
RE	*Paulys Realencyclopädie der classischen Altertums-Wissenschaft*, new revised edn by G. Wissowa (vol. I/1, Stuttgart 1893–); vol. I/1 (1893) to XXIII/2 (1959; with index of additions); XXIV (1963); I/A1 (1914) to X/A (1972); Supl. I (1903) to XIV (1974)

REA	Revue des Etudes Arméniennes, new series (Paris 1964–)
REB	Revue des Etudes Byzantines (vols. 1–3: Etudes Byzantines) (Bucharest and Paris 1944–)
REG	Revue des Etudes Grecques (Paris 1888–)
RESEE	Revue des Etudes Sud-Est Européennes (Bucharest 1963–)
RH	Revue Historique (Paris 1876–)
RHSEE	Revue Historique du Sud-Est Européen (Bucharest 1924–46)
RJ	Rechtshistorisches Journal (Frankfurt am Main 1982–)
RN	Revue Numismatique (Paris 1836–)
ROC	Revue de l'Orient Chrétien, ser. 1, vols. 1–10 (Paris 1896–1905); ser. 2, vols. 1–10 (Paris 1906–1915/17); ser. 3, vols. 1–10 (Paris 1918/19–1935/6): vols. I–XXX
RSBN	Rivista di Studi Bizantini e Neoellenici, new series (Rome 1964–)
SBB	Sitzungsberichte der bayerischen Akademie der Wissenschaften, phil.-hist. Klasse
SBN	Studi Bizantini (vols. 1–2) e Neoellenici (vols. 3–10) (Rome 1925–) (cont. as RSBN)
SBÖ	Sitzungsberichte der österreichischen Akademie der Wissenschaften, phil.-hist. Klasse
SOF	Südost-Forschungen (Leipzig, Vienna and Munich 1936–)
T.Usp.	Taktikon Uspenskij (see Bibliography: Primary sources)
TM	Travaux et Mémoires (Paris 1965–)
Varia	Varia Graeca Sacra, ed. A. Papadopoulos-Kerameus (St Petersburg 1909)
VSW	Vierteljahreschrift für Sozial- und Wirtschaftsgeschichte (Leipzig and Wiesbaden 1903–)
VV	Vizantijskii Vremmenik, vols. 1–25 (St Petersburg (Leningrad) 1894–1927); new series (Moscow 1947–)
ZK	Zeitschrift für Kirchengeschichte (Gotha 1877–)
ZRVI	Zbornik Radova (vols. 1–6; Vizantološki Institut, kn. 1–6 = Srpska Akademija Nauka, Zbornik Radova, kn. 21, 36, 44, 49, 59, 65) Vizantološkog Instituta (from vol. 7 (1961)) (Belgrade 1952–)

The sources

The sources for the period with which we shall be dealing are, in comparison with those for the sixth century, or the tenth and eleventh centuries, for example, both limited in number and difficult to use. But I should like to stress at the outset that these difficulties ought not to be overestimated, nor should they be used as a justification for refusing to ask questions. In fact, it is less the paucity of the sources than their nature which is problematic. There are, effectively, only two 'histories' of the period compiled by Byzantines, both of which date from the early ninth century, although based in large part on earlier material. One, the Brief History of the patriarch Nicephorus, has virtually nothing to say on the reign of Constans II (641–68). While both use what may well be material contemporary with many of the events they describe, it is an immensely difficult task to sort out the different and sometimes very contradictory traditions bound up in the two histories. The other, the Chronography of the monk Theophanes the Confessor, was compiled between A.D. 810 and 814, and continues the Chronicle of George the Sygkellos. It is written around a carefully worked-out chronological framework, divided into sections by the year on an annalistic basis, at the head of each of which Theophanes lists the year according to the age of the world, from the birth of Christ, and according to the lengths of the reigns of the emperor, caliph, the pope and the four patriarchs of the East. It has been shown that the dates are one year out for the entries from the year 6102 (A.D. 609–10) to 6265 (A.D. 772–3), except for the period 6207 (A.D. 714–15) to 6218 (725–6), as the result of an incorrect division in the text. But this is the only blemish on a fundamental text, upon which our own chronology of the seventh and eighth centuries is based.[1]

---

[1] See G. Ostrogorsky, 'Die Chronologie des Theophanes im 7. und 8. Jahrhundert', *BNJ* 7 (1930), 1–56; Ostrogorsky, art. 'Theophanes', in *RE* V/A2 (1934), 2127–32; for further discussion and literature, see H. Hunger, *Die hochsprachliche profane Literatur der Byzantiner* (2 vols. Handbuch der Altertumswissenschaft XII, 5.1 and 2 = Byzantinisches Handbuch 5, 1

The Brief History of Nicephorus (patriarch from 806 until 815) covers the period from 602 to 769, apart from the gap already mentioned for most of the reign of Constans II. It is based in part on the same sources as the Chronography of Theophanes. The gap seems to be the result of a loss of some folios from the manuscript tradition. Nicephorus wrote also a Short Chronicle which is of only limited historical value, covering the period from Adam to 829, in which year he died.[2]

Last, and for the beginning of our period, there is the so-called Paschal Chronicle, originally covering the period from Adam to the year A.D. 629 but, due to the loss of the final folios, ending in 628. It was compiled by a priest or monk in the 630s and built around a chronological framework intended to fix the Easter cycle and the reckoning for a purely Christian chronology.[3]

These Greek sources can be supplemented from a very wide range of other sources in other languages. And, indeed, one of the difficulties facing the historian of this period is precisely this wide range of material, often later in date, but again using sources contemporary with – or almost contemporary with – the events described: chronicles, or fragments from chronicles in Arabic, Syriac, Armenian, Coptic and Latin, for example, all provide vital material which must be assessed. Among the most important of these are the much later Chronicle of Michael the Syrian, Jacobite

---

and 2, Munich 1978), vol. 1, pp. 334–59; and also I. Rochow, 'Die monenergetischen und monotheletischen Streitigkeiten in der Sicht des Chronisten Theophanes', *Klio* 63 (1981), 669–81. On the debate over the authorship of the Chronographia, see C. Mango, 'Who wrote the Chronicle of Theophanes?', *ZRVI* 18 (1978), 578–87; and I.S. Čičurov 'Feofan Ispovednik – publikator, redaktor, avtor?', *VV* 42 (1981), 78–87. Detailed analyses and historical-philological commentaries of various sections of the text of Theophanes can be found in P. Speck, 'Die Interpretation des *Bellum Avaricum* und der Kater Μεχλεμπε', in *Varia II* (Poikila Byzantina VI. Bonn 1987) 371ff., idem, *Das geteilte Dossier. Beobachtungen zu den Nachrichten über die Regierung des Kaisers Herakleios und die seiner Söhne bei Theophanes und Nikephoros* (Poikila Byzantina IX. Berlin–Bonn 1988); idem, *Ich bin's nicht, Kaiser Konstantin ist es gewesen. Die Legenden vom Einfluß des Teufels, des Juden und des Moslem auf den Ikonoklasmus* (Poikila Byzantina X. Bonn 1990), and idem, 'Der "zweite" Theophanes. Eine These zur Chronographie des Theophanes', in *Varia V* (Poikila Byzantina XIII. Bonn 1994), pp. 433–83; I. Rochow, *Byzanz im 8. Jahrhundert in der Sicht des Theophanes* (BBA LVII. Berlin 1991). See also L.I. Conrad, 'Theophanes and the Arabic Historical Tradition: Some Indications of Intercultural Transmission', *BF* 15 (1990) 1–44; and L.M. Whitby, 'The Great Chronographer and Theophanes', *BMGS* 8 (1982–83) 1–20. For a good, brief introduction and assessment of the various types of source dealt with in the following, see W. Brandes, F. Winkelmann, eds., *Quellen zur Geschichte des frühen Byzanz* (BBA LV. Berlin, 1990).

[2] See especially P.J. Alexander, *The Patriarch Nicephorus of Constantinople. Ecclesiastical Policy and Image Worship in the Byzantine Empire* (Oxford 1958) on Nicephorus and his writings; and Hunger, *Profane Literatur*, vol. 1, pp. 344–7. See also C. Mango, 'The *Breviarium* of the Patriarch Nicephorus', in *Byzantion: Tribute to Andreas N. Stratos* (Athens 1986), II, pp. 545–8; and *Nicephorus, Patriarch of Constantinople. Short History*, ed. and trans. C. Mango (Washington D.C. 1990).

[3] See Hunger, *Profane Literatur*, vol. 1, pp. 328–30.

The sources xxiii

patriarch of Antioch, and the Chronicle falsely ascribed to Denis of Tell-Mahré; in addition, the mostly lost chronicle which was actually composed by the latter and upon which that of Michael the Syrian draws heavily, as does Bar Hebraeus and one of the anonymous chronicles.[4] A number of lesser Syriac chronicles, all anonymous, compiled mostly in the tenth, eleventh and twelfth centuries, cover events up to the years 724, 813 and 846.[5] Particularly important sources are the Armenian history compiled by the bishop Sebeos, probably in the early 660s; and the Chronicle of John, the bishop of Nikiu in Egypt, compiled in Coptic towards the end of the seventh century.[6] Both present events from their own, localised perspective, but Sebeos especially sheds much light on the political and ecclesiastical history of the empire and the capital city. Sebeos' history is supplemented partially by that of the later chronicler Ghevond (Łewond).[7] Of the Latin historical sources, the most useful are the chronicle compiled by the bishop John of Biclar, and the Liber Pontificalis, although a number of minor chronicles and annals are also valuable.[8] The history of the Goths, Vandals and Suevi of Isidore of Seville, and its continuations, as well as his Chronica maiora, are also valuable for the history of the eastern Mediterranean up to the 620s, as well as for Spain and the West.[9] Finally, the Arab histories (dating mainly from the later

---

[4] J.-B. Chabot, La Chronique de Michel le Syrien, Patriarche jacobite d'Antioche (4 vols., Paris 1899, 1901, 1905, 1910 and 1924). On the history and structure of the text, see vol. I, pp. xxiv–xxxvii; and J.-B. Chabot, Pseudo-Denys de Tell-Mahré, Chronique (Paris 1895). For the Syriac material in general, see S.P. Brock, 'Syriac sources for the seventh century', BMGS 2 (1976), 17–36; and G.J. Reinink, 'Pseudo-Methodius und die Legende vom römischen Endkaiser', in The Use and Abuse of Eschatology in the Middle Ages, eds. W. Verbeke, D. Verhelst and A. Welkenhuysen (Leuven 1988), 82–111, see 84ff. on the as yet mostly unpublished but very important seventh-century history of Johannan bar Penkaye. For editions and translations of Bar Hebraeus, see Brock, art. cit., 22f. For the oriental sources for the seventh century, see also the papers in Av. Cameron, L. Conrad, eds., The Byzantine and Early Islamic Near East I: Problems in the Literary Source Material (Studies in Late Antiquity and Early Islam 1, I. Princeton 1992).

[5] See J.-B. Chabot and E.W. Brooks (eds.), in CSCO scriptores Syri, ser. 3, vol. IV (Chronica Minora II, 4, pp. 63–119; III, 1, pp. 185–96; II, 5, pp. 123–80) and for a chronicle to the year 1234, ed. J.-B. Chabot, CSCO scriptores Syri 56, pt. 1. In addition, there are the chronicles of Elias of Nisibis (vol. I, ed. E.W. Brooks, CSCO scriptores Syri, ser. 3, vol. VII; vol. II, ed. J.-B. Chabot, ibid., ser. 3, vol. VIII); and the minor anonymous Chronicon Maroniticum, ed. and trans. E.W. Brooks and J.-B. Chabot, CSCO scriptores Syri, ser. 3, vol. IV (Chronica Minora II, 3, pp. 35–7).

[6] F. Macler, Sébéos, Histoire d'Héraclius (Paris 1904) and R.H. Charles, ed. and transl., The Chronicle of John, Bishop of Nikiu (London 1916).

[7] G. Chahnazarian, ed., Ghévond: histoire des guerres et des conquêtes des Arabes en Arménie (Paris 1856).

[8] John of Biclar's chronicle is in MGH (AA) XI, 2, pp. 211–20; the Liber Pontificalis is edited by L. Duchesne (2 vols., Paris 1884–92).

[9] Isidori Iunioris Episcopi Hispalensis Historia Gothorum Wandalorum Sueborum ad An. DCXXIV, in MGH (AA) XI, 2, pp. 267–303 (text); Continuationes Isidorianae Byzantina Arabica et Hispana, in ibid., pp. 334–68; Chronica Isidori Iunioris, in ibid., pp. 424–81.

eighth century and later, but often dependent upon much earlier material), especially those of Balādhurī and Ṭabarī. The latter are especially important for the Muslim invasions and the occupation of the eastern territories of the empire.[10] All of these varied sources are valuable, but each must be carefully weighed as to its textual background, its sources, the question of contamination and interpolation – in other words, as to its value and reliability as a historical source.

But quite apart from these more obviously 'historiographical' forms of evidence, there is a vast range of other material: official documents issued or drawn up on behalf of the state (edicts and *novellae*, for example);[11] imperial letters (sent, for example, to foreign rulers, leading secular or ecclesiastical officials and to generals); ecclesiastical documents (patriarchal letters, letters and documents concerning matters of dogma and Church business, the appointment of clerics, convening of synods and so forth, as well as the acts of the Church councils – chiefly the acts of the Lateran council of 649, of the sixth ecumenical council of 680–1 and of the 'Quinisext' council of 692;[12] lists of episcopal sees and descriptions of ecclesiastical administration, and so on);[13] epic poems and encomia, such

[10] See Balādhurī, *Kitāb futūḥ al-Buldān. The Origins of the Islamic State*, trans. Ph. Hitti (London 1916 and Beirut 1966); and M.-J. de Goeje, ed., *Annales quos Scripsit Abu Djafar Mohammed Ibn Djarir al Tabari cum Aliis* (3 vols., Leiden 1879); and also Th. Nöldeke, *Geschichte der Perser und Araber zur Zeit der Sassaniden aus der arabischen Chronik des Tabari* (Leiden 1879) for the period up to the end of the Sassanid empire. On these sources see E.W. Brooks, 'The Arabs in Asia Minor (641–750) from Arabic sources', *JHS* 18 (1898), 182–208; E.W. Brooks, 'Byzantines and Arabs in the time of the early Abbasids', *EHR* 15 (1900), 728–47. On the Arab historiographical tradition, see G. Strohmaier, 'Arabische Quellen', in Brandes, Winkelmann, *Quellen zur Geschichte des frühen Byzanz*, pp. 234–44; and in general A. Noth (with Lawrence Conrad), *The Early Arabic Historical Tradition. A Source-Critical Study* (Princeton 1994).

[11] These will be discussed in greater detail in chapter 3 (esp. in regard of the so-called 'Farmers' Law') and chapter 7 (imperial legislation and codification).

[12] For the Lateran, see R. Riedinger, ed., *Concilium Laterananse a. 649 Celebratum* (Acta Conciliorum Oecumenicorum, 2nd ser., vol. I. Berlin, 1984) (this edition replaces the text in Mansi X, 863–1170). In addition, see the article by R. Riedinger, 'Die Lateransynode von 649 und Maximos der Bekenner', in *Maximus Confessor. Actes du Symposium pour Maxime le confesseur* (Fribourg, 2–5 Sept. 1980) eds. F. Heinzer and Chr. Schönborn (Fribourg, 1982), pp. 111–21 (= *Paradosis* 27); for the council of 680, Mansi XI, 190–922 and F.X. Murphy and P. Sherwood, *Constantinople II et Constantinople III* (Paris 1974), pp. 133–260; and for the Quinisext council, Mansi XI, 921–1005; and V. Laurent, 'L'Œuvre canonique du concile in Trullo (691–2), source primaire du droit de l'eglise orientale', *REB* 23 (1965), 7–41. New edition of the acts of the council of 680: *Concilium universale Constantinopolitanum tertium*, ed. R. Riedinger, 2 vols. (Acta Conciliorum Oecumenicorum II/2. 1–2) (Berlin 1990/1992).

[13] In particular the description of George of Cyprus: see E. Honigmann, *Le Synekdémos d'Hiéroklès et l'opuscule géographique de Georges de Chypre* (Corpus Bruxellense Historiae Byzantinae I, Brussels 1939); H. Gelzer, *Georgii Cyprii, Descriptio Orbis Romani* (Leipzig 1890); and the Pseudo-Epiphanius Notitia, in H. Gelzer, 'Ungedruckte und ungenügend veröffentlichte Texte der *Notitiae Episcopatuum*. Ein Beitrag zur byzantinischen Kirchen- und Verwaltungsgeschichte', in Abhandlungen der bayerischen Akademie der Wissen-

The sources xxv

as those in praise of the Emperor Heraclius by George of Pisidia, or to celebrate and give thanks for the victory over the Persians and Avars in 626 by Theodore the Sygkellos;[14] private letters, whether of laypeople or Churchmen; semi-official documents incorporated into 'official' collections, such as the accounts of the trials of Maximus Confessor or Pope Martin or the account of the seizure of power by Philippicus Bardanes;[15] theological and dogmatic writings, such as the apocalyptic tracts or the collections of 'questions and answers', especially that attributed to Anastasius of Sinai;[16] hagiographical writing – a particularly important source;[17] epigraphic

schaften, phil.-hist. Klasse, XXI, 3 (Munich 1900). More recent edition, with analysis, of all the Notitiae, in J. Darrouzès, *Notitiae Episcopatuum Ecclesiae Constantinopolitanae* (Paris 1981).

[14] The poems of George of Pisidia deal with the Persian wars of Heraclius, the siege of 626, the character and mission of the emperor himself, the role of the *patricius* Bonus: see A. Pertusi, ed., *Giorgio di Pisidia, Poemi* I: *Panegirici epici* (Studia patristica et Byzantina VII, Ettal 1959); and the discussion in Claudia Ludwig, 'Kaiser Herakleios, Georgios Pisides und die Perserkriege', in *Varia III* (Poikila Byzantina XI. Bonn 1991), pp. 73–128; the sermon of Theodore the Sygkellos, *skeuophylax* of the Hagia Sophia, was edited by L. Sternbach, *Analecta Avarica (Rozprawy Akademii Umiejetnosci Wydzial Filologiczny*, ser. 2, vol. XV Cracow 1900), pp. 297–334 (= L. Sternbach, *Studia philologica in Georgium Pisidam* (Cracow 1900)).

[15] For Maximus: *Maximi Confessoris Relatio Motionis*, in *PG* XC, 109–29; *Gesta in Primo Eius Exsilio*, in *PG* XC, 135–72; see C.N. Tsirpanlis, 'Acta S. Maximi', *Theologia* 43 (1972), 106–24. For Martin: *Commemoratio*, in Mansi X, 853–61 and *PL* CXXIX, 591–600; and see R. Devreesse, 'Le Texte grec de l'hypomnesticum de Théodore Spoudée', *AB* 53 (1935), 49–80. These slightly later accounts seem to be based on Martin's own letters 16 and 17 (*PL* LXXXVII, 201–4 and Mansi X, 860–4). For Philippicus, see the account of the deacon Agathōn in Mansi XII, 189C–196C.

[16] In particular the Apocalypse of Pseudo-Methodius: A. Lolos, ed., *Die Apokalypse des Ps.-Methodius* (Beiträge zur klassischen Philologie LXXXIII, Meisenheim am Glan 1976) and the literature in Haldon, *Ideology and Social Change*, 168 and n. 74; see chapters 9 and 11 below. Further discussion in W. Brandes, 'Die apokalyptische Literatur', in Brandes, Winkelmann, *Quellen zur Geschichte des frühen Byzanz*, pp. 305–26. For Anastasius of Sinai, see G. Dagron, 'Le Saint, le savant, l'astrologue. Etude de thèmes hagiographiques à travers quelques recueils de "Questions et réponses" des V°–VII° siècles', in *Hagiographie, cultures et sociétés (IV°–VII° s.)* (Etudes Augustiniennes, Paris 1981), pp. 143–55 (repr. in Dragon, *La Romanité chrétienne en Orient* IV (London 1984). Among the most important texts of Anastasius are the *interrogationes et responsiones* (*PG* LXXXIX, 311–384) and his third sermon (*PG* LXXXIX, 1152–80); new edition ed. K.-H. Uthemann, *Anastasii Sinaitae Opera. Sermones Duo In Constitutionem Hominis secundum Imaginem Dei necnon Opuscula adversus Monotheletas (Corpus Christianorum series Graeca* XII. (Turnhout 1985), pp. 55–83). See J.F. Haldon, 'The Writings of Anastasius of Sinai: a key source for seventh-century East Mediterranean history', in: *The Byzantine and Early Islamic Near East* I: *Problems in the Literary Source Materials*, eds. Averil Cameron, L. Conrad (Princeton 1992), pp. 107–47.

[17] Hagiography and miracles constitute a vital source for the social and cultural life of the period. Among the many texts which are especially important are: the Lives of the patriarchs John the Almsgiver in Alexandria, Eutychius in Constantinople, of Pope Martin, Maximus Confessor (originally in Syriac), the *Hypomnesticum* or commemoration of Theodore Spoudaios (on Pope Martin), the Lives of Theodore of Sykeon and of

material – inscriptions on city walls, for example, or on tombstones;[18] numismatics; and last, but certainly not least, sigillographic material – the seals used by both officials and private persons to validate and secure letters or merchandise. And in addition to this predominantly 'documentary' material, we must also bear in mind the considerable archaeological evidence, particularly where settlement patterns on the one hand and architectural forms on the other (Church buildings, fortifications and so on) are concerned; as well as that of late Roman and Byzantine forms of visual expression – icons, frescoes, mosaics – essential to our understanding of some of the assumptions of Byzantine culture, its perception of the world and of the relationship between both emperor and people, and between God and humanity.[19]

Anastasius of Persia, the miracles of St Demetrius in Thessalonica, of Artemius and Therapon in Constantinople, the fictional Life of Andrew the Fool, the miracles of St Theodore at Euchaita. For literature see note 19 below; full references will be found in the bibliography.

[18] Most of the relevant material is to be found in the major collections: *Corpus Inscriptionum Graecarum*, ed. A. Böckh (vols. I and II) and I. Franz (vols. IIIff.) (Berlin 1828–); *Monumenta Asiae Minoris Antiqua*, eds. W.M. Calder, J. Keil et al. (Manchester 1928–62); *Inscriptions grecques et latines de la Syrie*, eds. L. Jalabert, R. Mouterde et al. (Paris 1929–); *Inscriptions grecques et latines de la Syrie*, ed. W.H. Waddington (Paris 1870 and Rome 1969 = *Inscriptions grecques et latines recueillies en Grèce et en Asie Mineure* III, 1/2. Paris 1870 and 1876); *Supplementum Epigraphicum Graecum*, eds. J.J.E. Hondius and A.G. Woodhead (Leiden 1927–); see also F. Cumont, 'Les Inscriptions chrétiennes d'Asie Mineure', in *Mélanges d'archéologie et d'histoire* 15 (1895); V. Beševliev, *Spätgriechische und spätlateinische Inschriften aus Bulgarien* (Berlin, 1964); H. Grégoire, *Recueils des inscriptions grecques chrétiennes d'Asie Mineure* (Paris 1922); E. Popescu, *Inscripţiile Greceşti şi Latine din Secolele IV–XIII descoperite în România* (Bucharest 1976). For further publications, see J. Karayannopoulos, *Πηγαὶ τῆς Βυζαντινῆς Ἱστορίας*, 4th edn (Thessaloniki 1978), pp. 195–97.

[19] The critical literature on the types of sources listed here is, of course, enormous. For the main groups of both literary and non-literary sources the following compendia, handbooks and bibliographies will provide a basic and fairly full survey by period and genre of the sources themselves and the problems connected with them: G. Ostrogorsky, *Geschichte des byzantinischen Staates* (*Handbuch der Altertumswissenschaft*, XII, 1.2 = *Byzantinisches Handbuch*, 1, 2, Munich, 1963), pp. 72–5; Gy. Moravcsik, *Byzantinoturcica*, vol. I, 3rd edn (Berlin 1983); Hunger, *Profane Literatur*, vols. I and II (for historiography, secular poetry, epistolography, military handbooks, law); J. Karayannopoulos and G. Weiss, *Quellenkunde zur Geschichte von Byzanz (324–1453)* (2 vols., Wiesbaden 1982) for a survey of all the literary genres and discussion of their value, as well as of the non-Byzantine sources, esp. vol. II, pp. 302–18; H.-G. Beck, *Kirche und theologische Literatur im byzantinischen Reich* (*Handbuch der Altertumswissenschaft*, XII, 2.1 = *Byzantinisches Handbuch*, 2, 1, Munich 1959), esp. pp. 430–73 for a detailed survey of theological and related writings in the seventh century (dogma, polemic, liturgical poetry, sermons, hagiography, mystical and exegetical works); on hagiography see also I. Ševčenko, 'Hagiography of the iconoclast period', in A.A.M. Bryer and J. Herrin (eds.), *Iconoclasm* (Birmingham 1977), pp. 113–31, and Ševčenko, 'L'Agiografia Bizantina dal IV al IX secolo', in *La civiltà Bizantina dal IV al IX secolo* (3 vols., Bari 1977, 1978 and 1982), vol. I, pp. 87–173. For a brief introduction to the Syriac material see S.P. Brock, 'Syriac sources for seventh-century history', *BMGS* 2 (1976), 17–36; for numismatics, the introductory comments of M.F. Hendy, *Studies in the*

The problems posed by all these sources are considerable. Many of them are in need of modern editions and commentaries; few of them have been studied in detail or have been internally analysed. Where written texts are concerned in particular it must be apparent that no source can be taken at face value. It is sometimes difficult to date a source at all – a classic example is the very valuable but fictional account of the Life of Andrew the Fool, dated by different scholars to both the later seventh or the later ninth century.[20] Where the date is certain, the value of the information provided both explicitly and implicitly by a text needs to be carefully considered – what was the purpose or context of the original compilation, for example, and what were its possible sources of information? Often, literary texts refer only indirectly and allusively to a particular state of affairs or development, or use technical terms from the period of their own compilation of earlier events – both have led, and continue to lead, to conflicting views about the precise significance of the references in question. Similar reservations apply to the question of the date of certain works of art, too, so that some of the Mt. Sinai icons which are so crucial for an understanding of pre-iconoclastic art are variously dated from the end of the sixth to the middle of the seventh century – a period over which substantial changes occurred – and for a knowledge of the evolution and origins of which these artifacts are central. Likewise, the use and exploitation of sigillographic as well as numismatic materials bring with them a number of equally formidable problems, and it is important that the historian as well as the readers of works of history are aware of these difficulties. For differences in interpretation usually rest on two supports: conflicting views of how and what a given source or type of source can divulge about a specific question; and conflicting or contradictory interpretational frameworks.

This brief list of types of source highlights the mosaic-like complexity of the historian's task. It also demonstrates the constraint upon interpretation imposed by the sources and the importance of keeping some general principles of analysis – some theoretical guidelines – in mind. For without

---

Byzantine Monetary Economy, 300–1450 (Cambridge 1985), pp. 2–18; and Karayannopoulos and Weiss, *Quellenkunde*, vol. I, pp. 172–8; for seals, see the valuable comments in the introductory section to F. Winkelmann, *Byzantinische Rang- und Ämterstruktur im 8. und 9. Jahrhundert* (BBA LIII, Berlin 1985), pp. 17–18; and W. Seibt, *Die byzantinischen Bleisiegel in Österreich*, I: *Kaiserhof* (Vienna 1978), pp. 36f.; with Karayannopoulos and Weiss, *Quellenkunde*, vol. I, pp. 178–83. All these materials are surveyed in the collective Brandes, Winkelmann, *Quellen zur Geschichte des frühen Byzanz*.

[20] See the conflicting views of L. Rydén, 'The *Life* of St Basil the Younger and the *Life* of St Andreas Salos', in *Okeanos. Essays presented to Ihor Ševčenko on his sixtieth birthday by his colleagues and students* (= Harvard Ukrainian Studies, 7 1983 (Cambridge, Mass. 1983)), pp. 568–86; and C. Mango, 'The Life of St Andrew the Fool reconsidered', *Rivista di Studi Bizantini e Slavi* II (= Miscellanea A. Pertusi II, Bologna 1982), pp. 297–313 (repr. in C. Mango, *Byzantium and its Image* VIII (London 1984)).

some organising framework, the 'evidence' becomes simply overwhelming; or, what is perhaps worse, too readily fitted into an ill-considered or preconceived notion of what late Roman and early Byzantine society was 'really' like. I shall try to avoid these two extremes. But I shall also avoid a detailed analysis of each source employed, since this would require more than a volume to itself. Instead, I will refer, where appropriate, to relevant discussions of the problems associated with the deployment of a particular source or group of sources and comment only at those points where a particular difficulty in connection with a specific source is encountered.

For the historian of the seventh century, the interrelationship between evidence and hypothesis plays a more than usually central role. The American philosopher W.V. Quine once wrote: 'I see philosophy and science as in the same boat – a boat which ... we can rebuild only at sea while staying afloat on it.' Among others, the history of the seventh century is also in that boat.[21]

[21] W. V. Quine, 'Natural Kinds', in *Ontological Relativity and Other Essays* (New York 1969), pp. 114–38, see p. 127.

Introduction

The seventh century was a time of fundamental transformation throughout the eastern Mediterranean and Balkan world; and the most powerful political entity in that world experienced a succession of major upheavals. Entering the seventh century as the dominant political formation, stretching from Spain to the Euphrates and from the Danube to the Atlas mountains, it had been reduced by the end of our period – the year of the accession of Leo III in A.D. 717 – to a rump of its former self: East Roman rule in Egypt and North Africa, in Syria, Iraq and in eastern Anatolia had been swept away by the conquests of Islam, the new and vigorous world religion which was to provide the biggest threat to Christianity for the next thousand years. In the Balkans, Slavs and Bulgars had reduced Roman-controlled territory over the same period to the coastal areas and a few fortified settlements; while in Italy, the exarchate which had been established under Tiberius Constantine on the foundations of Justinian's reconquest was by the reign of Leo III all but extinguished. At the same time, new and powerful foes replaced older, traditional enemies: the expansion and the power of the caliphate centred at Damascus radically altered the balance of power in that area; in the Balkans, the establishment and consolidation of the Bulgar khanate posed a constant threat to Constantinople itself; while in the West, the increasingly independent see of St Peter was compelled to loosen its ties with Constantinople in order to preserve its own position as both leader of the Western Church and defender of its immediate hinterland. The East Roman empire which we observe at the beginning of the seventh century has, by the time of Leo III, been transformed into the 'Byzantine' empire of the Middle Ages, and along with it its institutions, its social relations and the dominant elements of political and popular belief systems.

The seventh century, traditionally, belongs to the 'Dark Ages', in the fullest sense of the phrase, a period when both the sources available to the historian are fewer than in earlier or later times, and when the exigencies of the struggle to survive (or, in more analytic terms, when social, economic and cultural transformations were in full swing) made the production of a widely based secular literature both less relevant to the cultural identity of the dominant elite – the imperial establishment and its bureaucratic and military representatives – and subordinate to the demand for political and theological certainties. In fact, as a cursory examination of the relevant bibliographies will quickly show, while there is an absolute decline in secular literary production, this is not the case with theological or political-theological writings, hagiography and homiletic writings, collections of *erōtapokriseis* (questions and answers on everyday or theological concerns), apocalyptic and eschatological tracts and similar texts, all of which reflect the immediate concerns and foremost worries and interests of seventh-century society. In this sense, at least, this is by no means a 'dark age' – the light is there, but it shines on different areas, more selectively. Indeed, the very term 'dark age', or 'ages', is itself suspect, as has been noted before now.[1] Where we read in the literature about this period of economic 'decline' or political 'collapse' we should perhaps substitute 'political and economic transformation' – if only to avoid examining the society in question purely in terms of a reflection of the language and perceptions of those members of it able to express themselves in literature.

This is not a total history of Byzantine culture and society during the period in question. Rather, I want to look at the basic 'shape' of this early medieval social formation as it might be seen in the early seventh century and to follow the process of change over the following one hundred or so years. But I shall not simply describe the changes in question – as far as we can see them through the interrogation of the available sources – I shall also try to suggest what lay behind them, why they occurred at the time and in the form that they did, and why they had the results which they had. I shall be trying in the process to determine what particular characteristics differentiate the later Roman and early Byzantine world from its eastern and western neighbours, what in particular governs the development of its specific cultural forms and modes of expression. At the same time as trying to provide a useful survey of the Byzantine world at this time, I shall also be concentrating on some of the key problems of Byzantine history as currently identified in recent historiographical work. This book is therefore a contemporary document, in the sense that it contains a statement both of problems of history as they are perceived today, and of

---

[1] See especially F.-G. Maier, 'Die Legende der "Dark Ages"', in F.-G. Maier, ed., *Die Verwandlung der Mittelmeerwelt* (Frankfurt a.M. 1968), pp. 10ff.; and D. Talbot Rice, 'The myth of the Dark Ages', in D. Talbot Rice, ed., *The Dark Ages* (London 1965), introduction.

what has been achieved; and one of historiographical desiderata – what still remains to be done.

Because of this format, the chronological narrative has been kept to a minimum: chapter 2 provides a brief survey of the political history of the period, which remains the most useful measure against which to 'fix' other developments, even if it occasionally leads to a rather inflexible schematisation and even if it is often regarded as no longer a primary moment in historical analysis; the politics of a state or its rulers are as much the product of the cultural, social and economic relationships which determine the shape of a society as any other aspects of its existence and evolution.

The remaining chapters – with the exception of chapter 1 (which provides a general background for the whole) – will each deal with a particular theme, as can be seen from the headings and sub-headings, which will be treated both structurally and chronologically. That is to say, the developments in time within a specific problem area will be presented and described, while at the same time an examination of the key aspects of the theme to be dealt with will be undertaken. In this way, I hope that I can provide the reader with both a descriptive and an analytic account of the movement and transformation of the early Byzantine state and its society through time. I have also tried to make the book accessible to both specialists and non-specialists, by incorporating within a general account the detailed debates and analyses which will be relevant to the former.

The seventh century has received a great deal more attention over the last twenty years than in the years prior to about 1965. This shift in interest is partly a reflection of an awareness of the former neglect to which the period and its problems were consigned, which in turn represented the difficulties experienced in dealing with the sources. More importantly, it reflects also a shift in research priorities and interests together with a reappraisal of the methods and the theories that might be invoked in examining such a period. Thus, if we exclude articles in journals, of the six or so publications that have dealt specifically with the seventh century, only two appeared before 1965: volume III of Kulakovskij's classic *Byzantine History*, covering the period from 602 to 717; and the selection of papers on the seventh century in volume 13 of the *Dumbarton Oaks Papers*. The five-volume history of Andreas Stratos, *Byzantium in the seventh century*; the Berlin symposium on the same period, out of which two major publications appeared and a third is currently in press; and the recent book by T.K. Louggis on Byzantium in the so-called dark ages have all appeared since 1965.[2] But there is much disagreement between these various works

---

[2] See J. Kulakovskij, *Istoria Vizantii* (Kiev 1915 and London 1973) vol. III; A.N. Stratos, *Byzantium in the Seventh Century* (Engl. transl.) I: 602–34 (Amsterdam 1968); II: 634–41 (Amsterdam 1972); III: 642–68 (Amsterdam 1975); IV: 668–85 (Amsterdam 1978); V:

on fundamental questions – the nature of the social relations of production, the role of the army in society, the relationship between the state and large landholding, between tax and rent, and so on. In what follows, some idea of these debates will be given and some solutions will be suggested, as part of the process of providing a general survey of the development of East Roman society and culture during the seventh century.

Inevitably, I have not been able to deal with everything that might seem desirable in such a general survey. The history of Byzantine Italy and its particular socio-cultural, economic and institutional evolution during this period represented too different and too distant a world to be directly relevant to the history of the central lands of the empire – although its political and military importance, its ideological significance (Rome in particular, of course) and its effect on Byzantine state and ecclesiastical politics have been taken into account. In addition, of course, good surveys of Italy in this period are available, and in several accessible languages. It would be pointless to duplicate their results.[3] Similar considerations apply to Byzantine Africa, a political and social formation about which all too

---

686–711 (Amsterdam 1980); F. Winkelmann, H. Köpstein, H. Ditten and I. Rochow, *Byzanz im 7. Jahrhundert. Untersuchungen zur Herausbildung des Feudalismus* (BBA XXXXVIII, Berlin, 1978) and H. Köpstein and F. Winkelmann, eds., *Studien zum 7. Jahrhundert in Byzanz. Probleme der Herausbildung des Feudalismus* (BBA XXXXVII, Berlin 1976); for the Dumbarton Oaks sumposium, see *DOP* 13, (1959). See further T.K. Louggis, *Δοκίμιο για την κοινωνική εξέλιξη στη διάρκεια των λεγομένων σκοτεινών αιώνων* (Athens 1985), a somewhat reductionist interpretation which takes issue with a number of traditional interpretations without really demonstrating a convincing alternative (and which seems to assume that all historians in the Soviet Union or Eastern Europe are 'Marxist', whereas those elsewhere are not – see pp. 87ff.). In addition, the introduction (by V. Vavřínek) and contributions to the collection *From Late Antiquity to Early Byzantium*, ed. V. Vavřínek (Prague 1985), provide useful guides to recent debates and literature among both Soviet/East European and West European/North American historians. Other works might be mentioned which deal only partly with aspects of seventh-century history. These will be referred to as they become relevant and are listed in the bibliography. For a recent treatment of the sources for the period, see the important collective work *Quellen zur Geschichte des frühen Byzanz* ed. F. Winkelmann (BBA LV, Berlin, 1989); and for the seventh-century city, W. Brandes, 'Die byzantinische Stadt Kleinasiens im 7. Jahrhundert – ein Forschungsbericht', *Klio* 70 (1988), 176–208; W. Brandes, *Die Städte Kleinasiens im 7. und 8. Jahrhundert* (BBA LVI, Berlin 1989).

[3] Apart from the older works, see T.S. Brown, *Gentlemen and Officers. Imperial Administration and Aristocratic Power in Byzantine Italy A.D. 554–800* (Rome 1984); and more recently T.S. Brown, 'The interplay between Roman and Byzantine traditions and local sentiment in the Exarchate of Ravenna', in: *Bisanzio, Roma e l'Italia nell'alto Medioevo* (Settimane di Studio del Centro Italiano di Studi sull'alto Medioevo XXXIV, Spoleto 1988), 127–60. C.J. Wickham, *Early Medieval Italy. Central Government and Local Society, 400–1000* (London 1981); A. Guillou, *Régionalisme et indépendance dans l'empire byzantin au VIIe siècle: l'exemple de l'exarchat et de la pentapole d'Italie* (Istituto storico italiano per il medio evo, Studi storici 75–6, Rome 1969); O. Bertolini, 'Riflessi politici del'controversie religiose con Bisanzio nelle vicende del sec. VII in Italia', in *Caratterri del secolo VII in Occidente* (Spoleto 1958), pp. 733–89 (= Settimane di studio del Centro Italiano di Studi sull'alto Medioevo V (1957)).

little is known after the middle of the seventh century. In this case, however, the only major work on the subject is the now very old, but still essential, survey of Charles Diehl, whose study on the exarchate of Africa was first published in 1896.[4] This can be supplemented by a number of works dealing with particular aspects of the history of North Africa, but a detailed analysis of the literary, religious and social-economic history of Byzantine Africa from the reign of Heraclius up to the fall of Carthage in the last decade of the seventh century is still not available. Fortunately, recent work promises to fill some of these gaps, although there is still a great deal of detailed research, especially archaeological work, to be done before the later history of the isolated Latin culture of North Africa becomes reasonably clear; and there remains a dismal lack of source material. Again, Byzantine Africa was an important consideration in the eyes of the government at Constantinople, which did its best, with limited resources, to maintain its political and military hold, as well as its ideological authority. It consumed wealth in the form of military and naval resources, although the degree of its contribution to the fisc in general is unclear; and it remained a part of the Byzantine world, from the Constantinopolitan perspective, until the end – the expedition to retake Carthage in 698 is demonstration enough of this. In this respect, and in as far as the general course of North African history is concerned, it will be dealt with in this book. Anything more would involve a study in its own right.[5]

[4] Ch. Diehl, *L'Afrique byzantine: histoire de la domination byzantine en Afrique (533–709)* (2 vols., Paris 1896). See also R. Goodchild, 'Byzantines, Berbers and Arabs in seventh-century Libya', *Antiquity* 41 (1967), 114–24; R. Goodchild, 'Fortificazione e palazzi bizantini in Tripolitania e Cirenaica', in *XIII Corso di Cultura sull'Arte Ravennate e Bizantina* (Ravenna 1966), pp. 225–50; Ch.A. Julien, *Histoire de l'Afrique du Nord des origines à la conquête arabe*, 2nd edn (Paris 1951); M. Restlé, art. 'Byzacena', in *RbK* I (1966), 837–66; also E. Kirsten, *Nordafrikanische Stadtbilder, Antike und Mittelalter in Libyen und Tunisien* (Heidelberg 1966); and P. Goubert, *Byzance avant l'Islam* II/2 (Paris 1965), pp. 185–236 (for the period up to 610 only).

[5] See the various articles published in connection with the University of Michigan excavations at Carthage, esp. vol. VII (1982), notably the important contribution of Averil Cameron, 'Byzantine Africa – the literary evidence', *ibid.*, 29–62, with the older literature. See also D. Pringle, *The Defence of Byzantine Africa from Justinian to the Arab Conquest* (BAR, Oxford 1981); N. Duval, 'Influences byzantines sur la civilisation chrétienne de l'Afrique du Nord', *REG* 84 (1971); W.H.C. Frend, 'The Christian period in Mediterranean Africa c. A.D. 200–700', in *Cambridge History of Africa*, vol. II (Cambridge 1978), pp. 410–89; W.H.C. Frend, 'The end of Byzantine North Africa. Some evidence of transitions', *Bulletin archéologique du Comité des Travaux Historiques et Scientifiques*, new series, 19 (1985), 387–97 (IIe Colloque international sur l'histoire et l'archéologie de l'Afrique du Nord, Grenoble, 5–9 Avril, 1983); M. Brett, 'The Arab conquest and the rise of Islam', in *Cambridge History of Africa*, vol. II (Cambridge 1978), pp. 490–555, esp. pp. 490–513. For further literature and discussion, see N. Duval, 'L'Afrique byzantine de Justinien à la conquête musulmane. A propos de travaux récents', *Moyen-Age* 89 (1983), 433–9; as well as the work of J. Durliat, *Recherches sur l'histoire sociale de l'Afrique byzantine: le dossier épigraphique (533–709)* (Thèse du troisième cycle, Université de Paris I, Paris 1977); *Les Dédicaces d'ouvrages de défense dans l'Afrique byzantine* (Collections de l'école française de

There are other topics which I have not dealt with in depth, chiefly because they are adequately treated elsewhere. The (primarily theological) literature of the seventh century *as literature* has been left to others, for example; similarly, the history of the art and architecture (again, the surviving material is almost entirely religious in character) of the period, which presents certain very important characteristics and shifts, has been dealt with predominantly on the basis of work done by others – although, for reasons which will become clearer in the relevant discussion (in chapter 11), a great deal more emphasis has been placed upon visual representation than on architecture.

Historians rarely preface their work with statements of theoretical intent – perhaps much to the relief of many readers, but this is not necessarily always a good thing. For every work of historiography relies on sets of assumptions; and 'theories', however implicit they might be, are inescapable. I will mention here some of my own basic assumptions.

The main point to make is that this book is conceived and written within a historical materialist framework – that is to say, it is written from a 'Marxist' perspective. I place the word Marxist in quotation marks advisedly: the word can mean, and is regularly in debate within the social and historical sciences used to refer to, such a wide variety of subtly or not-so-subtly differentiated views and approaches, that to refer to oneself as a Marxist is of only limited help in determining which of a variety of perspectives within a range of possibilities is actually meant. For while Marxism has a relatively short history as a philosophical and political movement, it is nevertheless immensely ramified and has been enormously influential.

One may ask, of course, why it should be at all necessary to justify one's terms of reference or indeed to situate oneself in a particular historiographical tradition. Surely it should be enough to base oneself firmly in the sources and to apply one's historical common sense to their interpretation and to the possible shape of a given set of historical developments? The answer, and the justification, is not difficult to grasp. Theories are, in effect, sets of premises – whether they are implicit or explicit is unimportant at this point – which condition both the mode of interpretation as well as (crucially) the mode of appropriation of knowledge (in other words, the very way in which we permit ourselves to 'know' something). Such premises or assumptions are, as I have said, implicit in every piece of

---

Rome, Rome 1981); 'Les Finances municipales africaines de Constantin aux Aghlabides', in *Bulletin Archéologique du Comité des Travaux Historiques et Scientifiques*, n.s. 19 (1985), 377–86 (as above); 'Les Grands propriétaires africains et l'état byzantin', Cahiers de Tunisie XXIX (1981), 517–31; 'L'Administration civile du diocèse byzantin d'Afrique (533–703)', *Rivista di studi bizantini e slavi* 4 (1984), 149–78.

analysis, whether it be of literary texts or of historical sources. Theory, in this sense, is inescapable; and there is no use in appealing to an objective, fact-based history, for such does not, and indeed cannot, exist. It is better to admit that this is the case and to make these underlying assumptions explicit, for this allows at least the possibility of seeing where inconsistencies and contradictions might lie, inconsistencies which are inevitable in any process of intuitive and *ad hoc* reasoning. Theory is, from this point of view, highly desirable, since it is impossible to analyse that of which we have no, or only indirect, experience (either personally or culturally) without setting up a theoretical framework within which we can justify and direct our evaluation of the data.[6] I can do no better than to quote the linguist Noam Chomsky:

> The search for rigorous formulation has a much more serious motivation than mere concern for logical niceties or the desire to purify well-established methods of ... analysis. Precisely constructed models ... can play an important role, both negative and positive, in the process of discovery itself. By pushing a precise but inadequate formulation to an unacceptable conclusion, we can often expose the exact source of this inadequacy and, consequently, gain a deeper understanding of the ... data ... Obscure and intuition-bound notions can neither lead to absurd conclusions nor provide new and correct ones ... those ... who have questioned the value of precise and technical development of theory may have failed to recognise the productive potential in the method of rigorously stating a proposed theory and applying it strictly to [the] material with no attempt to avoid unacceptable conclusions by ad hoc adjustments or loose formulation.[7]

Of course, Chomsky is talking here of socio-linguistic data, the analysis and interpretation of which is subject to different principles from those applied to historical evidence. But the point he is making is equally relevant.

The search for rigorous formulation is not, therefore, a pointless exercise. Indeed, if we are to be able to deal effectively with our data, in such a way that we can order it according to the structure and function of the argument we wish to make, then an awareness of our basic assumptions is essential. For historians within the Marxist tradition, the need for rigorous

---

[6] For the foundations of my approach, see my remarks in 'Ideology and social change in the seventh century: military discontent as a barometer', *Klio* 68 (1986), 139–90, esp. 142–55. For a good general survey of current Marxist historical thinking from an explicitly realist and materialist epistemological standpoint, see G. McLennan, *Marxism and the Methodologies of History* (London 1981). See further the comments in J.F. Haldon, '"Jargon" vs. "the facts"? Byzantine history-writing and contemporary debates', *BMGS* 9 (1984–5), 95–132, esp. 96, 101f.; and idem, *The State and the Tributary Mode of Production* (London 1993), esp. 1–109, 140–58.

[7] N. Chomsky, *Syntactic Structures* (Janua Linguarum, series minor IV, The Hague and Paris 1976), p. 5. Compare the remarks of the Marxist historian Eric Hobsbawn: one must 'try to structure (memory) by fitting it into an explanatory or theoretical scheme. It's one of the advantages of being a Marxist ... Things which might otherwise be "trivial pursuit" actually get fitted into a pattern ...' (*The Guardian*, Friday 26 Feb. 1988, p. 25).

formulation and careful application of theoretical principles is crucial; and this involves determining the content and theoretical weight of the concepts invoked, either as abstract or concrete descriptive categories. For it is precisely through such categories that causal relationships – whether of socio-economic relationships or political ideological developments – can be specified and understood, and tied in to longer-term transformations.

Technical terms such as mode of production, social formation, symbolic universe and so on will thus occur from time to time in this book more especially in the context of analyses of the ways in which Byzantine society actually worked and changed. These, and a number of other terms, are part of a wider theoretical framework, a set of assumptions about the fundamental social, economic and cultural relationships which provide the dynamic for every human society, the generative syntactic structures, to borrow once more from linguistics, which constitute the grid within which social-cultural causation is to be understood. Such terms also imply a particular epistemology, of course, in this case a realist and materialist philosophy which provides a framework for and limitations to the ways in which knowledge of the world, past or present, can be appropriated and employed. But that is another story.

CHAPTER I

The background: state and society before Heraclius

It is all too easy to forget that every human society, whatever its achievements and the ways in which it impresses itself upon its natural context, is closely bound to its geographical and climatic conditions of existence in ways which may at first seem insignificant, or so obvious as to need no further consideration. Not only methods of agriculture and the production of social wealth, but modes of dress and the technology of clothing, for example, are subject to these conditions, although it is not always possible to determine exactly how the relationship operates. This is no less the case for the late Roman state and for late Roman society and culture, which occupied and dominated the east Mediterranean basin, the Balkans and much of the north African littoral up to the middle of the seventh century. The many local cultures and their histories which were incorporated into that state and were subject to its administrative and political machinery consequently varied very greatly in their appearance one from another, inasmuch as the geographical and climatic features of the zones in which they were located varied. It is useful to emphasise this perhaps obvious point at the outset. For while we shall be dealing with the general social, economic and cultural history of the Roman and Byzantine world during the seventh and early eighth centuries, it is important to remember that beneath the uniformity often imposed by contemporary descriptions, the apparatuses of the state and its official ideology, there continued to exist a variety and range of local cultures and of ways of doing and thinking which, while they may not necessarily have been in conflict with the umbrella of Roman and state culture, official orthodoxy and imperial ideology, were nevertheless often very different from one another and from the urban society and culture of the capital.[1] It is perhaps easier to see this

[1] See for example P. Charanis, 'Observations on the demography of the Byzantine empire', XIIIth International Congress of Byzantine Studies, Main Papers XIV (Oxford 1966), pp. 1–19; and the essays in P. Charanis, Studies on the Demography of the Byzantine Empire (London 1972). See also the important discussion in J. Koder, Der Lebensraum der Byzantiner (Darmstadt 1984).

during the sixth century, when Egypt, along with the wealthy elite cities of the east Mediterranean, such as Antioch or Tyre, clearly represented (beneath their common Hellenistic veneer) cultures of very different origins and appearance. But even in the later seventh century, when the empire consisted of little more than central and western Anatolia and Thrace, local differences and cultural variation continued to play a role.

Climatic variation within the empire was considerable. The political world of the later Roman state was dominated by three land masses: the Balkans, Asia Minor and the Middle East zone as far east as the Euphrates and as far south as Egypt; by the two seas which both separated and united them, the east Mediterranean and the Aegean, and the Black Sea; and by the geographically, but by no means politically, peripheral areas of Italy and the North African possessions of the empire. From the middle of the seventh century it is Anatolia and the Balkans that dominate, as the remaining territories are progressively lost; and from this time Italy and the Ionian Sea, on the one hand, and the Crimea and its hinterland, on the other, set the outer limits to what was thereafter 'Byzantine'.

Before the loss of these eastern lands, the empire as a whole was relatively rich in exploitable arable land and had access to regular and (usually) sufficient supplies of grain. Egypt, Thrace and the coastal plains of north-west and west Anatolia were all grain-producing areas.[2] But the loss of Egypt involved a major re-adjustment and an increased dependency of Constantinople on Thrace and the Anatolian sources, supplemented by produce from the city's own immediate hinterland. Of the three land masses referred to already, therefore, it is the Balkans and Anatolia which, after the loss of Egypt, determine the parameters within which the Byzantine economy, in the widest sense of the word, had to function. A recent estimate has put the total revenue loss to the empire in the seventh century at something in the order of seventy-five per cent of its sixth-century income – a dramatic loss which must have affected all aspects of the state administration fundamentally.[3] It was from this much-reduced area that the state now drew its revenues and manpower resources, and it was these areas – the Balkans and Anatolia – which had to be defended. It was the requirements of defence and revenue extraction within these areas which moulded the administrative apparatus of the state and which we shall look at in greater detail below.

---

[2] Procopius, *Historia Arcana* xxii, 137 (Thrace, Bithynia, Phrygia); cf. M. Rostovtzeff, art. 'frumentum', *RE* VII/1, 126–87, esp. 129 and 137.

[3] M.F. Hendy, *Studies in the Byzantine Monetary Economy c. 300–1450* (Cambridge 1985), pp. 619, 625–6.

Roman and Byzantine society was predominantly rural and agricultural. Settlements – villages and cities – were supplied almost without exception from their immediate hinterlands as far as all essential items – food, drink, clothing, the raw materials of everyday life, housing – were concerned. Only the larger cities, or the wealthiest individuals, had the resources to import goods, and these were chiefly luxury items for the landed elite who dwelt there.[4] Only Rome and Constantinople imported foodstuffs over long distances and on a large scale, and this was possible only because the state took complete responsibility for the financial burden entailed. Before the loss of Egypt, Constantinople drew its grain supplies almost entirely from that region, occasionally turning to Thrace or the nearest regions of Anatolia. After the 640s and 650s, it has been shown that Thrace, Paphlagonia and to a degree the Pontus, and north-west Asia Minor – Bithynia – were the chief sources of supply. Similarly, livestock, vegetables and other commodities were procured from these areas; although it is highly likely that, with the exclusion of its grain supplies, Constantinople could support itself from its immediate hinterland during much of the seventh century.

The nature and extent of long-distance trade was not dependent on the demand from a few major urban centres alone, however, and the problem of the extent of a trans-Mediterranean commercial network has led to a rich discussion among economic and social historians of the middle and later Roman periods. Wine, oil and ceramics (the latter often for functional reasons of transportation) were widely exported in the late Roman period from North Africa, for example. And these exports depended to a degree, at least, on commercial demand and competitive prices. But it seems that the extent of this trade was also related to the extent of imperially funded shipping and transport; so that although an established pattern of commercial exchange in certain goods (which may also have included textiles and clothing, for example) did exist, it too was in several ways parasitic upon the activities of the state.[5]

[4] See A.H.M. Jones, *The Later Roman Empire 284–602: A Social, Economic and Administrative Survey* (3 vols., Oxford 1964), vol. I, p. 465, vol. II, pp. 770, 840f., 850; A.H.M. Jones, *The Greek City from Alexander to Justinian* (Oxford 1940), pp. 259ff.; E. Kirsten, 'Die byzantinische Stadt', in *Berichte zum XI. Internationalen Byzantinisten-Kongress* (Munich 1958), pp. 10f.; D. Claude, *Die byzantinische Stadt im 6. Jahrhundert* (Byzantinisches Archiv XIII, Munich 1969), pp. 176f. For a general discussion with literature, see J.F. Haldon, 'Some considerations on Byzantine society and economy in the seventh century', *BF* 10 (1985), 75–112, see 78–80; note also J. Teall, 'The Byzantine agricultural tradition', *DOP* 25 (1971), 34–59; and for a detailed analysis, J. Durliat, *De la ville antique à la ville byzantine. Le problème des subsistances* (Collection de l'école française de Rome 136. Rome 1990).

[5] See the detailed summary with literature in R.-J. Lilie, *Die byzantinische Reaktion auf die Ausbreitung der Araber* (Miscellanea Byzantina Monacensia XXII, Munich 1976), pp. 201–27; Hendy, *Studies*, pp. 49, 51 and esp. 561–4; J. Teall, 'The grain supply of the Byzantine empire', *DOP* 13 (1959), 87–139. For the middle and early empire, see especially K. Hopkins, 'Taxes and trade in the Roman Empire (200 B.C.–A.D. 200)', *JRS*,

This pattern of supply, of course, reflects the costs and availability or otherwise of transport, as well as its efficiency. Transport by sea was considerably less expensive than by land; it was also generally much faster. This in itself can explain the reliance on Egyptian corn. But while the exigencies of transport by land meant that long-distance conveying of foodstuffs, either by cart or on pack-animals, was usually out of the question, it does not mean that the empire was poor in such resources. Rather, the expense of transport meant that settlement patterns tended to conform to the limits of what was locally available – although this then depended upon a number of variables, such as security, disease and epidemic, climatic fluctuations (drought, flooding) and so on. Only the major cities, with outlets to sea-borne transport, such as Constantinople or Antioch, could extend beyond this.[6] Population density was similarly subject to these considerations.

Resource availability affected directly the distribution of military forces, of course: where local resources were inadequate, or where the presence of soldiers posed a clear threat to the livelihood of a tax-paying population (and where this was perceived), supplies had to be brought in, at considerable expense, from further afield. Hence Justinian's establishment of the *Quaestura exercitus*, which provided the Danubian forces, by sea, with supplies from the Aegean islands and western Anatolia; and hence Maurice's ill fated attempts to have the same forces winter across the Danube in hostile territory and away from the stricken and impoverished frontier regions of Illyricum.[7] As we shall see, the provision of supplies for large concentrations of soldiers was always problematic, and the state had to develop new ways of dealing with the difficulties this posed during the seventh century.

The provision of livestock for transport and for military purposes also

70 (1980), 101–25; and for a summary of some aspects of the debate for the period from the fourth to the sixth century, see C.J. Wickham, in *JRS* 78 (1988), 183–93 (review of A. Giardina, ed., *Società romana ed impero tardoantico* III. *Le merci. Gli insediamenti* (Rome and Bari 1986); and the essays in *Hommes et richesses dans l'Empire byzantin* 1: *IV*ᵉ–*VII*ᵉ *siècle* (Paris 1989), and in *The Byzantine and Early Islamic Near East* V: *Trade and exchange in the late antique and early Islamic Near East*, eds. L.A. Conrad, G.R.D. King (Studies in Late Antiquity and Early Islam 1, V. Princeton forthcoming).

[6] Jones, *LRE*, vol. II, pp. 712ff. and map V; pp. 841–7; Haldon, *Some Considerations*, 79–80. For the distribution of cities relative to their geographical hinterland, see Hendy, *Studies*, pp. 78–90 (Balkans) and pp. 90ff. (Anatolia). The technology of agricultural production is equally important in this context, of course, although I will not discuss it in detail here. For good general surveys, see K.D. White, *Agricultural Implements of the Roman World* (Cambridge 1967); K.D. White, *Roman Farming* (London 1970); and esp. A.A.M. Bryer, 'Byzantine agricultural implements: the evidence of medieval illustrations of Hesiod's *Works and Days*', *ABSA* 81 (1986), 45–80. See also Jones, *LRE*, vol. II, pp. 767ff.; Koder, *Der Lebensraum der Byzantiner*, pp. 55–7.

[7] Hendy, *Studies*, p. 404; Jones, *LRE*, vol. I, p. 482, vol. II, pp. 661, 844 (*quaestura exercitus*), 678 (Maurice); see also W.E. Kaegi, jr., *Byzantine Military Unrest 471–843: An Interpretation* (Amsterdam 1981), p. 110.

played a significant role. Mules and horses were crucial to the imperial forces at all times, although little is known of the ways in which they were raised, maintained or supplied. Imperial estates in Asia Minor, particularly in the provinces of Phrygia, Lydia, Asia and Cappadocia, were important in the ninth century and after, as well as in the later Roman period. Both types of animal were raised and, in the ninth and tenth centuries at least, for which the evidence is reasonably clear, the regulations governing their issue were complex and strict. But the state relied heavily from the seventh century, if not already before, on the raising of animals by levy on landowners and estates. From the later seventh century (at the earliest), soldiers supported by state subsidies (fiscal exemptions, for example) of one sort or another, provided their own mounts. Since both horses and donkeys, and consequently mules, were indigenous throughout the empire, this will have been a ready source of such animals in times of need.[8]

Apart from its resources in arable products and livestock, and the derivatives therefrom (leather, horn, glue and felt, as well as food products) the lands of the later Roman state also provided a variety of metal ores, both precious and base. In Anatolia, the Caucasus region and to a degree also the Taurus, along with the eastern Pontus, were sources of gold, silver, lead and iron, as well as copper; in the Balkans, especially in the inner mountain regions, the same ores were to be found. But the evidence is scarce for the Byzantine period proper, and while iron, for example, was certainly extracted from several areas throughout the period with which we are concerned, political control over these areas was often uncertain. The availability of iron for weapons and farming implements may at times have been very problematic; and Byzantine regulations concerning the export and import of gold are to be seen also in this context, as well as in the wider context of international supply and demand in precious metals and the demands of state finance.[9]

Late Roman society presents an often confusing picture of landowners, senators, freedmen, slaves, semi-servile and free peasants, state and Church officials, and soldiers of differing statuses. It is possible to describe

---

[8] For the stud-farms in Cappadocia, see Jones, *LRE*, vol. II, p. 768; for imperial stud-farms in Asia, Phrygia and Lydia in the eighth century, see J.F. Haldon, *Byzantine Praetorians: An Administrative, Institutional and Social Survey of the Opsikion and Tagmata, c. 580–900* (Poikila Byzantina III Bonn 1984), p. 597 and n. 988 (also for raising animals through compulsory levies in the same period). Note also Hendy, *Studies*, pp. 311, 610–12.

[9] The most accessible general surveys are those of Lilie, *Die byzantinische Reaktion*, pp. 255ff. with literature and esp. the statistical chart at pp. 258–62; and Sp. Vryonis, jr., 'The question of the Byzantine mines', *Speculum* 37 (1962), 1–17. See on later supplies for the army Haldon, *Byzantine Praetorians*, p. 321 and n. 978 (pp. 593–4). For late Roman sources and evidence, Jones, *LRE*, vol. II, pp. 838–9. On gold see most recently Hendy, *Studies*, pp. 257ff.; and Koder, *Der Lebensraum der Byzantiner*, pp. 59–61.

this picture in several different ways, and each of these will have a certain validity according to the purpose of the description. The most obvious approach is to begin from the sources themselves, and to see how these different groups were described in juridical terms, in the legal sources, for example. What definitions are used, how are these related to one another and how are they related to the laws of property, the functioning of Church and state administration, and to the emperor. Another approach would be to look at the relationship of the various groups within society to land and to property, and the ways in which these relationships determined their status. These two approaches are, of course, quite compatible, indeed necessarily so if we are to have any chance of understanding how the society actually functioned.[10]

In the following pages, I will look at the general shape of the late Roman social formation and at the contradictions and tensions within it which provide the foundation for the developments of the seventh century.

The state itself was a complex structure of interlocking administrative functions whose primary purpose, as it had developed over the preceding centuries, was to defend and where possible extend imperial territory; to provide for the maintenance and equipping of the soldiers and officials of the administration and the imperial household; and to extract the necessary resources in the form of taxation in kind, in cash and in services for the fulfilment of these functions. At its head stood the emperor, the state embodied and, in Christian terms, God's chosen representative on earth. From the point of view of the 'official' ideology of state and Church, the state represented also the realm of the Chosen People on earth, the Christians who had hearkened to the message of Jesus Christ. The emperor, therefore, played a crucial role as leader and guide of this people, as defender of right belief or orthodoxy, as intercessor with Christ for his people and as protector of the rights of Christians everywhere. It was also incumbent upon him, where conditions permitted, to extend the territory of the empire and thus promote the orthodox faith; where physical poli-

[10] The best general survey remains that of Jones, *LRE*; see also F.H. Tinnefeld, *Die frühbyzantinische Gesellschaft. Struktur – Gegensätze – Spannungen* (Munich 1977); and for the fiscal administration of the state, see Hendy, *Studies*. Other accounts from different perspectives include the excellent survey of P. Brown, *The World of Late Antiquity* (London 1971); the essays in A. Momigilano, ed., *The Conflict between Paganism and Christianity in the Fourth Century* (Oxford 1963); A. Piganiol, *L'Empire chrétien* I (325–395). *Histoire romaine*, vol. IV, part 2 (Paris 1947); E. Stein, *Histoire du Bas-Empire*, vol. I (Paris and Bruges 1959 and Amsterdam 1968). Stein's work parallels Jones, *LRE*, but provides a much fuller political history and goes into a number of detailed questions more deeply; see also J. Vogt, *The Decline of Rome* (London 1965) and P. Brown, 'The later Roman empire', in Brown, *Religion and Society in the Age of St Augustine* (London 1972), pp. 46–73.

tical incorporation was impractical, conversion of those outside the bounds of the empire was an alternative strategy.[11]

During the sixth century, the Emperor Justinian had, of all the emperors since the extinction of the Western empire in the later fifth century, been able to put the key elements of that political ideology into effect. The reconquest of North Africa from the heretical Vandals, of Italy from the Ostrogoths (short-lived though these successes ultimately proved to be) and of parts of south-eastern Spain from the Visigoths were symbols of the might of the Roman state and its ruler at their most powerful. They were also clear expressions, and to some degree a vindication, of Roman claims to world empire and to orthodoxy.[12] But they also reflected the different fates of the eastern and the western halves of the empire during the fifth century. The dominant position which the East Roman state enjoyed throughout the sixth century, in spite of the constant conflicts along its frontiers, was a result of very much longer-term developments, just as the political and social structure of the Eastern empire represented the evolution of several centuries. During the fifth century the unified Roman world empire, which stretched from Scotland to the Sahara and from Gibraltar to the Euphrates, was replaced by a polycentric system of barbarian successor kingdoms in the West, facing and contrasting with the cultural and political unity, at least superficially, of the Hellenistic world of the East Roman empire, in which the old order was still represented, however

---

[11] For late Roman imperial ideology, see Jones, *LRE*, vol. I, pp. 321–9; O. Treitinger, *Die oströmische Kaiser- und Reichsidee nach ihrer Gestaltung im höfischen Zeremoniell* (Jena 1938); the essays in H. Hunger, ed., *Das byzantinische Herrscherbild* (Wege der Forschung, vol. CCCXXXXI, Darmstadt 1975); J.F. Haldon, 'Ideology and social change in the seventh century: military discontent as a barometer', *Klio* 68 (1986), 139–90, esp. 139–61; F. Dvornik, *Early Christian and Byzantine Political Philosophy* (2 vols., Washington D.C. 1966), vol. II, pp. 614ff., 652f.; A. Pertusi, 'Insegne del potere sovrano e delegato a Bisanzo e nei paesi di influenza bizantina', in *Simboli e simbologia nell' alto medioevo* (Settimane di Studio del Centro Italiano di Studi sull'alto Medioevo XXIII, Spoleto 1976), pp. 481–563; N.H. Baynes, 'Eusebius and the Christian empire', *AIPHOS* 2 (1934), 13–18 (repr. in Baynes, *Byzantine Studies and Other Essays* (London 1955), pp. 168–72).

[12] See Jones, *LRE*, vol. I, p. 270. But this is not to say that Justinian's reign was free of cultural and ideological conflict and contradictions. On the contrary, while acceptance of the imperial system provided the elements of uniformity and harmony at some levels, there existed a range of critical and oppositional elements which were clearly expressed through the literature of the period. Although such criticism seems to have been limited, on the whole, to literate elements of society, especially among those connected with the administration of the state or the palace (such as Lydus or Procopius, for example), it did on occasion find echoes in popular hostility, as in the Nika riots; or less openly, in the rumours and stories about Justinian being either a secret heretic or indeed a tool of the devil himself. For the best modern account of some of these tendencies, see Cameron, *Procopius*, pp. 242ff.; and the detailed analysis of Chr. Gizewski, *Zur Normativität und Struktur der Verfassungsverhältnisse in der späteren römischen Kaiserzeit* (Münchener Beiträge zur Papyrusforschung und Antiken Rechtsgeschichte LXXI, Munich 1988), pp. 131–47.

dimly. The reasons for the ultimate survival of the eastern half of the empire and the disappearance of the western half are complex and still debated. But the higher degree of urbanisation in the East, its apparently greater resources in both materials and in manpower, its greater agricultural and commercial wealth, its more deep-rooted, albeit very diverse, cultural identity and, not least, the less disruptive and factional effects of the senatorial aristocracy in the government, and on the economy as a whole, must lie at the heart of any answer which we might offer. A more effective bureaucracy, more able efficiently to extract the resources and revenues necessary for the state's survival, was also a fundamental factor. Thanks to its favourable cultural and political situation and a sound economic base, the Eastern empire was able to withstand and to stave off the disasters that befell the West. State unity and political stability were preserved.[13]

It was on this foundation that Justinian was able to launch his massive programme of reconquest. His achievements cannot be denied. The empire extended at the end of his reign once more across the whole Mediterranean; the Church of the Holy Wisdom marks one of the first and greatest achievements of Byzantine art and architecture; the Corpus Iuris Civilis established the basis for the development of European law. The essential prerequisites for these achievements were, as we have seen, the strong economic base of the Eastern empire, the effective repulse of the barbarians to north and west, together with the fragile internal stability of the successor kingdoms. But Justinian cannot be mentioned without reference also to his gifted subordinates and associates – Belisarius, Narses, Tribonian, John the Cappadocian and last, but certainly not least, his consort, the Empress Theodora. Her dubious background, her intrigues and her nepotism, quite apart from her questionable and, indeed, potentially treasonable monophysite tendencies, were enough to inspire the historian Procopius to write one of his most vicious caricatures in the Secret History. But even he could not deny her political insight and ability, nor her

---

[13] The most useful account of these developments from a political history viewpoint is Jones, *LRE*, vol. I, pp. 173ff., esp. also pp. 1025ff.; see also Jones, *The Roman Economy: Studies in Ancient Economic and Administrative History*, ed. P. Brunt (Oxford 1974), esp. chapters 4 ('Over-taxation and the decline of the Roman empire', originally in *Antiquity* 33 (1959), 39–43), 8 ('Taxation in antiquity') and 9 ('Inflation under the Roman empire', originally in *Econ. Hist. Review* 5 (1953), 293–318); and for a useful general survey, P. Anderson, *Passages from Antiquity to Feudalism* (London 1974), pp. 97–103 with literature. See also Brown, *The World of Late Antiquity*, esp. pp. 42–4; and W.H.C. Frend, 'The monks and the survival of the East Roman empire in the fifth century', *Past and Present* 54 (1972), 3–24; and N.H. Baynes, 'The decline of the Roman power in western Europe: some modern explanations', *JRS* 33 (1943), 29–35 (repr. in Baynes, *Byzantine Studies and Other Essays*, pp. 83–96); also E. Stein, 'Paysannerie et grands domaines dans l'empire byzantin', *Recueils de la société Jean Bodin* II: *Le Servage* (Brussels 1959), pp. 129–33.

stubborn determination and pride, a pride which saved the emperor himself and his authority at the height of the Nika riot: 'For one who has been an emperor', she is reported to have said, 'it is unendurable to be a fugitive. May I never be separated from this purple, and may I not live that day on which those who meet me shall not address me as mistress.'[14] Justinian and Theodora are two among many examples of social mobility within late Roman society.[15] Thanks to his uncle Justin (518–27) Justinian received the best of educations and, during the reign of the former, an intimate acquaintance with diplomacy, statecraft and palatine politics. He mastered the intricacies of the bureaucracy with an eye for detail and with great energy. His insistence on determining personally every aspect of state policy, down to the tiniest detail, was even in his own time a legend. He was known as 'the emperor who never sleeps'. He was an autocrat, and he tried to realise the ideals of imperial office and the imperial ideology.[16]

Justinian's great ambition was the *renovatio imperii*, the restoration of the world empire of Rome. The requirements for this task were considerable: the reconquest of lost territories; the establishment of Chalcedonian orthodoxy and religious unity throughout the empire; the reorganisation of the administrative and judicial machinery; a planned economic policy designed to support the increased demands of his military undertakings; and a grand scheme of building and renewal in both civil, ecclesiastical and military spheres. Such policy aims were inevitably quite unrealisable in a number of respects. The partial reorganisation of the administration and the fiscal establishment of the state, the partially successful policy of reconquest, the vast expense of the long-drawn-out wars, especially in Italy, and the partial nature of the building programmes, all point to ultimate failure. The resources available were simply not adequate to the task. Apart from this, the practical realities of sixth-century politics and the actual strengths of the successor kingdoms in the West cannot be ignored. The fundamental principle enunciated from Constantinople, of a single legitimate emperor and empire, was as taken for granted as the notion of a single Christian Church. Even Germanic rulers recognised the emperor at Constantinople as the highest source of legitimacy. But their idea of imperial authority did not involve actual reincorporation into the political

[14] Procopius, *De bello Persico* I, 24.33f. (trans. H.B. Dewing).
[15] Numerous accounts of Justinian's reign have appeared. See in particular Stein, *Bas-Empire*, vol. II, pp. 275–780; and Jones, *LRE*, vol. I, pp. 269–302, for detailed analyses with sources and literature. See also R. Browning, *Justinian and Theodora* (London 1971); B. Rubin, *Das Zeitalter Iustinians* I (Berlin 1960); J.W. Barker, *Justinian and the Later Roman Empire* (Madison 1960).
[16] See, for example, Procopius, *Historia arcana* XII, 27; XIII, 28ff. On Justinian's character and personality see the short account in Stein, *Bas-Empire*, vol. II, pp. 275–83; Jones, *LRE*, vol. I, pp. 269ff.; and M. Maas, *John Lydus and the Roman Past* (London 1992).

Map I The empire in A.D. 565: approximate extent

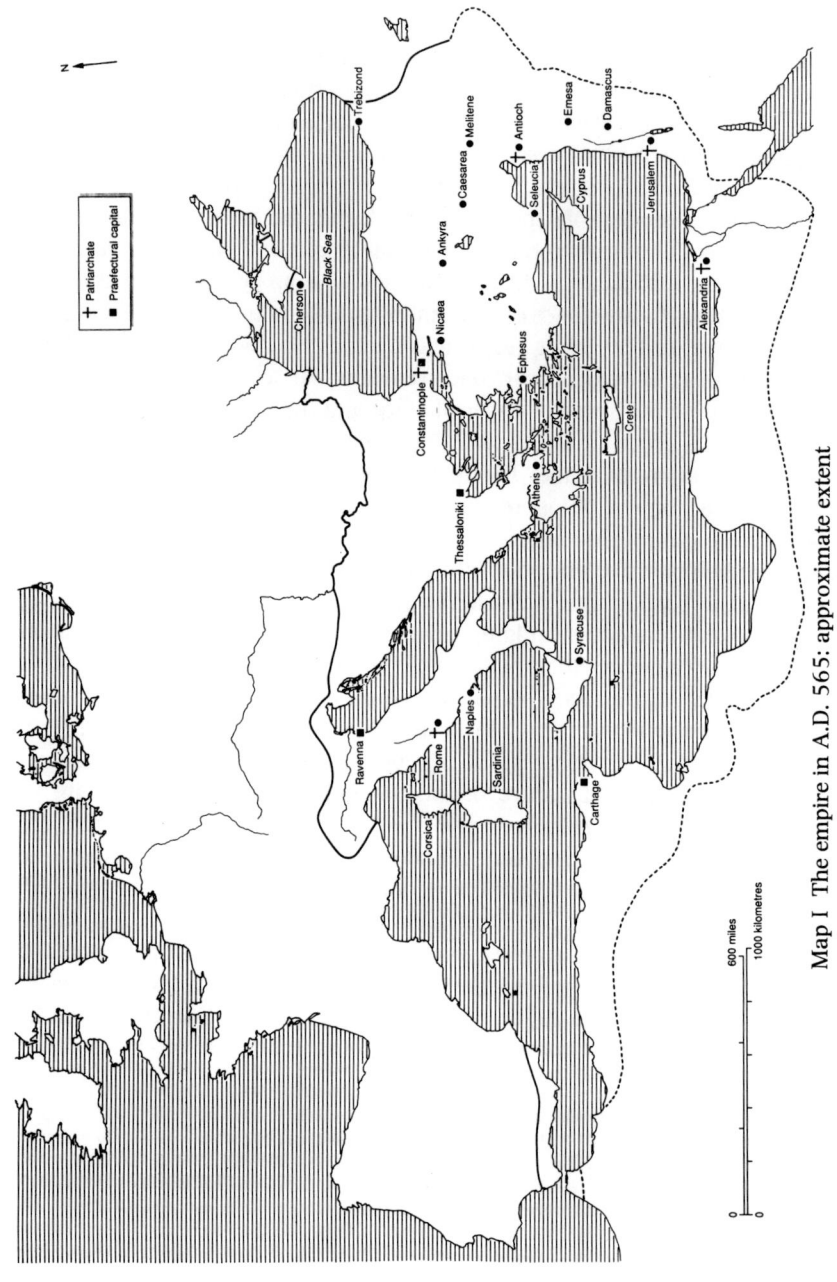

Plate 1.1 Justinian. Copper *follis*

framework of the Roman state, and Justinian's attempts to turn ideological theory into pragmatic politics met with universal, if not always particularly successful, opposition. A second element of the ideological equation was likewise not to be realised in practical terms; for while Justinian saw his role and that of any Roman emperor as entailing the liberation of orthodox subject-populations in the West from the rule of heretics, the practicalities of finance and politics meant that he was unable to put his theory into practice. But his position was made abundantly clear in several contemporary statements, notably at the beginning of the Corpus Iuris Civilis:

> Through the might of God we rule the empire, which was passed on to us by the heavenly majesty; we wage wars with success, secure peace, and we maintain the edifice of the state. We likewise exalt our spirit in contemplation, through the help of the almighty Godhead, so that we place our trust not in our arms, nor in our soldiers, nor yet in our own abilities; but we found all our hopes in the all-seeing protection of the all-highest Trinity alone, from which derive all elements of the Universe which lend order to the whole world.[17]

It was the precarious stability of the successor kingdoms which gave Justinian the opportunity to promote his policy of *renovatio* on the foreign political plane. Both the Vandal and the Ostrogothic kingdoms were rent by actual or latent conflict, and they were in any case unable to offer any co-ordinated opposition to Eastern Roman attack.[18] But the empire faced

[17] Justinian, *Digesta*, 'Constitutio Deo Auctore' (*CIC* I, p. 8).
[18] On the successor kingdoms, see esp. E.A. Thompson, 'The barbarian kingdoms in Gaul and Spain', *Nottingham Medieval Studies* 7 (1963); C.J. Wickham, *Early Medieval Italy*

powers other than the relatively recently formed states of the West. The Sassanid Persian empire presented a constant threat to the provinces of the Roman East. Persian political ideology likewise provided its rulers with an instrument and an excuse for aggression, namely the long-nurtured hope of recovering all the territories which had once belonged to the great empire of the Achaemenids destroyed by Alexander.[19] After many years of relative peace, the reign of Justinian saw an increase in hostilities between the two powers. Chosroes I (531–79), Justinian's contemporary and equal in statecraft and organisational enterprise, pushed through a series of administrative and military reforms that brought the Sassanid state to the height of its power and influence. War broke out in the East in 527, but lasted only briefly until in 532 an 'everlasting' peace was agreed. This was crucial to Justinian's plans, for East Roman resources were not adequate to the task of funding warfare in East and West simultaneously. Roman diplomacy played a crucial role in averting this eventuality – through 'subsidies', tribute, territorial or trading concessions, as well as through espionage, intrigue, the fomenting of unrest among client states and so on. Buffer states and client princes – from the Ghassanids in the Syrian desert to the Christian Armenian principalities in the Caucasus – were supported by border garrisons and settlements and protected the length of the north-eastern and eastern frontiers, from the Black Sea down to the Arabian desert. But the 'eternal' peace did not last long: in 540 renewed Sassanid incursions took place, aimed primarily at extracting tribute and booty from the cities of the eastern provinces. Those that refused to pay up – such as Antioch – were sacked. Chosroes was eventually bought off in 545; and a second truce was signed in 551, although desultory conflicts continued in the northern zone (where Romans and Persians were keen to control the Armenian principalities and the districts of Lazica and Suania, out of both strategic interest and on account of the mineral wealth of the region) until in 561 a ten-year truce was arranged. This was not to last much longer than Justinian himself.

The course of the wars of reconquest is too well known to need more than a brief survey here.[20] Between 533 and 534 Vandal Africa was

(London 1981); J.M. Wallace-Hadrill, *The Barbarian West 400–1000* (Oxford 1966); and J.M. Wallace-Hadrill, *The Long-Haired Kings* (London 1962); M. Wes, *Das Ende des Kaisertums im Westen des römischen Reiches* (The Hague 1967); E.A. Thompson, *The Goths in Spain* (Oxford 1969); P.A.B. Llewellyn, *Rome in the Dark Ages* (London 1971). There is, of course, a much wider literature, but further bibliography will be found in these works. See also C. Courtois, *Les Vandales et l'Afrique* (Paris 1955), pp. 353ff.

[19] See A. Christensen, *L'Iran sous les Sassanides*, second edn (Copenhagen and Paris 1944); and R. Frye, *The Heritage of Persia* (London 1963) for a general survey.

[20] Jones, *LRE*, vol. I, pp. 271–8, 287–94; and Stein, *Bas-Empire*, vol. II, pp. 283–96, 311–18, 339–68, 485ff., 560ff., provide detailed narrative accounts. See further J.B. Bury, *The Later Roman Empire 395–565* (2 vols., London 1923), pp. 124ff.

returned to imperial control. But these wealthy provinces were to prove almost as difficult a problem as were the Vandal rulers who had been overthrown. Constant attacks from the Berber tribes in the interior meant constant military preparedness, the construction of forts and a considerable drain on resources.

In 533 Belisarius began the reconquest of Italy from the Ostrogoths. Sicily fell quickly. But the Romans underestimated both Ostrogothic opposition and the disastrous effects of continuous warfare on the Italian countryside and population; apart from this, the constant need for troops on the eastern front, deliberate underfunding and undermanning by Justinian for fear of rebellion by over-successful generals, particularly Belisarius, and lack of resources and irregular pay for the troops meant that the war dragged on until the 550s. Indeed, the last Gothic garrisons surrendered or were destroyed only in 554. Simultaneously with these last actions, Roman forces wrested control of south-east Spain from the Visigoths (in 552), thereby increasing the empire's strategic control of the western Mediterranean, but extending also the limited resources at its disposal.[21]

A possible third front in the Balkans did not materialise until towards the end of Justinian's reign, in 559 and after.[22] The raids of Slavs and of Turkic peoples across the Danube, which threatened Constantinople itself, seemed to be little more than short-term problems. The arrival of the Avars north of the Danube could not yet be perceived for the threat it was to become. But the regular withdrawal of troops from Thrace and Illyricum to serve on the eastern front or in Italy or Africa left these areas without adequate protection. In consequence, the whole Balkan region, from the Adriatic to the Black Sea and south to Thessaloniki and even Constantinople, was subject to regular devastation – the economic consequences for the state are apparent.[23]

For contemporaries, however, whatever the criticisms voiced by Procopius or a faction of the senate at Constantinople, the brilliance of Justinian's achievements and the scope of his programme concealed the discrepancy between reality and ideological wish-fulfilment.[24] The real

---

[21] See P. Goubert, 'Byzance et l'Espagne wisigothique', REB 2 (1944), 5–78; P. Goubert, 'L'Administration de l'Espagne byzantine I', REB 3 (1945), 127–42; 'II', REB 4 (1946), 71–134. See also F. Görres, 'Die byzantinischen Besitzungen an den Küsten des spanisch-westgotischen Reiches', BZ 16 (1907), 515–38.
[22] See, for example, Stein, Bas-Empire, vol. II, pp. 535–40.
[23] See Stein's account, Bas-Empire, vol. II, pp. 521–5, 541–5; Jones, LRE, vol. I, pp. 293.; Obolensky, The Byzantine Commonwealth, pp. 44ff.; G. Ostrogorsky, Geschichte des byzantinischen Staates (Munich 1963), pp. 68–70.
[24] See F. Tinnefeld, Kategorien der Kaiserkritik in der byzantinischen Historiographie (Munich 1971), pp. 191ff., and J. Irmscher, 'Justinianbild und Justiniankritik im frühen Byzanz', in

situation became clear to most only during the reigns of his successors, who had to struggle with a situation they had inherited and on the whole did so with only limited success. The reconquest of the West had far-reaching consequences for the history of Western Europe and Italy as well as for Byzantium. The continued Byzantine presence in Italy, for example, the destruction of the Ostrogothic kingdom, the arrival of the Lombards (which the Byzantines, to a certain extent, brought upon themselves), all contributed towards the development of the medieval papacy. Most importantly for Byzantium, however, the state which Justinian bequeathed to his successors had only limited resources to cope with the enormous problems it now faced in its over-extended imperial possessions. It was inevitable that the structure should collapse at some point.

The state and its apparatus

Justinian's internal policies were, no less than his reconquests, determined largely by his ideology of renewal. But behind the façade of world conquest lay considerable social and economic difficulties. The Nika riot in 532, whatever its immediate background and the political motives of those members of the senate who tried to use the hippodrome factions for their own ends, is evidence of longer-term and deeper-seated social discontent and alienation.[25] Justinian was certainly aware of some of these problems. His intention was to reform the administration, strengthen the rural economy and establish unity of belief. As his many *novellae* and *edicta* illustrate, he knew of the failings and conflicts within the administrative machinery of the state. He clearly felt that part of his task lay in the establishment of a just society for his subjects, a task with which he had been privileged by God.[26] But he did no more than reform – the system of government and administration in all its complexity and with all its weaknesses was the system he inherited from the past. His task was merely to make it function properly, justly, efficiently; not to change it in any fundamental way.

The late Roman state had the structure of an autocratic absolutism, a structure which had evolved gradually during the long history of the principate, culminating with the establishment of the dominate under Diocletian and his successors. Nothing, according to Justinian's express

---

H. Köpstein and F. Winkelmann, eds., *Studien zum 7. Jahrhundert in Byzanz. Probleme der Herausbildung des Feudalismus* (*BBA* XXXXVII, Berlin 1976), pp. 131–42.

[25] E. Patlagean, *Pauvreté économique et pauvreté sociale à Byzance, 4e–7e siècles* (Paris 1977), pp. 215ff.; Stein, *Bas-Empire*, vol. II, pp. 449ff. for the Nika riot itself.

[26] Jones, *LRE*, vol. I, pp. 269–70; Stein, *Bas-Empire*, vol. II, pp. 277ff.; and esp. M. Maas, 'Roman history and Christian ideology in Justinianic reform legislation', *DOP* 40 (1986), 17–31.

view, was greater or more sacred on earth than the imperial majesty.[27] Titles, symbols of office and the imperial court ceremonial served to express and to enhance the God-given nature of imperial authority and power. The ideological system in which the formal political system was given its rationale had grown slowly out of a synthesis of Christian and Roman imperial traditions, both in their turn determined by the philosophical and symbolic traditions of the late ancient world. The 'objective idealism' of late ancient philosophical thought, which can be followed in the thinking of Plotinus and Philon through to the hierarchical world-view of Pseudo-Dionysius, together with the conflict between both Christian theology and Hellenistic philosophy on the one hand, and within the Church itself on the other, constitute the background and determining context for this evolution.[28] Court, civil administration, justice and the army depended upon the emperor, from whom they received their legitimation and their competence. The political system, with it formal ideology and its assumption of God-given jurisdiction provided a focus for unity in a culturally, linguistically and economically diverse world, in a way that few autocracies have succeeded in doing.[29] The 'price' of this, of course, lay in an absolute political orthodoxy which permitted no open criticism of the system or its principles as such, and which also involved a far-reaching state intervention in economic and demographic matters in the interests of the maintenance of resources and the ability of the state to defend its territories and revenues.

The complex administrative establishment, together with the military establishment and the armies, constituted the heart of the state structure.[30] The system was based upon the principle of centralisation, of a

[27] *CJ* I, 14.12.
[28] See especially the discussion with literature of Averil Cameron, 'Images of authority: élites and icons in late sixth-century Byzantium', *Past and Present* 84 (1979), 3–35, see 6ff.; also O. Kresten, 'Iustinianos I, der "Christusliebende" Kaiser', *Römische Historische Mitteilungen* 21 (1979), 83–109; S.S. Averincev, in chapter 2 of Z. Udal'cova, ed., *Kul'tura Vizantii, IV-pervaja polovina VII v.* (Moscow 1984); and esp. J. Shiel, *Greek Thought and the Rise of Christianity* (London 1968), pp. 18ff., 39–89.
[29] See the discussion and comments of C. Capizzi, 'Potere e ideologia imperiale da Zenone a Giustiniano (474–527)', in *L'Imperatore Giustiniano, storia e mito*, ed. G.G. Archi (Circolo Toscano di Diritto Romano e Storia del Diritto V, Milan 1978), pp. 3–35 with further literature.
[30] The best detailed surveys of the administrative and fiscal structures of the late Roman state can be found in Stein, *Bas-Empire*, vol. II, esp. pp. 419ff., 735ff.; Jones, *LRE*, vol. I, pp. 278–85, with 321ff., a general analysis of the state's government and administrative structures from the fourth to the sixth centuries; see further Hendy, *Studies*, pp. 371ff. and notes 1 and 2 with literature; A.E.R. Boak, *The Master of Offices in the Later Roman and Byzantine Empire* (New York 1919), in A.E.R. Boak and J.E. Dunlop, *Two Studies in Late Roman and Byzantine Administration* (New York 1924); M. Clauss, *Der Magister Officiorum in der Spätantike (4.–6. Jahrhundert): das Amt und sein Einfluss auf die kaiserliche Politik* (Munich 1980).

division between civil and military spheres of competence, and of a meritocracy in its staffing. Its officials underwent a regulated training (although in the very loosest sense), and its personnel occupied posts which were arranged in a fixed hierarchy of authority and status, with exact functions, competences and duties attached to each position. The sixth-century writer John Lydus has left us a vivid picture of the operation of this system, of its evolution according to contemporary understanding, and of the *esprit de corps* (or lack of it) among its members. His writings represent probably the best and most illuminating examples of an insider's view on the Roman state administrative machinery, with all its strengths and weaknesses, and they provide invaluable evidence for the ways in which the whole structure actually worked.[31]

The state and the Church

Justinian's interest in religious and Church affairs forms an integral part of his approach to governing the empire. The successes of the state depended, as we have seen, upon God's favour and, therefore, upon the strict observation of right belief in all senses: whether in the administration of Church and clergy, or in the observance of the Chalcedonian creed and the application of the principles enunciated through it. Unorthodox belief was a direct challenge to the emperor's authority and position, as well as to God; it was likewise a threat to the stability of the state.[32] Throughout his reign, Justinian attempted to bring conformity of belief and creed to the empire, both by persuasion as well as by force – conversion, threat of permanent exile, death. Clashes of opinion were often resolved ultimately in the crudest of ways, as was demonstrated in the so-called Three Chapters controversy, in which Justinian eventually got his way through bullying and bribery.[33] The greatest problem, however, one which no emperor succeeded in solving, was that of the Eastern monophysites, who formed a large part of the populations of Eygpt and Syria, but existed throughout the east, and whose adherence to their beliefs constituted a direct challenge to imperial authority. Persecutions and forced conversions failed dismally to resolve the issue, and it ceased to be directy relevant only when

---

[31] *Ioannis Lydi De Magistratibus Populi Romani Libri Tres*, ed. R. Wünsch (Leipzig 1903); and the commentary of T.F. Carney, *Bureaucracy in Traditional Society: Romano-Byzantine Bureaucracies Viewed from Within* (Lawrence Kan 1971).

[32] See, in general, Jones, *LRE*, vol. I, pp. 285–7; Stein, *Bas-Empire*, vol. II, pp. 369–402, 623–83 for a detailed treatment.

[33] See esp. Stein, *Bas-Empire*, vol. II, pp. 632ff.; Jones, *LRE*, vol. I, pp. 296–7; D.J. Constantelos, 'Justinian and the Three Chapters controversy', *Greek Orthodox Theological Review* 8 (1962–3).

those territories were conquered by Islam in the middle of the seventh century.[34]

Justinian's interest and concern, while it may have been more intense than that of many emperors, is certainly not to be seen as unusual, however. For it is worth emphasising that it was only in and through the vocabulary of Christianity, which described the 'symbolic universe' of the East Roman world, that Justinian and his contemporaries were able to apprehend their world and act in and upon it. Their symbolic universe – their 'thought-world' – was by definition a 'religious' one, in which human experience and perception of their world, both secular and spiritual, had necessarily to be expressed through this religious vocabulary. Politics are thus always 'religious', and religion is always 'political', however implicit this may be; and for a Roman emperor, religious matters were as much a key element of the everyday political and civil administration of the empire as were the affairs of the fisc or the imperial armies. It is important to stress this perhaps rather obvious point, since it is all too easy to impose a division between 'religious' and 'political' or 'secular' in modern terms which bears little or no relation to either the theory or the practice and understanding of late Roman or Byzantine culture, and serves only to obfuscate the underlying structures of its belief and practice.

The 'Corpus Iuris Civilis'

Only in the field of the law did Justinian succeed in carrying out one of his major projects. The codification of the civil law of the empire, compiled in the years 528–33, replaced all earlier codifications. The first section, the *Codex Iustinianus*, contained all imperial edicts and promulgations from Hadrian to 533 which were regarded by the compilers as relevant; Justinian's promulgations after this date are separately collected in the volume of *Novellae Constitutiones*, drawn up after his reign. The second section, the Digest or Pandects, consisted of a revised selection of comments from Roman jurists, intended to complement the codex; while the third section, the *Institutiones*, represented a sort of handbook and reference work for the

---

[34] The best brief survey of religious politics, the relationship between state and Church, and the role of the emperor in this sphere is to be found in F. Winkelmann, *Die östlichen Kirchen in der Epoche der christologischen Auseinandersetzungen (5. bis 7. Jahrhundert)* (Kirchengeschichte in Einzeldarstellungen I/6, Berlin 1980), esp. pp. 103ff. Note also W.H.C. Frend, 'Old and new in Rome in the age of Justinian', in D. Baker, ed., *The Relation between East and West in the Middle Ages* (Edinburgh 1973), pp. 11–28; also J. Meyendorff, 'Justinian, the empire and the Church', *DOP* 22 (1968).

imperial jurists who formed the backbone of the central administrative apparatus.[35]

The *Corpus Iuris Civilis* embodies in many respects the ideal world which Justinian sought to achieve through his expansionist and reformist policies. The continued emphasis on the absolute power of the emperor, holding his authority through God's will and grace – as well as the stress on the Christian idea of the all-powerful ruler within yet prescribing the law, in contrast to the classical tradition – is a clear demonstration of this. In particular, the theories underlying much of Justinian's reforming and administrative activity stand out. It is perhaps ironic that the theory of *renovatio* survived in a practical form to influence the development of European legal and constitutional history so deeply, yet its political results failed to survive much more than a generation after the death of one of its most successful exponents.

Social structure and economic relations

As has been stated many times, the basis of the later Roman state and its economy was agricultural production. The greater part of the population were rural, agricultural and represented a subsistence peasant economy. Something like ninety-five per cent of the state's income was probably derived from tax or other expropriations on the land. Agriculture was the basis of state, Church and private wealth. Since the costs of inland transport were high, trade in agricultural produce, except on the most highly localised basis, was virtually non-existent. The only exception was for the state-funded movement of grain, for example. Otherwise, local self-sufficiency was the rule, and only where cheaper forms of transport were available and a reasonable livelihood based on market exchange could be assured was commercial monoculture practised – the production of oil or wine, for example, where access to sea-borne trade was easy. It is in this respect that the importance of the North African export of oil and wine, for example, must be taken into account, as well as that of Egyptian goods accompanying the state-funded shipping of grain to Constantinople.[36]

---

[35] For general and more detailed treatments, see Jones, *LRE*, vol. I, pp. 278ff. and Stein, *Bas-Empire*, vol. II, pp. 402–17; and esp. P.E. Pieler, 'Byzantinische Rechtsliteratur', in Hunger, *Profane Literatur*, vol. II, pp. 343–480, see 411ff.

[36] Jones, *LRE*, vol. I, p. 465; vol. II, pp. 769–70 for tax; and on the agricultural population, *ibid.*, pp. 767–823. For transport and trade, *ibid.*, pp. 827ff., and Hendy, *Studies*, pp. 554ff. For the Mediterranean trade in wine, oil and related products, see note 5 above. There is a huge literature on the subject of late Roman social-economic structures. General surveys in Jones, *LRE* and Tinnefeld, *Die frühbyzantinische Gesellschaft*, pp. 18–58 (landowners and agricultural producers) and 59–99 (the senate); see also Stein, *Bas-Empire*, vol. II. For a more recent Marxist assessment, see G.E.M. de Ste Croix, *The Class Struggle in the Ancient Greek World* (Oxford 1981), pp. 453ff. Debate on the role and

The class structure of the late Roman social formation is, in spite of the often confusing array of contemporary technical terms, reasonably clear. The contrast between *humiliores* and *potentiores*, however nuanced by social change or legal context, appears throughout the legislation of the fifth and sixth centuries.[37] The dominant social group was represented by a numerically relatively small class of land-owning magnates, for the most part members of the senatorial aristocracy. Together with the Church, which by Justinian's time had become a substantial landowner, and the fisc – which in the form of imperial and state lands was also a major landowner – this class exercised a more or less complete control over the means of production of the empire. In opposition stood the vast mass of the rural and urban populations, the greater part of which stood in relationships of varying degrees of dependence or subservience to the landowners,

decline of slavery as a significant feature of Roman and late Roman relations of production, the development of the colonate, of large senatorial estates or *latifundia*, and the role of the state in the economy, has been lively, in both Soviet (and Eastern European) and Western (both Marxist and non-Marxist) historiography. Soviet historians in particular have been keen to emphasise the causes of the decline of the slave mode of production, the rise of the colonate and dependent peasantry, and of feudal or proto-feudal relations of production in the Roman period (second to fourth centuries and beyond), although the debate within Soviet historiography has itself been lively – one school of thought preferring to locate the origins of feudal relations of production in the later Roman period, another placing it later, in the Byzantine period proper (ninth and tenth centuries). For representative surveys, see E.M. Štaermann, *Krizis rabovladel'českovo stroya v zapadnykh provinciyakh Rimskoi imperii* (Moscow 1957) (German trans. W. Seyforth, *Die Krise der Sklavenhalterordnung im Westen des römischen Reiches* (Berlin 1947)); Štaermann, *Krizis antičnoi kul'tury* (Moscow 1975), arguing for a synthesis of Roman and Germanic cultural forms and social relations. See also the literature cited in Haldon, *Some considerations*, 99 and n. 59; and esp. Z.V. Udal'cova and K.A. Osipova, 'Tipologičeskie osobennosti feodalizma v Vizantii', in *Problemy social'noi struktury i ideologii srednevekovogo obščestva* I (Leningrad 1974), pp. 4–28. This perspective has been criticised on the one hand by those historians who reject the notion of synthesis altogether, such as M.Ya. Siuziumov, 'Zakonomernii perehod k feodalizmu i sintez', *Antičnaya drevnost'i srednie veka* 12 (1975), 33–53, and by those who see the structural impasse between ancient slavery and developing feudal relations as being resolved by synthesis in the West and by the continued existence of the centralised state in the East, such as G.G. Litavrin, *Vizantiiskoe obščestvo i gosudarstvo v X-XI vv* (Moscow 1977), and esp. A.P. Každan, *Vizantiiskaya kul'tura* (Moscow 1968) (German trans. *Byzanz und seine Kultur* (Berlin 1973)). For the Western literature, see esp. M.I. Finley, *Ancient Slavery and Modern Ideology* (London 1980); Finley, *The Ancient Economy* (London 1973); R. Remondon, *La Crise de l'empire romain* (Paris 1964); the essays of M. Bloch, *Slavery and Serfdom in the Middle Ages*, Eng. trans. W.R. Beer (Berkeley 1975); K. Hopkins, *Conquerors and Slaves* (Cambridge 1978); M. Mazza, *Lotte sociali e restaurazione autoritaria*, second edn (Bari 1973), esp. pp. 119–216; Anderson, *Passages from Antiquity to Feudalism*, pp. 18–103; and the critiques of P.Q. Hirst, 'The uniqueness of the West', *Economy and Society* 4 (1975), 446–75 and C.J. Wickham, 'The other transition: from the ancient world to feudalism', *Past and Present* 103 (1984), 3–36; see also O. Patterson, 'On slavery and slave formations', *New Left Review* 117 (Sept.-Oct. 1979), 31–67; and de Ste Croix, *The Class Struggle in the Ancient Greek World*, esp. pp. 205ff. and 453ff.

[37] Patlagean, *Pauvreté économique*, pp. 11ff. with literature, discusses the terms and the changes in meaning they underwent during the fourth to the sixth centuries.

whether institutional or individual. Of the agricultural population, the great majority were *coloni* of varying status, tied in a more or less rigid way to their holdings. Communities of free peasants continued to exist, often in substantial numbers, especially in certain regions of the Balkans, Anatolia and Syria. During the fourth, and particularly the fifth, centuries many specific groups within the empire's population had been incorporated into what has been termed the *Zwangswirtschaft* of the later Roman empire, that is, the compulsory tying of individuals according to their status and occupation to their functions. This affected particularly the urban curial class, soldiers, members of some trading and craft occupations, who became hereditary members of their various *collegia* or corporations. And although the state seems in fact to have had only limited success in making these restrictions and regulations work (for it is doubtful whether the legislation, which seems anyway to have been intended for the West more often than the East, could be effectively applied outside the state apparatus itself) they have reinforced the impression that late Roman society was tantamount to a caste system, a position which has now generally been abandoned.[38] Certainly by Justinian's reign some of the better-known fixed relationships – in the army, for example – seem to have been dissolved or were ignored by the state. There is no evidence, for example, that the *comitatenses* or field troops were still conscripted on this basis; although those in the *limitanei*, where service in the unit was still viewed as a privilege, were.[39]

The taxes and revenues needed by the state were extracted in a variety of ways. Extraordinary levies on foodstuffs or raw materials formed an important element, especially in respect of the supplying and provisioning of garrisons or of troops on the move. Similarly, corvées or compulsory labour duties might be imposed on a community (and taken into account in the regular tax-assessment) for the maintenance of bridges, roads and so on. But the chief form of revenue extraction, carried out by officials of the prefecture at the provincial tier, was the land-tax, based on the amount and nature of the land, and the number of persons cultivating it. Referred to in general terms in its late third- and fourth-century form as the *annona* or, on the principle of assessment (area of land, number of persons farming it) as the *capitatio/iugatio* assessment, this was an inclusive tax to which all cultivated land was subject. The principles of assessment were straightforward. A unit of land, or *iugum*, was taxed only if a corresponding unit of

---

[38] See Jones, *LRE*, vol. I, pp. 68–70, vol. II, pp. 861ff., and also Jones, 'The caste system in the later Roman empire', *Eirene* 8 (1970), 79–96 (repr. in *The Roman Economy*, pp. 396–418, with emendations and additions), and R. MacMullen, 'Social mobility and the Theodosian code', *JRS* 54 (1964), 49ff.

[39] J.F. Haldon, *Recruitment and Conscription in the Byzantine Army c. 550–950: A Study on the Origins of the stratiotika ktemata*, in SBÖ 357 (Vienna 1979), pp. 20–8.

manpower (*caput*) was available to cultivate it. Since both *iugum* and *caput* were, in the first instance, notional units of assessment, and *caput*, indeed, signified originally merely the liability for assessment, the two were sometimes used interchangeably. Contrary to the views of some historians, however, neither *caput* nor *capitatio* denoted a poll tax, as has now been convincingly demonstrated.[40] The system was not very flexible, and a number of measures had to be introduced to deal with the problems which resulted from demographic decline and consequent desertion of agricultural land. The slow process of binding the agricultural labour force to the land was one solution. Another was to make individuals and communities collectively responsible for adjacent land or land within their fiscal census district, and consequently for the revenues due from such land, if it were deserted or abandoned. This system, known as *adiectio sterilium*, or ἐπιβολὴ (τῶν ἀπόρων) in Greek, was increasingly invoked as the sixth century progressed, so that Procopius claims (albeit with some exaggeration) that the landowners of the empire were entirely ruined as a result.[41]

Capitatio/iugatio assessment also provided the basis for the calculation of the rate of conscription of peasants for the army. By the middle of the fifth century, and certainly throughout most of the sixth century, the imposition was commuted into a tax payable in gold, although it was not necessarily always collected in this form. It was assessed and collected from all free owners of land, whatever their wealth or status. Landlords were held to be fiscally responsible for their slaves and for the adscripted or semi-free tenants on their land (on these categories, see below). Increasingly, as the colonate spread, and as more and more agricultural communities became tenants on larger estates, tax was paid to the landlord first, from whom the state then collected it. During the sixth century, the state regularly delegated some of its functions to private persons, who were expected to carry out the appropriate tasks. The collection of the revenues due from large estates seems regularly to have been attributed to the landlords of such properties, including even the lands of the Church. Similarly, there is some evidence to suggest that soldiers were often

---

[40] The debate is complex because the technical terminology of the codes is often obscure and contradictory. See W. Goffart, *'Caput' and Colonate: Towards a History of Late Roman Taxation* (*Phoenix* suppl. vol. XII, Toronto 1974) for a detailed discussion. While I do not accept all of Goffart's conclusions, he quite rightly questions the traditional interpretation of *caput/capitatio* as a revised equivalent of an early poll-tax.

[41] See Procopius, *Historia arcana* XXIII, 15–16; and the description and analysis of Jones, *LRE*, vol. II, pp. 813–15. Fiscal responsibility was allocated by Justinian's time on the basis of the land belonging, or having belonged, originally to a single owner or to the same census district (ἐπιβολὴ ὁμοδούλων and ἐπιβολὴ ὁμοκήνσων respectively). See esp. Justinian, *Nov.* 128, 7 and 8 (a. 545). For the technical terms see Jones, *LRE*, vol. II, p. 815 n. 105; M. Kaplan, 'Les Villageois aux premiers siècles byzantins (VIème-Xème siècle): une société homogène?', *BS* 43 (1982), 202–17, see 206f.

maintained on a similar basis, their supplies and costs being deducted from the tax revenue collected by the landlord responsible for the lands or districts in which they were based. Other taxes – on trade and on commercial activity – brought in only very limited revenue. As we have seen, Jones' calculation of something like ninety-five per cent of total state income from the land, while it may only be an approximate guess, gives some idea of the dominant and crucial role of agricultural production to the late Roman state.[42]

The economic class-divisions within late Roman society are not difficult to perceive. In contrast to the vast mass of the population, peasants carrying on a subsistence agriculture (or, in coastal regions, for example, fishing and related activities) with limited freedom of movement and with limited rights of alienation in respect of their holdings, whether subject directly to the fisc or to their landlords, stood the dominant class of landed magnates and the service elite of the state bureaucracy, alongside the Church and the state itself. The cities, while they certainly contained a large population of free persons, offered only limited opportunities to those of humble social origins, chiefly as craftsmen, occasional labourers or as beggars – which, as in any pre-industrial social formation with a relatively advanced social division of labour, was the regular occupation of a number of people. The one obvious route out of poverty was to enter at some level or other the state apparatus or the Church; or to win a position in the retinue of a powerful person. And it is worth making the point here that while a measure of social mobility did exist in late Roman and early Byzantine society, it has often been given more prominence than it really deserves: the individuals who succeeded in rising to positions of power and authority received the attentions of their contemporaries precisely because they were exceptions. Their total number is tiny. Late Roman society represents a social formation in which class divisions were otherwise fairly firmly drawn, and in which access to power through wealth and state service excluded the great mass of the population from anything but the subsistence economy of the peasantry.

It must be said, however, that the oppression of the agricultural population and indeed the polarisation of interests between exploiting and exploited classes was much clearer in the West than in the East. Again, the

[42] In general, see Jones, *LRE*, vol. I, pp. 449–62, 464–9; vol. II, pp. 773–5; Jones, 'Capitatio and iugatio', *JRS* 47 (1957), 88–94 (repr. in *The Roman Economy*, pp. 280ff.); Goffart, *'Caput' and Colonate*; A. Cerati, *Caractère annonaire et assiette de l'impôt foncier au bas-empire* (Paris 1974); the essays in C.E. King, ed., *Imperial Revenue, Expenditure and Monetary Policy in the Fourth Century A.D.* (BAR Int. Series 76, Oxford 1980); Stein, *Bas-Empire*, vol. I, pp. 74ff., 441–3 and note 44. See also the comments of A. Guillou, 'Transformations des structures socio-économiques dans le monde byzantin du VIe au VIIIe siècle', *ZRVI* 19 (1980), 71–8, see 72ff. with sources and literature cited.

reasons for this are complex and have received much attention. Peasant revolts in the West in the fifth century are nowhere paralleled in the East and do seem to reflect the higher degree of impoverishment and oppression of the Western colonate, both at the hands of their landlords and of the state. The Eastern landed elite, powerful as it was, never dominated both urban and rural life and economic relations to the extent that seems to have occurred in the West; power in the East remained more diffuse, the state always managed to retain an effective fiscal control, and the rural population, while oppressed and exploited, remained both more diverse and heterogeneous in social and economic terms than in the West.[43] This is not to say that peasant opposition to the state or to private oppression was absent in the East. On the contrary, the existence of the so-called *Scamares* in the Balkans, for example, in an economic and physical context not too different from that of the Gallic *Bacaudae* (that is, state oppression together with military and economic insecurity on a generalised scale), is illustrative. Brigandage as a widespread form of communal opposition to both state and private oppression is well attested during the sixth century in Lycaonia, Phrygia, Pisidia and the Pontus.[44] While it may not reflect a direct reaction to the oppression of a landlord, it does demonstrate the fact that many communities regarded acceptance of state authority and the consequent fiscal demands as unacceptably oppressive.[45]

Justinian's successors

The contradictions and weaknesses within this vast social and political structure were made apparent by the last years of Justinian's reign and during the reigns of his successors Justin II (565–78), Tiberius Constantine (578–82), Maurice (582–602) and Phocas (602–10).[46] In the first place, the conflict of interest between Chalcedonian orthodoxy, represented by the state along with the Western and Anatolian provinces, and the monophysitism of a large part of the population of Syria, Egypt and eastern

[43] See esp. E.A. Thompson, 'Peasant revolts in late Roman Gaul and Spain', *Past and Present* 2 (1952), 11–23 (repr. in M.I. Finley, ed., *Studies in Ancient Society* (London 1974), 304–20); de Ste Croix, *The Class Struggle in the Ancient Greek World*, pp. 474ff., a good general survey of peasant and 'popular' opposition and of the degree of exploitation of the rural population. See also note 4 above.
[44] See Justinian, *Nov.* 24, 1 (a. 535, for Pisidia); *Nov.* 25, 1 (a. 535, for Lycaonia); *Edict.* 8, proem.; 3. 1 (a. 548, for Pontus). Note also Justinian, *Nov.* 30, 7.1 (a. 536, for Cappadocia).
[45] On the Scamares, see esp. A.D. Dmitrev, 'Dviženie Skamarov', *VV* 5 (1952), 3–14; Jones, *LRE*, vol. I, p. 294; vol. II, p. 656 on Anatolia.
[46] For the political history of the period, see Jones, *LRE*, vol. I, pp. 303–17; Ostrogorsky, *Geschichte*, pp. 66–72; *Cambridge Medieval History*, vol. IV, revised edn (2 parts, Cambridge 1966), I, pp. 28–30; P. Goubert, *Byzance avant l'Islam* (3 vols., Paris 1951–65); and Stein, *Studien*.

Plate 1.2 Justin II. Gold *solidus*

Anatolia, was brought into the open more clearly than ever as the ultra-orthodox Justin II – quite 'correctly' adhering to fundamental elements within the imperial ideology – tried to impose orthodoxy through mass persecutions and forced conversions.[47] Under Justinian, especially while Theodora lived, imperial policy had been less strongly delineated, although formal state opposition to monophysitism was quite clear. Now the conflict broke out into the open again, revealing how precarious the ideological unity of the state actually was.

In the second place, Justin's notion of his position and that of the empire failed to take into account the real threat posed by the Avars in the north and the Persians in the East. In his haughty refusal to continue paying the subsidies to the Avar khagan which Justinian had consented to, he earned the hostility of a powerful and extremely dangerous foe who, at the head of large numbers of migrating Slav communities, was over the following forty years to destroy much of Roman civilisation and political authority in the Balkans and most of what is now modern Greece. While hostilities did not commence immediately, and while Justin, through deft political manoeuvring at the expense of the Gepids (settled in Pannonia Secunda, south of the Danube) was able to recapture the Danubian fortress-city of Sirmium, lost some thirty years earlier, the arrival of the Avars in the Balkan–Danubian political forum had ultimately disastrous consequences.[48] For the Lombards, settled to the north-west of the Gepids, had asked the Avars for their assistence in their war with the latter. The result was the destruction of the Gepids; but the Lombards, frightened by their dangerous new allies, decided to emigrate westwards. In 568 they, together with a number of other Germanic groups, marched into north-east Italy, quickly conquering and occupying the plain of Venetia and most

---

[47] See in particular Averil Cameron, 'The early religious policies of Justin II', Studies in Church History XIII (1976), 51–67; I. Rochow, 'Die Heidenprozesse unter den Kaisern Tiberios I. Konstantinos und Maurikios', in *Studien zum 7. Jhdt.*, pp. 120–30.

[48] For a useful summary, see A. Avenarius, *Die Avaren in Europa* (Bratislava 1974), esp. pp. 67ff.

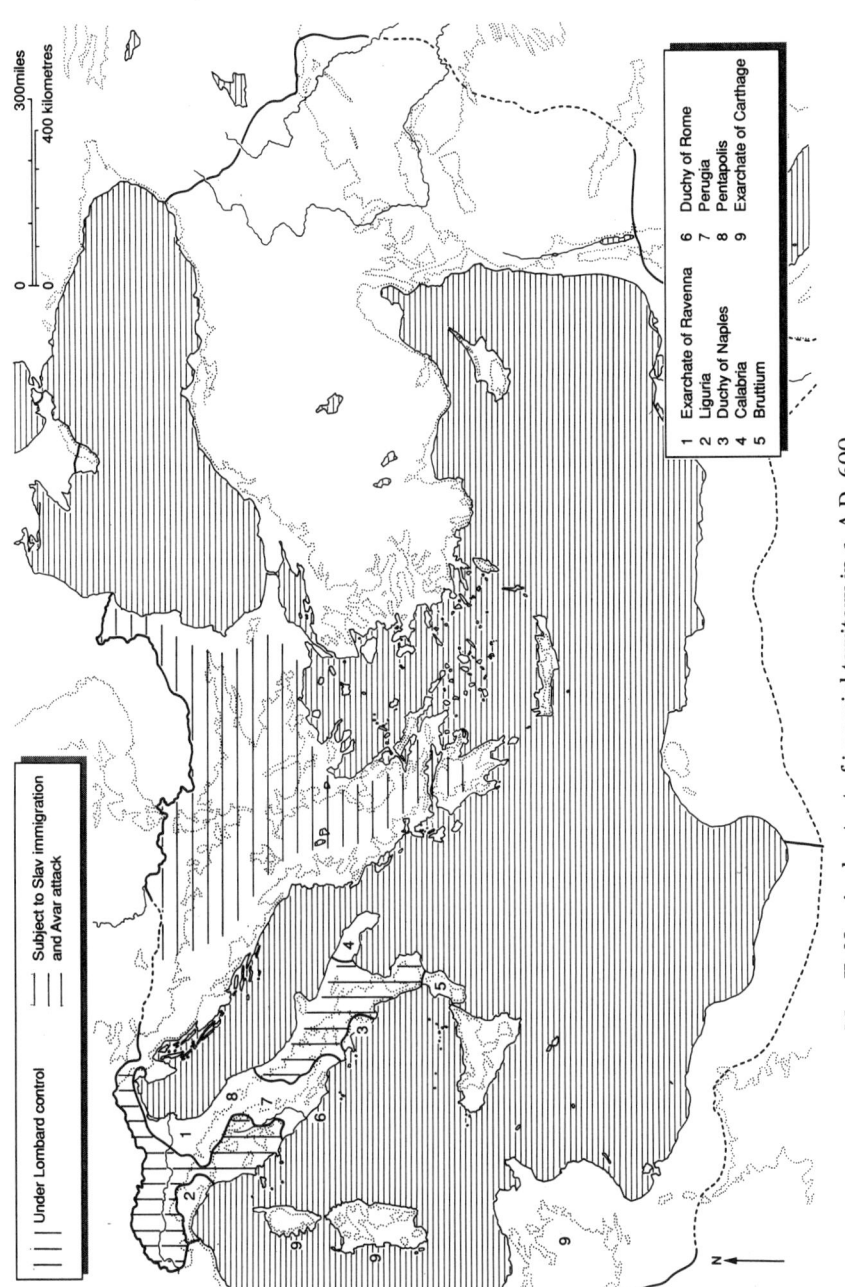

Map II Nominal extent of imperial territory in *c.* A.D. 600

Under Lombard control
Subject to Slav immigration and Avar attack

1 Exarchate of Ravenna
2 Liguria
3 Duchy of Naples
4 Calabria
5 Bruttium
6 Duchy of Rome
7 Perugia
8 Pentapolis
9 Exarchate of Carthage

Plate 1.3 Tiberius Constantine. Copper *follis*

Plate 1.4 Maurice. Gold *solidus*

of Liguria. By 572 they were masters of much of northern Italy and threatened to destroy the newly established prefecture and the results of Justinian's expensive reconquests.[49]

In Africa, serious Berber revolts had meant considerable temporary losses and great expense to the treasury;[50] while in Spain Visigothic forces began the gradual reconquest of the territories expropriated by Justinian. By 629 these Spanish possessions had been lost entirely. Justin then refused to pay the Persian subsidy due in 572; and in spite of initial successes, Roman forces suffered several defeats in the ensuing warfare, and a number of cities were sacked, notably Apamea in 573. The empire was thus engaged in conflict on several fronts at once, and the one crucial weakness in Justinian's strategy must have become apparent: the terri-

---

[49] See I. Dujčev, 'Bizantini e Longobardi', in *Atti del Convegno Internationale sul tema: la civiltà dei Longobardi in Europa* (Rome 1974), pp. 45–78.

[50] See in general, D. Pringle, *The Defence of Byzantine Africa from Justinian to the Arab Conquest* (BAR, Oxford 1981); P. Goubert, *Byzance avant l'Islam*, vol. II, 2: *Rome, Byzance et Carthage*; and the literature in notes 4 and 5 in the Introduction, above.

tories were simply too widely dispersed and too extended, and the resources needed to defend them under such conditions were simply not available. The war in the East continued to drain the treasury until 591, when civil war in Persia enabled Maurice to intervene to help Chosroes II and at the same time to conlcude an extremely favourable peace agreement. The war in the Balkans dragged on, the Romans registering some successes after 592. But the whole area had from the 580s been deeply infiltrated by migrating Slav settlers, and the indigenous population in the countryside was often either overwhelmed by these newcomers or driven out. While a number of cities held out, their existence was precarious; and once Roman military support had been removed, they could no longer survive. Only coastal cities such as Thessaloniki survived, but even here under considerable military and economic pressure.[51] In 602 the mutiny that led to Maurice's deposition took place; and during the reign of Phocas the strategy which had helped to stabilise the situation in the Balkans to Roman advantage was effectively abandoned. The whole area north of the Thracian plain, with the exception of the stronger fortresses and cities and coastal tracts, was lost to the authoritiy of the empire.

Maurice's deposition and murder in 602 gave the Persian Great King Chosroes II the chance he needed; and on the pretext of avenging his benefactor, his forces invaded the eastern provinces, ostensibly in support of anti-Phocas elements in the eastern field armies. Thus began a war which lasted until 626–7 and deprived the Roman state of huge areas – eventually including all of Egypt and Syria – for many years.[52]

The new and threatening situation which developed after the death of Justinian demanded new methods of dealing with it. Under the Emperor Maurice two new administrative circumscriptions appear, the exarchates of Ravenna and Carthage. These were effectively militarised districts, the old pretorian prefectures, in which for reasons of defence and military security, and of resource allocation, supreme civil and military authority was vested in a single military governor, or exarch. In many respects, the principle of their organisation foreshadows the later Byzantine *themata* (or

---

[51] Obolensky, *The Byzantine Commonwealth*, pp. 48ff.; G. Gomolka, 'Bemerkungen zur Situation der spätantiken Städte und Siedlungen in Nordbulgarien und ihrem Weiterleben am Ende des 6. Jahrhunderts', in *Studien zum 7. Jhdt.*, pp. 35–42 with literature; B. Zástěrová, 'Zu einigen Fragen aus der Geschichte der slawischen Kolonisation auf dem Balkan', *ibid.*, pp. 59–65; H. Ditten, 'Zur Bedeutung der Einwanderung der Slawen', in F. Winkelmann, H. Köpstein, H. Ditten and I. Rochow, *Byzanz im 7. Jahrhundert. Untersuchungen zur Herausbildung des Feudalismus* (BBA XXXXVIII, Berlin 1978), pp. 73–160, esp. 84ff. and 98ff. with extensive literature; also P. Lemerle, 'Invasions et migrations dans les Balkans depuis la fin de l'époque romaine jusqu'au VIIIᵉ siècle', *RH* 78 (1954), 265–308.

[52] See the account in Stratos, *Byzantium in the Seventh Century*, vol. I, pp. 58–68.

themes) but equally, precedents for them can be found in Justinianic legislation to deal with internal security in provinces such as Phrygia, for example. Institutionally, therefore, they are hardly new and seem simply to represent the obvious functional response of the state and its resources to a specific military threat. The reasons for their establishment at this time are not hard to see: the changed situation in Italy brought about the arrival and initial successes of the Lombards; and the constant threat and damaging attacks of the Berbers in North Africa.[53]

The economic situation of the empire also deteriorated after Justinian. Justin seems to have achieved a reasonable reserve in the treasury, but at the cost of cutting down his expenditure on the army and fortifications and ceasing the subsidies to the Avars and Persians. Tiberius went to the other extreme, although his policies are perhaps easier to understand. On his formal accession in 578 he remitted an entire year's taxes (by reducing the usual demand by twenty-five per cent over the next four years). He spent money freely on the army and carried through a vast recruitment campaign. He also renewed the payment to the Avars, which bought peace for a few years. But events in Italy demonstrated the scarcity of resources under which the empire suffered. In spite of pleas for military aid in 578 and 580 from the senate in Rome and later from the pope, Tiberius merely sent some cash and suggestions for diplomatic action to stem the incursions of the Lombards.[54] Neither cash nor troops were available in great supply, primarily because of the need to keep large armies in the Balkans and in the East. Even here, however, resources were scarce. Maurice tried to reduce the regular pay of the field units by twenty-five per cent which led to a mutiny in 588; and although the situation was recovered, similar attempts to save cash and resources by ordering the Danube forces to winter over the river in hostile territory led to further mutinies, until in 602 the troops, led by their elected leader Phocas, marched on Constantinople. Maurice fled, and after some days of confusion, Phocas was eventually proclaimed emperor.[55]

The reign of Phocas, which lasted until his overthrow by Heraclius in 610, was both militarily and economically a disaster. Persian successes in the east meant that the state was able to exact with only the greatest difficulty the revenues from Syria, Phoenicia and neighbouring districts. Asia Minor was raided and economic and social life disrupted, again with

[53] For the exarchates, see Jones, *LRE*, vol. I, pp. 312f.; Brown, *Gentlemen and Officers*, pp. 48ff.; Goubert, *Byzance avant l'Islam*; Ostrogorsky, *Geschichte*, p. 68 and note 1; and Ch. Diehl, *Etudes sur l'administration byzantine dans l'Exarchat de Ravenne* (Bibliothèque des écoles françaises d'Athènes et de Rome LIII, Paris 1888), esp. the opening chapter.

[54] See Menander Protector, frg. 49 (*Exc. de Leg.*, II, p. 469); Haldon, *Recruitment and Conscription*, pp. 25f., 28.

[55] See Kaegi, *Military Unrest*, esp. pp. 66–73 and 101–19.

Plate 1.5 Phocas. Gold *solidus*

the inevitable effects on the ability of the state to raise revenue. Pay and supplies for the army must also have been affected. The withdrawal of large numbers of troops, albeit temporarily, from the Danube front, gave the Avars and their Slav confederates and vassals a free hand to establish themselves securely south of the Danube, to devastate the countryside, isolate the cities and towns, and generally render the whole area untenable. Civil strife following Maurice's death, constant plots against Phocas in the capital, the resulting repression and the discontent of large sections of the populace of Constantinople, meant that Phocas was quite unable to maintain a uniform policy to deal with these problems.[56]

The extent to which the wars in the east and the Balkans influenced the basic structure of East Roman society is difficult to determine, of course. Undoubtedly, massive insecurity in the Balkans meant that regular agricultural production must have suffered considerably. Similarly, large tracts of Anatolia must have been affected by Persian military operations. Political repression and the expropriation of senators under Phocas must also have meant the accumulation in state hands, or the redistribution, of considerable amounts of landed property in the provinces. All these developments heightened people's awareness and perception of their situation in significant ways, as they likewise affected the administrative structure of the empire in these regions. Fundamental features of a Byzantine, rather than a late Roman culture and ideology had begun to form already, features which these diasters highlighted, but which were apparent even in the last years of Justinian's reign and throughout the reigns of his successors.

From the last years of Justinian the empire entered what might be perceived as a period of ideological reorientation. Late Roman culture demonstrates at this time a loss of confidence or trust in the traditional symbols of authority and the establishment, a drift away from the sym-

[56] Ostrogorsky, *Geschichte*, pp. 70–2.

bolism of the heaven-endowed earthly empire – the imperial cult and hierarchies of state and Church – and its apparent fallibility, towards embodiments of heavenly power of a less fallible nature: the cults of saints, the cult of the Virgin, the icon; symbols, in short, of heavenly intercession.

This change in emphasis affected equally the imperial establishment, which promoted aspects of the change as a means of refocusing the divergent trends within the symbolic universe of late Roman society around the specifically imperial, Christian and orthodox ideology of the state, centred about the Christ-loving, God-protected rulers at Constantinople.[57]

Late Roman society, thoroughly Christian, became increasingly introverted. Marginal groups were no longer tolerated as they had been, in spite of the persecutions which occasionally occurred, in the earlier sixth century.[58] At the same time, Constantinople, the city of the court and the bureaucracy, became more and more the focal point of the empire politically and culturally, a process which was accelerated after the loss of Antioch, Jerusalem, Alexandria and, lastly – and much later – Carthage, during the course of the seventh century. The decline and eventual collapse of the older provincial municipal institutions both administratively and socially completed this process.[59] It is possible to detect a transfer of social and economic interest away from the provincial cities to Constantinople, the former having lost not only their corporate and administrative identity, but thereby also their social relevance and attraction. It was this new emphasis upon the centre, Constantinople, which began to emerge in the late sixth century and which the emperors used as a means of reinforcing their own authority.[60]

The reorientation of this period appears most clearly in the official stress upon the heavenly guardians of the emperor and the state, and imperial ceremonial, which focused in a particularly evocative way on the figures of the emperor and the symbolism of imperial authority. In the changed situation of the later sixth century, one of the results of this new emphasis, as we shall see in chapter 9, served also to point out the frailty of earthly power and to direct attention away from God's representative upon earth

[57] For a summary and discussion of these developments, see Haldon, 'Ideology and social change', 161ff., and Cameron, 'Images of authority', 4ff.

[58] See especially P. Brown, *Religion and Society in the Age of St Augustine* (London 1972), p. 55; J. Nelson, 'Symbols in context: rulers' inauguration rituals in Byzantium and the West in the early Middle Ages', Studies in Church History XIII (1976), 97–119, see 115f.

[59] J.F. Haldon and H. Kennedy, 'The Arab-Byzantine frontier in the eighth and ninth centuries: military organisation and society in the borderlands', ZRVI 19 (1980), 79–116, see 87ff.; Haldon, 'Some considerations', 86–8; H. Hunger, *Reich der neuen Mitte. Der christliche Geist der byzantinischen Kultur* (Vienna, Graz and Cologne 1965), pp. 42ff.

[60] Haldon, 'Ideology and social change', 171–3, for a summary of these developments with further literature.

to God Himself.[61] Evidence for local and civic saints' cults increases sharply at this time and, together with the developments noted already, suggests strongly that ordinary people were transferring their attention away from the worldly and physical authority of the emperor and the state, distant and ineffective as it often was, towards a more immediate and tangible power, a power and authority invested in heavenly guardians and intercessors directly by God. Given the close links deliberately fostered by the emperors themselves between their authority and its sources, such a development is not really surprising in the context of shifting political horizons and military and social vulnerability.[62] These developments had important repercussions in the middle and later seventh century.

The later sixth and early seventh century witnessed a series of dramatic changes in the late Roman world: politically the empire suffered a series of major blows to its prestige and authority; economically, it was able to maintain its resources, although much reduced, only with considerable difficulty. Socially, it was rent by divisions within the Church, while the vast majority of the producing population was maintained at a subsistence level for the benefit of the state and its bureaucracy, and the wealthy social elite which dominated it. Many contemporaries were fully aware of the dangers of the situation, and debates about the likely outcome of the long-term political crisis which engulfed the Roman world during and after the reign of Phocas were not unusual. As Jacob, the Palestinian Jew who was forcibly baptised at Carthage under Heraclius in 634, remarked, the future of the empire seemed most uncertain:

From the Ocean, that is of Scotia [i.e. Ireland], from Britannia, Hispania, Francia, Italia, Hellas and Thrace and Egypt and Africa and upper Africa, the boundaries of the Romans and the statues of their emperors were seen until our times; for all peoples submitted to them at God's command. But now we see Romania reduced and humbled.[63]

A telling picture of the situation after Maurice's death is given in the collection of the miracles of St Demetrius, written down not long after the events they claim to portray:

For you all know what clouds of dust the Devil stirred up during the years of the successor of the emperor Maurice, of blessed memory, when he smothered love, and sowed mutual hatred in all of the East, in Cilicia, in Asia, in Palestine and the neighbouring lands up to Constantinople itself. The demes were no longer content merely to spill the blood of their comrades on the streets; they broke into one

[61] See Cameron, 'Images of authority', 15–21.
[62] Averil Cameron, 'The Theotokos in sixth-century Constantinople: a city finds its symbol', *JThS* 29 (1978), 79–108, see 102ff.
[63] *Doctrina Iacobi nuper Baptizati* (ed. N. Bonwetsch, in Abhandlungen der königlichen Gesellschaft der Wissenschaften zu Göttingen, phil.-hist. Klasse, XII, 3, Berlin 1910), p. 62. 4–12.

another's homes and slew the occupants mercilessly. Women and children, old and young, those who were too weak to save themselves by flight, they hurled from the windows of the upper floors; like barbarians they plundered their fellow citizens, their acquaintances and their relatives, and put their homes to the flame.[64]

The picture may be overdrawn, but it neatly encapsulates one aspect of the mood of the Eastern empire during the early years of the seventh century.

[64] *Miracula S. Demetrii* (ed. Lemerle), 82 (I, 112.11–113.7). For the general development of late Roman society through the period from the late fourth to later sixth centuries, see the useful survey of Averil Cameron, *The Mediterranean World in Late Antiquity AD 395–600* (London 1993), in which a wide range of work up to the date of publication on the literary sources and the archaeological material is cited and taken into account.

CHAPTER 2

The East Roman world c. 610–717: the politics of survival

HERACLIUS 610–641

The reign of the 'tyrant' Phocas demonstrates the degree to which the Justinianic expansion of the sixth century had over-extended the resources of the state, and how crucial the stability of the central authority was to the well-being of the empire as a whole. Phocas, a subordinate officer from the Danube forces, seems to have had neither the ability nor the experience needed of a ruler in the situation in which the late Roman state found itself. His reign is remarkable chiefly for the plots and attempts on his life which he managed to avoid during the eight years of his reign in Constantinople, and for the disastrous collapse of the empire's defences, especially in the East. A long series of unsuccessful, senate-inspired plots eventually culminated in the expedition sent by Heraclius the Elder, the exarch of Africa based at Carthage, under his son Heraclius and his nephew Nicetas; the former with a squadron of ships with Byzantine and Moorish troops to Constantinople, the latter marching in 608 via Egypt, which quickly joined the rebellion.[1] Heraclius with his fleet appeared off Constantinople on 3 October in the year 610; he had been greeted enthusiastically en route wherever he had stopped; and the story was repeated at Constantinople. Phocas' supporters deserted him, Heraclius was let into the city, and the tyrant was executed. His last words testify both to the situation of the empire after eight years of directionless government, and to Phocas' own desperate incompetence. As Heraclius confronted him before his execution he asked: 'Is it in this manner that you have governed the state?' Phocas replied: 'Will you be able to do any better?'[2]

Heraclius was crowned by the patriarch Sergius in the chapel of St Stephen in the palace on 5 October. His accession was acclaimed by the

---

[1] On the reign of Phocas, see Ostrogorsky, *Geschichte*, pp. 70–2; Stratos, *Byzantium in the Seventh Century*, vol. I, pp. 48–91 for a detailed political history; and J. Herrin, *The Formation of Christendom* (London 1987), pp. 187ff. for a summary. A detailed account: D. Olster, *The Politics of Usurpation in the Seventh century: rhetoric and revolution in Byzantium* (Amsterdam 1993).

[2] John of Antioch, frg. 5, 38; *Exc. de Insid.*, 150.

Plate 2.1 Heraclius. Gold *solidus*

demes, the palace guards and by the senate according to tradition; and there is no doubt that it was a popular accession. Phocas had been almost universally detested by the end of his reign; and it is interesting that the one quarter where his rule was popular was in the papal chancery at Rome. Since the early sixth century, the patriarchs of Constantinople had been wont to call themselves also ecumenical, a title to which Pope Gregory I took fierce objection. While the Emperor Maurice stayed out of the debate, Phocas quickly made clear his support for the papal position and in 607 issued a document which recognised the apostolic Church of St Peter as the head of all the Churches. His popularity in Rome is therefore easily understood; but it was the only foundation of such popularity.[3]

Heraclius is popularly, and probably quite justifiably, regarded by both modern historians and by Byzantines as one of the empire's greatest rulers. But his accession saw no immediate change for the better in the situation of the state. Indeed, things became decidedly worse, so much so that in 618 the emperor planned to abandon Constantinople, which seemed too open to attacks by Avars and Slavs in the north and the Persians from the east, and move the seat of empire to his old home, Carthage.[4] But the response to this plan from the populace of the city, and the arguments of the patriarch Sergius, dissuaded him from this action. Instead, he began to develop plans to restore the situation. In the East as in the West, however, he met with only limited success and a number of failures.

In 611, the Persians were driven out of Caesarea in Cappadocia; but Byzantine counter-attacks in Armenia and Syria were unsuccessful, and after defeats in 613, the Persians marched once more into the Anatolian provinces.[5] They also occupied Damascus, and in 614 Jerusalem itself was

---

[3] For the edict, see Dölger, *Regesten*, no. 155; and on the disagreement over titles, see E. Caspar, *Geschichte des Papsttums* (2 vols., Tübingen 1935), vol. II, pp. 452ff.; V. Laurent, 'Le Titre de patriarche œcuménique et la signature patriarcale', *REB* 6 (1948), 5f.

[4] Nicephorus, 12, 10.

[5] See esp. W.E. Kaegi, jr., 'New evidence on the early reign of Heraclius', *BZ* 66 (1973), 308–30, see 313ff.; Sebeos, 65.

taken, a particularly heavy blow to Byzantine morale: not only was the Church of the Holy Sepulchre destroyed, but the True Cross was carried off to Ctesiphon. At the same time, the Persians partly occupied Cilicia, and the important city of Tarsus was taken. Armenia likewise fell to Persian attack, and the Byzantine forces of the *magister militum per Armeniam* were pushed westwards and northwards. In 615 further attacks into Asia Minor took place, and in 616 Persian troops reached the Bosphorus.[6] Byzantine troops seem to have retained some cohesion, however. The armies of the *magister militum per Armeniam* were still operational; forces of the *magister militum in praesenti* and of the *magister militum per Orientem* seem to have been active in Cilicia and Isauria.[7] Troops from Africa and Egypt under Heraclius' cousin Nicetas were operating in Syria and in Egypt itself; although Persian invasion and occupation of these territories between 616 and 620, followed by the consolidation of Persian authority in Syria and Palestine, terminated this oppositional activity.[8] This was again a major blow for the Byzantines, for the 'granary of the empire' and the chief supplier of grain to Constantinople was now lost to the enemy.

In the north and west, meanwhile, the empire slowly lost control over much of the Balkan region. The partial withdrawal of troops from the Danube front in 602 has traditionally been taken as the moment from which this process began in earnest. It has been assumed that there was thereafter little to hinder the Slav populations north of the Danube from moving south and overrunniung considerable areas. But, in fact, the evidence suggests that throughout most of the reign of Phocas only minor incursions took place – it was the civil wars between Heraclius and the supporters of Phocas which actually necessitated the withdrawal of substantial forces from the Balkans and which expedited the real collapse. This was especially the case after 613 when the war with the Persians took a turn for the worse.[9] The actual occupation of the Balkans seems to have

---

[6] See the account of Theophanes on Persian inroads from the year 612: 299.32–3, 300.1–6, 20–21 (for 614); 300.30sq. (615); 301.9sq. (616–17).

[7] See Haldon, *Recruitment and Conscription*, p. 29, note 29; and for a temporary mint established first at Seleucia (615–17) and then at Isaura (617–18) see Ph. Grierson, *Catalogue of the Byzantine Coins in the Dumbarton Oaks Collection and in the Whittemore Collection*, vol. II: Phocas to Theodosius III, 602–717 (Washington D.C. 1968), pp. 327f. It must reflect the minting of coin specifically to pay the troops of the region. An otherwise unattested arms factory at Seleucia is also evidence of local military operations. See G. Zacos and A. Veglery, *Byzantine Lead Seals*, vol. I, parts 1–3 (Basel 1972), no. 1136.

[8] See the account of Stratos, *Byzantium in the Seventh Century*, vol. I, pp. 113f.; F. Winkelmann, 'Ägypten und Byzanz vor der arabischen Eroberung', BS 40 (1979), 161–82, esp. 169–70 with literature. Winkelmann shows that, *pace* Stratos and others, the Persians were probably not greeted with open arms, nor hailed as liberators of the Coptic and monophysite population.

[9] See esp. the discussion of R.-J. Lilie, 'Kaiser Herakleios und die Ansiedlung der Serben', *SoF* 44 (1985), 17–43 and the literature cited. For the traditional position, see P. Charanis,

been a very slow process, lasting some fifty years: in 582, the Avars – who exercised a political-military hegemony over the numerous Slav clans and tribal groups – captured Sirmium and occupied the surrounding region, an event which effectively opened a door into Byzantine lands south of the Danube. In 626, after the defeat of the Avaro-Slav attack on Constantinople, Avar domination of the Slav peoples began to loosen, and the independent *Sklaviniai* of the Balkans henceforth figure as the main opponents of Byzantine rule in the area, at least until the arrival of the Bulgars in the 680s. Both the literary sources and the numismatic evidence – finds of hoards which represent a response to invasions and attacks – provide a general framework for the chronology of these events. Between about 576 and 586/7 a number of invasions and raids penetrated into the south Balkans, past Thessaloniki and into the Peloponnese.[10] Again, from about 609 until the 620s, further hoards together with less precise literary references – that is, of dubious or inexact chronology – attest to raids deep into Greece and the Peloponnese.[11] The pattern suggests an initial series of raids and invasions, beginning probably before 577, but ending temporarily in the late 590s, until the last year of Phocas, when a second wave began. The permanent settlement of Slavs in the north and central Balkans begins already in the 570s, of course, on a very small scale; the Miracles of

'Ethnic changes in the Byzantine empire in the seventh century', *DOP* 13 (1959), 23–44, see 37ff.

[10] For the literary sources, see Menander Protector, frgs. 47 (p. 209.3sq.) and 48 (p. 468.36sq.); John of Ephesus, III, 25 (from 577/8 to 583/4). Note also the reference to clerics having to abandon their sees as a result of barbarian attacks in the letters of Gregory I. See E. Chrysos, 'Συμβολὴ στὴν ἱστορία τῆς Ἠπείρου κατὰ τὴν πρωτοβυζαντινὴ ἐποχή (Δ' – ΣΤ'αἰ.)', *Ἠπειρωτικὴ Χρονική* 23 (1981), 72–7, with literature. Note also the Chronicle of Monemvasia, which mentions the conquest of the Peloponnese and the expulsion of its indigenous population in 587/8 – something of an exaggeration: P. Lemerle, 'La Chronique improprement dite de Monemvasie. Le contexte historique et légendaire', *REB* 21 (1963), 5–49. In spite of the Chronicle's claims, Monemvasia seems in fact to have been established in 582/3. See P. Schreiner, 'Note sur la fondation de Monemvasie en 582–583', *TM* 4 (1970), 471ff.; P. Schreiner, ed., *Die byzantinischen Kleinchroniken* (2 vols., *CFHB* XII 1 and 2, Vienna 1975 and 1977), vol. I, p. 319, nos. 41a and b; vol. II, pp. 77f. For the numismatic material see B. Athanassopoulou-Penna, 'Θησαυρὸς νομισμάτων 6ου αἰῶνα μ.Χ. ἀπὸ τὴν περιοχὴ τῶν Θηβῶν', *Ἀρχαιολογικὴ ἐφημερίς* (1979), 200–13; D.M. Metcalf, 'The Slavonic threat to Greece circa 580: some evidence from Athens', *Hesperia* 31 (1962), 134–41; T.L. Shean, 'The Athenian Agora: excavations of 1972', *Hesperia* 42 (1973), 395–8; and esp. the general survey of A. Avramea, 'Νομισματικοὶ "θησαυροὶ" καὶ μεμονωμένα νομίσματα ἀπὸ τὴν Πελοπόννησο (ΣΤ'–Z' αἰ.)', *Σύμμεικτα* 5 (1983), 49–89. See also M. Nystazopoulou, 'Συμβολὴ εἰς τὴν χρονολόγησιν τῶν Ἀβαρικῶν καὶ σλαβικῶν ἐπιδρομῶν ἐπὶ Μαυρικίου (582–602)', *Σύμμεικτα* 2 (1970), 149; and Th. Olajos, 'Contribution à la chronologie des premières installations des Slaves dans l'empire byzantin', *B* 55 (1985), 506–15.

[11] Literary evidence: see P. Lemerle, *Les plus anciens recueils des miracles de St. Démétrius*; I. *Le Texte* (Paris 1979), II. *Commentaire* (Paris 1981), see 179–94 (I, 175. 1sq.); II, pp. 85f. for an invasion of 614–16; and for coin finds, see Avramea, '*Θησαυροί*', 77f.; D. M. Metcalf, 'The Aegean coastlands under threat: some coins and coin hoards from the reign of Heraclius', *ABSA* 57 (1962), 14–23.

St Demetrius attest to permanent Slav groups in the region of Thessaloniki in the early seventh century; but the penetration and occupation of the Peloponnese, for example, seems only to have commenced on a permanent basis after 609/10.[12]

The immediate danger to the Byzantine state, however, came from the Avars, who by the time of Heraclius exercised authority over a considerable area, from the Danube plain eastwards into the south Russian steppes, ruling a confederacy or empire which had considerable resources in manpower at its disposal. Already in the years 615–16, as both Persians and Avars approached Constantinople in a joint effort to force the surrender of the City, the extreme danger was apparent. In 617, in an attempt to meet the Avar khagan, Heraclius was ambushed near the Long Walls in the area of Heraclea and nearly captured.[13] By 619, however, he had been able to arrange a truce with the khagan, which enabled him to transfer troops from Europe to Asia Minor. In a series of campaigns, beginning 622 and lasting until 628, Heraclius was able to outmanoeuvre the Persian forces in Anatolia and Armenia and take the war to the heart of the Sassanid empire.[14] The Avars, who were bought off again in 623, bided their time until 626, when a Persian counter-attack and a major Avar offensive against Constantinople endangered the capital of the empire itself. Not to be distracted from the campaigns in the East, Heraclius

[12] See Lemerle, *Les plus anciens recueils*, 100–15 (I, 124.1sq.) II, p. 69ff.; and Sp. Vryonis, jr., 'The evolution of Slavic society and the Slavic invasions in Greece. The first major Slavic attack on Thessaloniki, A.D. 597', *Hesperia* 50 (1981), 378–90; Vryonis, 'Review essay of Michael W. Weithmann, *Die slawische Bevölkerung auf der griechischen Halbinsel* (Munich 1978)', *Balkan Studies* 22 (1981), 405–39; and for the occupation, M. Kordoses, 'Η σλαβική εποίκηση στήν Πελοπόννησο με βάση τα σλαβικά τοπωνύμια', *Δωδώνη* 10 (1981), 388–421; and see also J. Ferluga, 'Untersuchungen zur byzantinischen Ansiedlungspolitik auf dem Balkan von der Mitte des 7. bis zur Mitte des 9. Jahrhunderts', *ZRVI* 23 (1984), 49–61; and the older work of M. Vasmer, *Die Slawen in Griechenland* (Berlin 1941 and Leipzig 1970), esp. pp. 118ff. In general, see Ostrogorsky, *Geschichte*, pp. 77ff.; Obolensky, *Byzantine Commonwealth*, pp. 52ff.; Ditten, 'Zur Bedeutung der Einwanderung der Slawen', p. 95f.; *idem*, *Ethnische Verschiebungen zwischen der Balkanhalbinsel und Kleinasien vom Ende des 6. bis zur zweiten Hälfte des 9. Jahrhunderts* (BBA LIX. Berlin 1993), pp. 45ff.; Stratos, *Byzantium in the Seventh Century*, vol. I, pp. 118ff.; and the most recent brief survey, M. Nystazopoulou-Pelekidou, 'Les Slaves dans l'empire byzantin', in *17th International Byzantine Congress, Main Papers* (Washington D.C. 1986), pp. 345–67, see 346–51. For another view, see M.W. Weithmann, *Die slawische Bevölkerung auf der griechischen Halbinsel* (Munich 1978).
[13] See N.H. Baynes, 'The date of the Avar surprise', *BZ* 21 (1912), 110–28; also Stratos, *Byzantium in the Seventh Century*, vol. I, pp. 145ff., who argues for a later date, namely 623.
[14] See the brief summary in Ostrogorsky, *Geschichte*, pp. 86f., and N. Oikonomidès, 'A chronological note on the first Persian campaign of Heraclius (622)', *BMGS* 1 (1975), 1–9; A. Pernice, *L'Imperatore Eraclio* (Florence 1905), pp. 111ff.; most recently Stratos, *Byzantium in the Seventh Century*, vol. I, pp. 135–44, 151–72, 197–234; and note Haldon, *Byzantine Praetorians*, pp. 169–71 with notes 333–41; and C. Zuckermann, 'The reign of Constantine V in the Miracles of St Theodore the Recruit (BHG 1764)', *REB* 46 (1988), 191–210, see 206ff.

reinforced the Constantinoplitan garrison with troops from the field forces under his brother Theodore; and with the help of an imperial fleet, which destroyed the Slav attack on the sea-walls of the city, the siege was defeated and the Avar khagan, followed shortly thereafter by the Persian forces, withdrew.[15] The retreat of the Persian forces under Šahrbaraz to Syria, and the defeat of a second Persian column under Šahin, shortly before this, and at the hands of Heraclius' brother Theodore, signalled the final failure of Persian attempts to force the surrender of Constantinople. The war ended effectively in early 628, when, after the crushing defeat of his forces in the Caucasus and near Nineveh in 627, Chosroes was deposed and murdered and replaced by his son Kavadh (called Siroes in the Greek sources), who immediately negotiated a peace with the Romans. The agreement of 591 was brought back into force, and over the following year the Persian army withdrew from Egypt and all the territories it had occupied since the opening phases of the wars.[16] The course of events was complicated and influenced in addition by Byzantine plans to bring about the conversion of the Persians, initially in the context of the war through the general Šahrbaraz, a plan which achieved a certain degree of success before the Arab conquests put an end to Byzantine hopes.[17] Following on his triumphal return to Constantinople in 628, when he was met at Hiereia on the Asia Minor coast by the senate, clergy, the patriarch Sergius, his son Constantine and sections of the populace, the crowning achievement of the reign was the return of the True Cross to the city of Jerusalem on 21 March in 630. Thus ended what has sometimes been seen as the first crusade, symbolised in ceremonial enactment.[18]

In the West, the Avars' retreat in 626 had equally far-reaching consequences. Uprisings of subject Slav peoples soon followed, and within a few years an independent west Slav confederacy had appeared, under the leadership of a certain Samo, a Frankish merchant by origin. This was a direct result of the revolt against Avar domination and the diplomatic

[15] See F. Barišić, 'Le siège de Constantinople par les Avares et les Slaves en 626', B 24 (1954), 371–95; and in particular P. Speck, ed., *Zufälliges zum Bellum Avaricum des Georgios Pisides* (Miscellanea Byzantina Monacensia XXIV, Munich 1980), with literature and discussion; V. Grumel, 'La Défense maritime de Constantinople du côté de la Corne d'Or et le siège des Avares', BS 25 (1964), 217–33; Herrin, *Formation of Christendom*, pp. 198f.

[16] See the account of Stratos, *Byzantium in the Seventh Century*, vol. I, pp. 210ff.; and the literature in note 14 above.

[17] See C. Mango, 'Deux études sur Byzance et la Perse Sassanide, II: Héraclius, Šahrvaraz et la vraie croix', TM 9 (1985), 105–18

[18] Cf. A. Frolow, 'La Vraie croix et les expéditions d'Héraclius en Perse', REB 11 (1953), 88ff.; Frolow, 'La Dédicace de Constantinople dans la tradition byzantine', *Revue de l'histoire des religions* 127 (1944), 61ff.; Stratos, *Byzantium in the Seventh Century*, vol. I, 237ff., esp. 252–5.

activity and support of Constantinople.[19] At about the same time, according to later Byzantine tradition, Heraclius reached an agreement with two Slav groups, the Croats and the Serbs, inviting them to attack the Avars in the west Balkans, south of the Danube, and officially granting them permission to occupy the regions they were able to recapture for the empire. They were also converted to Christianity, according to the tenth-century account of the Emperor Constantine VII, although this was clearly a short-lived state of affairs. Nevertheless, according to the later tradition, it enabled the Byzantines to reassert, formally and in theory, their authority over these regions. In fact, it has been shown that Heraclius was able to do very little to recover the situation in the Balkans, and it was really during his reign that Byzantine power in that region effectively disappeared.[20]

A third blow to Avar hegemony was the rebellion some time between 619 and 635 – probably in the 630s – of the Onogur 'Huns' or Bulgars under their leader Kovrat, who with his uncle Organa had visited Constantinople in 619, where he had been baptised and where the Byzantines mediated in establishing a treaty with the Avars. The Onogur revolt was certainly supported from Constantinople, and in return for confirming the treaty he had witnessed in 619, Kovrat received the title of *patrikios*. The Onogur-Bulgars occupied an area in and around the Kuban region and on the east coast of the Sea of Azov, their territory being referred to as 'old Great Bulgaria'. While their successful rebellion against the Avars was welcome news in Constantinople, the later history of this people, in particular the branch led by one of Kovrat's sons, Asparuch, was to have a crucial impact on Byzantium.[21]

By the early 630s, therefore, the empire had been able to restore its eastern territories in full and, to a limited extent at least, to stabilise the

---

[19] See esp. A. Avenarius, *Die Awaren in Europa*, pp. 123–38; Ditten, 'Zur Bedeutung der Einwanderung der Slawen', pp. 127ff. with discussion and full bibliography; V. Chaloupecký, 'Considérations sur Samon, le premier roi des Slaves', BS 11 (1950), 223–39; Obolensky, *The Byzantine Commonwealth*, p. 59; Obolensky, in *CMH* IV.1, p. 482; Stratos, *Byzantium in the Seventh Century*, vol. I, p. 316.

[20] Avenarius, *Die Awaren in Europa*, pp. 138–47; Obolensky, *The Byzantine Commonwealth*, pp. 59f.; Stratos, *Byzantium in the Seventh Century*, vol. I, pp. 325–37; Ditten, *Zur Bedeutung der Einwanderung der Slawen*, p. 129 with literature: Ostrogorsky, *Geschichte*, pp. 87f.; V. Popović, 'Aux origines de la Slavisation des Balkans: la constitution des premières Sklavinies macédoniennes à la fin du sixième siècle', *Compte-rendu de l'Acad. des Inscriptions et Belle-Lettres* (Paris 1980), pp. 230–57; and the literature and discussion in Lilie, *Kaiser Herakleios und die Ansiedlung der Serben*, esp. 18ff. and note 3, and 29ff. Note also J. Čangova, 'Les Slaves aux environs de Preslav aux VIIe–VIIIe siècles d'après les données archéologiques', *Studia in Honorem Veselin Beševliev* (Sofia 1978), pp. 363–8; J. Ferluga, 'Untersuchungen zur byzantinischen Ansiedlungspolitik auf dem Balkan von der Mitte des 7. bis zur Mitte des 9. Jahrhunderts', *ZRVI* 23 (1984), 49–61.

[21] Nicephorus, 12.20; 24.9; Avenarius, *Die Awaren in Europa*, pp. 153–7; Obolensky, *The Byzantine Commonwealth*, pp. 62–3; R. Grousset, *L'Empire des Steppes* (Paris 1939), pp. 229–30; Ostrogorsky, *Geschichte*, p. 87 and note 3.

position in the Balkans. The Avar power was destroyed; and while the Slav population of the Balkans and the Peloponnese made Byzantine authority rather an empty concept, a more-or-less peaceful situation had been won, which gave the land and population time to recover from the years of warfare and devastation.

The monophysite problem and the rise of Islam

Heraclius' achievement was remarkable. The result of these years of constant warfare and effort was a restored empire. But it was a greatly weakened empire. All the resources of Church and state had been swallowed up in the war effort; and while the eastern provinces were safe and could once more provide the revenues needed to maintain the imperial armies and the corn to feed Constantinople, Thrace and what other Balkan possessions remained in Byzantine hands took much longer to recover. Heraclius was further burdened with the considerable debt he owed the Church, for it was only through borrowing and confiscating considerable amounts of silver and gold plate, bronze statues, and other forms of wealth, that he had been able to raise the cash with which to pay the troops.[22] Despite the ending of hostilities, a substantial army still had to be maintained; imperial generosity in the rebuilding of cities and fortresses and the rewarding of the soldiers who had fought against the Persians meant further drains on limited resources; while the disruption of warfare in parts of Asia Minor must have seriously affected the ability of many regions to pay the taxes demanded from them after their restoration to Imperial control. The Persians had pillaged many of the cities of the East and had removed the treasures of the Church and the reserves of local administrative capitals, such as Alexandria.[23] In short, and in spite of external appearances, the empire was economically in a parlous condition.

The situation was not helped by Heraclius' efforts to solve the question of the split between the Chalcedonian and monophysite communities. The varied cultural and linguistic make-up of the empire as well as the demands of the imperial ideology made unity in orthodoxy an essential and urgent matter of practical state politics. Together with the patriarch Sergius and the Chalcedonian archbishop of Alexandria, Cyrus (from 631), the formula of the single energy was worked out, intended to provide a bridge for Chalcedonian theology to approach the monophysite position. In the context in which it was invoked and elaborated, it functioned as a compromise intended to meet the criticisms which the monophysites had raised against the traditional dyophysitism of Chalcedon, according to

[22] Hendy, *Studies*, pp. 231, 494–5; Ostrogorsky, *Geschichte*, p. 83.
[23] Winkelmann, *Ägypten und Byzanz*, 169.

which the two natures of Christ, human and divine, operated through a single energy. But it is important to note that the debate was not begun by this political need. On the contrary, discussion over the nature of the energies of Christ had begun among theologians already in the sixth century, albeit with the intention of bringing the neo-Chalcedonian and the monophysite positions closer.[24]

But even though Heraclius led the negotiations himself, only partial and temporary successes were gained. Pope Honorius lent his support to the project; but even the agreement reached by Cyrus in 633 with the Theodosianites, a group of monophysites in Egypt, was short-lived. Once again, the imperial government was impelled to employ force in order to gain acceptance for its views. But Chalcedonians themselves soon began to express doubts about the theological validity of the argument, doubts expressed particularly strongly by Sophronius, patriarch of Jerusalem from 634. The result was that an alternative, emended position was developed, primarily, it would seem, by the patriarch Sergius. Partly encouraged by the rather reserved position of the pope, he argued that the crucial element was not the single energy, but the single will – *thelēma* – of Christ. In 638, Heraclius issued the famous Ekthesis, in which further discussion of the problem of one or two energies was forbidden, and the new, monothelete, formula was set out. It was put up for all to see in the narthex of the Hagia Sophia. But the new policy was likewise rejected by a large number of Chalcedonian churchmen, particularly in the West, as well as by the monophysite Churches. And although Sergius was replaced after his death in 638 by the keen monothelete Pyrrhus, it continued to meet with opposition, now from the successor of Pope Honorius in Rome also. The compromise had merely caused another division within the Church. But it also had important consequences for the imperial ideology itself and for the position of the emperors, as we shall see. And in the meantime, both Syria and Palestine had been conquered by the Arabs.[25]

The arrival on the historical stage of Islam and its initial bearers, the

---

[24] See F. Winkelmann, 'Die Quellen zur Erforschung des monenergetisch–monotheletischen Streites', *Klio* 69 (1987), 515–59, esp. 555f., following S. Helmer, *Der Neuchalkedonismus. Geschichte, Berechtigung und Bedeutung eines dogmengeschichtlichen Begriffes* (Bonn 1962), see p. 223.

[25] For the background to these developments see Ostrogorsky, *Geschichte*, pp. 90–1; Winkelmann, *Die östlichen Kirchen*, pp. 106–7; Haldon, 'Ideology and social change', 161ff.; and esp. V. Grumel, 'Recherches sur l'histoire du Monothélisme', *EO* 27 (1928), 6–16, 257–77; 28 (1929), 272–83; 29 (1930), 16–28; H.-G. Beck, *Kirche und theologische Literatur im byzantinischen Reich*, 2nd edn (Munich 1977), pp. 292–4; Herrin, *Formation of Christendom*, pp. 206ff.; the source analysis of J.-L. Van Dieten, *Geschichte der Patriarchen von Sergios I. bis Johannes VI. (610–715)* (Amsterdam 1972), pp. 179ff. ('Die griechische Überlieferung über die Anfänge des Monotheletismus'); and esp. that of Winkelmann, 'Die Quellen'.

nomadic tribesmen of the Arabian peninsula, demonstrated just how weak the long-drawn-out conflict between the two great powers had left the empire. Syria was finally lost in 636, Palestine in 638, Mesopotamia in 639/40, Armenia in the same year and Egypt by 642. Initially intending to direct the destruction of the invaders from his headquarters at Antioch, Heraclius abandoned the struggle in 636 after the disastrous defeat at the battle of the Yarmuk and returned to Constantinople.[26] Byzantine forces held out most effectively in Palestine, where the patriarch Sophronius inspired the defence of Jerusalem. Elsewhere, however, it seems that an underlying apathy in the bulk of the monophysite population to Byzantine rule – in Egypt and Syria especially – deprived the defenders of any otherwise committed popular support they might have hoped for and also made the Islamic invaders less unacceptable. This is not to say that they were welcomed with open arms. Merely that the morale of the imperial troops was low, the population not always particularly supportive, and resources were anyway overstretched.[27] In addition, it seems clear that neither the Persians nor the Byzantines fully realised the nature of the danger facing them. In spite of their larger than usual scale, it must have seemed difficult to believe that these raids were anything more than a temporary occurrence, producing temporary set-backs. That the Arabs were here to stay, however, soon became apparent; for already by the time of their attack on Egypt, the Sassanid empire had been virtually destroyed. The new Arab empire was in the making.[28]

[26] The best and most recent account is that of Lilie, *Die byzantinische Reaktion*, pp. 40–6 (Syria, Palestine, Mesopotamia); 46–52 (Egypt); 52–6 (Armenia). See also F. Gabrieli, *Muhammad and the Conquests of Islam* (London 1968), pp. 143–74 with literature; and Winkelmann, 'Ägypten und Byzanz', esp. 161ff.; W.E. Kaegi, jr., 'Heraklios and the Arabs', *Greek Orthodox Theol. Review* 27 (1982), 109–33; F. Donner, *The Early Islamic Conquests* (Princeton 1981), pp. 55ff.; and, for a general survey, A.G.K. Savvides, *Τὸ οἰκουμενικὸ Βυζαντινὸ κράτος καὶ ἡ ἐμφάνιση τοῦ Ἰσλάμ. 518–717 μ.Χ.* (Athens 1985).

[27] The question of monophysite 'nationalism' and hostility to Constantinople in the relatively rapid Arab conquest of the Eastern provinces has been much discussed. See the comments of Winkelmann, 'Ägypten und Byzanz', 162ff., 176–8; and in general W.H.C. Frend, *The Rise of the Monophysite Movement. Chapters in the History of the Church in the fifth and sixth Centuries* (Cambridge 1972); Frend, 'Heresy and schism as social and national movements', *Studies-in Church History* IX (1972), 37–56, see esp. 45ff.; and the summary of Stratos, *Byzantium in the Seventh Century*, vol. II, pp. 117–33, who surveys the modern literature. In fact, as Winkelmann's careful analysis suggests, internal weakness as a result of social tension (between big landowners and peasantry, for example) together with administrative and military incompetence, were as much to blame. For further discussion, see F. Winkelmann, 'Die Stellung Ägyptens im oströmisch-byzantinischen Reich', in *Graeco-Coptica: Griechen und Kopten im byzantinischen Ägypten*, ed. P. Nagel (Halle 1984), pp. 11–35, see pp. 14ff.; also Kaegi, 'Heraklios and the Arabs', 127; and J. Moorhead, 'The monophysite response to the Arab invasions', *B* 51 (1981), 579–91.

[28] For the Arabian background to the expansion of Islam, and for the life of Muhammad, see Gabrieli, *Muhammad and the Conquests of Islam*, pp. 25–90; and the brief summaries in Ostrogorsky, *Geschichte*, p. 92; Lilie, *Die byzantinische Reaktion*, pp. 34–9. For the conquest

The East Roman world: the politics of survival   51

Heraclius' last years mark a sad end to what had been a glorious reign. The Arab victories deprived the empire once again of territories that had only recently been won back with such difficulty and sacrifice. He suffered from a nervous disorder which meant that he could not bear to look upon water. His natural son John Athalarich was involved in plots to remove him from the throne;[29] and while the conspirators were betrayed and punished, the plot itself was symptomatic of the strong hostility felt by the populace of the city and many people in the ruling circle towards Heraclius' second wife, his niece, Martina. The marriage had been unpopular from the start, regarded as incestuous and contrary to the civil law of the state; and in spite of Martina's courage in accompanying the emperor on his campaigns against the Persians, her interest in securing the succession for her own sons with Heraclius, as well as for his son from his first marriage, Constantine, seems to have aroused a great deal of suspicion. The events in Constantinople surrounding the last years of the old Heraclius are confused, and the sources are often contradictory.[30] But in order to secure the succession fairly for the children of both first and second marriages, Heraclius raised his eldest son with Martina to the imperial dignity on 7 July 638, making David, the next son with Martina, Caesar. On Heraclius' death on 11 February 641, therefore, he was succeeded by the fifteen year old Heraclius, known as Heracleonas, and the twenty-eight year old Constantine. Martina was explicitly given a role to play, in so far as she was to be regarded by both half brothers as mother and empress. But the arrangement was destined not to work. To begin with, a strong opposition, expressed particularly vocally through the senate, to Heraclius' will quickly became apparent which, while accepting the half-brothers as co-emperors, rejected Martina as unworthy of representing the empire or

of Persia, see Gabrieli, *Muhammad and the Conquests of Islam*, pp. 118–42. On the Arab conquests in general for this period, see Lilie, *Die byzantinische Reaktion*, pp. 60–162; H. Ahrweiler, 'L'Asie Mineure et les invasions arabes', *RH* 227 (1962), 1–32; E.W. Brooks, 'The struggle with the Saracens 717–867', in *CMH* IV, 1st edn (Cambridge 1923), pp. 119–38; M. Canard, 'Byzantium and the Muslim world to the middle of the eleventh century' in *CMH* vol. IV.1, 2nd edn (Cambridge 1966), pp. 696ff., see 698–9; D.R. Hill, *The Termination of Hostilities in the Early Arab Conquest, A.D. 634–656* (London 1971); J. Wellhausen, *Die Kämpfe der Araber mit den Romäern in der Zeit der Umaijaden*, in Nachrichten der königl. Gesellschaft der Wissenschaften zu Göttingen, phil.-hist. Klasse IV (1901), pp. 1–34. For further literature see D.J. Constantelos, 'The Muslim conquest of the Near East as revealed in the Greek sources of the seventh and eighth centuries', *B* 42 (1972), 325–57; and Donner, *The Early Islamic Conquests*.

[29] See Stratos, *Byzantium in the Seventh Century*, vol. I, p. 219; vol. II, p. 136; Ostrogorsky, *Geschichte*, p. 93; for the plot involving Athalaric and a number of the Armenian officers in Heraclius' entourage, see Stratos, *Byzantium in the Seventh Century*, vol. II, pp. 137ff. with literature.

[30] The most useful general survey of these years, although not always the most objective interpretation, is that of Stratos, *Byzantium in the Seventh Century*, vol. II, pp. 139ff., 176ff. On the texts for these events, see esp. Speck, *Das geteilte Dossier*; and idem, 'Der Kater Μεχλεμπέ', 374ff.

of receiving foreign ambassadors, since she was a woman.[31] Two hostile factions developed around the two half-brothers, but with Constantine's death on 25 May 641 (according to one rumour, by poison), Heracleonas and Martina seemed to have won the day.[32] Constantine's supporters were now banished, but opposition seems only to have been strengthened. The senatorial establishment, as well as the population of the city, and significant elements of the army, were opposed to Martina's regency. The rumours that Constantine had been poisoned received widespread acceptance, and there was a demand that his son, also Constantine, usually named Constans, should be made co-emperor with Heracleonas. As troops of the Anatolian armies appeared at Chalcedon, Heracleonas was forced to accede to this demand. But even so, Heracleonas and Martina, along with her other sons, David Tiberius and Marinus, were deposed, mutilated and exiled (the first two to Rhodes) in September 641. Constans II began to rule as sole emperor.[33]

Heraclius' reign thus ended in confusion and political and military uncertainty. But in spite of the catastrophes of his last years, his achievements remain clear. His great wars of reconquest restored the empire in the East to the borders of Maurice's day, greater even than in the time of Justinian; and while the effective loss of the Balkans to Slav peoples changed the centre of gravity within the empire, Heraclius was nevertheless able through skilful diplomacy to reassert Byzantine imperial authority, however superficially, in a way that might have seemed impossible at the end of the reign of Phocas.

Heraclius seems also to have carried through a number of administrative reforms, chiefly connected with the needs or with the results of his wars with Persia.[34] Changes in military organisation reflected both the needs of the Persian wars on the one hand and the transfer of troops to meet the demands of the war with the Arabs on the other.[35] By the same token, a fiscal reform was undertaken, which reflected the beginnings of the process through which the system familiar from the eighth century and later came to be established.[36] These changes again seem to reflect the needs of the 'war economy' of much of Heraclius' reign. In this connection, of course, Heraclius' introduction of the silver hexagram must be considered, part of his overall response to the dramatic scarcity of cash

---

[31] See Nicephorus, 27.13; 28.5.
[32] Ostrogorsky, *Geschichte*, p. 94; Stratos, *Byzantium in the Seventh Century*, vol. II, pp. 179–85.
[33] Ostrogorsky, *Geschichte*, p. 95; Stratos, *Byzantium in the Seventh Century*, vol. III, pp. 2ff.; Herrin, *Formation of Christendom*, pp. 213–17.
[34] These will be discussed in detail in chapter 5.
[35] Haldon, *Byzantine Praetorians*, pp. 142–50, 164–82.
[36] Hendy, *Studies*, pp. 417ff.

resources during the first fifteen to twenty years of his reign, an innovation which, as has also been noted, served its immediate purpose but, owing to the inflexibility of the relationship between gold and silver which was operated by the state, did not in the end prove stable.[37]

Apart from this material and Heraclius' interest in the administrative affairs of the Church and in canon law – reducing and subjecting to a more rigorous central control the clergy of the larger churches, and especially of the Hagia Sophia[38] – there is very little evidence to support the often repeated notion of a major administrative reform during his reign. Numerous administrative changes there certainly were, and most seem to have been the result of considered policy plans designed to facilitate his military operations or to alleviate the chaos of the years before 628. But there is no reason to think that he introduced the 'theme system' or was responsible for a major shift in recruitment policy for the army. I will return to these questions in the following chapters.

CONSTANS II, 641–668

Constans II was only eleven years old when he became sole ruler, and it is clear that he had to rely upon the senate, both formally and informally, during his first years. The senate itself, representative of the Constantinopolitan bureaucracy and the provincial landowning class, seems to have experienced a considerable increase in its influence and prestige during these years, a development which contrasts sharply with the rather subservient position it occupied during much of the sixth century. Its power may have been concealed in constitutional and legislative matters during the sixth century, because the economic interests of its members were not threatened; but it is interesting to note that it was at times of political and economic insecurity or chaos that the senate as a body reasserted itself – during the reign of Phocas, for example, and during the last years of Heraclius, the reign of Heracleonas and Constantine, and the opening part of the reign of Constans II. As has been shown, however, the senate assumed a new position in the affairs of the state from this time on, as a higher court and as a source of advice and advisers to the emperors too. The reasons for this must be sought in both the political situation and the prevailing ideological tendencies of the time, as well as in the actual make-up of the senate and the social origins of its members.[39]

---

[37] See esp. Hendy, *Studies*, p. 494ff.
[38] See J. Konidares, 'Die Novellen des Kaisers Herakleios', FM V (1982), 33–106.
[39] Ch. Diehl, 'Le Sénat et le peuple byzantin aux VIIe et VIIIe siècles', *B* 1 (1924), 201–13; H.-G. Beck, *Senat und Volk von Konstantinopel. Probleme der byzantinischen Verfassungsgeschichte*, in SBB VI (1966), 1–75; Ostrogorsky, *Geschichte*, p. 95f.

Plate 2.2 Constans II. Gold *solidus*

Constans' first years were dogged by the political difficulties inherited from the reign of his half-uncle Heracleonas and his step-grandmother Martina. The general Valentinus, who seems to have held the command of the *Opsikion* forces, but may also have exercised the functions of an overall commander of operations on the eastern front, had been made count or *comes* of the *excubitores*, a small, elite palace guards unit, by Heracleonas and Martina in an attempt to buy his loyalty; and there is some evidence that he also had himself proclaimed co-emperor or Caesar (or that he tried to do so). Although he had been one of the prime movers in Martina's downfall, he was clearly keen to maintain his position of authority under Constans II. But in attempting to impose his will in Constantinople through his troops, he sparked off a popular riot which resulted in the routing of his soldiers and his own lynching, probably in 644 or 645. Constans was left in sole charge, aided and guided by his own officials and the members of the senate.[40]

He did not have a particularly auspicious start to his reign. The external situation of the empire was once again precarious. Byzantine troops evacuated Alexandria in September 642 as part of the agreement reached by the patriarch Cyrus with the Arabs, on Martina's instructions, according to which Byzantine troops and others who wished to leave would do so over a specific period. On 29 September the victorious Arab leader ᶜAmr entered the city and began systematically from that time on to extend Muslim authority along the North African coast westwards. The Pentapolis quickly followed and, in 643, Tripolis also. And in spite of a temporary Byzantine reoccupation of Alexandria in 645, following ᶜAmr's recall, the Arabs were able to expel the Byzantines for good in 646. The return of Byzantine authority and official Chalcedonian policy had not been entirely welcome – indeed, the monophysite patriarch Benjamin greeted the Arab leaders on their return at the head of a rejoicing proces-

---

[40] For Valentinus and his role, see Haldon, *Byzantine Praetorians*, pp. 178ff., and Stratos, *Byzantium in the Seventh Century*, vol. III, pp. 11–13.

sion of Copts; and Egypt was henceforth to remain permanently in Muslim hands.[41]

Under a leader just as able as ᶜAmr, Arab forces began in the early 640s to raid Anatolia. From 642 to 643 raids into Armenia began in earnest; and in 647 Muᶜawiya raided Cappadocia and besieged Caesarea. Phrygia was raided from there, and Amorium was also attacked. No attempt to hold key points or establish permanent bases was made; but enormous booty was taken back to Damascus, where the future caliph received a hero's welcome.[42] Up until this point, and indeed until 655, Byzantine control of the sea had been unchallenged. As they reached the Mediterranean, however, the Arab leadership realised that to pre-empt Byzantine counter-attacks and also to extend their conquests they would need a fleet. Muᶜawiya was the first who seems to have recognised this, and in 649, after the construction of a small fleet, the first Arab naval expedition took place, directed against Cyprus. The capital Constantia was taken by storm; and although a three-year truce was negotiated, Arab naval construction proceeded apace. In 654 Rhodes was devastated (the fallen Colossus being sold off to a merchant from Edessa); Cos was taken; Crete was pillaged. In 655, the Byzantine fleet, in an effort to put an end to this naval threat, and under the personal command of the emperor, was decisively defeated by Muᶜawiya's navy, and Constans barely escaped with his life.[43]

The civil wars which now developed upon the murder of ᶜOthman in 656 between Muᶜawiya, proclaimed caliph in Syria, and ᶜAli, in Medina, the son-in-law of Muhammad, gave the Byzantines a breathing-space. In order to concentrate his energies in defeating ᶜAli's party, Muᶜawiya agreed to a truce with the Byzantines in 659, which lasted until 661/2.[44] And while hostilities, regular raids and attacks upon Byzantine fortresses and settlements in Asia Minor continued thereafter with equal fierceness and regularity throughout the 660s, this truce had important consequences. To begin with, it enabled Constans to turn his attention to the Balkans, where

[41] On Cyrus and Benjamin, see Winkelmann, *Ägypten und Byzanz*, 170–5, with literature; and for the attempted reconquest under the general Manuel (launched from the Byzantine base in Rhodes), see Stratos, *Byzantium in the Seventh Century*, vol. III, pp. 35–8; A.J. Butler, *The Arab Conquest of Egypt and the last thirty years of the Roman Dominion* (Oxford 1902), pp. 194ff.; Lilie, *Die byzantinische Reaktion*, pp. 48–52.
[42] See Lilie, *Die byzantinische Reaktion*, pp. 54ff., for a detailed account of these raids, their frequency, direction and effects.
[43] See Theophanes, 346.9sq.; Stratos, *Byzantium in the Seventh Century*, vol. III, pp. 48–55; Lilie, *Die byzantinische Reaktion*, pp. 67–8. On Arab sea-power see Stratos, vol. III, p. 38ff.; Lilie, pp. 64ff.; and esp. E. Eickhoff, *Seekrieg und Seepolitik zwischen Islam und Abendland* (Berlin 1966); A.M. Fahmy, *Muslim Sea-Power in the Eastern Mediterranean* (London 1950).
[44] For the civil war and its background, see Gabrieli, *Muhammad and the Conquests of Islam*, pp. 94–8; and for its results for Byzantine strategy, Stratos, *Byzantium in the Seventh Century*, vol. III, pp. 135–41, 187ff.

Byzantine forces had been on the defensive since the beginning of his reign. In 658, as internal strife among the Arabs relieved the pressure on the eastern front, Constans undertook an expedition into the *Sklaviniai*, the regions of the Slavs, where – according to Theophanes – he defeated many tribes and took many prisoners.[45] The result was the transportation of several thousands of prisoners with their families to devastated or unoccupied areas of Anatolia and the probable recruitment of Slav soldiers into the Byzantine forces there,[46] beginning a policy which was to be pursued with vigour by both Constantine IV and Justinian II. It was also part of a wider change in the constitution of the population of Asia Minor itself and, more particularly, it hints at significant changes in methods of recruitment and maintenance of the imperial forces in the provinces.

The monothelete controversy

Constans' internal policies and administration were dogged throughout his reign by the problems inherited from his grandfather with regard to the doctrines of monenergism and monotheletism. At his accession the Ekthesis of Heraclius was still displayed in the narthex of the Great Church and continued to represent the official policy of the state. Monotheletism had already met with almost universal rejection in the West, both in Rome and, much more significantly as it turned out, in Africa, where one of the most important theologians of the orthodox Church, and certainly the most important in his own time, Maximus the Confessor, was active in the debate. In Syria and Palestine, in contrast, the neo-Chalcedonian communities seem to have espoused the formula of monotheletism with some enthusiasm, as later evidence would suggest, and it is clear that this fact in itself must have been a significant factor in persuading Constans and his advisers to maintain the policy as the official line.[47]

Early in 646, a number of local synods were held in the cities of the exarchate of Carthage, probably in response to Maximus' campaign against monotheletism; and the result was the condemnation of the

---

[45] Theophanes, 347.6.
[46] For example, Theophanes, 348.18 (for 665): a group of 5,000 Slavs which deserted to the Arabs in that year and which may have consisted of soldiers. See Lilie, *Die byzantinische Reaktion*, pp. 70, 237ff.; Ditten, 'Zur Bedeutung der Einwanderung der Slawen', pp. 147ff.; Ditten, 'Slawen im byzantinischen Heer', in *Studien zum 7. Jhdt.*, pp. 77–91, see 86ff.; P. Charanis, 'The transfer of population as a policy in the Byzantine empire', *Comparative Studies in Society and History* 3 (The Hague 1961), 140–54, see 143; and see also Lemerle, *Les plus anciens recueils* II, pp. 130f.
[47] The adherence of the patriarch of Antioch Makarios, along with a seemingly large number of his clergy and the non-monophysite population to monotheletism after the Arab conquest and up to the sixth council of 680 (in which Makarios was formally deposed), is good evidence for this. See Winkelmann, 'Die Quellen', 555–6 and sources.

imperial policy as heresy. The exiled monothelete patriarch of Constantinople, Pyrrhus, debated publicly with Maximus, under the chairmanship of the exarch himself, Gregory, but had to acknowledge defeat; and it may have been the solidarity of the North African bishops and population against the imperial policy that encouraged the exarch to declare his opposition to Constans' rule in 646/7 and have himself proclaimed emperor – perhaps in conscious imitation of the great Heraclius. This short-lived attempt met with failure when in the following year Gregory was killed fighting Arab raiders near Sufetula.[48] The raiders withdrew, but imperial authority was quickly reasserted, although this had little effect upon the internal political and ecclesiastical situation. In an effort to reach yet another compromise, the patriarch Paul issued the famous Typos in 648, and in the name of the emperor, in which it was decreed that the Ekthesis should be removed from the narthex of Hagia Sophia, but that at the same time no further discussion of the issue was to take place: neither was the question of the single will or energy of Christ to be debated, on pain of punishment. A prohibition on discussion, however, designed to prevent further disagreement, and to reinforce imperial authority, which was by now deeply bound up with the monothelete doctrine, was unlikely to lead to an acceptable solution. And indeed, at the Lateran council held in Rome in 649, under the newly elected Pope Martin, the 105 bishops (chiefly from the West) condemned both Ekthesis and Typos, along with the three patriarchs Sergius, Pyrrhus and Paul (then occupying the patriarchal throne). The results were circulated throughout the Church, in East and West, as well as to the emperor himself. Maximus even described the council as the sixth ecumenical council – a direct challenge to the emperor's traditional authority as convenor of such meetings; and recent research has made it clear that the acts of the council were carefully written up by Maximus and his supporters with the express intention of achieving the greatest possible propaganda effect. The council itself seems to have been orchestrated and dominated by Maximus and his confederates, and there can be little doubt that the later (anti-monothelete) orthodox tradition relied for its acounts of the events and the history of the controversy on these 'biased' reports.

The challenge to imperial authority could not be overlooked. It was a total rejection of the imperial policy – and by implication therefore of the emperor's orthodoxy – and his fitness to rule. Constans ordered Olympius,

---

[48] For Gregory's rebellion and the opposition of the African clergy to monotheletism, see Averil Cameron, 'Byzantine Africa – the literary evidence', pp. 56–9; I. Rochow, 'Zu einigen oppositionellen religiösen Strömungen', in *Byzanz im 7. Jhdt.*, pp. 225–88, see 263–4; Diehl, *L'Afrique byzantine*, pp. 555ff.; Stratos, *Byzantium in the Seventh Century*, vol. III, pp. 62–73.

the exarch of Ravenna, to arrest Martin and to compel the bishops then assembled in Rome to accept and sign the Typos. Like Gregory in Africa, however, Olympius seems to have found it more acceptable to rebel and to have himself proclaimed emperor. The imperial government, thoroughly involved in the worsening situation in the East, did nothing. But, also like Gregory, Olympius' independence was short-lived. He died in 652, and in June 653 the new exarch with his troops was able to carry out Constans' orders and arrest the pope. Martin arrived in Constantinople in December, when he was immediately arraigned before the senate. The case against him was based on political evidence – Olympius' rebellion providing the most damning proof of his treasonable conduct. In spite of his protestations, Martin was refused permission or opportunity to speak on the subject of the Typos. He was found guilty and condemned to death, later commuted by Constans to exile in Cherson, where he died – he had already been ill at the time of his arrest – in 656. Maximus suffered a similar fate, arrested and brought from Italy, imprisoned, tried and eventually – after the failure of successive efforts to change his mind, in which the desire of the imperial government for a public recognition from Maximus that the emperor's authority was absolute was made strikingly clear – mutilated and exiled, dying in 662 in the fortress of Schemarion in Lazica, in the Caucasus.[49]

The imperial victory which was thus secured treated some of the symptoms only, however, of a much deeper malaise within the political-ideological world of East Rome. Imperial authority had been forcefully and, in the eyes of many, effectively placed under a question mark. The rights of emperors to define dogma and to approve or disapprove of synodal and other ecclesiastical gatherings of similar status had been queried. But at an even deeper level, the public political debate represented by the monothelete controversy reflected also widespread shifts within the whole framework of the formal imperial ideology and indeed beyond this, within the symbolic universe of Byzantine culture itself. The central position of the emperor in respect of certain key questions had been thrown into relief; his

[49] For Olympius and Italy, see Stratos, *Byzantium in the Seventh Century*, vol. III, pp. 104–11; Stratos, 'The exarch Olympios and the supposed Arab invasion of Sicily in A.D. 652', *JÖB* 25 (1976), 63–73; and for the history and development of the monothelete controversy, the roles of Martin and Maximus, and the outcome of their trials, see esp. Beck, *Kirche*, pp. 430–73; Van Dieten, *Geschichte der Patriarchen*, pp. 179–218; P. Verghese, 'The monothelite controversy – a historical survey', *Greek Orthodox Theol. Review* 13 (1968), 196–211; V. Grumel, 'Recherches sur l'histoire du monothélisme', *EO* 27 (1928), 6–16, 257–77; 28 (1929), 19–34, 272–83; 29 (1930), 16–28; Herrin, *Formation of Christendom*, pp. 255–9, 263–5; and the fundamental studies of R. Riedinger, 'Aus den Akten der Lateransynode von 649', *BZ* 69 (1976), 17–38; 'Griechische Konzilsakten auf dem Wege ins lateinische Mittelalter', *Annuarium Historiae Conciliorum* 9 (1977), 253–301; 'Die Lateransynode von 649. Ein Werk der Byzantiner um Maximos Homologetes', *Byzantina* 13 (1985), 519–34; with further literature and discussion in Winkelmann, 'Die Quellen', 515–59, see 538.

relationship to God and his function as God's vicegerent had also, in some respects, been re-examined. By the later 640s, of course, the territories for whose predominantly monophysite populations the imperial monotheletism of the court and the Constantinopolitan patriarchate had been originally intended were lost to the empire. No doubt it was felt that attempts might be made in the future to bring them back into the empire, and so monotheletism retained its political-religious relevance in this respect. But essentially, monotheletism, and more particularly the efforts of the emperor to impose a monothelete imperial policy on the Chalcedonian clergy, were responses to a different set of developments. As we shall see in a later chapter, these developments and the tendencies noted above were fundamental to the later social and political history of the Byzantine state in the later seventh and eighth centuries.[50]

The Sicilian connection

In 654, Constans had crowned his son Constantine co-emperor; in 659 his two younger sons, Heraclius and Tiberius, were likewise raised to the imperial dignity. With this move Constans took the final step in passing over his younger brother Theodosius; and in 660 he had Theodosius tonsured and shortly afterwards murdered. It may well be that Theodosius was involved in a plot of anti-monothelete groups to depose Constans. However that may be, his treatment of Martin and Maximus, and finally of his brother, seems to have roused the hostility and dislike for him of the population of Constantinople. He was branded as a second Cain; and whether or not he had also long-term strategic reasons for the move, this seems to have encouraged him to transfer the seat of his government from Constantinople to the West. It is indeed interesting, for – as Ostrogorsky noted – the idea does seem to represent a continuity with the plans of both Maurice and Heraclius.[51] Whether this was conscious, or reflected merely the common-sense strategic requirements of a government under intense pressure, must remain uncertain. What it does illustrate is that there was clearly no thought that the West at this time was in some way less central or important to the empire. Indeed, it suggests on the contrary that Constans himself saw the West as both a strategically and politically safer

---

[50] Maximus was the first to have argued that the emperor, as a layperson, had no jurisdiction in questions of belief: see, e.g., *PG* XC, col. 117B–C. This was, of course, to prove an extremely important argument in later debates involving the relationship between secular and ecclesiastical authority in both East and West. For the implications of this controversy and an analysis of its context, see Haldon, 'Ideology and social change', esp. 166ff.

[51] Ostrogorsky, *Geschichte*, p. 101. On the murder of Theodosius, see Stratos, *Byzantium in the Seventh Century*, vol. III, pp. 191ff.; and Theophanes, 347 and 351.

seat of government and administration. The empire was still in the eyes of its subjects and its rulers the Roman empire – Rome itself and Italy (in spite of the Lombards) were a fundamental element of that empire – and, in spite of Islamic naval threats, the empire was still united in its parts by the Mediterranean Sea. Constans' move is a striking testimony to that set of beliefs – even if it is also a testament to the beginning of the disintegration of that pan-Mediterranean world and its culture, and an attempt to reaffirm what was all too rapidly becoming a facet of the glorious past.[52]

It is clear from Constans' activities in Italy, however, that he intended originally to subjugate the Lombards and at the same time to reorganise the defence and administration of Africa against impending Arab attack. He left Constantinople in 661/2, stopping at Thessaloniki, marching on to Athens and Corinth and, embarking again from Corinth or possibly Patras, sailed to Otranto. From here he opened his campaign against the Lombards, at first with considerable success, although failing to take Benevento. As his forces began to suffer from lack of supplies, he eventually had to abandon the siege and retire to Naples, whence he briefly visited Rome. For twelve days he participated in celebrations and prayer, greeted and entertained by Pope Vitalian. Thereafter he returned to Naples and finally established his headquarters in Sicily, at Syracuse. From that point his intention was to set up the defences of the island and of southern Italy against Arab sea-borne attack, and to reassert imperial authority in Africa, which may still have been at that time hostile to his rule, following Gregory's failed rebellion.[53]

Constans' rule in Sicily rapidly became extremely unpopular. He seems to have been in considerable financial difficulties and had to ask for money from the Church of Ravenna. In 666 the see of Ravenna was granted independence from Rome – autocephaly – by Constans (partly, it has been suggested, in response to the generosity of the Church there). But the presence of large numbers of troops of the imperial armies was an enormous burden on the resources of the island and indeed of all southern Italy. While the strategy which led him there seems to have been entirely logical, his desire to transfer his headquarters there on a permanent basis met with a great deal of opposition. His wife and three sons were prevented from joining him by officers of state and by members of the demes. Finally, in 668, he became the victim of an assassination plot. On 15 September he was murdered in his bath by a *cubicularius*, and shortly thereafter the

---

[52] A good description of the campaigns up to the emperor's establishment in Italy can be found in Stratos, *Byzantium in the Seventh Century*, vol. III, pp. 197ff.

[53] The march to Italy, the campaigns undertaken en route, and Constans' stay in Sicily have been the subject of much discussion. See Ostrogorsky, *Geschichte*, pp. 101–3; Stratos, *Byzantium in the Seventh Century*, vol. III, pp. 209–17, vol. IV, pp. 8f. and esp. P. Corsi, *La spedizione Italiana di Costante II* (Bologna 1983)

Armenian general Mzez Gnouni, or Mizizios, as he is called in the Greek sources, count of the *Opsikion*, the praesental army of the emperor, was acclaimed emperor. He seems to have had little actual or serious support, for the arrival of the exarch Gregory with his troops put an end to the usurpation. Mzez was executed.[54] Constans' body was returned to Constantinople, where it was interred in the Church of the Holy Apostles.

The coup which ended the reign of Constans, when he was only thirty years of age, was in itself not an entirely unexpected turn of events. As we have seen, the treatment he meted out to his brother and to Martin and Maximus and their followers had not added to his popularity. In addition, there surfaced from time to time in the background of Constans' reign a faction or factions within the senate and the ruling military circles which were hostile to him. He had already at the beginning of his reign been threatened by the power of Valentinus; but the latter seems to have been checked by the senate and other factions and interests in the capital. He had been fortunate in the failure of first the exarch Gregory and then Olympius, in Africa and Italy respectively. Both were areas where the combination of civil and military authority in the hands of a single governor made opposition to Constantinople a possibility; both were areas where cultural and linguistic differences made the development of a localised and occasionally – depending upon the political and ideological context – anti-Constantinopolitan feeling inevitable.[55] Already in 616 and 619, and again in 642, there had been mutinies or rebellions in Italy; and while the first seems to have been little more than a mutiny over pay in the army, those of 619 and 642 were clearly of a more political nature.[56] Equally problematic for Constans seems to have been the Armenian military faction, whose members dominated the chief military posts at this period. A plot in 652 involving members of the senate and of the Armenian military aristocracy, some of whom held commands in the forces then in Thrace, was betrayed to Constans while he was himself in Armenia, and he was able to arrest the conspirators in good time.[57] This plot in particular may represent senatorial hostility to the no longer malleable young

---

[54] See Haldon, *Byzantine Praetorians*, p. 179 and note 377 for Constans' troops in Italy and Sicily. For Mzez, see *ibid.*, p. 359 and note 1091; and Stratos, *Byzantium in the Seventh Century*, vol. IV, pp. 8–14; Ostrogorsky, *Geschichte*, pp. 102–3; Guillou, *Régionalisme*, p. 160; T.S. Brown, 'The Church of Ravenna and the imperial administration in the seventh century', *EHR*, 94 (1979), 1–28, esp. 17; for the grant of autocephaly, *ibid.*, 11ff.
[55] See Guillou, *Régionalisme*, esp. pp. 231ff. and 236ff. comparing Egypt, Africa and Italy; and the comments of T.S. Brown, 'The Interplay between Roman and Byzantine Traditions', 148ff. and 151–4.
[56] See Ch. Diehl, *L'Exarchat de Ravenne*, pp. 340f.; Guillou, *Régionalisme*, pp. 204ff.; Stratos, *Byzantium in the Seventh Century*, vol. I, pp. 121–2, vol. III, pp. 76–9; Brown, *Gentlemen and Officers*, pp. 159–63.
[57] See Stratos, *Byzantium in the Seventh Century*, vol. III, pp. 190–1.

emperor, who had been under the influence of his advisers since his accession, but who was by this time clearly beginning to assert his independence with increasing confidence.

Constans seems throughout his reign to have been the target of conspiracies, and these were, in many respects – and as I have argued elsewhere – a reflection or symptom of deeper changes in attitudes to the person of the emperor and to his role, as well as of the often confused situation in which the empire found itself at this period. Rebellions in Armenia were an important political factor for the government, for the nationalism and the clan traditions of the powerful Armenian princely and noble houses meant that the area was easily alienated. The continued conflict between Chalcedonian and monophysite Churches there, and the vested interests of both the caliphate (which now replaced the Sassanids in this role) and the Byzantines, meant that Armenia was a constant source of conflict and a potential threat to imperial security. In 648 or 649 Constans issued an order that the Armenian Church should accept its subordination to the Church of Constantinople and the Chalcedonian creed. In response, the Armenian clergy and many princes, including the Byzantine governor, Theodore Rstuni, met at the synod of Dvin in 649, where the imperial order was condemned and rejected.[58] The result was an agreement between Armenia and the Arabs by which the former threw off Byzantine authority and accepted Muslim overlordship. Constans was persuaded to march against the rebellious princes and, in a short campaign, suceeded in forcing the rebels to withdraw. But he had to return to the West in 652 in order to deal with the plot in Thrace in that year, leaving as commander-in-chief the general Marianus who, after the Armenian rebels had received Arab reinforcements, was defeated and his troops routed. Armenia remained semi-independent and under Muslim domination until after the murder of the Caliph Othman; upon which the Armenian Prince Hamazasp Mamikonian once again brought Armenia back into the Byzantine fold.[59] This was not the end of the problem, however. A rebellion of the *stratēgos* of the *Armeniakōn* district, the Armenian Šahpur (Saborios), took place in 668 while Constans was in the West. Again, the issue was resolved by the untimely death of the rebel, whereupon the troops of the region reaffirmed their loyalty to the empire. But it is once more symptomatic of the sort of difficulties facing the government at this time in respect

---

[58] For a summary of Byzantine–Armenian relations and the Arab attacks in the Caucasus see Stratos, *Byzantium in the Seventh Century*, vol. III, pp. 19ff.; and for the attempt at union and subsequent developments, *ibid.*, 26–31; Winkelmann, *Die östlichen Kirchen*, pp. 129–30.

[59] On these events see Stratos, *Byzantium in the Seventh Century*, vol. III, pp. 27–31; Kaegi, *Military Unrest*, pp. 162–3.

of the complex interrelationship between local identities, state politics and religious issues.[60]

Constans' reign is in many ways the most crucial of the seventh century, although we are often able to interpret with difficulty the developments reflected in the rather limited source materials. It was during his reign that the limits of Muslim expansion into Anatolia were reached and that what was to become for the next two centuries the 'frontier zone' was attained. It was during his reign, in all probability, that the basic elements of thematic provincial and military administration came into being. He was the first emperor to realise the potential of transplanting large numbers of Slav prisoners to devastated areas of Anatolia, both to provide manpower for the army and to repopulate the regions most affected by Arab raiding. He had to deal with the Arab threat on both a naval and military basis; and it was also during his reign that the importance of the Armenian noble clans and of Armenians in Byzantine service takes on a real significance. Most importantly, perhaps, Constans represents in many respects the ruler who epitomised the struggle of the emperors to retain their absolute authority in both Church and state affairs on the Justinianic and traditional model. Thereafter, the role of the emperors in Church matters and the position of the emperor in the relationship between God and humanity, as theorised in formal ideology and popular conception, underwent a series of subtle changes which were to have important consequences for his successors.

CONSTANTINE IV, 668–685

Constans was succeeded by his son Constantine, during whose reign the first great siege of Constantinople took place. The Arab offensive had been renewed in 663, shortly after Mu^{c}awiya's victory over ^{c}Ali, and this time the general outline of a coherent strategy became apparent: together with constant raids along the frontier and raids deep into the Anatolian provinces, designed to disrupt economic activity and the defensive capabilities of the Byzantine armies, Mu^{c}awiya's ultimate aim was clearly the capture of Constantinople itself and the overthrow of Islam's only remaining foe of any consequence in the Mediterranean.[61] Cyprus, Rhodes, Cos and Cyzicus had all been occupied by Arab naval forces by 670, thus securing a firm base from which to mount the final assault on the city. In 672 another squadron occupied Smyrna and set up another, temporary, base; and in 674 the main action commenced. A large Arab

---

[60] See Stratos, *Byzantium in the Seventh Century*, vol. III, pp. 236ff.; Kaegi, *Military Unrest*, pp. 166f.
[61] For a detailed analysis, see Lilie, *Die byzantinische Reaktion*, pp. 69–97; and note Gabrieli, *Muhammad and the Conquests of Islam*, pp. 232–3

Plate 2.3 Constantine IV. Gold *solidus*

fleet arrived off Constantinople and blockaded the city. Each summer for the next four years the same fleet blockaded Constantinople, withdrawing to shelter off Cyzicus for the winter season; and each year the defence held firm. During the final naval battle the Byzantine fleet used its terror weapon, mentioned in the sources for the first time, the deadly Greek fire. Supposedly invented by the Syrian architect and mechanic Callinicus, who had fled from his homeland to Constantinople, this seems to have consisted essentially of crude oil, possibly with a few extra ingredients (various inflammable and 'sticky' resins, for example) which when heated was expelled through a siphon at enemy vessels. It was, in effect, a sort of primitive napalm. The result was a major Byzantine victory. At the same time, Byzantine land forces were able to surprise and defeat one of the major Arab columns in Anatolia; and Muʿawiya was forced to withdraw his armies and ships and sue for peace. A thirty-year peace was signed, and the caliph undertook to make a yearly payment of 3,000 gold pieces, together with fifty Byzantine prisoners and fifty stallions.[62]

The effects of this defeat were enormous. It signalled the end of Muʿawiya's plans to take Constantinople and incorporate Rūm into the caliphate. It immediately increased Byzantine prestige in the Balkans and the West, so that both the khagan of the Avars (now confined effectively to the plain of Hungary) and the princes and chieftains of the Balkan Slavs sent ambassadors to Constantinople bearing gifts and recognising Byzantine supremacy.[63] In the East, peace with the caliphate meant that the Byzantines could now concentrate properly on their northern and western fronts. At the same time, internal dissension within the caliphate after Muʿawiya's death in 680 and the accession of Yazid I meant the end, for

---

[62] For the siege and the eventual Byzantine victory, see Lilie, *Die byzantinische Reaktion*, pp. 76–82; Dölger, *Regesten*, no. 239; Stratos, *Byzantium in the Seventh Century*, vol. IV, pp. 29–39; Ostrogorsky, *Geschichte*, pp. 103–4. On Greek fire see J.F. Haldon and M. Byrne, 'A possible solution to the problem of Greek fire', *BZ* 70 (1977), 91–9.

[63] Cf. Theophanes, 356.2sq.; Nicephorus, 33.6sq.

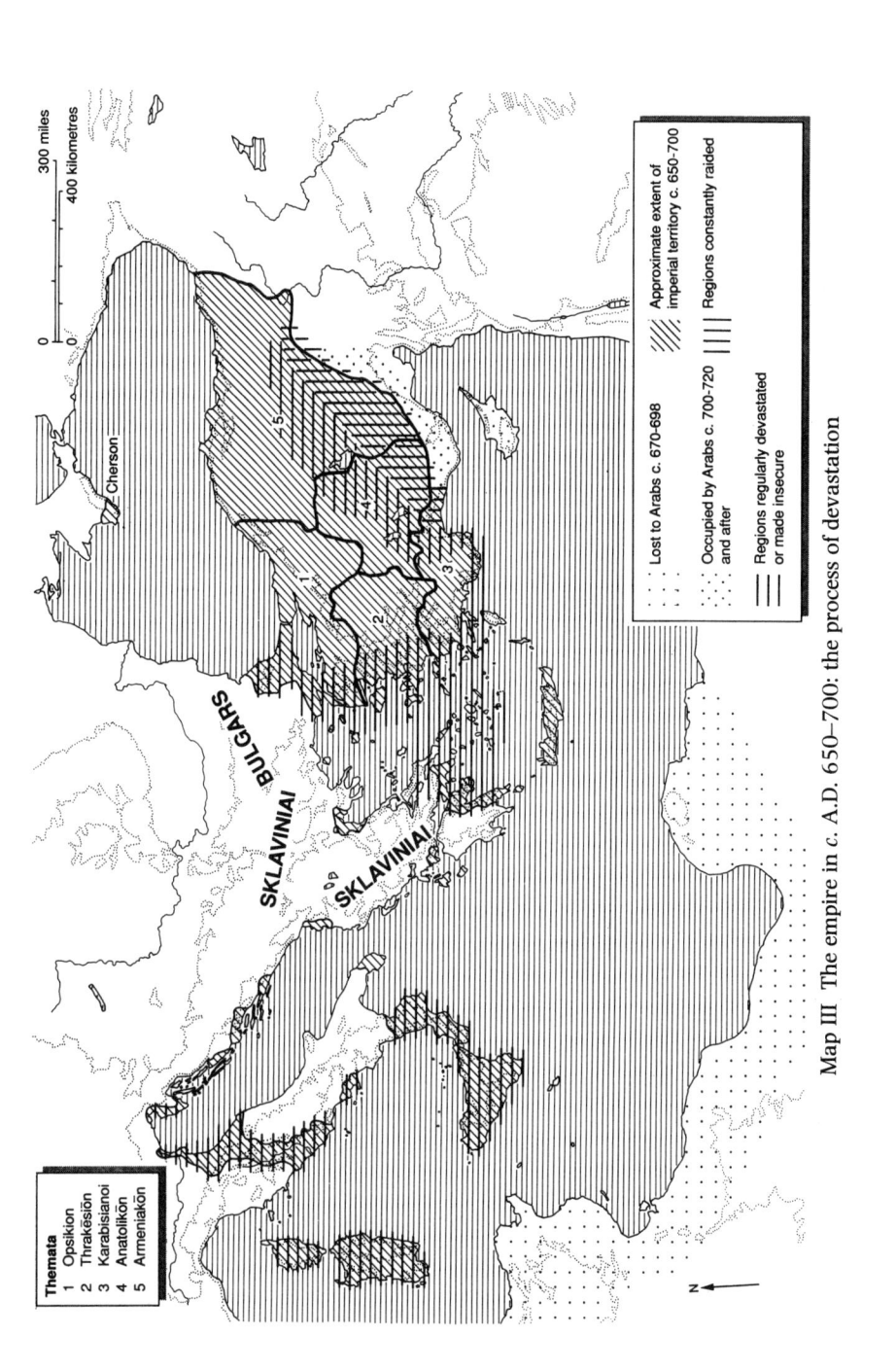

Map III The empire in c. A.D. 650–700: the process of devastation

the time being, of the Arab threat.[64] The Anatolian provinces were given a short time to recover from the economic and demographic devastation they had suffered, while the empire was able to consolidate the administrative and organisational changes that had taken place since the 640s.

The Bulgars

In the Balkans, however, the empire was soon faced by a new and equally dangerous enemy. While a notional suzerainty was still exercised by the Byzantines over much of the peninsula south of the Danube, this was limited in real terms to some coastal and riverine settlements and fortresses and certain littoral strips, particularly in Greece and the Peloponnese, but also in Dalmatia. The extent inland of actual Byzantine authority remains unclear, although the subject is still hotly debated. Numerous attacks were directed by the Slavs against Byzantine fortresses and towns, and in particular on Thessaloniki, which continued throughout the century to lead a precarious existence. It was besieged in 675–6 and 677; while Slav pirates raided other Byzantine coastal lands in 678–9, for example.[65] The number of punitive expeditions mounted by the emperors in the last third of the seventh century suggests that imperial control can have been neither very great nor at all secure.[66] The situation changed dramatically, however, with the advent of the Bulgars. The khanate of old Great Bulgaria, a confederation of Onogur–Bulgar clans, had already entered into friendly relations with Byzantium in the first half of the seventh century, as we have seen; and it was with Byzantine support that its ruler,

[64] Lilie, *Die byzantinische Reaktion*, pp. 97ff. The question of the involvement of the Mardaites in compelling the Arabs to treat with the Byzantines is also relevant, of course. These mountain brigands – whether or not they were encouraged by official Byzantine policy – were a real threat to the internal security of the Lebanon and north Syria; and it seems that the Byzantines were able to use them as a further inducement for the caliphate to come to terms. See Stratos, *Byzantium in the Seventh Century*, vol. IV, p. 39ff.; Lilie, *Die byzantinische Reaktion*, pp. 99, 101f. On the civil war in the caliphate, see G. Rotter, 'Die Umayyaden und der zweite Bürgerkrieg (680–692)', Abhandlungen für die Kunde des Morgenlandes, XXXXV, 3 (Wiesbaden 1982).

[65] See Ditten, 'Zur Bedeutung der Einwanderung der Slawen', pp. 149f.; and P. Lemerle, 'Invasions et migrations dans les Balkans depuis la fin de l'époque romaine jusqu'au VIIIe siècle', *RH* 211 (1954), 265–308, see 301f.; Stratos, *Byzantium in the Seventh Century*, vol. IV, pp. 63ff.

[66] See the excellent discussion with literature of Ditten, 'Zur Bedeutung der Einwanderung der Slawen', pp. 132–6 with 113–19. Note also Obolensky, *The Byzantine Commonwealth*, p. 59; Stratos, *Byzantium in the Seventh Century*, vol. I, pp. 332ff.; Ostrogorsky, *Geschichte*, pp. 87–8; and Lemerle, *Les plus anciens recueils*, II, p. 128. Important gains were made, of course. After the expedition of Constantine IV in 678 some degree of Byzantine control seems to have been accepted by Slav tribes in the Thessaloniki region. The political events of the period 682–4 and the Kouber/Mauros episode seems to confirm this. See Lemerle, *Les plus anciens recueils*, II, pp. 138–62 (and I, pp. 222–34 for the text).

Kovrat, threw off the Avar yoke. About the middle of the century this loose amalgam was broken up by the arrival of the Chazars. Some of the Bulgars were incorporated into the Chazar khanate; other groups fled, mostly westwards. Among them was a group under the leadership of Asparuch, one of the sons of Kovrat, who appeared north of the Danube delta in the years after 670, intending to settle in 'Byzantine' territory across the Danube and to exploit the fertile pasturelands to the south. The Byzantines certainly recognised no threat in the Bulgars' arrival; but they were nevertheless unwilling to permit them to enter what was, in political theory if not in actuality, Byzantine territory. In 680 a fleet was despatched with troops to the mouth of the Danube, while a cavalry force marched up from Thrace, intending to expel the Bulgars from their stronghold in the delta. The Bulgars avoided open battle, but were able to take advantage of a Byzantine withdrawal to take the imperial forces by surprise and inflict a substantial defeat upon them. In 681 Constantine IV concluded a treaty with Asparuch which recognised the Bulgar occupation of the territories already held and agreed to an annual tribute or subsidy.[67] As a result of this arrangement, the Byzantines lost control of a number of Slav groups who had hitherto recognised Byzantine overlordship in the area about the lower Danube from the Dniester to the Balkan range itself, including part of the plain of Walachia, south Bessarabia, the Dobrudja, and the older province of Moesia Inferior. The so-called 'seven tribes', the Severi, and several other groups in these regions now came under Bulgar overlordship, and from this time the development of a Bulgaro-Slav state in the north-eastern Balkan zone can be followed. The capital of this new khanate was established at Pliska, strategically placed to control the approaches to the Dobrudja, and the route from the Danube via Anchialus to Constantinople itself. From this time on, the existence of an independent and often hostile Bulgar power was to be the cause of some of the greatest difficulties faced by the empire and was to have a decisive influence on the course of Byzantine history.[68]

The end of monotheletism

These new developments in the Balkans coincided with a major shift in Byzantine policy regarding monotheletism. As we have seen, Constans had enforced the observance of his Typos of 648 and had eventually bullied the

[67] See Ostrogorsky, *Geschichte*, p. 105; Stratos, *Byzantium in the Seventh Century*, vol. IV, pp. 93ff., 101–13; Avenarius, *Die Awaren in Europa*, pp. 171ff.; Lilie, *Die byzantinische Reaktion*, pp. 99–100.
[68] See Obolensky, *The Byzantine Commonwealth*, pp. 63f.; Ditten, *Zur Bedeutung der Einwanderung der Slawen*, pp. 135 and 150; Stratos, *Byzantium in the Seventh Century*, vol. IV, pp. 101ff.; Ostrogorsky, *Geschichte*, p. 106.

orthodox opposition to his policies into silence. With his death, and more importantly with the pragmatic recognition that the relevance of this compromise was now lost, along with the majority of the monophysite provinces, while Rome and the West retained their political and strategic significance for the empire, Constantine IV decided that the time was ripe for a reconciliation between the imperial and the Western Churches. With the agreement of Rome, the sixth ecumenical council was convoked and met from 3 November 680 until 16 September 681. Its main task was to rescind the doctrines of monenergism and monotheletism and return the Christian world to doctrinal unity. Those who were held responsible for its introduction and spread were anathematised: the patriarchs Sergius, Pyrrhus and Paul, together with Pope Honorius. Altogether the council held eighteen sittings, mostly presided over and led by the emperor himself; and at its final meeting he was hailed as the 'new Marcian' and the 'new Justinian', the destroyer of heretics.[69] The sixth council represents an important moment in East–West relations and in the history of the Church; it represents also a recognition on the part of Constantine that the split in the Church, which had without any doubt been promoted by his father, was injurious to his own position, as orthodox ruler and defender of the faith, and his authority in theoretical and theological terms. In practical respects, of course, this was unquestioned. But as long as an argument based upon his 'heretical' stand as a monothelete could be voiced, his position was threatened.[70] Constantine took some time to reach his final decision on the convening of a council, however; and in his letter to the patriarch George I (679–86), with whom he had replaced the less malleable Theodore I in 679, he explains the long delay in the calling of a synod as a result of the many cares and problems he had had to deal with in view of the hard-pressed military situation.[71] While this was certainly the case, it is reasonable to suppose that Constantine deliberated over his change of policy for some considerable time.

Internal conflict on the political-ideological plane was not lacking, however. In order to secure his own position and that of his young son Justinian, Constantine decided to deprive his two younger brothers, Heraclius and Tiberius, crowned during Constans' reign, of all rights to the throne and the imperial dignity. This met with immediate opposition from

[69] Mansi XI, 656; Riedinger, 798.10–11.
[70] For the council, see L. Bréhier, in A. Fliche and V. Martin, eds., *Histoire de l'église depuis les origines jusqu'à nos jours* V: *Grégoire le grand, les états barbares et la conquête arabe (590–757)* (Paris 1938), pp. 183ff.; F.X. Murphy and P. Sherwood, *Constantinople II et Constantinople III* (Paris 1974), pp. 133ff.; Winkelmann, *Die östlichen Kirchen*, pp. 110–12. See also Stratos, *Byzantium in the Seventh Century*, vol. IV, pp. 115–31; Herrin, *Formation of Christendom*, pp. 275–81.
[71] See Mansi, XI 201C–D; Riedinger, 10.21–25.

the army and the senate, who already in 670 had extracted a confirmation of his brothers' rights from Constantine; and in 681 troops from the *Anatolikōn thema* appeared at Chalcedon demanding that Constantine respect the position and status of the two brothers. 'We believe in the Trinity', Theophanes reports them to have said, 'and we wish to see three crowned emperors.'[72] Constantine brooked no opposition. He deprived his brothers of their titles and shortly afterwards had their noses slit. The leaders of the *Anatolikōn* mutineers were arrested and executed, and the troops returned to their bases. Imperial authority had once again been restored. It has been noted that Constantine's action was similar in its effects to that of Constans against his brother Theodosius, a move tending to reinforce the growing tradition of single rule passed on to an eldest son; so that while sons of emperors are crowned as equals in theory, in practice power was exercised only by the *autokrator* himself. This is an important development, for it sees the gradual ending of the traditional 'college' of emperors which had been the norm in the later sixth century and under Heraclius.[73]

Constantine's last years were marked by a relatively stable situation on both the northern and eastern fronts. In 684/5 he personally led an expedition into Cilicia, threatening north Syria, and compelled the caliph ᶜAbd al-Malik to pay a tribute of 1,000 *nomismata* per day, together with a symbolic horse and a slave, in return for the Byzantines halting their advance.[74] In Italy the reconciliation with Rome (in spite of the long-term results of the agreement, which were again to cause dissension between Rome and Constantinople over their respective ecumenical status), together with a peace arranged through the papacy with the Lombards,[75] brought a situation of relative unrest to an end; while in Africa, in spite of Arab successes in regularly raiding the Byzantine provinces and, more importantly, in beginning to outflank them through the large-scale forced conversion of the Berber population to Islam, the key fortresses and cities of the exarchate still held firm. Indeed, during Constantine's last years the Byzantines were able to take advantage of an alliance with the Berbers to defeat a major Arab force under the great leader ᶜUqba. The Arabs were

---

[72] For the confirmation of 670, Dölger, *Regesten*, no. 236. For the demands of the *Anatolikōn*, see Theophanes, 352.15 and see Stratos, *Byzantium in the Seventh Century*, vol. IV, pp. 135–40, who argues that the brothers were in addition involved in a plot, together with troops from the *Anatolikōn thema* who had recently been defeated by the Bulgars, to maintain state monotheletism.
[73] See the comment of Ostrogorsky, *Geschichte*, pp. 107f.
[74] See Lilie's account, *Die byzantinische Reaktion*, pp. 100f.; and Stratos, *Byzantium in the Seventh Century*, vol. IV, pp 165ff.
[75] For a summary of the events, Stratos, *Byzantium in the Seventh Century*, vol. IV, pp. 55–62.

Plate 2.4 Leontius II. Gold *solidus*

forced to evacuate the territories they had occupied in Tripolitania and Byzacene and withdraw to the Libyan littoral, where the Pentapolis had been in Muslim hands since the 640s. And while this situation lasted only a few years, it demonstrated that the conquest of North Africa would not be as easy as that of Egypt. On the other hand, it is also clear that the Byzantines themselves contributed very little to Arab difficulties, withdrawing to their cities and fortresses and, on the whole, passively awaiting the outcome. One by one the Berber clans were converted to Islam, the remaining, isolated Byzantine fortresses and settlements fell, until Carthage itself was taken in 697 and then, after a temporary Byzantine success in retaking it, definitively in 698.[76]

JUSTINIAN II, 685–695 AND 705–711

Constantine, who was only thirty-five years old when he died, was succeeded by his seventeen-year old son, Justinian II, in September 685. He seems to have been a despotic and arrogant young man, not gifted with his father's tact or willingness (under certain conditions) to compromise. He has been compared, unfavourably, with his autocratic grandfather Constans. He was an able ruler, however, and in his first year exploited the internal situation of the caliphate greatly to his advantage. The threat of new attacks and a renewed Byzantine offensive persuaded the Caliph ᶜAbd al-Malik to confirm the arrangements he had previously made with Constantine IV. Not only were the tribute payments increased, but he agreed also to share the income from the island of Cyprus, and that from Armenia and Iberia, with the Byzantines. Cyprus remained a shared territory for many years thereafter; while Iberian and Armenian revenues

[76] Gabrieli, *Muhammad and the Conquests of Islam*, pp. 180ff.; Averil Cameron, 'Byzantine Africa – the Literary Evidence', pp. 59f.; J. Durliat, 'Les Attributions civiles des évèques byzantins: l'exemple du Diocèse d'Afrique (533–709)', *JÖB* 32, 2 (1982), 73–84, see 78ff. (= Akten des XVI. Internationalen Byzantinisten-Kongresses II, 2); Diehl, *L'Afrique byzantine*, pp. 576–92; M. Brett, 'The Arab conquest and the rise of Islam in N. Africa', in *Cambridge History of Africa*, vol. II (Cambridge 1978), pp. 490–555, esp. 503–13. See also Av. Cameron, 'Gelimer's laughter: the case of Byzantine Africa', in F.M. Clover, R.S. Humphreys, eds., *Tradition and Innovation in Late Antiquity* (Madison 1989) 171–90 (repr. in eadem, *Changing Cultures in Early Byzantium* [Aldershot 1996] VIII).

were in fact no great loss, since these territories were barely under the caliph's authority at that time, owing to the civil war. In return, the Mardaites, who had been a thorn in the flesh of the Muslim authorities in north Syria and Lebanon, using their mountain fastnesses as a base from which to plunder and raid the surrounding countryside, were transferred to western Asia Minor.[77] The Byzantine general Leontius marched against the forces of Ibn az-Zubair, the common enemy now of both the caliph and the emperor, in Armenia, Iberia and Caucasian Albania, devastating wide areas and taking many prisoners. This occurred in 688/9.

The truce in the East, and the relatively favourable position of the empire, meant that Justinian could turn his attention to the Balkans. In 687/8 troops were transferred from Anatolia to Thrace, and in the following year Justinian himself led the expedition against the Slavs and Bulgars, breaking through to Thessaloniki and subjecting a large number of Slavs to Byzantine rule. The real situation in the Balkans is reflected in the fact that the emperor had to fight his way through from Thrace to Macedonia. Most significant for the empire was the transfer of large numbers of Slavs to Asia Minor, in particular to Bithynia and Cappadocia, where they seem to have been eventually drafted into the provincial armies, as a number of lead seals of the officials who dealt with them demonstrate.[78] Justinian also undertook the transfer of a section of the population of Cyprus to the area of Cyzicus, hard-hit by the Arab occupation of 674–8 – as well as of the Mardaites, mentioned already, to the Peloponnese, parts of the south-west coastal region of Asia Minor, the island of Cephallenia and the region around the important port of Nicopolis in Epirus.[79]

The transfer of the Cypriots seems to have been a breach of the agreement whereby the island was to remain neutral, although it is unclear as

---

[77] Lilie, *Die byzantinische Reaktion*, pp. 102–8; Stratos, *Byzantium in the Seventh Century*, vol. V, pp. 19ff.; R.J.H. Jenkins, 'Cyprus between Byzantium and Islam, A.D. 688–965', in *Studies Presented to D.M. Robinson* (St Louis 1953), pp. 1006–14, see 1006ff.; C. Mango, 'Chypre, carrefour du monde byzantin', *XVe Congrès International d'Etudes Byzantines. Rapports et co-rapports* V, 5 (Athens 1976), pp. 3–13, see 4ff.

[78] See Theophanes, 364 and Ostrogorsky, *Geschichte*, p. 109, notes 2 and 3; Lilie, *Die byzantinische Reaktion*, pp. 237ff.; Ditten, 'Zur Bedeutung der Einwanderung der Slawen', pp. 152f.; Charanis, 'The Transfer of Population', 143. See also Ai. Christophilopoulou, Βυζαντινὴ Ἱστορία, vol. II, 610–867 (Athens 1981), pp. 365f., and esp. H. Köpstein, 'Zum Bedeutungswandel von σκλάβος/sclavus', *BF* 7 (1979), 67–88: the fact that Byzantine seals refer to the Slav settlers as prisoners of war/slaves may lie behind the development of the equivalent Slav – slave. See chapter 6 below.

[79] See Stratos, *Byzantium in the Seventh Century*, vol. V, pp. 59f.; Lilie, *Die byzantinische Reaktion*, p. 105f.; Ditten, 'Zur Bedeutung der Einwanderung der Slawen', p. 156; Ostrogorsky, *Geschichte*, p. 110; Charanis, 'The Transfer of Population', 143–4. The Cypriots in fact returned to their island shortly after (see Theophanes, 365; Michael Syr., vol. II, 470) and their settlement, Justinianoupolis (see Mansi XI, 961), was abandoned. Justinian is also reported to have settled 'Scythians' in east Macedonia in the Strymon region: cf. Constantine Porphyrogenitus, *De Thematibus*, 88f.

to whether the caliph took it as a serious cause of offence. In 692/3, however, Justinian decided to break the truce and to attack the Arab forces in Iraq, newly pacified by ᶜAbd al-Malik, and therefore a weak link in the Arab defences. ᶜAbd al-Malik had to go on to the offensive, but as a result of the mass desertion of the recently drafted Slav troops, the Byzantine forces were soundly defeated. A second Byzantine attack in the following year was also thrown back. The immediate result was the submission of the Armenian princes once again to Muslim overlordship and the beginning of a new series of regular raids into Anatolia, which had barely begun to recover from the previous forty years of devastation. Justinian's desire for military glory, and his foolhardiness, did not have by any means a satisfactory outcome for the empire.[80]

According to Theophanes, Justinian had the remaining Slavs and their families massacred in revenge for the betrayal, although this seems to be a later and not very reliable accretion to the account. What is known is that the Arabs settled the deserters in Syria, where they entered Arab service and proved extremely valuable owing to their knowledge of some of the localities that formed targets for the yearly Muslim raids.[81] Justinian's policy of transferring large numbers of Slavs to Asia Minor to repopulate devastated areas figures large in the historiography of the seventh century. Its importance in revitalising or in maintaining the economy of considerable areas of agriculturally valuable land must certainly have been great. The policy was in itself not new. Already during the reign of Justinian I such transfers of population had occurred. Under Maurice, Armenians were transferred to Thrace. Goths and Vandals had been likewise settled in Anatolia during the later fourth and fifth centuries; while in the eighth and ninth centuries the policy was continued by both Constantine V, for example, and Basil I, among others.[82] Already by the reign of Justinian II the system of military districts, or *themata*, under their generals, or *stratēgoi*, seems to have become established; and there is no reason to doubt that the resettlement of Slavs in, for example, Bithynia, was designed also to

---

[80] See Lilie, *Die byzantinische Reaktion*, pp. 109ff.; Stratos, *Byzantium in the Seventh Century*, vol. V, pp. 30–9, and see pp. 24–27 on Armenia. For a general survey of the role of Armenia between Byzantium and Islam in the seventh century see P. Charanis, 'The Armenians in the Byzantine empire', *BS* 22 (1961), 196–240; H. Manandean, 'Les Invasions arabes en Arménie (notes chronologiques)', *B* 18 (1946–8), 163–95; and J. Laurent, *L'Arménie entre Byzance et l'Islam depuis la conquête arabe jusqu'en 886* (Paris 1919).

[81] Theophanes, 366; Lilie, *Die byzantinische Reaktion*, p. 111 note 22; Ditten, 'Zur Bedeutung der Einwanderung der Slawen', p. 153.

[82] See esp. Ditten, 'Zur Bedeutung der Einwanderung der Slawen,' pp. 155–7, and 'Slawen im byzantinischen Heer von Justinian I. bis Justinian II.', in H. Köpstein and F. Winkelmann, eds., *Studien zum 7. Jahrhundert in Byzanz*, pp. 77–91.

boost the available manpower for these locally raised forces. I will discuss this in greater detail in the next chapters.

The Quinisext council of 692

Justinian's religious policy followed on from that of his father with, however, a very much more pronounced emphasis on the independence and supremacy of the see of Constantinople, the one question on which Constantine IV had compromised with Rome. Justinian presented himself as particularly orthodox, and in placing the motto *servus Christi* on his coins, together with a bust of Christ, he emphasised both the source of his authority and his own subordination to that source.[83] In a letter of February 687 to the pope, the emperor again stressed his function as God's representative and chosen guardian of orthodoxy;[84] and in confirmation of his role he summoned in 692 the so-called Quinisext or Troullan council, thus named because it dealt with and confirmed matters treated at the fifth and sixth ecumenical councils (in 553 and 680/1 respectively) and was held in the Troullos or domed hall of the imperial palace. In addition to dealing with matters of dogma and ecclesiastical politics, the Quinisext dealt also with matters of clerical and lay discipline, problems of provincial Church and parish administration, and popular practices and beliefs. It provides in this respect a crucially important insight into provincial life and customs; but its canons also demonstrate the extent to which Arab raids and the state of almost uninterrupted warfare in the frontier areas of Anatolia especially had disrupted the patterns of both normal rural and urban life.[85]

Perhaps the most significant decisions of the council, however, were those which dealt with the jurisdiction and traditions of the sees of Rome and Constantinople and their relationship. The marriage of priests was permitted, in contrast to the traditions of the Roman Church (canons 3 and 13); the Roman Saturday fast, observed during the Lenten period, was rejected (canon 55); canon 82 prohibited the representation of Christ as a lamb – an increasingly popular form in the West – insisting that he be presented in human form, thereby stressing the greatness of his suffering and his sacrifice, as God made man, for humankind. But even more explicitly, canon 36 took up canon 3 of the council of Constantinople of 381 and canon 28 of the council of Chalcedon of 451 in stressing the

---

[83] J.D. Breckenridge, *The Numismatic Iconography of Justinian II (A.D. 685–95, 705–711)* (New York 1959); cf. also A. Grabar, *L'Empereur dans l'art byzantin. Recherches sur l'art officiel de l'empire d'Orient* (Paris 1936 and London 1971), p. 164.
[84] Cf. Mansi, XI. 737f.; Riedinger, 886f.; Dölger, *Regesten*, no. 254.
[85] See, for example, Haldon, 'Some considerations', 91f. On the Quinisext and its canons, see Chapter 8, p. 318 and n. 113 below.

equality of the sees of Rome and Constantinople in all matters except the date of their establishment, and having precedence over the sees of Alexandria, Antioch and Jerusalem.[86]

The papacy, of course, rejected the canons of the council as not ecumenical and rejected them in their entirety. Justinian, perhaps thinking of his grandfather Constans and Pope Martin, ordered the *prōtospatharios* Zacharias to Rome, to arrest the pope and return with him to Constantinople. But the troops of Rome, as well as those of Ravenna, opposed this, and indeed the imperial officer escaped the Roman mob only through the good offices of the pope himself.[87] Justinian was unable to respond to this opposition and the humiliation he had suffered; for shortly afterwards, towards the end of 695, a coup in the city deprived him of his throne. His unpopular and harsh fiscal policies, put into practice by the general logothete Theodotus and the *sacellarius* Stephen, had already made him an unpopular ruler. He seems also to have paid little heed to the will or the authority of the senate and the leading officers of state, while his policies in general seem to have won him the hostility of the provinces. In the coup, the Blue deme (one of the two chief hippodrome supporters' organisations) acclaimed Leontius, the recently appointed general of the *thema* of Hellas, as emperor and, with the assistance of elements of the senate, together with the connivance of the city and palatine troops, they were able to seize Justinian and his hated subordinates. Theodotus and Stephen were executed; Justinian had his nose and tongue slit, and was banished to Cherson, where some forty years earlier his grandfather had sent the hapless Martin.[88]

Justinian's successors

The Emperor Leontius ruled for just three years and presided over the final extinction of Byzantine power in Africa. Little is known of his policies, but he seems to have been a popular ruler.[89] In 697 he despatched elements of the fleet – chiefly made up of units of the Kibyrrhaiotai – to retake

---

[86] See L. Bréhier, in Fliche and Martin, eds., *Histoire de l'église*, V, pp. 194ff.; the canons: Mansi XI, 921–1005. For a brief summary, Winkelmann, *Die östlichen Kirchen*, pp. 112–13. On the purpose of the council, in particular the implicit intention of reinforcing Constantinopolitan as opposed to both Roman and other practice, see V. Laurent, 'L'Œuvre canonique du Concile in Trullo (691–692), source primaire du droit de l'église orientale', *REB* 23 (1965), 7–41, see 10ff.'

[87] See F. Görres, 'Justinian II. und das römische Papsttum', *BZ* 17 (1908), 432–54, see 440ff.; Stratos, *Byzantium in the Seventh Century*, vol. V, p. 53–6; Guillou, *Régionalisme*, pp. 209–11; Herrin, *Formation of Christendom*, 282–7.

[88] See Ostrogorsky, *Geschichte*, pp. 117f.; Stratos, *Byzantium in the Seventh Century*, vol. V, pp. 66–74 (although the account is in parts somewhat eccentric); and Kaegi, *Military Unrest*, pp. 186ff.

[89] Grierson, *DOC*, vol. II, p. 610; J.B. Bury, *The Later Roman Empire from Arcadius to Irene (395–800)*, 2 vols. (London and New York 1889), vol. II, pp. 352f.

Plate 2.5 Tiberius III Apsimar. Gold *solidus*

Plate 2.6 Justinian II (second reign). Gold *solidus*

Carthage, under the command of the *patrikios* John. The city and some neighbouring forts were retaken, but the garrisons placed in them were soon driven out again in a second Arab attack, and in 698 the city fell a second time, never to be retaken. While waiting in Crete for reinforcements, and new orders, however, John was deposed by the soldiers of the Kibyrrhaiot fleet, who proclaimed their own commander, the *drouggarios* Apsimar, emperor. The fleet sailed to Constantinople and landed at the port of Sykai on the Golden Horn. Although the city was ravaged by the plague at that time, Leontius held out for some months before some of the garrison units were persuaded to open the gates to soldiers of the besieging forces. After a short period of plundering and disorder, Apsimar brought his troops under control; Leontius was mutilated to disqualify him from the imperial position, and banished to the monastery of Psamathion near the Xerolophus district of Constantinople. Apsimar altered his name to Tiberius, a move designed to give him some legitimacy and to associate him with the house of Heraclius.[90] It is worth noting that the demes or factions of the Blues and the Greens seem to have played a role in these political changes, for Leontius was supported (it would seem) by the Blues, Tiberius Apsimar by the Greens. But too much has been made of these affiliations

[90] On these events see Theophanes, 370.27sq. and Nicephorus, 39f. Cf. Grierson, *DOC*, vol. II, p. 624; Stratos, *Byzantium in the Seventh Century*, vol. V, pp. 85f.; Kaegi, *Military Unrest*, pp. 188f. For Carthage, see Brett, 'The Arab Conquest and the Rise of Islam in N. Africa', pp. 505ff.; Diehl, *L'Afrique byzantine*, pp. 582ff.

and involvements and, while it is certain that particular emperors favoured a particular team and therefore its supporters' club, and that the hostilities and rivalries that might emerge from such explicit commitments to the fortunes of a given hippodrome team spilled over into the street and into the political life of the city and the court, there are few grounds for thinking that the hippodrome factions represented clear social class divisions, still less religious-doctrinal orientations. Undoubtedly, such alliances were formed, but these were determined by temporary and fluid conjunctures, rather than by the structure of social relations of production as such.[91]

Tiberius Apsimar reigned from 698 until 705. His reign saw the continuation of Arab incursions into Asia Minor and a continuous loss of frontier districts to Muslim forces. No attempt was made to reconquer the lost North African provinces; in Asia Minor Tiberius' brother Heraclius was given command of the main thematic cavalry forces and waged a moderately successful campaign, although he was unable to alter the basic situation in any fundamental way. Armenia played a significant role throughout, rebelling in 703 and calling in Arab assistance; but in 704 rebelling again, against the Arabs, calling on Roman support in the struggle. Tiberius may also have undertaken action in the south Balkans against various Slav peoples, although little is known of this.[92] He certainly presided over the resettling in Cyprus of a number of those who had been removed to the Cyzicus region some years earlier. It was he, too, who put the sea-walls of Constantinople back into good repair, for they had apparently been allowed to collapse and decay.[93]

JUSTINIAN II AGAIN

In spite of his relatively peaceful internal government and his moderate successes against the Arabs, Tiberius ruled only seven years. For in 705 the exiled Justinian returned and, with the help of the Bulgar Khan Tervel, with whom he had reached an agreement, managed to enter the city and take back his throne. His banishment in Cherson had been cut short when the authorities there, worried by his plotting, had determined to hand him back to the emperor. But he was warned of their intentions and fled to the khagan of the Chazars, who received him with great honour, and whose daughter he married. Tiberius' envoys demanded that he be handed over,

---

[91] See A. Cameron, *Circus Factions: Blues and Greens at Rome and Constantinople* (Oxford 1976), pp. 126ff., 297ff., and see 267–8; Ostrogorsky, *Geschichte*, pp. 117f.
[92] Lilie, *Die byzantinische Reaktion*, pp. 112ff.
[93] A. Guilland, *Etudes de topographie de Constantinople byzantine*, 2 vols. (Berlin and Amsterdam 1969), pp. 263f.

and the Chazar khagan, wishing not to endanger the long-standing alliance between the two powers, agreed. But Justinian was once again able to forestall his enemies, and fled, this time to the Bulgar Khan Tervel. Accompanied by a considerable Bulgar and Slav army, Justinian arrived in the autumn of 705 before the land walls of Constantinople. The defences were too strong for an assault, but Justinian and a few supporters crept in through one of the ducts of the aqueduct. Tiberius and his supporters, surprised, fled in panic, and within a few hours Justinian had been able – with the help of a not inconsiderable faction which favoured his return – to re-establish himself. It is interesting to recall that the young Leo, later Leo III, was among Justinian's most enthusiastic supporters. In order to cement his authority, both Leontius and Tiberius, who had not been able to escape, were publicly executed.[94] Justinian was then able to bring his wife from Chazaria, together with his young son Tiberius, who was crowned co-emperor.

In return for his assistance, meanwhile, Tervel received the title of Caesar and the salutations of the populace of Constantinople. Those who had opposed Justinian, however, were ruthlessly executed or otherwise punished, including the patriarch Callinicus, who had crowned Leontius in 695: Justinian had his eyes put out.[95] Unfortunately for the empire, these were only the opening stages of a reign of terror and revenge, in which Justinian appears to have concentrated most of his resources and attention in avenging himself on those whom he perceived to be his enemies. But he was able to restore good relations with the papacy, and in 710/11 Pope Constantine visited Constantinople, where a compromise arrangement was reached, although no written accord was drawn up.[96] Justinian has been generally assumed to be responsible for despatching a punitive expedition against Ravenna at this time, to avenge the hostile attitude of the city at the time of his overthrow in 695; in fact, it seems that there had been some attempt at a coup against Pope Constantine, which involved Felix, the archbishop of Ravenna and a number of others in both Rome and Ravenna. Upon hearing that the exarch had met with Constantine at Naples (where he was *en route* for Constantinople) late in 710, and had had those involved in the plot at Rome arrested and punished, the Ravenna plotters rebelled openly, and were able to kill the exarch upon his return to the city. Justinian's naval expedition, despatched from the local forces based in Sicily, was in fact intended to deal with this situation, and it was

---

[94] See Ostrogorsky, *Geschichte*, p. 119; Stratos, *Byzantium in the Seventh Century*, vol. V, pp. 103–29. See the useful account of I. Dujčev, 'Le Triomphe de l'empereur Justinien II en 705', in Βυζάντιον. Ἀφιέρωμα στὸν Ἀνδρέα Ν. Στράτο, 2 vols. (Athens 1986), vol. I, pp. 83–91.

[95] Nicephorus, 42; Theophanes, 375. See Ostrogorsky, *Geschichte*, p. 120.

[96] See *Liber Pontificalis*, I, 389; cf. Paul the Deacon VI, 31.

the misleading and much embroidered version of Agnellus, chronicler of the Church of Ravenna, which was responsible for the alternative – and, in the event, barely plausible – account of events.[97]

Shortly after this expedition, however, Justinian did send a fleet against Cherson, the city of his former exile, and had his personal enemies punished – although the strategic logic behind the expedition was the reassertion of Byzantine control over the city and its hinterland, which had come increasingly under Chazar domination. After the departure of the expedition, however, and for reasons which must remain unclear, the Chersonites rebelled, and with Chazar help. The expeditionary force returned on Justinian's order, but was unable to take the city, which with the aid of its new allies and under the command of the exiled officer Bardanes – who had been proclaimed emperor – was now well defended.[98] There followed a mutiny of the fleet and the army it was transporting, which also accepted Bardanes as emperor and which sailed back to depose Justinian. The latter left the city in order to raise the troops of the *Opsikion* and *Armeniakon* districts in his support; but he was deserted by all but his closest friends, and both he and his son, whom he had left in Constantinople, were killed.[99] Bardanes, who now took as his imperial name Philippicus, deposed the patriarch Cyrus and appointed in his place John, by whom he was crowned.[100]

THE RISE OF LEO III, 717–741

With the death of Justinian II and his son Tiberius, the dynasty of the Heraclids was finally extinguished, a rather sad conclusion to what has been seen as the first truly 'Byzantine' dynasty. What followed was further political confusion and, as the deacon Agathon – a contemporary of the events in question – described it, a period in which the emperor's authority counted for nothing, in which the empire had been reduced and humbled, and tyranny – that is usurpation and violent changes of power – was the order of the day.[101]

In a desperate effort to evoke the glories of the past, to restore imperial authority and to cement his own position, Philippicus issued an edict soon

---

[97] See Stratos, *Byzantium in the Seventh Century*, vol. V, pp. 135ff.; C. Head, *Justinian II of Byzantium* (Madison 1972) and 'Towards a reinterpretation of the second reign of Justinian II', *B* 40 (1970), 14–32; for Agnellus' account, see *Liber Pontificalis Ecclesiae Ravennatis*, 368; and cf. Guillou, *Régionalisme*, pp. 216–18.

[98] Bardanes had been exiled in 711 and sent out with the first expedition. See Theophanes, 372ff.; Mansi XII, 192. See also A.A. Vasiliev, *The Goths in the Crimea* (Cambridge, Mass. 1936), pp. 83ff.

[99] Kaegi, *Military Unrest*, pp. 189f.; Stratos, *Byzantium in the Seventh Century*, vol. V, pp. 171ff.

[100] Theophanes, 381.   [101] Mansi XII, 192A.

Plate 2.7 Philippicus Bardanes. Gold *solidus*

Plate 2.8 Anastasius II. Gold *solidus*

after his accession which condemned the acts of the sixth ecumenical council of 680, which had rejected monotheletism, and officially reintroduced the doctrine of the single will. The representation of the sixth council in the imperial palace, as well as a commemorative inscription on the Milion gate of the palace, were removed and destroyed. In place of the inscription, portraits of the emperor and the patriarch Sergius appeared.[102] Philippicus was of Armenian background, and the monophysitism which he may well have found familiar is surely behind this move. It seems to have been not unpopular among the clergy, including both the later patriarch Germanus and the theologian and homilist Andrew of Crete.[103] The new policy met with stiff opposition in Rome, of course, especially in view of the recent entente between Justinian and Pope Constantine. The latter now returned Philippicus' portrait, which had been sent to Rome by the new emperor, and rejected his monothelete declaration of orthodoxy. His name was excluded both from the prayers of the Church and from the date of documents. And as an added gesture of defiance and

---

[102] Mansi, XII, 192D–E; Riedinger, 899.10ff.; see A. Grabar, *L'Iconoclasme byzantin: dossier archéologique* (Paris 1967), pp. 48f.

[103] Beck, *Kirche*, pp. 474, 500. For Andrew see S. Vailhé, 'Saint André de Crète', *EO* 5 (1902), 378–87, based on the earliest extant life, dating probably to the eighth century. See Papadopoulos-Kerameus, *Analekta* V, 169–79; and I. Ševčenko, 'Hagiography of the Iconoclast Period', 127 and note 105b.

self-assertion, the pope had pictures of all six ecumenical councils put up in St Peter's.[104] Whatever the success of Philippicus' new policy among the clergy, however, he seems not to have commanded much military support.

Throughout the second reign of Justinian, the Balkan provinces had been at peace, with the exception of occasional raids, a peace due primarily to Justinian's agreement with Khan Tervel. In Anatolia, in contrast, Arab raids continued on a yearly basis. In 707/8 the important fortress town of Tyana fell after a major Byzantine force was defeated. In 711 the frontier town of Sisium was finally abandoned by its citizens, who could no longer withstand the constant harassment. At the same time it seems that the Byzantines were gradually losing their hold in Cilicia, fortress by fortress, in spite of the occasional counter-attack or the naval expedition against Damietta in 709. The situation continued to deteriorate under Philippicus. In 712 Amasia and Misthia fell, along with other forts around Melitene; and in 713 Antioch in Pisidia was taken. The long-term effects of this constant raiding was, it has been suggested, effectively to empty the frontier areas of population, as the local peasantry and townspeople were either killed, carried off into slavery or driven to seek refuge in areas far from the conflict zone.[105] In the Balkans, Justinian's defeat and deposition gave Khan Tervel a pretext for invasion to avenge his friend and ally, and his forces ravaged Thrace up to the walls of the city itself. When Philippicus began to organise his troops to oppose these attacks, however, a mutiny broke out among the *Opsikion* troops. On 3 June 713 he was deposed and blinded, and succeeded by the *prōtoasēkrētis* Artemius, a palatine clerical official, who became emperor with the name Anastasius II.

Anastasius' first act was the restoration of Chalcedonian orthodoxy, rejection of monotheletism and the rehabilitation of the sixth council. He was an active emperor who took immediate measures to defend Constantinople against an imminent Arab attack. The walls of the city were repaired, and a fleet was commissioned, in an effort to attack the Arab naval forces in their ports and pre-empt the siege.[106] Unfortunately, the *Opsikion* division mutinied once more while on Rhodes, where the expedition was assembling, crossed back to the mainland and, together with the corps known as the Gothograeci, probably the *optimates* of an earlier period,[107] acclaimed as emperor an unknown fiscal official named Theodosius. The latter sensibly tried to run away, but was apprehended and forced to accept the dubious honours bestowed upon him. The provincial

---

[104] *Liber Pontificalis* I, 391.
[105] See the list and summary of Lilie, *Die byzantinische Reaktion*, pp. 116–21, 137ff.
[106] Theophanes, 383.10sq.; Nicephorus, 49.5sq.; Mansi XII, 192ff.; Riedinger, 900.12ff. See Kaegi, *Military Unrest*, p. 191.
[107] Haldon, *Byzantine Praetorians*, pp. 201f.

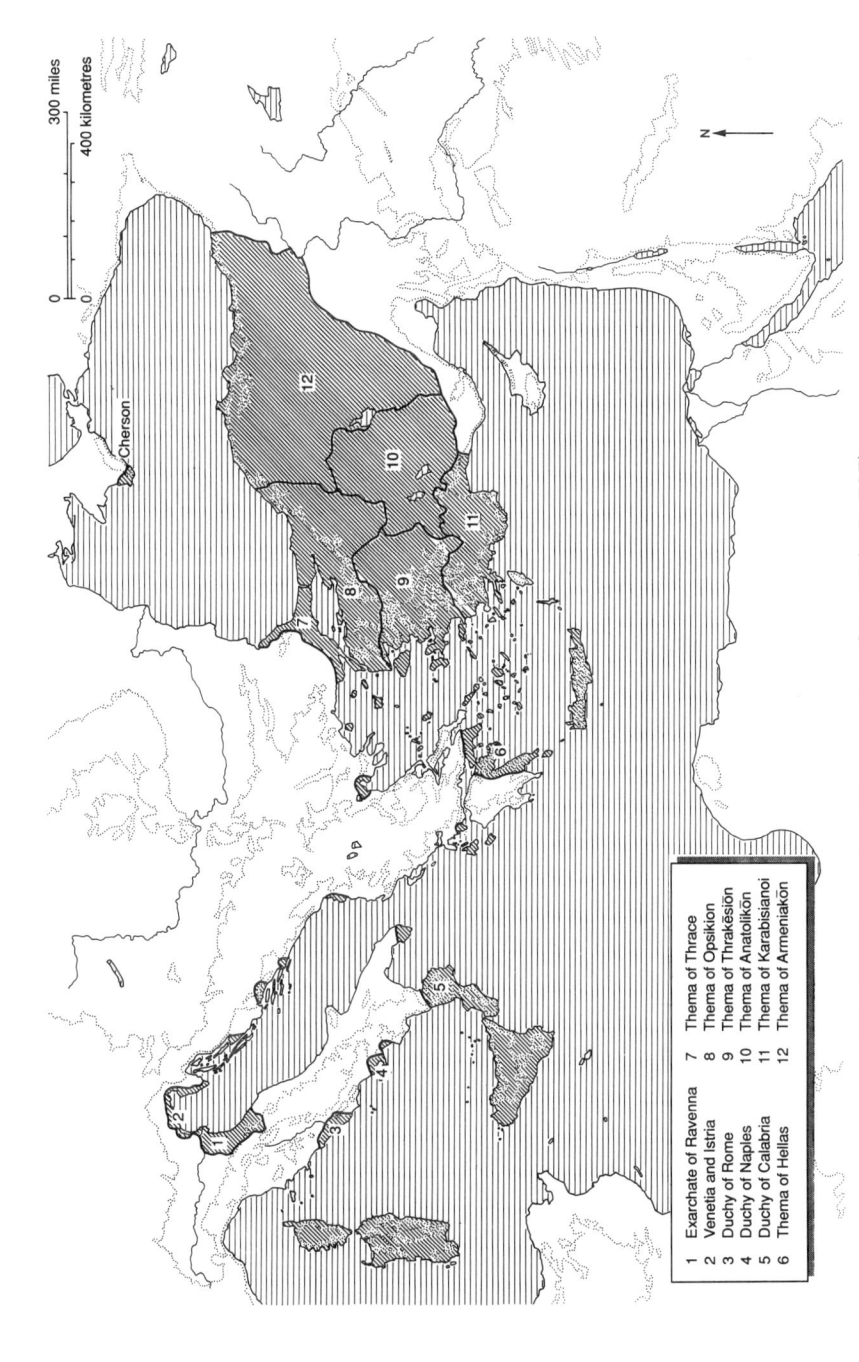

Map IV The empire at the accession of Leo III (A.D. 717)

1 Exarchate of Ravenna
2 Venetia and Istria
3 Duchy of Rome
4 Duchy of Naples
5 Duchy of Calabria
6 Thema of Hellas
7 Thema of Thrace
8 Thema of Opsikion
9 Thema of Thrakēsiōn
10 Thema of Anatolikōn
11 Thema of Karabisianoi
12 Thema of Armeniakōn

Plate 2.9 Theodosius III. Gold *solidus*

troops then marched to Constantinople which, after some months of desultory siege warfare, capitulated. Anastasius had meanwhile fled to Nicaea, but he soon abdicated and retired as a monk to Thessaloniki.[108] His successor Theodosius III occupied the throne for just over twelve months. Almost immediately after news had reached the provinces of his accession, the *stratēgos* of the *Anatolikōn* region, Leo, together with the *stratēgos* of the *Armeniakōn*, Artavasdus, rebelled against the new emperor. The alliance was strengthened by Artavasdus' marriage to Leo's daughter; and the conflict took the form of a struggle for precedence between the two great Anatolian *themata* of *Anatolikōn* and *Armeniakōn*, on the one hand, and that of the *Opsikion* on the other. Theodosius' son and retinue were captured in Nicomedia in Leo's rapid advance towards the capital; and, having secured a promise of personal safety for himself and his family, Theodosius abdicated and took up the monastic life at Ephesus.[109] His most lasting achievement was probably the treaty he agreed with the Bulgars in 716, which fixed a formal frontier between the two powers along a line through northern Thrace, from the Gulf of Burgas across to the Maritsa between Philippoupolis and Adrianople, a frontier which illustrates the extent and power of the khanate of the Bulgars by this time.[110]

In March 717 Leo was crowned emperor in the Hagia Sophia by the patriarch Germanus. Shortly after the second great siege of the capital of the once mighty East Roman state began.[111]

Leo III won his throne largely because he was able to present himself as the most able general who could deal effectively with the Arab threat to the empire and especially the capital. For the invasion had already begun when Leo was finally admitted to the city. His rise to power had started

---

[108] Theophanes, 385.18sq.; Nicephorus, 51.2sq.; Kaegi, *Military Unrest*, pp. 192f.; G.V. Sumner, 'Philippicus, Anastasius II and Theodosius III', *GRBS* 17 (1976), 291ff.
[109] See Kaegi, *Military Unrest*, pp. 192–4.
[110] See Obolensky, *The Byzantine Commonwealth*, pp. 65f.
[111] See R. Guilland, 'L'Expédition de Maslama contre Constantinople (717–718)', in *Études byzantines* (Paris 1959), pp. 109–33, see 114.

when, as a young soldier, he had been commissioned as a *spatharios* during the second reign of Justinian II.[112] Appointed to the post of *stratēgos* of the *Anatolikōn* by Anastasius II, it was ostensibly in support of Anastasius that he rose in rebellion against Theodosius III.[113] During his campaign against Theodosius and his negotiations with the capital, he had been able to outwit the leaders of the invading Arab forces: he was able to persuade the Arab commander Suleyman, who invaded from Cilicia and marched towards Amorion in 716, that Amorion would be handed over to the invaders. Instead, he succeeded in getting a garrison into the defenceless fortress town, upon which the invaders had to fall back again. An Arab fleet was meanwhile ravaging parts of western Asia Minor; while the main force, under the brother of the caliph (also Suleyman), Maslama, waited for word of the commander Suleyman. As the latter began to withdraw, however, Maslama marched into Roman territory through Cappadocia and, upon discovering Leo's deception, attacked and took Sardis and Pergamum, wintering in the latter. The fleet wintered in Cilicia.

In 717 Maslama ordered his fleet up, while he and his forces crossed the Dardanelles from Abydus, laying waste in the following weeks all of Thrace, and closely investing the city. The fleet blockaded Constantinople from the sea. But the capital was well defended and adequately provisioned, chiefly thanks to the measures taken by Anastasius II. With the help of its terror weapon, Greek fire, and a well-thought-out strategy of counter-offensives, Leo's forces – helped by the attacks of the Bulgars, the onset of winter, the cutting-off of Arab supply sources, the outbreak of disease in the Arab camp and a timely victory over the Arab forces in Bithynia – were able to defeat the blockade and hold Maslama's forces in check. In August 718 the new Caliph ʿUmar II (Suleyman died in 717) ordered Maslama's withdrawal. The army in Thrace was embarked on his ships, but Byzantine naval attacks and bad weather resulted in the loss of many vessels on the return voyage. Arab sources claim 150,000 Muslim deaths during the campaign, a figure which, while certainly inflated, is nevertheless indicative of the enormity of the disaster in medieval eyes. This was to be the last Arab attempt to take Constantinople itself, and it is possible to follow a change in Arab strategy after this time. The caliphate had finally come to terms with the existence of the Byzantine empire and, while long-term Byzantine counter-attacks were still a thing of the future,

---

[112] For the contemporary importance of this corps, see Haldon, *Byzantine Praetorians*, pp. 182ff.

[113] See Theophanes, 386–97 for Leo's early career; and for his 'Caucasian adventure' under Justinian II, see B. Martin-Hisard, 'La domination byzantine sur le littoral oriental du Pont Euxin (milieu du VIIe–VIIIe siècles)', *Byzantinobulgarica* 7 (1981) 141–54.

the defeat of this expedition marks an important moment in Byzantine–Arab relations.[114]

LEO III AND IMPERIAL ICONOCLASM

In spite of this major set-back, Arab attacks all along the border and well into the very deep 'frontier' zone continued throughout Leo's reign. From 720 until his death in 741 there were yearly attacks, in which the border areas were repeatedly devastated, fortresses and settlements taken, retaken and lost again, with both sides suffering regular losses. Only in 740 were the Byzantines able to lure Arab forces on to unfavourable terrain and win a major victory near Acroinum.[115] Only one of three Arab columns was actually destroyed, however, and the victory was perhaps more significant as a shock to Muslim morale and as a heartening triumph for the beleaguered Byzantines. Arab raids went on until 744, but the civil wars which led to the overthrow of the Umayyads and the installation of Abbasid rule, along with the transfer of the centre of power to Baghdad, soon interrupted the regularity and reduced the devastating nature of the attacks; in addition to which Leo's son and successor, Constantine V, went over to the offensive in the 750s, and the nature of the warfare between the two sides began, slowly but surely, to change both in character and in its effects.[116]

In the north, meanwhile, Leo cemented the friendly relations enjoyed by the empire with the Chazars through the marriage of his son Constantine to a daughter of the Chazar khagan in 733;[117] while in the Balkans, as a result of the arrangement of 716, peace reigned. Two rebellions at the beginning of his reign were quickly crushed. In 717/18 Sergius, the *stratēgos* of Sicily, rebelled before news of the successful outcome of the siege of Constantinople had reached him and set up a rival emperor by the name of Tiberius. Upon receiving news of Leo's victory, along with the imperial letters proclaiming his accession, the soldiers handed the rebels over to the emperor's envoy, the *chartoularios* Paul and his troops.[118] In 719 a second coup was foiled. The *magistros* Nicetas Xylinites, together with the exiled ex-emperor Anastasius and with assistance from the Bulgar Khan Tervel, attempted to dethrone Leo. The plotters inside Constantinople

---

[114] For accounts of the siege, see Theophanes, 395–8, 399; Nicephorus, 53–4; and the discussion of Lilie, *Die byzantinische Reaktion*, pp. 125–33; E.W. Brooks, 'The campaign of 716–718 from Arabic Sources', *JHS* 19 (1899), 19–31.
[115] See Theophanes, 411; Lilie, *Die byzantinische Reaktion*, pp. 152–3 with literature and sources.
[116] The best survey of these wars, their nature and their effects is to be found in Lilie, *Die byzantinische Reaktion*, pp. 144–55, with discussion at pp. 155–62. For the period from 750, see ibid., pp. 162ff.
[117] Vasiliev, *The Goths in the Crimea*, p. 87. [118] Theophanes, 398–9.

Plate 2.10 Leo III. Gold *solidus*

were unable to rally the support of the troops and officers manning the walls; while Tervel's soldiers seem to have abandoned Anastasius at the last minute, handing him over to Leo. All the plotters were executed.[119] Leo's quick and firm handling of these revolts enabled him to secure his position and at the same time dissuade others from repeating the mistakes of Sergius and Anastasius.

Leo's reign is probably best known for two great events: the introduction of an official imperial policy of iconoclasm and the issue of the Ecloga. The latter has been traditionally dated to 726; in fact, it appears that it dates to the end of his reign, to the year 741.[120] It represents in essence a revised and very much abridged version of the Justinianic codification, with particular emphasis on family, property and inheritance, and penal law. Its practical intention was to provide the administrators with a handbook and reference work, although it hardly replaced the older codifications. But substantial changes were also introduced, changes which reflect in particular the powerful influence of canon law, especially with regard to marriage and the power of the husband over wife and children; there were also changes in the system and nature of punishment: while capital punishment and fines dominate the Justinianic codes, the Ecloga, on the pattern of the Old Testament, introduces a system of corporal mutilations – slitting of the nose, tongue and so on – which had become increasingly common in the course of Byzantine history during the seventh century, but which were quite foreign to Roman legal tradition. Such changes may well be based on the formal incorporation into the legal framework of the state of elements of local customary law.[121]

---

[119] See Theophanes, 400.18sq.; Nicephorus, 55.19sq. and see Kaegi, *Military Unrest*, pp. 212f.

[120] For the older view see V. Grumel, 'La Date de l'Eclogue des Isauriens: l'année et le jour', *REB* 21 (1963), 272–4; D. Simon, 'Zur Ehegesetzgebung der Isaurier', FM I (1976), 40–3; P.E. Pieler, *Byzantinische Rechtsliteratur*, p. 438 and notes 97ff. For the year 741 see now Ecloga (ed. Burgmann), pp. 10–12 with literature.

[121] *Ecloga* (ed. Burgmann), pp. 4–7; T.E. Gregory, 'The Ekloga of Leo III and the concept of Philanthropia', *Byzantina* 7 (1975), 271–5.

But in spite of its later partial rejection or condemnation by anti-iconoclastic polemicists, the Ecloga exercised an important influence on the development of Byzantine and Eastern medieval legal theory, and marks an important stage in the history of Byzantine law.[122] It marks equally the determination of Leo himself and his son Constantine, in whose joint names it was promulgated, to come to grips with the problems of Byzantine society at an official level and to address the changes which had taken place in both social and property relations, as well as in ideas and morality since the sixth century. The prologue to the work therefore stresses both the need to preserve the law as the basis of God's will on earth, of human society, and of imperial competence and success, as well as the pressing need to make it clearer and more easily understood and accessible to the judicial authorities. Corruption and bribery were to be combated, hence the legal representatives of the state's justice are to be properly salaried. And interestingly, the emperors note that the law has been frequently difficult of access and comprehension among lawyers and judges far from Constantinople – a reflection of the difficult conditions, bad communications, and disruption of urban life during the previous one hundred or so years.[123]

The introduction by Leo of an official policy of iconoclasm has given rise to a debate among modern historians, as well as among Leo's and Constantine's contemporaries, of a very different nature. The background to the whole debate lies already in the later sixth and seventh centuries, as the cult of relics and the associated use of holy images became more and more prominent, and as both icons and relics were brought more and more centrally into the arena as the focus of popular devotion, both publicly and privately, as channels of direct access to the heavenly realm. At the same time, both as a direct result of the collapse of the empire and the massive territorial losses of the period up to the 660s – in which the 'failure' of the emperors and the state were clearly implicated, the more so in view of the 'heretical' policies of the monothelete Emperor Constans and the patriarchs associated with him and with Heraclius – imperial authority itself came under pressure as political failure followed political failure. The development in the 'cult' of icons worked together with the events of the political and economic world to encourage a serious questioning of the authority and abilities of individual emperors. Thus the armies of the provinces were encouraged to take up arms in favour of one or another candidate for the throne who it was felt would best answer their needs and those of the state. The attempt of Philippicus Bardanes – with the blessing of certain leading Churchmen – to reintroduce monotheletism is an interesting and important illustration of the perceived need both to reassert imperial and official

[122] See the comments of Ostrogorsky, *Geschichte*, p. 132 with literature.
[123] See *Ecloga* (ed. Burgmann), 'Prooimion', 11.21sq.

Church authority, and at the same time unify the disparate religious-ideological elements within the empire. Monotheletism harked back to the explanations of an earlier epoch. Iconoclasm identified a different source of the problem.[124]

Iconoclastic, or anti-image, sentiment was, of course, nothing new in Christian thought. The debate on the nature of icons had long been part of Christian doctrinal discussion and argument, although no developed theory of icons yet existed. Iconoclastic groups may have existed in seventh-century Anatolia; while the crucial question as to whether icons should be seen as graven images or as representations *through* which, rather than *to* which, prayer could be directed, had never been formally confronted by the Church.[125]

During the 720s, however, an iconoclastic perspective seems to have been espoused by some provincial churchmen, the best known of whom – Constantine, the bishop of Nacolea – was later regarded as the founder of Byzantine iconoclasm and appropriately reviled by the iconophile camp. Leo III was himself originally from Syria; but whatever contemporary or later iconophile commentators claimed, the extent to which Leo was influenced by either Islamic or monophysite thinking (the caliphs ʿUmar II (717–20) and Yazid II (720–4) had both issued orders condemning the use and production of images representing living beings as idolatrous)[126] or by Jewish theology[127] must remain unclear. What is probable is that Leo seems genuinely to have regarded the iconoclastic case as a strong one and believed that it was 'idolatry' and the sins of the Chosen People – the Romans – which had brought about their downfall and, as an integral causal element in that downfall, the decline in, and contempt for imperial

[124] See Haldon, 'Some remarks', esp. 176–84 and 'Ideology and social change', 161ff., where these developments are discussed in greater detail. See also P. Brown, 'A Dark-Age crisis: aspects of the iconoclastic controversy', EHR 88 (1973), 1–34; E. Kitzinger, 'The cult of images in the age before iconoclasm', DOP 8 (1954), 85–150. For a recent survey of the origins and cause of official iconoclasm, see Herrin, *Formation of Christendom*, pp. 319ff., 325–43. See esp. M.-F. Auzépy, L'évolution de l'attitude face au miracle à Byzance (VIIᵉ–IXᵉ siècle)', in *Miracles, prodiges et merveilles au Moyen Age* (Paris 1995), 31–46, and J.F. Haldon, 'The Miracles of Artemios and Contemporary Attitudes: Context and Significance', in *The Miracles of Saint Artemios: Translation, Commentary and Analysis*, by J. Nesbit, V. Crysafulli (Leiden–New York–Köln 1997), 33–73.

[125] See Kitzinger, 'The cult of images before Iconoclasm', 129ff.; S. Der Nersessian, 'Une apologie des images du septième siècle', B 17 (1944/5), 58ff.; N.H. Baynes, 'The icons before iconoclasm', *Harvard Theol. Review* 44 (1951), 93ff.; Haldon, 'Some remarks', 182, note 64.

[126] See esp. Grabar, *L'Iconoclasme*, pp. 103f.; D. Stein, *Der Beginn des byzantinischen Bilderstreites und seine Entwicklung bis in die 40er Jahre des 8. Jahrhunderts* (Miscellanea Byzantina Monacensia XXV, Munich 1980), pp. 139–41 with literature.

[127] See J. Starr, *The Jews in the Byzantine Empire, 641–1204* (Athens 1939), esp. on Leo's persecutions, and A. Sharf, *Byzantine Jewry, from Justinian to the fourth Crusade* (New York 1971); cf. Theophanes, 401.22. For monophysitism, which seems to have played little or no role in the affair, see S. Brock, 'Iconoclasm and the monophysites', in A.A.M. Bryer and J. Herrin, eds., *Iconoclasm: Papers given at the ninth Spring Symposium of Byzantine Studies*, University of Birmingham, March 1975 (Birmingham 1977), pp. 53–7.

authority which seemed so clear to contemporaries.[128] The two were bound up closely together.

In 726, a dramatic earthquake and volcanic eruption occurred on the islands of Thera and Therasia, an event which Leo seems to have taken as a sign of God's anger and as a direct signal for him to take action. As an immediate result, he appears to have had an icon of Christ on the Chalke gate of the palace removed and replaced with a cross, a reflection of his belief that the holy cross and the wood of the cross represented symbols of salvation for emperor and people, whereas icons, being made by human hands, were transient symbols of human frailty. But Leo's action was also a reflection of his personal response to the situation, and it does not begin any official persecution of icons at this time.

At about this time, the bishop Constantine of Nacolea had been preaching that icons should not be the objects of *proskynēsis* or worship, since this was idolatrous. As a result of this activity, he had been disciplined by his superiors and the patriarch Germanus. Leo may have been aware of these debates and seems eventually to have decided that the iconoclastic viewpoint – given the historical background to his own reign and those of his predecessors, together with the eruption on the islands – had greater validity. The public debate, therefore, began only in 726. But the context for this debate, and the reasons for Leo's eventually adopting an iconoclastic position, had a longer history. After some four years of discussion, in which a split within the clergy between pro- and anti-icon parties developed, Leo made a first public move, putting Germanus in 730 in a position where he was forced either to accept an iconoclastic declaration of faith or to resign. He chose the latter and was replaced as patriarch by Anastasius, his former *sygkellos*. Contrary to generally received opinion, however, there seems to have been no official edict issued prohibiting the use of icons. Instead, Anastasius issued an iconoclastic declaration of faith in which the cross was presented as the true symbol of Christ's passion and the salvation of humanity, whereas icons were to be cast out. As these developments took place, a rebellion of the Helladic troops under their *stratēgos*, who set up a pretender to the throne, had occurred; but it was decisively defeated in a naval engagement by the imperial fleet near Constantinople in April 727. Again, contrary to the often accepted view that the rebellion was an iconophile response to Leo's policies, this was not the case.[129] In the first place, Leo had as yet made no official pronouncement; in the second place, the rebellion seems to fit well into the general pattern of coups and revolts which had plagued the empire. It was the third in Leo's reign itself, and although it failed, it illustrates the continuing state of internal insecurity

[128] See Nicephorus, 52.2–6; Mansi XII, 192A.
[129] See, for example, Ostrogorsky, *Geschichte*, p. 135.

and ideological uncertainty, and the lack of confidence in and respect for the imperial authority.

It is equally clear that the conflict of interest between the empire and Rome over the increased rates of taxation for Italy and Sicily had nothing to do with the iconoclastic policies of Leo from the 730s. The refusal of Pope Gregory II to pay the taxes was in 723/4; the rebellion of the army of the exarchate and the cities of Italy shortly after the exarch Paul's failure to arrest the pope as ordered by Leo took place in 725/6; as did the unsuccessful naval expedition sent by the emperor. Order was restored only with the arrival of the new exarch Eutychius in 727/8, who formed an alliance with the Lombard King Liutprand. Indeed, Gregory's general support for the empire is clear from his opposition to the usurper Petasius, who rebelled but was defeated by Eutychius shortly after. Iconoclasm played no part in these events.[130]

There is no reason to doubt that Leo's eventual espousal of iconoclasm represents a genuine religious and theological commitment on his part, and that of a majority faction within the clergy. But these personal actions and beliefs must also be set firmly within the context of the political and ideological developments of the time. Iconoclasm seemed to provide answers to a number of questions of direct concern to those who perceived the dangers of a world in which both official Church and imperial authority had been challenged, at a variety of levels, by the events of the previous century. While the use of icons, the authority vested in them, and the consequent tension between two different sources of authority, seemed to lie at the root of the problem, they were in fact but symptoms of a much more complex set of developments which had come to a head in the debates of Leo's reign.[131]

[130] See O. Bertolini, 'Quale fu il vero oggiettivo assegnato da Leone III "Isaurico" all' armata di Manes, stratego dei Cibyrreoti?', *BF* 2 (1967), 15–49; Guillou, *Régionalisme*, p. 219f.; Brown, *Gentlemen and Officers*, pp. 156, note 24 and p. 180. Cf. *Liber Pontificalis*, I, 403; Theophanes, 404.

[131] The debate on the origins and background to iconoclasm is, as may be imagined, immense. For its immediate context and development under Leo, however, the excellent analysis of Stein, *Bilderstreit*, offers a detailed survey of much of the earlier literature, as well as a demonstration of the argument outlined here, and upon which I have relied. See esp. pp. 138ff of *Bilderstreit* and also H.-G. Beck, 'Die griechische Kirche im Zeitalter des Ikonoklasmus', in *Handbuch der Kirchengeschichte*, vol. III, part 1 (Freiburg 1966), pp. 31–66; St. Gero, *Byzantine Iconoclasm during the Reign of Leo III* (Louvain 1973) and *Byzantine Iconoclasm during the Reign of Constantine V* (Louvain 1977); the collected articles in Bryer and Herrin, eds., *Iconoclasm*; Kitzinger, 'The cult of images before iconoclasm'; P. Schreiner, 'Legende und Wirklichkeit in der Darstellung des byzantinischen Bilderstreites', *Saeculum* 27 (1976), 165–79; idem, 'Der byzantinische Bilderstreit: kritische Analyse der zeitgenössischen Meinungen und das Urteil der Nachwelt bis heute', in *Bisanzio, Roma e l'Italia nell'Alto Medioevo* (Settimane di Studio del Centro Italiano di Studi sull'Alto Medioevo XXXIV [Spoleto 1988]) 319–427; P. Henry, 'What was the iconoclastic controversy about?', *Church History* 45 (1976), 16–31. These all contain surveys of the literature and fuller bibliographies than can be accommodated here.

The results of Anastasius' declarations of faith were soon to be made clear. In 731 Gregory III summoned a synod which met at Rome in November. A general condemnation of the new tendency – there is not enough evidence to support the notion that it was an official 'policy' – coupled with the threat of excommunication for those who promoted it, was pronounced, the arguments being founded upon a collection of Scriptural and patristic texts established by Gregory. There is no evidence of any condemnation of either the patriarch Anastasios or the emperors Leo and Constantine. The conflict of interest between the two patriarchates of Rome and Constantinople and between pope and emperor was becoming clearer. And although there is no evidence of an official condemnation of Constantinople from Jerusalem, the latter may have produced a condemnation of iconoclastic ideas and of the patriarch Anastasios, but not the emperor Leo himself. The effects were an increasing ecclesiastical political isolation of Constantinople. As the gulf between the Churches widened, so Byzantine political influence and authority gradually diminished. The transfer of the papal patrimonies of Calabria, Sicily, east Illyricum and, probably, Crete, from Roman to Constantinopolitan jurisdiction may have occurred shortly thereafter, although a later date, in the reign of Constantine V, is also possible.[132] What is clear is that the move represents an attempt to secure ecclesiastical and political jurisdiction over regions which might otherwise become permanently alienated from the

[132] The council of 769 in Rome (see Mansi xii, 713–22) used the acts of 731 (which otherwise do not survive) for the establishment of its own arguments: see the brief account in Herrin, *Formation of Christendom*, p. 348 and n. 15. See *LP*416.5–15. Stein, *Bilderstreit*, p. 217 n. 98, discusses the other surviving fragments of this synod and shows that only the most general condemnation was issued. For the lack of evidence for a condemnation by the patriarch John of Jerusalem and the eastern bishops (Theoph., 408.29–31), and the possible confusion which may have led Theophanes to incorporate this story, see Stein, *Bilderstreit*, 211ff. and M.-F. Auzépy, 'L'Adversus Constantinum Caballinum et Jean de Jérusalem', *BS* 56 (1995) 323–38 (ΣΤΕΦΑΝΟΣ. *Studia byzantina ac slavica Vladimíro Vavrínek ad annum sexagesimum quintum dedicata*). In respect of the transfer of Calabria, Illyricum, etc., there are no references to this in the contemporary record; letters of Hadrian I (772–95) and Nicholas I (858–67) refer to the events; the first reference, in a letter of Pope Hadrian I to Charles the Great, written between 787 and 794, offers no specific chronology for the transfer (see *MGH Ep.* V. *Epist. Karol. Aevi* iii, 57.5ff.), and L.M. Hartmann, *Geschichte Italiens im Mittelalter*, II, 2, pp. 112–14; M.V. Anastos, 'The Transfer of Illyricum, Calabria and Sicily to the Jurisdiction of the Patriarchate of Constantinople', *SBN* 9 (1957) 14–31. But for a different interpretation, see D.H. Miller, 'Byzantine–Papal relations during the Pontificate of Paul I: Confirmation and Completion of the Roman Revolution of the Eighth Century', *BZ* 68 (1975) 47–62; and Darrouzès, *Notitiae*, p. 249 for the statement that these sees were transferred 'because the Pope was in the hands of the Heathen' (i.e. the Franks). While this statement also reflected contemporary political concerns in respect of Byzantine–Frankish relations (see Schreiner, 'Bilderstreit', 376 n. 291) the fact that no contemporary Byzantine or western source refers to this major event for the 730s is significant. See V. Grumel, 'L'annexion de l'Illyricum oriental, de la Sicile et de la Calabre au patriarcat de Constantinople', *Recherches des Sciences Religieuses* 40 (1951–52) 191–200 (who places the event in the years 752–757).

Constantinopolitan Church and the imperial government. On ideological grounds alone, this would not be permitted.

Leo III died on 18 June 741.[133] His son and successor Constantine soon found himself fighting a desperate struggle for survival with his brother-in-law Artavasdus,[134] and although the eventual outcome was a complete victory for Constantine, the civil war demonstrated still that the difficulties faced by the emperors in Constantinople both ideologically and in terms of the practical distribution of power to the provincial *stratēgoi* were by no means resolved by Leo's policies, his military successes, or his reaffirmation and confirmation of his personal imperial authority. Leo's greatest achievement lies in the very fact of his success in defeating his rivals and in maintaining his authority over some twenty-three years, during which the external and internal problems he had to deal with were hardly less pressing than those which faced his predecessors. But it should be recalled in the end that Leo was, after all, a successful usurper. His reign marks only the tentative beginnings of a reconstruction of imperial authority, and, through the political struggle which the iconoclastic debate engendered, of a relocation of the imperial position within the wider framework of the official, imperial ideological system of the Byzantine state.

Leo's reign is significant in one other respect, however. This chapter began with an account of late Roman political history in the early seventh century; it ends with an account of the history of the Byzantine state in the early eighth century: Byzantine, because our map shows a very different state territorially; because shifts in the ideological world, in the 'symbolic universe' of the people and culture of this state, had taken place, which lent to it a vastly different character from that of late Roman culture; and because, whatever the continuities one may detect, the functional apparatuses of this state were already very different from those of the later sixth century. Precise dates at which a social formation or a state can be said to deserve one descriptive title as opposed to any other are always liable to criticism. It seems reasonable to conclude this chapter by suggesting simply that it was during the seventh century that the transformation from late Roman to Byzantine society, culture and institutions took place. The evidence for this assertion is presented in the following chapters.[135]

---

[133] Theophanes, 413.
[134] On the background, development and results of the civil war, see P. Speck, *Artabasdos, der rechtgläubige Vorkämpfer der göttlichen Lehren* (Poikila Byzantina II, Bonn 1981).
[135] For recent literature and discussion of the question of the Slav occupation of the southern Balkan region, see also J. Karayannopoulos, *Les Slaves en Macédoine. La prétendue interruption des communications entre Constantinople et Thessalonique du 7ème au 9ème siècle* (Centre d'Etudes du Sud-Est Européen, no. 25 (Athens 1989)); and Ph. Malingoudis, *Oi Slaboi sti Mesaioniki Ellada* (Athens 1988).

CHAPTER 3

Social relations and the economy: the cities and the land

The study of the relations between dependent and independent peasant communities on the one hand, and their landlords – ecclesiastical or secular, private or state – on the other, has long been the source of much thought-provoking debate among historians of the early Byzantine period. The discussion and the variety of often contradictory answers given by different historians to the questions which the period poses illustrates the main problems: there are simply not enough written sources for the period to enable a clear and detailed picture of social relationships in the provinces (for example) to emerge. We cannot expect the sort of information available for the sixth century, therefore, and the sorts of results it is possible to extract from such material are not forthcoming for the seventh century. But the problems are not insoluble. It is possible to build up the basic outlines of the developments of the seventh century from archaeological, epigraphic, sigillographic and numismatic sources, among others, which can complement the available literary documentation. By employing these materials within a coherent framework or set of models, it is possible to obtain a shadowy picture of seventh-century social and economic relations, within which the available evidence can play a role without contradictions and upon which an understanding of developments in the subsequent period can be reached.

The essential elements in any analysis of seventh-century society are represented by the relationships between the state and the sources of its revenue, and by that between the rural population and their means of production – land, livestock and tools – and those who owned or controlled those means of production. It will be useful to take these elements separately, to begin with, and in the following chapter I will look first at the role played by cities in the late Roman and early Byzantine world, both as centres of administration, as well as of economic activity.

THE BACKGROUND

In the last thirty or so years, debate on the nature and function of the city in the seventh century and later has been extensive. In essence, two opposing points of view can be discerned. The first, which represents a reaction against views held until the 1950s, argues that the seventh century saw a more or less total collapse of antique urban organisation, and of social and economic life. The cities of the period up to the sixth century disappeared as a result of the Arab onslaught and the rapid ruralisation of the empire; the lack of small denomination bronze and copper currency from the archaeological record in the second half of the seventh century confirms the disappearance of market exchange and illustrates therefore the end of the market function of the towns in the provinces.[1]

The opposing view argues that cities did survive physically; that, while they may have shrunk and often have been confined to their citadels as a result of constant enemy harassment, they nevertheless retained their role as centres of market- and exchange-activity, petty commodity production and administration. The evidence cited in support of this line of reasoning includes both the clear continuation of occupation on many sites, attested archaeologically and in literary sources – as well as the occurrence of gold coins on many sites, regardless of size or importance.[2]

Between these two poles, a number of alternatives or modifications have been suggested. In a series of articles which seemed to strengthen the case for a total eclipse of urban life after the first decade of the seventh century, Clive Foss argued that the archaeological evidence was not only fuller, but also more reliable and explicit, than the relatively sparse literary material; and that it was the disastrous results of the Persian invasions and partial occupation of Anatolia from 615 on, which sealed the fate of the cities of Asia Minor.[3] There have been a number of criticisms of this position; in

---

[1] For a basic statement, see A. Každan, 'Vizantiiskie goroda v VII–IX vv.', *Sovietskaya Arkheologiya* 21 (1954), 164–88; and for further literature, Haldon, 'Some considerations', 78f.

[2] See G. Ostrogorsky, 'Byzantine cities in the early Middle Ages', *DOP* 13 (1959), 47–66; Sp. Vryonis, jr., *The Decline of Medieval Hellenism in Asia Minor and the Process of Islamization from the Eleventh through the Fifteenth Century* (Berkeley, Los Angeles and London 1971), p. 7; R.S. Lopez, 'The role of trade in the economic re-adjustment of Byzantium in the seventh century', *DOP* 13 (1959), 69–85; see Haldon, 'Some considerations', 78 and 82 with literature.

[3] Clive Foss, 'The Persians in Asia Minor and the end of Antiquity', *EHR* 90 (1975), 721–43; 'The fall of Sardis in 616 and the value of evidence', *JÖB* 24 (1975), 11–22; *Byzantine and Turkish Sardis* (Cambridge, Mass. and London 1976), pp. 275ff.; 'Late antique and Byzantine Ankara', *DOP* 31 (1977), 29–87; 'Archaeology and the "twenty cities" of Byzantine Asia', *Amer. Journal of Archaeology* 81 (1977), 469–86; and *Ephesus after Antiquity: A Late Antique, Byzantine and Turkish City* (Cambridge 1979).

particular, that it concentrates on cities which may not represent the typical case and that it fails to situate the cities in question in the context of their social and historical environment.[4] Most importantly, both for the case presented in the work of Foss, and in the arguments outlined above, the long-term development of the city and its changing functional relevance within the structure of late Roman social and economic relations has not generally been adequately taken into account. The crucial point is, quite simply, that the Byzantine 'city' was different from its classical antecedent because it no longer fulfilled the same role, either in the social formation as a whole or in the administrative apparatus of the state. This difference would have persisted whether or not there had been any Persian invasion or Arab attacks; and it is this underlying *structural* development which must be understood if we are to grasp the nature of the changes from the fifth and sixth centuries which affected urban and rural life. Once this has been understood, the question of whether or not urban sites continued to be occupied, and the exact causes of their immediate destruction or shrinkage, become less crucial; and it can be seen from this perspective, therefore, that much of the debate – that part which argues for or against the continuity of urban life purely or predominantly on the basis of the archaeological evidence for destruction caused by hostile military action – is in fact quite misguided. The question becomes one of recognising the underlying structural tendencies in the evolution of cities in the context of the late Roman state and its society, and determining the extent to which the political events referred to in the literary sources and evidenced in the archaeological record intensified or otherwise affected that process. That it was already under way seems to me undeniable.[5]

[4] See in particular the review by W. Brandes, 'Ephesos in byzantinischer Zeit', *Klio* 64 (1982), 611–22, with a detailed discussion and extensive bibliography; and the comments of F. Trombley, 'The decline of the seventh-century town: the exception of Euchaita', in *Byzantine Studies in Honor of Milton V. Anastos*, ed. Sp. Vryonis, jr. (Malibu 1985), pp. 65–90, esp. 75ff. For further literature arguing for discontinuity, see Kirsten, 'Die byzantinische Stadt', 1–35; C. Bouras, 'City and village: urban design and architecture', in *Akten des XVI. Internationalen Byzantinisten-Kongresses*, 1 (Vienna 1981), pp. 611–53 (= *JÖB* 31); D. Zakythinos, 'La Grande brèche', in Χαριστήριον εἰς Α.Κ. Ὀρλάνδον (3 vols., Athens 1966), vol. III, pp. 300–27. For a recent comment on the debate, see J.C. Russell, 'Transformations in early Byzantine urban life: the contribution and limitations of archaeological evidence', in *17th International Byzantine Congress, Major Papers* (New York 1986), pp. 137–54.

[5] See the comments of A.P. Každan, in Βυζαντινά 9 (1977), 478–84; and in particular J.F. Haldon and H. Kennedy, 'The Arab-Byzantine frontier in the eighth and ninth centuries: military organisation and society in the borderlands', *ZRVI* 19 (1980), 79–116, esp. 87ff.; Haldon, 'Some considerations', 77–89 with literature; also E. Frančes, 'La Ville byzantine et la monnaie aux VIIe–VIIIe siècles', *Byzantinobulgarica* 2 (1966), 3–14 for a summary of the debate and full bibliography. For a detailed analysis, see G.L. Kurbatov, *Osnovnye problemy vnutrennego razvitiya vizantiiskogo goroda v IV–VII vv.* (Leningrad 1971). For a fuller survey of the literature and the debate, see Brandes, 'Forschungsbericht'.

The extent to which demographic factors – decline or stability, for example, as affected by plague or similar occurrences – can be taken into account in this schema is very difficult to determine. It has been pointed out, for instance, that one area – in north Syria – clearly experienced a rural-based economic and demographic upswing during the sixth century, a boom which is not reflected in the literary sources at all, only in the archaeological record. On the other hand, there is clear evidence of population decline in regions such as Thrace during the second half of the sixth century which, constantly ravaged and threatened by hostile action, seems to have suffered greatly. Different regions thus suffered or not according to often highly localised factors. The important point to make in this context is that demographic decline is not the cause of urban decline, even if it does have an effect when it takes place.[6]

Within this general context, then, it seems entirely reasonable that we should expect the continued occupation, if on a smaller scale, of some sites, the abandonment of others, and even, for specific reasons, the preservation of certain cities within their original limits, rare though this might be. The city of Euchaita, for example, which has been singled out as such an exception, may have survived through the seventh century, although its population and clergy were often forced to seek refuge from Arab raiders in the citadel or fortified section of the town, which included an acropolis. The city was the home of St Theodore Tiro, of course, and as such remained an important cult centre and an attraction for pilgrims. The cycle of miracles which describes life in the city in the later seventh and eighth centuries along with the miracle-working acts of the martyr preserves an important account of the effects of hostile attacks and economic insecurity in the town at this period; but the presence of the cult itself seems to provide the main reason for its survival and its relatively populous nature.[7]

Such exceptions, in areas both subject to and free from regular attack, do not disprove the central thesis: namely, that the structural and functional position of the 'city' in the totality of social and economic relationships of the late Roman state was changing and that it was these changes in function which lie at the heart of any development – whether of decline or continuity – in the history of the seventh- and early eighth-century city.

In many respects, the crucial changes had already taken place by the end of the sixth century. As has been noted in chapter 1, the decline of the curial order, both as a social group with independent economic resources and as the competent governing element within municipal administra-

---

[6] See Patlagean, *Pauvreté économique*, pp. 301ff.; and esp. H. Kennedy, 'The last century of Byzantine Syria: a reinterpretation', *BF* 10 (1985), 141–83.
[7] See the detailed discussion of F. Trombley, *The Decline of the Seventh-Century Town* (cited in note 4 above) and Haldon, 'Some considerations', 96.

tions, had several consequences. The cities lost their role as crucial fiscal intermediaries in the extraction by the state of its revenues. Under the principate, the income of a city had been drawn from several sources. Rent on city lands, local taxes and dues, customs duties, interest of endowments (although Jones has estimated that most of the income from this source was lost during the great inflation of the third century), along with the voluntary donations of members of the governing body and the citizenry, all contributed to the municipal treasury. The proportion of these different sources of income varied from city to city, according to its character: whether it was chiefly commercial, an ancient foundation and so on. The first blow to civic economic independence was struck by Constantine I and Constantius, who confiscated the civic lands and their revenues. Julian restored them, but Valens and Valentinian confirmed Constantine's action. The *res privata* now administered these lands and their income; but after 374 it was decreed that the cities, which had protested that they could not cope without this revenue, should receive back one third of the income from their former lands, as well as being made responsible for the management of the lands themselves; furthermore they were to get back one third of their civic taxes, which had been administered in the meantime by the *sacrae largitiones*. Eventually, the management of these taxes, together with the rents from urban sites and buildings, was also returned to the cities. Some cities were able to increase their lands through purchase or inheritance, of course, and the richer cities, which derived their wealth as much from taxes and duties on commerce and so on, often suffered less than those which were dependent entirely on their rural hinterland. But the latter made up the majority, and it is clear from the fourth-century legislation that the cities became increasingly unable to cope with their own maintenance, quite apart from the administration of the revenues of the state.[8]

As a result of this loss of civic economic independence, the *curiales* no longer directed the fiscal administration of the state at the municipal level. Instead, centrally appointed officials – the *curator* or *pater civitatis* – representing in theory locally elected officers, but constituting in practice part of the vast machinery of the state bureaucracy, took over this role; these officials were later complemented by the establishment under Anastasius of *vindices* in each *civitas*, responsible for the collection of imperial revenues in each city, who seem also to have taken over the administration of the civic revenues.

---

[8] The evidence is fully discussed by Jones, *LRE*, vol. II, pp. 732ff.; see also J. Durliat, 'Taxes sur l'entrée des marchandises dans la cité de Carales-Cagliari à l'époque byzantine (582–602)', *DOP* 36 (1982), 1–14; and more particularly the discussion of F. Millar,

The cities and the land   97

The cities thus lost in both economic and social status. That these developments were already well advanced by the later fifth century is generally admitted; and the role of the local bishop, who acted and was recognised as a potential protector of the city and its populace in respect of both the landed magnates and the state, is illustrative. A law of Zeno, repeated in the *Codex Iustinianus*, suggests as much.[9] And while the bishop also represented – as local agent for the estates of the Church in his region – one, often the foremost, of the powerful landlords and *principales* of the municipality, there is no evidence that bishops ever had any formally constituted civic duties within the framework of the city administration, as has sometimes been assumed, on a pattern similar to that of the towns of the early medieval West.[10]

The decline of the curial order (the wealthier or luckier members obtaining exemption from civic duties through membership of the senate, the poorer increasingly unable to shoulder the burden of both state and civic liturgies) was halted for a while, although not reversed, by the state assuming control of the cities' lands and incomes from the middle of the fourth century. Henceforth, the magistrates and decurions had to administer only the affairs of their city. Even in the later sixth and early seventh centuries there are enough references to the city fathers of certain cities to make it clear that not all *curiales* were either poor or indifferent to their duties.[11] But, as has been pointed out, even contemporaries were aware of

'Empire and city, Augustus to Julian: obligations, excuses and status', *JRS* 73 (1983), 76–96.
[9] See *CJ* I, 3.35; and for the *curator civitatis* note 10 below. For the *vindices*, Jones, *LRE*, vol. II, pp. 759 ff. and notes.
[10] See Claude, *Die byzantinische Stadt im 6. Jhdt.*, 135 and 157f. Note the cogent arguments of A. Hohlweg, 'Bischof und Stadtherr im frühen Byzanz', *JÖB* 20 (1971), 51–62; G. Dagron, 'Le Christianisme dans la ville byzantine', *DOP* 31 (1977), 3–25, see 19ff. A law of Anastasius of 505 (*CJ* I, 55.11 (= i, 4.19)) repeating a law of 409 for the West, however, set up a new assembly, including the bishop and clergy, chief landowners and decurions, which was henceforth to elect the *defensor civitatis* – supposedly the protector of the citizens against official oppression – instead of the city council alone. The measure was designed chiefly to compensate for the fact that the *curiales* were no longer the wealthiest or the most powerful in the city, and might easily fall prey to the provincial governor. Anastasius' law also gave this assembly the duty of electing a corn-buyer in times of need, as well as the right to elect the *curator* or *pater civitatis*, the official appointed originally by the central government to supervise and regulate civic finances. See Jones, *LRE*, vol. II, pp. 726f. and 758f., and esp. J. Durliat, 'Les Attributions civiles des évêques byzantins: l'exemple du diocèse d'Afrique (533–709)', in *Akten des XVI. Internationalen Byzantinisten-Kongresses*, II, 2 (Vienna 1982), pp. 73–84 (= *JÖB* 32); A. Guillou, 'L'Evêque dans la société méditerranéenne des VIe–VIIe siècles: un modèle', *Bibliothèque de l'Ecole des Chartes* 131 (1973), 5–19 (repr. in Guillou, *Culture et société en Italie byzantine (VIe–XIe siècles)* II (London 1978).
[11] See, for example, *Vita Theod. Syk.*, 25, 6 and 45, 2–3. For a good discussion of the decline of the curial class, see de Ste Croix, *The Class Struggle in the Ancient Greek World*, pp. 465–74.

the decline of the cities and their councils, as a novel of Justinian for the year 536 implies.[12] Civic autonomy had all but disappeared, in fact, by the later sixth century. The town councils seem, on the whole, to have either ceased to exist, or to have been bypassed and become ineffectual. Power resided with the imperial revenue officials, in particular with the *vindices* – and with the assembly of bishops, clergy and magnates. But even the authority of the latter was tempered by the fact that provincial governors regularly appointed their own representatives to the cities in their province, representatives who acted, in effect, as city governors, tending to assume responsibility for civic buildings, walls, water supply, and the like, and who, together with the *vindices* of the bureau of the praetorian prefecture, now dominated city administration. The *curiales* continued to function, however, if only in their capacity as simple collectors of state and civic revenues under the supervision of the imperial establishment.[13]

By the later sixth century, therefore, there is sufficient evidence to demonstrate that the cities of the empire had lost their fiscal, economic and political independence to a very large extent to the state; and that the dominant administrative and legislative body within each city was now made up of the bishops and clergy, the richer landowners, some of the centrally appointed officers of the imperial fiscal bureaux, along with the now relatively unimportant *curiales*. Of course, richer *curiales* still were to be found in many cities; but the general tendency is clear enough, and even the extraction and administration of local civic revenues and their expenditure came under the supervision and sometimes direct control of imperial officials. In the richer cities – such as Alexandria, Antioch, or Ephesus, for example, where wealthy merchants or landowners who had invested in shipping were to be found or in those cities where local magnates retained an interest in the well-being of their cities – a certain degree of civic autonomy survived.[14] And, of course, this gradual reduction in the relevance of the cities to the fiscal and political administration of the state did not always have negative effects on local economic activity, whether small-scale artisan production, services or market exchange. What is important is the shift in the function of cities, from self-governing,

[12] Justinian, *Nov.* 38, proem.
[13] See Jones' comments, *LRE*, vol. II, p. 759ff.; and see J. Durliat, 'Les Finances municipales africaines de Constantin aux Aghlabides', in *Bulletin archéologique du comité des travaux historiques et scientifiques*, new series, 19 (1983), 377–86; and note also Zacos and Veglery, nos. 400, 1462, 2890, all datable to the seventh century, of decurions and, in the last case, the community (*to koinon*) of the city of Sinope – perhaps a reference to the municipal council or the municipality itself. Such seals say nothing, of course, about the functions of their users.
[14] But even a city such as Alexandria was financially under the thumb of the *vindex*, as Justinian, *Edict.* XIII, 15 makes clear; and see the remarks of Durliat (see note 13 above), 378–80 with literature.

The cities and the land 99

economically independent, local fiscal and administrative agencies, acting for the state as well as on their own behalf, to dependent urban centres with no real role in the imperial fiscal administrative system and no autonomous economic existence.[15]

By the early seventh century, civic autonomy existed in name only. The state effectively passed the towns by as far as revenue administration was concerned. They still functioned as administrative centres for imperial provincial officials, of course, as well as for the Church. As long as there was no threat to local trade or exchange activity, they will have continued to serve as market centres or centres of small-scale commodity production. But while the later Roman and early Byzantine notion of culture and civilisation were still inseparable from the concept of the city, with all that that entailed in both practical terms (public facilities and services, for example) and in ideological respects, few urban centres had the income or the independence of their former selves; none were essential to the actual functioning of the state.

THE FATE OF URBAN SETTLEMENT AND MUNICIPAL CIVILISATION IN THE SEVENTH CENTURY

Thus far the term 'city' or 'town' has been used without distinction to define urban centres of population; but no attempt has been made to define more precisely what is meant by these terms. And it is this undifferentiated application of the term 'city' to both late Roman and Byzantine urban settlements that has led to both misunderstandings and confusion in the debate.

Since the later nineteenth century, there has been much discussion on the question of defining what exactly is meant by the term 'city', and a

[15] The changes summarised have been analysed in much greater detail by a number of scholars. See Jones, *LRE*, vol. II, pp. 726f., 732–4, 737–63 and *The Greek City from Alexander to Justinian*, pp. 148ff. and 267ff.; Kirsten, 'Die byzantinische Stadt', 23ff.; W. Liebenam, *Städteverwaltung im römischen Kaiserreiche* (Leipzig 1900 and Amsterdam 1967), pp. 476ff.; H. Aubin, 'Vom Absterben antiken Lebens im Frühmittelalter', in *Kulturbruch oder Kulturkontinuität von der Antike zum Mittelalter*, ed. P.E. Hübinger (Darmstadt 1968), pp. 203–58, see esp. 213ff.; Kurbatov, *Osnovnye problemy*, pp. 46ff. and 154ff., and 'Razloženie antičnoi gorodskoi sobstvennosti v Vizantii (IV-VII vv.)', *VV* 35 (1973), 19–32 (where he documents the alienation of civic lands to private persons, the state and the Church); F. Vittinghof, 'Zur Verfassung der spätantiken Stadt', in *Studien zu den Anfängen des europäischen Stadtwesens* (Reichenau 1956). For a detailed discussion of the earlier literature, both in the Soviet Union and elsewhere, see Frančes, *La Ville byzantine et la monnaie*; and more recently, the excellent discussion in Brandes, *Die Städte Kleinasiens*, pp. 17–22. H. Kennedy, 'The last century of Byzantine Syria: a reinterpretation', *BF* 10 (1985), 141–84, and H. Kennedy and J.H.W.G. Liebeschuetz, 'Antioch and the villages of northern Syria in the fifth and sixth centuries A.D.: trends and problems', *Nottingham Medieval Studies* 32 (1988), 65–90 present valuable surveys of the pre-Islamic decline in key aspects of urban culture in the sixth and early seventh centuries. For further literature, see the bibliographical notice at p. 476 below.

number of very different ways of using it has been suggested. The issue is obviously complicated by the fact that modern attempts to define what a city should mean in social, economic and political terms – which may be based (as with Max Weber) on analyses of Western medieval cities – may not always coincide with what either Romans or Byzantines, for example, considered to be a city or with the character of those settlements which were, sometimes very loosely, referred to in the sources as *civitates* or *poleis*.[16]

The term 'city' in the Roman world was essentially a legal administrative definition applied by the Roman state as it expanded to communities which, as we have seen, were in origin autonomous and responsible to the state only in respect of the supervision and collection of the state's revenues. These might be either urban communities proper, real centres of distinct *territoria*, or they might be groups of villages, attributed jointly with the administrative responsibility and the constitutional forms of the classical *civitas* or *polis*.[17] But behind this lay also a complex web of cultural meanings which the term evoked for a member of late Roman society. The city symbolised Roman, or Greco-Roman, civilisation; it evoked ideas about both local tradition and imperial context, of literacy and 'letters' in general, of physical space and a certain economic order.

The term 'city' – *civitas* – thus referred in the first instance to both the

[16] The approaches to the problem are many and varied. On the whole, simple definition based on legal status alone, or the existence of a circuit wall, for example, have proved unsatisfactory. Weber's approach to the problem was to establish models of urban communities, which might help to elucidate the historical realities as constructed through the sources. But the debate about the use, application and validity of these 'ideal types' remains. See G. Korf, 'Der Idealtypus Max Webers und die historisch-gesellschaftlichen Gesetzmässigkeiten', *Deutsche Zeitschrift für Philosophie* 11 (1964), 1328ff., and Max Weber, 'Die Stadt. Begriff und Kategorien', in *Die Stadt des Mittelalters* I: *Begriff, Entstehung und Ausbreitung*, ed. C. Haase (Darmstadt 1969), pp. 34–59, together with a number of other valuable contributions in the same volume. See also the article of D. Denecke, 'Der geographische Stadtbegriff und die räumlich funktionale Betrachtungsweise bei Siedlungstypen mit zentraler Bedeutung in Anwendung auf historische Siedlungsepochen', in *Vor- und Frühformen der europäischen Stadt im Mittelalter*, eds. H. Jankuhn, W. Schlesinger and H. Steuer (Abhandlungen der Akad. der Wissenschaften in Göttingen, phil.-hist. Klasse III, 83 (1973), 1, pp. 33–55); C. Goehrke, 'Die Anfänge des mittelalterlichen Städtewesens in eurasischer Perspektive', *Saeculum* 31 (1980), 194–239; M.I. Finley, 'The ancient city: from Fustel de Coulanges to Max Weber and beyond', *Comparative Studies in Society and History* 19 (1977), 305–27; and the comments of G. Warnke, 'Antike Religion und antike Gesellschaft: wissenschaftshistorische Bemerkungen zu Fustel de Coulanges' *La Cité antique*', *Klio* 68 (1986), 287–304. For a recent detailed discussion, see Brandes, *Die Städte Kleinasiens*, pp. 23–43.

[17] See Jones, *LRE*, vol. II pp. 712ff., and 'The cities of the Roman empire: political, administrative and judicial functions', *Recueils de la Société Jean Bodin* VI (1954), 135–73 (repr. in *The Roman Economy*, pp. 1–34), 1ff., for example; also the useful survey and discussion of J. Koder, 'The urban character of the early Byzantine empire: some reflections on a settlement geographic approach to the topic', in *17th International Byzantine Congress, Major Papers*, pp. 155–89.

centre and its dependent *territorium*; *polis* was understood in the same way, a point which hardly needs to be demonstrated. In the second place, the term refers to a cultural symbol which points to notions about the past and the present through which individuals could identify themselves. It is important to recall, therefore, that while a definition of a city or town based on predominantly economic and social considerations is essential (that is, a town is a settlement, in which the dominant form of exchange activity occurs through market transactions, where some elements of petty commodity production are present and necessary, and where market-exchanges constitute a fundamental element for the existence of the community),[18] it must equally be remembered that many of the 'cities' of the Roman world were in origin little more than villages with elements of the local state administration present; and that while the presence of the latter may also have attracted or stimulated some market-exchange and small-scale commodity production, this economic activity was in effect a secondary phenomenon. In times when communications are unhindered and a stable small-denomination coinage available, such activity will be favoured; in times of political and economic insecurity, this activity may well disappear, although the primary administrative function of the settlement may remain.[19]

When a late Roman or Byzantine source refers to a *polis*, therefore, these considerations must be borne in mind: *polis* may refer to a thriving centre of commercial and exchange activity; it may equally refer to an unimportant provincial settlement which serves merely as an administrative convenience and a shelter for the local populace. Each case must be taken, so far as is possible, on its merits. Indeed, the situation is complicated by the varied terminology used in the sources. On the whole, modern historians have added to the problem by reading the term *polis* uniformly as 'city' or 'town', thus translating the medieval use of the term into a context where it must necessarily be, at the very least, ambiguous. This is an important point, since it is clear that the use of the term *polis* by Byzantine writers did not always have the meaning we understand by the term. On occasion, indeed, it may be used merely for effect or to demonstrate a writer's familiarity with ancient terminology; and it is certainly clear from the use of terms such as 'fortress' or 'castle' and *polis* side by side and often interchangeably among medieval Greek writers that what was meant by *polis* often bears no relation to either the ancient or the modern concept

---

[18] See, for example, K. Marx, *Pre-Capitalist Economic Formations*, ed. E. Hobsbawn (London 1964), pp. 71f. and 77.
[19] For the character of such activity, see J.P. Sodini, 'L'Artisanat urbain à l'époque paléo-chrétienne (IVe–VIIe siècles)', *Ktema* 4 (1979), 71–119; and the section on Korykos, in Tinnefeld, *Die frühbyzantinische Gesellschaft*, pp. 215ff.

associated with the term.[20] Sometimes, a writer deliberately differentiates between a city and its acropolis or castle, and here it can be argued, as has been done for Euchaita, for example, that a larger urban settlement is meant by the *polis*, not just a fortress.[21] On other occasions, the physical description of a settlement as a *kastron* is qualified by the remark that the place in question was also a *polis*, that is, it possessed the juridical status and constitutional form – the corporate personality – of a city.[22] On the whole, the juridical distinction between a *polis*, with its attendant status and rights, and other settlements, is retained up to the seventh century. From this time on, however, the term *polis* begins to lose its technical meaning, as we shall see. It is thus essential that modern historians differentiate also between *poleis* which had an independent economic existence and a market character, and those which represent primarily administrative centres or settlements that obtained the title and privileges of a city for social-cultural – ideological – reasons.

Anatolia and the eastern provinces

Up to the middle of the second decade of the seventh century the majority of the urban settlements of the eastern provinces had suffered no permanently damaging attacks on their lands or their *territoria*, with the exception of the fortress settlements of the eastern *limes* most open to attack from the Persians during the wars of the sixth century. Antioch, for example, which was destroyed by an earthquake between 526 and 529, was rebuilt with imperial aid (by this time a normal procedure – even the wealthiest cities could not raise the resources necessary for such major building programmes without imperial assistance, an important illustration of their economic dependence once their lands were no longer entirely under their control). But apart from occasional Persian successes, the eastern provinces suffered only minor discomfort at enemy hands.

This is not to say, of course, that the cities and towns of the empire had not experienced hostile attacks, or suffered considerable destruction, in previous centuries. In the 250s and 260s, for example, attacks from both the Goths on the one hand and the Sassanids on the other penetrated as far as the Pontic coast, Bithynia, Pamphylia, Cappadocia, capturing or sacking many cities, including Satala, Caesarea in Cappadocia, Comana, Sebastea, Trebizond, Pergamum, Nicomedea, Nicaea, Prusa, and Apamea.[23] Other

[20] See Haldon, 'Some considerations', 90 and note 36.
[21] See Trombley, 'The decline of the seventh-century town'.
[22] See, for example, Malalas, 302, 22sq.
[23] For Antioch, see Jones, *LRE*, vol. I, p. 283. For the Persians, D. Magie, *Roman Rule in Asia Minor* (Princeton 1950), pp. 708 and 1568f. and pp. 1566–8 for the Goths; see also

areas of Anatolia suffered at the hands of Isaurian brigands throughout the fifth and much of the sixth century, as the legislation of the *Codex Iustinianus* and Justinian's novels demonstrate. The Huns similarly raided eastern Anatolia from the Caucasus region in 515; while the Persian wars of the sixth century certainly caused widespread devastation in the regions around the key fortress cities along the Armenian front and in the diocese of Oriens.[24] The construction of walls around the formerly open and undefended cities of the empire was a phenomenon which began already in the later second century, however, gathering pace through the troubled years of the third century. By the fifth and sixth centuries towns or cities without defences of some sort were a rarity; but the need to maintain them was a constant drain on limited resources, and itself contributed to the changed circumstances which forced the municipalities to turn increasingly to local and central imperial sources for financial aid.[25]

These developments inevitably affected the towns and cities of the areas in question, at least for the duration of the perceived danger. They thus contributed also to the overall pattern of decline in urban fortunes over this period. But it seems clear from both literary and archaeological evidence that it was the constant and regular devastation of the seventh century which hastened the end – inevitable anyway in structural terms – of the towns of both Anatolia and the Balkans.

From 610, following the rapid conquest of much of Syria, successful Persian attacks on the Anatolian cities of Satala, Nicopolis, Theodosioupolis and Caesarea took place; and although Caesarea was retaken a year later, the Persians left it in ruins.[26] After the failure of the Byzantine counter-offensive in 613, Tarsus and Melitene were taken; but in the following years, as the Persians directed their attention toward the conquest or consolidation of Syria, Palestine, and Egypt, it was the urban centres of these regions which suffered.[27] From 615/16 Anatolian cities suffered once again, as the Persians turned their attention to Constantinople. From 615 onwards, Chalcedon, Sardis, Ancyra and a number of

F. Hild and M. Restle, *Tabula Imperii Byznatini*, II: *Kappadokien* (Kappadokia, Charsianon, Sebasteia u. Lykandos) (Vienna 1981), p. 66.

[24] For Justinian's legislation, see Jones, *LRE*, vol. 1, pp. 280ff.; for the Huns, Stein, *Bas-Empire*, vol. 2, p. 105; and for the Persian wars, see the summary in chapter one above and the literature cited in note 23 above.

[25] On the walling of cities, see Trombley, 'The decline of the seventh-century town', 76f.; J.W. Eadie, 'City and countryside in late Roman Pannonia: the *Regio Sirmeinsis*', in R.L. Hohlfelder, ed., *City, Town and Countryside in the Early Byzantine Era* (New York 1982), pp. 25–42, see 31; T.E. Gregory, 'Fortification and urban design in early Byzantine Greece', *ibid.*, pp. 43–64; F.E. Wozniak, 'The Justinianic fortification of interior Illyricum', *ibid.*, pp. 199–209.

[26] See Foss, 'The Persians in Asia Minor', 722f.; Kaegi, 'New evidence'; Sebeos, 61ff.; *Vita Theod. Syk.*, 153, 3sq.: *TIB*, vol. II, p. 194.

[27] See, for example, Sebeos, 65 and 67.

other cities were sacked by Persian forces,[28] and the devastation of wide stretches of central and western Anatolia seems to have been repeated in the following year. Only with Heraclius' counter-attack and successes from 622/3 on did it cease.

The cities of Asia Minor thus received a substantial blow to their physical structure and to their hinterlands, although hostile action was not the only cause. A great earthquake in the years 612–16 seems effectively to have destroyed much of the old city of Ephesus, a disaster from which it never recovered. The seventh-century settlement was limited to a fortified area around the old theatre and to a fortified settlement around the church of St John on the hill of Aya Solük. As the seventh century progressed, the latter seems to have become more and more important, although the theatre area had the harbour at its disposal. While urban activity certainly did not cease, the earthquake seems to have been the final blow to an ancient *polis* and its extensive suburbs.[29]

The urban communities of both the Anatolian and the eastern provinces generally had little time to recover their fortunes before the beginnings of the Arab attacks on Roman territory and the subsequent conquest of Syria, Palestine, Egypt and eventually the rest of Roman North Africa. The cities of these latter areas suffered one of two fates: either they surrendered unconditionally – generally being left more-or-less unmolested, although under new political masters – or they resisted and were either taken by storm or eventually starved into surrender. The penalty for resistance was the sack of the town, the death or enslaving of much of the population, and the destruction of all fortifications and defensive structures.[30]

From the 640s until the 740s, on the other hand, the towns and cities of Anatolia, both in those regions which were now to become frontier zones and in the heart of the empire, were subject to a continuous series of raids, major and minor attacks and plundering expeditions. These have for the most part been well documented by historians, and I will detail them only very briefly here. But the evidence from both literary and archaeological sources is graphic; and it is quite clear that the massive and constant insecurity which was a result had far-reaching consequences for both the rural and urban populations. Communications became uncertain, the sowing and harvesting of crops, and certainly their consumption, was frequently impossible, especially in the most exposed zones; market

---

[28] See the account in Foss, 'The Persians in Asia Minor', 724 with literature; Foss, *Sardis*, pp. 53ff. and 'Ankara', 62ff.

[29] See Foss, *Ephesus*, pp. 103ff. for a detailed discussion and analysis of the sources. He dates the event to 614.

[30] See the brief account in chapter 2 above; and Gabrieli, *Muhammad and the Conquests of Islam*, pp. 143–80. The best analysis of the history of urban centres in Anatolia in the seventh and eighth centuries is now Brandes, *Die Städte Kleinasiens*.

activity, which depended both upon the safety of local transport at least, as well as on the existence of secure centres of exchange and the availability of a suitable medium of exchange, was extensively disrupted and, where it continued, was limited either to large emporia secured and supported by the state or to barter and gift-exchange in kind on a highly localised basis between rural producers and consumers and local administrative or military personnel. What is important to recall is the fact that, while these 'external' factors – essentially, the existence of a constant and real military threat – were without doubt instrumental in the demise of classical civic life and institutions, they were so only in so far as they dealt the final blow. There is no evidence to suggest that any of the cities affected by these developments would have recovered its ancient dynamism had these attacks not occurred. Indeed, many cities not directly affected, or only very occasionally affected, by hostile action or its results, nevertheless suffered ultimately the same fate as the rest. The already existing tendency outlined above underlies the developments of the seventh century.[31]

The following list illustrates clearly enough the activities of Muslim forces – whether on major expeditions, as, for example, against Constantinople in the years 674–8 or 717–18, or on the yearly spring or winter raids.[32] Importantly, a larger city often weathered a siege or attack – unless it was the specific target of an expedition. But the surrounding countryside was almost invariably devastated, and it was the destruction of local resources in foodstuffs, livestock and materials, or the impossibility – indeed the pointlessness – of attempting to maintain local agricultural or pastoral activity, which must have led to the rapid decline in the population of many exposed or frequently attacked cities.[33] The larger cities shrank in size – to a defensible area – and their character changed as their hinterland became insecure. Only those centres which could be both easily defended and which had access to the sea, for example, could continue to thrive – and the best example, exceptional for many reasons, was Constantinople itself.

In the following, an asterisk and a numeral denotes the capture of a city and the number of times it was taken; otherwise its presence in the list

---

[31] For a similar conclusion, see A. Každan and G. Constable, *People and Power in Byzantium: An Introduction to Modern Byzantine Studies* (Washington D.C. 1982), p. 57; C. Mango, *Byzantium: The Empire of New Rome* (London 1980), pp. 60ff. for a more detailed survey of the development of urban life from the fourth to the ninth centuries.

[32] On these, see Haldon and Kennedy, 'The Arab-Byzantine frontier', 113; 'Kudama b. Djaᶜfar', 199f.

[33] See the apposite comments of Lilie, *Die byzantinische Reaktion*, pp. 190ff. and 305f., who points out that, while Caesarea and Euchaita were each taken for a short while in the opening phases of the warfare, as later was Trebizond, Ancyra (654) and Amorium (669) – all quickly re-taken – it is almost entirely the smaller and less important urban centres which were permanently or regularly captured.

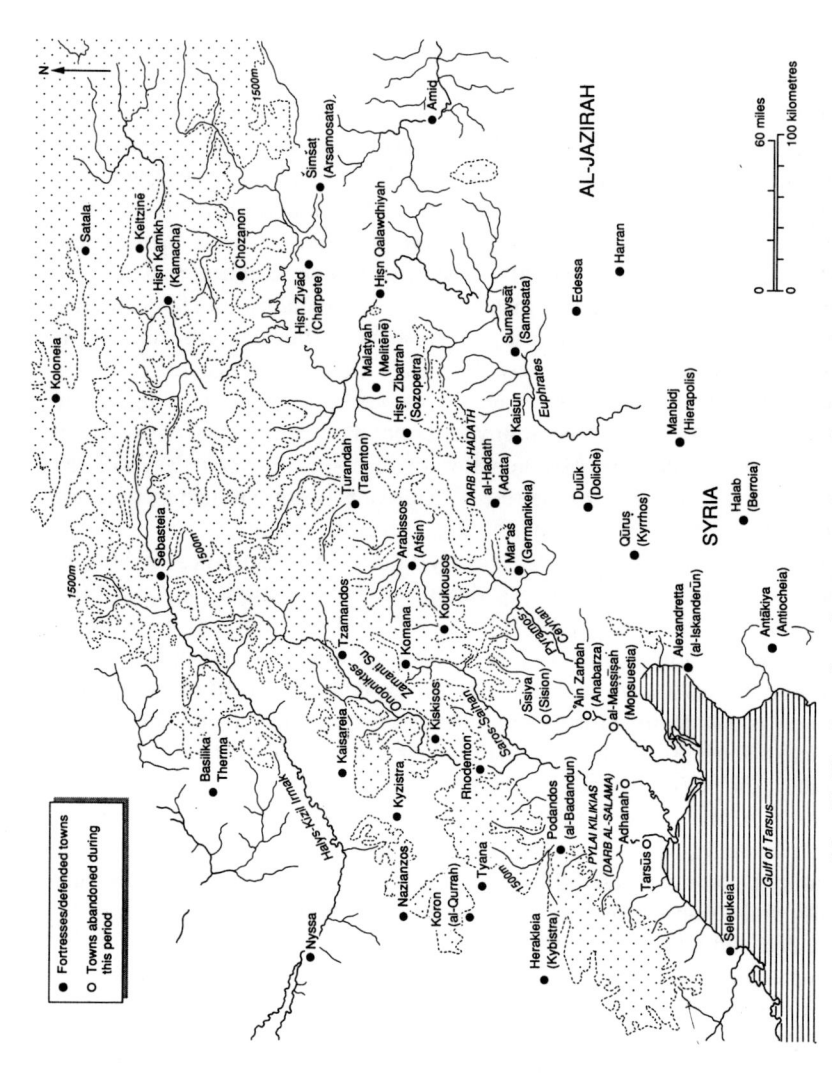

Map V The Anatolian frontier region in the seventh and early eighth centuries

refers to a siege and the accompanying devastation of its hinterland. The list covers the period from 636 to 740.

Abydus (* 1), Acroinum (* 3), Amasea (* 1), Amastris, Amisus, Amorium (* 8), Ancyra (* 3), Antioch (Pisidia) (* 4), Antioch (Isauria) (* 1), Chalcedon (* 4), Chrysoupolis (* 1), Dorylaeum (* 2), Ephesus (* 1), Euchaita (* 1), Gangra (* 2), Heraclea (* 3), Iconium (* 1), Caesarea (* 4), Kamacha (* 4), Camuliana (* 1), Koloneia (* 1), Cyzicus (* 1), Melitene (* 7), Misthia, Mopsuestia, Myra, Neocaesaraea (* 1), Nicaea (* 2), Nicomedia, Nicopolis (* 1), Pessinus (* 1), Pergamum (* 3), Podandus (* 1), Sardis, Satala (* 1), Sebastea (* 1), Sebaste (* 1), Sinope, Sisium (* 1), Smyrna (* 3), Synnada (* 1), Tarenta (* 2), Tarsus (* 3), Trebizond (* 1), Tyana (* 3).

These towns or fortresses,[34] along with many others, were thus the target of specific attacks on a number of occasions; and they were affected by the raids which bypassed them on their way elsewhere even more often. The frontier areas – Armenia II and IV, Cappadocia, Isauria, Pisidia, Lycaonia – were raided virtually every year for over a century; the regions behind them – Phrygia, Galatia, Helenopontus; and then Lydia, Bithynia and Paphlagonia – were traversed or reached almost as often. Frequently Arab forces wintered deep in Byzantine territory: yearly from 663 to 668, from 670 to 672, 679 and so on. And it must be realised that there were probably many raids or targets not explicitly mentioned in any source.

Even taking into account the occasional truce between empire and caliphate – as in the late 680s – the effects of these raids and attacks on the economy of Asia Minor must have been considerable. It is difficult to calculate or quantify, of course, with any degree of accuracy. Comparative evidence can be adduced; while the archaeological material, where it is available, can help to flesh out the bare bones of our narrative and other literary sources.

For comparative material, we might usefully turn to the effect of Türkmen raids on Byzantine settlements in western Anatolia in the last forty or so years of the eleventh century, where it has been demonstrated very clearly how the livelihood of the 'cities' or fortresses and their dependent rural populations was very rapidly disrupted and then destroyed by regular, but very often quite small, raids. The local agricultural population, where they were not spared in return for supplying the raiders, was generally forced to abandon its lands, tenaciously though the peasants tried to hang on to their livelihoods, fleeing first to the nearest fortress towns and, when these became too obvious a target – or indeed when they

---

[34] The best comprehensive survey, year by year and raid by raid, is that of Lilie, *Die byzantinische Reaktion*, who gives full documentation and discusses the chronology of the attacks.

became too overcrowded and unable to support the influx of refugees – further afield. The result was the destruction of the town's resources and, unless relieved or resupplied by a military expedition, its forced capitulation or capture and sack.[35]

The archaeological record suggests a similar pattern for many of the cities of Anatolia in the seventh century. It demonstrates initially a general shrinkage of the area covered by the original settlement – a shrinkage which, it must be emphasised, begins already in the later fifth and sixth centuries, a result of the structural developments outlined already – and entailing the abandonment of much of the city and most or all of its suburban districts; together with the fortification, usually involving the extensive use of spolia robbed from the older settlement, of a much smaller area, more often than not on a hill or promontory or some other such easily defended position. This is certainly the case with Ephesus, Magnesia on the Maeander, Sardis, Priene, Miletus, Heraclea, Aphrodisias, Laodicea, Hierapolis, Myra, Tius, Apollonia, Patara, Side, Ancyra, Nicopolis, Heraclea (Pontica), Assus, Pergamum, and very many others.[36] Alternatively, some

[35] See Vryonis, *The Decline of Medieval Hellenism*, pp. 144ff.
[36] For Ephesus, see Foss, *Ephesus*, pp. 103ff. with further literature and Brandes, in *Klio* 64 (1982), 611–22; for Magnesia: Foss, 'The Persians in Asia Minor', 742, and 'Archaeology and the "twenty cities"', 483; for Sardis: Foss, *Sardis*, pp. 53ff. (and see Každan, in *Βυζαντινά* 9 (1977), 478–84); for Priene: Foss, 'Archaeology and the "twenty cities"', 479 with further literature; for Miletus: Foss, *ibid.*, 477–8; for Heraclea: A. Peschlow-Bindokat, 'Herakleia am Latmos: vorläufiger Bericht über die Arbeiten in den Jahren 1974 und 1975', *Archäologischer Anzeiger* (1977), 90–104; W. Müller-Wiener, 'Mittelalterliche Befestigungen im südlichen Ionien', *Istanbuler Mitteilungen* 11 (1961), 5–122, see 14; for Aphrodisias: see K.T. Erim, 'Recent discoveries at Aphrodisias', in *Proceedings of the Tenth International Congress of Classical Archaeologists* (3 vols., Ankara 1978), pp. 1077ff. and Erim in *Anatolian Studies* 21–4 (1970–3) and 32 (1981) for yearly reports; and R. Cormack, 'The conversion of Aphrodisias into a Byzantine city', in *Abstracts of Papers of the 5th Annual Byzantine Studies Conference* (Washington D.C. 1979), pp. 13–14; for Laodicea: Foss, 'Archaeology and the "twenty cities"', 484, and literature; for Hierapolis: P. Verzone, 'Le ultime fasi vitali di Hierapolis di Frigia', in *Proceedings of the Tenth International Congress of Classical Archaeologists* (3 vols., Ankara 1978), pp. 1057ff.; Verzone, in *RbK* II (1971), pp. 1203–23; for Myra: (the centre of the cult of St Nicholas, of course) see G. Anrich, *Hagios Nikolaos. Der heilige Nikolaos in der griechischen Kirche* (2 vols., Leipzig and Berlin 1913), vol. II, p. 518; for the excavations, see J. Borchhardt, ed., 'Myra: eine lykische Metropole in antiker und byzantinischer Zeit', *Istanbuler Forschungen* 30 (1975); for Tios: see W.W. Wurster, 'Antike Siedlungen in Lykien', *Archäologischer Anzeiger* (1976), 23–49, see 30ff.; for Apollonia: see Wurster, *ibid.* 38ff.; also R.M. Harrison, 'Upland settlements in early medieval Lycia', in *Actes du Colloque sur la Lycie antique* (Paris 1980), pp. 109–18; for Patara: G.K. Sams, 'Investigations at Patara in Lycia (1974)', *Archaeology* 28 (1975), 202–5; for Side: A.M. Mansel, *Die Ruinen von Side* (Berlin 1963), pp. 13ff. with literature; for Ankara: Foss, 'Ankara', 30ff. and 62ff.; for Nicopolis: F. and E. Cumont, *Studia Pontica* II (Brussels 1906), esp. 304–11; Heraclea Pontica: W. Hoepfner, *Herakleia Pontike – Ereğli. Eine baugeschichtliche Untersuchung* (Vienna 1966), esp. pp. 35–48; for Assus: Foss, 'The Persians in Asia Minor', 740f.; J.M. Cook, *The Troad* (Oxford 1973), pp. 240ff. and 369; for Pergamum: see Claude, *Die byzantinische Stadt im 6. Jhdt.*, 23; Foss, 'The Persians in Asia Minor', 742f. and 'Archaeo-

The cities and the land 109

urban settlements were abandoned more or less completely, the population, or part of it, transferring to a nearby and more defensible site. This was the case with Colonae, for example, one of the best-known instances. Here, the population simply moved to the nearby fortress of Chonae, situated on a rocky promontory. Similarly, the site of the antique city of Faustinoupolis was abandoned for the fortress site of Loulon, some eight km. to the south; that of Prymnessus for Acroinum; Aurelioupolis in Lydia (the classical Tmolus) seems to have lost its population to an ancient but much more defensible site some five km. away; and Perge in Pamphylia was left for the better-defended fortress town of Syllaeum.[37]

Many smaller cities in the frontier-zone and their hinterlands were ultimately permanently abandoned. The extensive excavations at Anemurium in Cilicia show that the town, already in decline in the late third century following the Persian attack of 260, and after earthquake damage suffered in the 580s, had been reduced to a very humble settlement by the second half of the seventh century and may eventually have been abandoned, although this remains uncertain.[38] Tyana was likewise abandoned;[39] according to an account of the later eighth century, Euchaita was saved from abandonment in the 750s only by a timely miracle;[40] Sision

logy and the "twenty cities"', 479ff. This lists only some of the more recent publications. Further literature can be found in these works, and in Brandes, *Die Städte Kleinasiens*, pp. 81–131, where a detailed analysis of both literary and archaeological evidence can be found.

[37] See Kirsten, 'Die byzantinische Stadt', 29ff.; for Chonai, see Beck, *Kirche*, p. 171; for Faustinopolis/Loulon: F. Hild, *Das byzantinische Strassensystem in Kappadokien* (Vienna 1977), p. 52; *TIB*, vol. II, pp. 223ff.; for Acroinum: Kirsten, 'Die byzantinische Stadt', 29 and Kirsten, in *RE* XXIII, pp. 1154ff.; for Aurelioupolis: C. Foss, 'A neighbour of Sardis: the city of Tmolus and its successors', *Classical Antiquity* 1 (1982), 178–201; and for Syllaion-Perge, see V. Ruggieri, S.J., F. Nethercott, 'The metropolitan city of Syllaion and its churches', *JÖB* 36 (1986), 133–56. For further analysis and literature, Brandes, *Die Städte Kleinasiens*.

[38] See the summaries and analysis of J. Russell, 'Anemurium 1976', *Anatolian Studies* 27 (1977), 25–9; 'Anemurium: the changing face of a Roman city', *Archaeology* 5 (1980), 31–40; 'Transformations in early Byzantine urban life: the contribution and limitations of archaeological evidence', in *17th International Byzantine Congress, Major Papers*, pp. 137–54, see 144–9.

[39] See Hild, *Strassensystem*, p. 46; *TIB*, vol. II, pp. 298f.

[40] See *Vita et Miracula Theodori*, in H. Delehaye, ed., *Les Légendes grecques des saints militaires* (Paris 1909), p. 198. 28–31; D. de F. Abrahamse, *Hagiographic Sources for Byzantine Cities* (Ann Arbor, Michigan 1967), pp. 347ff.; Trombley, 'The decline of the seventh-century town', 69. For the date of the attacks described in miracles 4, 6, 7, 9 and 10 (the 750s), see C. Zuckerman, 'The reign of Constantine V in the miracles of St Theodore the Recruit (BHG 1764)', *REB* 46 (1988), 191–210. Každan has pointed out that a careful reading of the text of the miracles shows evidence of little more than a stronghold, and a local economy based on cattle-raising; in addition, that Euchaita in the eighth-century version of the Vita of St Theodore is not a city but a ranch or an estate. See A. Každan, 'The flourishing city of Euchaita?', *Fourteenth Annual Byzantine Studies Conference, Abstracts of Papers* (Houston, Texas 1988), 4. In contrast, F. Trombley continued to argue for urban continuity at the economic level. But the examples he cited actually show no more than

provides another example of abandonment;[41] and there were undoubtedly a great number of smaller settlements, of which we know little or nothing, which suffered a similar fate. Towns well away from the most exposed areas were also abandoned. Cnidas in Caria seems to have suffered this fate in the middle of the seventh century; many others like it – with a relatively weak economy and no other administrative or functional significance – will have followed the same route to oblivion.[42]

Those cities which survived as active economic centres did so because of their particular position. While it was attacked on several occasions, Nicaea lay far from the frontier; it had been and remained an important centre of communications and a commercial nodal point.[43] Smyrna, with its harbour facilities, presents a similar picture, and like Nicaea eventually recovered from the effects of the seventh and eighth centuries to become once more a flourishing centre for trade and commercial activity by the later ninth century.[44] Trebizond, similarly, with its harbour, and lying well protected behind the Pontic Alps, also survived, although it, too, was not entirely free from attack. The town was thoroughly sacked by Arab and Armenian forces in 655; but by the ninth century Arab writers describe it as a flourishing trading entrepôt.[45] Finally, Attalia seems to have preserved its character as a harbour and market-town, although little is known of its history in the seventh and eighth centuries in detail.[46] These towns, and others like them, owed their physical and their economic survival to their geographical advantages; it has been plausibly suggested that many profited also from the influx of refugees from more exposed areas, an influx which, while it may have strained local resources, may

that sites continued to be occupied where the state and the Church placed their administrative establishments. See F. Trombley, 'The Akropolis and lower city of the Byzantine "Dark Age" town (7th–8th century): the cases of Gortyna, Soloi and Druinopolis', ibid., 40.

[41] See Lilie, Die byzantinische Reaktion, p. 119 and note 50 with sources.

[42] See I.C. Love, 'A preliminary report of the excavations at Knidos (1970)', American Journal of Archaeology 76 (1972), 61–76, and 'A preliminary report of the excavations at Knidos (1971)', ibid., 393–405; see also Ruggieri and Nethercott (see note 37 above).

[43] See J. Sölch, 'Historisch-geographische Studien über bithynische Siedlungen', BNJ 1 (1920), 263–337, see 278ff.; and A.M. Schneider and W. Karnapp, Die Stadtmauer von Iznik (Nicaea) (Berlin 1938) (= Istanbuler Forschungen, 9), esp. p. 42; W.M. Ramsay, The Historical Geography of Asia Minor (London 1890 and Amsterdam 1962), p. 45.

[44] Foss, 'Archaeology and the "twenty cities"', 480ff.; Magie, Roman Rule in Asia Minor, p. 796.

[45] See, for example, P. Lemerle, 'Notes sur les données historiques de l'autobiographie d'Anania de Shirak', REA, new series, 1 (1964), 195–202; H. Ahrweiler, 'L'Asie mineure et les invasions arabes', RH 227 (1962), 1–32, see 30 with literature. For its vital role as a commercial centre, see R.B. Serjeant, 'Material for a history of Islamic textiles up to the Mongol conquest, Chapter IV', Ars Islamica 10 (1943), 71–104, see 94.

[46] See Jameson, in RE S12 (1970), pp. 110ff.; E.G. Bean, Turkey's Southern Shore (New York 1968), pp. 41ff.

also have stimulated local market activity and reinforced the local agricultural labour-force.[47]

It seems clear from the archaeological and the limited literary evidence that whether or not sites were abandoned, the long-term decline of the classical city was completed during the seventh century by the attacks of the Arabs in Asia Minor and the consequent social and economic effects. Hostile activity was not the only contributory factor in this process, of course. A number of cities or towns suffered considerable damage from earthquakes, often so severe as to permanently end the life of the ancient settlement – the effect on Ephesus, for example, providing an interesting illustration;[48] and in several cases this may have occurred before the seventh century. A number of towns affected by such natural disasters never recovered their former position or wealth: Miletus,[49] Aphrodisias,[50] Laodicea,[51] Nicopolis,[52] and Anemurium, referred to already. While earthquakes did not cause the decline of the ancient cities, of course, they did constitute an important factor.[53] Similarly, the frequent outbreaks of plague which were a feature of early medieval history affected the population of the empire drastically, especially those dwelling in the (relatively) confined conditions of an urban settlement. The best-known epidemic is perhaps that which swept across the Mediterranean in the 540s; but further epidemics affected parts or all of the eastern Mediterranean world more or less continuously: Constantinople was affected, for example, in 555–6, 560–1, 572–3, 585–6, 592, 598–9, 608–9, and in 618; and it affected Persia, Syria, Palestine and Egypt at intervals thereafter.[54] It occurred again in Constantinople in 697–8 where it was endemic for a year or more.[55] It was a constant factor in the eastern Mediterranean

---

[47] Ahrweiler, 'L'Asie mineure et les invasions arabes'.   [48] Foss, *Ephesus*, p. 103.
[49] W. Müller-Wiener et al., 'Milet 1978–1979', *Istanbuler Mitteilungen* 30 (1980), 23–98, see 28ff.
[50] Claude, *Die byzantinische Stadt im 6. Jhdt.*, 18 with literature.   [51] *Ibid.*, 155.
[52] F. and E. Cumont, *Studia Pontica* II (Brussels 1906), p. 311.
[53] See the remarks of Mango, *Byzantium: The Empire of New Rome*, pp. 68f.
[54] See the detailed account with literature in Patlagean, *Pauvreté économique*, pp. 85ff.; P. Allen, 'The "Justinianic" plague', *B* 49 (1979), 5–20; and esp. J.-N. Biraben, *Les Hommes et la peste en France et dans les pays européens et méditerranéens* I. *La Peste dans l'histoire* (Paris 1975), esp. pp. 25ff.; and J.-N. Biraben and J. Le Goff, 'La Peste dans la haute moyen age', *Annales* 24 (1969), 1484–1510, see 1485ff.; D. Jacoby, 'La Population de Constantinople à l'époque byzantine: une problème de démographie urbaine', *B* 31 (1961), 81–109; M.W. Dols, 'Plague in early Islamic history', *Journal of African and Oriental Studies* 94 (1974), 371–83 and *The Black Death in the Middle Ages* (Princeton 1977), pp. 13ff. There is an enormous literature on the subject, which can be pursued through the works listed here. See the discussion in L.A. Conrad, 'Epidemic disease in central Syria in the late sixth century. Some new insights from the verse of Hassân ibn Thâbit', *BMGS* 18 (1994) 12–58.
[55] See Theophanes, 370. 26sq.; Nicephorus, 40. 4sq. and see Teall, 'Grain supply', 101.

basin throughout this period. The consequences for the population must have been drastic.[56]

The urban settlements of Asia Minor were already suffering from the long-term effects of the general shift in the economic relations within the later Roman empire between the wealthiest magnates of the senatorial establishment and their cities. And because of the change in the function of the cities with regard to the state, they experienced a radical upheaval in their circumstances during the seventh and early eighth centuries as a result of the combination of factors described above. This change affected their physical appearance, their extent, as well as their economic and social function. The nature of the change is well summarised by the anonymous tenth-century Persian writer of the book *The Regions of the World* and by the Arab geographer Ibn Hawkal, both of whom emphasised the scarcity of cities (in the Muslim sense of the term) at a time when the empire was economically much stronger and when its urban settlements had had a century or more to recover from the warfare of the seventh and eighth centuries. It is significant that Arab writers use the Muslim terms for castles (qila^c) and fortresses (husūn) of the Byzantine cities and towns they describe – significant because the difference between concepts such as village, town and city is important in Muslim geographical terminology. Arab writers differentiate carefully between types of settlement when describing Muslim lands. Clearly, the fact that they refer to many Byzantine cities in this way suggests that they did not regard such settlements as cities at all (Arabic madināh). They were not to be compared with Muslim centres such as Baghdad, for example, or Damascus, or even Constantinople itself, centres of commerce, market exchange, administration and so on.[57]

A comment of the chronicler Tabarī emphasises the point, for he men-

---

[56] Patlagean, *Pauvreté économique*, pp. 87ff. has demonstrated the effects of the plague of the 540s on the urban life of parts of the Eastern empire; see also H. Kennedy, 'The last century of Byzantine Syria: a reinterpretation', *BF* 10 (1985), 141–83, see 181ff.

[57] *Hudūd al-^{c}Ālam, The Regions of the World*, trans. V. Minorsky (Oxford 1937), p. 156f.: 'In the days of old, cities were numerous in Rūm, but now they have become few. Most of the districts are prosperous and pleasant, and have (each) an extremely strong fortress, on account of the frequency of the raids which the fighters for the faith direct upon them. To each village appertains a castle, where in time of flight (they may take shelter)'; Ibn Ḥawqal, *Kitāb Surāt al-Ard, configuration de la terre*, trans. J.H. Kramer and G. Wiet (Beirut and Paris 1964), p. 194 (text ed. J.H. Kramer (Leiden 1938), p. 200): 'Rich cities are few in their [the Byzantines'] kingdom and country, despite its situation, size and the length of their rule. This is because most of it consists of mountains, castles (qilā^c), fortresses (ḥusūn), cave-dwellings and villages dug out of the rock or buried under the earth.' For the Muslim terminology, see G. von Grunebaum, 'The structure of the Muslim town', in *Islam: Essays in the Nature and Growth of a Cultural Tradition* (London 1961), pp. 141–58, see 141f. (repr. in *Islam and Medieval Hellenism: Social and Cultural Perspectives* (London 1976)).

tions in connection with Ancyra and Amorion that there was nothing in the land of the Byzantines greater than these two cities. The results of archaeological investigations have shown that at this time – 838 – neither was much more than a well-defended and strategically important fortress. Even allowing for Tabari's probable desire to glorify and to magnify the deeds of the victorious caliph who took the cities, his comment is telling. Ancyra shrank to a small citadel within the walls constructed from spolia robbed from the old city during the reign of Constans II, probably between 656 and 661, a citadel whose walls contain an area of some 350 metres by 150 metres.[58] Amorium, likewise an important fortress and military base, and from the later seventh century probably the headquarters of the *thema* or military district of the *Anatolikōn*, was also very small. In 716 it was successfully defended against a major Arab attack by only 800 men, if the source is to be believed.[59] While it may well have lain in a pleasant and fertile district and been a flourishing administrative centre, and consequently probably attracted some commercial activity, it was hardly a city in the sense outlined above, certainly not in the eyes of a contemporary Arab.[60]

Whether defined in terms of their economic function, their position as centres of social wealth and investment, or in terms of their constitutional status, their administrative character and functions, or their role in the extraction of revenues on behalf of the state, the classical cities of Anatolia underwent a dramatic transformation in this period. Some were abandoned or destroyed; those that survived shrank to insignificance, often surviving merely as defended villages; others owed their continued existence – and the existence of a limited degree of commercial activity – to their function as military and administrative centres, of both Church and state; yet others to their geographical position in respect of trade-routes and distance from enemy threat.[61] When cities did recover their economic well-being, during the later ninth century and after, it was not as revived or reinvigorated classical or late antique *poleis*, but as medieval towns, owing their fortunes to the administrative and military intervention of the

---

[58] See Foss, 'Ankara', 74ff., 78.
[59] See Mango, *Byzantium: The Empire of New Rome*, p. 72; W.E. Kaegi, jr., 'Two studies in the continuity of late Roman and Byzantine military institutions', *BF* 8 (1982), 87–113 and 'The first Arab expedition against Amorium', *BMGS* 3 (1977), 19–22.
[60] For the region in which it lay, see Michael Syr., *Chron.*, vol. II, p. 441 (for the year 647).
[61] See Kirsten, 'Die byzantinische Stadt', 20 and 28f., for example; the exceptional position and history of the Crimean town of Cherson provides an illuminating example: see A.I. Romancuk, 'Die byzantinische Provinzstadt vom 7. Jahrhundert bis zur ersten Hälfte des 9. Jahrhunderts (auf Grund von Materialien aus Cherson)', in H. Köpstein, ed., *Besonderheiten der byzantinischen Feudalentwicklung* (BBA L, Berlin 1983), pp. 57–68 with literature.

state, the safety of local and long-distance commerce, and their role as centres of market-exchange and local society and culture.

The Balkans and Constantinople

While I have concentrated thus far on Asia Minor, the Balkans fared no better. Only Thessaloniki retained any importance as a centre for trade, and then only with great difficulty and on a very limited basis. Many older cities shrank, becoming simply fortresses and/or administrative centres. As in Asia Minor, many were abandoned or destroyed; only those with access to the sea and some potential for trading or supplying a local demand in crafts could hope to survive. The disappearance of the antique pattern of urban centres took place during the later sixth and seventh centuries, as in Asia Minor. It is clearly connected with the long-term effects of, in particular, the Avar and Slav incursions into, and occupation of, much of the Balkan area south of the Danube. Some cities, of course, survived, and for the same sorts of general reasons as those outlined for Anatolia.[62]

Until recently, it was argued by many scholars that the continuity of names evident for a number of Balkan urban sites was alse evidence of a continuity of occupation and traditional urban activity and life. But it has been shown that many classical names also survive in Anatolia, and there it is no guarantee that continuity in the strict sense was the case. Indeed, while continuity of name is an element of importance, the mere survival of a city name in a later form is no evidence that the site in question continued to house either an urban centre of any sort, still less the market and economic elements necessary to define it as such.[63] The results of an analysis of literary evidence and archaeological material seem to confirm the pattern outlined already, a pattern of long-term decline in urban and municipal fortunes, beginning in the third century, and ending with the eclipse of urban life – save a few exceptions – during the first half of the seventh century. Those 'cities' that survived – the harbour town of Odessus, for example, at the mouth of the Danube, or the Danube settlements of Durostorum and Bononia – did so as closed fortresses, similar in

---

[62] See the comments of B. Bašković, 'L'Architecture de la basse antiquité et du moyen age dans les régions centrales des Balkans', in *Rapports du XIIe Congrès Internat. des Etudes Byzantines* VII (Ochrid 1961), pp. 155–63.

[63] See, for example, V. Beševliev, 'Zur Kontinuität der antiken Städte in Bulgarien', in *Neue Beiträge zur Geschichte der alten Welt* II: *Römisches Reich* (Berlin 1965), pp. 211–21, who argues from continuity in toponymy to continuity in economic and urban life. This is a doubtful procedure; and other evidence has shown that many of these sites were little more than hamlets during much of the medieval period. See A. Petre, 'Quelques données archéologiques concernant la continuité de la population et de la culture romano-byzantines dans la Scythie mineure aux VIe et VIIe siècles de notre ère', *Dacia* new series, 7 (1963), 317–57.

many ways to the fortress towns of Byzantine Asia Minor, but not in Roman hands.[64]

The exception that proves the rule in this general argument is, of course, Constantinople. Here, all the archaeological and textual evidence points to a very considerable decline in population during the later seventh and eighth centuries. It seems likely that many of the buildings and monuments of the fifth and sixth centuries fell into disrepair or were abandoned, and that large areas of the city within the Theodosian walls were deserted.[65] The later plan of the city, as it is known from the tenth century, with its internal cemeteries, monastic gardens and orchards, private pastures and estates, suggests the reduction of the urban population to well below its sixth-century peak, probably the highest point it ever reached.[66] Only a very few major public works are mentioned for the whole of the second half of the seventh and the eighth centuries, and only two monasteries are recorded as having been founded at that time.[67] The public works included the building of a defensive wall around the palace precinct by Justinian II (a valuable indicator also of the political climate during his reign) and the repairing of the Theodosian circuit after an

[64] See the general summary of G. Gomolka, 'Bemerkungen zur Situation der spätantiken Städte und Siedlungen in Nordbulgarien und ihrem Weiterleben am Ende des 6. Jahrhunderts', in *Studien zum 7. Jahrhundert*, pp. 35–42; also A. Milčev, 'Der Einfluss der Slawen auf die Feudalisierung von Byzanz im 7. Jahrhundert', *ibid.*, pp. 53–8, see 55f. For a general political-historical survey, see also P. Lemerle, 'Invasions et migrations dans les Balkans depuis la fin de l'époque romaine jusqu'au VIIIe siècle', *RH* 211 (1954), 265–308; and Ostrogorsky, 'Byzantine cities in the early middle ages', 107ff., 111ff.; R.-J. Lilie, '"Thrakien" und "Thrakesion"', *JÖB* 26 (1977), 7–47, see 35ff. For an instructive parallel, the history of the garrison town of Sirmium is valuable, albeit for an earlier period: see Eadie, 'City and countryside in late Roman Pannonia' (cited note 25 above), 25ff.

[65] The best textual evidence for this comes from a later eighth-century compilation known as the 'Brief historical notes' (*Parastaseis syntomoi chronikai*), which repeatedly points out that a certain monument or building had once existed but was now destroyed or in ruins. Many other monuments had whole mythologies built up around them, their original purpose and function being entirely lost. See Th. Preger, *Parastaseis syntomoi chronikai*, in *Scriptores Originum Constantinopolitanarum* (2 vols., Leipzig 1901 and 1907, repr. New York 1975), vol. I, pp. 19–73. This edition has now been reproduced, accompanied by a translation into English and a commentary: see Averil Cameron and Judith Herrin, *Constantinople in the Early Eighth Century: the Parastaseis Syntomoi Chronikai* (Leiden 1984). In this context, see the comments in the introduction, pp. 31ff. and 45–53; and esp. C. Mango, 'Antique statuary and the Byzantine beholder', *DOP* 17 (1963), 53–75 (repr. in *Byzantium and its Image* V (London 1984)). For the most concise recent survey of the decline of the city in the seventh and eighth centuries, see C. Mango, *Le Développement urbain de Constantinople (IVe–VIIe siècles)* (Paris 1985), pp. 51–62.

[66] See D. Jacoby, 'La Population de Constantinople à l'époque byzantine: un problème de démographie urbaine', *B* 31 (1961), 81–109 (repr. in *Société et démographie à Byzance et en Romanie latine* (London 1975)) for the sixth-century population – estimated at about 400,000.

[67] See P. Charanis, 'The monk as an element of Byzantine society', *DOP* 25 (1971), 61–84 see 65f. for the monasteries.

earthquake in 740.[68] It has been argued that the fact that the main aqueduct of the city fell into disuse some time after 626 (when it was damaged or destroyed during the Avaro-Slav siege of that year) and was (apparently) only repaired in 766, is good evidence of a very low population for the capital throughout this period – it could clearly manage on the few internal cisterns and springs nearby.[69] The point is confirmed by the testimony of the 'Brief history' of the patriarch Nicephorus, who notes that after the plague of 747 the city was almost entirely uninhabited; the dead were disposed of within the Constantinian walls of the city in old cisterns, ditches, vineyards and orchards.[70] The city was struck by plague in 619 and 698 also;[71] and in the eighth century the Emperor Constantine V had to repopulate the city from Greece and the Aegean islands.[72] Incidental evidence reinforces this picture of contraction and abandonment of many parts of the previously inhabited area of the city, and the reduction of commercial and exchange activity. After the sixth century, the stamping of bricks, hitherto widespread, ceases (although its exact purpose remains uncertain); while the quality of the locally produced ceramics seems also to have suffered a decline.[73]

But in spite of the dramatic fall in its fortunes, Constantinople survived, primarily because it was both the seat of the emperors, the single source of social and political power and authority in the empire, and at the same time extremely well positioned and defended. And exchange- and market-activity clearly did continue. The fictional *Life of St Andrew the Fool*, many parts of which date to the later seventh century, as well as the collection of the miracles of St Artemius, compiled probably in the 660s, both refer on several occasions to the sale and purchase of vegetables, fruits, wine and clothing, as well as to the use of small denomination bronze coins. In addition, we also read of other aspects of city life – taverns, brothels, street-gangs, beggars, foreign merchants, candle-makers and so on. Payment in cash is taken for granted.[74]

From the later eighth century there is some evidence for a revival, a revival which can be detected also in other urban centres of the empire

---

[68] See Theophanes, 367. 12–14 and 412. 16–20 for Justinian II and Leo. Note that Leo had to impose a special tax to raise the labour-force.

[69] See Mango, *Le Développement urbain de Constantinople*, pp. 56f. But for a different view see Trombley, 'Byzantine "Dark Age" Cities', 435f.

[70] Nicephorus, 63. 1–64. 12, esp. 64. 10–12; Theophanes, 423. 4–29.

[71] Nicephorus, 12. 6–9; Theophanes, 371. 23.   [72] Theophanes, 429. 22–5.

[73] See J.W. Hayes, *Excavations at Saraçhane in Istanbul*, vol 2: *The Pottery* (Princeton 1992); see R.B.K. Stevenson, *The Pottery 1936–1937: The Great Palace of the Byzantine Emperors* (Oxford 1947), pp. 33ff., for the pottery; Mango, *Le Développement urbain de Constantinople*, for the bricks.

[74] See *Vita Andreae Sali*, 648D, 656B, 660A, 708D (drinking houses); 649A, 652C etc. (brothels, street theatres); 689C, 713D (purchase/sale of vegetables and fruit); 656B (purchase of vegetables, payment for entry to baths) and 653C, 656B, 777C for *lepta, follera, miliarēsia, tremissis*; *Miracula S. Artemii*, 32. 26–7; 26. 27, -28. 12.

from the same time. But the important point is this: that the developments which could clearly affect Constantinople, the most populous, well defended and administratively and socially most important city in the empire, in such a dramatic way, can hardly have been less drastic in their effects on provincial cities.

CITIES AND MARKET EXCHANGE

It remains to examine briefly the evidence for cities or other settlements as centres of economic activity, that is, as centres of market-exchange or of production. The evidence relating to this problem for the seventh and eighth centuries is slight. Literary texts are, as we have seen, difficult to interpret, given the regular Byzantine use of the term *polis* to describe something which was clearly often simply a fortress. Some texts are more explicit, however: by the end of the eighth century, according to the chronicler Theophanes, the fair at Ephesus produced market-taxes of some 100 lbs. of gold for the imperial fisc, a sum which, even if not accurate, suggests a wealth of market activity, at least on this occasion.[75] Fairs, of course, often connected with specific religious celebrations (in this case the feast of St John the Theologian) were not always annual; nor do they necessarily represent the normal state of affairs: in the eleventh century, for example, John Mauropous, the bishop of Euchaita, comments on the fact that the great feast of St Theodore, which attracted people 'from every nation', transformed the city from a 'wasteland' to a populous city with markets and stoas.[76] Clearly, the wealth and brilliance of the fair did not represent the day-to-day social and economic reality of life in Euchaita; and this was probably the case with most other such occasions.[77]

Other arguments have been adduced to demonstrate the nature and extent (and usually continuity) of urban economic activity at this time. The evidence of coins has played an important role in these debates.

There existed in the later Roman and Byzantine worlds in effect two currencies: a gold coinage designed primarily for the use of the state in redistributing its revenues and in collecting its income; and a low denomination copper or bronze coinage, tied at a nominal ratio into the gold system, issued for the purposes of both revenue and market transactions. Ostrogorsky, along with a number of other scholars, argued that the continued presence of gold coins on many Anatolian and Balkan sites

---

[75] Theophanes, 469f.; cf. H. Antoniadis-Bibicou, *Recherches sur les douanes à Byzance, l' 'octava', le 'kommerkion' et les commerciaires* (Paris 1963), pp. 107f.
[76] See P. de Lagarde and J. Bollig, *Johannis Euchaitarum Metropolitae quae Supersunt in Cod. Vaticano Graeco 676* (Berlin 1882), pp. 131–2; note also Hendy, *Studies*, pp. 141–2.
[77] For a list, see Vryonis, *The Decline of Medieval Hellenism*, pp. 39–41.

during the seventh century, while being fewer in quantity than in the sixth century or in the ninth century, nevertheless demonstrated the continued existence of a relatively healthy 'monetary' economy and a good level of commercial activity. While noting at the same time that there was a dramatic fall-off in finds of the copper coinage from the period in question, he argued that this was not a significant element.[78]

In fact, it is crucial. For the presence of gold coins has very little to do with the existence of a market economy, being a reflection rather of the needs of the state and its military, administrative and fiscal machinery. A decline in the number of copper coins, however, assuming that it is not merely a reflection of their lack of intrinsic value, the whim of collectors, or accidents of deposit and discovery,[79] must surely be ascribed to a reduction in the number of coins struck and consequently reflect a general decline in demand, or the perceived demand. In other words, such coins were required in smaller numbers (and only in certain places), because the market-transactions they were designed to facilitate no longer took place, or took place on a very much smaller scale than had previously been the case.[80] Coin finds from excavations on the one hand, and coins (both gold and copper) in collections on the other, tend to bear out the assumed results for the economic life of the towns and cities of the empire outlined already: after evidence of much hoarding in or around 615, presumably a result of the threat of Persian attack, followed by a gradual recovery in the use and circulation of both copper and gold coins, finds dateable to the last years of the Emperor Constans II virtually cease.[81] Athens and Corinth in the Balkans and a whole series of excavated sites in Anatolia (Ephesus, Sardis, Priene, Ancyra, Assus, Aphrodisias, Anemurium) demonstrate this feature.[82]

From the reign of Heraclius through the rest of the seventh century the

---

[78] See Ostrogorsky, 'Byzantine cities in the early middle ages', 50ff.; see, for example, also Vryonis, *The Decline of Medieval Hellenism*, p. 7 – they both argue against Každan, *Vizantiiskie goroda* (an argument repeated also in *Derevniya i gorod v Vizantii (IX–X vv.)* (Moscow 1960), pp. 264f.). But see the critique of Ostrogrosky by P. Grierson, 'Coinage and money in the Byzantine empire 498–c. 1090', in *Moneta e Scambi nell'Alto Medioevo* (Settimane di Studi del Centro Italiano di Studi sull'alto Medioevo VIII, Spoleto 1960), pp. 411–53, see 445ff.; and the detailed account of the literature in Brandes, *Forschungsbericht*, 192–200.

[79] See the comments of Grierson (see note 78 above).

[80] See the survey carried out by D.M. Metcalfe, 'How extensive was the issue of folles during the years 775–820?', *B* 37 (1967), 270–310, for a slightly later period, esp. 272ff., where similar points are made in respect of the function and quantity of low-denomination coins.

[81] See, for example, Foss, 'The Persians in Asia Minor', 721ff.

[82] See Foss, *Ephesus*, pp. 197f., with table; 'The Persians in Asia Minor', 736–42; and esp. C. Morrison, 'Byzance au VIIe siècle: le témoignage de la numismatique', in Ἀφιέρωμα στόν Ἀνδρέα Ν. Στράτο (2 vols., Athens 1986), vol. I, pp. 149–63, esp. 155ff. and tables.

copper coinage was depreciated: the *follis'* original weight of eleven grams was reduced in 615/16; it was then further reduced to some five grams; and while it later stabilised for a while, constant efforts to bolster up the copper system by various reforms point to its dubious reputation and unreliability as a means of generalised exchange.[83] The gold coinage, while it retained its integrity, and while it is also found hoarded,[84] played only an accidental role in commercial transactions: where it was available and relevant to the types of transaction taking place, it might tend to be drawn in to market exchanges. The copper coinage disappears more or less completely from the last years of the reign of Constans II, after about 658, as it became less relevant to the requirements of exchange activity: that is to say, as market exchanges of a day-to-day variety petered out in all but a few major emporia – such as Constantinople – or as it found other forms through which goods could be transferred from one person to another, such as gift-exchange and barter. The state continued to produce the small denominations, of course, but their distribution and their use seems to have been very limited.[85] Where finds of copper coins do occur, they are more often than not to be connected with the presence of soldiers, for it seems that from the early seventh century both copper and silver had to be brought into the payment system of the state due to a lack of adequate supplies of gold.[86] And it can be argued that the drastic disappearance of copper from archaeological sites after the last years of Constans II was due to the state increasingly financing its forces with produce, equipment and so forth in kind, rather than through the traditional medium of cash grants and salaries, and thus making the regular issue of coin for this purpose unnecessary or, at best, marginal to its fiscal needs. Even the limited amount of copper found after the reign of Constans, therefore, may not

[83] See Hendy, *Studies*, pp. 498f.; and Sp. Vryonis, jr., 'An Attic hoard of Byzantine gold coins (668–741) from the Thomas Whittemore collection and the numismatic evidence for the urban history of Byzantium', *ZRVI* 8 (1963), 291–300, see 292; P. Charanis, 'The significance of coins as evidence for the history of Athens and Corinth in the seventh and eighth centuries', *Historia* 4 (1955), 163–72; Foss, 'Ankara', 87.
[84] See the remarks of C. Morrison, J.N. Barrandon and J. Poivier, 'Nouvelles recherches sur l'histoire monétaire byzantine: évolution comparée de la monnaie d'or à Constantinople et dans les provinces d'Afrique et de Sicile', *JÖB* 33 (1983), 267–86, esp. 274f., where fluctuations in the purity of gold can be related to regional historical contexts and developments.
[85] In the fictional Life of Andrew the Fool, which dates probably to the later seventh century (see the chapter on the sources, note 20), the regular use of small-denomination copper coins in day-to-day transactions is taken for granted: see *PG* CXI, 653C, 656B, 777C. Compare the results of Metcalfe's analysis with regard to *distribution* (see note 80 above), 305ff. See also C. Morrisson, 'Byzance au VIIᵉ siècle: le témoignage de la numismatique', in *Byzantion: Tribute to Andreas N. Stratos* I (Athens 1986), pp. 149–63.
[86] See Hendy, *Studies*, pp. 640–3 for payment in copper. The question of supplying the armies in kind will be examined in detail below.

necessarily signify the existence of a generalised system of commercial exchange in urban centres at this time.

Lack of exchange activity through the money medium does not imply either a lack of exchange activity as such, of course, or the complete desertion of the sites in question – one of the mistaken inferences drawn by the first proponents of urban discontinuity.[87] Nor does the possibility that the cessation of finds of copper coins on most excavated sites might be a reflection of state policy (a response to both changes in patterns of demand and/or changes in the perceived need for such issues) imply that urban life continued just as before, but without money. On the contrary, there is every reason to believe that the fiscal policy of the state itself reflects the same conditions as those which affected urban culture so drastically, and which I have described already.[88]

Let me summarise. The evidence of texts, numismatics and archaeology all point uniformly in one direction: the effective disappearance of the late antique urban economies which had survived up to the reign of Heraclius. What remained was instead a pattern of defended villages and fortresses, the strongest of which often came to serve as the administrative and military centres; and, on the coasts of the Black Sea, the Aegean, the Adriatic and in south-west Asia Minor, there are a few isolated ports and emporia. These represented the seeds of the future medieval towns of the Byzantine world, very different in both social character and urban structure from their classical antecedents. But in practice, only Constantinople, the centre of the imperial administration, the seat of the emperors and the site of the major imperial mints, was able to maintain its identity as a city in the late ancient sense of the term. But even there, what began to develop from the middle of the seventh century was a medieval town, not a classical *polis*.

There were undoubtedly some exceptions to this general pattern, but they hardly affect its overall validity. Even Euchaita which, it has been argued, retained much of its original civic area along with some of the public buildings which occupied it, was hardly a flourishing *polis*. The citadel to which citizens fled during Arab attacks had become synonymous with the term *polis* for the hagiographer who describes it in the eighth century; and while the lower (late antique) town still stretched out within the Anastasian walls of the early sixth century, there is no evidence to suggest that the population was particularly large, nor that any degree of

---

[87] See the apt comments of P. Charanis, 'A note on the Byzantine coin finds in Sardis and their historical significance', *EEBS* 39–40 (1972–3), 175–80 and 'The significance of coins as evidence' (cited in note 83 above), 164ff.; and for gift-exchange, see Haldon, 'Some considerations', 84 and note 18.

[88] See, for example, the comments of J. Russell, 'Transformations in early Byzantine urban life' (note 38 above), 142. For state fiscal policy, see chapter 5 below.

market exchange was a usual feature of its life. It was essentially a rural settlement and pilgrimage centre. The comments of its eleventh-century bishop referred to already – long before it began to suffer under the Türkmen nomads – places it in its real context.[89]

The history of the seventh-century Byzantine town is concerned, therefore, not with the question of whether or not life in the classical cities ended; nor whether the cities themselves were abandoned. It is concerned rather with the changed conditions in which they found themselves from the fourth and fifth centuries and after. That many – possibly the majority – of the 'cities' continued to be occupied (if only as centres of refuge or as military and administrative bases) is not in doubt. Some were abandoned, certainly; and the economic and market role of many was also ended under the changed conditions of the seventh century. On the other hand, some cities certainly continued to function as both centres of population and market exchange activity, where their provisioning could be assured. What is crucial, and what indeed had actually occurred before the physical destruction of the seventh century, is the change in the function of cities or towns within late Roman society and economy. They were quite simply no longer relevant to the state or to the greater part of the ruling elite. Where they survived, therefore, it was either because they could fulfil a function in respect of the institutions of Church or state (as an administrative base, for example) or in respect of genuine economic and social patterns of demand. The numerous episcopal cities must still have supported a degree of exchange activity, however limited and closed, for example, in order to meet the needs of the clergy and ancillary personnel. The same will have applied to sites where civil or military officials were established. The occasional coin and the production of local imitations of formerly imported wares on a number of sites suggest as much. Where such demand was met in other ways, or ceased, the life of the urban centres ebbed away, too.[90]

There remain two categories of evidence which have not been mentioned so far, namely the various *notitiae* of episcopal sees and the lists of signatories to the ecumenical councils – in our period, those held at Constantinople in 680 and in 692. Neither source is of any value in telling us about the actual condition of the cities or sees in question; and of the two, the *notitiae*, as has often been pointed out, are of only limited use in

---

[89] See the article of Trombley, 'The decline of the seventh-century town', and note 76 above.
[90] See, e.g., J.W. Hayes, 'Problèmes de la céramique des VIIe–IXe siècles à Salamine et à Chypre', in *Salamine de Chypre, Histoire et archéologie* (Paris 1980), pp. 375–87, for the evidence of pottery. For the marked shifts in the organisation of the 'cultural space' of cities in the sixth and seventh centuries, the dramatic decline of urban culture as evidenced in artistic production, architecture and public buildings, for example, see especially the detailed discussion of Müller-Wiener, 'Von der Polis zum Kastron', esp. 451–62.

telling us which cities or sees were still within imperial territory or under imperial authority.[91] They represented rather a theoretical state of affairs, being often quite anachronistic, particularly for the period with which we are concerned here, when territory was being lost, or fought over, constantly, and when the political status of a city might change within a very short period. The conciliar lists of signatories are more useful, since they represent the signatures of clerics who actually attended the meetings in question, and they might be useful on that basis in arguing for the continued occupation of their respective cities and their being still within imperial territory – although it must be remembered that representatives from other patriarchates such as Antioch or Jerusalem, clearly outside the imperial jurisdiction at the time of the sixth and Quinisext councils, were also present. The use to which these lists has been put has varied. The question of whether or not there was an exact equivalence of city and see needs to be borne in mind; while the reliability and completeness of the documents themselves in their edited form is problematic: as Ostrogorsky pointed out, there are some 174 signatures to the acts of the sixth council; yet Theophanes, writing some 130 years later, had information that there had been 289 bishops present. It has likewise been argued that the lists of signatories may include absentee bishops whose sees were only nominally within the empire.[92] On the other hand, the archaeological evidence for the continued occupation of many urban sites, at however limited and lowly a niveau, does show that such settlements, even when lying in very exposed areas, were seldom entirely deserted or permanently abandoned. Part of the reason lies in their actual location, often an ancient site with access to both routes and amenities, chiefly water; and in the agricultural resources at their disposal.[93] The lists of signatories, while they certainly

[91] For a detailed discussion, see H. Gelzer, 'Ungedruckte und ungenügend veröffentlichte Texte der Notitiae Episcopatuum', Abhandlungen der bayer. Akad. der Wissenschaften XXI (Munich 1901), pp. 534ff.; and now the edition and commentary of J. Darrouzès, *Notitiae Episcopatuum Ecclesiae Constantinopolitanae* (Paris 1981). See also Ostrogorsky, 'Byzantine cities in the early middle ages', 105 and notes.
[92] Theophanes, 360. 2 and Ostrogorsky, 'Byzantine cities in the early middle ages', 53 and notes; a point taken up also by C. Foss, *Byzantine Cities of Western Asia Minor* (Cambridge Mass. 1972), pp. 28f. and Lilie, '"Thrakien" und "Thrakesion"', 35; see also J. Darrouzès, 'Listes episcopales du Concile de Nicée (787)', *REB* 33 (1975), 61. For a counter-critique, see F. Trombley, 'A note on the See of Jerusalem and the synodal list of the sixth œcumenical council (680)', *B* 53 (1983), 632–8; R. Riedinger, 'Die Präsenz- und Subskriptionslisten des VI. ökonomischen Konzils (680/1) und der Papyrus Vind. gr. 3', Abhandlungen der bayerischen Akademie der Wissenschaften, phil.-hist. Kl., n.F. LXXXV (Munich 1979); and H. Ohme, *Das Concilium Quinisextum und seine Bischofsliste. Studien zum Konstantinopeler Konzil von 692* (Arbeiten zur Kirchengeschichte LVI. Berlin–New York 1990); and for the equivalence of city and see, A.H.M. Jones, *Cities of the Eastern Roman Provinces* (Oxford 1937), pp. 519f.
[93] The close relationship between continuity of site and occupation, and geographical/climatic situation has been emphasised by Guillou, *La Civilisation byzantine*, pp. 19ff., 41ff., followed by Hendy, *Studies*, pp. 90–100 (Anatolia) and 78–85 (Balkans).

seem to be incomplete, might support this evidence, and suggest that the bishops in question were indeed normally resident in their 'cities'. It might be objected, of course, that conditions in some areas must have led to abandonment, even if temporary – a point made explicitly in the record of the Quinisext council.[94] And while it has been argued that, since more bishops attended the Quinisext than attended the council of 680, there may have been a recovery in the fortunes of cities in parts of Asia Minor as a result of the truce with the Arabs made in 679, the evidence of Theophanes referred to above casts some doubt on this. In addition, the truce, which came into force in 680, will just as probably have facilitated the movement of Churchmen to Constantinople for this council, a point demonstrated by the fact that news of the empire's Bulgar war reached Apamaea in Syria II without difficulty.[95] But the truce itself only lasted until 692, and while it certainly made communications between Constantinople and the provinces easier, it was hardly long enough for any sort of urban economic recovery. The statement regarding clerics who had left their cities and abandoned their flocks was made in 692 at the Quinisext, some twelve years *after* the truce had first taken effect. This hardly suggests that conditions had improved dramatically. Even if more bishops did attend the council of 692, this reflects travel conditions only. The fact that it may imply that bishops were, on the whole, resident in their sees, says nothing at all about the 'cities' themselves.[96]

The point made already must be stressed: the crux of the matter is, surely, that the debate has wrongly assumed an intimate connection between the question of whether classical urban life continued or died and that of whether or not its sites were abandoned or deserted. The evidence we have surveyed makes it clear that both questions are to a large extent misguided. Classical civic life was already on its death-bed before the seventh century; what was replacing it was provincial town life of a very different character, on a very much less wealthy and less physically extensive basis. Hostile attack and harassment speeded up the former process and almost smothered the latter. But the organisational needs of the church alongside local cultural and economic tradition kept many sites alive, even if chiefly because of the shelter they offered. What survived was an 'urban' culture of a sort; but it bore little or no relation to the antique cities on whose sites it evolved, whatever the occasional exception may suggest.

[94] Mansi, XI, 952B–C (canon 18).
[95] See Mansi, XI, 617A–B; and note the comments of Trombley, 'A note on the See of Jerusalem', 636f.
[96] The evidence adduced by Hendy, *Studies*, pp. 76f. (letters, occasional references in narrative and other sources) for provincial bishops normally residing in their sees in peace time, is hardly relevant to the debate, which is concerned with the specific conditions prevailing towards the end of the seventh century.

Finally, it is worth emphasising the fact that the walled urban settlement was an important element in Byzantine perceptions of their culture. Towns or 'cities' which were destroyed were regularly rebuilt;[97] new 'cities' were established, often specifically to provide shelter for a newly immigrant community under imperial auspices; settlements were given the title of 'city' and the accompanying ecclesiastical hierarchy, when they became important enough.[98] In other words, the fate of the Byzantine city is not simply a question of economic resources, market potential, exchange activity, or the administrative requirements of the state and the Church. It is intimately connected also with the ideology of the Byzantine world and its perception of self. Cities served not just as refuges or fortresses, markets or administrative bases. They constituted an important element of Byzantine self-identity. The continuity of site and settlement from the sixth and seventh centuries right through to the end of the empire is surely related to this.[99]

[97] Eirene rebuilt the towns of Thrace after 784 (Theophanes, 417. 6–11); emperors were regularly involved in the reconstruction of city walls throughout the empire (cf. Theophanes, 481. 9 for Ancyra, Thebasa, Andrasus).

[98] E.g. Nicephorus, 66. 11; Theophanes, 429. 26 for Constantine V's construction of 'towns' in Thrace for the Syrians and Armenians transported from Anatolia. The city of Gordoserbon in Bithynia, which appears in the list of conciliar signatories for 680, was probably a settlement of Serbs from the great population transfer carried out under Constantine IV. See Ramsay, *Historical Geography*, p. 197 and table. In general, see Ostrogorsky, 'Byzantine cities in the early middle ages', 62f.

[99] Hendy, *Studies*, pp. 90ff. and maps 20–3. For an important comment on the changing cultural and economic function of late antique towns, see now also J.-M. Spieser, 'L'Evolution de la ville byzantine de l'époque paléochrétienne à l'iconoclasme', in *Hommes et Richesses dans l'Empire byzantin* I: *IVe–VIIe siècle* (Paris 1989), pp. 97–106.

CHAPTER 4

Social relations and the economy: rural society

ESTATES AND LANDLORDS

Land, whether exploited by arable farming – cereals, vegetables, fruit and so forth – or by pastoral farming, constituted the dominant means of production in the Byzantine world, as indeed it does in all pre-industrial cultures. The relationship between those who work the land and produce the wealth from it, and those who own or control the land and the uses to which it is put, is crucial for an understanding of how late Roman and early Byzantine society worked. Even more so than in other areas, however, the limited number of sources which can be usefully employed in clarifying this aspect of early Byzantine history is a major hindrance. Apart from the legal texts of the later sixth century, particularly imperial novellae and apart from the late seventh- or early eighth-century Farmers' Law (which is still very much debated with regard to its date, its origins and the extent to which its precepts can be generalised for the whole empire), we have to rely upon casual references in literary texts, the results of archaeological work on the economy of the urban settlements – referred to in the previous section – and upon inferences based on the situation as it is known in the earlier and later periods, and the possible logic of the changes which are implied. In this section, I will begin by looking at the situation in the later sixth century.

As we have seen, the state (in the form of the *res privata*, the *domus divinae* and the *fundi patrimoniales*)[1] along with the Church and the senatorial elite formed the most powerful grouping of landowners or landholders in the empire. The state especially, but other landowners also, sub-let their lands to tenants who received a rent from the actual cultivators themselves. The increasing use of emphyteutic leases to both larger land-

---
[1] See for the difference, Karayannopoulos, *Finanzwesen*, pp. 72–80; JGR I, coll. 1, nov. 1 (p. 2.8–9) (a. 566 = Dölger, *Regesten*, no. 4); grouped together, however, under Tiberius Constantine, see JGR I, coll. 1, nov. 12 (p. 2.6sq.) (a. ? = Dölger, *Regesten*, no. 67). On the issues dealt with in this chapter see now M. Kaplan, *Les hommes et la terre à Byzance du VIe au XIe siècle* (Byzantina Sorbonensia X) (Paris 1992).

owners and to smallholders, and its spread during the sixth century, is especially important in this connection, as we shall see.[2] Along with free emphyteutic tenants, land was farmed for the most part by dependent peasants of one category or another: *coloni adscripticii* and *liberi*, for example.[3]

Until the sixth century, these seem to have constituted the largest group. The latter were free persons restricted to their holdings for a period of up to thirty years, after which they were permitted to leave; the former were bound to their holdings hereditarily. The term *colonus* designated originally a free peasant farmer, then a free tenant of a holding, of equal legal standing to the landlord. From the middle of the third century, it began to be used not simply of one side in a contractual leasing arrangment, but of a cultivator-tenant of dependent status. By the middle of the fifth century the status of *colonus* was hereditary; and by the sixth century the majority were regarded as effectively unfree as far as their mobility was concerned, being classified as 'slaves of their land'. They could be released from their obligations only by their landlord, and only under certain conditions with regard to the land itself.[4] The term *adscripticius* refers to the fact that *coloni* of this type were entered in the land-tax register, along with their holdings, under the name of their landlord. The *coloni liberi*, while free in person, and free too to make wills and pass on and inherit property, were, from Anastasius' time, also forbidden to leave their holdings; but they continued to be entered in the tax-registers under their own names, paying land-taxes direct to the state, rather than through a landlord.[5] But this was in practice

---

[2] See M.V. Levčenko, 'Materiali dlya vnutrennei istorii vostočnoi rimskoi imperii V–VI vv.' in *Vizantiiskii Sbornik pod. red. M.V. Levčenko* (Moscow and Leningrad 1945), pp. 12–95, see p. 64; note that Justinian expressly recommended that such lessees should be relatively well-off (*euporos*): see *CJ* I, 2.24/5 (a. 530).

[3] In general on *coloni*, and the various sub-groupings, see Tinnefeld, *Die frühbyzantinische Gesellschaft*, pp. 45–55; Jones, *LRE*, vol. II, pp. 795–803; for a good general survey see also Patlagean, *Pauvreté économique*, pp. 263–340 ('La Terre et la société'); and A.H.M. Jones, 'The Roman colonate', *Past and Present* 13 (1958), 1–13 (repr. in *The Roman Economy*, pp. 293ff.); P. Collinet, 'La Politique de Justinien à l'égard des colons', *SBN* 5 (1936); de Ste Croix, *The Class Struggle in the Ancient Greek World*, pp. 226–59; M. Kaser, *Das römische Privatrecht*, vol. II: *Die nachklassischen Entwicklungen*, 2nd edn (Munich 1975), pp. 143–9; D. Eibach, *Untersuchungen zum spätantiken Kolonat in der kaiserlichen Gesetzgebung unter besonderer Berücksichtigung der Terminologie* (Cologne 1977), esp. pp. 47ff. For their status, see R. Günther, '*Coloni liberi* und *coloni originarii*: einige Bemerkungen zum spätantiken Kolonat', *Klio* 49 (1967), 267–71, and Eibach, *Untersuchungen*, pp. 132–204, critical of Jones' traditional perspective.

[4] See *CTh.* V, 17.1 (a. 332): *coloni* tied to the land; *CTh.* XIII, 10.3 (a. 357): land not to be sold without its *coloni* (= *CJ* XI, 48.2); *CJ* XI, 68.3: status of *coloni* hereditary; *CJ* XI, 52.1 (a. 393: the classical definition of a *colonus* as free in person, but 'slave of the land' on which they were born; cf. *CJ* XI, 48.21/1 (a. 530): Justinian asks what differentiates a slave from an *adscripticius*; cf. *CJ* VII, 24.4/1 (a. 531).

[5] For *adscripticii* see *CJ* XI, 48.22 (a. 531): *publici census adscriptio*; for the *liber colonus*, see *CJ* XI, 48.19; for the origins of the two categories, see Jones, *LRE*, vol. II, pp. 797ff.; but more

the only real difference between *coloni liberi* and *adscripticii*, for it seems that the latter (contrary to the traditionally held view) could also take out emphyteutic leases and act as legally independent and free persons. The fact that their *peculium*, or personal property, and the rights and duties attached thereto came under the authority of their landlords – traditionally taken to be a sure sign of their servile status – has now been shown to be a factor of their political-juridical position in respect of their landlords and the estates of which they were a part. For such estates owed revenue to the state and *munera* or civic burdens to the local municipality in whose territory they were situated. From this point of view, the distraint (or the possibility of distraint) by the landlord of the *peculium* of the peasants 'tied to the land' functioned in the same way as the distraint by the *res publica*, that is, the city, of the property of a member of the curial class who failed to fulfil his civic liturgies or duties – *munera*. It served in effect as a security on the returns from agricultural production, in which relationship the landlord functioned effectively as an agent of the city and thence, ultimately, of the fisc. It must in addition be remembered that, if the adscripted *colonus* had no freedom to leave his holding, neither had the landlord the freedom to move or to expel him, or to increase the basic rent or tax imposition on his holding. The relationship was regulated by the state to the mutual benefit of both parties – in theory if not always in practice – and, of course, and chiefly, for the securing of the state's revenue. The *adscripticius* thus received what the ordinary tenant-farmer or freeholder did not, namely security of tenure and the protection of state legislation.[6]

Alongside these two major groupings were free smallholders, often no different in economic condition than the *coloni*, with whom they might share a village and a community. Juridically and economically, of course, they were of slightly higher status, being both free in person and free to alienate their own properties; but since they were subject to pressure from both the state on the one hand, for taxes, and from the more powerful landlords around them on the other hand, their position was rarely secure. There is evidence for communities of such freeholders in most regions of the empire into the early seventh century,[7] and indeed Justin II expressly forbade the *curatores* and other officials of the imperial estates throughout

especially D. Eibach, *Untersuchungen zum spätantiken Kolonat in der kaiserlichen Gesetzgebung unter besonderer Berücksichtigung der Terminologie* (Cologne 1977), esp. pp. 132–204, critical of the traditional perspective set out by Jones.

[6] See J. Gascou, 'Les grands domaines, la cité et l'état en Egypte byzantine', *TM* 9 (1985), 1–90, esp. 22–7; and Goffart, *Caput and Colonate*, pp. 87ff., for the position of such *coloni* in relation to their landlords and the estates to which they were bound.

[7] See Jones, 'The Roman colonate', 294f. Note that the sixth-century legislation often treats such freeholders as subject to the same economic conditions and difficulties as the remaining smallholders – *coloni* – within the empire. Cf. *JGR* I, coll. 1, nov. 1 (p. 2.7sq.) (a. 566); nov. 11 (p. 18.4sq.) (a. 575 = Dölger, *Regesten*, no. 40); see Jones, *LRE*, vol. II, pp. 778ff.

the empire to lay claim to the nearby villages and their lands, whether these villages were of freeholders surrounded by civic lands or the estates of senatorial landowners or of the Church. They were also forbidden to exercise any form of patronage – *patrocinium* – over such communities.[8]

The extent to which this pattern of landownership and land-exploitation survived into and beyond the seventh century is difficult to say. It has often been argued that the civil strife under Phocas – followed, first, by the Persian and then by the Arab onslaught – was responsible both for the decimation of the senatorial landed elite in the provinces and the reduction in the numbers of latifundia-style estates in the eastern half of the empire.[9] There is, in fact, little evidence to demonstrate that this was the case and, indeed, little theoretical justification – in terms of how Byzantine society moved from the situation familiar from the sixth century to that which we find in the ninth century and later – for assuming this. Partly, the argument rests on methodological misapprehensions about the possibilities of generalising from the late seventh-century Farmers' Law, which does not mention such estates. But, as we shall see, there is no reason why it should; and negative evidence is hardly a suitable foundation for such an extensive explanatory edifice.[10]

Of the group of landowners referred to who dominate in the sixth century, there is no doubt that the Church and the state continued to be major landowners within the lands remaining to the empire after the

[8] *JGR* I, coll. i, nov. 12 (p. 20.33sq.). For *patrocinium*, see Tinnefeld, *Die frühbyzantinische Gesellschaft*, pp. 36–44; Jones, *LRE*, vol. II, pp. 775–8; Brown, *The World of Late Antiquity*, pp. 36–7; L. Harmand, *Le Patronat sur les collectivités publiques des origines au Bas-Empire* (Paris 1957), pp. 427ff. and 448ff. Patronage functioned quite simply: a community placed itself under the protection of a powerful person (at first, usually a military officer with troops at his disposal, sometimes even a whole garrison; later also private persons, such as a powerful landowner in the district), in order to obtain some protection from state officials or tax-collectors, or to render assistance in some local feud or conflict with another landlord. In return, the protector or patron received recompense in cash or kind; but he could extract greater returns, through the peasants' mortgaging their holdings to him, for example. Frequently, peasants found it simplest to hand over their land to their new landlord and receive it back again with security of tenure and tenancy, as his *coloni*. In this way, many originally independent and free smallholders became the tenants of more powerful landowners, including the Church.

[9] For example, Ostrogorsky, *Geschichte*, p. 112. Ostrogorsky's basic argument was that these developments promoted the more-or-less complete replacement of the traditional system of latifundia estates and the colonate by a patchwork of free peasant communities, from among whom the soldeirs of the *thema* forces were enrolled, a process set in motion by the Emperor Heraclius. See also Stein, *Studien*, pp. 157ff. This basic thesis was given a slightly different nuance, although the general idea remained, by the Soviet historian M.Ya. Siuziumov, 'Nekotorye problemy istorii vizantii', *Voprosy istorii* 3 (1959), 98–117, according to whom the seventh and early eighth centuries witnessed the final transformation from the slave mode of production to a proto-feudal state of development.

[10] See for example, F. Winkelmann, 'Zum byzantinischen Staat (Kaiser, Aristokratie, Heer)', in *Byzanz im 7. Jhdt.*, pp. 161–288, esp. p. 198; Tinnefeld, *Die frühbyzantinische Gesellschaft*, pp. 98–9.

territorial losses of the mid-seventh century. The insistence that Churchmen – bishops included – must return to their communities (which they had abandoned to avoid enemy attacks) in the records of the Quinisext council of 692 suggests also that the Church was keen not to lose control over its landed possessions in the more exposed provinces.[11] Bishops, who represented the landed elite as well as the Church in their sees, were also crucial to the running of the local administration, as well as to the welfare of their congregations. It was often the bishop who was responsible in directing municipal action regarding works of fortification and supplying a city in times of danger, even extending to the administration of public granaries and the provisioning of locally based troops. The departure of the bishop might thus have drastic results for both local fiscal and civil, as well as military, affairs, quite apart from his role in maintaining morale and confidence in the state.[12]

By the same token, the continued existence of the senate in Constantinople, the power and the authority it exercised on occasion during the seventh century, and its reinforcement through newcomers from the imperial bureaucracy and administrative apparatus, meant that large landed properties in all probability survived. The actual composition of the senate, and the degree of continuity from the sixth century in terms of families and specific estates, remains impossible to assess. From a detailed analysis of members of the senatorial and administrative elite during the seventh century, however, it seems that the older senatorial magnate families gradually lose in power to the rising service aristocracy of the Constantinopolitan establishment – in which the choice of individual emperors in promoting those they favoured or judged worthy of a particular office or honour was crucial.[13] At the same time, however, there is no reason to doubt that a large proportion of the old senatorial elite were assimilated to the new service elite of the second half of the seventh century; and whatever the origins of the military and civil officials of the period, personal wealth could only be secured beyond one generation through the acquisition of land. Landed property remained an essential

---

[11] See Mansi XI, 952B–C (Quinisext council, canon 18).
[12] Dagron, 'Le Christianisme dans la ville byzantine', 20ff.; Durliat, 'Les Attributions civiles des évêques' 77–8, notes 32–4 and literature (for the sixth century; but the institutional continuity is not to be doubted for the following period). For bishops responsible for fortifications, see Gregory I, Ep. IX, 121.
[13] See esp. the surveys of Winkelmann, Zum byzantinischen Staat, pp. 185–219 and Quellenstudien zur herrschenden Klasse von Byzanz im 8. und 9. Jahrhundert (BBA LIV, Berlin 1987), pp. 143ff.; and the articles of R. Guilland on 'Les Patrices byzantins' in Τόμος εἰς Μνήμην Κ.Ι. Ἀμάντου (Athens 1960), pp. 11–24 (the period 602–68); in Hellenika 23 (1970), 287–98 (the period 668–717) and in B 40 (1970), 317–60 (the period 717–829). The last two are repr. in Guilland, Titres et fonctions de l'empire byzantin VIII and IX (London 1976).

element in securing one's future and also in cementing one's position within the establishment. Marriage into older and established landed families on the one hand, and the purchase of land – from other landowners, including both Church and state in the form of perpetual leases,[14] or from impoverished or threatened peasant communities – must have made the continued existence of large-scale landed property a necessary element in seventh- and eighth-century society. It should also be recalled that it is the wealthier landowners or landholders who are able to survive natural or man-made disasters, for they have greater resources and reserves and hence greater economic flexibility. The importance of patronage, for example, and the effects of a drought or blight on the poorer farmers is enough to demonstrate this. In addition, it is clear from the later evidence that enemy raids had the most devastating effects on smallholders, not on the large estate owners. The tenth-century semi-official fiscal treatise dealing with the desertion of properties and the abondonment of smallholdings names enemy attacks as one of the chief causes of this. It was a development from which wealthier and more powerful landowners could always take advantage.

Military personnel in particular – the thematic officers, for example – will have been able to acquire land with relative ease, buying out impoverished peasants, arranging emphyteutic leases with absentee landowners, imposing their 'protection' on local rural communities, simple extortion through the use of their soldiers and, of course, taking over the property, where it existed, of their soldiers themselves. Military officers represented the only group which was in a position to maintain its interests under the sorts of conditions prevailing in areas regularly threatened by hostile action. They had not only the resources (the authority of state power) but the armed force necessary to impose their will on any opposition, and also to protect the area in which they were established. The 'protection' offered by military personnel must often have been welcomed, but as in an earlier period, *patrocinium* tended ultimately to favour the patron at the expense of the client.

Considerable areas of south and central Asia Minor, for example, must have been effectively lost to the control of those who had extensive lands there, whether lay or Church, at times. The Quinisext council, referred to already, explicitly mentions the abandonment of many congregations by the clergy due to fear of the Arab raids. This seems to include bishops also, among the most important landlords, albeit acting on behalf of the Church,

[14] The Church, for example, was permitted to sell off land both to the fisc and to private persons under specific circumstances – as when it had debts to make good. See Justinian, *Nov.* 46, proem; 1; 2; 6.2; 120.4; the Church could also sell land in order to raise funds for the release of prisoners from the enemy. See Justinian, *Nov.* 65 (a. 538).

Rural society 131

in any district. If bishops had left, it is unlikely that many lay landowners would have stayed to be killed or captured. But the abandonment of their lands made possible both the imposition of authority from a new source and the casting-off of the ties between landlord and tenants' obligations on the part of the peasantry. I will discuss this and related developments below.[15]

One of the most frequently cited texts in this debate is the ninth-century Life of St Philaretus the Merciful, a Paphlagonian landowner of some means who gave up his considerable wealth in charitable acts and who was compelled to surrender properties he could no longer adequately exploit, to the advantage of his neighbours, both richer landowners and the villagers of the area.[16] Even taking into account the probable exaggerations in the number of animals and properties Philaretus is supposed to have possessed (designed to emphasise the extent of his generosity and piety), it is clear that Philaretus stood for a landowner of considerable wealth, presumably a character not unfamiliar to those who read or heard the hagiographer's account. His livestock included 600 bullocks, 100 pairs of oxen, 80 pack-horses and mules/donkeys, 800 horses, 12,000 sheep; while he owned 48 large parcels of land distributed over a wide area, including also land in the areas of Pontus and Galatia. He was born, according to the Life, in 702; and it is reasonably clear from the description that his estates were for the most part inherited from his family.[17] His neighbours included other landowners,[18] as well as smallholders; and it seems equally logical to infer that the history of such estates reached back well into the seventh century. Philaretus himself was regarded by the small farmers and peasants around him as a powerful landowner; while it is clear from the rest of the narrative that the most powerful and wealthy elements of the ruling class, both in the provinces and in Constantinople, regarded him as their equal.[19]

---

[15] See Haldon, 'Some considerations', 97f., and 'Some remarks on the background to the iconoclast controversy', BS 38 (1977), 161–84, see 174f. For the relevant canons of the Quinisext, see Mansi XI, 945B–D (canon 8), 951B–C (canon 18), 960C–E (canon 37), 961A–C (canon 39). For the tenth-century evidence, see the Fiscal Treatise (ed. Dölger), p. 116.2–3; 118.42–119.1; and cf. 119.6–7.

[16] M.-H. Fourmy and M. Leroy, 'La Vie de S. Philarète', B 9 (1934), 85–170; and see also L. Bréhier, in B 1 (1924), 177–90.

[17] See J.W. Nesbitt, 'The Life of St Philaretos (702–92) and its significance for Byzantine agriculture', Greek Orthodox Theol. Review 14 (1969), 150ff.; H. Evert-Kappesowa, 'Une grande propriété foncière du VIIIe siècle à Byzance', BS 24 (1963), 32–40.

[18] Vita Philareti, 117.

[19] See H. Köpstein, 'Zu den Agrarverhältnissen', in Byzanz im 7. Jahrhundert, pp. 1–72, see 63f., although historians are divided as to whether Philaretus was a landed magnate or merely the son of a wealthy peasant family which made good. See, for example, M. Loos, 'Quelques remarques sur les communautés rurales et la grande propriété terrienne à Byzance, VIIe–XIe siècles', BS 39 (1978), 3–18, see 9ff.

That large private estates existed, therefore, side by side with the estates of state and Church in the late seventh and eighth centuries is clear. There seems no reason to doubt that they had continued to exist, and to come into being, throughout the seventh century. But Philaretus' own background and that of his family remains unknown, and a question mark must remain over the issue of the degree of physical continuity of such estates.

The text of the Vita Philareti also refers to the large estates of the Church as something that is taken for granted in provincial life; and it refers to villages of independent peasants, who own and farm their own holdings and who pay taxes directly to the state.[20] And this brings us to the next question, namely, what was the extent of such village communities within the empire? And what is the significance of the so-called Farmers' Law for this question?

VILLAGES AND TENANTS

The Farmers' Law is usually thought to date from the last twenty years or so of the seventh century or the first two decades of the eighth century. It appears to be a privately sponsored compilation, although this does not exclude the possibility of its having been consulted by officials with judicial authority, and it was designed to regulate property-relations and tenure within an agricultural-pastoral community – a village – the majority of whose occupants seem to have been independent smallholders, but among whom were to be found various categories of lessee and tenant, as well as domestic slaves and wage-labourers or journeymen. Its legal foundation is at least Justinianic, and some aspects may well be pre-Justinianic. The date, however, does remain very uncertain, and it may well be a compilation of a later period. In this respect, arguments based upon it must be treated carefully, although it is possible to argue that the relationships described therein can be applied with hindsight to the period with which we are concerned.

Now it has been argued by several historians that the Farmers' Law is good evidence for (a) the dominance of such free village communities in the Byzantine world at this time (and at the expense of the earlier dominance of large senatorial *latifundia*); and (b) the strong influence of Slav social institutions, in particular the *obščina* or commune, on Byzantine peasant society, a result of the settlement by the state of large numbers of Slavs from the Balkans in Asia Minor.[21]

---

[20] *Vita Philareti*, 117; for the Church estates, see *ibid.*, 15.26; 157.5 (Philaretus' grandsons handed their lands over to a convent).

[21] For the Farmers' Law (*nomos georgikos*) see W. Ashburner, 'The Farmers' Law', *JHS* 30 (1910), 85–108; 32 (1912), 68–95 (text, translation and commentary). There is a

Rural society   133

The first argument is based on the existence and widespread dissemination during the medieval period of the Farmers' Law itself and on evidence from the ninth and tenth centuries which suggests that communities of peasant proprietors subject directly to the fisc formed a central element in the rural population of the empire.[22] The second argument is based on the known introduction of Slav colonists into the empire and on a failure to consider adequately other elements which might have contributed to this apparent increase in peasant proprietorship which are internal to late Roman and Byzantine social and economic relations.[23]

In fact, as has been shown, the growth in the numbers of such communities, their increased importance to the economy of the state and the related changes in the basic system of taxation – from the late Roman *capitatio/iugatio* to the middle Byzantine land- and hearth-tax – can all be explained within the context of developments internal to the dynamic of relations of production in the late Roman social formation, although external factors – warfare on the one hand, immigration on the other – certainly played an important role.

We have seen that those who worked the land can be divided into a number of categories, both from the legal and from the economic point of view. But the proportion of free tenants paying both taxes and rents, of *coloni liberi* who were effectively treated as free tenants after they had cultivated their holdings for thirty or more years, and of small-scale

wide-ranging discussion. For the best recent survey of the problems and the literature, see Köpstein, 'Zu den Agrarverhältnissen', 40ff.; P. Lemerle, 'Esquisse pour un histoire agraire de Byzance: les sources et les problèmes', *RH* 219 (1958), 32–74, 254–84; 220 (1958), 42–94; see 219 (1958), 32–74; and the revised, English, translation: *The Agrarian History of Byzantium from the Origins to the Twelfth Century. Sources and Problems* (Galway 1979), pp. 32ff. For an attempt to date part of the contents of the Farmers' Law to sources of the pre-Justinianic period, see N. Svoronos, 'Notes sur l'origine et la date du Code Rural', *TM* 8 (1982), 487–500. Svoronos' analysis suggests that many features of the code or law predate the codification of Justinian I and are drawn from texts of an earlier period which were available to the compilers of the later seventh century. But this has been heavily criticised and shown to be based on dubious methodological suppositions. See L. Burgmann, 'Ist der Nomos Georgikos vorjustinianisch?', *Rechtshistorisches Journal* 1 (1982), 36–39.

For the arguments over Slavisation, see for example E.E. Lipšic, *Byzanz und die Slawen. Beiträge zur byzantinischen Geschichte des 6. -9. Jahrhunderts* (Weimar 1951), pp. 30ff. with literature; but see the detailed discussion of Ostrogorsky, *Geschichte*, pp. 113–14 and note 3. A more recent review of the problem is presented in R. Poptodorov, 'Sledi ot slavjanskoto pravo v'v Vizantijskoto', *Izvestija Črkov Noistorič. i Arkhiv. Institut, Sofija* II (1984), 126–37, which argues that both the Ecloga and the Farmers' law show traces of a barbarisation and Slavisation of classical Roman law; although, as with the earlier arguments, the methodological grounds upon which such conclusions are based are not very satisfactory.

[22] For text, tradition and dissemination of the Farmers' Law, see also the detailed comments of Ostrogorsky, *Geschichte*, p. 75 note 10; and J. Karayannopoulos, 'Entstehung und Bedeutung des Nomos Georgikos', *BZ* 51 (1958), 357–73.
[23] See Ostrogorsky, *Geschichte*, pp. 113f. and note 3.

peasant emphyteutees, paying a fixed and possibly very low rent (and often holding their leases, which were transferable, in perpetuity and hereditarily)[24] seems to have become increasingly important during this period, as the relevant imperial legislation demonstrates. Just as significantly, the later Byzantine term for a dependent peasant, *paroikos*, is to be found in this sixth-century legislation,[25] referring, however, to a lessee of land, a *locator* (or *colonus*, in one of its original meanings). This points the way to the gradual assimilation of all three categories of tenant smallholder into a single body of tenants, paying a rent to their landlord and tax to the state, bound to their properties according to late Roman law or to their lease (although, as we have seen, emphyteutic lessees could cede or sell the land – that is, the lease – to a third party, and were often regarded, at least in respect of non-Church lands, as the *possessor* and not simply the *locator*, or tenant).

It is important in this connection to note that the Ecloga of Leo III and Constantine V places a great deal of emphasis on this particular form of contractual relationship, which again seems to point to its importance at this period.[26]

In the first half of the seventh century, the Life of Theodore of Sykeon portrays a western Anatolian society of free peasant smallholders and communities, in which the community clearly plays a role as a corporate body; the Life refers likewise to peasant farmers fleeing from the tyranny of their landlords[27] and to the existence of large estates belonging to the Church of the nearby city of Anastasioupolis.[28] The late seventh-century Farmers' Law similarly refers to the village community – ἡ τοῦ χωρίου κοινώτης – and to the communal lands belonging to the village as a

---

[24] See above; and P. Lemerle, *The Agrarian History of Byzantium from the Origins to the Twelfth Century. Sources and Problems* (Galway 1979), p. 25.

[25] See Justinian, *Nov.* 7, proem, 1 (a. 535); *Nov.* 120.1 proem (a. 544); *CJ* I, 2.24. proem; I, 34.1. The term occurs earlier for *coloni* in a variety of documents, see A. Déléage, *La Capitation au Bas-Empire* (Paris 1945), pp. 182ff.

[26] See in particular the comments of M. Kaplan, 'L'Exploitation paysanne byzantine entre l'antiquité et le moyen age (VIᵉ–VIIIᵉ siècles): affirmation d'une structure économique et sociale', in V. Vavřínek, ed., *From Late Antiquity to Early Byzantium* (Prague 1985), pp. 101–5, see 102f., and 'Remarques sur la place de l'exploitation paysanne dans l'économie rurale', in *Akten des XVI. Internationalen Byzantinisten-Kongresses*, II, 2 (Vienna 1982), pp. 105–14 (= *JÖB* 32), see p. 107f. with references. Köpstein, 'Zu den Agrarverhältnissen', p. 66, argues that *paroikos* relates only to ecclesiastical lands and their leases. In fact, as Kaplan suggests, the term begins with this general meaning, but had by the early ninth century begun to acquire the meaning later attributed to it (a dependent peasant) as a result of the rapid spread of this system of leasing land, and its replacement of the colonate. See *Ecloga* (ed. Burgmann), 12.1–6.

[27] *Vita Theod. Syk.*, 147.49sq. (fleeing *colonus*); 98.1sq.; 114.1sq.; 115.2sq. etc. (free peasants); 143.1 (the village community).

[28] Ibid., 76.1sq.; and cf. 34.6–7 for the lands of the Church of Helioupolis in Bithynia.

whole.[29] There seems little reason to doubt that the Farmers' Law, compiled on the basis of extracts from the *Codex Iustinianus* and the customary law of part of the empire and designed to regulate the institutions of the independent peasant village, represents a relatively ancient tradition both socially and economically.[30] There is no reason to doubt either that such communities existed in an unbroken tradition throughout the seventh century; for although the point is still debated, it seems that the Farmers' Law presents nothing in its regulations or assumptions that is not already present in the late Roman village community.[31] But the terminology has undergone a certain evolution: the term *geōrgos* (γεωργός), which could refer to both *coloni adscripticii* or *liberi*, or yet again a free smallholder or a lessee (*locator*, ἐμφυτευτής) in the fifth and sixth centuries, occurs in the Farmers' Law to describe the members of the village. Since the latter clearly hold land, over which they have sole jurisdiction and which they are free to leave, the term can refer to the last three categories only.[32]

The Farmers' Law describes the relationships which might come before a court within the village community; it makes it clear that social differentiation was a normal element of the community: wealthier and poorer smallholders, and hired labourers, are mentioned, for example. It describes an economy of cereal, fruit and vine cultivation, of sheep and cattle raising; it also frequently refers to the sub-tenanting of holdings among the villagers, and to the fact that some villagers might also be the tenants of larger landowners – individuals or institutions – from outside the village.[33]

---

[29] See in particular on this question the old but still very valuable work of A.P. Rudakov, *Očerki Vizantiiskii kul'turi po dannim grečeskoi agiografii* (Moscow 1917 and London 1970), pp. 174ff. For the village community, see the *Farmers' Law*, art. 81.
[30] See the literature in notes 117 and 118 above; and St. Maslev, 'Die soziale Struktur der byzantinischen Landgemeinde nach dem Nomos Georgikos', in F. Winkelmann and H. Köpstein, eds., *Studien zum 7. Jahrhundert*, pp. 10–22, see 10–12.
[31] See the summary of the debate in Maslev, 'Die soziale Struktur', and Svoronos, *Notes sur l'origine et la date du Code Rural*, esp. the final comments on p. 500.
[32] See the evidence summarised by Köpstein, 'Zu den Agrarverhältnissen', pp. 41f. For the wide application of *georgos* – originally limited just to *coloni* – during the later sixth century, see P. Lemerle, *The Agrarian History of Byzantium from the Origins to the Twelfth Century* (see note 21 above), pp. 20ff.
[33] See the *Farmers' Law*, esp. art. 9 and 10 for the tenant (*mortitēs*) of the (larger) landowner or landholder. In general on the content of the Farmers' Law, see Köpstein, 'Zu den Agrarverhältnissen', pp. 41–8 and 49–53; Maslev, 'Die soziale Struktur' (note 30 above); and H. Köpstein, 'Zu einigen Aspekten der Agrarverhältnisse im 7. Jahrhundert (nach den juristischen Quellen)', in *Studien zum 7. Jhdt.*, pp. 23–34, see 29ff. The *mortē* arrangement, which involved a rent of only ten per cent on the income from the land, seems to represent in practice, if not in name, the earlier emphyteutic lease, designed to enable the landowner to keep land under cultivation by offering a relatively attractive arrangment with tenants. As we have seen, such leases were increasingly employed through the sixth century, see below, and note that the Ecloga knows only emphyteutic and ordinary leases. The term *mortē* does not occur, and it is tempting to assume that the *mortē* arrangement was the equivalent of the *emphyteusis*.

It refers to the common land of the village; and it refers to the practice of bringing abandoned land back into cultivation and dividing it among (some) members of the community. The common grazing of livestock on the fields after the harvest was also a feature – normal in many peasant societies, of course.[34]

The relationship between such a community and the state is referred to only obliquely: when a peasant is unable to gain a livelihood from his land, whether he has rented a part of his holding to another (being unable to farm it himself) in return for a portion (usually a half) of the resulting yield; or whether he has rented all of his holding, taking up work for others on a waged basis; or whether he has fled, unable to pay his taxes and his debts, then the burden of taxation was transferred to those who could maintain his plot. If no one was in a position to do this, the whole community was made responsible for the taxes owed, although possibly – as in the ninth and tenth centuries – a reduction in the total owing was made in order to avoid the impoverishment of the remaining members of the village. If, after a certain (unspecified) time, the land was still unoccupied, it was – along with other untenanted holdings – formally confiscated by the state and redistributed to members of the village collectivity.[35]

I will deal with this question in more detail in chapter 5. But there is no explicit evidence in the Farmers' Law that communal fiscal solidarity was firmly established.

The Farmers' Law therefore seems to represent a village community not too different from those known from Anatolia, Syria and other regions of the empire in the sixth century. The differences which have been noted provide no real objections to continuity of basic structure and social organisation. For example, there is evidence in the late Roman *mētrokomiai* (or extended villages) of Syria and Egypt for a regular redivision of holdings, an absence of family property and less emphasis on the rights of individuals to occupy and cultivate abandoned village land. In theory – although the legislation itself hints at the reality being rather different – such community land could not be held by an outsider. The village community of the Farmers' Law, in contrast, has both heritable family

---

For social differentiation in this sort of community, note the opposition between the 'landowners of the village' and the ordinary 'inhabitants' (tenants, leaseholders etc.) of the village in the *Vita Theod. Syk.*, 116; 118; for the 'leading men' of the village, see also *ibid.*, 114; and *Vita Philareti*, 137.23. Cf. Loos, 'Les Communautés rurales', 9 with references; Patlagean, *Pauvreté économique*, p. 265.

[34] For example, P. Stirling, 'A Turkish village', in T. Shanin, ed., *Peasants and Peasant Societies* (Harmondsworth 1971), pp. 37–48, see 40ff.; D. Thorner, 'Peasant economy as a category in economic history', *ibid.*, pp. 202–18; R.H. Hilton, *Bond Men Made Free* (London 1973), see pp. 71f.

[35] See Köpstein, 'Zu den Agrarverhältnissen', p. 53 note 1; Lemerle, *Agrarian History*, pp. 41–5.

property and outsiders in the village; it expressly permits the cultivation of abandoned land by neighbours; and it envisages no mass redivision of holdings. But the late Roman evidence is specific to Egypt and Syria, while the Farmers' Law represents a geographically and chronologically very different context. And the evidence of the Life of Theodore of Sykeon does suggest an Anatolian village economy and structure very similar to that described in the Farmers' Law, but for a period one hundred years earlier. In discussing the nature and evolution of rural communities, people who argue for and against continuity must also bear traditional regional variations and cultural differences in mind, as these examples suggest.[36]

The juridical character of the village community seems to have evolved also during the period from the sixth century to the later seventh or early eighth, and these are developments which are important for our understanding of the role played by village communities in the social relations of the seventh-century Byzantine world. Central to this question is the nature of the relationship between the state, the cities and the countryside.

This change in juridical status can be detected in the term used to describe and to define the village. In the late Roman period, certainly by the sixth century, two terms of equivalent value – *komē* and *chōrion*, the former the traditional word for a village of small proprietors, the latter for an inhabited holding or part of an estate within a single fiscal unit – were used to describe village communities.[37] The reasons for the semantic equivalence of the two, as has been demonstrated, lie in the fact that, as the development of the colonate and smallholding came to dominate on large

[36] See especially Każdan, *Derevniya i gorod*, pp. 31ff., for the *mētrokomiai*. Lemerle, *Agrarian History*, pp. 7f. believes that the *mētrokomia* with its collective liability for taxes was already in existence in the fifth century as the standard form of non-dependent village throughout the empire. M. Kaplan, 'Les Villageois aux premiers siècles byzantins (VIᵉ–Xᵉ siècle): une société homogène?' *BS* 43 (1982), 202–17 (see 206f. and note 31) argues in contrast that it was a limited phenomenon occurring in some eastern districts only. Partly, the debate revolves around the technical meaning of the terms ὁμόκηνσον and ὁμόδουλον in respect of the allocation of deserted lands (*epibolē*). But as Jones, *LRE*, vol. II, p. 815 note 105 points out, the terms refer to fiscal census units, not necessarily communities in the collective sense, thus supporting Kaplan's contention.

As far as concerns the area to which the Farmers' Law was originally intended to apply, it should be noted that pastoral activity occupies more than fifty per cent of the text's interests. Regulations concerning livestock, especially cattle, outnumber those dealing with agricultural activity. The Anatolian plateau, and especially the central and eastern sections, present themselves as obvious candidates. But this remains still in the realms of hypothesis.

[37] Original sense of *komē*: Libanius, *Discours sur les patronages*, ed. L. Harmand (Paris 1955), 15 (cap. 4) and 17 (cap. 11). For a comment, see G. Dagron, 'Entre village et cité: la bourgade rurale des IVᵉ–VIIᵉ siècles en Orient', *Κοινωνία* 3 (1979), 29–52. For the original sense of *chōrion*: Digest X, 1.4/5 (168); and for a comment, M. Kaplan, *Les Propriétés de la Couronne et de l'Eglise dans l'empire byzantin (Vᵉ–VIᵉ siècles)* (Paris 1976) – for *komē* = *vicus*, *chōrion* = *fundus*. See also Köpstein, 'Zu den Agrarverhältnissen', pp. 56ff.

estates (as opposed to the dominance of agricultural slavery), the smallholders and tenants themselves usually dwelt in village communities on their lands. As the social and juridical differences between free peasant smallholders in *kōmai* on the one hand and dependent peasants on the *chōrion* or *fundus* of their landlord on the other, were gradually ironed out, so the technical difference between the two terms vanished. *Chōrion* eventually predominates, both because it reflects an equivalent semantic use of the term, but also because it bore a fiscal significance, representing as it did in origin a single fiscal unit, the property of a landlord occupied by his tenants.[38] As the cities ceased to function as the administrative centres for the fiscal assessment of their regions, this role was transferred to the smaller, but more immediately relevant, unit of the village. *Chōrion*, with its original fiscal significance, as well as its meaning of village, replaced *kōmē*. But the development was a gradual one. Even in the Farmers' Law the term *chōrion*, while referring also to the village, still bears a wider significance.

These changes in terminology are important, however. For while it seems clear that the village community described in the Farmers' Law is in itself not new, it is clear that such villages now represented a more important element in the totality of the relations of production, especially with respect to the state and its revenue-raising apparatus. The compilation of the Farmers' Law and its wide dissemination themselves reinforce this view: both in Byzantine society in general and in the eyes of the state (and the officials who exercised judicial power in the provinces) the village community was, or was becoming, an economic and social element of much greater relative importance than had hitherto been the case.

Such communities existed throughout the later Roman world, and indeed the nucleated settlement was the usual form of settlement outside the cities, whatever the legal status of its inhabitants.[39] The qualitative change in their role does not necessarily imply that there were more of them. What it does suggest is that the village, and its individual landholders, were becoming the key element in the state's administration of its revenue-collection, in contrast to the later Roman period, when it had been

[38] This development has been admirably summarised by Kaplan, 'Les Villageois aux premiers siècles byzantins', 203ff.; see also Patlagean, *Pauvreté économique*, pp. 241f.

[39] For the settlement-pattern and the nucleated village, see Patlagean, *Pauvreté économique*, pp. 241ff.; Dagron, 'La bourgade rurale'; M. Kaplan, 'Quelques remarques sur les paysages agraires byzantins (VIe siècle – milieu XIe siècle)', *Revue du Nord* 62 (1980), 156ff. On social differentiation, see note 33 above; for an example of a village of tenants (*locatores, emphyteutai, coloni liberi* – albeit not specified so exactly) see *Vita Theod. Syk.*, 34, 76, 162 (villages on the estates of a landowner from Ankara). See esp. N. Svoronos, 'Sur quelques formes de la vie rurale à Byzance, petite et grande exploitation', *Annales* 11 (1956), 325–35 (repr. in *Etudes sur l'organisation intérieure, la société et l'économie de l'Empire Byzantin* II (London 1973).

the landlord and the city who had been the chief intermediaries. The evidence from the later period, when the village or *chōrion* as a fiscal unit and as a juridical entity played the key role, demonstrates the results of this evolution.[40] But the terminological changes evidenced by the increasing use of *chōrion* for village and then fiscal community, which begins in the sixth century and proceeds throughout the seventh, show that the social, economic and administrative shifts which this development represents were already under way.

The village community of the Farmers' Law is thus a traditional element of the rural economy. Indeed, the degree of social differentiation and dependence presented in the Farmers' Law suggests that such communities already had a long history. The important question, however, is how widespread such communities were in the Byzantine world. In the Farmers' Law, it is clear that the dominant element seems to be the independent smallholders who either own their land or rent it on a more or less permanent basis – the last point is hypothetical, but is supported by the context which we have described for the period. As we have also seen, Philaretus possessed a number of holdings which will have been farmed by his own tenants or by hired labourers. From later sources it is clear that such holdings will normally have been part of other village communities which had come under the sway of the landlord in question – the Farmers' Law already presents some evidence of this process, which was itself nothing new. According to the Vita Philareti, both the local big landowners and some of the villagers themselves were keen to occupy and cultivate the lands which Philaretus himself was unable to keep up, again a procedure implicit in the provisions of the Farmers' Law.[41] Together, the Farmers' Law and the Life of Philaretus show that both independent peasant village communities and large estates with interests in the surrounding villages – as well as, presumably, villages of a greater dependent status – were an integral part of the rural economy of later seventh- and eighth-century Byzantine society.

---

[40] For taxation in the tenth century (assessment, application, extraction), see F. Dölger, *Beiträge zur Geschichte der byzantinischen Finanzverwaltung besonders des 10. und 11. Jahrhunderts* (Byzantinisches Archiv IX, Leipzig 1927 and Hildesheim 1960); G. Ostrogorsky, 'Die ländliche Steuergemeinde des byzantinischen Reiches im X. Jahrhundert', *Vierteljahresschrift für Sozial- und Wirtschaftsgeschichte* 20 (1927), 1–108; Ch.M. Brand, 'Two Byzantine treatises on taxation', *Traditio* 25 (1969), 35–60; J. Karayannopoulos, 'Fragmente aus dem Vademecum eines byzantinischen Finanzbeamten', in *Polychronion. Festschrift Franz Dölger zum 75. Geburtstag* (Heidelberg 1966), pp. 317–33; N. Svoronos, 'Recherches sur le cadastre byzantin et la fiscalité aux XIe–XIIe siècles: le cadastre de Thèbes', *BCH* 83 (1959), 1–166 (repr. in *Etudes* III).

[41] For *proasteion*, see Lemerle, *Agrarian History*, and the Fiscal Treatise (ed. Dölger, *Beiträge*); see esp. M. Kaplan, 'Les Villageois', esp. 214, for the social differentiation in the *Vita Philareti*.

The increased importance of such independent communities – as implicitly evidenced by the Farmers' Law and as is made clear from later evidence (in the tenth century it is taken for granted that they represent the central element in the state's fiscal operations) – may suggest also that the number of such communities increased during this period. Some of the possible causes of such an increase have been argued at length: the abandonment by landlords of their country estates and the consequent assertion by the peasants of their independence;[42] the immigration of large numbers of Slav settlers with their community structure and organisation;[43] and the growing independence of peasant smallholders with perpetual, or long-term, heritable leases, paying low and fixed rents to landlords who may often have been permanently resident away from their estates and properties.[44]

There is little reason for doubting that the Slav immigrants, having been settled by the state, constituted communities which held and cultivated land to maintain themselves. Justinian II's explicit intention was to promote the availability of soldiers from this source, a point on which I will say more in chapter 6.[45] But it seems unlikely that these transfers of population affected the social structure of the rest of the empire in such a way as to bring about administrative changes in the fiscal system and at the same time promote a sudden development of free peasant communities.

Two fundamental causes seem to be operating. On the one hand, a development which we have already noted, the change in emphasis in the mode of exploitation of large properties: the gradual weakening of the adscripted colonate in favour of long-term and often heritable leases on state, Church and private lands tended to reduce the need for estate-owners to supervise either directly or indirectly the production process on their lands. As long as rents were collected, interference was unnecessary; and anyway the producers were responsible under the terms of the leases for the state taxes. This reduced both the administrative costs and the fiscal obligations of landowners to the state. It removed the need for bailiffs, except as rent-collectors. But it also weakened the landlords' direct control over their property, while reinforcing the relationship between producers and state. The juridical differences in status of the various types of producer – *coloni*, leaseholders, smallholders and peasant proprietors – will thus

---

[42] See Köpstein, 'Zu den Agrarverhältnissen', p. 59, basing her argument on the fact that evidence from the canons of the Quinisext in 692 for clerics fleeing their cities might also apply to secular landowners.

[43] Köpstein *ibid.* and literature; Charanis, 'Ethnic changes', 42f. and 'Transfer of population', 143.

[44] See above, pp. 134f.

[45] See Theophanes, 347f. (A.D. 658), 364 (A.D. 689); see Charanis, 'Transfer of population', 143f.

have become less significant to the fiscal requirements of the state, less relevant to the process of production and less relevant to the landowners themselves. The long-term cumulative result must surely have been a very considerable increase in the numbers of communities subject directly to the fisc, albeit made up of persons of very varied legal status. Most importantly, the great majority will have possessed freedom of movement and have been, in effect, *possessores*, even if not owners, of their holdings, whatever their original condition. The peasants of the Farmers' Law, as well as those in the Life of Theodore of Sykeon and those referred to in the Life of Philaretus, must not be taken to represent a uniform body of free peasant proprietors. They represent farmers with freedom of movement, freedom to transfer their land or to transmit it to their heirs. All of these provisions were possible within the terms of the normal emphyteutic lease, as well as straightforward proprietorship.[46]

On the other hand, we are probably dealing also with a change in emphasis – reflected in the sources from the Farmers' Law on – in government fiscal policy. The cities could no longer – and had been for some time unable to – cope with the problems of taking fiscal responsibility for their *territoria*. State officials had taken over the supervision and administration of these tasks since the fifth and sixth centuries. As we have also seen, landlords – estate owners – no longer played such a crucial role in this context either. The state had, as a result, to concentrate on the level at which wealth-production actually took place; in other words, on the land and the communities which farmed it. The centres of production were the villages, and these now replace the towns or cities in the fiscal administrative structure of the early Byzantine state. In a much more significant way than before, the village comes to occupy a central position in the society and the administration of the empire from the later seventh century onwards.

TAXATION AND THE LAND

The basic taxes had been assessed in the sixth century on the *capitatio/ iugatio* equation, according to which land was taxed relative to its productivity when under cultivation (or otherwise exploited), and the agricultural producers (or animals grazing on pasture land) were taxed only in association with productive land.[47] Supposedly, the last reference to this system

---

[46] See the remarks of M. Kaplan, 'Remarques sur la place de l'exploitation paysanne', 106f. with literature, and the comments on the rise of emphyteutic leasing in the sixth century above and in chapter one infra.
[47] See chapter 1.

occurs for Sicily during the first years of the first reign of Justinian II;[48] between then and the reign of Nicephorus I (802–11) a major change took place, when tax was no longer raised on the basis of the combined assessment of capitation and iugation, but by separate assessments, the *kapnikon*, or hearth-tax; and the *synōnē*, or land-tax. The former was, in effect, a tax on the household-property of the adult members of a household; the latter was a tax on productive land.

It has further been argued that a change took place at this time in the methods by which the state tried to maintain the continued productivity of the land. Abandoned or otherwise uncultivated holdings in the later Roman period had, from the fourth century at least, been transferred to the neighbouring landowners or landholders, who were made responsible for the taxed normally pertaining to it. This system, referred to as the *epibolē* (*tōn aporōn*), or *adiectio sterilium*, had by the later ninth century been replaced by a different system, in which the state intervened directly to exempt abandoned properties until the owner or his/her heirs could bring it back into cultivation again. If this had not happened within a period of thirty years, then the state simply took it out of its original register and fiscal district and gave it to a new owner.

Now, in spite of the arguments of several scholars, the old system seems still to be in operation in the Farmers' Law, although not explicitly referred to as *epibolē*. Thus, while there was a change in terminology, the new system does appear only from the second half of the ninth century.[49]

It has generally been assumed that the abandonment of the older system of assessment based on the *capitatio/iugatio* formula – which reflected the needs of the state to ensure that land was cultivated in order to secure its revenue – demonstrates that the lack of manpower which gave rise to it no longer existed; in other words, that manpower was no longer a problem. And it has been argued further that this is because of the growth in the number and extent of communities of free peasants, and in particular the

---

[48] See E. Stein, 'Vom Altertum zum Mittelalter. Zur Geschichte der byzantinischen Finanzverwaltung', *Vierteljahresschrift für Sozial- und Wirtschaftsgeschichte* 21 (1928), 158–70, see 150 and 152; G. Ostrogorsky, 'Das Steuersystem im byzantinischen Altertum und Mittelalter', *B* 6 (1931), 229–40, see 237; the references are in the accounts of the Lives of Popes John V and Conon (*Liber Pontificalis*, I 366.8–10; 368.19-369.2).

[49] See Haldon, *Recruitment and Conscription*, pp. 52f.; Lemerle, 'Esquisse', *RH* 219, 60f., 263f.; *Agrarian History*, pp. 46f.; and esp. J. Karayannopoulos, 'Die kollektive Steuerverantwortung in der frühbyzantinischen Zeit', *Vierteljahresschrift für Sozial- und Wirtschaftsgeschichte* 43 (1956), 289–322; Köpstein, 'Zu den Agrarverhältnissen', p. 47 and note 4. For the first reference to the *kapnikon*, see Theophanes, 486.29-487.1; and Theophanes cont. 54.4 for the rate at which it was raised (2 *miliarēsia* per household). In general, see Ostrogorsky, 'Die ländliche Steuergemeinde', 51ff.; Dölger, 'Beiträge', 52 (but with a different view on its origins from that of Ostrogorsky).

Rural society   143

drafting in of large numbers of Slavs, which made such a legislative tying of manpower to the land unnecessary.[50]

But this line of argument is weak: neither the Farmers' Law, nor the supposed thematic reforms of the Emperor Heraclius, nor the appearance of new districts in the provinces, nor indeed the much later evidence for smallholding on a widespread basis can actually prove this point.[51]

There can be no doubt that the system of *capitatio/iugatio* does reflect the interests of the state and its fiscal administration in ensuring that land was cultivated and that revenues could be appropriated from the maximum possible number of cultivators exploiting the maximum amount of productive land.[52]

But the Byzantine state of the seventh century was just as interested in this question, indeed, more so, given the loss of some two-thirds of the total revenue sources of the empire in a period of some sixty or so years.[53] Even assuming that the situation with regard to labour power had improved (which in the conditions of the seventh century can hardly be certain), it seems inherently unlikely that the state would voluntarily adjust its system of revenue calculation and assessment. Surely some other factors were at work here, which made it necessary for the state, in order to maintain or intensify the extraction of revenues from a much smaller territory, to reform its operation. A hypothetical increase in peasant freeholders and a hypothetical decline of large estates is hardly sufficient, and would in any case make no difference to the total income of the state derived from this source.

In fact, the conditions of the later and middle seventh century provide some clues to the real nature of the change. In the first instance, as we have seen, vast tracts of land stretching deep into Anatolia were made more or less permanently insecure for urban life. They will hardly have been any more conducive to rural and agricultural exploitation. The populations of the 'cities', whether they remained or whether they moved or fled to safer areas, were themselves almost entirely agricultural; the rural populations of the same areas will have been subject to equally or more insecure conditions, and they can hardly have remained or been able to extract a livelihood from their regularly pillaged and plundered lands and villages.

---

[50] See Ostrogorsky, 'Das Steuersystem', *passim*.
[51] See J. Karayannopoulos, 'Die vermeintliche Reformtätigkeit des Kaisers Herakleios', *JÖBG* 10 (1961), 53–7; Köpstein, 'Zu den Agrarverhältnissen', 59; W.E. Kaegi, jr., 'Some reconsiderations on the themes: seventh–ninth centuries', *JÖBG* XVI (1967), 39–53. Lemerle, *Agrarian History*, pp. 48ff., places great emphasis on the importation of Slav populations in relieving the labour-shortage. But see below.
[52] See, for example, the comments of Jones, '*Capitatio* and *iugatio*', 291f.; and esp. Goffart, '*Caput*' and *Colonate*, pp. 47ff.
[53] See Hendy's estimate, *Studies*, p. 620.

Several sources attest to the abandonment of such areas by the clergy (higher and lower), by the agricultural population and by town-dwellers.[54] Later sources detail the effects of enemy activity in a way which only reinforces this impression.[55] The seventh-century Apocalypse of Pseudo-Methodius, written in fact during and after the devastation of the Anatolian provinces but purporting to tell the future, gives a graphic account of the devastation of the eastern provinces of the empire, the capture, massacre or flight of the population and the abandonment of cities and villages. We must, of course, make allowances for the intentions and the rhetoric of the text; but even so, it must have had a recognisable basis in reality and therefore in the popular experience in order to achieve its aims.[56]

Given this basic context, it is difficult to believe that the seventh century really did witness a dramatic rise in the available labour force and a consequently less urgent need for the state to concern itself with the relations between land and labour. On the contrary, the flight of the rural population from many areas will have meant a considerable reduction in revenues; it must certainly have adversely affected the demography of the empire, for the effects of both warfare and endemic outbreaks of plague can hardly have done otherwise. The reinforcement of the population through the transfer of Slav peoples may well have helped to re-establish a certain demographic equilibrium; it certainly represents an enormous effort on the part of the state and hints at the magnitude of the problem. But it clearly also points to the dramatic consequences for the population of parts of Anatolia of the events of the second half of the seventh century. It is, moreover, to be stressed that these Slav immigrants were settled not just in districts which we might reasonably assume had been badly affected by warfare; but in areas also in the heart of the empire's territory. Thus there are seals referring to the Slav prisoners of war for the districts of Cappado-

---

[54] See above, the canons of the Quinisext, the miracles of St Theodore at Euchaita, the archaeological and narrative evidence for the abandonment of urban sites, the catalogue of Arab raids itself, year by year. Note also M. Kaplan, 'L'Economie paysanne dans l'Empire Byzantin du Ve au Xe siècle', *Klio* 68 (1986), 198–232, see 221–2, who surveys the disastrous effects of such hostile activity on peasant agricultural production; and cf. the Fiscal Treatise (ed. Dölger, *Beiträge*), 116.2–3, 119.1. Note especially canon 95 of the Quinisext, which notes that the ecclesiastical authorities were faced by a number of problems as a result of the large number of refugees coming out of Galatia (Mansi, XI, 984B–E). But see also Haldon, 'The Miracles of Artemios and Contemporary Attitudes', p. 34 and n. 8 for some problems with this text.

[55] The *Vita Philareti* (115) notes that Philaretus lost much of his livestock to Arab raiders; the Fiscal Treatise details enemy raids as the cause of insecurity and the abandonment of land by even the better-off peasants – see 116.2–3, 119.1.

[56] Ps.-Methodius, *Apokalypse*, see XI, 9–17 (the text makes explicit mention of the abandonment of cities, the enslavement of the population, the destruction of crops, as well as the decline in the population of the affected districts); Haldon, 'Ideology and social change', 168 note 74 with literature.

cia I and II, for Phrygia Salutaria, Caria and Lydia; but also for Bithynia, in the *Opsikion* district neighbouring Constantinople.[57] Areas such as Bithynia clearly suffered greatly during the Arab siege operations from 674 to 678, and the long-term effects of this warfare must have been apparent for many years. But Arab raids penetrated deep into Anatolia on many other occasions and, while frontier regions and areas where the Arab forces wintered or were regularly present will have been most affected, it would seem that nowhere was entirely free from harassment and economic and demographic disruption.[58]

The generally unquestioned assumption that there was a demographic increase in Anatolia at this time, therefore, seems to be fundamentally flawed, based on a set of hypotheses that have little foundation in the sources for the period, and which indeed are in clear contradiction to the logic of the situation which the sources do portray. Ostrogorsky's carefully developed thesis is based, in effect, on three elements: the destruction or disappearance of large estates; the supposed establishment under Heraclius of soldiers' lands; and the assumption that the Farmers' Law represents the generality of rural communities throughout the empire. None of these is, in fact, more than a hypothesis; the first two are extremely improbable, and there is certainly no evidence of any substance in their favour. The Farmers' Law, as I have suggested, does represent an increase in the importance of such communities and may represent also an increase in their numbers. But I do not think that this is enough to assume the veritable social and demographic revolution for which Ostrogorsky argued.[59] On the contrary, the evidence seems to point the other way; and while the transfer of Slavs in such large numbers must have improved or stabilised the situation, the fiscal response of the state, in eventually severing the link between land and labour for tax purposes, actually points in the opposite direction to Ostrogorsky and those who have followed his

---

[57] See Zacos and Veglery, vol. I, pt. 1, pp. 190f. table 33 (dated to the year 694/5).
[58] The best synoptic account of this warfare is to be found in Lilie, *Die byzantinische Reaktion*, see pp. 76ff.; also Haldon, 'Ideology and social change', 184.
[59] See Ostrogorsky, *Geschichte*, pp. 110ff.; Guillou, 'Transformation des structures', 77, also argues for increased agricultural productivity during the seventh and eighth centuries and into the early ninth. Over such a long period (during the later part of which the empire's lands were a good deal more secure than in the earlier part) he may be correct – but his argument rests partly upon the assumption that the state could only intensify its demand for revenues if productivity had increased, an assumption which is dubious. While it is true that a peasant subsistence economy has only a limited potential for quantitative extension before it collapses in on itself (see W. Kula, *An Economic Theory of the Feudal System: Towards a Model of the Polish Economy, 1500–1800* (London 1976) see pp. 28ff. and 165ff. for comparative data), the desperate situation of the Byzantine state in the later seventh and early eighth centuries must have made increased demand on limited resources inevitable. But it will have been the form that this demand took that was crucial to its potential success.

reasoning. Shortage of manpower can traditionally be met by landlords and/or tax-collecting institutions in one of two ways (dependent also, of course, on which options were available as cultural and political possibilities). The first is to tie the labour force to the land, a process which involves close supervision by the state, a stable population, the co-operation of the landowners and landlords, and – as far as possible – stable political conditions. This was the route taken by the Roman state during the fourth century, a process which continued into the fifth and sixth centuries with decreasing momentum. It was a pattern followed also in Eastern Europe, for example, from the fifteenth century, as population decline became apparent, and as the flight of peasants to hitherto unexploited lands outside seigneurial political control threatened to damage the economic interests of the feudal class of landlords.[60]

The second way is to attract labour power through offering or accepting land on conditions and terms relatively advantageous to the cultivator: low rents, for example, or a low rate of taxation, heritable tenures, freedom of movement, freedom to alienate the property or the lease and so on. This pattern was partly followed in England for a period after the devastation caused by the Black Death.[61] It seems also to have been followed in the East Roman world during the sixth century and after, and the popularity and spread of advantageous emphyteutic leases, or similar contractual forms, during this period certainly seems to represent already the awareness of landlords, institutional or private, of the advantages such leases had in retaining their agricultural labour force, and in bringing back uncultivated land into productive use.[62]

Now, in the seventh-century context described above, is it really likely that the state 'relaxed' its fiscal policy because sources of labour were plentiful? It seems most improbable. In fact, it must have been faced with a major difficulty in terms of the effectiveness of its legislation, for it was clearly simply impossible to enforce regulations which compelled *coloni*, for example, to remain on their holdings or to impose fiscal solidarity on communities of smallholders which may well have resulted in mass abandonment of the land, under the conditions we have described for many areas. Parts of Anatolia, and indeed of the Balkans (or those districts remaining in Byzantine hands), were at times full of refugees of one sort or

---

[60] See, for example, M. Dobb, *Studies in the Development of Capitalism* (London 1967), pp. 53ff.; R.H. Hilton and R.E.F. Smith, *The Enserfment of the Russian Peasantry* (Cambridge 1968), pp.1–27; and for a summary of developments throughout Eastern Europe, Anderson, *Passages*, pp. 252ff.
[61] See G. Duby, *Rural Economy and Country Life in the Medieval West* (London 1968), pp. 72ff.; and see M.M. Postan, 'The fifteenth century', *Economic History Review* 9 (1938–9), 160–7.
[62] See chapter 1, and pp. 134f. above.

another, seeking safety, or work, or both. Every Arab raid set elements of the population in motion, even if flight was only to a local fastness; many of the larger and safer urban centres in the west and north-west of Asia Minor must have contained far more people – who needed food and shelter – than they could adequately cope with. And even if this did not affect all areas at the same time and in the same degree, it represented a more or less continuous state of affairs from the 650s and 660s well into the first half of the eighth century. Not only *coloni*, whether *liberi* or *adscripticii*, but agricultural producers with freedom of movement, will have been affected.[63] The net result was that the close connection forged over the preceding centuries between a settled population and its land was, in many regions, broken. Land was abandoned, even if only temporarily, and this meant an immediate reduction in resources and, in particular, provisions for the personnel of the state – the army especially. Faced with the impossibility of enforcing the older legislation, and the need to find some alternative way of raising revenues, as well as of restoring abandoned land to productive use, here was reason enough for remodelling the traditional system of assessment, even if only selectively at first.

But a more compelling reason exists, and one which helps to locate the change in the middle years of the seventh century.

As we shall see in chapter 5, there are good grounds for believing that the greater part of the state's revenue had, from the late 650s if not already in the 640s, been assessed in kind, primarily in order to maintain and support the armies or *themata* which, from the early 640s, began to be cantonned across Anatolia. In itself, the procedure was not new, a part of the regular assessment of many areas having always been collected in produce for the provisioning of the army. But a result of the generalisation of this practice was that the land-tax itself came to be referred to by the term traditionally applied to a compulsory purchase or levy of provisions and materials for the state, especially the army. The term in question is *synōnē* or, in Latin, *coemptio*. The only context for such a shift, from a cash assessment and collection to one carried out mostly in kind, can reasonably be shown to be the period with which we are concerned, the 640s and 650s. That the change had occurred already by the later seventh or early eighth century is nicely confirmed by the Farmers' Law, where the regular land-taxes on a property are referred to as the *extraordina* of the public fisc (τὰ ἐξτραόρδινα τοῦ δημοσίου λόγου).[64] Now the term *extraordinaria* had referred exclusively to exceptional levies above the usual assessment and could in no way have applied in the sixth century, for example, to

---

[63] See in particular the 95th canon of the Quinisext already referred to (Mansi XI, 984B–E), regarding the refugee problem in Asia Minor.
[64] *Farmers' Law* art. 19 (JGR II, p. 66).

regular taxes. The *synōnē* or *coemptio*, on the other hand, was just such an extraordinary levy and would be perfectly well described in this way.[65] As the hitherto limited practice of collecting a portion of the state revenues in kind was thus applied throughout the empire to the land-tax, so the terms which had described extraordinary levies in kind seem to have been generalised and applied to the ordinary assessment on land. The common element was collection in kind.

There is indeed some evidence to suggest that a reorganisation of the land-tax assessment had taken place by the 660s. In about 667, an imperial *iussio* or command was issued, ordering the drawing-up of tax-rolls for the populations of Calabria, Sicily, Sardinia and Africa. The same *iussio* ordered also the registration of units of assessment – *capita* – and the raising of a ship-tax from the landowners of the said provinces.[66] The order coincides, of course, with the presence of the Emperor Constans II in Sicily and reflects accordingly the needs of the court, army and fleet at that time. In 681 another imperial *iussio* was issued, by which the number of *capita*, or units of assessment, and the rate of collection of the *coemptio*, along with other yearly assessments, was reduced for the population of the papal patrimonial lands in Sicily and Calabria.[67] These two texts together suggest a significant development. In the first place, the drawing-up of new tax-registers (*diagrafa*) implies a major reassessment or reorganisation of fiscal liabilities. In the second place, the *coemptio* – *synōnē* – is treated explicitly as a regular, yearly assessment, a character which it had never

---

[65] See the detailed discussion in J.F. Haldon, 'Synônê: Re-Considering a Problematic Term of Middle Byzantine Fiscal Administration', *BMGS* 18 (1994) 116–53 (repr. in idem, *State, Army and Society in Byzantium* [Aldershot 1995] VIII).

[66] *Liber Pontificalis*, I, 344.2; Dölger, *Regesten*, no. 234.

[67] *Liber Pontificalis*, I, 366.8; Dölger, *Regesten*, no. 250. Note also *Liber Pontificalis*, I, 368.19–369.2, according to which an imperial command to Pope Conon in about 687 reduced the taxes of the papal patrimony in Bruttium and Lucania by 200 *annonacapita* per annum. The term used strongly suggests a unit of assessment upon which the calculation of the tax – *annona/synōnē* – was based. By the 730s the system was well established. An edict of Leo III of 731 for Sicily and Calabria orders the increase of the taxed by thirty-three per cent and on the papal patrimonial lands the entering of adult male taxpayers and their heirs on the tax-registers. See Theophanes, 410.8: φόρους κεφαλικούς; Dölger, *Regesten*, no. 300. Whether this latter procedure can be taken as evidence for the existence of the *kapnikon* or its ancestor – since male heads of households only are to be registered – is uncertain. For the letter of Theodore the Studite (see p. 149 below), see *PG* IC, 929–33, esp. 932B, and the detailed discussion on the whole question of distributive and contributive tax-assessment in N. Oikonomidès, 'De l'impôt de distribution à l'impôt de quotité à propos du premier cadastre byzantin (7ᵉ – 9ᵉ siècle)', *ZRVI* 26 (1987), 9–19 – the first really to address this crucial issue. Of course, *miliarēsia* were first issued under Leo III so that, if the *kapnikon* or its ancestral form were already in existence as a cash levy, it would have been raised in either copper *folleis* or silver hexagrams. But neither the copper nor the silver coinages were particularly stable in the later seventh century, and this must have presented a number of problems. Possibly, then, it is to Leo III that the introduction of the *kapnikon* must be ascribed. For the coinage, see Hendy, *Studies*, pp. 494–6 and 498–501.

possessed in the late Roman period. The occurrence of *coemptio* and *capita* together, the former representing the actual tax, the latter the units of assessment, raised regularly, is good evidence for the existence by this time of the new procedure. The date of the two orders, applying to the West, would tend to support the date and the reasons suggested for its probable introduction in the East in the 640s or 650s. It also suggests the way in which the later *kapnikon* was to evolve, as a separate assessment on heads of families in fixed dwellings, calculated differently from the *capita/synōnē* system, but clearly fixed to the notion of residence, as the name implies.

The *synōnē* element of the later *kapnikon/synōnē* pair can thus be taken back with very great probability to the 640s or 650s. There is no reason to assume that the *kapnikon* element – whether under that name or not – was not originated at the same time. The older assessment was, after all, a land-tax which combined both agricultural land and livestock and other property in a single calculation; the new procedure may simply have meant the separate assessment of each. Given the preconditions described already, and the need to raise a very large part of its revenue in kind, it must have made good fiscal and administrative sense to add to the original assessment, based on both *capita* and *iuga* and now raised in kind, a second assessment. For while the collection of the land-tax in kind will have reduced some of the state's difficulties, it was also much less flexible than a collection based in cash; and the overall effect must have been a reduction in the amount of actual wealth thus expropriated. The introduction of a 'new' tax, raised on households – which is what the term *kapnikon* clearly implies – may have been intended to compensate for this by introducing a more flexible (for the state, at any rate) element into the equation, to be raised in cash.

A letter of Theodore the Studite, dated to the year 801, offers some valuable evidence in this context. Referring to the fact that the Empress Eirene had substantially lightened the burden of many tax-payers, it remarks in particular that the need for the poor to engage in extra (paid in cash?) work, not to free themselves from poverty, but to be able to pay the tax-collectors the levy 'which cannot be combined', is now over. This levy, it states, has existed for a long time; and it has been suggested that this is a reference to the *kapnikon*, a flat-rate hearth-tax, levied at a rate of two *miliarēsia* per household, which cannot be acquitted in kind or in any other way except in coin. Like any flat-rate levy, therefore, it probably hit the poorest members of the community hardest. As we have seen, the *kapnikon* is first explicitly mentioned for the reign of Nicephorus I, although the context implies that it was already then old and well established. It seems not unlikely that it, too, should be taken back into the seventh century, to the time when the state was obliged to split its major tax-assessment on land and persons into two portions.

A second point in this connection concerns the nature of the assessment itself. A recent study has pointed out that, whereas the late Roman assessment was *distributive*, that is to say, the state fixed its total revenue requirements (as far as it was able) in advance, and then distributed the demand across the different units of assessment, the middle Byzantine system was *contributive*, that is, taxes were assessed on the basis of the ability of individual units of assessment to pay. The assessment could vary, therefore, according to the wealth of the tax-payers as well as the demands of the state. The split between the assessment on land and the fixed rate on households which underlies the difference between *synōnē* and *kapnikon* may well represent the first step in this shift. Oikonomidès has collected evidence which suggests strongly that the weight placed by the state on oaths in respect of statements of property-value and wealth in the later seventh century and up until the early ninth century (again a situation changed by Eirene's reforms mentioned in the letter of Theodore the Studite and evidenced also in a novel ascribed to her reign) is a sign that such a system was possibly already in operation. A distributive system did not require such accurate information, since demands were issued according to state requirements only, not the amount of taxable wealth available. It is precisely the conditions of the seventh century which we have described – population movement, insecurity of agriculture and rural production in general in many areas – which may have forced the state to fall back upon a contributive assessment, secured on the basis of central assessments of the wealth available from specific regions and specific tax-payers. Censuses in this context will have been unavoidable.

The loosening of the direct tie between tax-liability and land with labour will have had several consequences. In the first place, it had the advantage for the state that refugee populations (which could hardly be punished as the old laws demanded) were no longer in breach of imperial legislation – a trivial point in some respects, but important with regard to the authority of the government. Secondly, it represented an effort to regain some at least of the 'lost' tax-payers – who, according to the traditional system of assessment, were only liable if they cultivated land – by making the 'hearth-tax' or *kapnikon* (in its ancestral form) independent and separate from the possession of land. Households or heads of households were henceforth liable to tax regardless of their relationship to the land. This alteration, while it must have been difficult to carry through, necessitating many detailed censuses throughout the empire, will also certainly have increased the tax-revenue, since it taxed the inhabitants of cities and non-agricultural communities, too, unless they received specific exemp-

Rural society 151

tion.[68] Thirdly, the change in the system of assessment must have recognised and at the same time thereby promoted greater mobility, since – although the state still required the maximum amount of land under cultivation – it was no longer possible rigidly to tie the agricultural population to the land, nor was it in many regions at all practicable. In recognising the change and in adjusting its methods of assessment, the state also averted the possibility that tied *coloni* on state lands or over-taxed freeholders would abandon their holdings and take up advantageous leases on Church or private estates.[69] Fourthly, the conditions which gave rise to these changes in fiscal practice must have promoted the frequent and widespread transfer of liability for taxes and/or the cultivation of the land – the old *epibolē* – as individuals and sometimes groups of peasants gave in to the pressure to escape hostile action or the effects of bad harvests, for example, both before and after the changes. The consequence was more regular supervision on the part of the fisc over the affairs of the rural communities and, if the sixth-century pattern is anything to go by, increased hardship on those landholders and communities who had to shoulder the extra burden.[70]

Finally, and given the options for dealing with demographic decline discussed already, it is highly probable – and the existence of the Farmers' Law, amongst the texts, is good evidence for this – that the state both reassessed the rate of taxation downwards and drew substantial numbers of refugees to its own estates (which were extensive) on attractive terms. Indeed, the considerable remission of taxes during the last years of the sixth century suggests that the state had come to recognise the potential increase in the total area of productive land and consequently of revenue which might thus be achieved. Perhaps this reflects the success of emphyteutic lessors in obtaining both labour for their land and in maintaining their own incomes.[71] A lessening of the tax-burden permitted the investment by peasant cultivators of a greater proportion of their resources in agricultural production, with a consequent increase in absolute terms of output and, indirectly, of population.[72]

[68] Note that censuses were carried out in the West in the 660s and in 730 – not exactly frequently, but illustrative of their importance to the fiscal administration of the state. See notes 66–7 above.
[69] The notion that such a reform also promoted mobility was first expounded by N.A. Constantinescu, 'Réforme sociale ou réforme fiscale?', *Bulletin de l'Académie Roumaine, section historique*, 11 (1924), 94ff., but was rejected by Ostrogorsky, *Geschichte*, p. 115 note 3.
[70] See chapter 1, p. 29 and Procopius, *Historia Arcana*, XXIII, 15–16. Cf. Kaplan, 'L'Economie paysanne', 229 (for the tenth century) and 202 (general).
[71] Tax evasion in the sixth century: Justinian, *Nov.* 147 (a. 553 for Oriens and Illyricum); JGR I, coll. 1, nov. 1 (Justin II, a. 566); nov. 11 (Tiberius Constantine, a. 575) (Dölger, *Regesten*, nos. 4 and 40).
[72] See, for example, Fiscal Treatise (ed. Dölger, *Beiträge*), 115.28–33 and the discussion in Kaplan, *L'Economie paysanne*: a reduction in tax/rent burden can result in the expansion of

All these changes amount to a series of fairly drastic organisational alterations in the late Roman system of tax-assessment and collection. Exactly where and how they were first implemented must remain unclear for the time being.

There is no reason to doubt that these changes in tax-assessment together with the conditions of economic disruption and dislocation which brought them about, can also have contributed towards an increase, at least in some areas, of independent peasant smallholders. Large estates, while their owners may have been able to take refuge, and whether ecclesiastical, imperial or private, must have suffered under the same conditions and the consequent shortage of labour; they will have been only too happy to maintain production on the basis of less oppressive contractual arrangements, long-term, short-term or perpetual. The flight of much of the rural population of the most exposed areas will have benefited safer regions and will also inevitably have promoted the gradual disappearance of the remaining legislative ties between land and peasants. Many peasants of relatively humble status must have escaped their former condition entirely in this way. The importation by the state of new elements to repopulate the countryside, whatever the scale on which it was done, will also have reinforced this tendency,[73] and the need for the state to recruit its soldiers from among the ordinary population of the provinces, and for the soldiers to provide at least a part of their own equipment during the later seventh century, is good evidence that by this time there existed a sufficiently numerous and prosperous source of volunteers or conscripts from among the rural population on which it could draw.[74]

The result of this brief survey, therefore, is that there does seem to have taken place an expansion of independent smallholding. This expansion was both a result of the changes in the relationship between agricultural producers and landlords, and to a degree also of the reorganisation of the system of fiscal assessment by the state, in turn brought about by the

---

the basic unit of production both in land and in demographic terms – in a growth, therefore, of productive capacity in the quantitative sense. The disadvantages are heritable partition of the family holdings and ultimately a reduction in the size and the viability of such units – which become as a consequence more vulnerable in adverse condition (drought, pestilence, warfare, bad harvests, etc.). It is nevertheless clear, as the Fiscal Treatise demonstrates, that the effects of a reduction in the overall burden of tax and rent were recognised by contemporary authorities.

[73] The question of where and how these settlers were accommodated, as well as that of the fiscal system of the state in general, will be dealt with in chapters 5 and 6. But note that the picture was further complicated by the movement of refugees from both inside and outside the empire. For the year 686, for example, Theophanes (364.3–4) notes that a famine in Syria forced many people from that region to flee to 'Romania', an event recorded also in a contemporary Syriac chronicle. See G.J. Reinink, 'Pseudo-Methodius und die Legende vom römischen Endkaiser', 95 and note 62.

[74] See Haldon, *Recruitment and Conscription*, pp. 72f.

dislocation of the warfare of the second half of the seventh century. The conditions promoted by war and constant insecurity cast a large number of the agricultural population adrift, as refugees – either from the tax-collector, the rent-collector and bailiff, or from the Arabs. They stimulated an increase in demographic mobility. The relocation of refugee populations to several different areas of the empire, in particular to a number of the Anatolian provinces, and – given the endemic shortage of labour power – under much improved conditions, completes the picture. The state, faced with a *fait accompli*, could only conform to the changed situation and adjust, to try to maximise the potential of the new conditions.

THE LANDED WEALTHY AND THE NEW ARISTOCRACY

The changes which I have outlined so far clearly did constitute a shift in the relations of production in the countryside. While labour power was scarce, cultivable land deserted and the state able to impose a uniform policy on the rural population with great difficulty – the latter an effect of the divergent interests of the older landowning element of the ruling class and the new, particularly the military, service meritocracy – the condition of the peasantry with regard to the assertion of its rights of tenure, and communal solidarity in respect of the fisc, had improved. But clearly, a number of factors militated against the disappearance of large estates and of social equilibrium in peasant communities.

In the first place, as we have seen, areas where a strong military presence was required will have been easy prey to the landed property ambitions of officers who, in return for protection from various threats – whether from the enemy or from government officials, for example – will have been able to gain power over smallholders and peasant communities and indeed over the property of both resident and absentee landlords without much difficulty. As in an earlier period, it would not have proved difficult to turn the 'protection' into a rent, until the patronage was effectively converted into one form of possession or another through lease, donation or sale.[75]

Social differentiation within peasant communities, the impoverishment of some smallholders to the advantage of others (clearly present in the Farmers' Law) and in particular the subdivision of holdings among heirs, leading to holdings which might eventually become too small to be economically viable, these factors must all have facilitated the encroachment of the wealthier peasant on the land of the poorer, and of the big estate owner on the lands of peasant communities in general.[76] Together

[75] See, for example, Haldon, 'Some considerations', 95–8; Jones, *LRE*, vol. II, pp. 776f.
[76] For the effects of these factors in the late Roman period, up to the later sixth century, see Jones, *LRE*, vol. II, pp. 773–81.

with poor harvests, seasonal or climatic fluctuation, natural disasters and similar perennially present elements, and in addition the demands of the fisc, of the local provincial or military administration and other departments of the state administration, such factors must always have left peasant farmers very vulnerable to fairly dramatic changes in fortune and sudden household economic failure.[77] The abandonment of holdings and the attribution of their tax-dues to their neighbours was clearly a normal occurrence for the compilers of the Farmers' Law. The speed with which Philaretus' community set about taking over his unworked holdings (quite apart from the greed of the larger landlords in simply taking Philaretus' property), together, presumably, with the taxes that went with those holdings, demonstrates several aspects of such a situation: both the process, described in the Farmers' Law, whereby unwanted land might be alienated (temporarily in the first instance) to a third party within the community who was responsible also for its taxes; and it demonstrates the ways in which a landholder or owner could lose his lands (although, in the case of Philaretus, a lack of prudence rather than of resources was to blame). In Philaretus' community, or in his neighbourhood, the needy peasant farmer was not uncommon – witness the number of animals or amount of other property that was given away.[78] On the other hand, the powerful local landowner, with estates spread over several regions or provinces was also present. Church and state continued to represent substantial landowning interests. And there is no reason to doubt that peasants of *colonus* status, bound to their land by private contract, continued to farm such estates, sharing villages with free tenants, emphyteutic leaseholders and so on.[79] In areas relatively free from enemy harassment, the well-established bond between land and tenant, whatever the legislative intervention of the state may have done to relax or sever the connection, probably remained, if only because the tenant farmer attained thereby a degree of economic security for himself and his family – as well as the (dubious) protection of a landlord. The advantages and dis-

---

[77] Compare the effects of the severe winter and bad harvests of the years 927/8 and 938/9, described in the novel of Romanus I which dealt with the results (Dölger, *Regesten*, no. 628; text: *JGR* I, pp. 205ff.). See Ostrogorsky, *Geschichte*, pp. 227ff.; R. Morris, 'The powerful and the poor in tenth-century Byzantium: law and reality', *Past and Present* 73 (1976), 3–27.

[78] The best summary of the provisions of the Farmers' Law is to be found in Köpstein, 'Zu den Agrarverhältnissen', pp. 40–53; for Philaretus, see *ibid.*, pp. 61–2 (summary of text); Kaplan, 'Les Villageois', 214f.

[79] The tenants of Church and monastic lands are referred to in the early ninth century as *paroikoi*, which may mean simply tenant or bear a more specific and technical meaning similar to that of *colonus liber* of the legislation of Anastasius and Justinian. See Theophanes, 486.30. For the technical meanings of *paroikos*, see Lemerle, *Agrarian History*, pp. 179–82.

advantages were, from a theoretical standpoint, evenly balanced. Indeed, it must be emphasised that while the conditions of the seventh century do seem to have resulted in a number of important and substantive changes, not all areas within the empire, nor all of the rural population, will necessarily have been affected in precisely the same way. Considerable room for regional variation should be allowed within the general explanatory framework.

And so, while the overall effect of the economic and social dislocation of the second half of the seventh century and of the opening years of the eighth century seems to have been to promote an increase in peasant mobility and in the numbers of peasant smallholders subject directly to the fisc, with all the contingent results for the state and its fiscal apparatus, already the age-old disadvantages which accompanied the subsistence economy of the peasantry were leading to a new phase of polarisation between estate owners and peasant communities, on the one hand, and within such communities on the other. The evidence of the Life of Philaretus, for the later eighth century, and of the measures taken by Nicephorus I with regard to the tax-burden of the impoverished peasantry, as well as those of Eirene in respect of taxes which affected the poorest members of society in the provinces and in the capital, make this much clear.[80]

The origins of the provincial landed elite, the 'aristocracy' of the ninth and tenth centuries and after, are to be sought for the most part in the same social and economic dislocation and turmoil as the increased mobility and numbers of the peasant freeholders. Whereas the latter were spread geographically throughout the empire (at least, there is nothing to contradict this assumption), the later evidence for the location of the more powerful provincial families suggests that it was precisely in areas of relatively low population density, and which formed the wide band of territory constituting the frontier zone, that this section of the ruling class had its origins.

It has already been demonstrated by several scholars that the dominant elements of the Byzantine ruling class in the period from the ninth to the eleventh centuries originated in the eastern *themata* of Anatolikōn, Kappadokia, Paphlagonia, Charsianon and *Boukellariōn*.[81] Out of the forty-seven

---

[80] Theophanes, 486.23–6; see Haldon, *Recruitment and Conscription*, p. 50 note 87. For Eirene's reforms, see the letter of Theodore the Studite of 801 (*PG* IC, 929–33) with note 67 above.

[81] See especially Sp. Vryonis, jr., 'Byzantium: the social basis of decline', *GRBS* 2 (1959), 159–78, see 161f.; Vryonis 'The internal history of Byzantium during the "Time of Troubles" (1057–1081)' (Diss., Harvard 1956), pp. 173ff. and 390f.; and *The Decline of Medieval Hellenism*, pp. 24f and list. See also A.P. Každan, *Social'niy sostav gospodstvuiuščego klassa Vizantii XI–XII vv.* (Moscow 1974), pp. 195, 204 and lists. More recently Winkelmann has shown how the development of *nomina gentilia* is, initially, to be found among these provincial families. The degree to which this reflects the bias of the sources

family names located by the sources either explicitly or by implication (ownership or large-scale estates), thirty derive from the districts of *Anatolikōn*, Kappadokia and Paphlagonia. Similarly, Kazdan's analysis of the origins of the eleventh- and twelfth-century civil elite shows that, whereas the great majority of the known members of the military elite came from central or eastern Anatolia and the Caucasus, with smaller percentages from Macedonia, Bulgaria and outside the empire, the majority of the civil elite hailed from Constantinople or its immediate hinterland, coastal Greece and coastal Anatolia, with the Aegean region.[82] The close connection between the homelands of the military elite, and the non-urban and plateau zone of Asia Minor, with its predominantly pastoral economy, and the concomitant identification of the greater part of the civilian elite with the urbanised or more densely populated regions of the empire, becomes immediately apparent.[83] Now it is significant that not only was the military elite drawn for the most part from areas of a chiefly pastoral economic character where towns had usually been limited to those districts in river valleys, for example, which could support them through a limited amount of arable exploitation;[84] they also represented those areas which, from the seventh to the later ninth century, formed the frontier, as mentioned above.[85] Their association with a pastoral economy was ancient,[86] and some were the site of large-scale imperial stud-farms in the later Roman period.[87] The same type of economic activity was still carried on in the tenth and eleventh centuries, as the Life of the magnate-turned-monk Michael Maleinus implies: the property he gave away on taking holy orders consisted chiefly of herds of cattle and flocks of sheep.[88] Cedrenus notes that the estates of Eustathius Maleinus in the themes of Boukellarion and Charsianon consisted mostly of large ranches;[89] and already in the fourth century (and therefore probably earlier) some senatorial magnates

---

and their interest in the political–military conflicts of the empire, on the one hand, and a more-or-less accurate picture, on the other, remains uncertain. But the general context of the growth of such families would suggest that they do illustrate an actual tendency. See Winkelmann, *Quellenstudien, passim* and pp. 211f.

[82] Každan, *ibid*. Clearly, a complete catalogue is not possible; but the bias of the sample offered by the sources is suggestive and is supported by other evidence discussed below.
[83] See Haldon, 'Some considerations', 95ff., esp. 97–8; Každan, *ibid*.; Hendy, *Studies*, pp.100ff.
[84] The best survey is that of Hendy, *Studies*, pp. 90–100.
[85] See Lilie, *Die byzantinische Reaktion*, map at p. 336; and cf. Hendy, *Studies*, map 25.
[86] See Strabo, *Geographica*, XII, 2.7ff.
[87] Jones, *LRE*, vol. II, pp. 767–9; E. Kirsten, art. *Cappadocia*, in *Reallexikon für Antike und Christentum* II (1954), cols. 869f.
[88] *Vie de S. Michel Maleinos* (ed. L. Petit, in *ROC* VII (1902), 543–603), see 557.31sq.
[89] Cedrenus, vol. II. 448.9–16; Scylitzes, 340.

lived not in cities, but on their fortified ranch-villas.[90] Just as significantly, there were areas in which the activities of local magnates in appropriating both imperial and private lands, farms and herds of horses had attracted the attention of the Emperor Justinian. As has been pointed out, the districts primarily involved were the Cappadocias, Helenopontus, Paphlagonia, Phrygia Pacatiana, Galatia I, Pisidia and Lycaonia, districts which were later to be subsumed within the themes of *Anatolikōn* (Phrygia Pacatiana, Pisidia, Lycaonia, part of Galatia), Kappadokia (Cappadocia I and part of II) and Charsianon (Cappadocia II and part of Galatia I).[91]

It seems clear, therefore, that the regions of central and south-eastern Anatolia from which the later provincial military magnates appear for the most part to have been drawn coincided with areas which were both geographically and climatically unsuited to arable exploitation, favouring instead a pastoral economy. They were areas which had always supported such an economy, and in which the extended 'ranch' had formed the traditional unit of exploitation. They were, furthermore, areas of relatively low population density and of few urban centres, as Hendy has most recently pointed out.

The fact that the later provincial magnates originated in large part in these districts is surely no accident. It seems to be a direct result of the coincidence of warfare, patterns of settlement and patterns of economic exploitation. And in the context of the dislocation of the seventh century it is worth noting in passing that unlike arable farmers, pastoralists and ranchers – given reasonable warning – may often be less vulnerable, requiring as they do much less manpower and being able to bring herds and flocks more quickly to safety.[92] It is significant that the later Byzantine aristocracy of the tenth and eleventh centuries placed more emphasis on their moveable wealth – whether in the form of livestock or jewellery or similar items – than on land itself, an illuminating indicator of the relative ideological values attributed to these two forms of investment in social wealth.[93] Contrary to the assumptions of some historians, therefore, a

[90] Cf. B. Treucker, *Politische und sozialgeschichtliche Studien zu den Basilius-Briefen* (Frankfurt and Munich 1961), p. 15.
[91] The arguments are well summarised by Hendy, *Studies*, pp. 103–4. For Justinian's legislation, see Justinian, Nov. 28 (Helenopontus), 29 (Paphlagonia), 24 (Pisidia), 25 (Lycaonia), 30 (Cappadocia), 8 (Galatia and Phrygia Pacatiana). For these reforms and their background, see Jones, *LRE*, vol. I, pp. 280ff.
[92] In the tenth-century treatise on guerrilla strategy, *De Velitatione Bellica*, it is predominantly livestock that the author envisages being taken to safety before raiders arrive, with the implication that the economy of the regions in question was predominantly pastoral or transhumant in character. See G. Dagron, *Le Traité sur la guérilla (De Velitatione) de l'empereur Nicéphore Phocas (963–969)* (Text G. Dagron and H. Mihăescu; transl. and comm. G. Dagron; Appendix J.-C. Cheynet) (Paris 1986), XII.8–9; XX.59.
[93] See the analysis of G.G. Litavrin, 'Otnošitel'nye razmeny i sostav imuščestva provincial'noi vizantiiskoi aristokratii vo vtoroi polovine XI v.' *Vizantiiskie Očerki* (Moscow 1971),

context of ongoing warfare and military conflict may well have been more, rather than less, conducive to the appropriation of lands and the evolution of large-scale landed property in the provinces during the seventh and eighth centuries, at least where a pastoral economy dominated.[94]

The implications of this concordance are considerable. In the first place, it seems that the dominant position won over the period up to the tenth century in these eastern and central Anatolian lands by this class of military magnates was not necessarily replicated in the more densely populated regions with a more strongly arable tradition. It has been demonstrated that the newly reconquered territories in south-eastern and southern Asia Minor and in northern Syria, taken in the period from the middle of the ninth to the middle of the eleventh century, were almost without exception kept firmly within state hands.[95] By the same token, the military elite seem never to have established themselves as firmly either in the European provinces or in the western and northern plains and littoral of Asia Minor, areas where the heavily agricultural and densely settled nature of the land made such a dominance much less straightforward.[96] This does not mean that large estates, relatively speaking, farmed by tenants of varying degrees of dependent status, did not develop. But it is clear that they did not develop on the same scale as in the East, undoubtedly a result of both lack of opportunity on the part of the local military and state establishment: western Asia Minor, for example, was never subject to the degree of population collapse and economic dislocation that typified the history of the eastern regions during the seventh and early eighth centuries. It also suggests that the geography of ownership in the predominantly agricultural zones, with a much greater parcellisation and subdivision of the land among both peasantry and estate-owning families, prevented the rapid consolidation of large tracts of land into estates. This was clearly the case in the sixth century and before. In western Asia Minor, for example, in the district of Magnesia on the River

pp. 164–8; and the comment of Každan and Constable, *People and Power in Byzantium*, p. 51.

[94] See Winkelmann, *Quellenstudien*, esp. pp. 28f., for example. But comparative evidence from the later period of Byzantine history – from the twelfth century in Asia Minor, along the Byzantine-Turkish frontier region, and from the middle of the thirteenth century, along the border regions between the empire of Nicaea and the Turks – suggests very strongly that warfare and economic insecurity are not incompatible with a pastoral economy and the growth of estates. See the comments of M. Angold, *A Byzantine Government in Exile: Government and Society under the Laskarids of Nicaea (1204–1261)* (Oxford 1975), p. 101; and also Vryonis, *Decline of Medieval Hellenism*, pp. 145–55. See also C. Cahen, *Pre-Ottoman Turkey: A General Survey of the Material and Spiritual Culture and History c. 1071–1330* (London 1968), pp. 143ff.

[95] See N. Oikonomidès, *Les Listes de préséance byzantines des IXe–Xe siècles* (Paris 1972), pp. 355f. and 363; and Hendy, *Studies*, p. 104.

[96] Hendy, *Studies*, pp. 85ff. (Balkans) and 132ff. (general discussion).

Maeander, and at Tralles, land-holdings and farms, whether on larger or smaller estates, or pertaining to village freeholders or to cities, were extremely fragmented in the early fourth century, as fragments from surviving census records illustrate; there is no reason to suppose that the picture changed through the later Roman period and into the seventh century. It is interesting also that this region later formed the southern section of the *Thrakēsiōn thema*, an area for which the late tenth-century evidence might imply a very similar pattern of property-holding.[97] The tenth-century evidence adduced by Hendy demonstrates that the state was more easily able to defend its interests in this region, among others, in maintaining peasant taxpayers independent of large landowners; and although it is a clear implication of the legislation that wealthy landlords already existed in the districts dealt with in the novels of Constantine VII and Romanus II (chiefly the *Thrakēsiōn thema*), they were clearly not landlords on the scale of the magnates of central and eastern Anatolia.[98]

There seems little doubt, therefore, that the rise to prominence of the military magnates of Anatolia which becomes apparent in the sources during the ninth century and after is predicated upon the events and developments of the second half of the seventh century. Whether through their power and authority alone, or whether also through legal and marital assimilation with the pre-existing civilian (senatorial) nobility, they became the dominant landowners in the East and represented a powerful faction at court. But their pre-eminence should not blind us to the existence of other wealthy landowners in other regions of the empire, nor to the fact that the power and wealth of the latter, where it was not inherited, was also, in origin, due to their position in the imperial establishment, their closeness to the palace and to the emperor's circle, and the

[97] See esp. A.H.M. Jones, 'Census records of the later Roman empire', *JRS* 43 (1953), 49–64 (repr. in *The Roman Economy*, pp. 228–56).
[98] See *JGR* I, coll. 3., nov. 6 (pp. 214–17, a. 947, Constantine VII; Dölger, *Regesten*, no. 656); nov. 16 (pp. 243–4, a. 962, Romanus II; Dölger, *Regesten*, no. 690). Compare Basil II's novel of 996 dealing with the vast estates of Eustathius Maleinus, *JGR* I, coll. 3, nov. 29 (pp. 264–5). For the landed elite of the period, see S. Stavrakas, *The Byzantine Provincial Elite: A Study in Social Relationships during the Ninth and Tenth Centuries* (Ann Arbor 1978); J.-F. Vannier, *Familles Byzantines: les Argyroi (IXe–XIIe siècles)* (Paris 1975), esp. pp. 16ff.; W. Seibt, *Die Skleroi: eine prosopographisch-sigillographische Studie* (Vienna 1976); I. Djurić, 'La Famille des Phocas', *ZRVI* 17 (1976), 195–291 (Fr. résumé 293–6); also Morris, 'The powerful and the poor', 16; and D. Papachryssanthou, in *TM* 3 (1968), 309–23 (for the Monomachoi); E. Honigmann, 'Un itinéraire arabe à travers le Pont', *AIPHOS* 4 (1936), 268ff.; H. Grégoire and N. Adontz, 'Nicéphore au col roide', *B* 8 (1933), 203ff.; and esp. M. Kaplan, 'Les grands propriétaires de Cappadoce (VIe–XIe siècles)', in *Le aree omogenee della civiltà rupestre nell'ambito dell'impero bizantino: la Cappadocia* (Galatina 1981), pp.143–8. See further H. Ditten, 'Prominente Slawen und Bulgaren in byzantinischen Diensten (Ende des 7. bis Anfang des 10. Jhdts.)', in *Studien zum 8. und 9. Jahrhundert in Byzanz*, eds. H. Köpstein and F. Winkelmann (*BBA* LI, Berlin 1983), pp. 95–119, see 100ff.

various networks of clientship and patronage which invariably develop as corollaries to a court and its apparatuses. However much influenced by the topoi of the hagiographical genre, the Life of Philaretus does make it clear that large-scale property accumulation or maintenance could take place or continue outside the state and its institutions. For the same period as this Life, other hagiographies similarly refer to the wealth of provincial landowners. The origins of such wealth, of course, must remain unknown – whether acquired by earlier members of the family while in imperial service, granted as a reward for such service, purchased gradually or obtained fraudulently, all are possible. But while a degree of continuity from before the seventh century may be present, it would seem on the basis of the admittedly very limited evidence not to have been very great.[99]

THE SENATORIAL ARISTOCRACY AFTER THE SIXTH CENTURY: SURVIVAL AND ASSIMILATION

The fate of the older landowning elite is uncertain, as we have seen, and it is equally impossible to relate its fortunes to particular regions of the empire or to specific patterns of landholding and their survival, or their decline from the sixth century. On the other hand, something can be said about the changes in the composition of the ruling class of the seventh-century world, from which certain inferences may be drawn.

The chief landowners of the late Roman period had usually been members of the senatorial order, which had since the fourth century undergone an enormous expansion, chiefly a result of the Diocletianic reorganisation, through which senators were initially excluded from all but a few minor civilian posts. The military and most civilian posts of the state were thenceforth supposed to be occupied by members of the equestrian order, membership of which depended upon office, granted by the emperor. The senate itself was a mostly hereditary body, although new members were regularly adlected by the emperor.[100] As a result of Diocletian's reforms, the senate lost much of its former political power, although as a body it still represented the old aristocracy of land and office in the West, and always had great social prestige.

This situation began to change during the fourth century, partly because Constantine I began to employ members of the senatorial order in the administrative machinery of the state on a much wider basis, effectively ignoring the restrictions imposed by Diocletian. Through large numbers of grants of senatorial status to outsiders the senate expanded;

[99] See the remarks of Winkelmann, *Quellenstudien*, pp. 29–31, with sources and literature, for the ninth century.
[100] For the procedure, see Jones, *LRE*, vol. II, pp. 530f.

Rural society   161

while both Constantine and his sons increasingly appointed senators to posts formerly reserved for members of the equestrian order. Many posts now came to be reserved for senators only, thus excluding the equestrian order. The senate in the East, of course, had neither the wealth nor the prestige of that in Rome; but it experienced similar changes and, while in the 350s there had been only some three hundred members, by the 380s there were some two thousand.[101] The reasons for the increase are not hard to find: as an ever greater number of posts were opened up to or reserved for senators, more and more outsiders were appointed to them and received senatorial status; since the occupancy of such offices was limited, the regular intake of newcomers was considerable. By the same token, an ever greater number of palatine officials received senatorial rank on retirement; while the emperors also made a great number of grants of honorary senatorial status. The long-term result was that senatorial rank became increasingly devalued, so that, as Jones pointed out, decurions who had held the high-priesthood of their city were also admitted.[102]

The result of the rapid expansion of the senatorial order was the complete devaluation and ultimate disappearance of the equestrian order, membership of which had depended on office.[103] Diocletian's reorganisation had improved the position of this order at the expense of the senate. Its membership increased greatly, but as the fourth century wore on it became more and more inflated and lost ever more in status and value to the newly expanding senatorial order, until it had effectively disappeared – only some officials in certain palatine bureaux retained the grades of the equestrian order.[104]

The senatorial order, as it expanded, was also regraded internally. Previously, all senators had been *clarissimi*; from the time of Valentinian I a revised system was introduced, in which, while senators by birth and newcomers admitted by a grant of the title, who held no office, still ranked as *clarissimi*, they were preceded in rank by those of *illustris* and *spectabilis* grade, the award of these titles being attached to the holding of imperial posts. The exceptions to the general rule were provided by the titles of consul and ex-consul, who had precedence over all senators – and by the revived title of *patricius*, reintroduced under Constantine I, awarded to

---

[101] Themistius, *Oratio* 34, 456.
[102] The process is well summarised by Jones, *LRE*, vol. II, 527; see also Tinnefeld, *Die frühbyzantinische Gesellschaft*, pp. 66–71.
[103] The order was divided into a number of grades: *egregius, centenarius, ducenarius* and *perfectissimus* (with *eminentissimus* for praetorian prefects) according to salary and post. See Jones, *LRE*, vol. II, p. 525.
[104] Jones, *LRE*, vol. II, pp. 525–7; Tinnefeld, *Die frühbyzantinische Gesellschaft*, p. 71.

individuals as a personal distinction.[105] This alteration was important, especially for the later development of the system of precedence, since its effects were to change the aristocracy of the state from one of birth to one of office. The son of a senator of *illustris* rank was still hereditarily a member of the senatorial order, of course, but he received only the generic title of *clarissimus*.[106] Higher status was attained by holding office or by an imperial grant. During the fifth century, the senatorial order became so enlarged that a tendency to increase the status and privileges of the highest grade, the *illustres*, at the expense of those of *spectabilis* and *clarissimus* rank, is clear. The latter, particularly if they were also *curiales*, were encouraged or indeed compelled to reside in their provinces; under Marcian, they were excused from being nominated for or holding the praetorship and praetorian games in Constantinople, which was their only remaining link to Constantinople and the senate body. By the time of Justinian, only *illustres* could belong to the senate proper and bear the title senator.[107] The title of *clarissimus* was still hereditary, and all sons of senators inherited it. *Spectabilis* was merely an honorific dignity, bearing only very few privileges and attached to a number of lowlier functions. Membership of the senate itself, which had thus once again become a relatively small body, was attained by imperial award of an office carrying the rank of *illustris*, whether active or honorary. This does not mean that the formal rules were always adhered to, since senators could still, often with success, petition the emperor for the title of *illustris* for their sons. The result was that the senate of the sixth century was still made up of a mixture of both hereditary members and those appointed by the emperor. The system was openly pluralistic.

The order of ranks and precedence was complicated still further by distinctions within the highest grade of *illustres*. Honorary offices, with illustrious rank attached, were granted, but with equivalent status to active offices, as opposed to the lower-ranking, purely honorary posts without such a title. The former were referred to as *illustres inter agentes* and were described as titular holders of actual offices (*vacantes*) in opposition to the *honorarii* who held the title as an honorific only.[108] Within the grade of *illustres* new, higher grades were established, those of *magnificus* and *gloriosus* (also as *gloriosissimus*), which in effect replace *illustris* in

---

[105] See *CTh.* VI, 6.1 (a. 382) for consuls; and Zosimus, vol. II, 40 for the title of *patricius*. The Emperor Zeno had insisted upon the rank of consul or the office of praetorian praefect in order for the title of *patricius* to be bestowed (see *CJ* XII, 3.3 proem), but Justinian withdrew this ruling in 537 (Justinian, *Nov.* 62, 2.5). See Stein, *Bas-Empire*, vol. II, p. 430.
[106] Cf. *CJ* XII, 1.11   [107] See *Digesta* I, 9.12 c.l and Jones, *LRE*, vol. II, p. 529.
[108] See Justinian, *Nov.* 62, proem and 1; *CJ* XII, 16.1 (a. 415 = *CTh.* VI, 23.1). Note Stein, *Bas-Empire*, vol. II, p. 429; Jones, *LRE*, vol. II, p. 535.

respect of most of the higher-ranking posts to which it was attached; while Justinian awarded the title of *illustris* to a number of provincial officials and even *curiales* who had previously borne only the ranks of *spectabilis* or *clarissimus*.[109] The reasons lie primarily in the distinctions between the *illustres inter agentes* and active *illustres*, or *gloriosi*, on the one hand, and the lower-ranking *illustres*, on the other.[110] The complexity of the system as a whole is demonstrated for an earlier period in a law of Theodosius II,[111] according to which the order of precedence is: (i) those who actually held offices with illustrious rank; (ii) those who received a titular office (*vacans*) while at court; (iii) those who had received such an office in their absence; (iv) those who received an honorary office at court; (v) those who received such an office in their absence. Members of the first group – the active office-holders – always ranked above the rest; but in groups (ii) to (v) position depended on the rank of the titular or honorary office held: thus an honorary office-holder, the position of whose office in the hierarchy of posts was higher than that of a titular office-holder, would have precedence.[112]

The expression 'senatorial aristocracy' should be used with care, therefore. It refers to both the hereditary group of those who held the title of *clarissimus*, which by Justinian's time must certainly have numbered several thousand, as well as to those lower-ranking *illustres* in the provinces. Many of these would have been landowners of small or middling status, whose property will have been dispersed among several villages and cities, mixed in with the properties of both local *curiales* and of much larger landowners. Some of those referred to above in the Maeander region will have been typical. But the term refers also to those of *magnificus* or *gloriosus* rank, holding actual titular or honorary offices of state (whether or not they resided at Constantinople or had permission to live in their province), men of much greater wealth and social standing. 'Senatorial aristocracy' is a term which, for the sixth and early seventh century at least, is perhaps better used of this group alone, since in relation to

---

[109] Justinian, *Nov.* 70 (a. 538).
[110] See P. Koch, *Die byzantinischen Beamtentitel* (Jena 1903), pp. 41ff. and 70f.; Stein, *Bas-Empire*, vol. II, pp. 429–32 with literature.
[111] *CTh.* VI, 22.8 (a. 425).
[112] All forms of service in the imperial establishment were covered by the general term *militia*; but a distinction was drawn in practice between its specific sense of service as a member of a particular department or unit in the army; and service in one of the higher posts, military or administrative, described also as *dignitates*, *honores* or *administrationes*. The former were filled by issuing *probatoriae* or certificates of appointment; the latter by an imperial codicil and at the emperor's pleasure. Even active positions in this group were regarded as dignities in the general sense, hence the great demand for titular and honorary appointments to such positions, and they were generally referred to as dignities rather than 'posts'.

wealth, power, the patronage of the court and the administration of the government, both in the civil and the military spheres, they constituted the ruling elite – the governing elite within the ruling class – of the empire.

By the late sixth century, and in spite of the reduction in the size of the senate proper which had taken place, the granting of titular and honorary senatorial offices had once again increased its numbers. Justinian, as mentioned already, decreed that only *patricii*, ex-consuls, *illustres* and *illustres inter agentes* could sit on the senate; he also decreed that all members of the consistory (usually all senatorial offices) should be present during senate meetings – and that all senators should participate at judicial sittings of the consistory.[113] The active *illustres*, consisting of those generally referred to as *gloriosi* or *gloriosissimi*, formed the supreme group of senatorial dignities in the civil and military establishment. And while their rank could on occasion, and upon application to the emperor, be conferred upon their sons, such positions were not hereditary and depended to a very great extent upon the emperor. Of course, once a senatorial family had established both contacts to the palace and a basis in landed wealth, it was able to further the interests of its offspring and promote their careers, so that offices and titles could eventually be received by successive generations as their services and suitability were brought to the attention of the emperor or the appropriate officials. But such a system left a great deal of leeway for the emperor or his advisers to promote outsiders, and it left the way open for persons of quite humble rank to rise to positions of considerable power.[114]

In spite of some alterations, it is evident that the system of ranking

---

[113] See Justinian, *Nov.* 62, 1 and Stein, *Bas-Empire*, vol. II, p. 432 and literature. Justinian also decreed (*Nov.* 62, 2, a. 537) that *patricii* were henceforth to have precedence over those with consular titles and that precedence among this group was to be determined on their having held one of the variety of consular offices (whether titular, honorary or whatever). According to this novel, the prefect of the city (*praefectus urbis*) was now to have first place, followed by the 'other' *patricii*, then the consuls and *consularii*, and then the praetorian prefects, *magistri militum*, and other *illustres*. The consistory (*consistorium*) included leading members of the senate and the civil and military establishment appointed *ad hominem*: the *magister officiorum*, *quaestor*, *comes sacrarum largitionum*, *comes rei privatae*, praetorian prefect (when present), *comes domesticorum*, *comes excubitorum*, *magister militum praesentalis*, along with other former and titular holders of offices, as well as those who were not formally members of the senate but whom the emperor wished to consult. See Jones, *LRE*, vol. I, pp. 333ff. By the early seventh century, the *sacellarius* seems also to have played a key role: he is referred to as the highest-ranking of the senators present at the interrogation of Maximus Confessor (see *PG* XC, 88C; 101A-B; 113A-B). A description preserved in the tenth-century Book of Ceremonies (*De Cerimoniis*), 628.10–14 for the year 638 describes a senatorial procession of the *endoxotatoi patrikioi*, along with those of *apo hypaton* rank and others of senatorial grade down to simple *illustres*.

[114] See Jones' commentary, *LRE*, vol. II, pp. 551ff.; and for evidence of continuity, especially in the West, see Arnheim, *Senatorial Aristocracy*, pp. 103ff. and 155ff.

senatorial offices does not change dramatically through much of the seventh century. The titles of *patrikios*, *hypatos* (consul) and *apo hypatōn* (ex-consul) continue to be awarded by the emperor or claimed by officeholders of the appropriate rank. The development is complicated, however, by the increase in importance and status of titles conferring membership of a number of palatine *ordines*, both civil and military, which are used together with the traditional titles of rank as well as with titles of offices. Concomitantly, the value of several titles and their status seems to decline gradually during the seventh century. Most obvious is the title of *stratēlatēs* or *magister militum*, originally designating one of the leading military commands, already by the reign of Justinian awarded to relatively humble commanders of contingents, both on an active, and a titular and honorary basis.[115] During the seventh century, the title of *stratēgos* came to be applied to the actual commanders of the provincial forces – the *themata* – and this further depressed the value of *stratēlatēs*, which now signified no active duties or competence. Like *stratēlatēs*, the general descriptive terms for members of the senatorial establishment – *gloriosus/ gloriosissimus*, or *endoxotatos* in Greek – continue in use, to define the members of the Constantinopolitan senate as determined by Justinian in novel 62.[116] But the fact that titles and the system of precedence demonstrate a great deal of continuity tells us little, if anything, about continuity in the senatorial class itself – whether defined in the narrower sense or in the more general meaning of all the *clarissimi* and *spectabiles* as well.

A hint may be supplied by looking at the names of those mentioned in the various sources who occupy positions of power, and by looking at the relationship between names, titles and offices.

To begin with, even a superficial prosopographical survey of the period shows a marked increase in the number of non-Latin and non-Greek names among palatine officials, imperial advisers, and especially among military personnel. Charanis has shown how central a role was played by Armenians at this time, for example, who already from the later sixth century seem to have become increasingly important. By the end of the reign of Heraclius, and during the reigns of his son Heraclius Constantine and grandson Constans II, members of Armenian noble families occupy key positions in both the central and the provincial military administration

---

[115] For example, the *magister militum vacans* Martinus, in 535; and the three *magistri militum vacantes* under the command of Belisarius in Sicily in the same year. See Stein, *Bas-Empire*, vol. II, pp. 323–4 and note 1; p. 430 and note 3.
[116] For a more detailed analysis of titulature, see chapter 10 below.

of the empire, often endowed with titles of senatorial rank.[117] But persons of Iranian, Slav and Germanic origins were also to be found.[118]

At the same time, while there seems little reason to doubt that many of the leading officers and persons mentioned in the sources in this connection did hold senatorial dignities, whether or not this was made explicit, the position and role of the senate changes over the period under examination here. Traditionally, the senate had played, since the fifth century, a central role in the selection and ratification of a new emperor – and during the events surrounding a succession in general. It has been shown that this was the case during the fifth and sixth centuries, as well as in the events surrounding the election of Heraclius and his immediate successors.[119] And while, according to Justinian's novel 62, the senate had by that time entrusted its executive functions to the emperor,[120] it is clear that the senate as a body, made up in part at least of active officials of state of considerable power and wealth, along with other members of the landed wealthy elite of the empire, continued to exercise a very great *de facto* authority. Those who were included among the group of leading advisers to the emperor had formed a cabinet within the older consistory and were referred to as the *proceres sacri palatii*. They represented the real power at the court. The senate and the consistory themselves – which from Justinian's time were effectively equivalent bodies with a shared membership – had few opportunities formally to intervene. Only at times of crisis, such as when a problem over the succession arose, for example, were they able to function as an independent body, usually to represent, as well as their own

[117] See P. Charanis, 'The Armenians in the Byzantine empire', *BS* 22 (1961), 196–240, esp. 205f. and 'Ethnic changes', 32ff. See also W. Seibt, *Die byzantinischen Bleisiegel in Österreich I, Kaiserhof* (Vienna 1978), p. 165; Winkelmann, *Quellenstudien*, pp. 203ff. and literature at p. 230 note 849. But note the more reserved position of S. Gero, 'Armenians in Byzantium: some reconsiderations', *Journal of Armenian Studies* 2 (1985), 13–26.

[118] See Winkelmann, *Quellenstudien*, pp. 199ff. (mostly eighth century or later); H. Ditten, *Prominente Slawen und Bulgaren*, pp.100ff.; R. Guilland, 'Les Patrices byzantins de la première moitié du VIIe siècle', Τόμος εἰς μνήμην Κ. Ι. Ἀμάντου (Athens 1960), pp. 11–24 (repr. in R. Guilland, *Recherches sur les institutions byzantines* (2 vols., Berlin and Amsterdam 1967), pp. 162–9) and 'Patrices de Constantin IV à Théodose III', *Hellenika* 23 (1970), 287–98 (repr. in *Titres et fonctions* VIII).

[119] See the detailed studies of Ch. Diehl, 'Le Sénat et le peuple byzantin aux VIIe et VIIIe siècles', *B* 1 (1924), 201–13; H.-G. Beck, *Senat und Volk von Konstantinopel. Probleme der byzantinischen Verfassungsgeschichte*, in *SBB* (1966), pp. 1–75 (repr. in *Ideen und Realitäten in Byzanz* XII (London 1972).

[120] Justinian, *Nov.* 62, proem: 'Antiquissimis temporibus Romani senatus auctoritas tanto vigore potestatis effulsit, ut eius gubernatione domi forisque habita iugo Romano omnis mundus subiceretur, non solum ad ortus solis et occasus, sed etiam in utrumque latus orbis terrae Romana dicione propagata ... Postea vero quam ad maiestatem imperatoriam ius populi Romani et senatus felicitate reipublicae translatum est, evenit ut ii, quos ipsi elegerint et adminstrationibus praeposuerint, omnia facerent quae vox imperialis eis iniunxisset ...'

interests, those of the population of Constantinople and the ruling administrative circles.[121] The occasions on which senatorial intervention was important during the sixth century are illustrative: the selection and acclamation of a successor to Anastasius in 518; during the Nika riot in 532; during the reign of Maurice, when the senate formally advised the emperor to treat with the khagan of the Avars; and before and during the revolution which led to the downfall of Phocas.[122] In addition, of course, the senate was present and played a formal role at all accessions and acclamations; but its power as a body was, on the whole, less important than the power exercised by its members as individuals within the government.

In the seventh century this general pattern is repeated. The senate appears to have played a formal role as one of the three constitutive elements in every imperial election (senate, people and army): in the accession of Phocas,[123] of Heraclius,[124] of Heraclius Constantine – in the last case the Armenian chronicler Sebeos emphasises the fact that Heraclius placed his son's future in the care of the senate, a fact which may suggest the reason for the central role played by this body in the events that followed, and hints also at the differences between the various factions surrounding Heraclius on the one hand, and his wife and niece Martina on the other.[125] In the confused events following the death of Heraclius Constantine, the deposition of Martina and Heracleonas, the rebellion of Valentinus and the accession of Constans II as sole ruler, the senate again plays a crucial role and is, according to the words of the young Constans, reported by Theophanes, the adviser to the emperor and the protector of the people. Sebeos also notes the central role of the senate and lays stress on the fact that it was the latter body which worked against the plans of the general Valentinus to have himself confirmed as co-emperor.[126] Heraclius seems to have placed a great deal of value on the senate and its support, both in the proceedings against Priscus, the son-in-law of Phocas (and a member of the senate himself) and in his dealings with the Avars.[127] The

---

[121] See Jones, *LRE*, vol. I, p. 325.
[122] See the brief summary of Tinnefeld, *Die frühbyzantinische Gesellschaft*, pp. 77ff. with references and literature; Jones, *LRE*, vol. I, pp. 267f. and 271f.; Stein, *Bas-Empire*, vol. II, pp. 219ff. and 449ff.; and Diehl, 'Le Sénat et le peuple byzantin' (cited in note 119 above). For the embassy to the khagan, see Theophylact Simocatta VII, 15.8; Theophanes, 279.20sq.
[123] Cf. Theophylact Simocatta VIII, 10.2 and 3.15.   [124] Nicephorus, 5.14–16.
[125] Sebeos, 67, 80. Sebeos' reliability is, of course, open to question, writing as he was well away from the scenes he reported.
[126] Theophanes, 331.3sq., 341.24–7, 342.15sq.; Sebeos, 105.
[127] Nicephorus, 6.9–11; see A. Pernice, *L'imperatore Eraclio, Saggio di storia bizantina* (Florence 1905), pp. 48f.; Stratos, *Byzantium in the Seventh Century*, vol. I, p. 100; and *Chron. Pasch.* 706.17sq.

interrogations of both Pope Martin and of Maximus Confessor were carried out before the senate, and it was senators who continued the examinations afterwards – the patrician and *sacellarius* Troilus and the patrician Epiphanius played a major role as intermediaries.[128] Some continuity of family and position is suggested in the account of the trial of Maximus, where Theodore, the son of John the *candidatus* and brother-in-law of Platon the *patricius* is brought as a witness against Maximus.[129] Sergius, the *epi tēs trapezēs*, is also a leading member of the senatorial opposition. Similarly, the patrician Troilus may be the father of Andreas, the member of the retinue of Constans II responsible for his death in 668; while the *patricius* Justinian, the father of the later patriarch Germanus, was also involved in the same plot.[130] During the reign of Constantine IV the senate seems to have supported the emperor in opposing the wishes of the soldiers of the *Anatolikōn* district that the emperor's brothers should be equal co-emperors with him;[131] and again under Justinian II the senate supported his preparations against Cherson.[132] The senate seems also to have supported the attempt of Philippicus Bardanes to reintroduce monotheletism; but it was equally involved, although to what extent is difficult to say, in the deposition of Philippicus and the accession of Anastasius II.[133] The senate, or members of it, may well have been behind the rebellion of Leontius against Justinian II in 695; and it was the senate, together with the city troops, which in all probability called upon Theodosius III to abdicate in favour of Leo III in 717.[134]

As a formally constituted body, therefore, made up of the chief palatine officials, both civil and military, the senate seems to have continued to play the role which it had in the sixth century throughout the seventh and well into the eighth century. This is hardly surprising, since it included all the most powerful advisers and officials of the imperial administration in

---

[128] See *PG* XC 88C; 113A-B: the *sakellarios* Troilus ranked highest among the senators. For possible seals, see Seibt, *Bleisiegel*, no. 132, a seal of Troilus *patrikios*; and Zacos and Veglery, no. 3061, seal of Troilus, *apo hypatōn*. See also *PG* XC 101A-B (Troilus and Epiphanius, both *patrikioi*). Other senators of consular rank named include Paul and Theodosius (*PG* XC, 96D; and see 109D, 113A-B, 137B).

[129] *PG* XC 113C. See also note 139 below.

[130] *PG* XC, 120B. For Andreas, the son of Troilus, see Seibt, *Bleisiegel*, at no. 132; Theophanes, 351.29; and P. Peeters, 'Une vie grecque du Pape S. Martin', *AB* 51 (1933), 259 and note 1. For the *patricius* Justinian, see Guilland, *Recherches*, vol. 2, p. 166.

[131] Theophanes, 352.19sq. See Diehl, 'Le Sénat et le peuple', 208; also Michael Syr. XI, 13 (vol. II 455f.).

[132] Nicephorus, 44.16–20.

[133] Nicephorus, 48.12–14; Zonaras XIV, 26; Agathon Diac., 192. See Beck, *Senat und Volk*, p. 31.

[134] For Theodosius III see Theophanes, 390.20sq.; Nicephorus, 52.15sq. On these events, see Beck, *Senat und Volk*, pp. 31ff.

Rural society   169

Constantinople.¹³⁵ And that some degree of continuity of family and personnel existed is suggested by the few examples mentioned just now.¹³⁶ But the increasing number of newcomers to the ranks of the senate as imperial officials in the reigns of Justinian II and his successors especially suggests that by this time the relative proportion of 'old' senatorial families to 'new' members was shifting in favour of the latter. As I have said, membership of the clarissimate had been hereditary; that of the higher grades – *spectabiles, illustres* and *gloriosi* – more limited, although evidence for imperial concessions of a father's rank and title to his son upon formal request exists, at least for the sixth century, as Jones has shown.¹³⁷ Even without this element, however, a relatively high degree of continuity might be expected, given the wealth, power and contacts of the senatorial establishment in Constantinople and its richer associates, certainly up until the 650s, as our evidence might suggest.

The names of those with the title *patrikios* collected by Guilland for the years up to 668 compare and contrast interestingly with those for the following period up to 717. Of forty named *patrikioi* known from 602 to 668, only three have non-Greek or non-Latin names, two of which are Persian and one Armenian. For the period to 717, however, thirty-four named *patrikioi* are known, of whom three have Armenian or Caucasian names, and eleven are given epithets – such as Myakios, Rizokopos, Bouraphos, Pitzigaudes and so on. Guilland's list and figures can be supplemented from the seals now available, and they do not appreciably alter this picture. This evidence suggests the arrival of 'outsiders' on the scene, whose advancement is a result of imperial favour and promotion; as well as the need to differentiate among them by the use of such descriptive terms. It suggests, in effect, the increasing importance of men from outside the older establishment and the older circle – however large it may have been – of senatorial families.¹³⁸ Of course, it provides only the crudest of

---

[135] All those with the title of *patricius* will have been senators; in addition, the leading palatine officers were members (see note 113 above), and by the early eighth century some of their staff as well. There is no reason to doubt, for example, that the various officials involved in the interrogation of Maximus were also senators (see, for example, PG XC, 88C: the *sakellarios*; and 120B: the ἐπὶ τῆς τραπέζης τῆς βασιλικῆς, and note 226 above); while the officials present at the sixth council in 680 (Mansi XI 209ff.: master of offices, count of the *Opsikion*, military logothete, curator of the imperial House of Hormisdas, the lieutenant of the count of the excubitors, quaestor, *dioikētēs* of the Eastern provinces, domestic of the imperial table and five others with no named functions) will all have been *endoxotatoi* and senators. In the proem to the Ecloga of 741 the quaestor and his staff are counted as *endoxotatoi*, the former being a *patrikios*, the latter merely *hypatoi* (see *Ecloga*, ed. Burgmann, 104f., 162.40–2).
[136] See Haldon, *Byzantine Praetorians*, pp. 156f and 158f.
[137] Jones, *LRE*, vol. II, pp. 529–30.
[138] The lists are to be found in the articles of Guilland cited in note 118 above; and see the comments of Winkelmann, *Zum byzantinischen Staat*, pp. 204ff., and 'Probleme der

guides: many newcomers will certainly have borne traditional Greek or Latin names, while some of the epithets – such as *strouthos*, for example, the sparrow – may simply have been popular nicknames. But the comparison is suggestive, in spite of the methodological uncertainty.[139] And it is important to bear in mind also that this development seems to represent only the opening stage of the genesis and formation of a new ruling class, marked during the later eighth and ninth centuries in particular by the appearance of some 150 family names – *nomina gentilia* – and the clear appearance in the sources of an elite whose social and political power is based upon both imperial service, as well as clan property in land. In this

gesellschaftlichen Entwicklung im 8. und 9. Jahrhundert', in *17th International Byzantine Congress, Major Papers*, pp. 577–90, see 581f. and note 34. The evidence of the names used on seals, which represents a much wider variety of offices, is also telling: there is an increase in the number of names of non-Greek and non-Latin origin, through the seventh and into the eighth century, which, while hardly conclusive, is evidence of their introduction from a variety of sources (particularly Armenian) into the Greek cultural milieu. Names such as Vasakios (Seibt, *Bleisiegel*, no. 1335; Zacos and Veglery, nos. 721, 1089, 1672), Vaanes (Zacos and Veglery, nos. 1086, 1671, 2569), Arazat (Zacos and Veglery, no. 590A), Arsakios (Zacos and Veglery, no. 591), Mouselios/Mousilios (Zacos and Veglery, nos. 662, 946, 947), Arsaphios (Zacos and Veglery, nos 1115, 1420), Rostom (Zacos and Veglery, nos. 2343, 3046), which illustrate the degree of Armenian influence – as well as those such as Baianos (Zacos and Veglery, no. 594), Tourganēs (Seibt, *Bleisiegel*, no. 199) or Oulid (Zacos and Veglery, nos. 1566, 1567, 3042), of Turkic and Arabic origin respectively – demonstrate the penetration of the early Byzantine establishment, both military and civil, by 'new' elements on a considerable scale, and in stark contrast with the sixth century, when such elements – whether Germanic, Turkic or Iranian – were limited for the most part to the military. See also Winkelmann, *Quellenstudien*, pp. 146ff. on nick-names which became *nomina gentilia*, and pp. 197ff. on names of non-Greek origin.

[139] Equally tantalising is the appearance of seals in the later seventh and eighth centuries of individuals, sometimes with their title (usually *hypatos, apo hypatōn, patrikios*, but including also those of *kandidatos* and *spatharios*) along with an expression of a familial relationship: son of ... (e.g., Zacos and Veglery, nos. 363, 388, 370, 531, 782, 879, 1827, 2229, 2336, 2641, 3040, 3117, and possibly nos. 2126, 2060, and 1460). Might these represent the efforts of older senatorial families to emphasise their lineage? Or of persons whose fathers were newly established (and thus in their time well known), among the elite of the state establishment?The question has been addressed by J. Nesbitt, 'Double names in early Byzantine lead seals', *DOP* 31 (1977), 111–21, see 109ff. and by Winkelmann, *Quellenstudien*, pp. 144–6, with further examples from the eighth century, from literary sources. On the whole, such references would seem to back the second rather than the first suggestion, depending as they do on the person or persons named on the seal being known to the reader. Of course, as Winkelmann's detailed treatment has demonstrated, the generalisation from the specific 'son of' to 'of the line/family of' (which is what the phrase ὁ κατὰ τὸν/τοὺς most probably is meant to convey, cf. *Quellenstudien*, pp. 151f.) is evidence for the establishment of specific families with an awareness of their lineage identity. But the great majority of the known examples seem to represent families evolving in the eighth century and after – there is no real evidence for continuity here. Interesting is the possibility that a seal of John, *kandidatos*, son of Hadrian (dated c. 600–50) may have belonged to the John, *kandidatos*, nicknamed Chilas, whose son Theodore, the brother-in-law of the *patrikios* Plato, was a witness during the interrogation of Maximus (*PG* XC, 113C). For the seal (the reading of which is, however, problematic) see Zacos and Veglery, no. 370.

respect, the later seventh century seems to mark a real transformation, with the subsumption of the older establishment into the nascent service aristocracy of the middle Byzantine period.[140]

The sum of this evidence suggests, therefore, that the older senatorial establishment, in the narrower sense as defined above, survived, in spite of some confiscation during the reign of Justinian after the Nika riot and in spite of the supposed mass execution of many senators during the reign of Phocas, more or less intact into the seventh century.[141] It continued to dominate the administration of the state as a class; but, as the dramatic changes of the second half of the seventh century began to take their toll, it became increasingly populated by newcomers whose arrival served to strengthen its essential character as an elite of service rather than of birth or cultural tradition, and to weaken the cultural-political hegemony of the older aristocracy. That some families may have survived is quite probable, of course, and an element of continuity in landed property and family ideology is not to be excluded, especially in areas least affected by the physical disruption of the times. Such a family may have been that of Botaneiates, a name which occurs as early as the sixth century, although the family (if it is the same, and not a coincidence) is best known from the eleventh century.[142] It is unfortunately impossible to generalise either in favour of or against continuity from this single example; it is difficult to know whether the limited sources reflect the historical situation or their own limitations.

In terms of the social relations of production in the empire as a whole, therefore, the seventh century marks the emergence of a new factor within the ruling class, formed from among the members of the provincial and Constantinopolitan service elite. It also witnessed the beginnings of a process of assimilation between the two groups dominating the social and political life of the state, the older 'senatorial' establishment and the newer 'service' elite. I will discuss some of the implications of this in chapter 10 below. Large estates continued to exist, probably on a very similar scale to that of the sixth century; but the growth in long-term leases on estates at the expense of the older colonate, together with increased mobility among the rural populations of the empire, a change in the system of tax-assessment and collection, and the increased availability of land and the arrival

---

[140] In this respect, Winkelmann's survey in *Quellenstudien* of the names for the eighth and ninth centuries is extremely important, and it illustrates a caesura in the nomenclature of the elite between the late Roman and middle Byzantine periods very clearly. See esp. pp. 143ff.: 'Symptome und Tendenzen der Konsolidierung einer Magnatenschicht'.

[141] For confiscations after 532, see Procopius, *Historia Arcana* XII, 12f.; and for the events of the reign of Phocas, see above, and Tinnefeld, *Die frühbyzantinische Gesellschaft*, pp. 97–9.

[142] See G. Buckler, 'A sixth-century Botaneiates?' *B* 6 (1931), 405–10, and Winkelmann, *Quellenstudien*, pp. 158 and 181.

of imported labour power, all promoted the importance and the numbers of communities of independent peasant smallholders subject directly to the fisc. By the early eighth century the sum total of all these changes and developments adds up to a very different set of relations of production within the Byzantine world of Asia Minor and the Balkans.

CHAPTER 5

The state and its apparatus: fiscal administration

THE LATE ROMAN SYSTEM

In chapters 3 and 4, I outlined the chief developments in the relations between cities and their hinterlands on the one hand, and between landowners and the rural agricultural population of the empire on the other. These developments provide the backdrop to the subject of this chapter and the next, that is, the administrative structures of the Byzantine state, its mode of revenue extraction and distribution, and its military machinery. For the fiscal and military establishments form the two central and interrelated elements of the state administrative apparatuses which secure both its physical defence and its political and institutional reproduction. Contingent upon these are the mode of civil provincial administration and the conduct of foreign policy, and it is to these areas that I shall turn in this chapter.

Let me begin, therefore, with the machinery of revenue extraction. The changes that took place in the organisation of this aspect of state administration during the seventh century were considerable; and the best way to illustrate this, and then to attempt to demonstrate the causes of change and their process, will be to sketch out briefly the systems of the later Roman period (up to about 600) and of the Byzantine period (of about 800–900), respectively.

During the sixth century the extraction and administration of revenues had been organised under the auspices of three departments: the praetorian prefectures, the *comitiva sacrarum largitionum* and the *res privata*. The *res privata* was responsible for the administration and collection of rents from state lands; it included all lands which lapsed to the state, as well as lands which had been inherited from the previous rulers of districts as they had been incorporated into the empire. Properties bequeathed to the emperors, the family property of those who had occupied the imperial throne, former public and civic lands, estates confiscated for one reason or another, all these lands were administered by this department, whose staff, therefore, was considerable. Often, large tracts of whole provinces – as, for example, much of Cappadocia I or Bithynia – belonged to the imperial domain. The administration of this property was headed by the *comes rei privatae*. His bureau (*officium*) was divided into a number of subdepartments or *scrinia*, each responsible for specific functions: grants of lands, rents, leases and so on. In each diocese and province were provincial staffs to collect and supervise rents, and to administer the various consolidated or dispersed estates. The revenues drawn from this source were employed in the first instance in the maintenance of the imperial household, being dispensed probably through its treasury, the *scrinium largitionum privatarum*. But the emperor could also draw upon the *res privata* as a source of reserves for purposes of state or the granting of largesses.

Anastasius formalised this arrangement by setting up a new department, separate from the *privata*, called the *patrimonium*, at the disposal of the emperor and subordinate to the department of the *sacrae largitiones* (see below) – the *privata* continuing to be used as a source of state and fiscal income. Already in the later fourth century, the estates in Cappadocia (the *domus divina per Cappadociam*) had been transferred directly to the charge of the *praepositus sacri cubiculi*, the palatine official directly responsible for the imperial household and its administration. Under Justinian, further marking-off occurred, with the result that the *res privata* was divided by 566 into some five branches: the original *res privata*, the *patrimonium*, the *domus divina per Cappadociam*, the *domus dominicae* (two sections, each under *curatores*, administering estates whose revenues were allocated apparently to the personal expenses of the rulers) and the *patrimonium Italiae* under its *comes* (following the reconquest of Italy: it seems to have been constituted of land confiscated from the Ostrogothic nobility and rulers, as well as of older imperial lands).[1]

---

[1] For a full and detailed treatment, see Jones, *LRE*, vol. I, pp. 412–27; Stein, *Bas-Empire*, vol. I, pp. 174 and 341; vol. II, p. 67 and note 1, pp. 423ff., 472–3 and 748ff.; note also J.B. Bury, *The Imperial Administrative System in the Ninth Century, With a Revised Text of the Kletorologion of Philotheos* (British Academy Suppl. Papers I, London 1911), p. 79, who assumes the *curator* mentioned in a novel of Justin II (*JGR* I, coll. 1, nov. 1; a. 566 = Dölger, *Regesten*, no. 4) to be an independent official in charge of both the Cappadocian lands and the *domus dominicae*, a forerunner of the later *megas kourator* (cf. Oikonomidès, *Préséance*, p. 318). According to a novel of Tiberius Constantine (*JGR*, I, coll. 1, nov. 12; a. 578–82 = Dölger, *Regesten*, no. 67) the *domus divinae* included also the *patrimonium* for practical administrative purposes; and although several *curatores* are referred to in this novel, there is every reason to suppose that the system was again centralised during the seventh century – possibly before the Arab wars, possibly as a result of them. There may in any case, as Bury supposes, have been several *curatores* under the disposition of a (*megas*) *kourator* at Constantinople, perhaps that in charge of the estates of Hormisdas. See Jones, *LRE*, vol. I, p. 426; Stein, *Studien*, p. 98 and note 7: the *curator* of the estates of Hormisdas was clearly one of the leading officials in charge of imperial properties. See also the

The department of the *sacrae largitiones* administered bullion from gold and silver mines, as well as the mines themselves, together with the mints, the workshops where parade armour was decorated with precious metals, the production and collection of clothing (for historical reasons) and the state dye-works. During the fourth century the armour-decorating workshops were transferred to the supervision of the *magister officiorum*. The count of the sacred largesses (*comes sacrarum largitionum*) also issued the donatives in silver and gold which the soldiers received. As with the *res privata* there was a central bureau with provincial staffs. The central *officium* consisted of ten departments or *scrinia*, responsible for general clerical matters, revenues, accounts, messengers, military donatives, bullion, diocesan reserves of gold, and mints; as well as the imperial wardrobe, silver and silver coin, palatine silversmiths, copper, and (originally) arms and armour decorators. Each diocese had a representative from the department, and there were a number of regional treasuries where gold, silver and finished clothing could be stored. The mints were supervised from these points. In addition, the *sacrae largitiones* had representatives in the cities, responsible for administering the revenues drawn from confiscated civic lands; it also had its own transport service (like the *res privata*); and it was responsible for the controllers of foreign trade, the *comites commerciorum*. The income of the *largitiones* derived from the surviving cash taxes in gold and silver, customs and import duties, the donations made by cities and the senate on the occasion of an imperial accession (the *aurum coronarium* and *aurum oblaticium*) and quinquennial celebrations, as well as the commutations received in lieu of recruits, the *aurum tironicum*, and of military horses, each rated at about 25–30 gold *solidi*. A cash assessment on land may also have provided some funds, although the rate of assessment is unknown, as is the extent of application of such an assessment.[2]

The mints were probably the most important element in the administrative machinery of the *largitiones*. They were run by *procuratores* and staffed by *monetarii*, who constituted a hereditary group from the fourth century, often quite wealthy, although by origin they were mostly imperial slaves. Following the reconquests of Justinian's reign, there were mints at Con-

---

discussion of D. Feissel, 'Magnus, Mégas et les curateurs des "maisons divines" de Justin II à Héraclius', *TM* 9 (1985), 465–76, esp. 474f.; and M. Kaplan, 'Quelques aspects des "maisons divines" du VIe au IXe siècle', in *Mélanges N. Svoronos* (Paris 1986), pp. 70–96. For the *scrinium largitionum privatarum*, see *Notitia Dig.*, occ. XII, 4. Bury surmises (*Administrative System*, pp. 81–2) that part of the income from this source also went into the emperor's private treasury, the *sacellum*. See below.

[2] See Jones, *LRE*, vol. I, pp. 427–34; Stein, *Bas-Empire*, vol. II, pp. 426f., 761f. and 766–9; J.P.C. Kent, in E. Cruikshank-Dodd, *Byzantine Silver Stamps* (Dumbarton Oaks Studies VII Washington D.C. 1961), pp. 35ff.; and the contribution of R. Delmaire, in *Hommes et richesses* I, 265–77.

stantinople, Thessaloniki, Carthage and Ravenna, the last two acquired by reconquest, all producing gold coin; and at Nicomedia, Cyzicus, Antioch, Alexandria (and temporarily also at Rome, Salona, Carthagena, and Cherson) producing copper. During the reign of Maurice, a mint was set up in Sicily, at Catania; and during that of Heraclius, temporary mints were established at Constantia in Cyprus and at Seleucia in Isauria (later at Isaura itself) (from 582/3, and in 615 to 618 respectively).[3] The mints themselves were organised at the diocesan level, and although this had not been the original intention, since several of the mints actually pre-dated the reforms of Diocletian and Constantine through which the dioceses were established, the result in the sixth century was that the major dioceses had each one mint for copper; while the minting of gold was limited to prefectural capitals or their equivalents, that is, Constantinople, Ravenna and Carthage.

The bullion for the coinage came from levies in kind where the land was ore-bearing, from mining and panning, from confiscated plate (not always inconsiderable amounts) and, chiefly, through the recycling of gold coin via the fiscal machinery of the state back to the *largitiones*. From Valens and Valentinian onwards gold coin was melted down in the provinces before being shipped back to the capital, or the imperial *comitatus*, in bullion form for re-minting. The export of gold was strictly prohibited, as was the clipping of any coin, in particular gold. By these means the state tried to recover the gold it issued in coin, although inevitably it was not entirely successful. But as Jones notes, the frequent re-minting of the gold must have constituted a crucial factor in the maintenance of the weight and purity of the *solidus*.[4]

In spite of their sizeable incomes and their functions, both the *sacrae largitiones* and the *res privata* were over-shadowed by the praetorian prefectures. The prefecture comprised a specific territorial area, subdivided into dioceses, under *vicarii*, and then into provinces under local governors with a variety of titles (*moderatores, rectores* and so on), each comprising a group of *civitates*. The office of the prefecture was responsible for the corn supply for the capital(s) and certain other cities, as well as for the costs incurred in transporting this by the guild of state shippers or *navicularii*; it was responsible for the rations or ration allowances, in kind or in cash, for the army, civil service, and related departments of state, as well as the

---

[3] Jones, *LRE*, vol. I, pp. 374 and 437ff.; A.R. Bellinger, *Catalogue of the Byzantine Coins in the Dumbarton Oaks Collection and in the Whittemore Collection*, vol. I, *Anastasius I to Maurice, 491–602* (Washington D.C. 1966), pp. 64f.; M.F. Hendy, 'On the administrative basis of the Byzantine coinage, *c*. 400–900, and the reforms of Heraclius', *Birmingham University Historical Journal*, 12/2 (1970), 129–54, see 140ff.; Ph. Grierson, *DOC* II, 1, pp. 209 and 327–30.

[4] Jones, *LRE*, vol. I, p. 435f.

fodder allowance of officers and troopers in cavalry units and their civilian counterparts. It was also responsible for the maintenance and operation of the public post; for that of the state arms workers along with their materials (although not for the arms factories or *fabricae*, which came under the authority of the *magister officiorum*); and for the public works of the provinces, levying labour and materials from local communities for roads, bridges, granaries, post stations and so on. From Diocletian's time the rate of assessment in kind (later commuted into cash) and the estimates needed to meet this wide range of needs had been systematised into a single general levy, raised each year, referred to as the *indictio*. The rate might vary from year to year, however, according to need, and the assessment was at least in theory not a fixed tariff. As the greater part of this indictional levy was commuted to gold during the last years of the fifth century, in the East, so the prefectures were able to build up reserves to meet exigencies and thus, to a degree, make the maintenance of a single established rate possible.

Until Justinian's reign, there were two prefectures in the eastern part of the empire, that of Illyricum and that of Oriens, the former based at Thessaloniki, the latter at Constantinople. The size and wealth of the latter gave it a pre-eminent position. During the reign of Justinian, the prefectures of Italy (based at Ravenna) and Africa (based at Carthage) were re-established (in 537 and 534 respectively), and as we have seen, the *quaestura exercitus* was also set up. Map VI illustrates the diocesan and provincial composition of the empire *c.* 565.[5]

Since it is of some importance for an understanding of the development and origins of the later provincial and central administration, it is worth pausing for a moment to examine in greater detail the structure of the prefecture of the East. Each diocese was represented by a *scrinium* (although Egypt, which was otherwise an independent diocesan district under the *Praefectus Augustalis*, was included in the *scrinium* for Oriens, to which it pertained); there was further a *scrinium* for Constantinople, for public works, for arms (the assessment and collection of materials for the state factories) and other departments for the purchase of corn for Constantinople and other cities; for the assessment and collection of the *annonae* (rations) for the troops (referred to as the *stratiōtikon*); and there was also a prefectural treasury or *arca*, divided into two sections on account of the size and complexity of the fiscal operations of the Eastern prefecture, the general and the special bank (*genikē trapeza, idikē trapeza*). The special bank was responsible for the assessment of the *collatio lustralis*, the tax on merchant and craft sales introduced by Constantine I, but

[5] See Jones, *LRE*, vol. I, pp. 370–2 and 448f. For map VI see p. 228 below.

abolished by Anastasius. The other prefectures had a similar, if less ramified, bureaucracy. The diocesan *scrinia* were headed each by two *numerarii*, assisted by an *adiutor* and a *chartularius* or accountant; the staff consisted of *tractatores* or *trakteutai*, each responsible for the accounts of one province, assisted in turn by a clerical member of staff who dealt with correspondence. Supervisory staff were despatched to each province to advise on the collection of the indictional assessment and to help with the extraction of arrears, the latter referred to as *compulsores* or *expelleutai*.

The calculations for the indiction depended upon returns submitted by the competent state officials: those responsible for the military, civil and administrative staffs of all branches of the state apparatus. While allowances were fixed, yearly requirements often varied according to circumstances, so that the indiction was not always adequate. In this case, *superindictiones* on the whole prefecture, or on a single diocese or province, could be imposed to raise the necessary shortfall in supplies or cash. In addition corvées, or *munera sordida* (such as providing bread for the troops quartered in the district, supplying stone or timber, craftsmen and labour for public works, billetting and providing animals for officials of the state and so forth), were also levied, although certain privileged groups were exempted from such duties, such as senators, for example. In short, the assessment of tax was based on the principle of a distributive allocation: the state calculated its needs first, and then proceeded to assess tax-payers at a rate which would, as far as could be predicted, ensure the meeting of those targets.[6]

The actual assessment of the indiction was based upon the *capitatio/ iugatio* calculation, described in chapter 4, although the rates varied from province to province with regard to both the size and the number of units of land and labour power in question. Thus the total needs for each province would be calculated in accordance with the number of *capita* and *iuga*, together with a variety of other factors regarding the economic situation of the territory in question, the amount of arrears that might be owed and so forth. The prefecture then circulated the assessment to the diocesan *vicarii* and provincial governors. From then on the municipal officers appointed by the town councils were responsible for the issue of tax-demands to tax-payers, and for their collection by the curial *susceptores/ hypodektai* and *procuratores/epimelētai*. The *vindex* appointed from the time of Anastasius to each city was effectively a collection-manager and tax-farmer, who continued to employ the curial collectors, but who was responsible directly to the prefecture. While unpopular, they were apparently very efficient, and this system was retained through Justinian's

[6] Jones, *LRE*, vol. I, p. 449 and pp. 450–3. For the difference between distributive and contributive modes of assessment, see Oikonomidès, 'L'Impôt de distribution', 9–11.

reign.[7] But the tendency of provincial governors to appoint their own officials to govern cities on the one hand, a development which, although frowned upon by the emperors, led to the eventual disappearance of the town councils as governing bodies, and on the other hand, of the *vindices* to take over the administration of the city revenues, as well as the imperial taxes, meant that by the time of Justinian, and certainly by the end of the sixth century, the cities had suffered an almost complete loss of civic autonomy in both local administrative and fiscal matters – even though the curial order continued to exist, and its members were still called upon to collect the taxes and to bear personal liability for their return. Parallel to this, of course, the state also delegated the collection of taxes to estate owners, including the Church, a practice which saved it (or the local provincial governor) the cost of organising and supporting the fiscal officials who would otherwise have been responsible for this task.[8]

The greater part of these taxes had, until the later fifth and early sixth centuries, been collected in kind and then distributed by local officials of the prefecture to the various points of consumption – chiefly military units and centres of the civil administrative establishment. From this time on, however, the bulk of the assessment was commuted into gold, although at rates which varied over the prefectures, usually according to local conditions and costs. From the reign of Justinian there is some evidence that a standardisation was taking place, and it seems likely that by the end of the sixth century this process had been completed.[9] Military supplies could still be demanded in kind, of course, and the *coemptio*, or compulsory purchase of corn, was a regular imposition in some areas. Part of the land-tax seems also still to have been raised in kind for distribution to the army.[10]

As will by now be clear, the three departments responsible for revenue collection were, at various points, closely related. The income of the *sacrae largitiones* was normally collected by the *susceptores* and similar officials appointed by the cities to collect the prefectural taxes; the rents of the lands of the *res privata* were often collected by officials of the provincial governors, supervised by officials deputed from Constantinople.[11] At the same time, the diocesan level of prefectural administration seems certainly by Justinian's reign to have become less important and relevant to the civil, and to some extent the fiscal, administration of the state, and indeed may have ceased to function as an effective intermediate instance of government. The territorial prefecture with its constituent provinces made up the

---

[7] *Ibid.*, pp. 453–8.
[8] *Ibid.*, vol. II, pp. 759f.; and chapter 3 above, pp. 95–9. For the *procuratores* in the later sixth and early seventh centuries, and the delegation of fiscal obligations, see Guillou, 'Transformations des structures', 72f.
[9] Jones, *LRE*, vol. I, pp. 458ff.   [10] *Ibid.*, vol. II, pp. 671–4.
[11] *Ibid.*, vol. I, pp. 414 and 434.

key elements, with only a few exceptions where the diocesan level was retained for specific purposes.[12]

THE MIDDLE BYZANTINE SYSTEM

This system of revenue extraction and administration seems to have continued to operate uninterrupted until the early seventh century. From the reigns of Phocas and Heraclius, however, a number of changes seem to have taken place and, together with the events of the seventh century and the drastic loss of revenues and territory, the whole system underwent a transformation. I have already noted that a shift occurred in the mode of tax-assessment in this period, from the late Roman distributive to the middle Byzantine contributive pattern. I will look next at the chief elements of the state's fiscal establishment in the ninth century before attempting to trace more closely the course and the nature of the transformation. As in the case of the later Roman administration, that represented in the sources for the ninth century and later has been examined by a number of scholars, and I shall refer to the results of their analyses for what follows.

In contrast to the tripartite division of competences between prefecture, *sacrae largitiones* and *res privata*, the fiscal administration of the ninth century is represented by a number of departments, or *sekreta*,[13] of more or less equal status, subject directly to the emperor. These comprise the *genikon* (*logothesion*), the *eidikon* (or *idikon*) (*logothesion*), the *stratiōtikon* (*logothesion*), the first and last coming under the authority of a *logothetēs*, the *idikon* under an official known as the *epi tou eidikou*, or simply the *eidikos*; and the *sakellion* and *vestiarion*, each under a *chartoularios*. According to the *Kletorologion* of Philotheus, from the year 899, and in which these bureaux are detailed, the *sakellarios* was the general supervisor of all these departments, presumably having achieved this distinction by virtue of having been originally in charge of the emperor's own treasury, which was left as an independent bureau under the authority of his assistant, the *chartoularios*.[14] The origins of these departments are not difficult to discern: the large *officia* of the prefecture, of the *sacrum cubiculum* (imperial bedchamber, which meant in effect the imperial household), as well as of the *magister officiorum* and the *res privata* and *sacrae largitiones*, seem to have been divided into groups of *scrinia*, which, under the officials immediately subordinate to the former departmental heads, became independent *sekreta*. The *genikon*, *idikon* (or *eidikon*) and *stratiōtikon* derived from the

---

[12] Ibid., pp. 374f.
[13] For the origins of the term, see Bury, *Administrative System*, pp. 83f.
[14] See *T.Usp.*, 47.12, 49.22, 51.1, 3, 7, 8, 53.21, etc.; *Klet. Phil.* 113.23–115.4, 12–20, 121.3–26, 123.7–10; Dölger, *Beiträge*, pp. 16ff. and 27.

general, special and military departments of the praetorian prefecture of the East;[15] the *sakellion* from the old *sacrum cubiculum* subdepartment of the *sacellum*;[16] and the *vestiarion* from the department of the *sacrum vestiarium* within the *sacrae largitiones*.[17] In a similar fashion, the department of the public post, originally under the praetorian prefect and supervised by the *magister officiorum*, had become an independent bureau under the *logothetēs tou dromou*;[18] while the old *praepositus gregum* under the *comes rei privatae* became independent as the *logothetēs tōn agelōn*.[19] A number of other departments developed similarly out of older and larger bureaux. But from the fiscal-administrative standpoint, the changes also meant a concentration and centralisation in Constantinople, since the bureaux in question had their own officials in each provincial circumscription, or *thema*, during the ninth century, and there was only one level of administration, as opposed to the civic, provincial and diocesan levels of the later Roman period. The department of the *sakellion* under its *chartoularios* directed local thematic civil and fiscal administration through its *prōtonotarioi*, and liaised with the local officials of the *genikon*;[20] the department of the *stratiōtikon* likewise directed local military administrative matters, the assessment of supplies and provisions, and so on, through its thematic representatives, the *chartoularioi tōn thematōn*;[21] while the bureau of the quaestor in Constantinople, whose tribunal formed the penultimate court of appeal before that of the emperor, supervised the thematic *kritai*, or judges.[22]

---

[15] See the original analysis of Stein, *Studien*, pp. 149ff.; also Bury, *Administrative System*, pp. 86, 90 and 98; and emending Bury's identification, Oikonomidès, *Préséance*, pp. 313–14 and 316 with literature; Hendy, *Studies*, p. 412; V. Laurent, *Le Corpus des sceaux de l'empire byzantin*, vol. II: *L'Administration centrale* (Paris 1981), pp. 129–30 and 303ff.

[16] Hendy, *Studies*, p. 412; cf. Jones, *LRE*, vol. II, pp. 567f. on the *sacrum cubiculum*; Oikonomidès, *Préséance*, pp. 314f.; Laurent, *Corpus*, vol. II, pp. 383ff.

[17] Bury, *Administrative System*, pp. 95f.; Jones, *LRE*, vol. I, p. 428. This department should not be confused with the *oikeiakon vasilikon vestiarion* under the *epi tou oikeiakou vestiariou* or *prōtovestiarios*, descended from the palatine *comitiva sacrae vestis* of the *sacrum cubiculum*. See Oikonomidès, *Préséance*, p. 305 with literature; Bury, *Administrative System*, pp. 95f. and 125; Hendy, *Studies*, pp. 412–13; Seibt, *Bleisiegel*, p. 184.

[18] Jones, *LRE*, vol. I, p. 369, vol. II, pp. 832ff. for the *cursus publicus*, its administration and supply by the praetorian prefecture, and the inspectorate exercised by the master of offices. See Bury, *Administrative System*, pp. 91–2; Oikonomidès, *Préséance*, p. 311; D.A. Miller, 'The logothete of the drome in the middle Byzantine period', *B* 36 (1966), 438–70; Hendy, *Studies*, p. 608 and note 240.

[19] Jones, *LRE*, vol. I, p. 414; Bury, *Administrative System*, p. 111; Oikonomidès, *Préséance*, p. 338; Laurent, *Corpus*, vol. II, pp. 289–99.

[20] *Klet. Phil.* 121.6; Oikonomidès, *Préséance*, pp. 314f. and literature; H. Ahrweiler, 'Recherches sur l'administration de l'empire byzantin aux IXe–XIe siècles', *BCH* 84 (1960), 1–109, see 43.

[21] *Klet. Phil.* 15.15; Oikonomidès, *Préséance*, p. 314; Ahrweiler 'Recherches', 43; Dölger, *Beiträge*, pp. 21f.

[22] See Ahrweiler, 'Recherches', 67ff.; 43–4.

The function and responsibilities of the various fiscal *sekreta* of this period are reasonably clear, although the sources of revenue for departments such as the *eidikon*, for example, are difficult to determine. The *genikon*, through its officials deputed to the provinces – *epoptai*, *exisōtai* and *dioikētai* (only the last group of whom seem actually to have been based in the *themata*) – was responsible for the calculation, assessment and collection of the chief public taxes, the *dēmosia*, primarily the land-tax and the *kapnikon*, or hearth-tax.[23] The *stratiōtikon* was responsible for calculating the regular and expeditionary requirements of the troops, who were paid through it, and through the thematic *prōtonotarios* and *chartoularios* from the *genikon*.[24] The later *eidikon*, in its original form of the *idikē trapeza* of the praetorian prefecture of the East, had probably functioned as a central and provincial clearing-house for assessments in kind – ores, weapons, clothing and so forth – before passing on the materials to the relevant departments: iron, for example, to the state arms-factories under the praetorian prefects, later supervised by the *magister officiorum*;[25] clothing (assessed and collected by the department of the *largitiones*, although the prefecture played a key intermediary role), passed on at provincial and diocesan level to the actuaries of the military units.[26] In the same way, the *sacrae largitiones* had stored and sold off bullion excess to the state's requirements.[27] The later *eidikon* seems to have retained these functions (as the regular use of both the forms *idikon*, special, and *eidikon*, dealing in items in kind, suggests)[28] and certainly controlled the imperial arms storehouses and was responsible, via the *prōtonotarioi* and *stratēgoi* of the *themata*, for the production and distribution of weapons and other military equipment.[29] The public *vestiarion*, once an element within the *largitiones*, had inherited that department's function with regard to mints and bullion, as well as, apparently, the stores for the imperial fleet and iron for other items of military hardware.[30] The *sakellion* exercised a general fiscal

---

[23] See esp. Dölger, *Beiträge*, pp. 14ff. and 47; Laurent, *Corpus*, vol. II, pp. 129–30.
[24] See Haldon, *Byzantine Praetorians*, pp. 314–18 with literature.
[25] The *scrinium armorum* of the prefecture was responsible for this function: see Lydus, *De Magistratibus* III, 4–5.
[26] See *CJ* XII, 1–4 (three constitutions addressed to the praetorian prefect, one to the *comes sacrarum largitionum*).
[27] See Cruikshank-Dodd, *Silver Stamps*, pp. 23ff.
[28] See Stein, *Studien*, pp. 149–50; Dölger, *Beiträge*, pp. 19–20 and 35–9; Laurent, *Corpus*, vol. II, pp. 191–3; and esp. Hendy, *Studies*, pp. 628–9.
[29] See Haldon, *Byzantine Praetorians*, pp. 316–17, 320–2 with sources and literature.
[30] See *Klet. Phil.* 121.15–26; Oikonomidès, *Préséance*, p. 316; Bury, *Administrative System*, pp. 95–7; Hendy, *Studies*, p. 412; Seibt, *Bleisiegel*, pp. 184–5; Laurent, *Corpus*, vol. II, pp. 353ff. The *vestiarion* may also have continued to operate weaving establishments or supervise the production of cloth, as the existence of *magistri linteae vestis* in the old *officium* of the *comes sacrarum largitionum* might suggest: cf. *Notitia Dig.*, Or. XIII, 14; *CJ* XI, 8.14; although the majority of such establishments now came under the *eidikon*.

supervision in the *themata* through the protonotaries; but it seems also to have supervised some of the imperial charitable institutions, which it presumably supported.[31] In addition to these bureaux, the imperial private treasury, or *koitōn*, the private *vestiarion* and the imperial estates under the (great) curator (*megas kouratōr*) also provided funds in cash and materials from a variety of sources: the last-named from imperial estates throughout the empire and representing the surviving elements of the former *res privata* minus the estates of the *praepositi gregum* (now under the *logothetēs tōn agelōn*);[32] the *koitōn* under the *parakoimōmenos* (originally the chief *koitōnitēs*), which was itself originally a department of the *sacrum cubiculum* under the *praepositus sacri cubiculi*;[33] and the related *oikeiakon vasilikon vestiarion*, or imperial private wardrobe, under the *prōtovestiarios*, received resources allocated from the *genikon*, as well as the income from tribute and some income from the imperial estates in addition. Both the last-named departments had treasuries, from which donatives and largesses might be issued; and the private *vestiarion* was also a storehouse for precious silks and other items of imperial or ceremonial clothing and vestments, jewels and plate.[34]

THE PROCESS OF CHANGE

The later system of fiscal and economic management, while clearly derived directly from that known in the sixth century, has obviously undergone a series of changes – changes which produced a less hierarchical and very much more centralised set of institutions. It is the evolution from one to the other that concerns us here.

In the first place, the central role of the *sakellion* and the *sakellarios* deserves attention. The subdepartment of the *sacellum* within the *sacrum cubiculum* had acted as a personal treasury for the emperors from the later fifth century, possibly earlier, although the first reference to a *sacellarius* is for the reign of Zeno.[35] Thereafter the proximity to the emperor and

[31] *Klet. Phil.* 121.3–14; Oikonomidès, *Préséance*, pp. 314f. Its income derived in the first instance from the *res privata* – the properties later under the *megas kouratōr*.
[32] *Klet. Phil.* 123.11–20; Oikonomidès, *Préséance*, p. 318; Bury, *Administrative System*, pp. 100–3; cf. Jones, *LRE*, vol. I, pp. 425–7; the *megas kouratōr* seems to have been a new creation of Basil I, associated with the estates of the Mangana; although a single *curator* had remained in charge of imperial estates (excluding those of Cappadocia) since the later sixth century. See Kaplan, 'Maisons divines', 83ff.
[33] Bury, *Administrative System*, pp. 124–5; Oikonomidès, *Préséance*, p. 305.
[34] For the *prōtovestiarios*, see note 17 above. The *koitōn* was embraced within the *oikeiakon vasilikon vestiarion*, although it constituted an independent section. For tribute, see *DAI* (*De Administrando Imperio*) 50.53. See also Hendy, *Studies*, p. 227 and note 41; and Dölger, *Beiträge*, p. 25 note 3.
[35] John of Antioch, frg. 214.4. *Sacellarius* was a title applied to a number of officials serving in the capacity of treasurer to a particular department or individual, in the Church, for

consequent importance of the imperial *sacellarius* meant that officials entrusted with this post occupy a more significant position in the imperial administration than the position alone might warrant. *Ad hominem* appointment of particular persons not formally connected with them to military commands or other such specialised tasks was a common feature of imperial administrative practice; and the *sacellarius* was on several occasions entrusted with such missions. Narses was Justinian's *sacellarius* between 530 and 538, and went on to high office;[36] the *sacellarius* Rusticus was entrusted by Justinian with the delivery of money for the army in Lazica;[37] the former *sacellarius* of Phocas was killed in 610;[38] the *sacellarius* Theodore Trithyrius is referred to during the reign of Heraclius by later chroniclers as leading imperial troops (in 635) in Syria;[39] while the *sacellarius* Philagrius was entrusted by the Emperor Heraclius Constantine with the protection of his son, the future Constans II, as well as with considerable funds in cash.[40] *Sacellarii* were thus becoming increasingly important during the later sixth and the first part of the seventh century; and indeed during the reign of Constans II, the *sacellarius*, referred to as the leading dignitary of the palace, led the interrogation of Maximus Confessor and appears to have been one of the emperor's most trusted political aids.[41]

Not only was the *sacellarius*, therefore, one of the leading officials in the imperial personal retinue, he and his department seem to have been increasingly involved from the time of Justinian in the fiscal affairs of the state: the delivery of pay to the troops, which seems to have been regarded as part of his regular functions,[42] or (with a similar supervisory mission in respect of military pay and recruitment) actually commanding military

---

example, or in the army: the *sacellarius* of the general Peter, *magister militum* in Numidia (see *PG* XC, 112A, 113A) is mentioned during the interrogation of Maximus Confessor in the mid-seventh century. See Bury, *Administrative System*, pp. 80f.

[36] Procopius, *De Bello Persico*, I, 15.31 (a. 530) and *De Bello Gothico*, II, 13.16 (a. 538).

[37] Agathias III, 2; see Bury, *Administrative System*, p. 85; Stein, *Studien*, p. 146.

[38] *Chron. Pasch.* 701; Nicephorus, 5.6.

[39] Theophanes, 337.23, 338.3; Nicephorus, 23.12; see Lilie, *Die byzantinische Reaktion*, p. 42; Stratos, *Byzantium in the Seventh Century*, vol. II, pp. 64ff.

[40] See Nicephorus, 28.12; John of Nikiu, 192. See Laurent, *Corpus*, vol. II, no. 740, a seal of Philagrius, *koubikoularios* and *sakellarios*. Philagrius is referred to by Nicephorus as ὁ τῶν βασιλικῶν χρημάτων ταμίας, as is Theodore Trithyrius at Nicephorus, 23.12, Leontius, at *ibid.*, 5.6, and Stephen, the *sakellarios* of Justinian II at *ibid.*, 37.13, all of whom are otherwise referred to by the specific title of *sakellarios* (Theophanes, 337.23; 338.3; 367.15; *Chron. Pasch.* 701), as we have seen. The seal provides final confirmation of the views of Bury (*Administrative System*, pp. 84–5) and Stein (*Studien*, p. 146) that the phrase ὁ τῶν βασιλικῶν χρημάτων ταμίας is equivalent to *sakellarios*.

[41] *PG* XC, 88C, 89A, 113B.

[42] See notes 37 and 40 above; note Hendy, *Studies*, pp. 410–11, who points out that Pope Gregory claimed to be acting as imperial *sacellarius* in paying the expenses of the local troops in 595. See Greg. I, *epist.* V, 39 (*MGH*, Ep. I, p. 328).

forces.[43] The importance of the *sacellarius* in the central fiscal administration had clearly become very great; and by the reign of Justinian II, if not well before, the *sacellarius* had, together with the general *logothete*, become one of the chief fiscal officers of the state.[44] In the process, his department seems also to have taken on responsibility for the administration of its chief's duties, probably including also the supervision of the other fiscal bureaux. It is interesting that the *sacellarius* (*sakellarios*), as a confidant of the emperor as well as an official of state, was regarded as the chief of a trustworthy and more easily controlled department; that at least is the impression gained from the proem to the Ecloga (741), where the emperors note that the *quaestor* and the judiciary are henceforth to be paid direct from the *sakellion*, to avoid the possibility of bribery.[45]

The role of the *sakellarios* during the seventh century suggests in the first instance, therefore, a more direct intervention in a closer control of the state finances by the emperors, the tool of this intervention being the *sakellion*, that is, the relevant department of the *sacrum cubiculum*. This impression is reinforced in other respects, as other sections of this department came to prominence: the increasing importance of the corps of *spatharioi* through the middle and later seventh century, both as soldiers in the emperor's presence and as imperial agents in a variety of duties; the increased use and higher worth attached to the dignity of *spatharios*; and the increased importance and similarly increased bestowal of the title *cubicularius* (*koubikoularios*) over the same period.[46] Both the *spatharioi*, and the *sakellarios* and his staff, constituted originally subdepartments of

[43] See note 39 above. [44] Theophanes, 367.15sq., 22–30; cf. 369.26–30.
[45] *Ecloga* (ed. Burgmann), proem. 166.103–9.
[46] Haldon, *Byzantine Praetorians*, pp. 182ff., where the textual and sigillographic evidence is discussed. The *spatharii praesentales in actu* increasingly seem to replace the older corps of the *excubitores*, which appears to become a parade-ground force only. See *ibid.*, pp. 161ff. See also Guilland, *Recherches*, vol. I, pp. 275ff. for a prosopographical list of some important *cubicularii*. A sample from the sigillographic collection of Zacos and Veglery is illustrative: of some 42 officials bearing the title *cubicularius* for the period *c.* 500 to 900, 7 belong to the period before *c.* 650, 21 to the period from *c* 600 to *c.* 750, and 10 to the eighth century; of the approximately 256 or so officials bearing the title *spatharius* or imperial *spatharius*, 3 belong to the period up to *c.* 600, whereas there are some 26 for the period *c.* 600 to 750, and the remaining 227 belong to the late eighth or ninth centuries. Other collections, such as that of Schlumberger, of Pančenko and of Laurent, bear out the same pattern. The spread of seals reflects both the incidence of finds and collections, of course, as well as the historical fact that seals became increasingly popular, and their inscriptions increasingly detailed, from the seventh to the tenth century. But the results of this breakdown of the date and the numbers of seals bearing the titles *cubicularius* and *spatharius* is borne out also in the literary sources, and it does point to a dramatic increase in the role and importance of the imperial *cubiculum* and the titles to which it gave rise. Whether or not the greater part of the seals represents titles rather than offices (and from the later seventh century this seems to be the case), it is significant that it is titles connected with the *cubiculum* that demonstrate this increase in use, and they reflect therefore the corresponding increase in the importance of this palatine department.

the *sacrum cubiculum*, a connection which is clearly reflected in the seals of *sakellarioi* of the period, the majority of whom bear also the dignity of *koubikoularios*.[47] Similarly, as we have seen, the (later) important department of the private imperial *vestiarion* (*oikeiakon vasilikon vestiarion*) was descended from the *comitiva sacrae vestis* of the *sacrum cubiculum*. The importance of the personnel of the sacred bedchamber and its various subdepartments in the central government, therefore, seems to have increased dramatically at this time, an impression reinforced also by the fact that the official in charge of the imperial table, the *epi tēs trapezēs*, had also become an officer of considerable importance by the middle of the seventh century: Sergios Eukratas, who held this position (*epi tēs trapezēs tēs vasilikēs*), was centrally involved, along with the *sakellarios*, in the interrogation of Maximus Confessor; the *domestikos tēs vasilikēs trapezēs*, Leontius, was one of the leading officials of state present at the sessions of the sixth ecumenical council in 680/1.[48] The post of *epi tēs trapezēs* was descended from that of the *castrensis* of the sacred table, with his staff, who formed a section of the department of the *castrensis sacri palatii*, also within the *sacrum cubiculum*.[49]

This process of centralisation and supervision through the departments of the imperial bedchamber and household was well under way by the second half of the seventh century, but seems to have begun during the reign of Heraclius, if not earlier.[50] As has been shown, the civil wars which followed the accession of Heraclius, and the exigencies of the long war with Persia, resulted in a number of changes in imperial administrative practice, both in fiscal administration as well as in other fields – for example, military organisation – which mark the beginnings of this tendency. Particularly significant is the organisation of mints, which underwent considerable restructuring during the period 627–30. The mints of the exarchates of Ravenna and Carthage, along with that of Alexandria, remained in operation, but those of Thessaloniki, Nicomedia, Cyzicus, Cyprus, Antioch and Catania in Sicily were closed down. The effects of this

---

[47] See, for example, Zacos and Veglery, nos. 747: seal of Antiochus, *koubikoularios, vasilikos chartoularios* and *sakellarios* (7th cent.); 911: seal of Leontius, *koubikoularios, chartoularios* and *sakellarios* (7th cent.); 932: seal of Mauricius, *koubikoularios*, imperial *chartoularios*, and *sakellarios* (650–750); 1365: seal of Philagrius, *koubikoularios* and *sakellarios* (7th cent., and cf. 747, above; and 750: seal of Antiochus Philagrius, *c.* 550–650); 1678: seal of anon., *koubikoularios* and *sakellarios* (7th cent.).

[48] *PG*, XC, 120B; Mansi XI, 209C.

[49] For the *castrensis sacri palatii*, see *Notitia Dig.*, Or., xvii; and for a καστρήσιος τῆς θείας τραπέζης, see *Vita Danielis Styl.*, 25; for the same official under Justinian: Jones, *LRE*, vol. 2, pp. 567–8 note 7.

[50] The autonomy and the momentum of organisation demonstrated by the establishment of the imperial estates and the *patrimonium* in the later sixth century, independently of other institutions, has already been noted by Kaplan, 'Maisons divines', esp. 92.

development were to terminate effectively the role of the *sacrae largitiones* in the dioceses, with a consequent further reduction in the relevance of the diocesan level of administration for the praetorian prefectures.[51] As we have seen, the diocesan element had already lost much of its administrative significance by the time of Justinian. This change in the administration of mints must have removed one of the last remaining supports to its continued existence. From c. 630 there was only one mint for the prefectures of Illyricum and Oriens, that at the capital, Constantinople, with the exception of that at Alexandria. The new system constitutes, therefore, a fairly radical break with the past. Gold continued, as before, to be minted at the prefectural level of administration, at Constantinople, and at Carthage and Ravenna for the two exarchates. The diocesan level seems to disappear from the record entirely, and the production of copper coins for these areas from then on depended upon the prefectural mints as well. The Constantinopolitan mint now produced copper in fixed quantities for particular destinations, sometimes minting the coins specifically for the destination in question.[52] As Hendy has noted, this is a reversal of the traditional late Roman procedure. And it implies several important consequences: in the first place, a clear centralisation of the minting, and the distribution, of coin, both gold and, for the first time, copper; and in the second place, a reorganistion and possibly the disappearance of the *sacrae largitiones*, and the assumption of their functions and remaining administrative personnel by another department. The last explicit mention of a *comes sacrarum largitionum* is to Athanasius, *komēs largitiōnōn*, for the year 605.[53] A logothete is referred to for the year 626, and while claims for his being a *logothetēs tou stratiōtikou* seem improbable,[54] the reference to the title is significant. Already in 602/3 Constantine Lardys is described as ex-praetorian prefect, logothete and curator of the imperial estates of Hormisdas.[55] Since *logo-*

---

[51] This development, and the numismatic evidence for it, has been fully analysed by Hendy, 'Administrative basis'. Justinian had effectively abolished the separate vicariates (diocesan governorships) of Asiana, Pontica and Oriens by combining them with the provincial governorships of Phrygia Pacatiana, Galatia I and Syria I respectively; those of Pontica and Asiana were effectively restored after 548. See Jones, *LRE*, vol. 1, pp. 280ff., 294.
[52] Hendy, 'Administrative basis', 147–52, and *Studies*, pp. 417–20. The temporary mints at Jerusalem and Alexandretta, at Constantia in Cyprus, at Seleucia and Isaura in Isauria, are to be explained in terms of the exigencies of the warfare of the period 608–26/7 (Hendy, *Studies*, pp. 415f.).
[53] *Chron. Pasch.*, 696 (cf. Theophanes, 297.20 who mentions his execution in 609).
[54] *Chron. Pasch.* 721: Θεοδόσιος ὁ ἐνδοξότατος πατρίκιος καὶ λογοθέτης. For his identity as a military logothete, see R. Guilland, 'Etudes sur l'histoire administrative de l'empire byzantin: les logothètes', *REB* 29 (1971), see 25–6 and note 9; N. Oikonomidès, 'Les premiers mentions des thèmes dans le chronique de Théophane', *ZRVI* 16 (1975), 1–8, see 6 note 23; Hendy, 'Administrative basis', 154; *Studies*, p. 413. Against this, see Haldon, *Recruitment and Conscription*, p. 34, note 43 with literature.
[55] See *Chron. Pasch.* 694.8.

thetēs is a Greek equivalent of the Latin technical title *numerarius* (or *scriniarius*), the chief of a *scrinium*, the important position and high rank attributed by the sources to these officials at this time is significant.[56] It suggests that they were already persons of high standing and that they may already be heads of independent bureaux. Constantine Lardys was an ex-praetorian prefect, and both he and Theodosius were *gloriosissimi*, both therefore belonging to the topmost group of officers of state. The older *scriniarii*, while they had been important officials in their departments, had not attained this elevated status. And there are other high-ranking *logothetai*, connected with the customs and trading depots or *apothēkai*, also known from the reigns of Maurice and Phocas.[57]

We have, therefore, at least the possibility that by the reign of Heraclius, from 610, the fiscal departments of the praetorian prefecture were becoming, or had already become, independent bureaux supervised by high-ranking officials. Such a development would immediately involve also a reassessment of the relationship between the *largitiones* and the special, general and military departments of the praetorian prefects (who certainly continued to operate, at least in a general capacity, until 629 if not beyond),[58] and the eventual result seems to have involved the organisation of the mints on a single, centralised level and the absorption of responsibility and authority for this operation into the single bureau of the *sacrum vestiarium* within the *largitiones* which, with its much reduced staff (no longer needing regional or urban representatives or staffs, merely the central staffs of the mints themselves, and the officials in charge of receiving the bullion for coining) could now handle all the demands made upon it. The local affairs of the *largitiones* had in any case been handled by officials of the prefecture or by officials seconded from Constantinople.[59] The later establishment of the general *logothesion* seems to reflect this fact, for its staff includes *chartoularioi tōn arklōn*, sometimes called *chartoularioi* of the *exō arklai*, that is, chartularies of the provincial treasuries formerly under the *largitiones*.[60]

The prefectures had each had, of course, a central fisc (two for Oriens, as we have seen, the special and the general), but they had never had local

---

[56] Stein, *Studien*, pp. 148–50, *contra* Bury, *Administrative System*, p. 83. These were the *numerarii* of the *scrinia* – see Jones, *LRE*, vol. I, pp. 450 and 589. See, for example, Justinian, *Edict* XIII, 10. proem; 11.1; 13 for *scriniarii* = members of *scrinia*, including the chiefs also.

[57] See Jones, *LRE*, vol. II, p. 589; and for other *commerciarii* see Zacos and Veglery, p. 214, nos. 3 and 6, with earlier literature: Στέφανος, ἐνδοξότατος ἀπὸ μαγίστρων, θεῖος λογοθέτης καὶ κομμερκιάριος Τύρου; and Ἰωάννης, ἐνδοξότατος ἀπὸ ὑπάτων πατρίκιος, λογοθέτης καὶ βασιλικὸς (probably κομμερκιάριος).

[58] *JGR* I, coll. 1, nov. 25, 2 (a. 629 = Dölger, *Regesten*, no. 199).

[59] See above, and Justinian, *Edict* XIII, 11.2; 3; XIII, 20.

[60] For example, *Klet. Phil.*, 113.29; *De Cer.*, 694.18.

Fiscal administration

treasuries or reserves, such as those operated for the *largitiones* at diocesan level by the *praepositi* or *comites thesaurorum*.[61] It seems highly likely, as Bury long ago suggested,[62] that the later chartularies of the *arklai* (Lat. *arcae*) were in fact these diocesan officials of the *largitiones*, absorbed into the bureau of the general bank of the prefecture of the East – that is, into that section of the prefecture's activities handling public and general taxes. The *praepositi thesaurorum* had, after all, received the income from minor taxes on land, for example, which were owed to the *sacrae largitiones*, and it was to these local depots that such revenues were delivered. In the same way, gold, silver and other goods for which the *largitiones* was responsible were also delivered there (usually by officials of the prefecture), before being passed on to the capital. Similarly, the *commercia*, and the diocesan *comites commerciorum*, were also absorbed into the bureau of the general bank.[63] It seems probable, then, that this element of the organisation of the *largitiones* was absorbed in its entirety into the structure of the general bank of the prefecture, a development which will also have enhanced the status and power of the latter bureau. While the mints continued to be administered separately at a later date, within the bureau of the public *vestiarion*, the vestigial remnant of the *largitiones* (the name alone reminds of its origins, and the loss of its wider fiscal and administrative functions),[64] they received recirculated gold coin and bullion now entirely through the medium of the general *logothesion* and the *eidikon*.[65]

The reorganisation of the mints in the period 627–30, thus, must have involved also the transfer of their regional depots, along with full responsibility for the original cash revenues of the *largitiones*, to the relevant branch of the praetorian prefecture, chiefly the *genikē trapeza* under its *numerarii*. The greatly increased importance of the *sacellarius* at the same period, it may be guessed, was in some way connected with this rearrangement; and it seems not unreasonable to suggest that, whatever vestigial authority the praetorian prefect retained, the relative independence of at least two, and possibly three, of his former departments – the general, special and military banks – goes back to the reign of Heraclius

---

[61] For the operation of their regional chests, see Jones, *LRE*, vol. I, pp. 428–9.
[62] Bury, *Administrative System*, p. 87. These officers are clearly not to be connected with the prefectural (i.e. central) *arcae* as such, *pace* Stein, *Studien*, p. 150.
[63] Jones, *LRE*, vol. I, pp. 428–33. For the *comitiva sacrarum largitionum*, see *Notitia Dig*, Or. XIII; and see below.
[64] Its function appears to have been twofold: the minting of coin (distribution via the other fiscal bureaux) and the storage and provision of naval equipment – although the origins of this aspect of its role is unclear.
[65] See, for example, Dölger, *Beiträge*, pp. 19ff. and 35ff.; Laurent, *Corpus*, vol. II, pp. 191ff.; but the *komēs tēs lamias* (κόμης τῆς Λαμίας) has nothing to do with mines, being in fact in charge of the Constantinopolitan granaries. See J.F. Haldon, 'Comes horreorum – komēs tēs Lamias?', *BMGS* 10 (1986), 203–9.

and that the supervisory authority of the *sacellarius* and his department is similarly to be dated to this time, if not slightly earlier. In consequence, the rationalisation of the remaining functions of the *largitiones* into the 'new' and independent bureau of the *vestiarion*, likewise under the general supervision of the *sacellarius*, must also date to approximately the same time.[66] While this scheme is, to a degree, hypothetical, the implications follow directly from Heraclius' proven reorganisation of the system of minting quite logically, although the later sources, such as the so-called Taktikon Uspenskij and the *Kletorologion* of Philotheus, both from the ninth century, present an already evolved structure which may no longer exactly represent the original form of these new departments. But the mention of two *logothetai*, for the years 602/3 and 626, demonstrates that the Greek title for the head of the chief fiscal bureau was already current.[67] Heraclius' reorganisation of the mints, therefore, may reasonably be taken, at least partially, to reflect a wider process of fiscal administrative reorganisation, a process which seems already to have commenced before his reign, however, and which this reorganisation may have completed.

The causes of this process of centralisation are more difficult to locate and can on the whole only be guessed at. The precarious economic position of the empire in the last years of the sixth century certainly provides a context.[68] But inherent structural tendencies within the organisation of the fiscal-civil administration may equally well have been working themselves out.[69] The result seems to have been that the greater autonomy of

[66] It is significant that the traditional system of control-stamps on silver plate associated with the *largitiones* begins to break down at about this time, a point emphasised by Hendy, Studies, p. 413. See Cruikshank-Dodd, *Silver Stamps*, pp. 31 and 45f. It is also significant that the single *zygostatēs* in the bureau of the *sakellion* in the ninth century and later (see T.Usp., 61.12; Klet. Phil., 121.8; 153.29; Oikonomidès, *Préséance*, p. 315 with sources and literature; Hendy, Studies, pp. 317f.), responsible probably for controlling the purity and weight of the coinage, appears on a seal of the seventh century (Zacos and Veglery, no. 2803: John, *skribōn* and imperial *zygostatēs*). *Zygostatēs* is here clearly an office, and the epithet 'imperial' is therefore all the more significant. Whether the seal dates to the period with which we are concerned here or to the later part of the seventh century, it is evidence already that the functions of the earlier municipal *zygostatai* under the supervision of the praetorian prefecture (see CTh. XII, 7.2 = CJ X, 73.2, emended; and cf. Justinian, Edict XI) had probably been centralised within the bureau of the *sakellion* at an early stage; given the mint reforms discussed by Hendy for the years 627–30, the latter date is very probably the moment at which such a centralisation might have occurred. For the system of control-stamps, and especially the gradual transfer of their administration to the city prefect of Constantinople, as the department of the *largitiones* was progressively fragmented, see D. Feissel, 'Le Préfet de Constantinople, les poids-étalons et l'estampillage de l'argenterie au VIᵉ et au VIIᵉ siècle', *Revue Numismatique* 28 (1986), 119–42.

[67] Note also the reference to a certain George, *chartoularios* of the sacred *logothesion*, mentioned in a story from the last years of the reign of Heraclius or the first years of Constans II: see *Miracula S. Artemii* 25.29.

[68] See chapter 1; and the summary of Jones, LRE, vol. I, pp. 298–315, esp. 305ff.

[69] The development of two separate reserves within the Oriental prefecture, for example, which appears in the last decades of the fifth century as a response to the fiscal

Fiscal administration 191

the two banks of the oriental prefecture on the one hand, and the increasing intervention in, and supervision of, fiscal affairs by the *sacellarius*, the emperor's personal treasurer, on the other hand – an effect of the lack of cash resources and the multiplicity of demands on the limited revenue available – coincided. The political-military collapse of the reign of Heraclius before 622–6 may have encouraged attempts to reorganise the state's fiscal administration, to recognise some of the changes which had become effective in the interim, and to continue and extend the process of central supervision and control in respect of revenues, resources and expenditure. As a corollary of Heraclius' reorganisation of the mints, it is therefore likely that the departments of the general, special and military *logothesia*, under the general supervision of the praetorian prefect and the *sacellarius*, together with those of the *vestiarion* and the *sakellion*, appeared in a form which was recognisably that of the Byzantine rather than of the later Roman state. The concomitant disappearance of the *largitiones*, and, with them, of the final significant prop of the diocesan level of provincial administration, together with the weakening of the power of the praetorian prefect, will have had important implications for the later development of the provincial civil administration, as well as the pattern of the palatine establishment.

The lack of direct evidence concerning these developments has, of course, turned this problem, and the related question of the origins of the military provinces or *themata*, into the major *vexata quaestio* of this period of Byzantine history. On the whole, it is now generally accepted that the processes of both civil and fiscal, as well as military, reform or change were gradual, beginning in the later sixth century, and concluded only during the second half of the eighth century at the earliest.[70] Apart from the

---

administrative exigencies of the times, is illustrative of such tendencies; there is no reason to suppose that the institutional framework of the state's fiscal administration did not continue to develop, that is, that it was not a fixed, static block of organisational relationships. For the fifth century, see Stein, Studien, p. 149 and Bas-Empire, vol. I, p. 221 and note 6.

[70] The literature, as is frequently pointed out, is considerable. For the most recent general surveys, see Lilie, Die byzantinische Reaktion, pp. 287ff. and 'Die zweihundertjährige Reform: zu den Anfängen der Themenorganisation im 7. und 8. Jahrhundert', BS 45 (1984), 27–39 and 190–201, see 27ff.; Haldon, Recruitment and Conscription, pp. 20ff.; Hendy, Studies, pp. 409ff. and 621ff. Of the older literature, the work of J. Karayannopoulos, 'Über die vermeintliche Reformtätigkeit des Kaisers Herakleios', JÖBG 10 (1961), 53–72, and Die Entstehung der byzantinischen Themenverfassung (Byzantinisches Archiv X, Munich 1959), esp. pp. 5ff. and 55–8; and Karayannopoulos, 'Contribution au problème des thèmes byzantins', L'Hellénisme contemporain 10 (1956), 458–78; and cf. A. Pertusi, 'La Formation des thèmes byzantins', in Berichte zum XI. Internationalen Byzantinisten-Kongress (Munich 1958), vol. I, pp. 1–40; and 'Nuova ipotesi sull' origine dei temi bizantini', Aevum 28 (1954), 126–50, are all still important. See also J. Toynbee, Constantine Porphyrogenitus and his World (London 1973), pp. 134ff. and 224ff.; and Oikonomidès, 'Les Premiers mentions'; Kaegi, 'Two studies'.

references to the *logothetai*, and to the *sakellarios* and his important role during the reign of Constans II already mentioned, the first references to the leading officers of the developed establishment occur for the year 680, when certain high officials accompanied the emperor at the sessions of the sixth ecumenical council. These are named in order as follows: Nicetas, most glorious ex-consul, *patricius* and master of the imperial offices; Theodore, most glorious ex-consul and *patricius, comes* of the imperial Opsikion and deputy general of Thrace; Sergius, most glorious ex-consul and *patricius*; Paul, also most glorious ex-consul and *patricius*; Julian, most glorious ex-consul, *patricius* and logothete of the military treasury; Constantine, most glorious ex-consul and curator of the imperial estate of Hormisdas; Anastasius, most glorious ex-consul, *patricius* and second-in-command to the *comes* of the imperial *excubitores*; John, most glorious ex-consul, *patricius* and quaestor; Polyeuctes, most glorious ex-consul; Thomas, also most glorious ex-consul; Paul, most glorious ex-consul and director of the eastern provinces; Peter, most glorious ex-consul; Leontius, most glorious ex-consul and domestic of the imperial table.[71]

Of the older establishment, the master of offices appears to have still exercised important functions and counted among the leading officials; and indeed he continued to exercise some of these functions well into the eighth century.[72] Likewise, the curator of the imperial estates of Hormisdas seems still to be functioning and may by this stage be the equivalent of the later *megas kouratōr*, in charge of other imperial properties formerly attached to the *domus divina* and the *res privata*.[73] The quaestor was also present, and although his functions were altered in some respects, his duties and authority remained much the same in the later period as in the

---

[71] Mansi, XI, 209A–C; Riedinger, 14.19ff.
[72] See the studies of Boak, *The Master*, pp. 49ff., and Bury, *Administrative System*, pp. 29f.; for the master in the eighth century, when he seems still to have exercised authority over the *scholae*, until the reforms of the guard units undertaken by Constantine V, see Haldon, *Byzantine Praetorians*, pp. 145–50 and 229ff.; and F. Winkelmann, *Byzantinische Rang- und Ämterstruktur im 8. und 9. Jahrhundert* (BBA LIII, Berlin 1985), p. 31.
[73] See above, note 1. The fate of the imperial estates of the *res privata*, the *patrimonium* and the *domus divinae* is unclear. The stud-farms and other livestock-farming estates came under the *logothetēs tōn agelōn*, descended from the older *praepositus gregum* (see above, note 19); the remaining properties may well all have been administered by the later (*megas*) *kouratōr*, and the income derived therefrom seems to have gone into the *koitōn*, the successor to the *sacellum* as the emperor's private chest, and the imperial private *vestiarion*. See Hendy, *Studies*, p. 199 note 235; Stein, *Studien*, pp. 168–85. By the early eighth century, seals of officials in charge of imperial estates demonstrate the new bureau's development. Cf. Zacos and Veglery, no. 3221, seal of anon., *hypatos* and *chartoularios tōn vasilikōn ktēmatōn*. See Bury, *Administrative System* p. 102; Oikonomidès, *Préséance*, p. 318.

Fiscal administration 193

sixth century.[74] He may well already have taken over by this time the *scrinia libellorum* and *epistolarum* originally under the disposition of the *magister officiorum*, since the Greek term *antigrapheis* represents the Latin *magistri scriniorum* and, as Bury noted, the *antigrapheis* are associated with the quaestor in the proem to the Ecloga.[75]

Leaving aside for the moment the military officials named, the remaining palatine officials there represent either new offices or give their titles only, but not their posts. The military logothete is represented, the head of the old bureau of military finance in the *officium* of the praetorian prefect, as we have seen, but from his high rank by now evidently an important independent official. His presence would argue indirectly also for the independence by this time of both the general and the special banks of the prefecture;[76] while the presence of the *domestikos* of the imperial table suggests that the subdepartment of the sacred table within the old *sacrum cubiculum* was by this time also an independent bureau.[77] If this conclusion is accepted, the further implication is that the *sacrum cubiculum* had by now devolved into its constituent parts, an inference which the clear pre-eminence of the *sakellarios* in the middle of the seventh century would tend to support.[78] Thus the *koitōn* under the chief *parakoimōmenos*,[79] the imperial private *vestiarion* under the *prōtovestiarios* (the old *comitiva sacrae vestis* under its *comes*), as well as the *sacellum* and the imperial table, were now all independent services in the palace.

References to the various officials of the central *sekreta* begin to occur in the literary sources for the later seventh century. Thus Theodotus, the monk, *genikos logothetēs* during the reign of Justinian II, is mentioned for the years 694/5, for whom there exists also a seal;[80] a seal of Paul, *apo hypatōn* and *genikos logothetēs* may date to the same period; while seals of

---

[74] See the detailed discussion of Bury, *Administrative System*, pp. 73ff.
[75] Bury, *Administrative System*, pp 75–6; *Ecloga* (ed. Burgmann), proem. 103–4. See *Klet. Phil.* 115.5–11; Oikonomidès, *Préséance*, pp. 321f. with literature; see also below, on the *epi tōn deēseōn*.
[76] A dated seal for the years 659–68 of Stephen, *apo hypatōn*, *patrikios* and *stratiōtikos logothetēs*, emphasises the independence of this bureau at a relatively early stage. See Zacos and Veglery, no. 144; and see p. 145, table 1.
[77] See above, note 49; Bury, *Administrative System*, pp. 125f.; Oikonomidès, *Préséance*, pp. 305f.
[78] See note 17 above with literature.
[79] Bury, *Administrative System*, pp. 124f.; Oikonomidès, *Préséance*, p. 305.
[80] Theophanes, 367.22–4; 369.27; cf. Zacos and Veglery, no. 1064A, seal of Theodotus, monk and *genikos logothetēs*. The description *genikos logothetēs* is used by Theophanes of the chief finance officer of the Caliph ᶜAbd al-Malik – Sergius, the son of Mansur – for the year 692. But it is difficult to know exactly what value should be placed on its use here. It may at least suggest that Theophanes' source used the term and thus suggest that it was already current among Greek-speakers for such an official. Cf. Theophanes, 365.24.

(another) Paul, *genikos logothetēs*, and of Michael, *hypatos* and *genikos logothetēs*, also belong to the second half of the seventh century.[81] Subordinate officials of the *genikon* are also evidenced by seals for this period.[82] Similarly, seals of officials for the imperial *koitōnion* and from the public *vestiarion* for the early eighth century suggest that this branch of the older *cubiculum* in its new form, as well as the public *vestarion*, were now well established;[83] while seals of officials described as *epanō tōn deēseōn* of the later seventh and early eighth centuries again demonstrate that this *sekreton*, formerly the *scrinium* of the *magister memoriae* under the disposition of the *magister officiorum*, was by now of independent status and probably – as in the ninth and tenth centuries – under the authority of the quaestor.[84]

THE FATE OF THE PRAETORIAN PREFECTURE: THE 'SUPERVISORS OF THE PROVINCES'

The evidence of these literary and sigillographic sources, while by no means definitive, does suggest that the basic framework of the fiscal administrative and palatine administrative systems known from documents such as the Taktikon Uspenskij and the *Kletorologion* of Philotheus, of the ninth century, were already well established by the year 700; and the earlier material, in particular the fact of Heraclius' reform of minting practice and the inferences which must logically follow from it, suggests

---

[81] See Zacos and Veglery, nos. 961, 3162, 2903; N.P. Lihačev, 'Datirovannye vizantiiskie pečati', *Izvestiya Rossiiskoi Akademii Istorii Material'noi Kul'tury* 3 (1924), 153–224, see 180, no. 11; V. Laurent, 'Bulletin de sigillographie byzantine, I', *B* 5 (1929/30), 571–654, see 607 note 3: seal of Cyriacus, *apo hypatōn* and *genikos logothetēs* (dated 696/7).
[82] For example, Zacos and Veglery, no. 1231, anon., *hypatos* and *chartoularios* of the *genikon logothesion*.
[83] Zacos and Veglery, no. 1093, seal of anon., *chartoularios tou vasilikou koitōniou* and *chartoularios tou vasilikou vestiariou*. See also nos. 1409 and 1714, of Andrew, *chartoularios tou vasilikou vestiariou*. All these seem to date to the early part of the eighth century. It is unclear whether no. 1093 belongs to an official of the *koitōn* who functioned also within the public *vestiarion*, or whether the private *vestiarion* is meant. The latter might seem more likely, in view of the origins of both departments within the *sacrum cubiculum*, although the later private *vestiarion* had no *chartoularios* in the ninth century and after (see Oikonomidès, *Préséance*, p. 305). The public *vestiarion*, on the other hand, was later in the charge of a *chartoularios*, and this official, and certainly the Andrew of the seals 1409 and 1714, may well represent this bureau. See Oikonomidès, *Préséance*, p. 316 and references.
[84] See V. Laurent, *Les Sceaux byzantins du médailler Vatican* (Medagliere della Biblioteca Vaticana I, Città del Vaticano 1962), no. 8; Zacos and Veglery, no. 2466; Bury, *Administrative System*, pp. 77f.; Oikonomidès, *Préséance*, p. 322. For a further comment on the fate of the *sacrae largitiones*, see R. Delmaire, 'Le Déclin des largesses sacrées', in *Hommes et Richesses dans l'Empire byzantin* I: *IVe–VIIe siècle* (Paris 1989), pp. 265–78.

that this pattern was probably already in existence much earlier, and by the end of his reign. But this in itself is no argument for a major transformation of either the principles or the practice of civil or military administration – at least not at this stage.

While the various bureaux of the prefecture dealing with financial affairs became increasingly independent, the prefecture seems still to have operated into the last years of the reign of Heraclius. In 629 the praetorian prefect of the East is referred to in a novel, issued at Jerusalem, on the juridical situation of the clergy, addressed to the patriarch Sergius.[85] Although no more explicit references to this official occur, other evidence suggests that the prefectures continued for a while to be the main civil administrative subdivisions within the surviving territories of the state. In the first place, the praetorian prefect of Illyricum continued to exist until the second half of the seventh century, although probably with only nominal uthority over much of his former prefecture, which was now mostly outside Byzantine imperial control.[86] In the second place, an early ninth-century ceremony, preserved in the tenth-century Book of Ceremonies of Constantine VII, lists the praetorian prefect and the quaestor (along with the eparchs of the *themata*) together.[87] While it is certainly true that only the title may have survived, as in many similar cases[88] (that of *stratēlatēs*, for example, or *anthypatos* or *magistros*), one might have expected it to have been generalised as a title in the system of precedence, just like these latter, which it was not, however; and it seems reasonable to suppose that, like the offices of quaestor and prefect of the *themata* which it accompanies, it, too, referred to an office, not a dignity alone. It may well be, of course, that the praetorian prefect exercised a nominal supervision only by this time. Already in the later sixth century he was referred to by the function for which his department was best known: τὴν ἡγεμονίαν τῶν φόρων τῆς ἑῴας ... ὃν ἔπαρχον πραιτωρίων εἰώθασιν ὀνομάζειν Ῥωμαῖοι,[89] that is, for the collection and assessment of revenues. And whereas, by the middle of the seventh century, the bureaux of the general, special and military *logothesia* had taken on an independent existence, this does not preclude the prefect's having still exercised overall authority.

---

[85] JGR I, coll. 1, nov. 25, 2 (a. 629 = Dölger, *Regesten*, no. 199).
[86] See E. Stein, 'Ein Kapitel vom persischen und vom byzantinischen Staate', BNJ I (1920), 50–89, see 83; Ch. Diehl, 'L'Origine du régime des thèmes dans l'empire byzantin', in *Etudes Byzantines* (Paris 1905), pp. 276–92, see p. 290; H. Gelzer, *Die Genesis der byzantinischen Themenverfassung*, Abhandlungen der königl. sächsischen Gesellschaft der Wissenschaften, phil.-hist. Klasse (Leipzig 1899 and Amsterdam 1966), see pp. 35f.; Bury, *ERE*, pp. 223 and 234 note 1; Lilie, 'Die zweihundertjährige Reform', 35.
[87] See Stein, 'Ein Kapitel', 71ff.; most recently, Kaegi, 'Two studies', 98ff. Cf. *De Cer.* 61.25; and see below.
[88] See Lilie's objection, 'Die zweihundertjährige Reform', 35.
[89] Theophylact Simocatta, VIII 9.6.

The praetorian prefect had charge also, of course, of the local civil and judicial administration, and the provincial governors and their staffs; and the late Roman provincial geography continues to exist well into the eighth century, as the evidence of lead seals shows quite clearly. The provinces of the sixth century occur on seals of the later seventh and eighth centuries to the extent that, of those mentioned in the Justinianic legislation and whose territory was still within the empire in the later seventh and eighth centuries, twenty-six occur on seals of *kommerkiarioi* or *apothēkai* (on which see below) for the years *c.* 654–*c* 720.[90] While the traditional provinces continued to exist, therefore, their local administrative apparatuses probably continued to function as far as was possible.

In this respect, the seals of a large number of provincial *dioikētai* are significant. In the ninth and tenth centuries, the *dioikētai* were those officials responsible for supervising the collection of taxes, and they were responsible to the general logothete. They represent the earlier provincial *trakteutai* of the diocesan *scrinia*, responsible to the central clerks and *chartularii* of the prefectural bureau.[91] As such, it is likely that they were also closely connected with the chartularies of the provincial *arcae* taken over from the *largitiones*, although evidence for these officials occurs only from the ninth century.[92] But evidence for the continued existence of the *dioikētai* occurs through the seventh and eighth centuries and into the ninth century in an unbroken tradition.

From the second decade of the seventh century, general supervisors seem to have been appointed over a whole group of provinces, possibly over the whole of the Eastern prefecture. A seal of Theodore, *megaloprepestatos illoustrios* and *dioikētēs* of all (province names or designation illegible), dating to the years 614 to 631 demonstrates that this practice was known during the period of fiscal reorganisation under Heraclius;[93] while the mention of Paul, the *endoxotatos apo hypatōn* and *dioikētēs* of the eastern

---

[90] For the Justinianic provinces, see Jones, *LRE*, map VI. Including the islands, Cyprus and Honorias (which Justinian joined with Paphlagonia, but which seemed afterwards still to have been treated as an independent province), there were 27 such provinces. For the seals, see Zacos and Veglery, pp. 146ff. and tables 3ff. See below for seals of *dioikētai* bearing provincial names. There are seals for 23 Anatolian provinces, plus seals for the various isles making up the Justinianic *insulae*, and Cyprus. Armenia I and II are the only provinces not found.

[91] See, e.g., Theophanes, 367.27 for 694; and Bury, *Administrative System*, p. 89; Oikonomidès, *Préséance*, p. 313. See also Dölger, *Beiträge*, pp. 70ff.; N. Svoronos, 'Recherches sur le cadastre byzantin et la fiscalité aux XIe–XIIe siècles: le cadastre de Thèbes', *BCH* 83 (1959), 1–166, see 56f. For the earlier *trakteutai*, see, for example, *Vita Eutychii* 68; and Justinian, *Edict* XIII, 9–12; 27; 28. In the *Vita Eutychii*, they are described as τοὺς τὴν ἐπαρχίαν ... διοικοῦντας.

[92] See Oikonomidès *Préséance*, p. 313.

[93] Zacos and Veglery, no. 131.

provinces in 680 at the sixth ecumenical council; the seals of George and Theodore, each *apo hypatōn* and *dioikētēs* of the *eparchiai* (or provinces, unspecified), dated c. 650–700; of Marinus, *apo eparchōn* and *dioikētēs* of the *eparchiai*, dated 650–700; of Paul, *hypatos* and *dioikētēs* of the *Anatolikoi*, dated c. 700; of Leontius, *patrikios* and *dioikētēs* of the *eparchiai*, dated c. 650–700; and of Stephen, *apo hypatōn* and *dioikētēs* of the *eparchiai*, or *patrikios* and *dioikētēs* of the *eparchiai*, dated c. 650–700, demonstrates the continuation of the same practice.[94] Throughout the same period, officials issued seals bearing the title *dioikētēs* alone, without further elaboration, and these may represent the subordinate provincial officials placed under the authority of these general *dioikētai*.[95]

From the first half of the eighth century, a shift in the pattern becomes evident, as ordinary *dioikētai* or supervisors begin to issue seals with the name(s) of their provinces also. Thus there are seals for *dioikētai* of Thrace, Hellas, Sicily, Euboea, Seleucia, Cyprus, Lydia, Bithynia, Galatia.[96] But what is interesting is that seals for those fiscal officials bearing the general title 'of the provinces' are limited almost without exception to the second half of the seventh century and the first years of the eighth.[97]

[94] See Mansi XI, 209B; Riedinger, 14.32; Zacos and Veglery, nos. 821, 1031, 1178, 2290, 2897, 1008 and 1014, respectively.

[95] See Zacos and Veglery, nos. 1464, 1527, 1528 and 1439; K. Konstantopoulos, Βυζαντιακὰ μολυβδόβουλλα τοῦ ἐν Ἀθηναῖς Ἐθνικοῦ Νομισματικοῦ Μουσείου (Athens 1917), nos. 325a, b, g; 586; Zacos and Veglery, nos. 749, 1724, 1991, 2069, 2018, 3109, 885, 956, 2352, 3189, 3192, 1698, 1866, 2120, 2158, 2399, 1951, 1847, 1917, 2302, 2297, 2531 and 2139; V. Laurent, *Documents de sigillographie byzantine. La collection C. Orghidan* (Paris 1952), nos. 249 and 251; G. Schlumberger, *Sigillographie de l'empire byzantin* (Paris 1884 and Turin 1963), pp. 497–8, no. 13; p. 499, nos. 19 and 20; p. 536, no. 4; J. Ebersolt, *Musées impériaux ottomans. Catalogues des sceaux byzantins* (Paris 1922), nos. 362 and 364 and 'Sceaux byzantins du Musée de Constantinople', *RN*, 4th ser., 18 (1914), 207–43 and 377–409, see 361 and 363; W. de Gray Birch, *Catalogue of Seals in the Department of Manuscripts in the British Museum* V (London 1898), pp. 1–106, nos. 17, 615 and 17, 617. These date to the period c. 650 to c 900, the majority from the eighth century. For a fuller and more detailed list, see Winkelmann, *Rang- und Ämterstruktur*, p. 134.

[96] See Zacos and Veglery, nos. 1044, 2114, 2081, 2082, 2078, 2079, 2019, 2020, 1895, 2183, 2426, 1628, 1642 and 3189 all dating to the period c 700–850. The giving of more explicit detail may have reflected a personal fashion, as well, of course. Thus the Theodore, *dioikētēs*, of Zacos and Veglery, no. 3189, seems to be the same as the Theodore, Zacos and Veglery, no. 2426, who was also *dioikētēs* of Lydia. See Zacos and Veglery, p. 1778. There are for the same period a considerable number of seals of *dioikētai* which give the name of a town rather than a province. For a list, see Winkelmann, *Rang- und Ämterstruktur*, pp. 134f.

[97] That of Sergius, *hypatos* and *dioikētēs* of the *eparchiai* (Zacos and Veglery, no. 487), dated to the first half of the eighth century is the latest I have been able to find extant. From its style and lettering, however, it might equally belong in the years around c. 700. Similar considerations apply to Schlumberger, *Sigillographie*, pp. 499f., seal of Sergius, *dioikētēs* of the *eparchiai*; and to Konstantopoulos, *Molybdoboulla*, no. 326a, seal of Theophylactus, *hypatos* and *dioikētēs* of the *eparchiai* (in the first and last cases partially confirmed by the rank, *hypatos*).

Three further points deserve our attention. First, the use of what are clearly thematic circumscriptions begins to increase on seals of *kommerkiarioi* and *kommerkia* (customs officials and depots – but see below) from the early eighth century, suggesting that the military districts which had come to overlie the older civil provinces were becoming increasingly important from the general administrative point of view.[98] Second, a slight change in the formula expressing the titles of two *dioikētai* of the *eparchiai* suggests a shift from a prefectural to a thematic emphasis. The *dioikētēs* at the sixth council formulated his title, as we have seen, thus: Paul, *endoxotatos apo hypatōn, kai dioikētēs tōn anatolikōn eparchiōn*.[99] In contrast, the seal of Paul, *hypatos kai dioikētēs tōn Anatolikōn*, dated to the turn of the century,[100] seems clearly to name the *thema* of the Anatolikoi. The first Paul seems still to bear the hallmarks of the oriental prefecture – compare the usual title of the prefecture itself: τὰ ἀνατολικὰ πραιτώρια, in legislative documents.[101] He is thus in charge of the fiscal *dioikēsis* of the provinces of the prefecture of the East. The second Paul, however, was in charge of a smaller area, namely the provinces within the military district of the *Anatolikōn* army. The change in emphasis, if such it is, must reflect a recognition of a state of affairs in which the importance of new and developing provincial circumscriptions outweighed the relevance of the older establishment. Provinces – *eparchiai* – were being seen from the standpoint of which *thema* they belonged to, a point which the seals of the *kommerkiarioi, apothēkai* and *kommerkia* referred to already makes quite explicit. As the new thematic districts became more closely defined, and as officials of the central bureaux – the chartularies of the *genikon* in particular – were able to assume responsibility for provincial fiscal administration under the local governors, so the need to appoint officials to oversee large groups of provinces (perhaps a result of the obsolescence of the diocesan level of administration) within, or over all of, the prefecture, will likewise have diminished.[102]

---

[98] For example, Zacos and Veglery, no. 222, dated to the years 717–18, of anon., *genikoi kommerkiarioi* of the *apothēkē* of Colonea and all the *eparchiai* of Armeniakōn; no. 155, with table 18/2 (p. 164), seals of the *Armeniakōn* redated by Seibt, in BS 36 (1975), 209 to the early eighth century; no. 263, dated 745/6, of the *kommerkia* of the *eparchiai* of the imperial God-guarded *Opsikion*; and cf. nos. 242, dated 732/3, for the *Anatolikōn*; no. 261, dated 741/2, for *Thrakēsion*; nos. 258 and 259, dated 730–41, for Thrace; and so on.

[99] Mansi XI, 209B; Riedinger, 14.32.

[100] Zacos and Veglery, no. 2290. Lilie, 'Thrakien und Thrakesion', 12 would identify the two Pauls as one and the same, with an assumed promotion from *apo hypatōn* to *hypatos* in the interim. See Winkelmann, *Rang- und Ämterstruktur*, p. 35. But in view of the frequency of the name, this must remain hypothetical.

[101] E.g., JGR I, coll. 1, nov. 25, 2 (a. 629 = Dölger, *Regesten*, no. 199): τοῖς ἐνδοξοτάτοις τῶν ἀνατολικῶν ἱερῶν πραιτωρίων.

[102] A late seventh-century seal of an anon., *hypatos* and *chartoularios tou genikou* (Zacos and Veglery, no. 1231) shows that this bureau already had its officials responsible for provincial fiscal administration.

Fiscal administration 199

Finally, the fact that *dioikētai* responsible for 'the provinces' in a general and non-specific sense seem no longer to issue seals after the first years of the eighth century is extremely suggestive. It implies that officials with such a wide jurisdiction throughout the empire were no longer necessary to the fiscal administration. The fact that, with one dubious (and Western) exception, all the known seals of *dioikētai* of named provinces are dated to the eighth century and later, makes the conclusion that the two developments are somehow connected inescapable.[103]

The significance of these general *dioikētai* must now be apparent. The first of whom we have any mention is the Theodore whose seal, referred to already, was issued some time between 614 and 631, a period of fiscal and military crisis for the state. Thereafter, there are seals of six *dioikētai* 'of the provinces' datable to the period c. 650–750, and there is mention of a fifth, for the *eparchiai* of the East, in 680. Finally, for the years around 700, there is a seal of a *dioikētēs* of (the provinces of) the *Anatolikon*. All these officials, with two exceptions, are very high-ranking persons, with the titles of *hypatos, apo hypatōn* or *patrikios*, testifying to their importance.[104] It is surely no coincidence that the period in which these *dioikētai* functioned begins at the time of substantial fiscal reforms under Heraclius and ends, both as the *themata* begin to occur in literary sources and on seals *as administrative entities* and as individual provincial *dioikētai* start to (re)appear on issues of seals.

The solution to the problem of the general *dioikētai* is, therefore, an administrative and institutional one. If, as seems probable, the *genikē trapeza*, or *genikon*, had become more or less independent during the reign of Heraclius, whether already before his mint reform or, as seems more likely, as a result of the ramifications of that reform, then the close connection between this bank and the diocesan *scrinia*,[105] which actually dealt with the calculation and collection of the public taxes – a connection hitherto assured by the presence of all these bureaux within the same *officium* – will have been severed. Yet it is clear that in the developed *genikon logothesion* of the ninth century, the descendants of the officials of the former diocesan

[103] The exception is the seal of Theodore, *dioikētēs* of Hellas, dated to the period 650–750. But it, too, may well be of eighth-century date. See Zacos and Veglery, no. 1628.
[104] The two exceptions are the seals of Sergius (Schlumberger, *Sig.*, p. 499), described simply as *dioikētēs tōn eparchiōn* (which may suggest an earlier rather than a later date – the regular use of titles and rank increases during the seventh and especially the eighth century. See Winkelmann, *Rang- und Ämterstruktur*, p. 132); and of Marinus, *apo eparchōn* and *dioikētēs tōn eparchiōn* (Zacos and Veglery, no. 1178). *Apo eparchōn* seems to have been a relatively humble rank during the seventh century (see Zacos and Veglery, no. 142; Winkelmann, *Rang- und Ämterstruktur*, pp. 40f.).
[105] Diocesan describes, of course, the competence of these *scrinia*. They were physically located at Constantinople. For the *theion logothesion* at the end of Heraclius' reign, see note 67 above.

scrinia, and their several provincial controllers, assessors and collectors of taxes, were all within the general *logothesion* itself.[106] At some stage, therefore, the department of the general bank of the prefecture must have absorbed or otherwise been given administrative authority over these *scrinia*. Whether the diocesan *scrinia* themselves survived is difficult to say; but originally each *scrinium* had (usually) one *tractator* or supervisor of taxes for each of its provinces. The appointment within the general bank of a single supervising *dioikētēs* to oversee the operations of all the *scrinia* (which will eventually, if it did not happen through administrative fiat, have in practice brought the diocesan and provincial *scrinia* into the purview of the general bank) would be a logical step, both to maintain communication between the *scrinia* and the bank itself, and to co-ordinate the extraction of revenue throughout the prefecture. Once the *themata* had emerged as territorial administrative districts – in the last years of the seventh century – that is, as groups of provinces and once the functions of the old diocesan *scrinia* with regard to their constituent provinces had been fully assumed by the enlarged department of the *genikon* – which could now supervise the activities of the *epoptai* and *dioikētai* directly – then the general supervisors, the *dioikētai tōn eparchiōn*, became redundant. As we have noted, *themata* are clearly seen as consisting of groups of provinces by the early eighth century. At about this time, seals of general *dioikētai* cease to be issued; and seals of named provincial *dioikētai* begin to appear.[107] While the internal chronology of the process outlined must remain hazy, therefore, the limits to the transformation are set by the process of fiscal administrative reform and centralisation on the one hand, which seems to have begun in the last years of the sixth century and reached a definitive stage with Heraclius' reorganisation of the mint system in 627–30; and on the other hand, by the appearance of thematic provincial groupings, the cessation of references to general *dioikētai* and the concomitant appearance of individual provincial tax officials in the early eighth century.

[106] *Klet. Phil.*, 113.26–115.4. Of the staff of the *logothesion*, the *chartoularioi megaloi tou sekretou* represented the older *chartularii scriniorum*; the *chartoularioi tōn arklōn* (also called *exō chartoularioi*: see Oikonomidès, *Préséance*, p. 313) represented the former *praepositi thesaurorum* of the *comitiva sacrarum largitionum*; the *epoptai* and *dioikētai* represent the former *censitores* and *inspectores*, and *tractatores* for each province, responsible to the diocesan *scrinium* within which their province was located. The *koummerkiarioi* (sic), by this time simply customs and trade-regulation officials, are descended from the *comites commerciariorum* of the *sacrae largitiones*; while the *komēs tēs Lamias* represents the old prefectural *comes horreorum*. On the latter, see Haldon, 'Comes horreorum – Komēs tēs Lamias?'; for the other officials, see *Notitia Dig.*, or. XIII (*comes sacr. largit.*) and Jones, *LRE*, vol. I, pp. 449–51, 455.

[107] Of course, the sigillographic material itself cannot form an entirely solid basis for argument, since there may be seals which do not fit this pattern. But the seals known at the present time do support the argument; ar l statistically the sample does provide a sound basis for generalisation.

THE FATE OF THE PRAETORIAN PREFECTURE: EPARCHS AND PROCONSULS

Whether the praetorian prefect still had a role to play is, in view of the almost total lack of evidence in this regard, impossible to say with certainty. That the post continued to be filled, however, possibly as a civil administrative figurehead, is suggested by the existence of two seals of the period 650–700, of Marinus, ἀπὸ ἐπάρχων καὶ διοικητὴς τῶν ἐπαρχιῶν, and of the same Marinus, now promoted, ἀπὸ ὑπάτων καὶ ἔπαρχος τῶν...[108] It seems highly likely that the latter title should be completed πραιτωρίων; although a thematic title, such as Anatolikōn or Armeniakōn is a possibility. If the first suggestion is correct, then the praetorian prefect was still in existence in the later seventh century and, furthermore, probably still exercised a general authority over the departments formerly under his direct control.[109] That the office survived until the early ninth century is clear from its inclusion in a ceremony dating to the years 809–43, although the status of the title is open to question.[110] Like that of *magister officiorum*, the post of praetorian prefect of the East may have retained some vaguely defined supervisory capacity, as has already

---

[108] See Zacos and Veglery, nos. 1178 and 1179. A further three seals of Marinus, as *apo hypatōn kai dioikētēs tōn eparchiōn* exist. See Zacos and Veglery, note to no. 1178 (Konstantopoulos, *Molybdoboulla*, no. 58; N.P. Lihačev, *Istoričeskoe značenie italogrečeskoi ikonopisi Izobraženiya Bogomateri* (St Petersburg 1911), 117 (figs. 259 and 260).

[109] If the second suggestion is preferred, then Marinus may well have been one of the thematic prefects responsible for the provisioning of the provincial military at this time. See Kaegi, 'Two studies', 104ff., esp. 107ff.

[110] The history of the debate around this passage, first discussed in detail by Stein, 'Ein Kapitel', 70–82, has been briefly detailed by Kaegi, 'Two studies', 99ff. Stein based his date for the passage (which actually describes a ceremony for the feast of Easter, not for Pentecost as in the manuscript), on the presence of what he saw as a series of archaic Latin terms and titles. He concluded from this, and from the fact that a *dioikētēs tōn anatolikōn eparchiōn*, but not a praetorian prefect, appears in 680 at the sessions of the sixth ecumenical council, that the praetorian prefect had therefore ceased to exist by 680. He concluded further that the passage must itself date to the later seventh century, but before 680. The importance of the passage in the *De Cerimoniis* for Stein lay in the fact that both the praetorian prefect and the 'eparchs of the themes' occur among the list of dignitaries presented to the emperor. The passage in question reads: βῆλον τέταρτον · τὸν ὕπαρχον τῶν πραιτωρίων, τὸν κοιαίστωρα, ἀνθυπάτους τῶν θεμάτων καὶ ἐπάρχους (*De Cer.* 61.15–16).

Two sets of observations need to be made. In the first place, it must now be clear that, unless the passage has been very heavily interpolated (which would render it useless for Stein's argument also), it must date from after 809, since the *domestikos* of the *Hikanatoi* is listed also (*ibid.* 61.17, cf. also 67.23), a unit which was first established in that year (see Haldon, *Byzantine Praetorians*, pp. 245f.). Quite apart from this, the presence of tagmatic officers of the *scholai*, and of the *vigla*, the former established as a *tagma* only under Constantine V, the latter established probably by Eirene, makes it clear that the passage is at the earliest of the early ninth century (Haldon, *Byzantine Praetorians*, pp. 228ff. and 236ff.; note also Guilland, *Recherches*, vol. II, p. 70). In general style, and in respect of the

been suggested, perhaps over the provisioning and supplying of troops in the provinces: the thematic eparchs (see below), who do seem to have fulfilled this function until their replacement during the first half of the ninth century by thematic *prōtonotarioi* appointed from the *sacellium*, certainly came under the authority of the praetorian prefect.[111] And it may well be that the praetorian prefect who survives in this early ninth-century ceremony, equivalent in rank to the quaestor – with whom he was grouped – did retain a general authority over the administration of military supplies, through his subordinates, the *anthypatoi* and *eparchai* of the *themata*, exercised through a much-reduced *sekreton* at Constantinople, with a local bureau in each *thema*.

Now it has been suggested that the thematic *prōtonotarioi*, who begin to appear in the literary sources from the second quarter of the ninth century, and on seals shortly before this, were originally the local representatives of the office of these thematic eparchs who, when the praetorian prefecture and the dependent thematic eparchate were finally superseded, inherited the functions of the thematic eparch within the administration of the *stratēgos*.[112] But the *prōtonotarioi* were members of the *sakellion* at a slightly later date,[113] and it is probable that this reflects a long tradition, since it

palatine titles which occur, it could well be contemporary with the *Taktikon Uspenskij* of 842/3. The text can tell us little or nothing about the later seventh-century or indeed the early eighth-century establishment at all.

In the second place, where Stein assumed that the title *anthypatos*, which occurs in respect of two groups of dignitaries (*De Cer.* 61.13: πατρικίους τοὺς καὶ ἀνθυπάτους; 61.16. ἀνθυπάτους τῶν θεμάτων καὶ ἐπάρχους) signified, at least in the second case, two distinct functions, it seems more likely that one group is meant, the eparchs of the *themata* who were also *anthypatoi*. Note *De Cer.* 67.17: ἐπαρχίσας θεματικὰς ἀνθυπατίσας (the presentation of the wives of the respective officials on the same occasion); and cf. *T.Usp.* 51.25: οἱ ἀνθύπατοι καὶ ἔπαρχοι τῶν θεμάτων. The eparchs and *anthypatoi* clearly represent one group, and Stein's whole discussion of the question of the 'survival' of proconsuls therefore needs considerable revision. Guilland's attempt (*Recherches*, vol. II, p. 69 note 15) to emend the text of *De Cer.* 67.17, which he clearly thought problematic, in order to fit in with Stein's view, which he shared, by inverting the order so that it would read ἀνθυπατίσσας, θεματικὰς, ἐπαρχίσας, must be regarded with some suspicion. Correctly understood, such an arbitrary intervention in the text is quite unnecessary. It is worth noting that two seals dated to the first half of the ninth century, of Eustathius, imperial *spatharokandidatos* and *anthypatos* of the Anatolikoi (Zacos and Veglery, no. 1901); and of John, imperial *spatharios* and *anthypatos* of the Anatolikoi (Zacos and Veglery, no. 2049) do provide evidence for thematic officials bearing the title *anthypatos*, suggesting that there may well have been thematic *anthypatoi* acting as civil governors, even if by the time of the *Taktikon Uspenskij* they had been combined in practice with the position of thematic eparchs. Stein's argument is, therefore, partially vindicated.

111 Kaegi, 'Two studies', 106f., and *De Cer.* 61.15–16.
112 Kaegi, 'Two studies', 109ff., partly following and emending Stein, 'Ein Kapitel', 79ff. See especially Winkelmann, *Rang- und Ämterstruktur*, p. 142 with the evidence from both seals and literary sources cited there. See also Haldon, *Byzantine Praetorians*, pp. 215f.
113 *Klet. Phil.* 121.6; cf. Oikonomidès, *Préséance*, p. 315.

was the *sakellarios*, with his bureau, who in the late sixth and seventh centuries seems to have been responsible for the general fiscal supervision of state departments. More probably, the establishment of the *themata* as territorial administrative units from the early eighth century meant an increasing intervention in and supervision of the activities of the thematic eparchs by the *sakellarios*, and the consequent increasing irrelevance of the officials of the old prefecture in favour of those of the *sakellion*.

Two further arguments would favour this general hypothesis. In the first place, it has plausibly been argued that the eparchs of the *themata*, who occur in the ninth-century protocol in the Book of Ceremonies, and in the Taktikon Uspenskij (dated to 842/3), are the descendants of those *ad hoc* praetorian prefects appointed during the sixth and early seventh centuries to supervise the arrangements for supplying troops in transit.[114] The fact that they bear the title of *anthypatos*, however, deserves more attention. Stein believed that the title represented a separate office and argued that the *anthypatoi* of the *themata* were the civil governors, and that the eparchs were the governors of the provinces within the *themata*.[115] This line of reasoning then proceeds to argue that, since the ceremony is to be dated to the seventh century (which is, as we have seen, incorrect), the mention of these two groups of officials is evidence for a thematic civil administration by 680 at the latest, and therefore for the existence of the *themata* as both civil and military administrative units by this date. The argument is based on several misapprehensions and is now generally rejected.[116] But Stein was not entirely on the wrong track. For the fact that the eparchs are also *anthypatoi*, that *anthypatos* is not yet a title or rank, even in the Taktikon Uspenskij of 842/3, and that, crucially, thematic *anthypatoi* are evidenced, for the *Anatolikōn* at least, on seals of the early ninth century, is important.[117] Given the continued existence of a praetorian prefect in the early ninth century – whatever his exact functions – it is not entirely improbable that the posts of the former *ad hoc* prefects who had been responsible for military provisioning, and those of the leading civil governors of the provinces within the *thema* for which they were responsible, were eventually amalgamated. Both groups were at the disposition of the praetorian prefect; both would have fulfilled functions which were in practice very closely related. The fusion of the two, with the result that thematic prefects

---

[114] Kaegi, 'Two studies', 103ff.
[115] Stein, 'Ein Kapitel', 71f. Anthypatos had been the title of several provincial governors in the sixth century and earlier, although the majority of such governors bore titles such as *praeses, moderator*, or *consularis*. See Jones, *LRE*, vol. III pp. 386–9, table, col. 10.
[116] See the detailed critique by Karayannopoulos, *Entstehung*, pp. 55ff.
[117] See Oikonomidès, *Préséance*, pp. 287 and 294 with literature; Winkelmann, *Rang- und Ämterstruktur*, pp. 35f. and above, note 110, for the seals.

were also the civil governors of the bureau of the praetorian prefect in Constantinople, would not have been illogical.

In the second place, it is surely significant that, at approximately the time after which the thematic eparchs and *anthypatoi* are last mentioned (that is, in 842/3), both thematic *prōtonotarioi* and thematic *stratēgoi* bearing the title *anthypatos* appear in the sources.[118] It is tempting to see in these two developments a related phenomenon, namely, the phasing out (or abolition) of the skeletal residue of the old prefecture, with its thematic representatives (*anthypatoi* and eparchs combined), and the transfer of the civil governorships to the thematic *stratēgoi* – hence the use of the older functional title as a rank granted to the governor of a *thema*; and the concomitant establishment of representatives of the *sakellion* within the *themata*, the *prōtonotarioi*, to take up the role of the older eparchs in respect of provisioning and supplying the army, liaising with the central *sekreta* (the *genikon*, *eidikon* and, to a degree, the *stratiōtikon*), as the eparchs would have had to do before them. What was involved, therefore, was the removal of an intermediate administrative instance, that of the thematic proconsular eparchs; and the establishment of direct surveillance from the *sakellion*. That the *prōtonotarioi* replaced the eparchs/proconsuls functionally, but not in terms of power and rank, is evident from the fact that, whereas *stratēgoi*, and eventually other functionaries also, come generally to hold the rank of *anthypatos*, the *prōtonotarioi* in the *sakellion* remain fairly humble officials: mostly of the rank of *hypatos*, *spatharios*, *kandidatos* and

---

[118] The first mention of the title *anthypatos* as a rank seems to be that in Theophanes cont., 108.1 (cf. Guilland, *Recherches*, vol. II, p. 71; Oikonomidès, *Préséance*, p. 294; Bury, *Administrative System*, p. 28) for the reign of Theophilus. In the *Taktikon Uspenskij*, however, firmly dated to 842/3 (Oikonomidès, *Préséance*, p. 45) the term seems still to be a function, see *T.Usp.*, 51.25; with the possible exception of the entry ὁ πατρίκιος καὶ ἀνθύπατος which, it has been suggested, represents the position created for Alexios Mousele by Theophilus referred to in Theophanes cont. above (see *T.Usp.*, 49.1 and Bury, *Administrative System*, p. 28. For its still being a functional rank, see Winkelmann, *Rang- und Ämterstruktur*, p. 35). The dating of a number of seals of the early ninth century bearing the title *anthypatos*, on the other hand, suggests that it had already towards the end of Eirene's reign a titular value – see the seals of Gregory Mousoulakios, who appears to have held the ranks of *anthypatos*, *patrikios*, while also being *komēs* of the Opsikion (see Haldon, *Byzantine Praetorians*, p. 360 and note 1100; Zacos and Veglery, no. 3113A; and Seibt, *Bleisiegel*, no. 158). But Gregory may be, like Alexios Mousele after him, an exception. Other seals bearing the title are all to be placed in the middle decades of the ninth century or later: see the list and commentary of Winkelmann, *Rang- und Ämterstruktur*, pp. 35–6. By the later ninth century, in contrast, and certainly by the time the Kletorologion was compiled, all the *stratēgoi* of *themata*, as well as members of the central *sekreta* holding the higher posts, could be *anthypatoi*. See Guilland, *Recherches*, vol. II, pp. 71ff. for a prosopographical list.

the like.[119] Seals of *prōtonotarioi* are extant in considerable numbers, seals of *anthypatoi* are relatively few. Two, with specific thematic titles (of the *Anatolikōn*), have been mentioned. Others cover the period from the seventh to the early ninth centuries.[120] Whatever the explanation for the imbalance, there is nevertheless a clear continuity from the sixth century until the middle of the first half of the ninth century in the use of the title *anthypatos*, often in conjunction with other ranks, to denote an office, and not simply a dignity.

However uncertain the picture, therefore, there is good reason for believing that the praetorian prefect continued to exist until some time in the period of 809 to 842; and that his bureau, which was responsible for elements of the provincial civil administration and the supplying and provisioning of provincial troops was represented by *anthypatoi* and eparchs, who in the final stages seem to have been amalgamated as a single post in the *themata*. This amalgamation (with one such joint post for each *thema*?) is the more likely in view of the fact that both officials were responsible for exactly the same territorial circumscriptions. The general hypothesis is supported by the survival of the older provincial governors, or praetors, until the time of the Taktikon Uspenskij in 842/3, and their subsequent emergence as the leading judicial officials in the *themata*. Once more, a key element of the traditional civil and fiscal administrative apparatus continued to play a role into the ninth century; and it seems unlikely that all these titles represent no more than a fossilised echo of a past system. Within the framework I have outlined, they played an active, functional role in the state establishment.

A final point is worth making here. The boundaries of the original large *themata* in Asia Minor corresponded, as we shall see, fairly closely, and in most cases exactly, with older provincial boundaries. There was no agreement with diocesan boundaries, however, since the *themata* represented areas which could support a certain number of soldiers, as well as a degree of strategic planning. This will be demonstrated below. Each *thema*, however, did consist of a group of older provinces, and the question arises

---

[119] For example, Zacos and Veglery, nos. 3118, 2496, 3214, 1727, 2324 and many more. See the remarks of Winkelman, *Rang- und Ämterstruktur*, p. 142, with lists at pp. 120 and 122–31 where some 65 seals of *prōtonotarioi* are listed. By the ninth century, these formerly prestigious titles had been greatly reduced in status.

[120] Sée note 110 above. The other seals are: Zacos and Veglery, no. 2881, of John, *anthypatos* (550–650); no. 775, Konstantinos, *anthypatos* (550–650), no. 1085, Tryphon, *Stratēlatēs* and *anthypatos* (late seventh century); Schlumberger, *Sig.*, 438,4; David, *anthypatos* (eighth–ninth century); Konstantopoulos, *Molybdoboulla*, no. 295: John, *illoustrios* and *anthypatos* (seventh to eighth century); cf. also Schlumberger, *Sig.*, p. 438,2, seal of Andreas Botaneiates, imperial *spatharios* and *anthypatos*.

as to why the titles of *anthypatos* on the one hand (representing civil and fiscal administration) and praetor on the other (representing judicial administration), which in Justinian's time had equivalent status (both were *spectabiles*), came to have different statuses by the early ninth century and how the division of labour came to be attached to the two titles in this way. Other titles, such as *moderator* or *comes*, were also available, but were not retained. The only reasonable answer would suggest that some deliberate administrative/legislative decision was taken at a certain point in the later seventh or early eighth century; and that, perhaps for traditional reasons of association, the two terms were thus assigned, the paramount civil governorships being described as *anthypatoi*, the judicial functions being awarded to the praetors. But the Taktikon Uspenskij would not contradict the notion that, until this time at least, the term praetors of the *themata* referred to the civil governors of the individual provinces within each *thema*, while the *anthypatoi* and *eparchai* were responsible for the whole *thema*, including all its constituent provincial subdivisions.[121]

To summarise briefly the results of the foregoing analysis. The evidence points to a major restructuring of the fiscal administration of the state during the reign of Heraclius. While the reform and reorganisation of the system of mints constitutes the major single change, the logical consequence of this centralisation of administration for the provincial organisation of the *sacrae largitiones*, together with the evidence for the increasingly important role of the *sakellarios*, and the appearance of high-ranking *logothetai* during the reigns of both Phocas and Heraclius, seems to be that the *sekreta* of the *genikon*, *eidikon* and *stratiōtikon*, together with the *sakellion* and the *vestiarion*, already existed in their essential form by the end of Heraclius' reign. Apart from the reorganisation of the mints, however, which itself may well have been a response to pre-existing tendencies, exacerbated by the civil war and the war with the Persians, these changes – essentially a reversal of the pattern which had hitherto operated – evolved as logical and necessary consequences of each successive administrative alteration in the older establishment and follow quite consistently from one another. They also conform to the possibilities presented by the available evidence and represent the only coherent explanation for that evidence.

At the same time, shifts in the pattern of provincial fiscal administration occurred. In order to ensure a coherent policy, and to fill the gap left by the disappearance of the diocesan tier, general supervisors were appointed to oversee provincial tax-assessment and collection; and it is presumably not

---

[121] See *T.Usp.*, 53.3 (and note Oikonomidès, *Préséance*, p. 344, who makes a similar suggestion).

a coincidence that the first such official of whom we learn, Theodore, was appointed during the reign of Heraclius, and possibly at the same time as the reorganisation of the mints took place. By the early eighth century, however, the establishment of the provincial field armies in Asia Minor and the fixing of their boundaries lent to these new districts an administrative identity (the equivalent of a group of provinces) which provided an intermediate level of administration. They replaced, in effect, an administrative level similar to that represented by the older dioceses. In consequence, fiscal supervisors could be appointed to these districts, the *themata*, with their subordinate provinces, and the general (prefectural) supervisors were superseded. Similarly, while the praetorian prefect remained in existence, the civil provinces within the *themata* formed new groupings, placed under a senior civil official, the proconsul, again equivalent in many respects to the *vicarii* of the older dioceses; while the *ad hoc* prefects appointed from the sixth century to deal with troops in transit were made permanent as a result of the permanent presence in what had been predominantly civil provinces of the field armies. By the later eighth or early ninth centuries the functions of these two 'thematic' civil officials had come to be formally assimilated; while the gradual evolution of the various fiscal bureaux at Constantinople meant that their role was increasingly redundant. Eventually – some time after 842/3 – they were abolished, their function being assumed by the thematic *prōtonotarioi* of the *sacellium*, their high status being transferred to the thematic governors or *stratēgoi*, who were henceforth formally endowed with both civil and military authority.

This is only a part of the story, of course, and it is necessary now to turn to the military administration of the state, and to the vexed question of the military provinces themselves, the *themata*.

CHAPTER 6

The state and its apparatuses: military administration

THE THEMATA

As with most other aspects of the state's administrative machinery, its structures of military organisation also evolved along lines which resulted in a system of very different appearance in the eighth and ninth centuries from that which operated in the sixth and earlier seventh centuries. A number of processes, which form in practice an evolutionary whole, need to be clarified or explained. All, however, depend to a greater or lesser extent on one key problem: the origins and development of the so-called *themata* or military provinces and the phenomena associated with them – the mode of recruiting, equipping and supplying the soldiers, the methods of paying them, and the fate of the civil provincial government.

The differences between the late Roman army of the sixth century and that of the Byzantine state of the ninth century are not difficult to perceive. The late Roman system was characterised by a fundamental division between the civil and military spheres of administration: civil officials had no authority over the military, and vice versa. The armies were divided into two essential groups: those of the mobile field forces, technically referred to as *comitatenses* (although in their turn made up of a number of distinct types of unit, differentiated originally by their posting, their mode and source of recruitment and so on), and the permanent frontier or garrison units, described and known as *limitanei* (although again made up from units of widely differing origins).[1] But while in theory remaining mobile, many units of the *comitatenses* came to be based for long periods in

[1] For detailed descriptions and analyses of the late Roman army, see Jones, *LRE*, vol. II, pp. 607–86; D. Hoffmann, *Das spätrömische Bewegungsheer und die Notitia Dignitatuum* (Epigr. Studien VII, 1, Düsseldorf and Cologne 1969); R. Grosse, *Römische Militärgeschichte von Gallienus bis zum Beginn der byzantinischen Themenverfassung* (Berlin 1920); Th. Mommsen, 'Das römische Militärwesen seit Diocletian', *Hermes* 24 (1889), 195–279; A. Müller, 'Das Heer Iustinians nach Prokop und Agathias', *Philologus* 71 (1912), 101–38; G. Ravegnani, *Soldati di Bisanzio in età Giustinianea* (Materiali e Ricerche, Nuova Serie VI Rome 1988).

one area or garrison town, the soldiers putting down local roots, and even – as some examples from Africa, Italy, Egypt or Palestine demonstrate – taking up other occupations.[2] For the *limitanei*, recruitment was assured through hereditary conscription, and membership of these units was regarded as a privilege, in view of the favourable tax-status of soldiers who, while subject to the regular land-and-head tax, were exempted from all extraordinary burdens. It was further assured through various forms of voluntary recruitment for the regular units of the *comitatenses*.[3] Weapons, uniforms and mounts were provided by the state, which also issued cash allowances for their purchase, through the commissariat, and from civilian suppliers or – as in the case of weapons and some items of clothing – from the state factories or workshops.[4]

The system of command at the beginning of Justinian's reign was, in most respects, unchanged from that of the fifth century. The *limitanei* along the frontiers were divided into a number of independent commands, consisting of nine *duces* (of Palestine, Arabia, Phoenice, Syria, Euphratensis, Osrhoene, Mesopotamia, Pontus, Armenia) on the eastern frontier, a *comes rei militaris* in Egypt, three *duces*, of the Thebaid, Libya and the Pentapolis in North Africa; and five *duces*, of Scythia, Dacia, Moesia I and II and Pannonia II on the Danube. The field armies were similarly grouped into divisions, in this case five, two of them in and near Constantinople (in Thrace and in north-west Anatolia) under the two *magistri militum praesentales*, one in Thrace, one in Illyricum and one in the East. In addition, military officers entitled *comites rei militaris*, who had authority over civil governors also, were appointed to provinces where banditry was a problem, notably Isauria, Pamphylia, Pisidia and Lycaonia. While the master of offices exercised a general inspectorate over the *limitanei*, both they and the field troops were subject directly to the authority of their respective *magistri militum*. Justinian introduced several changes. The zone of the *magister militum per Orientem* was divided into two, and a new *magister militum per Armeniam* took over the northern section; new commands for south-eastern Spain, for Italy (*magister militum per Italiam*) and for Africa (*magister militum per Africam*) were established after the reconquest, the latter circumscription including also the isles of Sardinia and Corsica. A combined military civil command of the Long Walls (established by Anastasius under two *vicarii*, one civil and one military) under a praetor

---

[2] Italy: Brown, *Gentlemen and Officers*, pp. 101ff.; Egypt: Jones, *LRE*, vol. II, pp. 662ff.; Syria/Palestine: Patlagean, *Pauvreté économique*, pp. 255ff. and 313–15; Durliat, 'Les Finances municipales', 379 and 'Les grands propriétaires et l'état byzantin', 527f.
[3] For sources and literature, see Haldon, *Recruitment and Conscription*, pp. 20–8 and *Byzantine Praetorians*, pp. 103ff.
[4] See Jones, *LRE*, vol. II, pp. 671 and 834–7; Haldon, *Byzantine Praetorians*, pp. 114f. with literature.

of Thrace, was also established. The number of commands of *limitanei* was increased along the eastern front to deal with Persian incursions; and in the Armenian zone the two *duces* of Armenia and Pontus were replaced by five commands along a more advanced frontier. Similar commands were established along the African frontier, in Tripolitania, Byzacium, Numidia and Mauretania, Sardinia and in northern Italy. In general, Justinian maintained the division between military and civil spheres of authority; but in Asia Minor he combined civil and military authority to deal with brigandage (in Isauria, Pisidia and Lycaonia); in Egypt the position of *Praefectus Augustalis* and *dux* were combined; and the *dux* of the Thebaid was given civil administrative authority to deal with raids from the desert tribes.

Apart from these units and their dispositions, the emperors also had the palatine units of the *scholae* (by the sixth century a parade-force only) and the *excubitores*, created by Leo I, who replaced the *scholae* as the elite imperial bodyguard. In addition, the palatine corps of *protectores et domestici*, both horse and foot, under their *comites* (later a single *comes*) formed another parade unit.[5] Justinian's main strategic innovation was the establishment of the *quaestura exercitus*, comprising Caria and the Aegean isles, together with the Danubian provinces of Scythia and Moesia II. The aim was to secure supplies and a sound base for the frontier units which could thus avoid further impoverishing an already devastated region.[6]

After Justinian's reign, several administrative changes were made, and certain organisational reforms within the structure of the field armies took place. Most of these seem to have occurred in the reign of Maurice. Of the administrative changes, the establishment of the two exarchates of Ravenna and Carthage were responses to the arrival of the Lombards on the one hand, and to the constant raiding of the Berbers along the African *limes* on the other. This move was partially the formal recognition of what had hitherto been *de facto* the case, namely the greater importance of the *magister militum* in each of the two prefectures as a result of the prevailing political and military situation. Already both Solomon and Germanus had combined the offices of *magister militum* with that of praetorian prefect in Africa; and although the praetorian prefect continued to exist as an independent office separate from the exarch, the latter was officially endowed with supreme authority.[7] It has recently been demonstrated in addition that the mints of both Carthage and Ravenna began to produce (for the first time in the former case) a regular issue of dated *solidi*, those of Carthage dated indictionally, those of Ravenna by imperial regnal years.

[5] See Jones, *LRE*, vol. II, pp. 655-7; Haldon, *Byzantine Praetorians*, pp. 119-41.
[6] Jones, *LRE*, vol. I, p. 280. Cf. Justinian, *Nov.* 41 (a. 536) and Lydus, *De Magistratibus* II, 28-9 (pp. 83-5).
[7] See Jones, *LRE*, vol. II, pp. 655-6; Brown, *Gentlemen and Officers*, pp. 46ff.; Guillou, *Régionalisme*, pp. 150ff. For the older literature, see Diehl, *Etudes byzantines*, pp. 157-84; *L'Afrique byzantine*, pp. 484ff.

This occurred between December 581 and August 582. Some time between August 582 and August 583 a new mint, producing copper and possibly also gold, was established at Catania in Sicily, which had since 537 been under a separate jurisdiction jointly administered by the *quaestor sacri palatii* and the *comes patrimonii per Italiam*. The first reference to an exarch for Italy is for 584; the first for Africa, 591.[8] There is little doubt that this reorganisation of minting and the new issues which resulted reflected also the new statute of the affected prefectures, and these developments seem to have coincided with and reflect the establishment of the exarchates, with their greater political, military and fiscal independence.[9]

In the tactical organisation of the armies, reforms also took place, mostly during the reigns of Tiberius Constantine and Maurice. The numerous units of *foederati*, effectively by this time units of mixed – Roman and barbarian – regulars in the *comitatenses*, came to be brigaded together in a single corps. Similarly, the private *bucellarii* of the leading officers in the praesental forces were also brigaded together as an elite force and were incorporated into the state establishment, receiving pay and provisions on the same basis as the regular troops. Both developments seem to have occurred in the context of the wars in the Balkans in the 580s and 590s; and at the same period an elite 'foreign legion' of Germanic cavalry, the *optimates*, seems to have been established, made up chiefly of Gothic and Lombard mercenary soldiers at first, although later recruited from within the empire also. These changes were accompanied by reforms in the command structure of the armies, which represented the culmination of a long-drawn-out development in which the older internal structure of regular units dating back to the time of Diocletian and Constantine was replaced or modified by a system which more closely reflected the functional needs and the language of the late-sixth-century army.[10] Finally, there is some evidence that the old division between the two *magistri militum praesentales* and their armies ceased to have any practical significance, so that there came to be usually only one praesental force under a supreme commander, normally operating in Europe. This development was to have important consequences in Heraclius' reign and after.[11]

The system which is described in the sources of the ninth century is very different. The *magistri militum*, with their field armies, and the *limitanei* under their *duces* are no longer to be found. Instead, the territories

---

[8] See Pelagius II, *Ep.* I, 703–5 (*PL* LXXII); Greg. I, *Ep.* I, 59.
[9] For the most recent treatment, see Hendy, *Studies*, pp. 406ff., with sources and literature.
[10] On these developments see Haldon, *Byzantine Praetorians*, pp. 96ff. and 107ff; and *Recruitment and Conscription*, pp. 31–2.
[11] *Byzantine Praetorians*, pp. 176ff. See also idem, 'Administrative continuities and structural transformations in East Roman military organisation c.580–640', in *L'Armée romaine et les barbares du 4e au 7e siècle*, eds. F. Vallet, M. Kazanski (Paris 1993) 45–51 (repr. in *State, Army and Society in Byzantium*, V).

remaining in the empire (or regained since the seventh century) were divided up into a number of military provinces, or *themata*, each governed by a *stratēgos*, or general, who – at least in terms of general authority – held both civil and military powers; although the civilian officials and their spheres of action within each *thema* were closely supervised by their respective chief bureaux at Constantinople. The *themata* varied in size, but were subdivided for military purposes into *tourmai*, or divisions, each consisting of a number of *drouggoi*, or brigades, the latter in turn made up of several *banda*, or regiments. By the ninth century, the chief territorial division within the thema was the *bandon*, also called a *topotērēsia*; but it is clear that the older provinces of the late Roman period survived well into the eighth century and possibly into the early ninth. The *stratēgoi* were subject directly to the emperor, by whom they were nominated. They commanded mixed forces of infantry and cavalry, made up of volunteers and conscripted soldiers, the latter enlisted according to an hereditary personal obligation. The frontier districts were organised into 'passes', or *kleisourarchiai*, each under a *kleisourarch*.[12]

The thematic administration, which by the middle of the ninth century clearly included also the civil government of the areas encompassed by each *thema*, was controlled from Constantinople by the various fiscal administrative *sekreta* – the *genikon*, *eidikon* and *stratiōtikon*, supervised by the *sakellion* and the *sakellarios* – through their thematic representatives: the *prōtonotarios* for the *sakellion*; the *chartoularioi* of the provincial treasuries for the *genikon*, along with their subordinate fiscal officials – *dioikētai*, *epoptai*, *exisōtai* and so on – and the thematic *chartoularioi* of the *stratiōtikon*. The latter were attached directly to the staff of the *stratēgos*, who had his own corps of guards, and a staff of clerical officials, in addition to the military officers of his command.[13]

While the number of *themata* had multiplied during the eighth century and especially the ninth century, partly through the subdividing of older and larger *themata*, partly through the acquisition of new (reconquered) territories, there had been originally only four such regions: the *Opsikion*, the *Anatolikōn*, the *Armeniakōn* and the *Thrakēsiōn*; together with a fifth division, the fleet of the *Karabisianoi*, which included the islands of the Aegean and part of the south-west coast of Asia Minor. It is now generally agreed that the *Thrakēsiōn* army, which represented the older division of the *magister militum per Thracias*, had been established in the area later known as the *thema* of the same name some time during the middle years

---

[12] For a descriptive survey of the *themata*, see *CMH*, vol. IV, part 2, pp. 35ff.; Toynbee, *Constantine Porphyrogenitus*, pp. 134ff. and 224ff. For further literature on their origins see chapter 5, note 70 above.

[13] For a summary, see Oikonomidès, *Préséance*, pp. 341ff. with literature.

of the seventh century and that it is as old as the other original *themata*.[14] During the reign of Justinian II these five divisions existed alongside the forces of the exarchates of Italy and Africa; and, as has long been recognised, they were descended respectively from the armies of the *magistri militum praesentales, per Orientem, per Armeniam, per Thracias*, as we have already noted, and from the forces under the *quaestor exercitus*.[15]

The first reference to these divisions together occurs in the *iussio* of the Emperor Justinian II, sent to the pope in 687 in confirmation of the acts of the sixth ecumenical council of 680. As witnesses to the orthodoxy of the emperor and his subjects, the emperor lists the following:

deinceps militantes incolas sancti palatii, nec non et ex collegiis popularibus et ab excubitoribus, insuper etiam quosdam de Christo dilectis exercitibus, tam ab a Deo conservando Obsequio, quamque ab Orientali, Thraciano, similiter et ab Armeniano, etiam ab exercitu Italiano, deinde ex Caravisiensis et Septensiensis seu de Sardinia atque de Africa exercitu.[16]

By this date therefore the basic elements of the later system of thematic armies appears to have been established. It is the process of this establishment, the origins of the armies concerned, and the transformation from late Roman institutions and practices to which I shall now turn.

Two questions present themselves: When did these forces occupy Anatolia? And how were they recruited, organised and supported? Two related questions follow: What was the relationship between these forces and the civilian population, and between their commanders and the civil administration? And what was the relationship between the establishment of these forces in Asia Minor and the later system of military land-holding familiar from the legislation of the tenth century? The first and third questions are probably the most straightforward, and I will deal with them first.

The first explicit reference to the *Opsikion* (Latin *Obsequium*) division is for 680, when the *komēs* of the *Opsikion* is listed among the officers accompanying the emperor during the sessions of the sixth ecumenical council; although there is good reason to think that the *Opsikion* army existed

---

[14] See the now out-of-date but still important work of Gelzer, *Themenverfassung*, pp. 9f. and 19ff.; and also Ostrogorsky, *Geschichte*, pp. 80f., with map and literature; Lilie, *Die byzantinische Reaktion*, pp. 287ff.; Haldon, *Byzantine Praetorians*, p. 165. For the first references to the districts and armies of the *themata* in the sources, see Pertusi, *De Thematibus*, comm. pp. 104–11, 114–20, 124–30 and 149ff. For the *Thrakēsiōn thema*, Lilie, '"Thrakien" und "Thrakesion"', 22–7.

[15] See Pertusi, *De Thematibus*, comm. pp. 105f. and 149; Haldon, *Byzantine Praetorians*, p. 165 with literature; H. Antoniadis-Bibicou, *Etudes d'histoire maritime à Byzance, à propos du Thème des Caravisiens* (Paris 1966), esp. pp. 63ff.; Toynbee, *Constantine Porphyrogenitus*, pp. 235f.

[16] Mansi XI, 737f.; Riedinger, 886.20–25.

already in the 640s and before;[17] in addition, it is almost certain that the Armenian noble Mzez Gnouni – the Mizizios of the Greek sources – was *komēs* of the *Opsikion* in the 660s, and up to his death after the assassination of Constans II in 668.[18] Certainly by the late 680s this army was seen as occupying a defined region, as later sources testify, although the evidence of seals of *kommerkiarioi* show that the traditional provincial names continued to be employed by contemporaries as before.[19] The *Armeniakōn* and *Anatolikōn themata* appear in references for the years 667 and 669 respectively;[20] the *Thrakēsiōn thema* is that referred to as the *Thracianus exercitus* in the *iussio* of 687 referred to above;[21] while the *Caravisiani – Karabisianoi –* appear in the same document, and at approximately the same time in an account contained in the collection of the miracles of St Demetrius at Thessaloniki.[22]

The word *thema* is itself a problem. In the older literature, and in particular in the work of Ostrogorsky, it was argued that it bore a specific technical meaning, namely a definite region, occupied by a military corps commanded by a *stratēgos*, who was the governor-general of his region and in whose hands both civil and military authority were united.[23] This view has been challenged from a number of different perspectives, but most importantly, the earliest reference to the word *thema*, in the ninth-century Chronography of Theophanes Confessor, has generally been regarded as an anachronism, contemporary with the compiler of the chronicle, not with the events described. The case cannot actually be conclusively proved in either direction. In the last analysis, the most that can safely be said about the term in these earliest occurrences is that it refers merely to armies: it is clear that in mentions of *themata* from the later seventh century this is how the word is used.[24] That it was later applied to the districts where these forces were based is not in doubt. But this does not seem to happen until the later seventh century (according to the ninth-century historical sources) or the beginning of the eighth century (according to the

---

[17] Mansi XI, 209; Riedinger, 14.20–21; Haldon, *Byzantine Praetorians*, pp. 144f. and 175–80.
[18] Haldon, *Byzantine Praetorians*, pp. 179f.
[19] See Theophanes, 364; Nicephorus, 36. 20. For the seals, Zacos and Veglery, no. 186 (dated 694/5) of George, *apo hypatōn*, (for) the Slav prisoners of the *eparchia* of Bithynia; no. 187 (dated 694/5) of George, *apo hypatōn*, of the *apothēkē* of the Slav prisoners in Phrygia Salutaria; no 243 (dated 731/2), of the imperial *kommerkia* of Bithynia, Salutaria and Pakatianē; and so on. See Zacos and Veglery, tables.
[20] Theophanes, 348. 29; 352. 14–23.
[21] Mansi XI, 737; Riedinger, 886.23. See Lilie, ' "Thrakien" und "Thrakesion" ', 22ff.
[22] See the references assembled in Pertusi, *De Thematibus*, p. 149.
[23] See the classic summary of this position in Ostrogorsky, *Geschichte*, pp. 80ff., with the older literature up to 1960.
[24] For summaries of the debate and a critique of the Ostrogorsky thesis, see Lilie, *Die byzantinische Reaktion*, pp. 287ff.; Haldon, 'Some remarks', 167, and *Recruitment and Conscription*, pp. 30ff.

contemporary documentation).²⁵ Note that the traditional title of the regional military commanders – *magistri militum* – was still in use in 662, in the district of Lazica in the Caucasus.²⁶

The word *thema*, then, seems to be a term introduced during the seventh century – possibly right at the beginning, but by no means certainly – to mean an army or division. From its use in later sources, on contemporary seals and from the list of armies in the *iussio* of Justinian II of 687 it is clear that it was applied to the forces of the various *magistri militum*, each of whose corps was described as a *thema*. At some point during the seventh century, these forces occupied areas of Asia Minor on what was to become a permanent basis, each covering a number of provinces; so that by the early eighth century, the civil provinces could be counted on occasion in 'thematic' groups, that is, according to which army occupied them. From this time, therefore, the term *thema*, while retaining its original sense of army, could refer also to a distinct geographical area, and fiscal administrators could be referred to officially as supervising the provinces of such-and-such a *thema*.²⁷

THE OCCUPATION OF ANATOLIA

The process by which these armies arrived and were established in Asia Minor seems now generally agreed: the armies of the *magister militum per Thracias* were at some point transferred to Anatolia, either under Hera-

---

[25] Theophanes, 364, 14–16: εἰς τὰ τοῦ Ὀψικίου ... μέρη; Nicephorus, 36. 20: εἰς τὴν τοῦ Ὀψικίου λεγομένην χώραν. On the value of these later references and the problems of interpretation which accompany them, see the comments of Lilie, 'Die zweithundertjährige Reform', 30. For the first references in contemporary documents to *themata*, see the seals noted in chapter 5, note 98 above for the years 717/18 and later; and that of Paul, *dioikētēs* of the *Anatolikōn*, dated to c. 700 (Zacos and Veglery, no. 2290).

[26] See Devreesse, *Hypomnesticum*, 70. 1–2; it occurs also – as στρατηλάτης ἐν τοῖς ἀνατολικοῖς μέρεσιν – in the (probably late seventh-century) fictional Life of St Andrew the Fool: PG CXI, 632A.

[27] The origins and etymology of the word remain unclear: see the literature cited in Haldon, *Recruitment and Conscription*, p. 31 and notes 35 and 36. More recently it has been suggested that the term is an early seventh-century loan word, from the Chazar turkic word *tümen*, meaning a division of 10,000 soldiers, although I do not find this particularly convincing. See J. D. Howard-Johnston, 'Thema', in *Maistor. Classical, Byzantine and Renaissance Studies for Robert Browning*, ed. A. Moffatt (Byzantina Australiensia V, Canberra 1984), pp. 189–97. More convincingly, see J. Koder, 'Zur Bedeutungsentwicklung des byzantinischen Terminus *Thema*', JÖB 40 (1990) 155–65, suggesting that the term may already have been employed with the meaning 'designated region' before the middle of the seventh century. It has also been argued that the *themata* are to be identified with a number of districts which appear in the earliest Arab accounts of the conquest of Syria and which clearly predate the actual conquest of these areas. These districts are referred to as Junds (Arab. Jund, pl. Ajnād), and it has been argued that they actually represent the military zones of a Heraclian thematic reorganisation. See I. Shahîd, 'Heraclius and the theme system: new light from the Arabic', B 67 (1987), 391–403; and I. Shahîd, 'Heraclius and the Theme System: Further Observations', B 69 (1989), 208–43. In fact,

clius or shortly thereafter, to oppose the Arabs; those of the *magistri militum per Orientem* and *per Armeniam* were withdrawn in the late 630s as the Romans were forced to deal with the effects of the defeat at the Yarmuk in 636. The regions already occupied by the praesental forces, the *Obsequium/Opsikion*, from the later sixth century, formed the later district of the same name. When exactly the Thracian forces were established in Asia Minor is unclear, but it was probably at the same time as the troops of the *magister militum per Orientem* withdrew into Asia Minor, since we hear of a *magister militum per Thracias* commanding an army on this front and being sent with his troops to reinforce Egypt in 638.[28] Thrace seems to have come already under the occasional protection of the praesental forces, although it clearly had troops of its own. The more pressing threat in the East, together with the lack of resources in Thrace itself to maintain such an army, must lie behind the decision to billet at least a large proportion of the troops in western Asia Minor. The forces which remained in and were maintained in Thrace were established as a *thema*, together with its dependent region, only after 680, or so it would seem, as the threat from the Bulgars became serious.[29]

The process of withdrawal and of the distribution of the troops in their new garrisons and camps was in all probability completed by the mid-640s: already one Arabic source refers to a military unit called *Armeniakōn* for this period, suggesting that the forces of the *magister militum per Armeniam* were by this date established in their new districts; while it has been pointed out that Arab attacks on Amorium in 644 and 646 may reflect the new headquarters of the *magister militum per Orientem*, whose forces had by this time also been withdrawn.[30] The praesental forces of the *Opsikion* seem to have been active in north-west Anatolia at about the same time, under an officer who may have been their *komēs*.[31] As has been shown elsewhere, the term *Obsequium/Opsikion* applied to this

they probably represent the regions under the command of the *duces* of Phoenice Libanensis, Arabia and the three Palestines: see J.F. Haldon, 'Seventh-century continuities: the *Ajnād* and the "Thematic Myth"', in *States, Resources and Armies* (Studies in Late Antiquity and Early Islam 1, III), ed. Averil Cameron (Princeton 1995), 379–423. On all these developments and the evolution of the debate on the origins of middle Byzantine military structures, see *idem*, 'Military service, military lands, and the status of soldiers: current problems and interpretations', *DOP* 47 (1993) 1–67 (repr. in *State, Army and Society in Byzantium*, VII).

[28] Nicephorus, 24, 19. See Haldon, *Byzantine Praetorians*, p. 173 note 349.
[29] For the *Opsikion* and Thrace – Haldon, *Byzantine Praetorians*, pp. 194f., and note 442 for Thracian troops in the 650s; Lilie, '"Thrakien" und "Thrakesion"', 28–35.
[30] See W. E. Kaegi, jr., 'Al-Baladhuri and the Armeniak theme', *B* 38 (1968), 273–7, and 'The first Arab expedition against Amorium', *BMGS* 3 (1977), 19–22; Haldon, *Recruitment and Conscription*, p. 33 and note 40; Lilie, 'Die zweihundertjährige Reform', 36. The removal of Armenia from Byzantine control in 652–5 must have meant the establishment of the forces of the *magister militum per Armeniam* in their new districts by this date at the latest. See Stratos, *Byzantium in the Seventh Century*, vol. II, pp. 73f. and 108ff.
[31] Haldon, *Byzantine Praetorians*, pp. 191ff.

Military administration 217

army derives not from a description of the field armies themselves, but from the title of the officer who, during the reign of Heraclius, was appointed to command them on the emperor's behalf. This officer was the commander of the palatine corps of *domestici*, the *comes domesticorum*, also called the *comes Obsequii*.[32] Finally, the command of the *Caravisiani* (Καραβισιάνοι / ἡ στρατηγία τῶν Καράβων), constituted by the central and southern parts of the old *quaestura exercitus* (i.e. the Aegean islands and Cyprus) and probably based at Samos, must have attained its final form by about 654, if not slightly earlier, with the Arab conquest of Cyprus in that year.[33]

The fate of the *limitanei* in the Eastern and Armenian commands is unknown. Since, according to Procopius, Justinian had 'deprived them of the name of soldier', their status seems to have undergone some changes – possibly they were no longer granted the usual immunities and privileges of military status. At any rate, they formed for the most part a settled garrison force and participated in regular campaigns infrequently. It is quite possible that the great majority – certainly those of the frontier districts overrun most rapidly by the Arabs – simply stayed in their settlements and on their lands, where their security, and their families, were to be found. In the northernmost districts of the eastern frontier, units of *limitanei* may well have survived intact at first; but the changed situation, their loss of status, and the permanent establishment of the field troops around them, must have quickly led to their assimilation to the ordinary civil population and the loss of any vestigial militia or police functions.[34]

By the mid-650s, therefore, it seems probable that all the original *themata* – armies – had taken up their new positions. It has long been clear that these new quarters consisted in essence of groups of older civil provinces, so much so that later subdivisions of *themata* tended to follow the lines of late Roman provincial boundaries:[35] and where older provincial boundaries are not respected, there are usually specific reasons. For example, the splitting of the province of Phrygia Salutaris between the *themata* of the *Opsikion* and the *Anatolikōn* reflected the fact that the palatine units of *scholae* and *domestici protectores deputati* (that is to say,

[32] Ibid., pp. 174ff.
[33] Stratos, *Byzantium in the Seventh Century*, vol. III, pp. 39ff. and 44f. This command was later broken up, probably under Leo III, into its constituent drungariates (of Kibyrrhaiōtōn, Samos and the Aigaion Pelagos); but there is little doubt that it represents the Aegean section of the *quaestura*, which was also referred to in a novel of Tiberius Constantine (*JGR* I, coll. 1, nov. 11, a. 575 = Dölger, *Regesten*, no. 40; issued during the reign of Justin II) as the ἀρχὴ τῶν νησῶν (καὶ τῶν ἐπὶ Σκυθίας τε καὶ Μυσίας στρατιωτικῶν ταγμάτων). See Antoniadis-Bibicou, *Histoire maritime*, pp. 63–89. On Cyprus, see W. E. Kaegi, 'The disputed Muslim negotiations with Cyprus in 649', in *Fourteenth Annual Byzantine Studies Conference, Abstracts of Papers* (Houston, Texas 1988), 5–6 with literature and sources.
[34] For Procopius' account, see *Historia arcana* XXIV, 13; and Jones, *LRE*, vol. II, pp. 684, 649ff. and 661f.
[35] See the parallel chart in Gelzer, *Themenverfassung*, pp. 127–30.

those based outside Constantinople) were in part based in its northerly section (the cities of Cotyaeum and Dorylaeum), which seems to have represented also the territory occupied by the forces of the *magister militum praesentalis II*, and therefore the later *Opsikion* army. When the forces of the *magister militum per Orientem* arrived, or rather, when the state allotted new bases and quarters to the troops withdrawn from Syria, only the southern part of the province was occupied, and it thus fell to them.[36] The fact that provincial boundaries were generally observed, however, and that provinces continued to be named explicity or referred to indirectly on seals until well into the eighth century is significant, for it shows that, when the field armies were established in Asia Minor, they were established at a time when the older civil administration was still fully operational, and by officials who were aware of the boundaries of their provinces and their jurisdiction. In the first instance, therefore, the field forces were merely based throughout the districts into which they had been withdrawn, probably on exactly the same basis as field troops anywhere in the empire at the time. (See maps VI and VII.)

In contrast, the diocesan boundaries of Asiana, Pontica and Oriens were entirely ignored, suggestive of both the insignificance of this – effectively – defunct level of prefectural administration (the more so after the closure of the diocesan staffs of the *largitiones*) and also the way in which the troops withdrew into Anatolia: both the *magister militum per Armeniam* and the *magister militum per Orientem* simply withdrew into the provinces closest to their last field of action and were then distributed over a number of provinces able to support and maintain them. As we have seen, the praesental troops of the second *magister militum in praesenti* already occupied the regions later called the districts of the *Opsikion* which they had shared with some palatine units. The allocation of provinces between the Oriental and Thracian troops in the west of Anatolia probably reflected both the economic wealth of the provinces over which the troops were billeted and the total numbers in each corps, a point to which I shall return in a moment.

[36] A point elaborated by Hendy, *Studies*, pp. 623f. The pattern is not entirely preordained, however. There is evidence for units of *scholarii* in the provinces of Phrygia Salutaris (Dorylaeum, Cotyaeum), Bithynia (Nicomedea, Cion, Prousa) and Hellespontus (Cyzicus) – see Theophanes, 236. 16sq.; *Vita Theodore Syk.*, 156. 68; 159. 9–11, 38; for *domestici protectores* in Galatia I (Ancyra, Anastasioupolis) – see *Vita Theodore Syk.* 45. 3; 76.3; Procopius, *Historia Arcana* XXIV, 25. These areas were all to become part of the *Opsikion* district. But there is also evidence for *scholarii* and *domestici* in Cappadocia (Justinian, *Nov.* 30, 7.2 (a. 536)); and for *domestici* in Galatia Salutaris (*Vita Theodore Syk.* 101. 5, at Pessinus) as well as *scholarii* (Justinian, *Edict* VIII, 3 (a. 548). These areas later formed part of the *Anatolikōn* and *Armeniakōn* districts. *Scholarii* were for a time also based in Thrace: see Theophanes, 236. 16sq., and cf. Hoffmann, *Bewegungsheer*, vol. I, p. 298; Haldon, *Byzantine Praetorians*, pp. 128 and 135 and notes.

The actual date of the withdrawal and the stationing of the Armenian and Oriental forces seems to have been after the battle of Yarmuk in 636, in which the joint forces of both field divisions were heavily defeated. Heraclius withdrew with part of the Oriental force into southern Anatolia, leaving some units to garrison the cities of Palestine and north Syria that were still in Roman hands. The forces of the *magister militum per Armeniam* withdrew to their bases in Mesopotamia and Armenia. The remaining Oriental forces were withdrawn from Egypt under treaty in 641 after the fall of Alexandria.[37] Shortly after 636, Heraclius issued a general order to the Roman forces in the East, to maintain themselves in their quarters and bases and to defend their positions against the Arabs, but not to go over to the offensive or to risk open battle.[38] This is a significant development, for it clearly represents a first step in the process of permanently establishing troops in Asia Minor on the one hand, but implies on the other no more than that the troops should remain (in the districts under the *magister militum per Armeniam*, at least) in their traditional quarters and garrison towns; or (in the case of the troops of the *magister militum per Orientem*) in the regions which had been (temporarily) assigned to them in southern and eastern Asia Minor. By the same order, the troops in the cities and fortresses still in imperial hands in Palestine and Mesopotamia were also to adopt a purely defensive strategy.

From the later evidence of the tenth-century compilation *De Thematibus* ('On the *themata*'), compiled by the Emperor Constantine VII, it is possible to reconstruct, approximately, the areas occupied by these forces. The *Opsikion* division was already based in the provinces of Hellespontus, Bithynia, Galatia I, part of Phrygia Salutaris, and Honorias;[39] the *Anatolikōn* forces occupied eventually the southern part of Phrygia Salutaris, together with Phrygia Pacatiana, Galatia Salutaris, Lycaonia, part of Isauria, Pamphylia, Pisidia and Lycia;[40] those of the Thracian contingent the provinces of Asia, Lydia, Caria and a small part of Phrygia Pacatiana;[41] and those of the *Armeniakōn* the provinces of Cappadocia I and II,

---

[37] See Balādhurī, 207, 210 and 253; Michael Syr., vol. II, 424; and cf. Lilie, *Die byzantinische Reaktion*, p. 42 note 5 and pp. 300–1; and for Egypt, pp. 48–51 with literature and sources. See also Stratos, *Byzantium in the Seventh Century*, vol. II, pp. 88ff.

[38] See Dölger, *Regesten*, no. 210 with sources. The order was issued probably in 637. See also the discussion of W. E. Kaegi, jr., 'The frontier: barrier or bridge?', *17th International Byzantine Congress, Major Papers* (New York 1986), pp. 279–303; cf. Balādhurī (as in note 37 above).

[39] See Pertusi, *De Thematibus*, 128, 132 and 135; Jones, *Cities of the Eastern Roman Provinces*, app. iv, tables viii, xii, xiv, xix, xx.

[40] Pertusi, *De Thematibus*, 114f.; Jones, *Cities of the Eastern Roman Provinces*, app. iv, tables xi, xii, xiii, xv, xvi, xvii, xviii, xxx.

[41] Pertusi, *De Thematibus*, 125; Jones, *Cities of the Eastern Roman Provinces*, app. iv, tables vii, ix, x, xi: only the cities of Ierapolis, Laodicea and Colossae/Chonae from Phrygia Pacatiana – see *De Thematibus*, III, 36–7; and Pertusi, *ibid.*, 150.

Armenia I–IV, Paphlagonia and Helenopontus.[42] The naval division of the islands seems at this stage not to have had any mainland territory, although it is difficult to state with certainty whether Caria belonged entirely to the region settled by the *Thracianus exercitus/Thrakēsianoi*. It may be that the littoral of the province, or certain cities and ports along it, such as Corycus on the Gulf of Attalia, or Kibyra (Cibyra), from which the later naval *thema* of the *Kibyrrhaiōtai* takes its name, did form part of this command.[43]

It is possible that the two Cilicias, or parts of them, were originally intended to be included within the districts covered by the Oriental forces; but although Byzantines and Arabs continued to fight over these provinces, it seems clear that it was Heraclius who decided to withdraw to the Taurus mountains and to establish a new defensive line there, which was, in the event, to become the new frontier. Both Arabic and Syriac sources report that Heraclius evacuated the troops and the civil population alike from Cilicia, and indeed that he established a *kleisoura*, or several *kleisourai* there, on analogy with those existing already along the northeastern frontier.[44] These were garrisoned outposts designed to control access to the mountain passes into Roman territory and had been a normal feature of the Armenian frontier zone for many years. The establishment of such garrisons in the Taurus at this time – 638–40 – illustrates the fact that the Byzantines clearly recognised the danger which now threatened the provinces of Asia Minor.[45] It seems most likely, therefore, that the forces of the three *magistri militum* of Thrace, Oriens and Armenia were already in the areas which they were to occupy according to later seventh-century sources by about 640.

THE ARMIES IN ANATOLIA: MAINTENANCE AND PROVISIONS

The early relationship of these field armies with the civilian government and population is clearly a more difficult problem. What can be said at the outset, and which has already been demonstrated, is that the late Roman provinces continued to exist. Their fiscal administration was still super-

---

[42] Pertusi, *De Thematibus*, 118; Jones, *Cities of the Eastern Roman Provinces*, app. iv, tables xxii, xxiii, xxiv, xxv, xxvi, xxvii and xxxii. Paphlagonia has until recently been taken to belong originally to the *Opsikion* – see Pertusi, *De Thematibus*, 134 with references, 136f. But see W. Treadgold, 'Notes on the numbers and organisation of the ninth-century Byzantine army', *GRBS* 21 (1980), 269–88, see 286–7; and Hendy, *Studies*, p. 649 with note 414.
[43] See Pertusi, *De Thematibus*, 149–50; Jones, *Cities of the Eastern Roman Provinces*, p. 517; Antoniadis-Bibicou, *Histoire maritime*, p. 85; and the remarks of Hendy, *Studies*, p. 652.
[44] Balādhurī, 210 and 253; Michael Syr., vol. II, 424. For the *kleisoura*, see Michael Syr., vol. II, 422–3; and the discussion of Lilie, *Die byzantinische Reaktion*, p. 303 note 35.
[45] For the older *kleisourai*, see Karayannopoulos, *Entstehung*, p. 52 with note 1.

vised and organised from Constantinople, under the general supervision of a *dioikētēs* of the provinces; and, as the ninth-century evidence – together with some contemporary material – suggests, they continued to have local governors under the authority of the praetorian prefect. In the early years after the arrival of these troops in Asia Minor, it is likely that they were billeted in the traditional manner on the population of the towns or rural areas they garrisoned, or they were maintained in garrison fortresses.[46] Of course, this will have been a considerable burden on the populations of the areas where the troops were based and will probably have been regarded as a short-term measure – there is no evidence to suggest at this stage that the government did not intend to strike back as soon as it had consolidated its position. On the other hand, the size of the areas occupied by the different divisions does suggest, as we shall see, that the burden on the civilian population had been taken into account and that it was spread as equitably as was possible in the circumstances. In addition, it is quite clear that fiscal administrative changes were also introduced in order to cope with this new burden – in particular a shift towards full-scale maintenance of the troops through regular levies in kind, extraordinary or exceptional levies which eventually became regularised. I will discuss this below.

In these respects, there is no reason to assume otherwise than that the traditional and standard rules pertaining to the military in their civilian provinces will have applied, both in regard to legal matters and juridical authority governing civil–military relations, and to the provisioning of the soldiers.[47]

A good deal is known about supplying and provisioning troops in the fifth and sixth centuries. Rations and fodder were issued either in kind, or were commuted for cash, in which case the regimental commissary officers purchased supplies from local producers or landowners. According to the system as set out by Anastasius, a proportion of the land-tax was assessed in kind. Units received warrants or requisition orders (*delegatoriae*) from the office of the praetorian prefect, which the quartermaster of a unit could present to a local civil governor or his representative. The latter then issued orders to selected villages or estate owners to supply specified provisions to the quartermaster (*actuarius*); and in return, the *actuarius* provided a receipt, which entitled the supplier to deduct the appropriate quantities or values from their next tax-assessment. Where commutation was the norm, the regimental actuaries purchased the requisite supplies according to a schedule of fixed prices established at each indictional assessment by the

---

[46] For the system in the sixth century and before, see Jones, *LRE*, vol. II, pp. 630ff. and esp. *CJ* XII, 37.19f. See also Teall, 'Grain supply', 113f.
[47] For the legal situation, see Jones, *LRE*, vol. II, pp. 631f.; Haldon, *Byzantine Praetorians*, pp. 304ff. and notes 914–24.

prefecture.[48] Troops on active service, however, were usually issued rations in kind. The same applied to troops in transit, such as expeditionary detachments. In such cases, the route of march having been transmitted in advance to the governors of those provinces through which the troops were to pass, the local civil governors would be responsible for collecting the required supplies and depositing them at appropriate points – in cities or on estates – along the way. The actuaries of the regiments drew the rations in kind and issued receipts to the tax-payers, who could then have the respective amount deducted from their next assessment. Sometimes the amount requisitioned exceeded the normal assessment, in which case the province or the prefecture would repay the tax-payers in cash or credit them appropriately.[49] During the fifth and sixth centuries, an *ad hoc* praetorian prefect was often appointed specifically to organise the requisitioning and delivery of supplies; and in Justinian's reign, the temporary prefect on the eastern front became permanent, a result of the constant warfare. The practice of appointing such prefects seems to have continued through the seventh century.[50]

By the later sixth century, it is clear that garrison troops and those in winter quarters were usually paid in cash – a regulation of the Strategikon of Maurice, compiled probably in the 580s or 590s, stipulates that officers must ensure that the districts in which the forces winter can provide adequate supplies – in both foodstuffs, as well as clothing and mounts – for the soldiers to purchase;[51] but the rule for units on active service seems still to have been to supply provisions in kind.[52]

Now it is obvious that the events of the 630s and 640s must have dramatically affected this traditional establishment in Asia Minor, if only with respect to its ability to cope with the sudden arrival, however well planned and executed, of most of the field forces from the eastern front. As has been emphasised before, the effects of the loss of the greater and richer parts of the Eastern prefecture outside Asia Minor by the mid-640s (Egypt was lost by 642) on the revenue of the state were considerable. Something over half of the total revenue of the state from the Balkans and the eastern prefecture has recently been estimated to have been lost.[53] And whether this is entirely accurate or not – something which, given the available figures for resource potential on the one hand, and actual exploitation on

---

[48] For a detailed description, see Jones, *LRE*, vol. II, p. 672, with notes 150 and 151; Haldon, *Byzantine Praetorians*, p. 113 and note 111.
[49] Jones, *LRE*, vol. II, p. 673; see *CJ* XII, 37.1–3, 5–11, 14–19; 38.1–2; Justinian, *Nov.* 130, 1–8; cf. J. Maspéro, *Organisation militaire de l'Egypte byzantine* (Paris 1912), pp. 109ff.
[50] Jones, *LRE*, vol. II, pp. 673–4; Kaegi, 'Two studies', 103ff. with sources.
[51] Maurice, *Strategikon* I, 2. 16. See Haldon, *Byzantine Praetorians*, p. 113.
[52] Kaegi, 'Two studies', 106f.   [53] Hendy, *Studies*, p. 620.

the other, is impossible to arrive at – this estimate provides a reasonable idea of the implications of such losses.

The result of such developments must have presented the government with almost impossible problems. Not only was the maintenance of the army traditionally one of the most expensive items, if not the most expensive item, in the state budget;[54] the state was now faced with the difficulty of supplying and maintaining a disproportionately large number of troops in a much-reduced empire, both in territorial and in fiscal terms; and, in addition, it was faced with the effects of constant and debilitating warfare on its eastern frontiers and of economic and therefore fiscal disruption. Fortunately, recent work on some aspects of this problem makes it possible to obtain a clearer picture of how the state managed to respond to what was, in effect, a major financial and resource crisis.

In the first place, the *ad hoc* praetorian prefects seem to have continued to exist and to play a role up until the early ninth century. So much is suggested by their appearance in both the Taktikon Uspenskij of 842/3 and in a ceremony of roughly the same period. Since it is also reasonably certain that they were replaced by the thematic *prōtonotarioi*[55] and since the method of calculating the necessary provisions for troops in transit and for those based locally, and of reducing the tax-assessment of those who supplied the troops accordingly, is known to have been almost the same in the ninth and tenth centuries as in the sixth century continuity of practice in this respect is assured.[56] There seems no reason to doubt that units of soldiers on the move were provisioned in the same way in the seventh century as they had been in the sixth and were to be in the ninth and tenth centuries: the local military commanders sent in an assessment of requirements to the central bureaux; the latter then calculated the taxes in kind accordingly; and the provisions were deposited by the relevant prefects along the route. Tax-payers received receipts, which they could claim against the next assessment.

The longer-term maintenance of large numbers of soldiers, however, presented a more intractable problem, since the resources which had traditionally been available to pay the troops their cash *rhogai* were simply no longer available in sufficient quantity.

Up to this time, soldiers had been supported from two main sources: the

---

[54] Jones, *LRE*, vol. I, pp. 458 and 463; Hendy, *Studies*, pp. 158–9 and 172; note the anonymous sixth-century treatise *Peri Stratēgias* (ed. and trans. G. Dennis, *Three Byzantine Military Treatises* (CFHB XXV, ser. Wash., Washington D.C. 1985), 1–135, see 2. 18–21: The financial system was set up to take care of matters of public importance that arise on occasion, such as the building of ships and walls. But it is principally concerned with paying the soldiers. Each year most of the public revenues are spent for this purpose.
[55] See above, pp. 201–4.
[56] For a detailed account, see Haldon, *Byzantine Praetorians*, pp. 314ff.

issue of *annonae* and *capitus*, in kind or commuted into a cash equivalent (according to a fixed tariff); and the cash donatives issued on the occasion of an imperial accession and every fifth year thereafter, made up of five *solidi* and a pound in silver in the first case and five *solidi* only on the quinquennial occasions. In addition, new recruits received weapons and clothing through the commissariat, purchased with a cash allowance issued for the purpose, arms coming from the state weapons and arms factories, clothing from state weaving establishments or through levies in kind raised as tax.[57] During the reign of Maurice, attempts were made to reform the system, in the first instance to divide the regular commuted *annonae* into three parts, issuing clothing and weapons directly; and in the second attempting to reduce the sum of the *annonae* by twenty-five per cent.[58] Both seem to have misfired, but both represent the efforts of the government to reduce its cash expenditure and move towards a direct-issue system such as had operated before the later fifth century, at least in respect of clothing and equipment.[59] This shortage of cash reserves for military expenditure was, then, already a feature of the last years of the sixth century. During Heraclius' reign, it clearly became critical. Not only was the emperor forced to borrow and turn into coin the gold plate of the Church;[60] it is equally clear that the troops, while still paid in cash, had to be content with copper rather than gold – in itself a procedure that was not new, but which illustrates the dramatic lack of gold revenues in the conditions prevailing in the period after 610. So much is clear from the fact that Heraclius had a statue in Constantinople melted down and turned into coin to pay troops in the Pontus; and the fact that the temporary mints set up to produce coin for the army during the Persian wars up to 627 produced predominantly copper.[61] While Maurice probably failed to effect the twenty-five per cent reduction in cash emoluments which he attempted

[57] See Haldon, *Byzantine Praetorians*, pp. 113–15 with notes 113–23, and *Recruitment and Conscription*, p. 69 and note 123; Hendy, *Studies*, pp. 175–8 and 646ff. Procopius, *Historia Arcana*, XXIV, 27–9, claims that the quinquennial donative was allowed to lapse by Justinian, but it has been argued that this is unlikely. Jones, *LRE*, vol. II, p. 670 and vol. I, pp. 284–5, argued that it may have been incorporated at the rate of 1 *solidus* per annum into the commuted yearly *annona*. The accessional donatives survived until the seventh century, certainly, and there is no reason for suggesting that the quinquennial donatives for the field armies did not do so either. See Hendy, *Studies*, pp. 646ff.
[58] See Haldon, *Byzantine Praetorians*, pp. 113f.; *Recruitment and Conscription*, p. 69 note 123.
[59] For the original system, Jones, *LRE*, vol. II, pp. 624f., and see 670f.
[60] See Theophanes, 302–3.
[61] For the melting of the statue, Kaegi, 'Two studies' 90ff. (but see Haldon, *Byzantine Praetorians*, pp. 627–8); Hendy, *Studies*, pp. 415–17 (mints at Alexandretta, Constantia (Cyprus) and Jerusalem during the revolt of Heraclius; and at Seleucia (Isaura) and Constantia during the Persian war). Soldiers in the sixth century, and from the ninth century, were usually paid in gold (although not exclusively) – this was a fundamental element in the redistributive fiscal operations of the state. See Haldon, 'Some considerations', 80ff.

to introduce, Heraclius, faced by a much more drastic situation, actually did cut military and civil *rhogai* by fifty per cent, probably in 615; and, furthermore, calculated the payment of salaries largely in the newly introduced silver hexagram.[62] Finally, in 641 a donative probably issued to celebrate the accession of the young Constans II (or also the coronation of Heracleonas) was issued, consisting – according to a much later source – of only three *solidi*, that is, only one third of the traditional donative on such occasions.[63]

All of this points to a dramatic reduction in the gold reserves of the state and the available coined gold in circulation. If, in 641, the state was able to put together only one-third of the donative usually issued on the occasion of an imperial accession, while at the same time trying to finance roughly the same number of field troops as it had possessed before the loss of most of its Eastern territories, the finances must already have been near breaking-point. It is from this time on, therefore – the early 640s – that major shifts in the methods of paying and financing the armies are to be sought.

The most pressing problem, in the first instance, may have been to reduce the overall burden on the fisc. One of the solutions to this problem seems to have been to pay the various provincial forces on a rotational basis, rather than all at once, at least in so far as the payment of donatives was concerned. The system of paying the troops their *rhogai* on a four-yearly rotational cycle, described by Constantine VII in the tenth century as 'the old system',[64] has been plausibly shown to be tied in with the older quinquennial donatives (collected quadrennially, in the last year of each quinquennium). Since the rota presented by Constantine is clearly a developed form, it is highly likely that the original cycle concerned the four original *themata* in Asia Minor: the *Anatolikōn*, *Armeniakōn*, *Thrakēsiōn* and *Opsikion*; and it is also highly likely that it should be taken back to the seventh century, perhaps as early as the 640s and 650s.[65] This rotational system must have applied to donatives only, however, enabling the state to spread the burden of cash payments over a longer period and to extract the necessary revenue year by year to cover the cost; for while the next stage in reducing costs might well have been to cut down or cut out altogether the commuted *annonae* and *capitus*, the payment of reduced cash *annonae* on such a rotational basis cannot have been a practical solution, since such a cycle would run the risk on a regular basis of depriving the troops of their

---

[62] Chron. Pasch. 706. See Hendy, Studies, pp. 494–5.
[63] See Cedrenus I, 753 and Stratos, *Byzantium in the Seventh Century*, vol. II, pp. 187 and 217–18.
[64] De Cer. 493–4.
[65] The argument has been fully developed in Hendy, Studies, pp. 647–51.

livelihood before it was completed. Cutting down the numbers of troops may also have been considered, but there were obvious limits – in terms of the effectiveness of defence – to this alternative.

On the other hand, a reversion to the payment of the field forces largely or entirely in kind would have gone part of the way towards solving the problem. For, however the troops were quartered or housed, they still needed to be fed, clothed and supplied with weapons, horses and so on. The permanent establishment of an *ad hoc* praetorian prefect for each *thema* (or army), who supervised the calculation, extraction and delivery of the military *annonae* and *capitus* in kind, seems to represent part of the solution finally adopted by the state. As we have seen, such a permanent post had already existed for the Oriental forces in the sixth century. Similar posts may have been created for the other field armies, especially the Armenian division and the forces in Thrace, where providing adequate supplies had for long been a problem. That there was such an official for each *thema* is reasonably clear from the ninth-century material referred to already. And it seems a reasonable hypothesis that the withdrawal of the troops into Anatolia marks the point at which this system is most likely to have come into existence as a permanent arrangement.[66] Possible corroboration for this development comes from a reference in the 660s to the *annonae* of the *scholae*, parade-troops who, as far as is known, would normally have always been paid in gold, in the sixth century at least; and to a *manceps*, or baker, in charge of the bread-ration of these palatine soldiers.[67]

Corroboration also comes from the numismatic evidence in Asia Minor (which, as Hendy has shown, contrasts for specific institutional reasons with the Balkans) where finds of copper coins die out almost entirely during the last years of Constans II. Up to 658, it has been pointed out that the copper coinage is represented by small but regular quantities on a number of excavated sites in Asia Minor: Aphrodisias, Anemurium, Ancyra, Sardis, Priene, Ephesus and Pergamum. From 658 to 668, however, the copper coins peter out and effectively disappear from Anatolian sites until the ninth century.[68] A number of the groups of copper have been interpreted as coming from a military context, which would explain the physical concentration – on sites which might be associated with the presence of soldiers as a garrison, or in the construction of defences. The disappearance of copper coins from Anatolian sites has, however, usually been taken to reflect the removal of the military units stationed there and the effective abandonment of the sites in question. In fact, neither of these is necessarily a corollary, as Hendy has also demonstrated. Instead, it has been suggested that the disappearance of copper – which during the

[66] See above, pp. 201–4, 223.   [67] See Haldon, *Byzantine Praetorians*, p. 125 and note 164.
[68] The phenomenon is fully documented in Hendy, *Studies*, pp. 640ff.

seventh and early eighth centuries does seem to have been employed to pay the troops on a number of occasions – signifies more probably the abandonment of a system of cash payments to soldiers.[69] If this were the case, then a reasonably precise date can be ascribed to the implementation of these changes, that is to say, the last years of the reign of Constans II. This is, of course, some twenty years after the arrival of the field armies in Asia Minor. But the discrepancy need be more apparent than real – payments in copper, possibly at a reduced rate (in comparison with the sixth century), as well as occasional payments in silver and gold, were still made,[70] while the troops might already have been supported by supplies and equipment issued for the most part in kind.

That the extent to which the land could support the armies which occupied it was taken into account from the beginning is clear from the actual size of the districts which were allotted to each *thema* or army. As maps VI and VII will show, the forces occupying the most fertile zone received by far the smallest district in which to billet its troops and from which to draw its resources. In contrast, the Armenian forces, which fell back into eastern Anatolia, occupied the least fertile area made up of some of the most arid sections of the central plateau, and in consequence – although there is every reason to suppose that the *magister militum per Armeniam* commanded forces significantly less numerous than those of the *magistri militum per Thracias* or *per Orientem* – seem to have been allotted a much wider resource-area from which to support themselves. The district of the *Opsikion* is not part of this pattern, in so far as it existed in effect – as the area in which the praesental and some palatine forces had always been stationed – before the 640s and the withdrawal from the East. The *Anatolikōn*, on the other hand, occupied the area between the *Thrakēsiōn*, *Opsikion* and *Armeniakōn* armies, and once again its extent, contrasted with both the *Thrakēsiōn* and the *Armeniakon*, suggests the nature of the land from which it was intended it should support itself. While this line of reasoning is hardly conclusive by itself, it is very suggestive, and it is a further indication that the withdrawal of 637 and after was carefully organised and co-ordinated, and planned with a view to the problems of supplying and maintaining the armies in the future.[71]

There seems, therefore, to be good circumstantial evidence that the withdrawal into Asia Minor was, if not planned greatly in advance, nevertheless planned carefully; and that the provinces into which the

[69] Hendy, ibid., with sources and older literature.
[70] The cash issued to the troops in 641 was, according to Cedrenus, in gold; that put aside by Heraclius Constantine and entrusted to the *sacellarius* Philagrius was similarly (apparently) in the form of gold coins. See note 63 above: and Nicephorus, 28. 11sq.; John of Nikiu, 192. See Haldon, *Byzantine Praetorians*, pp. 191f. with note 427.
[71] See excursus to chapter 6, pp. 251–3 below.

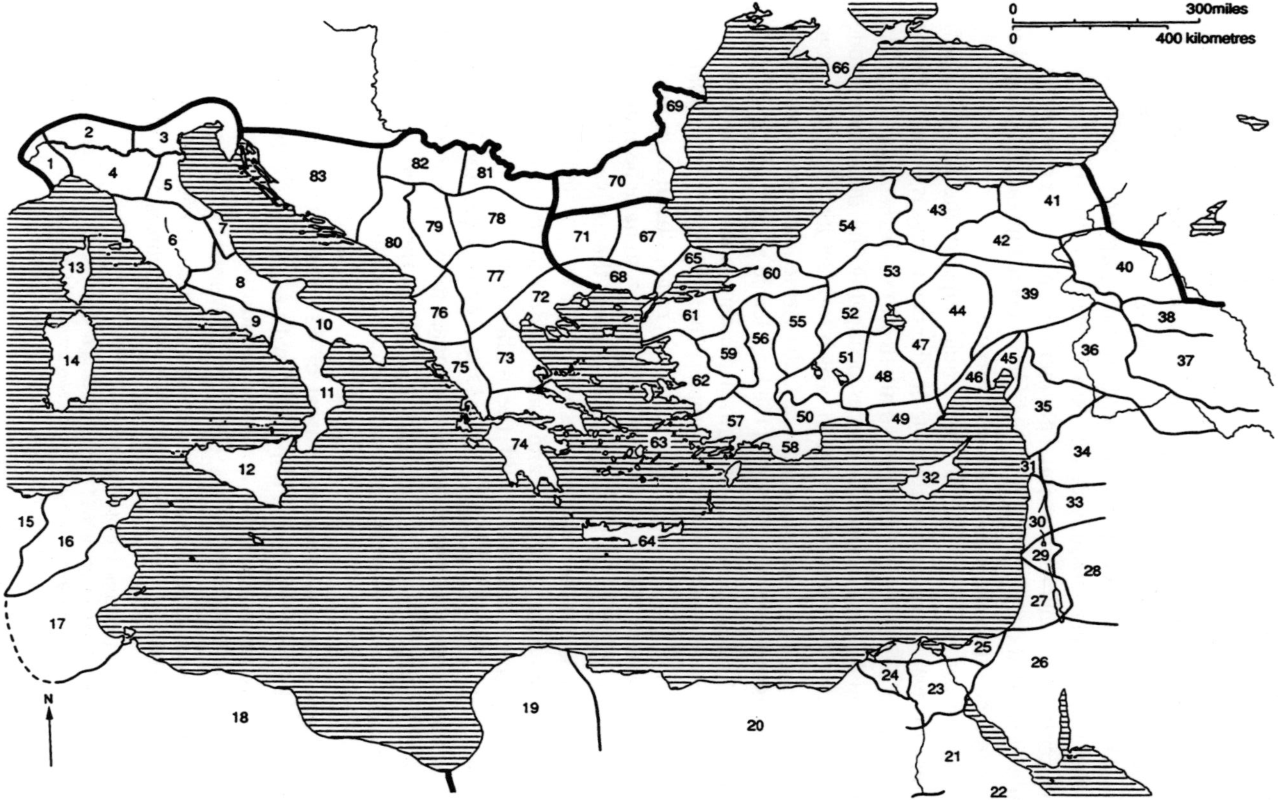

Map VI Justinianic prefectures and provinces c. A.D. 565

Military administration 229

armies withdrew were intended to be able to support them on the basis of requisitions of supplies and provisions in kind (the close relationship between size of army and size of districts occupied would be otherwise pointless). From the last years of Constans II the numismatic evidence suggests that payments in cash, even though in copper, were more or less entirely cut out, at least as a regular form of salary equivalent in (nominal) value to the *annonae* and *capitus* of the previous years. In other words, the state had come to rely entirely upon a system of supporting the armies through the levying of all requirements in kind. This implies that the greater part of the tax-burden also took the form of payment in kind. Similarly, the origins of the quadrennial cycle of payments for donatives also seem to lie in this period, although exactly when it might have been introduced is impossible to say.

There is one further piece of evidence to support this line of reasoning. As we have seen, up to the end of the sixth century at least, the armies were supported both by cash, with which goods, provisions and such like could be purchased, and by provisions in kind, for expeditionary or moving forces. Such provisions were part of the regular tax-assessment, and if

KEY

(a) Prefecture of Italy
1 Alpes Cottiae
2 Aemilia
3 Venetia (with Histria)
4 Liguria
5 Flaminia
6 Tuscia et Umbria
7 Picenum
8 Samnium
9 Campania
10 Apulia et Calabria
11 Lucania et Bruttium
12 Sicilia (under *quaestor sacri palatii*)

(b) Prefecture of Africa
13 Corsica
14 Sardinia
15 Numidia
16 Zeugitania
17 Byzacena
18 Tripolitania

(c) Prefecture of Oriens
19 Libya Pentapolis
20 Libya Inferior
21 Arcadia
22 Thebais Inferior
23 Augustamnica II
24 Aegyptus I and II
25 Augustamnica I
26 Palaestina III

27 Palaestina I
28 Arabia
29 Palaestina II
30 Phoenice
31 Theodorias
32 Cyprus (in *quaestura exercitus*)
33 Phoenice Libanensis
34 Syria II
35 Syria I
36 Euphratensis
37 Osrhoene
38 Mesopotamia
39 Armenia III
40 Armenia IV
41 Armenia I
42 Armenia II
43 Helenopontus
44 Cappadocia I
45 Cilicia II
46 Cilicia I
47 Cappadocia II
48 Lycaonia
49 Isauria
50 Pamphylia
51 Pisidia
52 Galatia Salutaris
53 Galatia I
54 Paphlagonia
55 Phrygia Salutaris

56 Phrygia Pacatiana
57 Caria (in *quaestura exercitus*)
58 Lycia
59 Lydia
60 Bithynia
61 Hellespontus
62 Asia
63 Insulae (*Aegean Isles* – in *quaestura exercitus*)
64 Creta
65 Europa
66 Bosporus
67 Haemimontus
68 Rhodope
69 Scythia (in *quaestura exercitus*)
70 Moesia II (in *quaestura exercitus*)
71 Thracia
72 Macedonia I
73 Thessalia
74 Achaea
75 Epirus vetus
76 Epirus nova
77 Macedonia II
78 Dacia Mediterranea
79 Dardania
80 Praevalitana
81 Dacia ripensis
82 Moesia I
83 Dalmatia

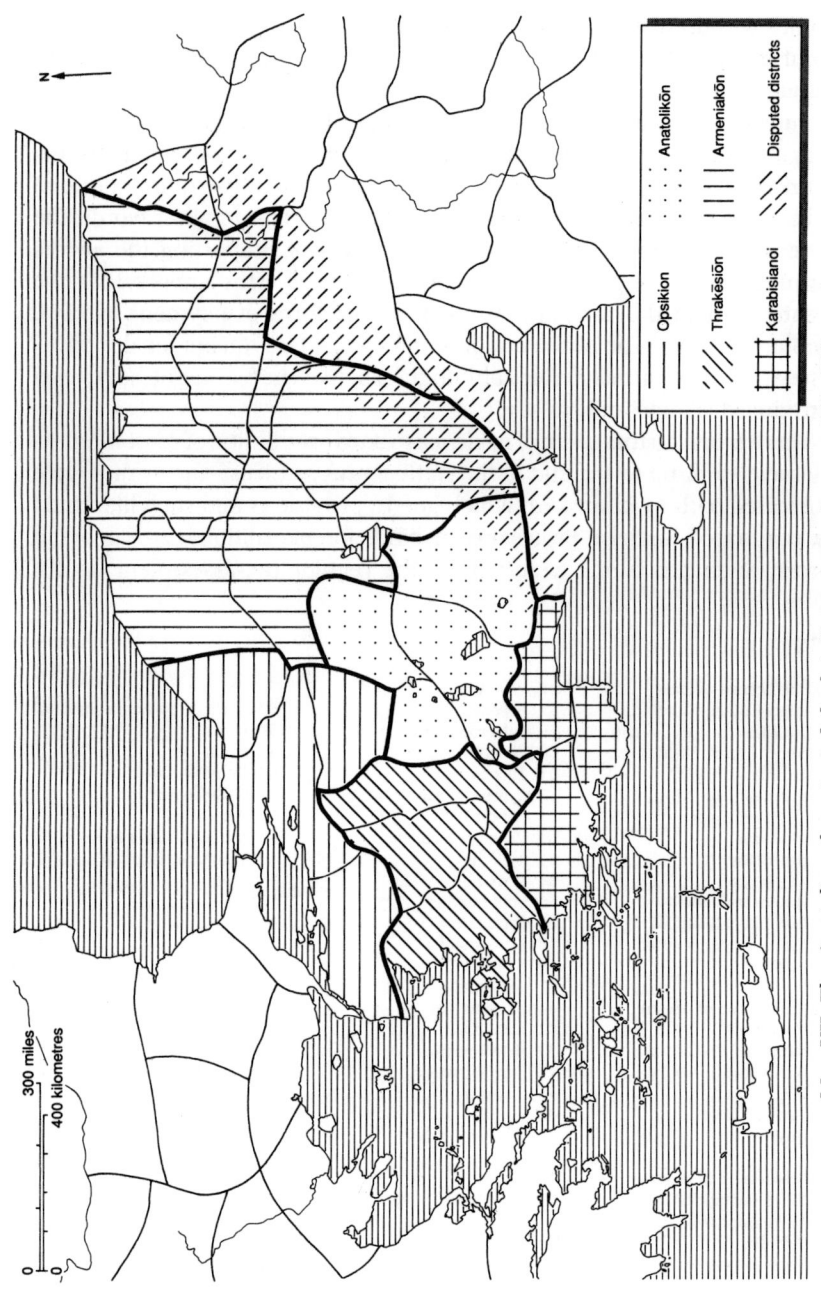

Map VII The Anatolian *themata* and the late Roman provinces *c.* A.D. 660

Military administration   231

extra supplies were needed, what was taken was set against the tax-assessment for the following years so that, in theory at least, the tax-payers were not unfairly exploited. The compulsory purchase of provisions – *coemptio* or *synōnē* – in addition to, or instead of this procedure, was, except in very special cases, strictly forbidden.[72] Only one area was exempted from this rule, namely Thrace where, as the relevant law of Anastasius states, because the revenue from the land-tax in gold was insufficient, due to disruption, population decline, and the devastations of the barbarians, the *coemptio* was the only reliable way of providing for the troops there.[73]

By the early ninth century, if not indeed much earlier, however, the term *synōnē* referred quite simply to the basic land-tax, raised by the state together with the hearth-tax or *kapnikon*. The *synōnē*, by the eleventh century at least, could be commuted into cash.[74] But in the early ninth century, without doubt, it was a regular yearly assessment which could be collected in kind.[75]

The question inevitably arises, by what process did a sixth-century technical term for a compulsory purchase of military provisions, applied only in exceptional circumstances, come to mean the standard land-tax, also collected in kind? The answer can only lie in the context outlined above, in which the state, faced by a drastic shortage of cash, was forced to return to a system of provisioning all of its troops in kind. The basic land-tax hitherto raised both in cash and in kind was now raised more regularly and on a widespread basis in kind alone; and the term henceforth applied to it was that already available describing precisely such a process, the *synōnē*.[76]

[72] Jones, *LRE*, vol. I, pp. 235, 460 and note 120.
[73] *CJ* x, 27.1 (a. 491) x, 27.2/5–10 (a. 491–505).
[74] See Ostrogorsky, 'Steuergemeinde', 49ff. and 60f., 'Steuersystem', 232, and *Geschichte*, p. 55 note 2. Contrast Dölger, *Beiträge*, pp. 51ff. and 78, who sees the *synōnē* still as a simple extra levy in kind. That *synōnē* = land-tax is clear from a number of sources, for example, *De Cer.* 695. 6–14, where certain households are to be exempt from all regular fiscal impositions, especially the *kapnikon* and the *synōnē*. This unusual exemption, granted for a specific purpose, was clearly intended to free such households from all the state taxes, including those not usually listed in such grants.
[75] See Haldon, *Byzantine Praetorians*, pp. 314f. and notes 950 and 951 (letters of the metropolitan Ignatius of Nicaea). Theophanes (443. 18–22) and Nicephorus (76, 5–14) refer to the raising of taxes in gold, which suggests that the state was by this time in a more favourable situation and could choose according to its needs whether to collect in gold or in kind. But whether this refers to the land-tax, the hearth-tax or both remains unclear.
[76] The system for supplying troops in transit in the fifth and sixth centuries detailed above, in which military supplies are taken from the tax assessment of each province in kind, is almost exactly the same in the ninth and tenth centuries, in which the thematic *prōtonotarios* supplies the troops from the *synōnē* in kind. The similarities are so obvious that it is clear once more that *synōnē* must be the Byzantine equivalent of the late Roman basic land-tax. By the later seventh century, this form of assessment seems to have been well established, for the Farmers' Law refers to the regular land-tax as the 'extraordinary tax of the public fisc' (τὰ ἐξτραόρδινα τοῦ δημοσίου λόγου). *Extraordinaria* had meant originally

The only context in which such a dramatic shift in the form of revenue collection is likely to have taken place – based as it is implicitly upon the assumption of a lack of, or shortage of, cash – is that of the seventh century; and the chief reason was, as we have seen, to support the armies and other state bureaux in the provinces. It is quite possible that the original arrangement actually involved both the usual tax-assessment, as well as a generalised supplementary *coemptio* for the newly-arrived armies. The gold or copper thus expended by the state in the process of the compulsory purchases would be recouped through the usual tax-payments (the Anastasian regulations on *coemptio* had envisaged the tax-payer being recompensed in gold coin).[77] But a proper *coemptio* as widespread as this would have demanded reserves of gold and coin which, as we have seen, the state does not seem to have possessed. As the state found itself unable to recompense tax-payers for the produce it needed, yet continued to demand the necessary provisions, the term will have become generalised and applied to the ordinary land-tax assessment also.

THE ROLE OF THE 'APOTHĒKĒ'

The final cessation of cash payments and allowances (for weapons and for clothing, for example) will have involved changes in the method of arming and equipping the troops, of course. In the sixth century, and probably up to the reign of Heraclius, soldiers received their initial uniform and issue of arms directly along with mounts for the cavalry troopers. Weapons and uniforms were delivered through the prefecture to the units, whose actuaries were responsible for submitting claims for what was needed, direcly from the state manufactories. Serving soldiers received a portion of their cash pay to cover the costs of purchasing new equipment or remounts; and it was the responsibility of the officers in each unit to check the soldiers' equipment and to order new material.[78] Part of this arrangement, of course, involved the issue of cash to the soldiers, which could be used to purchase material from the state, but which might also be spent unwisely on non-military items. Hence the unpopularity of Maurice's attempted reforms in the 590s. With the cessation of cash allowances altogether this

---

exceptional levies in addition to the regular taxes. Here in its Greek variant, *extraordina*, it clearly means the regular tax itself, presumably undergoing a similar terminological transformation to that of *synōnē*, which was itself originally classed among the *extraordinaria*. Note that, in spite of the fact that a large number of soldiers in the forces of the exarchate of Ravenna did possess land, the local military authorities still provided their supplies and rations, as a compulsory purchase (*coemptio*) of grain in 686 demonstrates: *Liber Pontificalis* I, 366; see Brown, *Gentlemen and Officers*, pp. 87–8.

[77] See note 73 above, and Haldon, 'Synōnē', for the detailed development of this argument.
[78] See Haldon, *Byzantine Praetorians*, pp. 113–15 and *Recruitment and Conscription*, p. 69.

clearly became impossible. And here another element in the pattern seems to fit into place.

A number of historians have noted that it is during this period that dated seals of *genikoi kommerkiarioi* suddenly become much more common, seals on which an association between an imperial *apothēkē* and a region or regions of the empire is apparent, and from which it is clear that one official often had jurisdiction over a number of widely dispersed areas. On the whole, this phenomenon has been explained in terms of imperial control over trading in luxury or other goods, since it is clear that the *apothēkai* were in origin state depots in which private merchants might also have an interest.[79] More recently, it has been shown that these *apothēkai* were very probably storehouses and also emporia for surplus produce from state factories, chiefly luxury goods such as silks, gold- and silverware, dyed cloths and so on.[80] It has further been argued that the division within the prefecture of the East between its general and special banks reflects this activity; for while the actual production of the items in question came under the supervisory authority of either the *magister officiorum* (dyeing and weaving) or the *comes sacrarum largitionum* (coin and plate), the raw materials were intially provided through the prefecture and were returned for sale or redistribution to a branch of the prefecture. The special bank seems to have fulfilled this function, and the later confusion in its name, between *eidikon* and *idikon* – 'things' and 'special' – may reflect this. The production of such goods certainly seems to have been controlled by the later *eidikon*, and it would seem that the newly independent special bank of the prefecture gained control of these aspects of state manufacturing in the 630s or 640s. The fact that officials in charge of the silk-producing establishments, for example, could also be *genikoi kommerkiarioi* reinforces this impression.[81]

But the sudden increased importance of *genikoi kommerkiarioi* holding high rank – the first clear example is dated to the years 654–9[82] – can have

[79] See, e.g., Antoniadis-Bibicou, *Douanes*, pp. 164ff.; R. S. Lopez, 'The role of trade in the economic re-adjustment of Byzantium in the seventh century', *DOP* 13 (1959), 67–85, see 73ff.; Lilie, *Die byzantinische Reaktion*, p. 282; and Zacos and Veglery, vol. I, pp. 135f. For the *apothēkai* as imperial depots, see Zacos and Veglery, no. 130bis (Tyre, late sixth century); Antoniadis-Bibicou, *Douanes*, p. 159; Hendy, *Studies*, p. 246 (Alexandria).

[80] Hendy, *Studies*, p. 628. That the *fabricae* were involved is, however, unlikely, *pace* Hendy, ibid. The production, transport and possession of weapons was strictly monopolised by the state and its personnel, i.e. the soldiers. Surplus weapons were stored in the imperial and municipal arsenals, and it is improbable that they were involved in open commercial exchanges. See Justinian, *Nov.* 85 (a. 539).

[81] For a detailed treatment, see Hendy, *Studies*, pp. 628–30; and see above, pp. 186ff., on the results of the fiscal reorganisation of Heraclius' reign. For seals of officials who were in alternate years both *genikos kommerkiarios* and *archontes tou vlattiou* (silk-weaving establishment), see Zacos and Veglery, tables 6/2, 8, 11 etc.

[82] Zacos and Veglery, no. 136, seal of Theodore, *hypatos* and *genikos kommerkiarios* of the *apothēkē* of Galatia.

had little to do with the sale of luxury goods at a time when the empire was in such political and fiscal straits. In fact, the *kommerkiarioi* and the *apothēkai* which they administered have been plausibly shown by Hendy to be connected with some aspects of the supplying of the imperial forces. On a number of occasions, dated seals of *kommerkiarioi* and *apothēkai* for specific regions can be related to specific military undertakings connected with those regions.[83] In view of this connection, and the original role of the *apothēkai* as stores for the produce of imperial factories, it has been argued that the main function of the *apothēkē* was to provide the troops with the necessary equipment for their expedition.[84] The *apothēkē* is thus seen as a derivative institution or system, rather than an actual storehouse – although these were certainly involved. The *apothēkē* of a province or group of provinces thus involved a process, the transport from the point of manufacture of certain goods, and their distribution to the soldiers of a given region for a specific purpose or campaign, a process supervised and directed by a general *kommerkiarios*. This connection is borne out by numerous other examples – campaigns in 687/8 in eastern Asia Minor are accompanied by the appearance of seals of the *apothēkē* in Cilicia, Cappadocia and Armenia; the campaign in Thrace in 689/90 is accompanied by the appearance of the *apothēkē* in Constantinople and Helenopontus, and in the Cyclades and Crete; the naval expedition to recover Carthage in 696/7 is similarly accompanied by the appearance of the *apothēkē* in the Cyclades and in Sicily. Examples can be multiplied, and while not every such seal can be so closely tied in with a specific example of an expedition in the literary sources, the connection is too strong to be a coincidence.[85]

[83] The clearest example is that for Justinian II's campaign against the Arabs in 692/3 and 694/5. Four seals, dated to the 8th indiction, that is, to 694/5, exist for a certain George, *apo hypatōn*, all connected with the Slav prisoners settled in Asia Minor by Justinian in 688/9 and, respectively, with the *apothēkē* of the provinces of Caria, Asia and Lycia, of Bithynia, of Phrygia Salutaris, and of the two Cappadocias. Theophanes reports Justinian's forced transfer of the Slavs to Asia Minor, specifically to the *Opsikion* district (i.e. Bithynia and Phrygia Salutaris) in 688/9, and two unsuccessful campaigns in the region of Sebastopolis, i.e. in Armenia, in 692/3 and 694/5. See Theophanes, 364. 11–366, 23. Whether or not Theophanes' dates are entirely correct, it is clear that the transfer of Slavs to Asia Minor, the establishment of a corps of Slav soldiers by Justinian from among the captive populations, the campaigns of 692–5, and the *apothēkē* of the regions in which the Slavs were settled, are closely connected. For the seals see Zacos and Veglery, nos. 2764, 186, 187 and 188, and table 33 (for Asia, Caria and Lycia, Rhodes and the Chersonnesos); and see table 18/2: the seal of George, *apo hypatōn* and *genikos kommerkiarios* of the (*apothēkē* of the) *Armeniakoi*, read by Mordtmann and followed by others (most recently Hendy, *Studies*, p. 631 note 340) for 694/5, is in fact for one of the regions of Armenia, not the district of the *Armeniakoi*. But it is connected with the first four seals mentioned above. See W. Seibt, review of Zacos and Veglery, in *BS* 36 (1975), 209.

[84] Hendy, *Studies*, pp. 631–3.

[85] For a detailed account, with both sigillographic and literary evidence, see Hendy, *Studies*, pp. 654–60 and 667–9.

This explanation, which represents a major advance in our understanding of the function of the *kommerkiarioi* and the *apothēkē* in the seventh century, has been challenged, however.[86] Several objections have been raised: first, no text refers explicitly to a connection between the supply of weapons and the *kommerkiarioi* or *apothēkē*; second, the chronology of the events of 688 to 694/5, which constitutes a central element in the demonstration of the validity of the argument outlined above, has been forced – in fact, the seals of the *kommerkiarioi* and of the Slav prisoners of the eighth indiction, i.e. 694/5, post-date the campaigns for which, according to Hendy, they were mobilised; third, the *kommerkiarioi* and the *apothēkai* were connected specifically with silk, its production and sale – the emperor's effigy on these seals was, like that on imperial coins, a validation of the purity of the product thus marked. According to this argument, the Slav prisoners and the seals pertaining to them can be more readily explained in terms of a mass distribution and sale of the rebellious Slavs in 694/5 as slaves in various provinces of the empire, a contract farmed out to the *kommerkiarios* George, who used the *apothēkē* system already in existence to fulfil it. The argument is underpinned with the assumption that the demand for silk in the seventh century was considerable enough to warrant a major investment and interest in its production; that this investment took place in the seventh century – from about 629 in Cyprus, in the period 641 and after in North Africa, and from about 654 in Anatolia – and that it was during this time that the silk industry 'grew and became one of the pillars of the empire's state economy'; and also that this growth took place chiefly in Asia Minor until the 730s and after, when it was transferred to Thrace and the south Balkan area.

Now there are a number of serious objections to this theory as it stands. There is no reason to doubt that the late sixth- and early seventh-century *kommerkiarios* may have been a contract-farmer who held a monopoly over the purchase and resale of silk within the empire; but there is no reason to doubt either that – as Oikonomidès in fact admits[87] – these official contractors also dealt in goods other than silk alone and had charge of the *apothēkai* in which they were deposited, a point already made by Hendy.[88] There are no grounds for assuming that this did not continue to be the case throughout the seventh century and the eighth century. The fact that seals bearing the emperor's effigy, and used to validate quality (and origin – in imperial workshops or imperial-controlled or supervised centres of production), are employed, is no argument that the goods in question involved silk alone: the products of the imperial arms factories

---

[86] N. Oikonomidès, 'Silk trade and production in Byzantium from the sixth to the ninth century: the seals of kommerkiarioi', *DOP* 40 (1986), 33–53.
[87] *Ibid.*, 34–5 and 38–9.   [88] Hendy, *Studies*, pp. 627ff.

had also been a state monopoly (like silk in the later sixth century), and such seals might equally serve to confirm the origin and legality of consignments of weapons produced in the state workshops or elsewhere under state licence. If Oikonomidès is correct as far as the Slav prisoners are concerned – that is, that the seals in question relate to a mass sale of Slavs through the *kommerkiarios* – this single example is alone sufficient to refute the notion that *kommerkiarioi* dealt only in silk, the more so since on one of the seals the *apothēkē* is specifically mentioned: if the *kommerkiarios* in question were bidding for the contract to sell slaves in his private capacity then it seems unlikely that he would put the *apothēkē* on his seal. In fact, it seems quite logical to assume that the emperor's effigy on the seals is simply a validation of the formal and imperially sanctioned nature of the transaction (whatever its exact nature), and that it need have nothing at all to do with silk – a point also tacitly conceded, although Oikonomidès wishes to argue that the example of the sale of slaves was probably an exception.

There are a number of other points to be considered, however. Even if Hendy is wrong as regards the sale of the Slav prisoners, the general hypothesis remains strong. The coincidence between the dated seals of *kommerkiarioi* and *apothēkai*, and known military expeditions, is really too marked to be written off as mere chance. In the second place, the argument relating *kommerkiarioi* to silk and to the importance of silk for the imperial economy in the seventh and eighth centuries depends upon a number of dubious assumptions about the nature of sericulture. Crucial to Oikonomidès' argument is the assumption that mulberry trees – which require a moderate climate – could flourish throughout Anatolia (except in Galatia I, for which no seal survives), in provinces as diverse as Asia or Caria, on the one hand, which have a relatively high rainfall and standard Mediterranean climatic conditions, and Lycaonia, the Cappadocias and the provinces of Armenia on the other, which have extreme seasonal variation between winter and summer, and very much lower rainfall. The mulberry tree (*Morus alba*) needs deep, well-drained and fairly rich loams to prosper, with adequate supplies of moisture. Eastern and central Anatolia can offer these conditions, when at all, on an extremely limited basis. On these grounds alone, therefore, the long-term production of silk in eastern Asia Minor, supposedly represented by the seals of *kommerkiarioi* and *apothēkai* for these provinces, is very doubtful. It is admitted, however, that the 'silk-producing areas' were forced to move westwards as a result of the effects of Arab raids and attacks – but only from the 730s and later.[89]

---

[89] Oikonomidès, 'silk trade', 44. In modern Turkey the very small silk industry is limited to the region around Bursa, in the north-west of Anatolia, and Antakya (Antioch on the

But Asia Minor, especially the central and eastern regions, was already subject to regular and devastating enemy action from the 650s if not a decade earlier. The evidence surveyed already (see chapter 3 above) is overwhelming. The stable political conditions for such an investment simply did not exist at this time. Even if one were to concede that isolated groves of mulberry trees could survive in certain secluded valleys, and that silk production could continue uninterrupted, this could hardly have provided the major source of silk – and imperial revenue – at this time. And indeed, one might also ask, where was the market for such large-scale production as is envisaged? Given the restrictive and redistributive nature of the state economy at this period, such sales can have brought in very little in net terms to the imperial fisc. It could be pointed out, of course, that silk – like gold – formed a major element in Byzantine diplomacy: used to buy off foreign powers, as gifts or bribes, as a form of payment and so on. Silk may well have been used in this way, and indeed in the ninth and tenth centuries military officers and others received silk vestments as a form of remuneration. But if silk were really on a par with gold, and indeed, almost replacing gold, why is it never referred to in this sense for this period in the sources? Gold and horses, and sometimes slaves, are mentioned as the usual forms of such gifts or tribute; precious silks, when they do occur, clearly occupy a relatively minor role. And the contention that the connection between the department of the *blattion* (the imperial silk-workshop) and some of the *kommerkiarioi* is a proof of this notion, is hardly a convincing argument – the fact that *kommerkiarioi* were (also) responsible for silk production is not to be doubted.

In the third place, Oikonomidès has argued that the westward movement of the 'silk-producing areas' in the eighth century illustrates a flight away from the war-zone – thus implicitly countering the idea that the *kommerkiarioi* and the *apothēkai* were connected with supplying the military. Two observations are relevant here. First, it is nowhere argued that the *kommerkiarioi* had to do only with the supplying of the troops with equipment – merely that this became one of their functions. Second, this function did not last much longer than the crisis which called it into being; and indeed, the movement westwards (that is to say, the appearance of fewer seals for *kommerkiarioi* and *apothēkai* for the Anatolian provinces, and a corresponding increase in the number of such seals for the Balkan districts) actually conforms to a real shift in the military strategy of the empire, as the Balkans became a more significant – and more contested – element in its political environment. Again, the close connection between known military undertakings and the seals of *kommerkiarioi* and *apothēkai*

Orontes) in the far south, both areas of Mediterranean climatic type. See J. C. Dewdney, *Turkey* (London 1971), pp. 135–6 and 182.

is compelling, and it is a relationship not challenged by the arguments put forward by Oikonomidès.[90]

While there is no reason to doubt, therefore, that the *kommerkiarioi* and the *kommerkia* or *apothēkai* were also connected with the sale and production of silk, there is every reason to reject the hypothesis that they were exclusively to do with this activity. The historical context, quite apart from the nature and demands of seventh- and eighth-century state fiscality, make it inherently unlikely. The evidence in favour depends in certain crucial ways upon arguments which can be shown to be false; while the evidence against it is enough to flaw it in fundamental ways. In respect of the sale of Slav prisoners in 694/5, Oikonomidès may well be right. But this neither supports nor detracts from his argumentation in any crucial way.

To return to the main argument once more. What seems to have happened, therefore, is that the state, having cut down to a bare minimum (the donative) the cash paid out to the armies, had to find an alternative way of supplying and equipping its soldiers. Supplies could be raised in kind, as we have seen. Hitherto, the troops had received initial grants of equipment free, and cash allowances thereafter for remounts, replacement weapons and so on. With the cessation of cash *annonae* and grants for such equipment, and the return to supplying the armies in kind, a system had to be found whereby weapons and equipment could also be supplied and distributed. The extension of the role of the *apothēkē*, which represented the central and provincial storehouses of the special bank of the prefecture – now the *eidikon/idikon logothesion* – offered an obvious solution.

But Hendy has also argued that the equipment involved – including weapons – was sold to the troops, partly on the grounds that the *kommerkiarioi* have generally been assumed to be tax-collectors, and that the pattern demonstrated by the seals – appointment by the year, dated by indiction, often alternating with similar appointments for different regions or for different spheres of imperial manufacturing – suggests that the *kommerkiarioi* were tax-farmers. Further, it has been taken for granted that the material to be distributed to the soldiers was the product of imperial workshops: the *ergodosia* in Constantinople and elsewhere, and the imperial arms-factories. But here we meet a number of problems.[91]

In the first place, while the state weaving- and cloth-factories had

---

[90] See Hendy, *Studies*, pp. 654ff. See also A. Dunn, 'The *Kommerkiarios*, the *Apotheke*, the *Dromos*, the *Vardarios*, and *The West*', *BMGS* 17 (1993) 3–24, at 11; and D. Jacoby, 'Silk in Western Byzantium before the Fourth Crusade', *BZ* 84/85 (1991/1992) 452–500, see 454 n. 7.

[91] See esp. J. W. Nesbitt, 'Double names on early Byzantine lead seals', *DOP* 31 (1977), 111–21, see esp. 115–17, and note 20; Hendy, *Studies*, p. 626 and note 310, and pp. 633 and 636.

originally supplied a considerable proportion of military clothing, they had never entirely covered the demand, which had been met by private producers whose products were handed over to the state as part of their tax-assessment.[92] Even after the commutation of much of this tax into gold – in the later fifth century – the soldiers were still equipped only partially by the state and were expected to purchase replacement items with their cash allowances.[93] As a result of the territorial losses suffered by the empire during the seventh century, however, the state must have found it impossible to cater for all but a very small proportion of these requirements. The majority of the weaving and clothing establishments of the later Roman state now lay outside the empire's control: only Heraclea in Thrace, Cyzicus in Hellespontus and Caesarea in Cappadocia, together with the workshops in Constantinople itself, remained; and of these, both Heraclea and Caesarea were in extremely insecure areas, subject to regular devastation. It is unlikely that their establishments remained in operation into the later 640s.[94]

Similar considerations applied to weapons, which had been a state monopoly. But by the 640s only five of the fifteen Eastern *fabricae* remained within imperial territory – at Nicomedia, Sardis, Adrianople, Thessaloniki and Caesarea in Cappadocia, together with the workshop which produced parade-armour in Constantinople.[95] Of these, those at Adrianople and Caesarea may well have ceased production due to their exposed position; while those of Thessaloniki and Sardis – if the latter survived at all – must have had production dramatically curtailed after the reign of Heraclius, if not before.

Now it is clear that the few establishments left to the state can hardly have catered for the requirements of field armies whose numbers, at a most conservative estimate, must still have attained some 80,000 soldiers in Europe, Africa, and Asia Minor in the 650s. The only option left to the state was to promote private production – whether or not this was supervised by government officials – of clothing and other items of equipment: boots, leatherwork, saddlery and so on, as well as weapons; and the latter constituted, of course, a radical break with the traditional system. What the *apothēkē* system and the *kommerkiarioi* represent, in fact, is not the transport of materials from Constantinople, for example, to the districts

---

[92] Jones, *LRE*, vol. I, pp. 433f.
[93] See Jones, *LRE*, vol. II, pp. 625 and 670–1; Haldon, *Byzantine Praetorians*, p. 113 and notes 113 and 114.
[94] For the workshops see Jones, *LRE*, vol. II, p. 836. Those at Tyre, Scythopolis, and in Phoenicia and Cyprus (together with others about which nothing is known, since no complete list (unlike for the West) exists) were lost to the empire by the 650s.
[95] There had been arms factories specialising in different types of production at Damascus, Antioch, Edessa, Marcianopolis, Naissus, Ratiaria, Irenopolis (Cilicia) and Horreum Margi. See *Notitia Dig.*, Or. XI, 18–39; and Jones, *LRE*, vol. II, pp. 834ff.

where they were needed, and the consequent sale of such material to the soldiers, but a much more fundamental shift.

If, as has been surmised, but need not necessarily have been the case, the *kommerkiarioi* are contract-farmers, dealing in materials (and it is worth noting that a number of their seals bear the impression of sacking on one side, implying their attachment to the actual goods)[96] and administering the requirements for specific military undertakings, then the accumulated evidence suggests the only viable option left to the state: they were contractors who were actually in charge of levying the equipment – weapons, clothing and so on – from local producers and craftsmen in the areas in which the troops were based. What must have operated was, in effect, a compulsory levy in kind, raised either in the form of an advance against future tax-assessments, or as a compulsory purchase at a low fixed price (although the emphasis placed by the state on avoiding cash transactions may argue against this) or as a variant of the simple *munera extraordinaria* or *aggareia*. The crucial point for the state was to minimise its own outgoings and maximise the extraction of resources from the population. And here the later system operated in the ninth and tenth centuries becomes relevant, for it is exactly the same procedure – albeit now under the supervision of the thematic *prōtonotarioi* and *stratēgoi* – that is to be found. In the account of the preparations for the expedition to Crete of 911 in the Book of Ceremonies of Constantine VII,[97] the method of raising arms for the thematic forces on a mass scale is abundantly clear: each local commander, or appropriate official, was required to ensure the production of a certain number of weapons (shields, arrows, lances and so on), which can only have been raised by compulsory levy from the local population.[98] This seems to have been the standard system from the ninth century on, and there is no reason for assuming that it is not the developed form of the *ad hoc* system introduced in the 640s and after to cope with the crisis which the state had to face in the production of weapons and clothing for its soldiers.

The *kommerkiarioi*, therefore, were contracted to arrange the production and delivery, and possibly the distribution of weapons and equipment from local craftsmen and producers to the soldiers in a given region or regions, as well as from the state's own factories and warehouses. Their contract will have lain in the state's offering them some form of return on excess production, which could be stored in the state *apothēkai* or *armamenta*; and in the *kommerkiarioi* undertaking to cover any shortfall out of their own resources. There was nothing at all new in this principle, except its

---

[96] Nesbitt, 'Double names', 115–17; Hendy, *Studies*, p. 626 note 310.
[97] *De Cer.*, 657. 12sq.
[98] For a detailed analysis, see Haldon, *Byzantine Praetorians*, pp. 319–22.

application to the production of military equipment.[99] And the reasons for the *kommerkiarioi* being commissioned in this sphere are quite straightforward: they had traditionally supervised the taxes and duties on the sale of finished goods produced by state workshops and disposed of through the special bank of the prefecture. The special bank, in its independent guise as the *eidikon/idikon logothesion*, continued to supervise these activities, gaining in addition control over the actual production establishments themselves, including – as the later evidence makes fairly clear – the production of weapons and other items of military equipment.[100] It was a natural extension of the role of the *kommerkiarioi*, as production began to be contracted out by force of circumstances to provincial workshops and craftsmen, that they should also supervise this aspect of the activities of the *eidikon*. And that this was the case is strongly suggested by the fact that on at least one occasion between 659 and 668 the general *kommerkiarios* of a provincial *apothēkē* was also *stratiōtikos logothetēs*, the official in charge of military finance and the assessments for military provisions.[101]

But such transactions could in no way have involved the *sale* of weapons and equipment to the troops. If the state had stopped paying the regular cash allowances to its soldiers, it could hardly have expected them to pay for their equipment with cash. Instead, the state returned to the system of the fourth century: supplies were raised in kind from the local population as part of the regular tax-assessment, supervised by the local prefects (of the *themata* or armies); equipment and clothing was now raised similarly, by levies on local producers, supervised by the *genikoi kommerkiarioi*, and for specific undertakings. The actual distribution of the material probably continued to be administered as before, regimental actuaries collecting and issuing it at the regular musters or *adnoumia*, as described in the Strategikon of the Emperor Maurice of the late sixth century, and in later hagiographies and military treatises.[102]

---

[99] For the classic example of tax-farming in the late Roman state, see Jones, LRE, vol. I, p. 457.

[100] See the evidence cited in Haldon, *Byzantine Praetorians*, pp. 320–2 and notes. The fact that the *kommerkiarioi* were in origin purely civilian officials is not a serious objection to this development. In the first place, there were neither juridical nor institutional hindrances to it; in the second place, the appointment of civil officials to military commands, for example, where the emperor placed particular trust in the individual concerned, was quite usual – cf. the example of the deacon John, *genikos logothetēs*, appointed to command the expedition assembling on Rhodes in 714 (see Theophanes, 385. 5sq. and the discussion of Hendy, *Studies*, pp. 657f.). In the crisis faced by the state at this period, such measures are only too easily explained.

[101] Zacos and Veglery, no. 144, seal of Stephen, *apo hypatōn, patrikios, stratiōtikos logothetēs* and *genikos kommerkiarios* of the *apothēkē* of ... (dated 659–68).

[102] See Maurice, *Strategikon* I, 2.11; and cf. Theophylact Simocatta VI, 6.4, VII, 7.1, VIII, 12.12; Haldon, *Byzantine Praetorians*, p. 104 and note 63. For the later *adnoumion*, see

By the same token, no loosening of state control over the production of weapons and, more significantly, the ownership of weapons need be implied (although this may have been an unavoidable result). The strict regulations on the shipment and possession of weapons in Justinian's novel 85 were retained in later legislation; and while the state therefore gave up its monopoly on production, it still intended to limit the possession of arms to its soldiers alone.[103]

There seems little doubt that by the time of the Ecloga of Leo and Constantine in 741 provincial soldiers were assumed to own the basic elements of their equipment – weapons, armour and, where relevant, horse. They were responsible for its maintenance in good condition and – certainly by the later eighth century – for the replacement of items, such as horses, which had been lost in the interim.[104] An eighth-century legal text also makes it clear that private persons were able, but not obliged, to contribute to the cost of equipping a soldier, thus emphasising the personal ownership of such material.[105] Equally, while the legal texts state that the soldiers did receive some cash emoluments, referred to as *rhogai*, they also received *annonae*, that is to say, provisions in kind. This suggests that the term *rhoga* had already come to be used of the donative (and, indeed, of any cash payment) – even though, as we have seen, this was issued probably on a four-yearly rotational basis by this time – and that the rations in kind were the main support of the armies.[106] The fact that the same texts refer to the *annonae* of civil officials makes the situation clear – the state had had to revert almost entirely to a system of payment in kind, in the provinces at least.

What appears to have been happening, therefore, was that the state

---

Leo, *Tactica*, VI, 15; Anon. Vári, 48 (28.3sq. Dennis); Haldon, *Recruitment and Conscription*, p. 63; and on the issue of weapons, see Haldon, *Praetorians*, pp. 114–15.

[103] See Justinian, *Nov.* 85 and cf. *Basilica* LVII, 9.1; *Procheiros nomos* XXXIX. That private production may have taken place – particularly in specialist production such as bows, or mail and lamellar armour – is suggested by the existence of a memorial stone of a bowmaker from the Attaleia region. See Grégoire, *Recueils*, no. 308 (= *CIG* 9239), of the seventh or eighth century.

[104] See Haldon, *Recruitment and Conscription*, pp. 67–72 for a detailed treatment and analysis of the relevant sources. The key text is *Ecloga* XVI, 2.

[105] See especially the (probably) mid-eighth-century text of a legal decision attributed by its editor to Leo III and Constantine V, in which a soldier's father-in-law is referred to as contributing to the expense of equipping the former: ed. D. Simon, 'Byzantinische Hausgemeinschaftsverträge', in *Beiträge zur europäischen Rechtsgeschichte und zum geltenden Zivilrecht. Festgabe für J. Sontis* (Munich 1977), pp. 91–128, see 94; see also Burgmann, *Ecloga*, 135–6. I have discussed this, and related texts, elsewhere: see J. F. Haldon, 'Military service, military lands, and the status of soldiers', 20ff.

[106] See *Ecloga* XVI, 4, where *rogai* are carefully defined as coming respectively from the emperor's hand (i.e. donatives or similar payments from the emperor's own treasury); whereas *annōnai* and *synētheiai* came from the *dēmosion*, that is to say, the public fisc.

issued soldiers with their basic equipment, as in the fourth century, which the soldiers were expected to look after and present in good order at musters and parades (*adnoumia*). This was produced partly in imperial workshops, but mostly under contract or by levy on the provincial populations. Whatever the initial legal status of such equipment may have been, it is clear that by the time of the Ecloga text, and certainly by the time of the writing of the Life of St Philaretus, the weapons and other material, including the soldier's horse, were regarded as his possessions, for which he was responsible. And while the state seems to have issued the basic requirements in the first instance, more expensive weaponry and armour was clearly available from private producers, or possibly from certain state workshops. This much is clear from the second legal text of the reign of Leo III and Constantine, referred to already. It is also evident from hagiographical sources, and from Theophanes' account of the second evil deed of the Emperor Nicephorus I that soldiers were expected to pay for and maintain their own equipment by the early ninth century.[107] The cumulative pay-scales, recorded by ninth-century Arab geographers, which may reflect the seventh-century situation or an evolution from it no doubt contributed to soldiers' ability to cover such additional expenditure, and may indeed represent this initial state issue when service was first begun and the increasing obligation of the soldiers as time passed to cater for their own equipment and mounts. But even in the ninth and tenth centuries, it seems that the state still equipped some soldiers and levied large amounts of military *matériel*, in addition to expecting thematic soldiers to provide for themselves.[108]

What this means in practical terms is that two complementary systems operated side by side. Troops raised for specific campaigns were armed and equipped by the state – this is presumably the chief function of the *eidikon* and its *apothēkai* in our period, and of the *eidikon* and the thematic *prōtonotarioi* in the ninth and tenth centuries. On such occasions, troops already available were mobilised, too, and were expected to turn out with their weapons, mounts and so on. Failure to do so had severe consequences, as the evident fear of the soldier Mousoulios in the Life of St Philaretus, as well as other, later examples, amply demonstrates.[109] But

[107] See *Vita S. Philareti*, 125, 34sq. and see Haldon, *Recruitment and Conscription*, pp. 50–1 and note 58 and pp. 58ff. For the reforms of the Emperor Nicephorus I, by which impoverished soldiers were to be equipped by their fellow villagers, Theophanes, 486. 23–6. For the Arabic source, see Ibn Khurradadhbīh, *Kitāb al-Masālik w'al-Mamālik*, in M.-J. de Goeje, *Bibliotheca Geographorum Arabicorum* VI (Leiden 1889), pp. 76–85, see p. 84.

[108] See *De Cer.* 657. 12sq., 658. 4sq.

[109] For Mousoulios, see note 107 above; and cf. the similar case of a horseless soldier reported in the Life of Eustratius (*Vita Eustratii*, 377. 3–6; see Haldon, *Recruitment and Conscription*, p. 51 note 88). Oikonomidès has argued plausibly that the four-yearly cycle

the state can hardly have expected soldiers whom it did not pay in cash to buy their equipment. On the other hand, those who could afford it would undoubtedly provide themselves with the best weapons and armour. And as the state, keen to minimise its own outgoings, and indeed the burden on local populations, insisted on the soldiers' responsibility for their weapons and mounts, so it would have encouraged private investment in such equipment, with the inevitable result that possession on the one hand, and legal ownership on the other, were assimilated.

THE PROBLEM OF 'MILITARY LANDS'

We can now turn to another aspect of the possible sources of support for the soldier, that is, the question of the military lands and the degree to which the state actually promoted a policy of providing soldiers with land from which they could support themselves and their duties.

It has been argued that, on the assumption that the state sold weapons and military equipment to the soldiers through the *apothēkē* system, and had also withdrawn regular cash payments to them except for the quadrennial/quinquennial donatives, it must have had to provide them with an alternative form of income; for how else could the soldiers have paid for the equipment available for purchase through the *kommerkiarioi*? Given the types of resources available, the only viable solution in such a situation, it is argued, would be to give soldiers land, which they and their families could cultivate, hence providing an income for their support.[110]

But there are a number of flaws in this argument also. In the first place, even if some soldiers and their families were given grants of land and the time required to bring it under cultivation, or at the least to achieve the minimum requirements in terms of autarky – let alone the production of the considerable surpluses necessary to support a soldier, purchase his equipment and maintain a sustained level of productivity – even if this were the case, it is inherently improbable that all soldiers could be supported in this way. Some would simply lack the requisite technical skill and knowledge; others might have no family adequate to farming the land. Quite apart from this, of course, is the fact that most campaigns took place at precisely the times of the year when agricultural production demanded

---

as it is described in the tenth century represents the state's rationalisation of a system whereby soldiers received cash (and other) emoluments due to them usually on the occasion of a campaign. See N. Oikonomidès, 'Middle Byzantine Provincial Recruits: Salary and Armament', in *Gonimos. Neoplatonic and Byzantine Studies presented to Leendert G. Duffy at 75*, eds. J. Duffy and J. Peradotto (Buffalo, N.Y. 1988), pp. 121–36, see 125–7.

[110] The argument is set out in detail in Hendy, *Studies*, pp. 634ff.

Military administration 245

the most attention and labour, in particular during harvesting.[111] Equally, if – as has been argued[112] – soldiers were originally given lands on imperial estates, complete with tenants to carry out the agricultural labour for them, it is very difficult to explain how such large holdings came to be reduced to the state of poverty implicit in the case of the soldier Mousoulios from the Life of Philaretus – for surely such an argument must presuppose a degree of state protection of such holdings against alienation and impoverishment (as was the case, for example, from the first half of the tenth century). The provision of soldiers with land, therefore, can at best have been a very slow and partial procedure.

In the second place, it is clear from the available evidence for the eighth, ninth and tenth centuries that there existed prior to the legislation of the mid-tenth century no legislation to bind soldiers, land and military service together; and if the state had given land to troops directly in return for military service, there would surely have remained some echo of this in the legislation or in some narrative source, somewhere. But the sources remain either quite silent on this point, or they positively assume otherwise. Indeed, neither of the two early eighth-century legal texts thus far referred to suggest any *obligation* upon soldiers' families to support them; and they actually make it quite clear that soldiers could leave their households and lands at liberty. This can only have been the case if the state, in principle at least, was still assumed to maintain its troops, if not also with a first issue of equipment and weapons, then certainly with regular *annonae* or provisions (and later cash *rhogai*). What the sources do make clear is that military service in the provincial, that is to say thematic, armies was, for many of the soldiers if not for all of them (for some continued always to be recruited on a mercenary basis and for the duration of a specific campaign)[113] a

[111] Soldiers were officially prohibited from engaging in farming for others. For the legislation and its relevance, see Haldon, *Recruitment and Conscription*, pp. 48–9 and note 83; 72–3 and note 128; Ahrweiler, 'Recherches', 8f. For an illustrative example, prohibiting soldiers from engaging in agriculture and trade, see *Leges militares* (ed. Koržensky), 80, 2. As Lilie, 'Die zweihundertjährige Reform', 194, has noted, the continued *official* emphasis on this ruling would tend to exclude an *official* promotion of the personal involvement of soldiers in such activities. On the other hand, the efficacy and purpose, as well as the date, of the 'Military Laws' remain unclear; while such prohibitions may have been intended to apply only to full-time salaried troops. See the remarks of Oikonomidès, 'Middle Byzantine Provincial Recruits', 133 note 36.

[112] W.T. Treadgold, 'The military lands and the imperial estates in the middle Byzantine empire', in *Okeanos. Essays presented to I. Ševčenko* (Harvard Ukrainian Studies, VII, Cambridge, Mass. 1983), pp. 619–31.

[113] See Haldon, *Recruitment and Conscription*, p. 79 note 145, and *Byzantine Praetorians*, pp. 216–20. This is undoubtedly also the implication of the comments of Theodore the Studite in a letter of the year 801 (ed. G. Fatouros, *Theodori Studitae Epistulae* (CFHB XXXI 1/2. Berlin 1992), ep. 7.61–63) to the effect that widows of soldiers need no longer 'lament bitterly at the piteous and inhuman demands made on their dead husbands' account'. The text suggests that the state continued to demand the equivalent of the husband's military

personal and hereditary obligation. Only in the tenth century was this obligation transferred to the land.[114]

It seems, therefore, unlikely that a great many soldiers were able to take up such an option on land, even if it were available. Yet all soldiers had been deprived of the greater part of their regular cash income and their cash allowances for weapons, clothing and other equipment. The notion that the *apothēkē* was in the business of selling weapons to such soldiers thus becomes even more unlikely. Soldiers in this position will have been simply unable to purchase weapons on this basis. And the only conclusion must be that the state, as I have surmised, did not sell weapons and equipment; it issued them directly, exploiting both urban and provincial craftsmen and skills, and thereby saving its own resources. The *apothēkē* system was a convenient and pre-existing means of widening and systematising the basis of production and distribution of military requirements. The fact that it is just such a system which operated in the ninth and tenth centuries (although no longer through the *kommerkiarioi*) lends strength to the argument.

An otherwise apparently powerful argument for the state's attribution of land to soldiers for their maintenance is thus crucially weakened. The state could clearly support and maintain its armies on a traditional basis of levies of provisions in kind, as it had always done for military expeditionary forces anyway, and as it had done during the fourth and much of the fifth centuries. It may well have attempted to lighten the burden by granting leave to soldiers who had families that could support them during the winter, for example, thus having to provision those soldiers who remained in camp or on active service only. There is some evidence, again from the Ecloga text (xvi, 1) that this was indeed the case.[115] As the *themata* became firmly established, so the probability that soldiers have families or relatives in the garrison area increases, and thus the possibilities for the state to transfer the leave-time support of the troops to the soldiers themselves will also have increased. Given the difficult situation, there is no reason to doubt that the state exploited such possibilities to the full.

None of this means that soldiers could not or did not hold or own land;

service in some other form, possibly cash or support for a replacement – the threat of the withdrawal of the special exempt status of soldiers' families in respect of certain fiscal and other dues will probably also have played a role.

[114] The question and the sources are analysed in detail in Haldon, *Recruitment and Conscription*, pp. 41–65. The clear evidence for a personal and hereditary military service in the ninth and tenth centuries, but one which was in no way formally and legally associated with land (until the legislation of Romanus I and Constantine VII) invalidates any line of reasoning which argues for a Heraclian origin for this relationship, of course. The argumentation of both Hendy and Treadgold is in this respect flawed. For a similar critique of Treadgold, see R.-J. Lilie, 'Die byzantinischen Staatsfinanzen im 8./9. Jahrhundert und die στρατιωτικὰ κτήματα', BS 47 (1987), 49–55, see 50–1.

[115] See the apposite comments of Lilie, 'Die zweihundertjährige Reform', 194 and note 77.

Military administration 247

nor that military service did not come to be supported by and associated with such holdings. Soldiers were clearly expected to be at least partially self-supporting by the later eighth, and certainly by the ninth century;[116] and some of the divergent views of historians who have examined this question can be partially reconciled in this respect.

For there is also no doubt that the state did give land to individuals, from whom it then expected to recruit soldiers. In the 590s, the Emperor Maurice is reported to have decreed the raising of 30,000 cavalry soldiers in Thrace, to which end he ordered the settling by forced transfer of the same number of Armenian families to Thrace. While the figures may no doubt be considerably inflated, the principle is clear.[117] Similarly, it is clear that the Slavs, whom Justinian II transferred to Asia Minor in 688/9 together with their families, were used as a source of recruits. Again, while the figure of 30,000 is no doubt inflated, along with that of the 20,000 who supposedly deserted (Syriac sources give for the latter a figure of a mere 7,000),[118] the principle seems to be clear: to draft in new populations (and not simply individuals, but whole communities and families) who, in the first case mentioned above certainly, and in the second case almost as certainly, were given land, and from among whom recruits could be conscripted. But it is important to note that these groups were ethnic bands and, if the Slavs are anything to go by, they were organised as such, under their own leaders, on a similar basis to that of late Roman *foederati*, or possibly the *laeti* (who had less independence as distinct groups), within the Western empire in the fourth and fifth centuries. They were intended by Justinian, just like the earlier federates, to operate as an independent corps which might fight in conjunction with Byzantine forces. The system they represent, therefore, is not a novelty,[119] but neither is it a generalised means of recruitment including the granting of land to soldiers, for which

[116] Haldon, *Recruitment and Conscription*, pp. 72ff. and the sources cited there. It is clear from the Italian evidence from the exarchate of Ravenna that after about 640 the majority of the garrison troops were, to a greater or lesser degree, able to support themselves; although vestigial cash payments such as *donativa* were still made. See Brown, *Gentlemen and Officers*, pp. 87f. For Africa, see Durliat, *Les grands propriétaires et l'état byzantin*, 527f. with sources and literature.
[117] See Sebeos, 54f.; and for the sixth-century examples, Charanis, 'Ethnic changes', 29f. and 32f.; and 'Transfer of population', 142.
[118] See in the last instance Hendy, *Studies*, pp. 631ff.; and Stratos, *Byzantium in the Seventh Century*, vol. V, pp. 34ff. Groups of Slavs had also been settled in Asia Minor by Constans II, as their reported desertion to the Arabs in 665 suggests. For these episodes, see Charanis, 'Ethnic changes', 42f., 'Transfer of population', 143, and 'The Slavic element in Byzantine Asia Minor in the 13th century', *B* 18 (1946–8), 69–83, see 70f.
[119] A point recognised by Hendy, *Studies*, p. 637; the settlement of Slavs to repopulate the land was not confined to the Byzantine empire only: in the eighth century the Duke of Istria also settled Slavs on deserted lands. See Brown, *Gentlemen and Officers*, p. 88 note 14; Guillou, *Régionalisme*, pp. 304 and 306 (Plea of Rizana).

there is no evidence at all. Indeed, the fact that these Slav 'prisoners' were probably given land on a 'federate' basis makes more likely the probability that, as has been suggested, they were settled on imperial estates.[120] For, of course, part of the purpose of introducing such populations as is sometimes made quite explicit in the sources, was the revitalisation of the local population and the bringing back into cultivation of abandoned or deserted lands.

There is no reason to doubt, therefore, that groups of barbarians such as the Slavs were settled in Asia Minor, under both Constans II and Justinian II, in order to provide auxiliary military support for the hard-pressed Byzantine corps and in order to reoccupy deserted agricultural lands. The terms on which the land was received are unknown, but if it was on the basis of a fixed relationship between land and soldiers, one would again expect to find echoes of the practice in the later sources. Much more likely – since it has been shown that the late Roman imperial estates in Cappadocia seem to disappear some time before the twelfth century and represent an area associated on the seals of *kommerkiarioi* with the captured Slavs[121] – is the probability that large tracts of imperial lands were granted to the new 'federates', perhaps on an emphyteutic basis: that is to say, the basis for their settlement was the provision of a corps of soldiers, but this was not tied directly to individuals and specific properties or holdings. This hypothesis is indirectly supported by the fact that under Justinian I authority over the Cappadocian estates, as well as those of the diocese of Pontica, was granted to the proconsul of Cappadocia, who was at the same time (and like several other Anatolian provincial governors) given military authority. The local administration was therefore already in a position to facilitate the establishment of new settlers on imperial lands.[122] Initially, the land may have been freed from all fiscal dues for three years – as was the practice with captive 'Saracens' in the tenth century and probably before – in order to permit them to reap an adequate return on their initial labour.[123] And emphyteutic leases will have meant ultimately that the

[120] Hendy, *Studies*, p. 637f.; a point made also, although for all soldiers, by W.T. Treadgold, *The Byzantine State Finances in the Eighth and Ninth Centuries* (New York 1982) and 'The military lands and the imperial estates' (cited in note 112 above).

[121] Hendy, *Studies*, pp. 637f., with pp. 104–6 and 133–5 and map 29; Kaplan, 'Maisons divines', 85.

[122] See Kaplan, 'Maisons divines', 85; Justinian, *Nov*. 30, 1.6 (a. 536); and Jones, *LRE*, vol. I, pp. 280ff.

[123] See *De Cer.* 694. 22–695. 14. For a brief summary of the principles upon which land was allotted to federates and to the barbarians in the West in the fifth century, see Jones, *LRE*, vol. I, pp. 249–53. Note that the land thus granted remained subject to the basic land-tax, whether it was granted in perpetuity or not. Perpetual emphyteutic leases of imperial lands, of the sort already common in the East in the later sixth and seventh centuries, would have provided the East Roman state with a means of both bringing land back into cultivation, recovering lost tax revenue, and a permanent source of recruits.

land so granted will eventually have come to be regarded as much as the property of those settled on it as that of the state. The disappearance of the Cappadocian estates might thus be explained.

There is therefore good evidence that the state could and did settle groups of immigrants on the land and in return demand military service from the first generation at least of such 'federates'. But such a system, as we have seen, can hardly have applied to the regular soldiery. Instead, the probability is that these continued at first to be garrisoned in camps, or be barracked or billeted on the population – supported by direct levies of provisions from the local provincial population. Where soldiers had their families in the region, they may have been encouraged to support themselves to a degree, certainly when on leave in winter quarters – so much is clear from the early eighth-century legal texts referred to. Gradually – I have argued this elsewhere – and just as in the earlier cases of Africa, Egypt, Syria and, differently, in Italy, as the armies became more permanently established across their cantonments, the soldiers will have inevitably become almost entirely recruited from local sources, as the first generation put down roots, intermarried with the provincials, obtained land or interests in other property and so on. Indeed, members of the army of the exarchate in Italy seem regularly to have taken out emphyteutic leases on Church properties, encouraged both by the Church, as a means of maintaining a steady income, and by the state, as a means of ensuring adequate support for the soldiers. The result in the East seems to have been that during the later seventh and the eighth centuries the local military command and the state were able to rely increasingly on the soldiers supporting their service at least partially out of their own or their families' pockets – especially in view of the fact that the property of soldiers and their immediate dependents had traditionally been, and continued to be, exempt from all but the basic public taxes.[124] In this respect, military service entailed privileged status for the soldier's household and family. This development implies no formal obligation, of course, but the legal stipulations of the Ecloga and the decision of Leo and Constantine discussed above accurately reflect a situation in which private support for military service was becoming usual. The only formal obligation was in respect of the hereditary nature of military service, probably reintroduced

---

[124] Haldon, *Recruitment and Conscription*, pp. 74ff. For the privileged position of soldiers' land (the possession of which, of course, did not necessarily imply their actual physical involvement in its exploitation) see *ibid.*, p. 54 and note 94, p. 73 and note 129, p. 60 and note 104; Brown *Gentlemen and Officers*, pp. 87f. for a similar situation in the exarchate of Ravenna. For emphyteutic leases to imperial troops, see *ibid.*, p. 177 and esp. pp. 105f.

under Heraclius, possibly later, but certainly during the seventh century.[125]

The state thus had at least one major, traditional and above all well-tried option open to it, through which it could continue to support and supply its armies. The granting of land, while it certainly occurred, was on the other hand neither the only available means of supporting soldiers, nor indeed a particularly effective one, given the difficult conditions of the time; nor again is there evidence for it, except indirectly – but undeniably – for the transplanted Slavs during the reigns of Constans II and Justinian II. Here, however, special circumstances prevailed, and the institutional conditions on which the latter were established approximates to those of the fifth-century *foederati* and *laeti*, rather than to those of the recruitment and maintenance of the regular soldiers in the imperial forces. For the latter, the state returned to a system similar to that which had operated in the fourth and fifth centuries.

One final observation needs to be made. All the developments outlined above seem to apply throughout the lands of the empire in the seventh and early eighth centuries (with the possible exception of the two exarchates), except for the methods of paying expeditionary forces in the Balkans. In Asia Minor, as we have seen, the evidence suggests that the state found it necessary to support and equip its troops almost entirely in kind, with the exception of donatives and other occasional cash payments. No doubt cash – gold – was still found with which to attract new recruits for specific campaigns, for example; but in general, cash was not the rule. On the other hand, and as Hendy has pointed out, excavations from Athens, where relatively high concentrations of copper coins of Philippicus and Leo III were found, all minted in Constantinople and associated both in time and in location with the presence of the military on specific campaigns or actions, suggest that cash still played a role in some aspects of the military administration of these regions, in contrast to Asia Minor.[126] It may well be a reflection of local conditions and the dearth of available resources in the Balkan lands still held by the empire at this time, which meant that the state found it easier to pay a part of the soldiers' salary in cash – rather than provide the supplies in kind – and to use coin as the medium of

---

[125] Haldon, *Recruitment and Conscription*, pp. 36ff. Against this, see Lilie, 'Die zweihundert-jährige Reform', 193 note 69. That hereditary service was introduced as late as the reign of Leo IV, however, seems improbable – *ibid.*, 199f. The fact that the hereditary nature of military service is not referred to in either *Ecloga* XVI, 2, or the decision attributed to Leo and Constantine (see Lilie, 'Die byzantinischen Staatsfinanzen' (cited in note 114 above), 51) is no evidence that hereditary service was not applied at that time – such an argument *e silentio* is hardly persuasive, the less so in view of the fact that neither text is in the least way concerned with this aspect.

[126] See Hendy, *Studies*, pp. 659ff., with sources and literature.

Military administration 251

exchange with local traders and producers. It may also reflect imperial administrative tradition in these districts.[127] But while this evidence does show that the state could and did employ coin on occasion, it does not appreciably alter the general picture drawn in this chapter, one in which the reversion to both the appropriation and redistribution of revenues in kind plays a major role.

The seventh century thus witnessed a major transformation in the fiscal and military administrative machinery of the state, in which the late Roman institutions inherited from the preceding period were recast to cope with a radically changed set of circumstances. It is important not to underestimate the degree of planning and foresight which this process demonstrates. For while the state was certainly responding to pressures which could hardly have been foreseen, it did not react blindly to circumstances. Both in the shape of fiscal as well as of military reorganization and readjustment, the late Roman and early Byzantine state demonstrates a remarkable functional coherence, an aspect which has perhaps been rather underplayed in recent debates.

EXCURSUS

The unequal allocation of territory to the different army corps, or *themata*, is more apparent when compared with the size of the field armies in question. These are difficult to estimate exactly, but the figures which can be obtained from the *Notitia Dignitatuum* for the East, which dates to about 420, where they can be corroborated by figures from the reign of Justinian or afterwards, suggest that the main field armies of the empire in the mid-sixth century were maintained at approximately the same strength as in the early fifth century. According to *Notitia Dig.*, Or. V-IX, the armies will have numbered very approximately as follows:

---

[127] See Hendy, *Studies*, pp. 418ff., 651ff and 662 for a detailed discussion and analysis. Hendy has also convincingly argued that the later (ninth- and tenth-century) differences in methods of paying Eastern as opposed to Western thematic *stratēgoi* and troops reflects the original late Roman pattern: the *themata* which occupied the territories of the praetorian prefecture of the East were paid from Constantinople on a four-yearly rotation which, as we have seen, was based on the old quinquennial issue of donatives. Their *stratēgoi* were paid annually also from Constantinopolitan funds. In contrast, the Balkan *themata*, which developed on the territory of the old praetorian prefecture of Illyricum, were maintained on a different basis, their soldiers and *stratēgoi* being paid from local funds, reflecting the late Roman source of cash, through the prefectural headquarters at Thessaloniki. Such continuities can also be shown to exist in the case of the naval *themata* which developed via the command of the *Karavisianoi* from the 'pseudo-prefecture' of the *quaestura exercitus*, with its bank (*arca/trapeza*) in Constantinople. The later *stratēgoi* of these *themata* were paid also from Constantinople in the ninth and tenth centuries. Likewise, the later thematic commander of the district of Mesopotamia was paid from the proceeds of the local *kommerkion*, just as the late Roman *dux* of the same command had received his salary via the local *commerciarius*. See Hendy, *Studies*, pp. 650–4.

magister militum praesentalis I	−20,500
praesentalis II	−22,500
per Orientem	−20,000
per Thracias	−23,500
per Illyricum	−17,500
total	−104,000.

Calculations depend, of course, on the strength of the various units, which is also difficult to assess − see the figures offered by Jones, *LRE*, vol. II, pp. 682f. and vol. III, p. 379, table xv. Figures for the sixth century suggest comparable numbers: in 499 an army of 15,000 was available to oppose a Bulgar attack in Illyricum (see Marcellinus *comes*, s.a. 499; Procopius, *De Bello Gothico* III, 29.3); in 530, after the new *magister militum per Armeniam* had been established, Belisarius commanded a reinforced Eastern army of 25,000; and of 20,000 in 531; while in 543 a total of some 30,000 men is recorded on the Persian front (Procopius, *De Bello Persico* I, 13.23, 18.5; II, 24.16). Procopius notes that a force of some 12,000 men operated in Lazica in 554 (*De Bello Gothico* IV, 13.8), and this must represent the greater part of the corps under the *magister militum per Armeniam*. The figure of 30,000 for 543 probably represents most of the combined field troops of both Eastern and Armenian commands. In Italy, the field armies numbered variously from 12,000 to 18,000 between 542 and 554 (Procopius, *De Bello Gothico* I, 5.2–4, III, 3.4; and Agathias II, 4); in Africa the field forces seem to have numbered about 15,000 (Procopius, *De Bello Vandalico* I, 11.2, 11–12, 19). Agathias also suggests, perhaps over-pessimistically, a grand total for Justinian's armies of about 150,000 in about 560 (Agathias V, 13). The size of the field armies suggested by this evidence (approximately 12,000 to 20,000, depending upon the theatre) seems to represent the norm at this period. See R. MacMullen, 'How big was the Roman imperial army?', *Klio* 62 (1980), 451–60; and H. Castritius, 'Die Wehrverfassung im 5. Jahrhundert n. Chr. und der Untergang des römischen Reiches', *Jahrbuch des Deutschen Evangelischen Instituts für Altertumswissenschaft des Heiligen Landes* 2 (1990). Also on numbers, and the relationship between size of army, civilian population and resource base, see J.-M. Carrié, 'L'Esercito: trasformazioni Funzionali ed economie locali', in *Società Romana ed Impero Tardoantico. Instituzioni, Ceti, Economie*, ed. A. Giardina (Rome 1986), pp. 449–88, 760–71, with further literature. The figures can also be revised downwards, to produce considerably smaller units and overall sizes: see the useful discussion in M. Whittow, *The Making of Orthodox Byzantium, 600–1025* (Basingstoke–London 1996), pp. 181–93 and, on the figures offered by Jones, *loc.cit.*, see R. Duncan-Jones, *Structure and Scale in the Roman Economy* (Cambridge 1990).

These figures suggest that in the period c. 500 to c. 550 at least, the field forces of Illyricum and Oriens numbered approximately the same as in the 420s; that the forces of the *magister militum per Armeniam*, which covered a much less extended area than those of the Eastern forces from which they had been separated, numbered about 12,000–15,000; that those of Italy and Africa numbered about 15,000 each; and that those of the praesental and Thracian forces numbered also about the same as in 420. The forces of the mid-sixth century must therefore have numbered as follows:

Military administration

magister militum per Illyricum	−17,500	} including troops of the *quaestura*
Thracias	−23,500	
Orientem	−25,000	
Armeniam	−15,000	
praesentalis I	−20,500	
praesentalis II	−22,500	
Africam	−15,000	
Italiam	−15,000	
total	−154,000	

This figure – granted its very approximate nature, the fact that troops were also based in Spain, and the estimate of Agathias – seems to be reasonably representative. There must have been some changes in the period from Justinian to Heraclius, of course, and the total was probably reduced. The command of the *magister militum per Illyricum*, some of whose units (and perhaps some from the army of Thrace as well) will have been separated to form the army of the Justinianic *quaestura*, had been effectively lost by the 630s and 640s – its vestiges may well have been incorporated into the praesental forces. The two praesental corps themselves seem to have been amalgamated (the maximum praesental force envisaged in the so-called Strategikon of Maurice is of 24,000 men: see Haldon, *Byzantine Praetorians*, pp. 96ff. and 546 note 782; and C. M. Mazzucchi, 'Le ΚΑΤΑΓΡΑΦΑΙ dello Strategicon di Maurizio e lo schieramento di battaglia dell'esercito romano nel VI/VII secolo', *Aevum* 55 (1981), 111–38, see 125ff.), and it is very likely that units were transferred from both to the Eastern, African and Italian armies. But given these changes, there is no reason to doubt that the Thracian, oriental and Armenian corps continued to be maintained at roughly their Justinianic strengths, that is, of some 20,000–25,000 for the first two, and some 12,000–15,000 for the last. The figures are, as we have said, hypothetical; but they do illustrate what must have been the proportional numerical relationship between the three armies. Thus regardless of whether or not the higher hypothetical totals for the armies arrived at by Jones and the smaller numbers supposed by Whittow actually pertained, the proportional difference between them remains more or less constant. The losses incurred in the war with the Persians, and with the Arabs, the probable desertion or disbandment of many units, particularly those which had been based in a given locality for many years and on a more or less permanent basis, will have meant ultimately the withdrawal of forces probably smaller than those previously enlisted. But the figures are indicative of the fact that the smallest division seems to have been allocated the most extensive region as its resource area in Anatolia.

CHAPTER 7

Society, state and law

STATE AND LEGISLATION

The study of Byzantine jurisprudence in the seventh and eighth centuries, of judicial procedures, the operation of the courts, the appointment and background of the judiciary and notarial staff, these are all areas which, on account of the sparsity of adequate sources, are particularly difficult to elucidate. Of the imperial legislation of the period, the novels of Justinian's immediate successors[1] and of Heraclius,[2] the Ecloga promulgated in 741,[3] together with the anonymous treatises or 'law books' known as the Farmers' Law[4] and the Rhodian Sea Law,[5] with the so-called 'mutiny act', or treatise on military discipline and punishment,[6] are all that we have. And the date of the last three texts – all very derivative and drawn from Justinianic or pre-Justinianic material – is still very much debated. Only with the help of casual references in other sources is it possible to say anything about judicial practice, the application of the law and the availability of justice. In this section, I shall make some attempt to see how

---

[1] See *JGR* I, Coll. I, 1–21.
[2] *JGR* I, Coll. I, 22–5; new edn by J. Konidaris, 'Die Novellen des Kaisers Herakleios', FM V (1980), 33–106 (text: 62–95).
[3] *Ecloga. Das Gesetzbuch Leons III. und Konstantinos' V*, ed. L. Burgmann (Forschungen zur byzantinischen Rechtsgeschichte X, Frankfurt a. M. 1983). For the date, see *ibid.*, pp. 10–12; and O. Kresten, 'Datierungsprobleme'. On the legal judgement appended in some Mss. to the Ecloga (as chapter 19), but which represents an independent legislative act, see D. Simon, *Byzantinische Hausgemeinschaftsverträge*, pp. 91–100.
[4] See the literature cited in chapter 3, notes 117–18; and Pieler, 'Rechtsliteratur', p. 440 and notes 115ff.
[5] W. Ashburner, Νόμος Ῥοδίων Ναυτικός. *The Rhodian Sea Law* (Oxford 1909 and Aalen 1976) (and in *JGR* II, 91–103). See Pieler, *Rechtsliteratur*, pp. 441f. For the two latter texts as 'law-books' rather than as formal legislation, see the literature in Pieler, 'Rechtsliteratur', p. 433 and notes 30 and 31.
[6] W. Ashburner, 'The Byzantine mutiny act', *JHS* 46 (1926), 80–109 (and in *JGR* II, 75–9); E. Koržensky, 'Leges poenales militares e codice Laurentiano LXXV', *Egypetemes Philologiae Közlöny* (Budapest 1930), 155–63, 215–18 (in *JGR* II, 80–9). For literature and discussion, see Pieler, 'Rechtsliteratur', p. 444, notes 147–50.

these aspects of the traditional and sophisticated system of jurisprudence and judicial practice fared during the period in question.[7]

The sixth century, and in particular the reign of Justinian, had been a Golden Age of late Roman legislative productivity and codification. This is, with hindsight, largely a reflection of the fact that the fifth and sixth centuries were the only period in Byzantine history when a professionalised legal apparatus existed, and in which a formal legal training and career-structure determined the nature of jurisprudence and the administration and activities of the court system.[8] The Codex Iustinianus, the Institutes and the Digest, along with the collection of novellae constitutiones of Justinian's reign (together with several novels of Justin II and Tiberius Constantine and three prefectural edicts) established some time after 575, constitute a milestone in late Roman and early Byzantine legal history.[9] Thereafter, and in spite of the possible loss of some legislation from the following century and a half, the amount of legislation promulgated in the traditional form of the novel dies to a bare trickle. Four novels and the Ekthesis of Heraclius, the Typos of Constans II, the Edict of 681 of Constantine IV,[10] the Ecloga and a judicial ruling probably from the reign of Leo III and Constantine V, and the three treatises referred to above,

---

[7] For the history of jurisprudence and legal literature in this period and later, see the older survey of Zachariä, *Geschichte*, pp. 5ff., esp. 11–15; L. Wenger, *Die Quellen des römischen Rechts* (Vienna 1953); B. Sinogowitz, *Studien zum Strafrecht der Ekloge* (Πραγ. τῆς Ἀκαδ. Ἀθηνῶν XXI, Athens 1956); also P.I. Zepos, 'Die byzantinische Jurisprudenz zwischen Justinian und den Basiliken', in *Berichte zum XI. Internationalen Byzantinisten-Kongress* V,1 (Munich 1958), esp. pp. 7–13; Pieler, 'Rechtsliteratur', pp. 429ff. For some general remarks on the relationship between law and state, albeit in an extremely formalised way, see P.E. Pieler, 'Verfassung und Rechtsgrundlagen des byzantinischen Staates', *Akten des XVI. Internationalen Byzantinisten-Kongresses*, I,1 (Vienna 1981), pp. 213–31 (= *JÖB* 31,1 (1981)). It must be stressed that the difficulties facing the historian in respect of law, justice and legal administration in this period are particularly great. The lack of sources makes definite conclusions about many aspects impossible, and hypotheses hazardous. I have tried to interpret this limited material through the context – cultural, social and ideological – already elaborated; and it is this context, therefore, which informs the suggested evolution outlined here.

[8] See the remarks of D. Simon, 'Νομοτριβούμενοι', in *Satura Roberto Feenstra Sexagisslmum Quintum Annum Aetatis Complenti ab Alumnis Collegis Amicis Oblata*, eds. J.A. Ankum, J.E. Spruit and F.B.J. Wubbe (Fribourg 1985), 273–83.

[9] See esp. P. Noailles, *Les Collections des novelles de l'empereur Justinien. La collection grecque des 168 novelles* (Paris 1914). The Justinianic codex is most easily consulted in the edition of Th. Mommsen, P. Krüger, R. Schöll and W. Kroll, *Corpus Iuris Civilis* (3 vols., Berlin 1892–95 and 1945–63), I: *Institutiones*, ed. P. Krüger and *Digesta*, ed. Th. Mommsen; II: *Codex Iustinianus*, ed. P. Krüger; III: *Novellae Constitutiones*, eds. R. Schöll and W. Kroll. For the most recent general survey, see Pieler, 'Rechtsliteratur', pp. 407–19.

[10] Ekthesis: Mansi X, 991B–997A; *Lateran*, 156.20–162.13 (Dölger, *Regesten*, no. 211); Typos: Mansi X, 1029C–1032D; *Lateran*, 208.15–210.15 (Dölger, *Regesten*, no. 225); edict of Constantine IV: Mansi XI, 697A–712D; Riedinger, 832.1–856.6 (Dölger, *Regesten*, no. 245).

dating to the later seventh or first half of the eighth century, are all that survive, and they probably represent in fact most of what was enacted.[11]

This lack of imperial legislative activity is significant. It reflects at the very least a change in the methods employed by the emperors in enforcing and publicising their policies. For we have already seen that a whole series of major administrative transformations took place, especially from the later years of the reign of Heraclius on, and it seems inherently improbable that all the novels of the emperors from Constans II to Leo III have been lost. The later tradition itself makes this unlikely, for there would surely, somewhere, in the codification of the Macedonian period, for example, be some reference to this legal and promulgatory activity.

It is, in fact, far more likely that no such activity took place, that is, that no novels (for example) were produced, because the matters of administrative organisation, civil law and Church affairs traditionally handled in this way were now dealt with quite differently. This change must have set in during the reign of Heraclius, for we would surely expect something of the legislative activity of this emperor – whose fiscal reorganisation, for example, introduced a whole series of major changes in the relevant areas of the state administrative machinery – to have survived if it had existed. But from Heraclius on, we have only a small group of novels dealing with matters of Church discipline and clerical organisation.[12] The seventh century, indeed, is a period of dramatic, often rapid, and certainly con-

[11] See the comments of Pieler, 'Rechtsliteratur', p. 434. Legislation which has survived only in accounts of other contemporary or later sources does not change this picture dramatically. The greater part is concerned with matters of ecclesiastical jurisdiction and/or fiscal policy. See Dölger, *Regesten*, nos. 174, 176, 182, 197, 205, 206, 227, 234, 237, 246 and 258, for example.

[12] Of the legislative activity of Justinian – the *Novellae Constitutiones* and related texts – some 50% deal with matters of administrative, fiscal and military organisation, problems of provincial government and so on. Some 30% deal with civil and criminal law, and the remaining 20% are concerned with Church property and related issues. See M.-Th. Fögen, 'Gesetz und Gesetzgebung in Byzanz. Versuch einer Strukturanalyse', *Ius Commune*. *Zeitschrift für europäische Rechtsgeschichte* 14 (1987), 137–58, see esp. 140ff., and N. van der Wal, *Manuale Novellarum. Aperçu systématique du contenu des Novelles de Justinien* (Groningen and Amsterdam 1964). For the novels after Maurice, see the remarks of P.J. Zepos, 'Die byzantinische Jurisprudenz zwischen Justinian und den Basiliken', 7. There are no novels after Heraclius until the reign of Eirene, and then of Leo V. Those of the latter, as well as those of Heraclius, are concerned exclusively with Church matters (Heraclius), divorce, or the question of the validity (and moral acceptability) of oaths. See L. Burgmann, 'Die Novellen der Kaiserin Eirene', FM IV (1981), 1–36; and Kresten, 'Datierungsprobleme'. It may justifiably be objected that the failure of legislation to appear in later sources or to survive in an extremely limited manuscript tradition is no guarantee that it did not exist – one of the known novels of Irene being a case in point (see Burgmann, 'Die Novellen der Kaiserin Irene'). On the other hand, while this may be true of one or two such items, a regular series of promulgations is most unlikely to disappear so completely, either from the later jurisprudential tradition or from the known manuscript tradition.

tinuous change, both in the administrative competence of various departments of state administration, in military organisation, in economic and fiscal structures, and in the conditions within which these organs had to function. Nowhere is this reflected or mentioned in a legislative text – although the passing reference of the Emperor Constantine IV to the effect that he and his armies had been so preoccupied with matters of civil and military importance that he had been unable to consider the question of summoning an ecumenical synod until 680 (to consider the pressing problem of monotheletism) is eloquent.[13] The Ecloga of Leo III and Constantine V deals exclusively with questions of property relations, marriage, divorce and inheritance, contracts, loans, leases and punishment. Nowhere does it touch explicitly upon the question of either a specific context for the legislation or the administrative framework within which the law is held to operate (although again, the introduction to the Ecloga speaks volumes about the background conditions with which the emperors were confronted in issuing the legislation).[14]

An initial conclusion from this data must be that emperors simply did not legislate in the same way as they had done previously. In other words, the novel was effectively abandoned as a way of intervening in matters of either judicial or civil-political interest. Two questions follow: what medium replaced the novel as a means of expressing and enforcing the emperor's will, on the one hand, and of affecting and modifying the operation and activity of the state apparatus, on the other? And what are the reasons for this sudden break? The answer to the second question, I believe, goes some of the way to providing an answer to the first.

In the first place, we must begin by recalling that the word 'law' depends for its strength very much on the context in which it is employed. There may, to begin with, be various forms of legislative activity which had the strength of 'law' in the modern sense – i.e. universally valid, regulatory and normative statements – but which are not referred to as 'norms' in medieval texts. Secondly, there may be a considerable difference between the promulgation of laws and their actual effectiveness, the more so if the law in question was not widely or sufficiently known. The latter is generally recognised to have been a major problem in the reign of Justinian and after; and it must be borne in mind that 'laws' may be ineffective both because they remained insufficiently known or understood, as well as because they were tacitly or explicitly ignored (that is, because they represented a theoretical or desired state of affairs too far removed from the reality of the times and impractical properly to enforce).[15]

---

[13] Mansi XI, 201C–D; Riedinger, 10.21ff. [14] Pieler, *Rechtsliteratur*, pp. 438–40.
[15] See especially F. Wieacker, 'Zur Effektivität des Gesetzesrechts in der späteren Antike', in *Festschrift für Hermann Heimpel zum 70. Geburtstag* (Göttingen 1972), pp. 546–66 (repr.

In the second place, the failure of laws, in pragmatic terms, their lack of effectiveness, does not mean that they remained without function.[16] On the contrary, a corpus of laws or legislative acts which enunciate a (more or less) consistent world view, a moral system, or whatever, regardless of its practical relevance in day-to-day terms, nevertheless constitutes a normative system and, where regularly invoked, acts as a symbolic referent, invoking also key aspects of the values of the culture in which it exists.[17] In Byzantine terms, of course, the invocation of the Justinianic legislation and codification played a crucial role throughout the history of the empire, recalling the commonality of orthodox Christianity, Roman civilisation, and the role and paramount position of the emperors. Just as significant was the figure of the Emperor Justinian himself in the later tradition.[18] The invocation of the Justinianic corpus in the Ecloga and in the 'Farmers' Law', quite apart from the codification of the ninth century and later,[19] is evidence enough of this. And it has been already demonstrated that the legislative activities of the Emperor Leo VI, for example, were grounded in the assumption that, whatever the changes which had actually taken place in the interim, it was still the legislation of Justinian which provided both the framework within which society had to be interpreted and understood and the law applied, and which determined the interpretation of Byzantine efforts to re-establish the Roman *oikoumene* as it had once been, as a valid enterprise.[20]

It is just this symbolic aspect which is, I would argue, crucial to the period with which we are concerned. The law, whether or not its detailed prescriptions and demands were understood or applied, symbolised the

in *Ausgewählte Schriften* I (Frankfurt a. M., 1983), pp. 222–40). For the later seventh and early eighth centuries this was clearly a major consideration. In the prooemium to the Ecloga (line 43) it is remarked that the members of the commission responsible for producing this new selection needed to collect the necessary texts together and that the laws are, for the most part, intellectually inaccessible. Whether even an imperial archive existed which possessed all the relevant material is a debatable point. See Pieler, 'Rechtsliteratur', p. 430; L. Burgmann, review of Pieler, in *Rechtshistorisches Journal* 1 (1982), 14 and n. 3.

[16] See Fögen, 'Gesetz und Gesetzgebung', 147.
[17] See P. Noll, 'Symbolische Gesetzgebung', *Zeitschrift für schweizerisches Recht* 100 (1981), 347–64, and G. Lanata, *Legislazione e natura nelle Novelle giustinianee* (Naples 1984).
[18] G. Prinzing, 'Das Bild Iustinians I. in der Überlieferung der Byzantiner vom 7. bis 15. Jahrhundert', FM VII (1986), 1–99.
[19] See A. Schminck, *Studien zu mittelbyzantinischen Rechtsbüchern* (Forschungen zur byzantinischen Rechtsgeschichte XIII, Frankfurt a. M. 1986), esp. p. 80 and note 136; pp. 103 and 107 (for Leo VI); and *Ecloga*, tit. lsq.; Farmers' Law, tit. 1 (ed. Ashburner, 85; JGR II, 63). See Pieler, 'Rechtsliteratur', pp. 440–1 and 449f. Note that the Justinianic motif occurs in other contexts – in the reign of Constantine IV, for example, whose son was so named (hardly an accident). Constantine was acclaimed in the final session of the sixth ecumenical council as the 'new Justinian': see Mansi XI, 656B.
[20] Fögen, 'Gesetz und Gesetzgebung', 148f.; Pieler, 'Rechtsliteratur', pp. 449f.

Roman state and everything that accompanied that notion. It symbolised the power of the emperor and his relationship to his subjects, and it acted as a symbol of his role and the tasks which he had to fulfil. It existed as the theoretical backdrop, as it were, to the practical ideology of the state and to the political-cultural beliefs and assumptions upon which people based their understanding and explanation of the world as they perceived it. Like the soteriological theology of orthodox Christianity, which provided one aspect of the theoretical understanding of the world, the law as an abstract but systematised structure represented another facet of that understanding, at least as far as it was available to the literate elements of society. And in this respect, of course, new legislation was not perceived as a need. What was required in the era after Justinian, and especially from Heraclius on, was conformity (assumed or real) to the norms set out by the system, or the reassertion and re-establishment of such norms, in so far as they were understood, of course (a major consideration in itself).

Seen from this perspective, the legal 'system' became less a practical instrument for intervening in the world of men in order to modify relationships or individual behaviour, but more a set of theories which represented a desired (if recognisably not always attainable) state of affairs. Emperors needed to issue no new legislation, therefore, but rather to establish (or to re-establish) the conditions within which the traditional system would once again conform to actual practice. Imperial action was thus not directed at emending laws to conform to reality, but rather at emending reality to conform to the inherited legal-moral apparatus.[21] The struggle to maintain imperial authority and imperial intervention (and insistence upon the right to intervene) in matters of dogma can be readily understood in this light.

What appears to have happened between the later years of the sixth and the middle of the seventh century, therefore, was in effect the exaltation of an interventionist, regulatory legal system, which concerned both administrative-functional aspects of the state's existence, as well as legal-ethical practices of its subjects, into an abstract and idealised 'world', in which the latter aspect attained a pre-eminence at the expense of the former. So much is clear from the concerns and preoccupations of Byzantines in the period from the end of the reign of Heraclius.[22] For the underlying reasons for this development are clearly connected with the

---

[21] This can be seen already in the second novel of Heraclius, A.D. 617, in which the explicit intention is to lend an older piece of Justinianic legislation new authority and practical relevance. See Konidaris, *Die Novellen des Kaisers Herakleios*, 74.22sq. and commentary, 100–2. It is even more clearly expressed in the Typos of Constans II issued in 648, which is specifically intended to re-establish the situation which prevailed before the conflict over the wills and energies of Christ developed: see *Lateran*, 208.19sq.

[22] See Haldon, *Ideology and social change*; and see chapters 9 to 11 below.

parallel developments in late Roman cultural attitudes already discussed. Indeed, the deliberately fostered gulf between emperor and court on the one hand, and the ordinary population on the other, emphasised by ritual and public ceremonial, must have been a major stimulus to this shift in attitude to the law and imperial legislation. Promoted coincidentally by the activity of the *antecessores* and *scholastikoi* (discussed below), and testified to by the collections of novels made during the period up to the end of the reign of Heraclius,[23] the Justinianic corpus became the measure against which all alternatives had to be assessed, a process that was furthered by the intervention of its originator himself, incorporated into the prooemia of the novels. For with some exceptions, where Justinian had to withdraw or emend his own legislation, the novels were intended to be relevant to all subjects of the empire, and for all times. The ban on interpretations of commentaries to the Digest reinforces the message.[24] Those novels which concern radical administrative measures form an exception, but even here the underlying assumption is that these 'specific' measures are short-term and should lead to the restoration of the 'healthy' situation, which had been originally intended.[25]

A system was thus erected which came to represent for the generations that followed, and particularly in the cultural context as I have described it, a perfect world, to which one could refer and direct one's energies but which, in practical terms, and in the terms of any perceived or day-to-day reality, was quite unreal. It was a world both emperors and subjects aspired to return to and that provided an invisible, taken-for-granted permanence against which experience and actual developments and situations were to be measured. Changing the framework laid down by Justinian was tantamount to tampering with the world as it really was, hidden, of course, behind the façade of the temporary set-backs of his-

[23] See Pieler, 'Rechtsliteratur', p. 431 and note 20, and 436f.; and note, for example, L. Burgmann and Sp. Troianos, 'Appendix Eclogae', FM III (1979), 24–125.

[24] See especially the discussion of Fögen, 'Gesetz und Gesetzgebung', 140ff. For the prohibition on writing interpretations of commentaries into legal manuscripts, see H.J. Scheltema, 'Das Kommentarverbot Justinians', *Tijdschrift voor Rechtsgeschiedenis* 44 (1976), 307–31, who shows that the legislation in question does not place a ban on commentaries to the Digest as such, as has usually been thought. See, for example, A. Berger, 'The Emperor Justinian's ban upon Commentaries to the Digest', *Quarterly Bulletin of the Polish Institute of Arts and Sciences in America* 3 (1945), 656–96.

[25] Cf. Justinian, Nov. 145 (a. 553), proem, 16sqq.: Τοῖς ἀεὶ παρεμπίπτουσι τὴν προσήκουσαν ἑκάστοτε θεραπείαν εὑρίσκοντες, ἐπειδὰν τὰ τῆς χρείας παρέλθῃ, πάλιν τῆς προτέρας γινόμεθα τάξεως, μέχρι μόνου τοῦ πεπονηκότος τὴν ἰατρείαν ἱστῶντες ('Since we find for all irregular situations the appropriate cure, so we return to the original state of things when the need is over, applying the cure only to the cause of the problem'.) Compare with the sentiments expressed in the proem to novel 29, on the restoration of the older administrative structure (A.D. 535).

In this connection, see in particular the important discussion of M. Maas, 'Roman history and Christian ideology in Justinianic reform legislation', *DOP* 40 (1986), 17–31.

torical change. Legislation that was enacted, therefore, represented 'temporary' responses to 'temporary' situations, the long-term intention being to restore the world of the Justinianic era. And already for the period beginning with Justin II, it has been suggested that the considerable decline in imperial legislative activity which sets in at this time reflects this unwillingness to tamper with Justinian's great edifice.[26]

By the reign of Constans II, as I will argue,[27] the situation had changed sufficiently, in terms of people's appreciation of what was happening and of their immediate political-ideological priorities and interests, that the moral-ethical aspect of their world and its meaning bore far more significance than problems of administration. Imperial 'legislation' of the period is concerned almost exclusively with such matters – problems of belief, of everyday observance, the avoidance of sin and the common responsibility for incurring the wrath of God, of the relationship between the earthly authority of the emperor and the Church and that of heaven – these are the dominant motifs of the times.

In ecclesiastical terms, the proceedings of the Quinisext, and in secular law, the Ecloga – itself explicitly based upon the Justinianic system – are key moments.[28] The major instances of imperial legislative acts for the period are, almost exclusively, similarly preoccupied with such matters – the Ekthesis of Heraclius, the Typos of Constans II, the Edict of 681 of Constantine IV, all mentioned above. The prefatory *sacrae* and the speeches before the sixth ecumenical council in 680 and the Quinisext prioritise, along with the difficulties faced by the emperor on the military front, just these issues, although at a higher level of abstraction.[29]

The administrative and functional legislation of Justinian and his immediate successors, however, finds no such echo. The last examples of such legislation concern the introduction of the silver hexagram in 615 and the abolition of the public bread ration in 618.[30] For the rest of the seventh century and much of the eighth, imperial interest in matters of administration and, especially, of fiscal affairs is expressed through the issue of imperial 'commands': *iussiones*, *keleuseis* or *prostagmata*. But even these are relatively few in number: only five are explicitly referred to by the literary sources up to the reign of Leo III, although there must have been considerably more.[31] The arbitrary nature of such references, of course, is no real guide to the frequency or infrequency of issues of such commands.

[26] See Zepos, 'Die byzantinische Jurisprudenz zwischen Justinian und den Basiliken', 7.
[27] See especially chapter 9 below.
[28] See *Ecloga*, 160–1.1–6 with comment at p. 4; Pieler, 'Rechtsliteratur', pp. 438–9.
[29] See Mansi XI, 201C–D; Riedinger, 10–12 (*sacra* to patriarch George); 195B–D; Riedinger, 2–10 (letter of the emperor to Donus, received by Agatho).
[30] Dölger, *Regesten*, nos. 167, 173 and 174.
[31] Dölger, *Regesten*, nos. 234, 249, 250, 255 and 256.

But the lack of legislative activity in the form of novels on the part of the emperors, and the fact that such matters seem henceforth to be dealt with by the issue of *iussiones* to the relevant parties, is suggestive of the nature of the change. The legal administrative framework of the Justinianic era now became the 'norm', whether it actually reflected the real situation or not. Legislative enactments intended permanently to emend this framework were therefore, and in principle, extraordinary. The novels of Heraclius provide an example, albeit on a very limited scale.[32] The emperors could modify the arrangements of their illustrious forebears by introducing 'temporary' measures, especially where these concerned fiscal policies and the appropriation of resources. Thus, even a major work of codification such as the Ecloga was compiled with the specific intention of making the Justinianic legislation more readily available and comprehensible. The modifications it introduced, especially in respect of divorce and marriage law, were clearly *perceived* as an attempt to strengthen the force of the older legislation and to reaffirm the already existing values of a Christian society.[33]

The various *iussiones* or *keleuseis* which do receive a mention in the sources are thus concerned with a range of matters, from fiscal policy to questions of imperial policy in respect of the Church, for example. But I suggest that the drastic and far-reaching changes which the administrative and military apparatuses of the state underwent at this time were perceived as (temporary) deviations from a structure that was still immanent in the legislative framework of the Justinianic era; and because these changes would ultimately be made good, there was no need for permanent legislation. Temporary modifications, carried out through specific commands, were all that was required. Most of these commands – and there must have been many hundreds of them – receive no mention in the sources because the sources are, by their very nature, not interested in such matters. Occasionally, as with the 'ten evil measures' of the Emperor Nicephorus I in the early ninth century, or the fiscal measures that affected the papal lands in southern Italy, they do attract the attention of a chronicler or commentator for specific ideological reasons.[34] But such examples are few.

A context thus developed in which legislative activity of the sort pursued

---

[32] See Konidaris, 'Die Novellen des Kaisers Herakleios', 64.39sq., where Heraclius notes that Justinian's arrangements are no longer in force due to the passage of time. See Konidaris' commentary, 94ff.

[33] Pieler, 'Rechtsliteratur', pp. 430–1 and 438ff.

[34] See Theophanes, 486–7, and Ostrogorsky, *Geschichte*, pp. 152ff.; Dölger, *Regesten*, nos. 234 and 250. Dölger (*Regesten*, nos. 372ff.) followed by Pieler, 'Rechtsliteratur', p. 434, assumes that many of Nicephorus' measures were in the form of novels. But there is no evidence for this at all.

by Justinian and his immediate successors became ideologically redundant. It was not only a question of a shift in the perception of the function and relevance of such legislation, however. The political-military environment was itself unfavourable to the promulgation of formal legislation such as Justinian had produced. In the first place, the question of the dissemination and the assimilation of legislative enactments, referred to already, had to be faced; and in the context of much of the reign of Heraclius, when the empire was to a greater or lesser extent harassed or occupied by enemies, when communications were vulnerable, and when the emperor himself was fully committed to managing the very survival of the state, the difficulties will have been so much greater. If this problem presented difficulties to the legislators of the (relatively) peaceful sixth century, how much more so will it have affected the situation in the middle and later seventh centuries? It is surely no accident that the four surviving novels of Heraclius all deal with the affairs of the Constantinopolitan Church, and of these only one addresses the question of the clergy in the provinces and their relationship with the civil and military authorities.

In the second place, the implementation of a legislative device such as a novel presupposed a degree of stability and continuity of both economic and especially of administrative institutions within the state. It assumed also the ability of the relevant imperial officials in the provinces, for example, to devote their attention to the matter in hand, unhindered by other major disturbances. Again, during much of Heraclius' reign, and in the remaining parts of the empire from the 640s on, this situation did not exist for many areas over considerable periods of time. Legislation of the Justinianic type was for the most part both too unwieldy and too slow to take effect, as well as being impossible uniformly to put into operation. It is not without significance that Justinian II overcame the problem in part by commanding the presence of the court, the representatives of the population of Constantinople and the leading military officers of capital and provinces in order to witness and sign their agreement to the acts of the sixth ecumenical council, which were read out to them in 687. By this means he could be sure that the key representatives of the state and the civil and military population of the empire were made aware of the formal acceptance of the decisions of the sixth council and the end of any monothelete policies.[35]

In the context of the rapid changes forced upon the state administrative and military machinery in the second half of the seventh century especially, therefore, the traditional form of interventionist imperial legislation must have become quite impracticable. In order to respond to the

[35] See Mansi XI, 737-8; Riedinger, 886-887.

multifarious demands of distant provinical officials, of the armies and their needs, of the state fisc and the central administration, it must have become much more efficient and effective to respond to each specific situation as and when it arose, a pattern of legislating which was, of course, already to hand. And the evidence that is available supports this hypothesis. No general legislation is recorded, but a large number of individually tailored imperial commands, edicts, letters to local officials, both military and civil, and so on do occur in the sources. The contrast could not be more obvious, and the total absence of the traditional legislative forms in this period is compelling. The vast array of changes – in fiscal administration, military organisation, the structure of the palatine bureaux – are nowhere dealt with in the traditional form. Legislative acts concerning them are entirely lacking, as are references in other sources to such acts. The changes themselves appear usually only obliquely, sometimes in more detail than others, in narrative sources and, indirectly, through the evidence of seals, coins and inscriptions.

The lack of legislative activity on the part of the emperors in the seventh and much of the eighth centuries thus becomes more easily comprehended. The effects of a shift in emphasis in the perception of the Justinianic codification and legislation, further affected by the radically changed economic and political environment of the seventh century, produced a very different view of the role and significance of imperial legislation. This view is reflected in practice in the Ecloga. It is a view in which the novel of the sixth century, as a convenient means of responding to and modifying a given situation, as well as a symbol of imperial authority, lost the former function to the advantage of the latter. In turn, the legislative framework of the Justinianic age became fossilised and hypostatised, representing an ideal, but lost (or at the least, 'hidden'), world which must be restored. If we put to one side the two novels of Irene and that of Leo V, the novel is only revived as an *effective* instrument of imperial authority in the tenth century.[36]

THE ADMINISTRATION OF JUSTICE

This major change in emphasis seems also to reflect, and may also be partially responsible for, what is generally recognised to have been a considerable decline in legal scholarship during the seventh century, although there was a clear distinction between imperial legislation on the one hand, and the activity of lawyers, jurists and legal scholars in general on the other. In the mid-sixth century a specialist legal education was

[36] Bearing in mind also the particular function of, and intentions behind, the novels of Leo VI: see Fögen, 'Gesetz und Gesetzgebung', 148ff.

available in several cities of the empire and represented one of the most reliable routes to rapid promotion in the imperial civil administration.

Professors of law were respected socially, and a career in the profession was greatly sought after.[37] The most famous law school was in Beirut, which flourished until the devastation of the city by an earthquake in 551. The curriculum established by the professors of law, or *antecessores*, lasted from five to six years, and it is chiefly on the basis of the paraphrases of and detailed notes on the Justinianic legislation established in their teaching that later curricula were based.[38] For whatever reason, the *antecessores* seem to have ceased their activity in the mid-560s, perhaps a result of the breaking off of imperial financial support after Justinian's death; thereafter legal education seems to have been conducted by the *scholastikoi*, practising lawyers or barristers. The principal difference lay in the method of teaching. The *antecessores* based themselves on the original texts – usually Latin – adding a loose translation and a series of exegetical notes for clarification and interpretation. In contrast, the *scholastikoi* based themselves on summaries of the original, or paraphrases, together with the Greek commentaries and text of the original legislation. In spite of the ban on certain types of exegetical commentary laid down by Justinian in the Digest, commentaries, interpretations and paraphrases of the Justinianic material continued to be produced, intended both as teaching materials and as exegetical texts for magistrates and judges, their form determined principally by the fact that Greek, rather than Latin, had by now become the dominant language of legal and administrative practice. Many of these commentaries, such as the paraphrases of the *antecessores* Stephanus and Theophilus, were in any case exempt from the ban, counting as 'indices' rather than as interpretations in the true sense.[39] A number of handbooks of a practical nature for actual use by lawyers were also produced, dealing with a variety of specific themes, although not all of these have survived or are known.[40]

From the reign of Phocas, however, the legislative activity of the emperors declined almost to nothing, and this seems to have been paralleled by a similar reduction in the activity of lawyers, commentators and interpreters. From the evidence of the Appendix Eclogae, a late eighth- or early ninth-century compilation based on the Ecloga of Leo III and Constantine

---

[37] See P. Petit, *Les Etudiants de Libanius* (Paris 1957), esp. pp. 166ff.
[38] See H.J. Scheltema, 'Byzantine law', in *CMH*, vol. II, part 2, pp. 55–77, see 55–60.
[39] H.J. Scheltema, *L'Enseignement de droit des antécesseurs* (Leiden 1970), esp. pp. 61–4.
[40] See the summary with literature of Pieler, *Rechtsliteratur*, pp. 434–8; and esp. Wenger, *Quellen*, pp. 682–92; Zepos, *Die byzantinische Jurisprudenz zwischen Justinian und den Basiliken*, 8f. Note also H.J. Scheltema, 'Korreferat zu P. Zepos, 'Die byzantinische Jurisprudenz zwischen Justinian und den Basiliken'', in *Berichte zum XI. Internationalen Byzantinisten-Kongress*, pp. 35–41, see 37–8.

V,[41] some evidence of the legalistic activity of the seventh century can be culled. Thus, references to excerpts from the Justinianic material, as well as to specific treatises, such as the *Poinalion* (based probably on the work of the Justinianic *antecessores*), occur, suggesting that a degree of juristic activity continued, in Constantinople at least, in this period, albeit limited chiefly to tracts on canon law or on punishment.[42] On the whole, however, the situation in the seventh century does not seem to have been favourable, either to the teaching of law or to an interest in its literary tradition. The situation up to the end of the reign of Heraclius may, in itself, have presented no major obstacles; although the failing fortunes of the provincial *civitates* and the lack of resources with which the state could finance the Constantinopolitan law school must have adversely affected the study of law.[43] Thereafter, with the loss of the Eastern provinces, and the devastation of much of the Balkans and Asia Minor, the *study* of law in the provinces must have been drastically affected.[44]

The *prooemium* of the Ecloga paints a gloomy picture. According to the emperors, the available legal literature (of which there must have been a reasonable amount in private possession at least in the capital)[45] was barely understood, if it was accessible at all, outside the capital. The purpose of the Ecloga and the commission which was constituted to compile it was, in the first instance, to collect the older texts and codifications, organise the material and select from it what was deemed relevant to the situation hinted at, and to compile this material in readily understood language into a concise reference-book. While the Ecloga did introduce a number of novelties, especially in respect of its dependence on canon law, it was based largely on pre-existing, that is, Justinianic, for the most part, precepts. The extent to which elements of local or regional customary law were also intended to be represented is difficult to say. But it is highly probable that the maintenance of the Justinianic system in the provinces was partial and heavily influenced by local custom. The fact that the older legal handbooks were neither easily available nor understood implies as much; and together with the nature and the explicit purpose of the Ecloga, this seems more than likely. Even in the sixth century, the population (and the officials) in frontier districts occasionally adopted the

---

[41] New edn by Burgmann, Troianos. See also Burgmann, *Ecloga*, pp. 134–5.
[42] See Pieler, 'Rechtsliteratur', p. 437; Burgmann, *Ecloga*, p. 2; Zepos, 'Die byzantinische Jurisprudenz zwischen Justinian und den Basiliken', 24ff.
[43] See Stein, *Studien*, pp. 3f. While the academy in Constantinople may have survived into the second half of the seventh century, there is no evidence that legal studies continued to be pursued there. See Scheltema, *L'Enseignement de droit des antécesseurs*, p. 63; and Pieler, 'Rechtsliteratur', 429.
[44] Note also C.E. Zachariä von Lingenthal, *Ὁ Πρόχειρος Νόμος* (Heidelberg 1837), XIII.
[45] See the remarks of Burgmann, *Ecloga*, pp. 2–3.

legal practices of neighbouring districts outside the empire; the situation must have been very much more difficult to control at times during the seventh century.[46] Particularly interesting is the intriguingly brief reference in the *prooemium* to the corruption of those entrusted with judicial functions, the influence of the powerful and the wealthy as compared with the poor. These are, of course, not unusual *topoi* in imperial legislation. But in the context of the *prooemium*, there is no reason to doubt either that they were meant to reflect a real situation.[47] Partly to ensure that the law was practised impartially, the emperors also undertook to secure the regular salary (from the *sakellion*) of the quaestor and the *antigrapheis* and all others appointed by the state to supervise and promote the execution of justice.[48]

The *prooemium* of the Ecloga, therefore, and the internal arrangement and contents of the compilation itself, are valuable pointers to the social and cultural situation of the Byzantine state in the early eighth century; and there is no reason to assume other than that they reflect a situation which had prevailed for several decades already – the fact that the emperors express the hope that the general applicability of imperial legislation might once again be re-established is indicative of their perception of the situation. The disappearance of the late antique cities, the economic and social disruption of the wars with the Arabs and the exigencies of state administrative and military reorganisation had produced a situation in which imperial legislation and Roman (Justinianic) jurisprudence were confined to those areas over which the imperial government had direct and constant supervision – effectively, Constantinople and its environs. No doubt the situation was, in theory at least, also controlled by imperial bureaucrats and officers in the provinces, but in practice, as the *prooemium* to the Ecloga implies, the judiciary was corrupt and venal and, to judge from the initial impetus behind the compilation, unable to understand or apply the traditional legislation in a competent or effective manner.

---

[46] Detailed analyses in Burgmann, *Ecloga*, pp. 3–19; Pieler, 'Rechtsliteratur', 438–40, as regards local traditions and customs. Note that Justinian also incorporated regulations for the application of regional customary law into the corpus of Roman law in the codex: see VIII, 52: 'quae sit longa consuetudo'; cf. *Digesta*, I, 3. For the adoption of 'foreign' law (regarding marriage), see Justinian, *Nov.* 154, 1; and the novel of Justin II of 566, *JGR* I, Coll. I, 3. On the ways in which Byzantine judges handled customary law, the existence of which was, of necessity, clearly recognised in the imperial legislation, see D. Simon, 'Balsamon zum Gewohnheitsrecht', in *Σχόλια. Studia ad Criticam Interpretationemque Textuum Graecorum et ad Historiam Iuris Graeco-Romani Pertinentia Viro Doctissimo D. Holwerda Oblata*, eds. W.J. Aerts, J.H.A. Lokin, S.L. Radt and N. van der Wal (Groningen 1985), pp. 119–33.

[47] *Ecloga*, prooemium, 52sq. Note in particular the hope, expressed in lines 87–95, that the changes which the Ecloga would inaugurate would also make possible the rehabilitation of the general applicability and acceptance of the imperial legislation.

[48] *Ibid.*, prooemium, 102–9.

What might loosely be termed the 'companion' texts to the Ecloga – the Farmers' Law and the military code in particular (texts probably produced at about the same period) – tend implicitly to bear out this conclusion. It remains unclear as to whether the Farmers' Law actually constituted a legally valid promulgation, or – like the military code, excerpted from the so-called Strategikon of the Emperor Maurice of the later sixth century, and from the Digest and the Codex Iustinianus – merely a legal handbook consisting of extracts drawn mostly from older sources.[49] The Farmers' Law in particular applied to a clearly provincial context and was expressed in an informal, albeit precise style closely paralleled by that of the Ecloga.[50] Again, while based on extracts from the Corpus Iuris, an element of customary law is evident which illustrates the fact that the monolithic Justinianic codification could no longer have been regarded as either accessible or easily understood in this provincial context, whatever its ideological import may have been.[51]

The evidence of the surviving legal texts, therefore, both legislation and handbooks, suggests that until some time in the middle of the seventh century the traditional legislative framework and its administrative basis continued to exist, although under rapidly changing circumstances. The extent to which the activity of the *scholastikoi* was maintained is impossible to say, although the references to the legal literature in contemporary or later texts suggests that from the reign of Phocas it was very restricted and – given the situation in the provinces after the 630s – probably limited almost entirely to Constantinople. This is also borne out by the remarks on the subject in the *prooemium* to the Ecloga. That *scholastikoi* continued to function after the middle of the century is suggested by canon 71 of the Quinisext council, which refers to their students as those who 'learn the civil laws', forbidding them to follow traditional (pre-Christian) custom such as going to the theatre or horse-races, wearing gowns and so on. The canon says nothing specifically of the location of this activity, of course, but Constantinople is almost certainly to be understood – the reference to theatres and horse-racing suggests as much. But these lawyers and their students appear in no contemporary legal text or literature.[52] After the 640s, and as a result of the withering away of municipal cultural life, the

---

[49] See Pieler, 'Rechtsliteratur', pp. 442–4 with literature; but see D. Simon, 'Provinzialrecht und Volksrecht', FM I (1976), 102–16, see 106.
[50] Pieler, 'Rechtsliteratur', p. 441.
[51] For a useful definition of 'popular' law – that is, as regional interpretations of imperial legislation, as opposed to something of quite different origins – see the remarks of Simon, 'Provinzialrecht und Volksrecht', 115–16.
[52] Mansi XI, 976A; but note that one manuscript tradition of the Ecloga mentions *scholastikoi* in the compilation of the text. Its reliability remains unclear. See *Ecloga*, prooemium, 42, and pp. 106f.

exigencies of warfare and defence, and the sharp contrast between provincial and Constantinopolitan life, it is highly likely that officials with judicial responsibilities had little or no legal training and were thrown back on their own resources for the resolution of judicial matters. The misinterpretation of late Roman law and the introduction of local and traditional modes of resolving certain types of case or conflict must have been an unavoidable consequence, and this is, in effect, the situation hinted at in the *prooemium* to the Ecloga.

As far as concerns the administration of justice at this period, there is virtually no evidence apart from one or two mentions in hagiographical literature pertaining to Constantinople.

In the sixth century, and probably well into the reign of Heraclius, the lowest courts had been those of the *defensores civitatis* in each city, who could try minor civil suits and could also hear and then refer minor criminal cases. The next level were the courts of the provincial governors, the *ordinarii iudices*; and above them, acting as courts of appeal, the courts of the diocesan *vicarii*, or *spectabiles iudicii*. The courts of the bishops were also empowered to act in civil cases parallel to the courts of the first instance, providing (after the reigns of Arcadius and Honorius) both parties involved had agreed to transfer the case from the secular to the ecclesiastical authority. Final appeal rested with the praetorian prefects, although a supplication could be made to the emperor if it was felt that an unjust decision had been reached (unjust, of course, very much determined by the context of the case in question and by the resources of the opposing parties!). Justinian himself introduced a number of reforms in an attempt to eliminate unnecessary appeals coming from the provinces to Constantinople; in Asia Minor especially, he increased the number of governors of *spectabilis* rank to bolster the intermediate courts of appeal, permitting some governors (those of Armenia I, Cappadocia, Palestine and Armenia III) to hear appeals from their own, as well as the neighbouring, province. In addition, the prefect of Constantinople heard appeals from certain provinces, as well as being responsible for the administration of justice in Constantinople and environs; and the provincial appeals of the *quaestor exercitus* were split on account of its peculiar geography: appeals from Scythia and Moesia were heard by the quaestor himself; those from Caria, Rhodes and Cyprus by his representative in Constantinople, who sat with the *quaestor sacri palatii*.[53]

This straightforward system of regular courts was complicated by the existence of a wide range of special courts which had jurisdiction over the

---

[53] The best general survey of judicial administration and the law in practice is still that of Jones, *LRE*, vol. I, pp. 479ff.; see also Stein, *Bas-Empire*, vol. II, pp. 467ff.; Bréhier, *Institutions*, pp. 219–24.

affairs of members of the various fiscal, administrative and military departments of the state, including the army. The relationship between the jurisdiction of such courts and the regular courts was very complex, and it was regulated by equally detailed and complex legislation. In general, the jurisdiction of special courts over their staff and dependents tended to prosper at the expense of the ordinary courts, partly because the state usually found it advantageous to privilege the activities of its own officials, partly because of the inherent institutional momentum, fuelled by the self-interest of the officials in question, which promoted such a privileged status. The system was further complicated by the existence of the privilege of *praescriptio fori*, according to which certain types of case were to be heard in specific courts only, and by which certain classes of persons could claim the jurisdiction of their own special courts, rather than that under which they would normally have come according either to domicile or (in criminal cases) the place of the crime.[54]

Many administrative bureaux possessed their own courts, chiefly the fiscal departments of the *largitiones* and the *res privata*, and those of military commanders and civil governors. The complexities and confusion which this proliferation of jurisdictions caused promoted in consequence an extension of the use of *praescriptio fori* wherever this right was granted, as a sure way of circumventing the maze of conflicting bureaucratic interests. The system inevitably favoured the privileged and the wealthy; and while the emperors made some effort to simplify the procedures involved and to disentangle the complex web of jurisdictional competences – including a limitation on the application of prescription of forum (later rescinded as impracticable!) – the system in its essentials seems to have survived into the seventh century.[55]

Since the majority of judges in the usual understanding of the term were attributed with their function by virtue of their position as governor, administrator or military officer, or as one of the heads of the great administrative departments at Constantinople, it is not surprising that most of them had little or no legal training. To ensure a degree of legal expertise, therefore, all magistrates with judicial duties had one or more assessors or advisers, selected usually by the officials in question themselves, but salaried by the state. These advisers were usually selected from barristers, and a career as assessor was one way of approaching a provincial governorship or magistracy. In Justinian's reign a panel of twelve

---

[54] Jones, *LRE*, vol. I, pp. 484–6.
[55] Jones, *LRE*, vol. I, pp. 487–94. For restrictions on the use of prescription of forum, see *CJ* III, 25.1 (a. 439); but note III, 23.2 (a. 440). For a graphic account of the way in which the administration of justice inevitably favoured the privileged, see Priscus of Panium Fragmenta (in *FHG* IV, 71–110), frg. 8 (86ff.).

trained lawyers and judges (the *iudices pedanei*) was re-established (it was originally instituted under Zeno) upon whom the emperor or leading officials could call to act as delegate judges. But in general, provincial judges remained relatively unlearned in the law – the majority purchased their office or obtained it through similar means – and were easily overawed by powerful local magnates or state officials of higher rank than themselves.

The imperial court and legal bureaux in Constantinople (as opposed to the courts of the urban prefect and other special jurisdictional courts) were administered by the *quaestor sacri palatii*, instituted by Constantine I, and the *magistri* of the *scrinia memoriae, epistularum* and *libellorum* (responsible respectively for imperial prescripts, references from judges to the emperor and the preparation of trials). The quaestor and the praetorian prefect of the East were delegated by the emperor to represent him in a great number of suits, but he also exercised his personal jurisdiction. In such cases, he sat together with the members of the consistory; and under Justinian, it became the rule that the full senate should be involved, in other words, that for important trials every meeting of the consistory should be regarded as a meeting of the senate.[56]

Barristers were attached strictly to the bar of the judge in whose court they were enrolled. They were trained in the law schools in Constantinople and Beirut, and could transfer out of their courts only by becoming an assessor to a magistrate. Higher office could be achieved by enrolment in one of the higher courts, as opposed to those of the provincial or municipal level. The law seems to have been a popular profession, bringing social status and possibly wealth and an official dignity as well. Many of the higher state officers of the fifth and sixth centuries rose through the bar and into the state administrative apparatus through service in Constantinople or in the court of a high-ranking official. By the sixth century, candidates for the bar had to produce certificates and evidence of their training and competence; but at the same time, as a strict limit on the numbers of barristers attached to each bar was enforced, retired lawyers began to claim priority for entry to the profession on behalf of their sons.[57] This was sanctioned by the state, but the effect was to turn the profession into a closed and almost hereditary caste. While a rigorous education in the law and in rhetoric (an indispensable element of an advocate's train-

---

[56] Jones, *LRE*, vol. I, pp. 499–507. For the ruling on *silentium* and *conventus* of the consistory and the senate respectively, see Justinian, *Nov.* 62, 1 (a. 537). See also Stein, *Bas-Empire*, vol. II, pp. 469f.; and esp. pp. 71–4 with notes. For the panel of judges, see Justinian, *Nov.* 82, proem and 1; and cf. *CJ* II, 7.25 (a. 519).

[57] For certificates and qualifications, see *CJ* II, 7. 11/2 (a. 460); II, 7. 22/4 and 24/4 (a. 517). For quotas and priority, *CJ* II, 7. 11 (460); II, 7. 22/5 (505); II, 7. 24/5 (517); II, 7. 26 and proem (524).

ing) remained a *sine qua non*, this development was not in itself damaging to the profession.[58] But in the conditions of the seventh century, its effect may well have been to promote a rapid decline in the number of barristers and in their standards of learning and competence.

As well as the lawyers, notaries were also an important, if lower-ranking, element in the legal profession. Notaries were very common, a fact which probably reflects the reasonable living that was to be made from the profession, since there was always a demand for the drawing up of wills, contracts, conveyances and so on. Notaries themselves and their assistants had to be registered, presumably to ensure that they possessed the requisite skills and knowledge. In Constantinople, according to novel 44 of Justinian, they were organised in offices or stations, where their assistants and apprentices worked.[59]

The extent to which this legal profession, and the jurisdictional system which supported it, survived beyond the middle of the seventh century is difficult to say. There is no evidence at all for the continued education of barristers after the early seventh century, although it is probable that a small number continued to train in Constantinople and to fill posts there.[60] Evidence for the continued activities of notaries is equally lacking. The *prooemium* to the Ecloga implies that provincial judges were either entirely ignorant of the Justinianic law, or unable to interpret it; but in doing so, it suggests that, as before, the system of provincial courts continued to function in the hands of local governors. This was certainly still the case in the reign of Heraclius, as a trial of a priest in Cyprus in 629, presided over by the local *archon*, or governor, demonstrates.[61] The Ecloga statement might also suggest that assessors were no longer available to assist the provincial governors, implying that the teaching of law had been very much reduced (and confined perhaps only to Constantinople).[62] On the other hand, there is good evidence, albeit for the ninth century and after, that the numerous special courts with jurisdiction over their staff (and their dependents) continued to exist, in other words, that the principles

---

[58] Jones, *LRE*, vol. I, pp. 514f.

[59] Jones, *LRE*, vol. I, p. 515. For the fees of notaries, see the table in the Edict of Diocletian, VII, 41 (they were paid by the line). See S. Lauffer, ed., *Diokletians Preisedikt. Texte und Kommentare* 5 (Berlin 1971), p. 120.

[60] See Burgmann, in *Ecloga*, pp. 106f., however, for a possible reference to *scholastikoi* in 741.

[61] *Ecloga*, prooemium, 52–95. For the trial in 629, see F. Nau, 'Le Texte grec des récits utiles à l'âme d'Anastase (le Sinaïte)', *OC* 3 (1903), 56–90, see 69f.

[62] The later *symponos* attached to the urban prefect appears to be descended from the late Roman *assessor*: see Bury's remarks, *Administrative System*, pp. 70–1; Oikonomidès, *Préséance*, p. 320. But this is no guarantee that assessors were still attached to provincial governors. The *consiliarius* (*assessor*) who was purportedly involved in negotiations between Maximus Confessor and imperial officials in 656 may have been such an official; but the context offers no certainty for such an identification: *PG* XC, 169B.

upon which the late Roman jurisdictional system had been based survived.[63] Whether or not prescription of forum continued to exist is difficult to say.[64]

Until at least the reigns of Heraclius and Constans II there is good reason for supposing that the system familiar from the sixth century continued to function, however. The collection of miracles of St Artemius, put together in the later seventh century and recording events dating from the reign of Heraclius to the 660s, refers to a number of officials familiar from the Justinianic period. The *commentariensis* of the prefect of the city, the *secretarius*, a *subadiuva* and the standard judicial procedures of the earlier period all occur.[65] In the same collection, reference is made to a *patrikios* and senator who was also one of the twelve judicial commissioners established in Constantinople. He is referred to in this text as a θεῖος δικαστής, the correct title. The narrator situates the story in the reign of Heraclius, and again it is clear that the system of the Justinianic period was still in operation.[66] In the reign of Constans II, the trial of Maximus the Confessor took place before the full senate and consistory, as was traditional.[67] The so-called Hypomnestikon, or *commemoratio*, written by Theodore Spoudaios shortly after the death of Maximus in exile in Lazica in 662, refers also to the judicial officer of the prefect of the city, in this instance called *protosecretarius*.[68] It can reasonably be assumed that notaries continued to be employed for much the same purposes throughout this period, since they appear again in the ninth-century Book of the Eparch, and a degree of continuity seems likely; although their organisation and the extent of their legal knowledge remain unknown. In the *Kletorologion* of

---

[63] See *Peira* LI, 29; and note *Basilika* VI, 1 for sixth-century legislation retained in later codifications. Cf. also *Procheiros Nomos* IV, 11, 18 and 24; *DAI*, 51.54–65. For the special jurisdiction as applied to soldiers, see Haldon, *Byzantine Praetorians*, pp. 304ff. The Ecloga also makes it clear that courts with differing jurisdictional competences continued to exist: see XIV, 7 (line 656sq.).

[64] See Haldon, *Byzantine Praetorians*, pp. 306f.

[65] *Miracula S. Artemii*, 22.26–23.27, probably of the later years of Heraclius. The *commentariensis* was an important official on the judicial side of all *officia* of leading state officers, civil and military, such as the praetorian prefect, the urban prefect, the *magister officiorum* and the *magistri militum*. There was usually only one such official attached to each *officium*; his superior was the *primiscrinius*, or *subadiuva*, of the judicial section, and above the latter came the *cornicularius* and the head of the section, the *princeps*. See *CJ* I, 27. 1/24 (a. 534); John Lydus, *De Magistratibus* II, 16; III, 8. For the duties of the *commentariensis*, who was responsible for the custody of prisoners, criminal proceedings and related matters: John Lydus, *De Magistratibus* III, 16 and 17; *CTh.*, IX, 40. 5 (a. 364), VIII, 15. 5 (a. 368) and IX, 3. 5 (a. 371). See also Jones, *LRE*, vol. II, p. 587. The *princeps* in this text seems to be represented by the *secretarius*, who would normally hear the case himself. In this example, the prefect happens to be present and intervenes personally (23.1sq.). Note the fee paid to the *secretarius* (8 hexagrams) and the *commentariensis* (3 hexagrams): *ibid.*, 23.23–4.

[66] *Miracula S. Artemii*, 17.10–12.   [67] *PG* CX, 88C and 109C.

[68] Devreesse, *Hypomnesticum*, 68.26–9.

Philotheus of 899 the *nomikoi* (or *tabellarioi*) are still under the authority of the urban prefect.[69] The judicial side of the urban prefect's bureau seems also to have survived, under a different nomenclature, in a developed form: the later *logothetēs tou praitoriou* is almost certainly to be identified with the older *princeps*, or *secretarius*, of the prefect's judicial department.[70] Similarly, the bureau of the quaestor can be followed – with less difficulty, since the post was an important one and is mentioned more frequently in the sources – from this period through to the tenth century.[71]

While the evidence is rather thin, therefore, it is possible to see a degree of structural continuity in the capital at least, in respect of the principles upon which justice was organised, administered and dispensed. The evidence of the Ecloga suggests that the study of the law and knowledge of the Justinianic and pre-Justinianic corpus were maintained in Constantinople, however difficult the circumstances – although it is worth noting that in the *prooemium* the legal texts from which the commission is to draw its material have first to be sought out before they can be collected together and excerpted; a fact which suggests that, if the law did continue to be studied (by *scholastikoi*, for example) it was on an individualised and private basis. No single library of legal texts seems, even in the palace, to have existed at that time.[72]

The pre-eminent position of the praetorian prefecture must have suffered, however, as the administrative changes which have already been discussed took effect, resulting in a diminution of the importance of the prefect's court. In its stead, the court of the urban prefect seems to have become the first court in the capital, alongside the imperial court and that of the quaestor – note that it is the prefect of Constantinople who is responsible for both Pope Martin and Maximus the Confessor after their arrest and trial, as well as for the brothers Theodore and Euprepius, who had also opposed imperial monotheletism.[73]

[69] *Eparchikon Biblion* I (περὶ ταβουλλαρίων), 13, 15, 16. See also *Klet. Phil.* 113.18; A. Dain, in *REB* 16 (1958), 166ff.; Noailles and Dain, *Les Novelles de Léon VI le sage*, p. 377; Bury, *Administrative System*, p. 72.

[70] See note 65 above. Bury believed that the *prōtokagkellarios* represented the older *princeps*; but this leaves then no room for the origin of the *logothetēs tou praitōriou*. The *prōtokagkellarios* is more probably to be associated with the late Roman *primiscrinius* or *subadiuva*. See Jones, *LRE*, vol. II, p. 587.

[71] See Oikonomidès, *Préséance*, pp. 321f.; Bury, *Administrative System*, pp. 73–7. Note the important position of the *quaestor* as one of the imperial officials accompanying Constantine IV at the sessions of the sixth ecumenical council (see, e.g., Mansi XI, 209B) and in the prooemium to the Ecloga, where he and his *antigrapheis* (the older *magistri sacrorum scriniorum*) are entrusted with the new codified selection and with the honest dispensation of justice. See *Ecloga*, pr., 40sq. and 102sq.

[72] *Ecloga*, prooemium, 40sq.

[73] Mansi X, 857B and E; *PG* CX, 104B and 172A. Cf. Devreesse, *Hypomnesticum*, 68.26–9; 72.26–73.2; 76.23–77.1. For Theodore and Euprepios, see *ibid.*, 71.17–18.

In the provinces, things seem from the 640s to have been very much less structured, that is, from the time when the Eastern armies are withdrawn into Asia Minor and Arab attacks begin in earnest. Civil governors (*archontes*) and judges (*dikastai*) are referred to in the Ecloga, although it is unclear as to whether the latter are based in the provinces also; and the civil governors were still clearly credited with the judicial authority they had formerly held.[74] Courts are mentioned in a matter-of-fact way, too, which suggests that the compilers of the Ecloga assumed the continued existence of the provincial courts, both ordinary and appeal courts, within the empire.[75] The fate of the civil courts of first instance, those of the *defensores civitatis*, is unknown; but it is highly likely that, in view of the fate of the municipalities and of civic culture generally during the seventh and eighth centuries, they fell into abeyance as they became less and less relevant, their functions being subsumed during the later sixth and seventh centuries by the courts of the bishops.[76] Similarly, the nature of the relationship between the episcopal courts, the courts of provincial governors and the generals of the territorial *themata* (as these became fixed during the later seventh and eighth centuries) remains obscure. There were clearly no thematic *kritai*, who appear much later, at this time. That pertaining between the first two presumably followed on from the earlier system with little change (except in respect of the knowledge and understanding of the law, and the degree to which local traditions and customs were used as a prism through which to interpret the Justinianic corpus); and it may be that the officials whom we have already encountered, the *anthypatoi* and eparchs, responsible for the civil government of these provinces, retained the judicial functions of the praetorian prefecture, representing up to the end of the seventh century a higher, prefectural, court of appeal.[77] Initially, the *stratēgoi*, who represented the older *magistri militum* under a different name, must likewise have exercised the jurisdiction over their troops and *officiales* familiar from the sixth century. But as the *themata* became territorially permanent, so the *stratēgos* seems to have gained a general authority over the civil government of the provinces within his *thema*. Thus the civil governors of the provinces, while they survived, will have continued to exercise their functions under the authority of the *stratēgos*, but within the jurisdiction also of the old prefecture which, as we have seen in chapter 5, continued to function.

---

[74] *Ecloga* VIII, 1. 6 (490); VIII, 3 (503); XVII, 5 (787); XVII, 21 (827) (*archontes*); VIII, 3 (504); XIV, 1 (638); XIV, 4 (645); XIV, 7 (656, 660 etc.) (*dikastai*).
[75] *Ecloga* IV, 4 (345) and XIV, 7 (658).
[76] See Hohlweg, 'Bischof und Stadtherr', 51ff.; and esp. K.L. Noethlichs, 'Materialien zum Bischofsbild aus den spätantiken Rechtsquellen', *Jahrbuch für Antike und Christentum* 16 (1973), 28–59.
[77] See chapter 5, above.

Now it is important to remember that the posts of proconsul, or *anthypatos*, and of the permanent, but originally *ad hoc*, praetorian prefect, or prefect of the *themata*, came to be amalgamated at some point during the later eighth or early ninth centuries; in other words, that the chief provincial governorships and the permanent prefectural officials responsible for military supplies were combined, continuing to fall within the jurisdictional competence of what was by then a supervisory prefecture in Constantinople, but coming under the general authority of their thematic *stratēgoi*. The title of praetor, however, also survives into the ninth century, for the praetors of the *themata* are mentioned in the Taktikon Uspenskij, although lower in the hierarchy than the *anthypatoi* and *eparchai*.[78] It seems quite probable that, until the general reorganisation which seems to have occurred shortly after 843 (the date at which the Taktikon Uspenskij was compiled), the praetors of the *themata* represented the ordinary civil provincial governors, with judicial as well as fiscal administrative functions, just as the *anthypatoi* and *eparchai* represented the general (and prefectural) civil and fiscal supervision of local administration. All will have come under the remnants of the prefectural office in Constantinople, as well as under the general authority of each specific thematic *stratēgos*. And just as the fiscal administration seems to have been reorganised under the *protonotarioi*, so the judicial administration of the *themata* seems to have been reorganised – perhaps at the same time – under the *kritēs* (still called praetor at times).[79] If this was the case – and the evidence does not contradict such a conclusion – then it can be assumed that the organisation and administration of justice in the provinces did carry on along very much the same lines as in the late Roman period, with the exception that the diocesan level of fiscal/judicial administration was replaced by the thematic level – under the *stratēgos*, together with the *anthypatos*, the permanent civil administrator of the groups of *eparchiai* that made up each territorial *thema* – below which came the provincial *praitores*. As I have argued in chapter 5, this picture remains hypothetical; but it does provide a more adequate explanatory framework for the appearance of thematic praetors, proconsuls and similar officials as late as the early ninth century.

THE FUNCTION OF THE LAW

The role played by the judicial system, and more particularly by the law at a symbolic level, in seventh-century society and ideology was central in the maintenance of a sense of Roman tradition and cultural identity. It was

---

[78] *T. Usp.*, 53.3.
[79] For the function and competence of the later *kritēs*, see Ahrweiler, 'Recherches', 67ff.; Oikonomidès, *Préséance*, pp. 323f.; and for *kritēs–praitōr*, see Leo VI, *Tactica*, 705.

also a crucial element in the maintenance of the Roman state itself, for it was through the law that provincial governors and officials could invoke and legitimate their authority, which flowed from the emperor and Constantinople. That emperors realised this is apparent from the *prooemium* to the Ecloga, where Leo and Constantine are concerned not simply with the clarification of the traditional jurisprudence, but its relevance and application to the provinces as well as to the capital city. The law embodied implicitly the assumption that the highest judge on earth was the emperor, who was himself chosen and protected by God; and the application of the law meant at the same time accepting and furthering the political ideology of the Roman state and all that this meant for contemporaries. Invoking the juristic and legal tradition, therefore, whether in Constantinople or in the furthest province, meant invoking also the political ideology of the orthodox Roman state.[80] The fact that, during the period with which we are concerned, the degree of ignorance or incompetence of local provincial governors in legal matters was such that the emperors felt eventually obliged to admit this state of affairs publicly and undertake action to correct it, does not in itself mean that the ideological strength of provincial government and the law was any weaker. As we have seen, 'the law' had a symbolic, an evocational value in itself. Whether it was applied according to the precepts and on the basis of the precedents of the Justinianic legislation, or on the basis of provincial interpretations which may have owed more to customary and traditional social practice, therefore, its force when described as the law of the Roman state was just as powerful.[81]

Quite apart from this consideration, however, another important aspect of judicial practice must be borne in mind. Modern legal systems, however they developed historically, are founded upon the assumption of normative prescription, precedents and interpretations, established by a judiciary whose members share the same technical education. More importantly, the judiciary strives to assert a normative framework within which civil and criminal cases can be handled and within which the evidence of witnesses, for example, can be processed on a consistent basis. Byzantine judges did not work in this way. On the contrary, attempts to make sense of the contradictions within Byzantine legal compilations (between apparently conflicting norms, for example) and especially between the formal legislation and the actual practice and decisions of judges, where these are known, have generally failed because of such assumptions. The enormous complexity of the legislative literature available to Byzantine judges, the corruption, the poor judicial training of judges, social and political vested

[80] *Ecloga*, prooemium, 9–31.
[81] See esp. F. Dölger, 'Rom in der Gedankenwelt der Byzantiner', in *Byzanz und die europäische Staatenwelt* (Darmstadt 1964), pp. 70ff., esp. 75–6.

interests – all these have been invoked as grounds for the apparent mismatch between legal theory and practice.[82] But as has now been shown, these conclusions were flawed because based upon entirely false assumptions. Byzantine judges worked within a widely respected normative judicial framework only at the most general level. They did not order and interpret their case material within a pre-existing normative system according to which the correct interpretation and the solution to a given problem could be read off. Their activity was seen instead as determined by moral-ethical considerations within a Christian framework, drawing upon the accepted principles of an orthodox culture and the accepted 'commonsense' understanding of the society as a whole.[83] Judges were selected according to their general literacy, moral standing, and according to their experience within the Church or state apparatus and appropriate administrative establishment. Judges were not, therefore, expected to fulfil their obligations through applying the law, in the modern sense. On the contrary, the law they applied was the morality of the society – this replaced the normative legal framework – interpreted through the prism of the inherited legislation on an *ad hoc* basis according to the needs of the particular case, the knowledge of the tradition of the judge in question, and the prevailing moral climate, as well as the personal feelings of the judge(s).[84] Ultimately, therefore, formal justice in the Byzantine world depended upon the moral preconceptions and ethical disposition of each individual judge, whose decision would be grounded in a selection of *topoi* drawn from the available legal literature. The decision would be legally grounded in so far as all legislation was, ultimately, ascribed to the emperors, who thus bore also the responsibility for its misapplication or misinterpretation. Challenges to a legal decision were thus based on an alternative and contradictory set of *topoi*, assembled to demonstrate the fallibility of the first decision. The success of an appeal, however, rested once more upon the personal morality and knowledge of the judges before whom the appeal was heard.

That some generally applicable normative legislation did serve the function of structuring social relations, of course, is apparent – marriage law, for example, to name one of many such areas. But this still left enormous scope for the moral personality of the judiciary. Even in the imperial court, it was clearly ultimately the moral universe of the emperor and his advisers which gave a particular slant or nuance to a decision,

---

[82] See Pieler, 'Rechtsliteratur', pp. 346f.
[83] The best discussion of this whole question is D. Simon, *Rechtsfindung am byzantinischen Reichsgericht* (Frankfurt a. M. 1973), see pp. 18ff.
[84] Pieler, 'Rechtsliteratur', p. 347.

rather than a consciously regulated intention to arrive at a decision which accorded in fact with the pre-given socially structuring framework.[85]

The breakdown of the traditional legalistic framework of the Roman state in the seventh century, at least in respect of the education of the judiciary and the accessibility of legal literature – while it may have introduced a number of qualitative changes into the administration of justice within the empire – does not seem to have had any dramatic effect upon the survival of the state or indeed upon the availability of 'justice' to the ordinary population. The ideological force of the concept of Roman law will hardly have been affected, for Roman law did not symbolise an abstract notion of justice alone, but rather the Roman state and the world order which that concept evoked.[86] 'Justice' and the law were by no means the same thing, of course, as is indeed the case in every state; and, as in the fifth-century account of Priscus of Panium, so in the later period, it was status, wealth and influence which usually ensured 'justice', rather than the neutral objectivity, theoretical or actual, of the law and the judiciary. The almost ritualistic complaints of emperors of corruption or bias in the judiciary, repeated in the *prooemium* to the Ecloga, speak for themselves.[87] Emperors who conscientiously interested themselves in justice were marked out in the popular imagination, as the legend of the emperor Theophilus demonstrates.[88] The personal element in law-giving and the application of justice is unmistakable, whether we are speaking of an emperor or an ordinary governor or judge.[89] None of this is to say, of course, that there were not also judges who, within the cultural limitations imposed by their world, did not strive for an 'objective' and as fair an assessment of the cases they heard as was possible. But those cultural limitations, rather than the individual, were the determining factor.

Roman-Byzantine law, therefore, and the legal-administrative apparatus which maintained it, plays a crucially ideological role in the Byzantine world of the seventh and eighth centuries and after. The law was invoked as a symbol of *Romanitas*, of continuity and Roman tradition, indeed as confirmation of Roman orthodoxy and the role of the new Chosen People. The maintenance of a judicial apparatus was essential for this to happen; and the fact that Roman-Byzantine law experiences both a renaissance, of

---

[85] Ibid., pp. 348–51; Simon, *Rechtsfindung*, pp. 15–32.
[86] Although this statement does not reflect the intention and the ideology of lawgiving and justice – see, for example, Hunger, *Prooemium*, pp. 184f. Even in the sixth century, however, it is very doubtful that the judiciary ever applied, or were able to apply, the prescriptions of the codes systematically. See Scheltema, in *CMH*, vol. IV, part 2, pp. 71f.
[87] *Ecloga*, prooemium, 52–68. Cf. Jones, *LRE*, vol. I, pp. 516ff.
[88] Ch. Diehl, 'La Légende de l'empereur Théophile', *Seminarium Kondakovianum* 4 (1931), 33ff.
[89] Cf. *Cecaumeni Strategicon*, 8.11sq., and note the comments of Bréhier, *Institutions*, pp. 224–5.

sorts, and a new vitality outside the Byzantine world from the ninth century onwards, demonstrates not only the fact that the early Byzantine state did manage, against remarkable odds, to restructure and reassess its resources and their potential; it demonstrates above all the potency of the law as a symbol of Roman power and claims to universal sovereignty within the imperial ideology.

CHAPTER 8

The imperial Church and the politics of authority

THE CHURCH AS INSTITUTION

The Christian Church constituted one of the most powerful economic and ideological institutions of the late Roman world, a role it continued to play in the barbarian successor kingdoms and in the Byzantine empire throughout its history. While there is no doubt that Christianity was not universally accepted throughout the lands of the later Roman state – enclaves of traditional, local non-Christian beliefs may have survived well into the seventh and eighth centuries, for example – it was certainly by the early seventh century the majority faith, in which traditional beliefs were subsumed and through which older ways of seeing the world came to be expressed. In theory, it represented a universalist soteriological belief system, with a highly developed and sophisticated theological-philosophical arsenal at its disposal. In practice, while its formal debates, its day-to-day teachings, and the political theory implicit in it, were represented by its clergy and by the literate minority within society, as the single and correct form of belief, it included also a plurality of ways of intepreting the world inherited from the cultural traditions amongst which it grew up and matured and upon which it was eventually superimposed. This syncretism existed throughout the empire and throughout its history, although the form of its expression and where it was expressed varied greatly. And while the formal, sanctioned directions of belief expressed by members of the orthodox establishment at any given moment (and depending upon which form of 'orthodoxy' prevailed) tend to monopolise the theological and political debates of the time, the underlying tensions out of which they were refined must never be forgotten. This is particularly true in the seventh century, for it was the period in which the contradictions which eventually led to the iconoclastic policies of emperors like Leo III became apparent, in which the possibility of 'pagan' survivals and heterodox belief had to be confronted and in which theologians came into direct conflict with the state and the emperor. And it was the latter conflict which perhaps more than anything else in these years points to the real nature of the political crisis within the Byzantine world.

Already in the fourth century, the crux of the matter had been summed up by two Churchmen: in his debate with the North African Donatists, Optatus of Milevis stated 'non enim respublica est in ecclesia, sed ecclesia in re publica, id est in imperio Romano'; while Ambrosius of Milan pointed out to the young Valentinian III: 'Imperator enim intra ecclesiam, non supra ecclesiam est.'[1] These two statements represent two potentially quite contradictory points of view, and they represent a tension between Church and state, emperor and patriarch, which subsisted throughout Byzantine history and was effectively resolved in the East only with the replacement of the Byzantine emperor by an Ottoman sultan. In the seventh century, they were to be invoked in a conflict which was, itself, to appear as symbolic of these two poles of opinion for later generations.

Let us stress two key points at the beginning. First, it should never be forgotten that the Byzantine Church, an organisational and doctrinal part of a much wider Christian whole, is part and parcel of the history of the Byzantine state and of Byzantine society and culture. Second, that its development, and its relations with the state, are dynamic: there is no static parallelism between emperor and patriarch, repeated in essence, albeit concealed by the nuances of the conjunctural politics of a given moment, throughout the course of Byzantine history. On the contrary, the Church and its clergy need to be seen in the perspective of their own society, responding and changing – or not – to the exigencies of temporary crises or permanent changes in their circumstances. The Church represents, therefore, a fundamental element in the history of Byzantine culture as a whole.

Perhaps the single most important determining feature of the Byzantine Church was its close political-ideological relationship with the position of emperor. These two institutions – priesthood and secular ruler – had been tied theoretically by the development of an imperial, Christian ideological system with its roots in the Roman and Hellenistic past, from the early fourth century. In its most idealised form, it was expressed as a relationship of mutual interdependence, and yet with a duty on the part of the secular authority – the emperor – to defend 'correct belief' and to protect the interests of the spiritual authority. The Emperor Justinian I gives a vivid statement of this position in a novel of the year 535:

---

[1] Opatatus Milevitanus, *Contra Parmenianum Donatistam*, in *CSEL*, vol. XXVI (1893), iii, 3; Ambrosius, *Sermo de Basilicis Tradendis*, or *Contra Auxentium*, in *PL*. vol. XVI, 875–1286, see 1007–18.

Mankind has been endowed by God from the mercy of heaven with two great blessings, those of priest and emperor. The former ministers to matters divine; the latter is set above, and shows diligence in, matters human. Both proceed from one and the same source, and both adorn the life of Man. For this reason nothing lies closer to the emperor's heart than honour and respect for the priestly office, while the latter is bound to pray constantly for the emperor. For when this duty is carried out without blemish and in true Godliness, and when in return the imperial power accepts the application of its secular authority justly and morally, then there exists harmony, and all mankind is blessed, and benefits.[2]

The passage continues with an expression of the conviction that the health of the state can be assured only if the traditions of orthodox belief are faithfully and correctly handed down and followed, a tradition bestowed by the Apostles of Christ, and protected and preserved obviously by the Fathers of the Church.

Clearly, this expression of the harmony of the secular and the spiritual spheres was a utopian statement. But it mirrors, although in a highly idealised form, the aims of imperial policy with regard to both orthodoxy in general and the fate of the empire, and to the ecclesiastical institutions and personnel of the Byzantine world in particular. And it is demonstrated in reality by the role of the emperor in the convening of synods and, more particularly, in the way in which the decisions of such ecclesiastical meetings were taken up in imperial legislation, where they received the added force of being backed by the secular authority and its judicial apparatus. From the time of Constantine I, the emperors had been involved in both the politics and the theology of the Christian Church, and imperial laws dealing with such matters ensured that, by the sixth century, emperor and Church, state and Christianity, were inextricably bound together. Justinian I presents in many respects the completion of this evolution, for it was he who first set about formulating clearly the extent of, and limits to, imperial authority in both secular and religious affairs. As God represented the only source of law, he argued, so the emperor, who was chosen and appointed by God to represent Him on earth, was the ultimate source of law in the earthly sphere.[3] The exact extent of this imperial authority,

---

[2] Justinian, Nov. 6, proem.
[3] I have necessarily simplified a much more complex political-theological ideology. See Haldon, 'Ideology and social change', 156f. and literature; and the survey of J.-M. Sansterre, 'Eusèbe de Césarée et la naissance de la théorie "césaropapiste"', B 42 (1972), 131–95 and 532–94. For Justinian's legislative statements, see esp. O. Mazal, Die Prooimien der byzantinischen Patriarchenurkunden (Vienna 1974), pp. 146ff., and note W. Ensslin, 'Der Kaiser in der Spätantike', Historische Zeitschrift 177 (1954), 449–68, see 463ff.; see also Beck, Kirche, pp. 36–7, and esp. K. Aland, 'Kaiser und Kirche von Konstantin bis Byzanz', in Kirchengeschichtliche Entwürfe (Gütersloh 1960), pp. 257–79 (repr. in Die Kirche angesichts der konstantinischen Wende, pp. 42–86, cited here); with the contribution of G.L. Kurbatov, in Z.V. Udal'cova, ed., Kul'tura Vizantii.

however, was an ill-defined area, which was to lie at the focal point of Church–state relations during the seventh century.

The close ties, both ideologically and institutionally, between Church and state, can be demonstrated in other spheres. Most notably, the role of bishops in the civil administration, especially in respect of municipal government and the regulation of revenue collection and distribution. As we have seen, bishops played a central role in this area, and not just as Churchmen – they were rather, by virtue of their position, regarded also as part of a single establishment which was divided into two mutually overlapping spheres, the spiritual and the material. There was nothing anomalous from this standpoint.[4]

By the same token, the increasing liturgification of imperial ceremonial and especially of the coronation[5] – a real break with the antique traditions of the Roman past – emphasised the officially sanctioned corporate identity of the secular and the spiritual spheres, their interdependence and their reciprocal influence. Increasingly, the Church within the East Roman empire became the East Roman imperial Church – the two were initially by no means the same. Church and state establishments worked together, and together they represented the formally sanctioned institutions of government. Faced with this monolithic concentration of authority, it is not surprising that oppositional tendencies were represented through a rejection of these poles of authority and a search for alternative routes of access to God and His spiritual authority from those of the emperor, the secular Church and the power of the state and its apparatuses.[6]

The unresolved tensions in the Justinianic formulation were expressed in practice through the weakest link in the chain, the relationship between imperial and patriarchal authority in day-to-day terms. The 'harmony' of Justinian's vision depended more or less entirely on the strength of per-

[4] See chapter 3. A particularly striking example is that of the African Church after the reconquest, where Justinian clearly intended to involve the Church very closely with the rebuilding of an imperial administration and the reincorporation of North African society, ideologically and politically, into the general framework of the empire. See esp. *CJ* I, 27 and Justinian, *Nov.* 37; with the remarks of R. Markus, 'Reflections on religious dissent in North Africa in the Byzantine Period', *Studies in Church History* III (1966), 140–9.

[5] Phocas' coronation in 602 marked the first such occasion actually in a church; coronations in 610 and 638 took place in the palatine chapel of St Stephen; and in 641 (and thereafter), coronation occurred in Hagia Sophia. The development illustrates the general tendency of late sixth- and early seventh-century cultural evolution, and the increasing 'exclusivism' of Christian imperial society; and it contrasts starkly with the militarised, secular and still pre-Christian-dominated coronations of the previous rulers, even when the patriarch had himself been directly involved. See Van Dieten, *Geschichte der Patriarchen*, pp. 2f.; and esp. Treitinger, *Die oströmische Kaiser- und Reichsidee*, pp. 7ff.; W. Ensslin, *Zur Frage der ersten Kaiserkrönung durch den Patriarchen und zur Bedeutung dieses Aktes im Wahlzeremoniell* (Würzburg 1948); the remarks of N. Svoronos, in *REB* 9 (1951), 125–9; Bréhier, *Institutions*, pp. 8–11 and 12f.

[6] See Haldon, 'Ideology and social change', 148f. and 161ff.

sonality of emperor and patriarch, together with the political and religious situation of the moment, for no formal and clearly demarcated division of competence was ever achieved. Emperors and clergy determined the limits of their power, therefore, in accordance with the exigencies of the moment, and with the abilities, strengths and weaknesses of those persons in power with whom they had to deal, and in the context of the factional interests of different power-groupings within the ruling and governing class.

Such tensions were most clearly evident when the state, in the person of the emperor, intervened directly in matters of ecclesiastical jurisdiction or of theology and dogma. This is not to say that they were not intellectually qualified to do so – on the contrary, many emperors were competent theologians in their own right. But they inevitably represented for the Church more than a merely neutral interest. The degree to which the church could tolerate such intervention depended, as we have seen, on the context in which it took place, and on its perceived repercussions. Emperors often found it easy to bully Churchmen into conformity, especially in Constantinople, where patriarchs could be threatened, or removed and replaced, when they failed to conform to the imperial line; although actually resolving the questions at issue was not always so easily achieved. The most coherent statement of the different competences of Church and state, and one which was to be invoked frequently by churchmen in later centuries, was that set out by Maximus Confessor during his trial and in his correspondence. Maximus' argument was directed at one particular aspect of the Church–state relationship, however. It was directed at the theoretical grounds upon which the emperors had attempted to justify their rights of intervention, and of directing debate, in matters of dogma and the nature of orthodoxy, grounds which – in the reign of Constans II at least – were presented by the imperial party as elements within Christian theology in the narrower sense. The central notion, the identity of the secular ruler as both emperor and priest, represented a position strongly refuted by Maximus, who queried likewise the emperor's claim to be the sole source conferring authority on synods and councils – a claim which was founded upon the model of Constantine I, but which was actually bound up with the refusal of the state to recognise the Lateran synod in 649.[7] While these arguments were henceforth to be reproduced in similar confrontations in later years, it was in the West, and particularly in the context of the political authority of the papacy during the later eighth century and afterwards that its importance for the development of the Church became most apparent. For the Byzantine world in the seventh century, it was a combination of perceived threats to imperial authority in the changed

[7] Haldon, 'Ideology and social change', 173ff. with literature; Winkelmann, *Die östlichen Kirchen*, pp. 133ff.; Aland, 'Kaiser und Kirche' (cited note 3, chapter 8 above), 65–7.

political, military and social climate of the times, together with the lack of any clear demarcation of spheres of influence and authority between Church and state which lay at the root of the further development of both the Byzantine Church and of the state itself.

Monophysites and dyophysites

The Constantinopolitan patriarchate, of course, was only one of five such archiepiscopal sees: Rome, Alexandria, Antioch and Jerusalem each had their apostolic traditions, and claims to equivalence and pre-eminence played an important role in the history of their relations with one another. But the patriarchate of Constantinople, by virtue of the loss of Alexandria, Jerusalem and Antioch to the Arabs in the 630s and 640s, took on a double significance for the development of Christianity after this time. On the one hand, it continued to vie with Rome for ecumenical status and pre-eminence, claims first expressed in the second council of Constantinople held in 381, and always strongly rejected by Rome.[8] On the other hand, it became the patriarchate of the capital city of the empire, which implicitly gave it an enhanced status in the Christian world generally, but which most importantly made its final transformation into an imperial Church inevitable. The disagreements with Rome thus received a very different nuance, for Rome remained politically and militarily – in practice if not in theory, and in spite of the few dramatic imperial interventions – an independent authority. Divisions within the Byzantine Church, therefore, which might otherwise have been resolved internally, could still be referred to Rome; and the result was, predictably enough, a further heightening of the built-in structural tensions within the Byzantine world between state and Church, and between factions within the Church itself.

The loss of the Eastern provinces was, in the event, in many respects the final solution to the intractable problems faced by the emperors, from the time of the council of Chalcedon in 451 and afterwards, of imposing orthodoxy (as it was there defined) on the increasingly recalcitrant and resentful monophysite populations in Syria, Egypt and in parts of Armenia. The establishment during the sixth century of independent monophysite Churches in Syria and in Egypt provided a focus for anti-Chalcedonian sentiment, and a framework through which the monophysite population of town and countryside could resist the efforts of Church and state to impose the Chalcedonian creed. From 543 the monophysite Jacob Baradaeus, as monophysite archbishop of Syria, pursued by the imperial

---

[8] See especially canon 3 of the council of 381 (Mansi III, 557f.) where Constantinople was placed second in the hierarchy after Rome, as the 'New Rome', and before both Alexandria and Antioch.

authorities, established a monophysite 'shadow' Church. During the period of Persian occupation it developed apace, so that by the time of Heraclius' first efforts at reconciliation (the synod of Hierapolis, 631) it was strong enough to reject his overtures, even though its leaders seem initially to have accepted a mononergite compromise formula.[9] In Egypt matters were complicated by competing factions within the monophysite camp. While local cultural identity, language and traditions gave Egypt its own very different and self-aware history, it was hardly surprising that the rejection by the council of Chalcedon of the Alexandrian – monophysite – position increased this feeling of difference, and that monophysitism took on also thenceforth the role of vehicle for local, regional – rather than separatist – expressions of independence. The varying fortunes of the monophysite Church depended, as in Syria, on the strength and determination of the imperial authorities and their success in repressing anti-Chalcedonian opposition. Many Syrians, indeed, took refuge in Egypt from just such repressive measures, and in 575 the Jacobite exile community in Egypt elected a Syrian archimandrite, Theodore, as anti-patriarch of Alexandria. The Coptic monophysites reacted by electing their own patriarch to succeed Peter IV (557–78), although the Chalcedonian patriarch John II was, of course, still in office. The matter was yet further complicated by the fact that a theological difference of opinion developed between the Syrian and the Egyptian monophysite communities as a result of the theology of the new monophysite patriarch of Alexandria, Damian (578–605).

This schism between Syrian and Egyptian monophysites was healed only in 616, when leading elements of the Egyptian landed elite and monophysite Church realised that unity was in their best interests. Once again, the Persian occupation of Egypt (from 619) could only favour the monophysite cause, since the Chalcedonian – Melkite – clergy, as representatives at the same time of the imperial Church, were forced to leave. Even after the departure of the Persians the Chalcedonian Church, under the imperial candidate for the see, Cyrus, a convinced supporter of the compromise formulae of the patriarch Sergius and the emperor, failed to recover the ground that had by then been lost. While the monophysite clergy, as before, was forced out of the city into the countryside – where it

[9] Van Dieten, *Geschichte der Patriarchen*, pp. 30ff. For the history and development of the Syrian monophysite – Jacobite – Church, see especially R. Devreesse, *Le Patriarcat d'Antioche depuis la paix de l'église jusqu'à la conquête arabe* (Paris 1945); D. Bundy, 'Jacob Baradaeus', *Le Muséon* 91 (1978), 45–86; E. Honigmann, *Evêques et évêchés monophysites d'Asie antérieure au VI⁰ siècle* (CSCO CXXVII, subsid. 17, Louvain 1951); W.A. Wigram, *The Separation of the Monophysites* (London 1923). For a general account of political-theological developments, see Beck, *Kirche*, pp. 288–91; Winkelmann, *Die östlichen Kirchen*, pp. 121–5, with sources and literature. On the regional and local feelings of independence in the monophysite areas, see Guillou, *Régionalisme*, pp. 236ff., and see above, chapter 2.

took refuge in the monasteries and sketes of the hinterland – by the imperial authorities, the Melkite Church remained for the most part distanced from the mass of the Coptic population. Only under archbishops of great ability and diplomacy did the 'establishment' Church meet with any success – the popularity of the Chalcedonian John III (610–19) in later monophysite sources is indicative. With the arrival of the Arabs, the efforts of the imperial Church to reassert its position finally ended.[10]

There is some evidence that the Chalcedonian clergy – including the patriarchs – did continue to reside in their sees in the areas taken by Islam from the 640s, attending the sixth ecumenical council and the Quinisext council, although the first unequivocal evidence suggests that it was finally only in 742 that the Chalcedonian patriarch of Antioch was allowed to take up his position, although the skeleton of a Melkite Church subsisted throughout the intervening years; and it was only in 706 and 744 that Chalcedonian patriarchs were elected once again in Jerusalem and Alexandria respectively. Again, the Chalcedonian Church subsisted, electing bishops and clergy and, when possible, sending representatives to the general councils, although its history is difficult to discern.[11]

In what follows, I shall frequently refer to the 'Chalcedonian' or dyophysite theology which had become the imperial orthodoxy by the later sixth century, in opposition to the monophysite theology of the Eastern provinces. This must not be taken to imply that there were not monophysites throughout the empire – merely that the majority tradition in the East was, by the later fifth century, a monophysite tradition. In addition, we should also speak more accurately of neo-Chalcedonian orthodoxy: from

[10] Most recent general survey: Winkelmann, *Die östlichen Kirchen*, pp. 114–21; also E.R. Hardy, *Christian Egypt* (New York 1952); D.C. Müller, 'Die koptische Kirche zwischen Chalkedon und dem Arabereinmarsch', *Zeitschrift für Kirchengeschichte* 75 (1964), 271–308; R. Rémondon, 'L'Eglise dans la société égyptienne à l'époque byzantine', *Chronique d'Egypte* 47, 93 (1972), 254ff.; M. Roncaglia, *Histoire de l'église copte* (Beirut 1966); P. Verghese, *Koptisches Christentum* (Stuttgart 1973); and for the relations between Greeks and Copts, the role of the Alexandrian patriarchate and the intervention of the state, F. Winkelmann, 'Die Stellung Ägyptens im oströmisch-byzantinischen Reich', *Graeco-Coptica. Griechen und Kopten im byzantinischen Ägypten* 48 (1984), 11–35, and 'Ägypten und Byzanz vor den arabischen Eroberungen', *BS* 40 (1979), 161–82. For Damianus and his followers, referred to as Damianites, as Angelitai and Tetraditai, see I. Rochow, 'Zu einigen oppositionellen religiösen Strömungen', in *Byzanz im 7. Jahrhundert*, pp. 225–88, see 264.

[11] See the account of L. Bréhier and R. Aigrain, in Fliche and Martin, *Histoire de l'église*, vol. V, pp. 479–84; Beck, *Kirche*, pp. 93–8; but for good circumstantial evidence that the patriarchs of Antioch and Jerusalem were in their sees, at least in the period of truce between empire and caliphate from 678 to 692, see F.R. Trombley, 'A note on the see of Jerusalem and the synodal list of the sixth oecumenical council (680–681)', *B* 53 (1983), 632–8. Note also Bréhier, *Institutions*, pp. 456–60; and especially H. Kennedy, 'The Melkite Church from the Islamic conquest to the Crusades: continuity and adaptation in the Byzantine legacy', *Seventeenth International Byzantine Congress, Major Papers* (New York 1986), pp. 325–43.

the late fifth century a division within the Chalcedonian camp developed. This was concerned chiefly with the position within dyophysite theology of the Antiochene tradition. The strict Chalcedonians wished to emphasise the twin aspects of Christ's two natures, and to retain the rich and sophisticated dyophysite tradition of the school of Antioch; the neo-Chalcedonians, in contrast, were concerned to incorporate the tradition of Cyril of Alexandria into Chalcedonian theology, and consequently to exclude its antithesis, the Antiochene theology. The debate was eventually resolved, as a result of direct imperial intervention through the affair of the Three Chapters, in favour of the second direction. By the end of Justinian's reign, neo-Chalcedonian theology dominated the dyophysite position.[12]

Wealth and administration

As we have said, the Church was a powerful economic force in the late Roman and early Byzantine world, not simply in respect of its own power and wealth, but also in the context of the economy of the state as a whole; for the Church also absorbed and consumed surplus wealth on a large scale, and thus directly affected the distribution of resources across the rest of society. It has been estimated that the resources consumed by the Church in the sixth century to support its charitable institutions, its clergy and episcopate, its buildings and its public ceremonial, surpassed that of the state and its administrative establishment (excluding the army) in both wealth and manpower.[13]

The wealth of the Church lay for the most part, of course, in land, although considerable amounts existed also in the form of precious plate and – last but not least – in buildings themselves. From the time of Constantine I the emperors had been the greatest benefactors of the Church. Property was obtained through private grants and gifts, as well as by donations from the state. It was protected by rulings on the inalienability of Church property – established by Leo I and extended to the whole empire by Justinian I – and by exemptions from certain forms of state tax or imposition.[14] Churches could receive property, in the form of willed legacies and from intestate estates, and from the time of Theodosius II also from individual members of the clergy who had no relatives entitled to inherit. Gifts of money or produce became a regular feature of the income of the

[12] For a brief summary, see Winkelmann, *Die östlichen Kirchen*, pp. 58–62; Beck, *Kirche*, pp. 372–84; G. Every, *The Byzantine Patriarchate (451–1204)* (London 1947), pp. 61ff.
[13] Already Valentinian III had legislated to limit the flow of decurions and others into the clergy; Justinian had limited the number of clergy attached to the Hagia Sophia to 525, a figure raised by Heraclius in a novel of 612 to 600. See Winkelmann, *Die östlichen Kirchen*, pp. 137–8; and esp. Jones, *LRE*, vol. II. pp. 933–4.
[14] See *CJ* I, 2.14 (a. 470) for Leo I; and Justinian, *Nov.* 7 (a. 535).

Church and its personnel, and Justinian even had to legislate to prevent the clergy from demanding such voluntary donations as an automatic right. The Church owned property in cities, too, and extracted wealth through rent and through the sub-letting of estates on an emphyteutic basis. By the time of Justinian, the Church was unable to manage all its property adequately, and the rapid expansion of the use of emphyteutic leases was the chief way in which this was made good. In practice, of course, the use of perpetual emphyteutic leases meant ultimately the effective loss of the estates or lands in question to secular landlords; but in spite of Justinian's legislation to protect the notion of the absolute inalienability of Church property, this type of lease continued to be the most effective way for the Church to continue to extract at least a limited revenue from its properties. But the fact of its widespread adoption by the Church throughout the empire is indirectly good evidence for the considerable extent of the property of the Church by this time.[15]

The seventh century was a century of devastation, demographic dislocation and decline, and of economic disruption for that part of the empire which remained after the initial expansion of Muslim power and the loss of the Eastern provinces. The extent to which the Church suffered in this, along with other landowners – both private citizens and the state – is difficult to say. But it has been plausibly suggested that the efforts of the ecclesiastical authorities to make sure that the clergy did not abandon their communities and sees – expressed most clearly in canon 18 of the Quinisext council[16] – were intended to ensure that Church property continued to be administered and, as far as was possible in the circumstances, exploited economically.[17]

The history of the Church of Ravenna provides interesting parallels. Although conditions were indeed more favourable to agriculture and economic activity in Italy in the seventh century than they may have been across much of Anatolia and the Balkans, the Church – unlike the secular landowning elite, which seems to have taken refuge in Constantinople and similar urban centres – was able to hold on to and even extend its landed wealth; so that it emerges from the 'dark ages' as an even more substantial

[15] On the economic organisation of the Church, and its property, see the general remarks in *CMH*, vol. IV, part 2, pp. 118ff.; Köpstein, *Zu den Agrarverhältnissen*, pp. 18–22; Bréhier, *Institutions*, pp. 518ff.; and esp. E. Wipszycka, *Les Resources et les activités économiques des églises en Egypte du IVe au VIIIe siècles* (Brussels 1972); G.R. Marks, 'The Church of Alexandria and the city's economic life in the sixth century', *Speculum* 28 (1953), 349–62; O. Grashof, 'Die Gesetze der römischen Kaiser über die Verwaltung und Veräusserung des kirchlichen Vermögens', *Archiv für katholisches Kirchenrecht* 36 (1876), 193–203; E.F. Bruck, 'Kirchlich-soziales Erbrecht in Byzanz', in *Studi in Onore di S. Riccobono* (3 vols. Rome and Palermo 1933ff.), vol. III, pp. 377–423; Beck, *Kirche*, pp.65–7; Jones, *LRE*, vol. III, pp. 894–90.
[16] Mansi, XI, 952B-C (canon 18).   [17] See Köpstein, *Zu den Agrarverhältnissen*, p. 65.

landowner than before.[18] It is this institutional tenacity in maintaining and reinforcing its hold on landed wealth which lies behind the above-mentioned canon of the Quinisext and which explains why the Church, unlike individual private landowners, was able to conserve its position where the latter were, more often than not, unable to do so with the same degree of success. What is clear is that, after the dislocation of the seventh and eighth centuries, the Church emerges still as the greatest institutional landowner next to the state.

One of the most significant aspects of Church and monastic finances, of course, was their charitable foundations. Since the beginning, the Christian communities had devoted a part of their income to charitable purposes. From the early fourth century the revenues from Church endowments could also be employed for such purposes, and the care of the sick, the elderly, of orphans and widows, along with the poor in general, became an important part of the pastoral work of the Church. As the available wealth grew, so orphanages, hospitals, almshouses and so on were endowed and built, maintained from the rents of Church lands, sometimes endowed also by a wealthy lay person. Such institutions often had their own lands, from which they could extract rents; others were maintained by monastic foundations, either as separate institutions or as part of the monastery itself. Still others were built and maintained by the state, and the imperial hostels in Constantinople provide illustration of this.[19] Under Justinian, care for the needy in society and a tutelary concern for society in general – both spiritual and physical well-being – were officially recognised, indeed promoted, aspects of the activities of the Church.[20] Such activity lent the Church both moral authority and political power – the eleemosynary activities of John the Merciful, patriarch of Alexandria from 610 to 619, for example, won the respect of monophysite as well as Chalcedonian communities and commentators, and indeed of the local officials of the state.[21]

The organisation and administration of the Church followed the pattern of late Roman administrative institutions. Below the patriarchs were metropolitans, autocephalous archbishops and bishops. The metropolitan was the senior bishop in each province, appointed by the patriarch. Bishops were elected by the provincial synods, although until the reign of

[18] See Guillou, *Régionalisme*, esp. pp. 181–7 and 232f.
[19] See Jones, *LRE*, vol. II, p. 901; and H.R. Hagemann, 'Die rechtliche Stellung der christlichen Wohltätigkeitsanstalten in der östlichen Reichshälfte', *Revue Int. des Droits ant.*, 3 ser., 3 (1956), 265–83; Bréhier, *Institutions*, pp.524–6; and esp. the account in D. Savramis, *Zur Soziologie des byzantinischen Mönchtums* (Leiden and Cologne 1962), pp. 25–38 with sources and further literature.
[20] See *CJ* I, 2.23 (a. 530) and Justinian, *Nov.* 65 (a. 538).
[21] See *Vita Joh. Eleemosyn.*, 8.16sq.

Justinian, the ordinary clergy and the citizens of the diocese also participated in the nomination of candidates for the election. Justinian curtailed these rights, and they were later restricted to the provincial bishops alone, although popular intervention – acclamations, for example, in support of one or other of the candidates – still took place. The bishop was the chief ecclesiastical authority in his diocese, and both clergy and monasteries were under his control. He was responsible for the maintenance of orthodoxy, the seeking out and destruction of heresy, and the imposition and application of the canon law of the Church. He was also the chief manager of Church properties, although in practice this was delegated to local managers and stewards – *oikonomoi* – and he supervised the distribution of Church revenues to his clergy and to Church foundations such as almshouses and orphanages. In respect of the clergy in his diocese he also presided over the ecclesiastical court and arbitrated at cases between laypersons and clergymen. From the reign of Heraclius (from 629) the privileges of the clergy in such legal proceedings were explicitly safeguarded, to prevent their being unjustly treated by the civil or military authorities. But one area in which conflict continued to arise – until the eleventh century, at least – was that of matrimonial law, where the civil law of the state encoded in the *Codex Iustinianus* and later collections, based as it was on traditional Roman law, was sometimes in conflict with canon law. Matrimonial cases were dealt with by the civil authorities, therefore, since civil marriages could be dissolved by the agreement of both parties, the legal question of the redistribution of property presenting the most difficult problems. According to the Church, in contrast, marriage was indissoluble (except in the case of adultery), and the conflicts which ensued – for example, the question of the fourth marriage of the Emperor Leo VI – were ultimately resolved only when the state ceded complete jurisdiction in such matters to the Church, with a ruling of the Emperor Alexius I in 1084.[22]

The bishop, of course, played a role not merely in the ecclesiastical organisation of his diocese, but in its economic and social life, too. From the sixth century, bishops were among the most important figures in municipal government, being entitled to sit also in civil courts and carry out civil-administrative functions. Bishops were, certainly at this time, drawn from among the social and economic elite of their cities or dioceses,

---

[22] See Dölger, *Regesten*, no. 1116. For the organisation of the Church and the relative positions of the patriarch, bishops, upper and lower clergy, rural and urban parishes, see esp. the survey in Beck, *Kirche*, pp. 67ff. and 79–86; *CMH* vol. IV, part 2, pp. 106–18; Jones, *LRE*, vol. II, pp. 874ff.; Bréhier, *Institutions*, pp. 477ff.; and G. Dagron, 'Le Christianisme dans la ville byzantine', *DOP* 31 (1977), 3–25 (repr. in *La Romanité chrétienne en Orient* (London 1984)), see pp. 19ff. On the question of matrimony and divorce, see Beck, *Kirche*, pp. 86–90.

and it is unlikely that this picture changed dramatically during the seventh century.[23] As such, they formed also an important element of the ruling class of late Roman society, in which they occupied a central position, acting as mediators of both the ideological interests of Church and state and the economic interests of the Church as a great landowner.[24]

The monasteries

Just as significant an element in the late Roman and early Byzantine world was the monastic community. During the period from the early fourth to the later sixth centuries, monasticism – confined originally to Egypt, Syria and parts of Palestine – experienced a dramatic expansion.[25] In spite of strenuous efforts on the part of the secular Church and the state to establish some form of control and authority over both the monastic communities themselves and their tendency to expand which was an important element in the decline of the urban economy and culture of the late Roman period, monasteries represented a source of independence and anti-authoritarianism to the regular establishment, and more particularly to unacceptable or novel departures in imperial policy with regard to the Church and dogma. In 451 the council of Chalcedon reached a number of decisions in respect of monastic property, the position of monks and monastic communities within the Church as an institutional body, decisions which were taken up and expanded by the Emperor Justinian I. The continued independence of such communities, however, and their tacit rejection of many such limitations on their size, their activities and their sources of recruitment is evidenced in the canons of the Quinisext, where the Church once again attempted to enforce some degree of generally recognised conformity.[26] Individual hermits and anchorites, 'holy men' of

[23] See the survey of A. Guillou, 'L'Evêque dans la sociéte méditerranéenne des VIe-VIIe siècles: un modèle', *Bibliothèque de l'école des Chartes* 131 (1973), 5–19 (repr. in *Culture et société en Italie byzantine (VIe-XIe siècles)* II (London 1978).
[24] See chapter 3; and Jones, *LRE*, vol. II, pp. 923ff.; Brown, *Gentlemen and Officers*, p. 176. Note also the comments and literature cited by F. Winkelmann, 'Kirche und Gesellschaft in Byzanz vom ende des 6. bis zum Beginn des 8. Jahrhunderts', *Klio* 59 (1977), 477–89, see 481ff. For a comprehensive general survey, see Beck, *Kirche*, pp. 120–40.
[25] See *CMH*, vol. IV, part 2, pp. 161ff. and 167ff.; and especially the discussion in Mango, *Byzantium: the Empire of New Rome*, pp. 105–24. On the types of monastic community, see also Beck, *Kirche*, pp. 120ff. with literature. On the expansion of monasticism, see Jones, *LRE*, vol. II, pp. 930ff.; Bréhier, *Institutions*, pp. 529ff.
[26] For Chalcedon and Justinian, see Beck, *Kirche*, p. 126; and esp. B. Granić, 'Die rechtliche Stellung und Organisation der griechischen Klöster nach dem justinianischen Recht', *BZ* 29 (1929), 6–34 and 'Die privatrechtliche Stellung der griechischen Mönche im V. und VI. Jahrhundert', *BZ* 30 (1930), 669–76; G. Dagron, 'Les Moines et la ville: le monachisme à Constantinople jusqu'au concile de Chalcédoine (451)', *TM* 4 (1970), 229–76, for a detailed analysis of the role of monks in ecclesiastical and imperial politics in the fourth and fifth centuries. For the Quinisext, see canons 40 to 49: Mansi XI, 939ff.

the type familiar from the late Roman period, remained even more difficult to control and continued to exercise considerable influence and authority among the ordinary rural population.[27]

Like the secular Church, monasteries could also own property, granted to them in the same ways. The efforts of the Church to retain some control over monastic foundations gave to bishops a pre-eminent role. Not only did bishops have to give their assent to the building of any new monastic establishment; monasteries were also obliged to pay them a regular episcopal tax, or *canonicum*, and to commemorate the local bishop in the liturgy. The bishop also supervised the election of the abbot of a monastery and consecrated him. Needless to say, these regulations were not always strictly observed, and conflicts between monasteries and the episcopate were not infrequent.[28] Monasteries were endowed by private persons, from the richest to the poorest, for the salvation of their souls – for which the monks waged a continuous battle in prayer – and by grants of property and wealth from the imperial government. The extent of monastic property is difficult to assess, although it must from early on have been considerable, to judge from the number of monasteries which existed in some regions of the empire: there were, over several centuries, some 300 establishments in Constantinople alone, endowed either with land or other property from which the monks could be supported, or given cash grants and provisions on a yearly basis from their patrons and/or founders. Monastic centres flourished in the Aegean area, in western Asia Minor, in Cappadocia, in the Pontus, in parts of the Balkans, to name only those areas still within the empire after the seventh century.[29]

Monasticism, beginning as an Egyptian phenomenon, reflects the degree of popular piety among the ordinary populations of the late Roman and Byzantine world, and its often turbulent history provides an accurate

---

[27] See the comments of H.-G. Beck, *Das byzantinische Jahrtausend* (Munich 1978), esp. pp. 214ff. The council of Chalcedon (canons 4 and 24) had ordered that all those following the monastic life should have a fixed abode, and that they should confine their activities to fasting and prayer. They should not intervene in politics or in the wider affairs of the Church. In his fifth novel, Justinian ordered that even anchorites and recluses should live in their own cells, but within the bounds of the monastery. But such rulings clearly had little effect at this early time and afterwards, until the later ninth century at least. For Justinian's legislation, see *CJ* I, 3.43 and 46; V, 3.7 and 133. For monks and 'holy men' in the seventh century, see below.

[28] See Mango, *Byzantium: The Empire of New Rome*, pp. 108ff. and 120ff.

[29] See especially P. Charanis, 'The monastic properties and the state in the Byzantine empire', *DOP* 4 (1948), 51–118, and 'The monk as an element of Byzantine society', *DOP* 25 (1971), 61–84; Savramis, *Zur Soziologie des byzantinischen Mönchtums*, esp. pp. 39ff. and 45–52; Bréhier, *Institutions*, pp. 553ff.; Beck, *Das byzantinische Jahrtausend*, pp. 214–15. See also the brief survey of F. Trombley, 'Monastic foundations in sixth-century Anatolia and their role in the social and economic life of the countryside', *Greek Orthodox Theol. Review* 30 (1985), 45–59.

measure of the intensity of feeling aroused within the Byzantine Christian world over key issues – the Christological debates of the fifth to the seventh centuries, iconoclasm, and so on. It is notable that both Maximus Confessor and Sophronius had spent their early years in monastic communities or as anchorites; and it is important to remember that it was just such people – men and women both – who demonstrated their piety and nearness to God by their ability to endure physical and emotional degradation and humiliation, gaining thereby a more direct and better felt access to the true source of the holy and who also fulfilled the half-pious, half-superstitious needs of ordinary people of all social strata in their day-to-day difficulties and personal problems, constituting thereby an alternative source of spiritual authority which was implicitly a challenge to the formally endowed authority of the secular clergy and the establishment Church.[30]

On the other hand, calculations of the size of monastic communities and the numbers of monks within the empire have often been absurdly exaggerated, and on very little evidence, to give the impression that the late Roman and Byzantine state was at times almost overrun with such monastic establishments and that vast revenues were lost to the fisc as a result of wide-ranging exemptions and other privileges granted by pious rulers to calculating abbots and monastic patrons. In fact, while the number of monks may at times have been considerable, and while the amount of monastic property may at times have attracted the attention of the state – one thinks of the policies of the Emperor Nicephorus II in the 960s – there was never the numerical superabundance of monks which this tendency implies. On the contrary, very many people adopted the monastic life only in their last years and after a secular career; others left the monastic life for the secular world once more; while, as at least one scholar has stressed, the greater the number of monks, the greater their variety and the more diverse and dilute their effects.[31]

The extent to which monastic property suffered during the seventh century is impossible to assess. One estimate has suggested that the basic pattern, at least as regards Constantinople and the less exposed areas of Asia Minor, remained essentially the same.[32] No doubt monasteries in exposed districts were abandoned, but their property – especially in land – could hardly be destroyed, and since it remained inalienable, it may have been taken over by the local diocese, where this survived administratively,

[30] See Haldon, 'Ideology and social change', 184 with literature; and P. Brown, 'The rise and function of the holy man in late Antiquity', *JRS* 61 (1971), 80ff. and 'A Dark-Age crisis: aspects of the iconoclastic controversy', *EHR* 346 (1973), 1–34, see 23ff.
[31] Charanis, 'The monk as an element of Byzantine society', 69.
[32] See Beck, *Das byzantinische Jahrtausend*, pp. 207–12; and in general on monasticism in its social, cultural and institutional effects, pp. 212–31.

or they were reclaimed at a later date. Monks do play an important role, even as refugees – the problems they caused for the North African Christians after the Arab conquest of Egypt, when large numbers of monophysite monks and nuns arrived, to the dismay of the local clergy, are well known.[33] Monks figure prominently in the events connected with the monothelete debate from the mid-630s on;[34] they seem often from the earliest times – a reflection (in theory, if not always in practice) of their more rigorous life and greater piety, which gave them a greater spiritual authority – to have acted as 'pressure-groups' on the secular clergy and the episcopate, partly, of course, through the greater respect afforded them by the ordinary people of their society and their ability consequently to influence the latter in one direction or another. Monks represented in the seventh century, as often before and in later years, the hardline and uncompromising element in the Christian community, standing up against imperial 'interference' in matters of the spirit. They play a central role in the cultural-ideological politics of seventh-century Byzantium; and from the early eighth century they begin to supply the Church with an increasing number of leading clergymen, both patriarchs and bishops.[35]

Through its administrative and economic activities and organisation, through its clergy, its ecclesiastical courts, its role of missionary, preacher and defender of orthodoxy, the Church in its widest sense, both monastic and secular, was intimately bound up with every aspect of later Roman and Byzantine society and culture. While it is to a degree inevitable that it should be studied and examined as a separate institution or set of institutions, within the framework of Byzantine society, it should nevertheless not be forgotten that it was itself a structured and structuring element of that society, in the history and development of which it played a fundamental role.

The relationship between imperial Church and imperial state was not, therefore, a fixed one. Social and political developments affected the structure of this relationship as they affected all other aspects of early Byzantine society. The political ideology of Church and state incorporated ancient traditions – Hellenistic, Roman, oriental and early Christian – each of which was invoked at any given time and in a particular situation in a particular way. The Church represented the implementation of a formal

[33] See below; and Van Dieten, *Geschichte der Patriarchen*, pp. 67ff.
[34] Both Sophronius and Maximus had begun their careers as monks; a large number of their followers likewise.
[35] See esp. L. Bréhier, 'Le Recrutement des patriarches de Constantinople pendant la période byzantine', *Actes du VI*ᵉ *Congrès Internationale des Etudes Byzantines*, vol. I (Paris 1956), pp. 221–7. The first patriarch from monastic circles was Cyrus (705–11) – see Van Dieten, *Geschichte der Patriarchen*, pp. 161ff.

and sophisticated theology, yet in a social and cultural context – a symbolic universe – in which different elements clearly had differential effects and in which heterodoxy and the cultural assumptions of a variety of pre-Christian cultural traditions played a central role. Christianity represented not just the formal political theology of the Greco-Roman state, it represented also a regional, local and personal-individual system of values, with its appropriate logic and explanatory efficacy.

Conflicts within Christianity, and the continued existence of varying degrees of explicitly non-Christian belief – 'paganism' – give the impression of an uneasy pluralism until the middle of the sixth century. From Justinian's reign, neo-Chalcedonian universalism and a single orthodoxy start to become the keynote values of early Byzantine society and the state. The marginalisation and exclusion of non-conforming groups becomes increasingly apparent under Justinian's successors. The unity of state and Church, the future salvation of the *oikoumenē*, depends upon their partnership in orthodoxy. To be different was dangerous. The long evolution of the imperial Church which began in the fourth century reaches its final stages in the reign of Justinian; thereafter, state and Church are inseparable. As the patriarch Antony IV puts it in his letter to Prince Basil I of Moscow in the last decade of the fourteenth century:

> My son, you are wrong in saying 'We have a Church, but not an emperor.' It is not possible for Christians to have a Church and not an empire. Church and empire have a great unity and community; nor is it possible for them to be separated one from the other.[36]

Much had changed in the intervening centuries, of course. But the political ideology which this statement represents was the result of the developments of the period from the fourth to the sixth centuries. The seventh century confirmed and finalised this evolution.

CHURCH AND STATE *c.* 610–717: AUTHORITY VS. LEGITIMATION

The origins of the monothelete conflict

Under the influence of his wife, the Empress Sophia, Justin II began his reign with an attempt to bridge yet again the gulf between Chalcedonian and monophysite Churches. Sophia, a niece of the Empress Theodora, had been brought up in the tradition of Severus of Antioch, the great monophy-

---

[36] The text is in F. Miklosich and J. Müller, *Acta et Diplomata Graeci Medii Aevi Sacra et Profana* I and II (*Acta Patriarchatus Constantinopolitani*) (Vienna 1860–2), vol. II, pp. 188–92; Engl. trans. E. Barker, *Social and Political Thought in Byzantium* (Oxford 1957), pp. 194–6.

site theologian of the first half of the sixth century.[37] Her influence over Justin became clear when he recalled and restored all the bishops exiled by Justinian I, and when in 566/7 he issued a document of unification, or Henotikon, in which the ecclesiastical policies of Justinian – with the important exception of the policies invoked and imposed during the Three Chapters controversy – were more or less entirely abandoned and in which a return to the position at the end of the reign of Anastasius (491–518) was evident. Unfortunately for Justin's initial efforts, this attempt was a failure, for the monophysite bishops who met at Kallinikon in 567 to debate and ratify the policy under the auspices of the imperial representative John in fact rejected it, since it did not manage actually to condemn dyophysitism, that is, the creed of Chalcedon.[38] In 571 a second Henotikon was promulgated in which Justin modified his position very slightly, stressing the fact that, however the question of the single or double natures of Christ (as man and God) might be resolved, He still occupied a single person and being, both God and man in one. In the same document, Justin also repeats and extends the basic position expressed in Justinian I's edict on correct belief, issued in 551. In practice, therefore, whatever his intentions or his hopes, the official position would be seen by the monophysites as one based fundamentally on Chalcedonian principles, in which two natures could still be admitted.[39] The result was, perhaps, predictable, and certainly typical: monophysite rejection of the principle of the Henotikon, followed by intensified state persecution. The majority of the monophysite bishops were forced to put their names to the document; those who refused were exiled.[40] The issue, therefore, remained unresolved, and the independent Jacobite Church organised by Jacob Baradaeus continued to develop.[41] Justin's short reign, which began with an attempt at compromise and unification, ended in persecution and repression.

Tiberius II and Maurice appear to have acted much more pragmatically, indeed the monophysite Church during Tiberius' reign seems to have been able to consolidate its organisational foundation, and monophysite sources

[37] See esp. W. de Vries, 'Die Eschatologie des Severus von Antiochien', OCP 23 (1957), 354–80; J. Lebon, Le Monophysisme Sévérien (Louvain 1909).
[38] See Michael Syr., vol. II, 289ff.; and Averil Cameron, 'The early religious policies of Justin II', Studies in Church History XIII (1976), 65ff. For Zeno's Henotikon, see Every, The Byzantine Patriarchate, pp. 50f.; Winkelmann, Die östlichen Kirchen, pp. 97f.
[39] See the long account in Evagrius, 199–200; and see, for the Justinianic position, E. Schwartz, 'Drei dogmatische Schriften Justinians', Abhandlungen d. bayer. Akad. d. Wiss., phil.-hist. Klasse, new series XVIII (Munich 1939). For a brief survey of Justinian's religious policies, see Every, The Byzantine Patriarchate, pp. 57–68.
[40] See Michael Syr., vol. II, 295ff.; John of Nikiu, 94; and especially John of Ephesus, I, 19sq.; II, 1sq.; II, 9sq.
[41] For the most useful general account, see W.H.C. Frend, The Rise of the Monophysite Movement (Cambridge 1972); and Winkelmann, Die östlichen Kirchen, pp. 122ff.

speak well of the emperor, who put an end, temporarily, to the persecutions.[42] But under Maurice, the policies of repression were once more applied, although their effect was again merely to drive the monophysite Church underground, but not to reduce its influence nor to damage its organisation.[43] And under Phocas the situation seems to have remained very much the same.

In contrast to the last years of the reign of Maurice, Phocas once more established friendly relations with the papacy and Rome. In the 590s the disagreement between the patriarch at Constantinople and the Pope in Rome over the former's use of the title 'ecumenical' resurfaced. Since Maurice took no action in the matter, his inactivity was assumed by Rome to signal his approval of the patriarch's position, and relations were considerably soured as a result. In contrast, Phocas recognised Roman authority over the whole Church, and in 607 he issued a decree in which he expressly forbade the Constantinopolitan use of the title ecumenical, recognising instead the supremacy of Rome.[44] Again, this question was to become one of the distinguishing features of later Byzantine ecclesiastical history in its relations with Rome and with the West in general.

The central question for the state, however, remained that of the schism between dyophysite Chalcedonians and the monophysites of the Eastern provinces. During Heraclius' wars with the Persians, the question naturally enough was relegated to a secondary position. Imperial Church and state worked together to restore the empire and to re-establish orthodoxy in the civilised world. The enormous loans made by the Church to finance Heraclius' armies, the central role of the patriarch Sergius during Heraclius' absence in the East, and especially during the great siege of 626,[45] all point to the close collaboration between the spiritual and political establishments of the Byzantine world. But in the provinces temporarily occu-

[42] Michael Syr., vol. II, 310.
[43] Although the repression was not as severe as it had formerly been – see Stratos, *Byzantium in the Seventh Century*, vol. I, p. 13. See R. Paret, in *REB* 15 (1957), 42ff.; and note the remarks of Michael Syr., vol. II, 372. In general on Church–state relations in this period, see I. Rochow, 'Die Heidenprozesse unter Tiberios II. und Maurikios', in *Studien zum 7. Jahrhundert*, pp. 120–30; Winkelmann, 'Kirche und Gesellschaft' 477ff.
[44] For Phocas' policies in respect of the monophysites, see John of Nikiu, chapter 104, for example; and Bréhier and Aigrain, pp. 71–2. On the Rome–Constantinople debate and the question of ecclesiastical supremacy, see Ostrogorsky, *Geschichte*, p. 71; V. Laurent, 'Le Titre de patriarche œcuménique et la signature patriarcale', *REB* 6 (1948), 5–26; Beck, *Kirche*, pp. 63f. with literature; Bréhier and Aigrain, pp. 64ff. and 70–1. For a brief summary of Byzantine–papal relations during the seventh century, see F. Dvornik, *Byzanz und der römische Primat* (Stuttgart 1966 = repr. of *Byzance et la primauté romaine* (Paris, 1964)), pp. 95–108; and Herrin, *Formation of Christendom*, pp. 206ff., 213–15, 250–67 and 274ff. For Phocas, *ibid.*, pp. 180f.
[45] See the account in Stratos, *Byzantium in the Seventh Century*, vol. I, pp. 126f.; Bréhier and Aigrain, p. 86. For the siege, see F. Barišić, 'Le Siège de Constantinople par les Avares et les Slaves en 626', *B* 24 (1954), 371–95; Van Dieten, *Geschichte der Patriarchen*, pp. 12–21.

pied by the Persians, things were very different. For here, the removal of Byzantine authority had permitted the open establishment and strengthening of the hitherto illegal monophysite Church. Whether or not Persian rule was regarded favourably, it certainly encouraged the self-confidence of the monophysite clergy and people; and upon the completion of the reconquest, it became evident that throughout the Eastern provinces – Egypt, Syria, Palestine and Armenia in particular – a potential or actual hostility to, and a resentment of, Constantinopolitan rule now constituted a real danger, both to the unity of the empire politically and ideologically, and to the authority of the emperor and of the Chalcedonian Church.[46]

In an effort to promote a reconciliation, the patriarch Sergius, the emperor and Cyrus, Chalcedonian patriarch of Alexandria from 631, adopted the 'doctrine of the single energy', known as monenergism. The real originator of this theological solution had been a certain Theodore, bishop of Pharan, towards the end of the sixth century, and the principal aim of his theology was to overcome the contradiction between the monophysite and dyophysite perspectives by pointing to the unity of effect of the natures of Christ, that is, the single energy which emanates from the *logos*. At the same time, he emphasised also the single will which was an inevitable corollary of the single energy.[47] The debate over one or two energies was thus in origin a purely theological issue reaching back into the sixth century arising out of the Christological debate around the question of the natures of Christ and expressed in the sophisticated vocabulary of Christian thinkers. And it was the position outlined in the writings of Theodore of Pharan that Sergius, Cyrus and Heraclius now tried to build upon, but with only limited success. Even though Heraclius himself led the discussion and negotiations, the monophysites could not be persuaded that this was not still essentially a dyophysite position; and in part they were correct, for Theodore of Pharan had grounded his theology in a dyophysite

[46] For the opening stages of the development of an imperial compromise solution, see the summary and literature in Stratos, *Byzantium in the Seventh Century*, vol. I, pp. 283–304; Van Dieten, *Geschichte der Patriarchen*, pp. 24ff. For Persian policy in the monophysite provinces, see Bréhier and Aigrain, pp. 88–90 and 111f. Heraclius was clearly already well aware of the nature of the problem: his *Edict on Faith* of 610, promulgated shortly after his accession, was firmly dyophysite, but was couched in terms intended to be acceptable to a monophysite reader, including a formulation of Cyril of Alexandria. See Michael Syr., vol. II, 402–3; Bréhier and Aigrain, pp. 86–7. The 'monophysite danger' should not, of course, be exaggerated: see chapter 2, and J. Moorhead, 'The Monophysite response to the Arab invasions', *B* 51 (1981), 579–91.

[47] See the summary of the complex argument in W. Elert, *Der Ausgang der altkirchlichen Christologie* (Berlin 1957), pp. 203ff. For the role of Sergius, see Bréhier and Aigrain, pp. 112ff.; and the agreement of 633, *ibid.*, pp. 117–18; Van Dieten, *Geschichte der Patriarchen*, pp. 24–31; Herrin, *Formation of Christendom*, pp. 206–11; and for the sources for and beginnings of the debate, see Winkelmann, *Die Quellen*, esp. nos. 1–11, and pp. 55f.

framework, and his argument inevitably allowed room for the possibility that there might be two natures. In spite of an agreement reached between Cyrus and the so-called Theodosiani, a monophysite sect in Egypt, formally announced in a document of union in June 633, no real resolution of the problem was reached. Pope Honorius, in a carefully expressed letter, made his agreement with the discussions for unity known; but the patriarch Sophronius of Jerusalem rejected the attempt out of hand, and his opposition – from a firmly dyophysite position – meant in effect the failure of the whole exercise, for it was announced in a local synod, held in 634 shortly after his accession to the patriarchal throne. The failure of this first attempt was made all the more apparent by its rejection from the Chalcedonian side. The rejection from Sophronius produced an edict in late 634 or early 635 from the emperor, supported by Cyrus and Sergius, to the effect that the question of the number of energies should no longer be debated at all, since union had now been achieved and since such debates would serve only to weaken the empire further. But the monophysites seem simply to have ignored the efforts of the emperor and his advisers. They were, far from being reunited with the Chalcedonian, now in the position of observers of a new schism within the ranks of the latter. And as first Syria (636), then Palestine (638) and finally Egypt (642) fell to the Arabs, the attempt lost much of its relevance for them, both from the theological and the political points of view.[48]

For the second time in his reign Heraclius now saw the Eastern provinces of the empire lost to an invader. In 638, perceiving that the monenergite doctrine had failed, he made a second attempt to attract the loyalty and support of the monophysites, but without stirring up Chalcedonian opposition, he hoped, and issued the Ekthesis, in which a monothelete doctrine was proclaimed, a doctrine which emphasised the single will of God, but which left the question of nature and energy to one side. Once again the debate on the question of the number of energies was strictly prohibited.[49] The Ekthesis was posted in the narthex of Haghia Sophia in

---

[48] Pope Honorius: Bréhier and Aigrain, pp. 121–3; and Mansi XI, 537–44; Riedinger, 548–58; Sophronius' opposition: Bréhier and Aigrain, pp. 118, 120–1 and 123–4; and his synodal letter, Mansi XI, 831–53. See also Van Dieten, *Geschichte der Patriarchen*, pp. 32ff. For the edict of 634–5 and its background, stimulated by a letter of the Pope to Sophronius, suggesting that the latter permit Honorius to handle the discussion personally with Sergius, see Dölger, *Regesten*, no. 205; Van Dieten, *Geschichte der Patriarchen*, pp. 39ff.; Bréhier and Aigrain, pp. 123–4.

[49] Dölger, *Regesten*, no. 211; V. Grumel, *Les Regestes des Actes du patriarcat de Constantinople* I: *Les Actes des patriarches*, vol. I (Paris 1972); vol. II (Chalcedon 1936); vol. II (Chalcedon and Bucarest 1947), vol. I, no. 292; Bréhier and Aigrain, pp. 131–2; Van Dieten, *Geschichte der Patriarchen*, pp. 47ff. For the text, see *Lateran*, 156.20–162.13 (Mansi X, 991–8); and for general historical context, Stratos, *Byzantium in the Seventh Century*, vol. II, pp. 141–9; and Van Dieten, *Geschichte der Patriarchen*, pp. 179–218 and 219–232.

Constantinople, and copies were sent to the patriarch Cyrus in Alexandria, and to the exarch of Ravenna for the successor to Pope Honorius, Severinus. In Constantinople Sergius convoked a council to approve the document and the statement of faith, but then he died in December 638. His successor Pyrrhus called a new council after his accession in January 639. All the attending bishops ratified the document. The new patriarch of Jerusalem, the monothelete Sergius of Joppa, also ratified it; while the Chalcedonian patriarch of Antioch, Macedonius, appointed shortly before by Sergius, stayed in Constantinople rather than occupy his see, and likewise ratified the Ekthesis.[50]

In Rome, meanwhile, Pope Honorius had died in October 638, and his successor Severinus seems to have come under direct pressure from the exarch to ratify the Ekthesis. In addition, his apocrisiaries were held up in Constantinople until they agreed to accept the document on the pope's behalf. This they refused to do, although they eventually agreed to persuade Severinus himself to accept it. The new pope was finally confirmed in his office by Constantinople in April of 640, but died shortly after in August of the same year. He never ratified the Ekthesis. His successor, John IV, seems to have been confirmed in his election relatively quickly, but immediately adopted a hostile position, calling a synod in Rome which rejected and condemned monotheletism and the Ekthesis.[51] Shortly before his death in April 641 Heraclius realised that his policies had failed to achieve their aims, indeed that they had created new divisions within the Church. In a letter to John IV he attributed the original authorship of the Ekthesis to Sergius and conceded also that it had brought further trouble to the Christian community.[52] His death did not end the matter, however, and it was in the reign of Constans II in particular that the divisions within Church and empire became critical. But monotheletism was itself not simply an ineffective and short-lived imperial compromise. Indeed, it seems from the later evidence – notably the adherence to monotheletism of the patriarch Makarios of Antioch and his supporters at the sixth ecumenical

---

[50] See Bréhier and Aigrain, pp. 132f.; Van Dieten, *Geschichte der Patriarchen*, pp. 47f. and 58–63; Stratos, *Byzantium in the Seventh Century*, vol. II, pp. 143f.; Grumel, *Regestes*, vol. I, nos. 293, 295 and 298.

[51] Bréhier and Aigrain, pp. 133f.; Van Dieten, *Geschichte der Patriarchen*, pp. 62–3; Dölger, *Regesten*, no. 214; Stratos, *Byzantium in the Seventh Century*, vol. II, pp. 146–7; Ostrogorsky, *Geschichte*, pp. 90–1. The split in the Chalcedonian community was ultimately founded upon much deeper cultural differences between East and West, of course, than these ecclesiastical–political disagreements suggest. See the discussion of P. Lemerle, 'L'Orthodoxie byzantine et l'écuménisme médiévale: les origines du "Schisma" des églises', *Bulletin de l'Association Guillaume Budé*, 4,2 (1965), 228–46 (repr. in *Essais sur le monde byzantin* VIII (London 1980). See also Herrin, *Formation of Christendom*, pp. 213–15.

[52] See Dölger, *Regesten*, no. 215.

council of 680/1 – that the monothelete doctrine was adopted, and probably on a widespread basis, in the neo-Chalcedonian communities of Syria and Palestine, where it appears to have taken firm root. The Syriac Life of Maximus Confessor in particular suggests that he and his followers did not find the massive support in the East which their own propaganda at the height of the controversy with the emperor and afterwards might suggest. On the contrary, it was only in Africa and in Rome that Maximus was really able to muster vocal and committed opposition to monotheletism. The explanation for this support, and the stubbornness of the Chalcedonian Syrian communities in adhering to the doctrine, must lie partly in the fact that from the 640s they were effectively cut off from the political body of the empire: one clear way of denoting their identity, for themselves and especially for their monophysite neighbours, was by sticking firmly to the official policy of the state to which they had once belonged – and might still belong again.[53]

While Heraclius' policies regarding the Church are dominated naturally enough by the great question of the relationship between Chalcedonian and monophysite Churches, the emperor concerned himself also with the less public matters of ecclesiastical administration, the organisation and regulation of monastic communities, and the Church hierarchy. Decrees issued in 612 and in 619 to regulate the numbers of the clergy in positions in the Great Church in the capital and in the Church of the Blachernai and others; and ordinances in 629 granting juridical privileges to the clergy, and in 638, on matters concerning both the Constantinopolitan and provincial clergy, are illustrative of this activity.[54] He was also very much concerned with the question of the Jews in the empire, particularly in view of the frequent collaboration of Jewish communities with the Persians. While initially granting an amnesty for their actions (issued at Tiberias in 630), he seems thereafter to have hardened his views, forbidding Jews to

---

[53] For Makarios, see below. For the Syriac Life of Maximus, see S. Brock, 'An Early Syriac Life of Maximus the Confessor', *AB* 91 (1973), 299–346, dated to the later years of the seventh century; and the comments of Winkelmann, *Die Quellen*, 552 and 557–9 on the propaganda effort of Maximus and his followers.

[54] See Dölger, *Regesten*, nos. 165, 175, 199, 212 and 213; Grumel, *Regestes*, vol. I, nos. 278 bis, 279 bis (with vol. III, 196); Van Dieten, *Geschichte der Patriarchen*, pp. 3–5, 10 and 22–3 for discussion. Heraclius' *genikos nomos* of 629 is particularly significant, for it marks a new stage in the privileges of the clergy and in Church–state relations. According to the decree, no layperson, including military officials, had henceforth the right to imprison any clerical person. Clergy who travelled to Constantinople to have their pleas heard now had the right to choose which court they wished to appear before – that of the praetorian prefect, that of the patriarch or of a specially delegated imperial judge. Lay courts no longer had any jurisdiction to alter the decisions of the Church courts; but for clerics who lay charges against non-clerics, the traditional and standard rule – that the plaintiff must accept the decision of the court under whose authority the defendant comes, was maintained. See Beck, *Kirche*, p. 82.

live within three miles of Jerusalem after the return of the True Cross.[55] There had on occasion been forced baptisms of Jews also, but in 634 he issued a general decree ordering the baptism of all Jews in the empire. Needless to say, such measures had little hope of even a limited success, and the loss of Syria and then Palestine to the Arabs by 638 made the decree irrelevant for these areas. But forced baptisms did occur in other parts of the empire, as the story of Jacob, 'the recently baptised', testifies.[56] If anything, of course, the decree made the Jewish communities in Palestine even more hostile to Roman rule and will have ensured, if not co-operation, then at least neutrality in the struggle against the Muslim invaders.

One further event of significance deserves mention, if only because of the consequences for the state after Heraclius' death and the attitude of later Byzantine writers to him: his marriage to his niece Martina. Heraclius' first wife, Eudocia, died on 13 August in the year 612 and was laid to rest in the Church of the Holy Apostles.[57] Shortly afterwards, the emperor decided to marry his niece, Martina. The Church clearly saw this marriage as contrary to canon law, and the patriarch Sergius tried to convince the emperor that his actions would also make him very unpopular. Heraclius replied politely, we are told, that Sergius was correct and had done his duty; but that he could leave the matter in the emperor's hands thenceforth. The marriage went ahead, indeed with the patriarch's blessing;[58] but although the temporary disagreement between Heraclius and Sergius was quickly forgotten in the troubles that followed – the emperor suffered a major military defeat in 613 at Persian hands; and in 614 Jerusalem fell and the Holy Cross was carried off to Persia – it remained a point of contention among both clergy and population, especially in Constantinople, where Martina was apparently very unpopular.[59]

The crisis of authority: Constans II vs. Maximus Confessor

Heraclius was succeeded by his eldest son Heraclius Constantine and by his first son with Martina, known as Heracleonas, who were to rule jointly according to his will.[60] In effect, Heraclius Constantine, usually referred to

---

[55] Dölger, *Regesten*, nos. 196 and 197.
[56] Dölger, *Regesten*, no. 206; and the account of Bréhier and Aigrain, pp. 110f.; see also Beck, *Kirche*, pp. 332–3 and note 1.
[57] See *Chronicon Paschale*, 702.19sq.; Ostrogorsky, *Geschichte*, p. 93.
[58] See Pernice, *L'imperatore Eraclio*, pp. 54f.; and Nicephorus, 14.11sq.; Theophanes, 30.25–8. For Sergius' baptism of the first child of the marriage, Constantine, in 613, see Theophanes, 30.6–7. See Grumel, *Regestes*, vol. I, no. 284.
[59] Nicephorus, 27; and see Ostrogorsky, *Geschichte*, p. 93.
[60] Dölger, *Regesten*, no. 216.

simply as Constantine, ruled alone at first, although Martina attempted to promote her own position and that of her son. Her unpopularity, however, and the fact that the patriarch Pyrrhus was accused of illicitly appropriating state funds for Martina's cause, together with the support of the senate and the army for the 'true' line of Heraclius and – in addition – Constantine's apparently anti-monothelete position[61] meant that she had to be content with a background role. Pyrrhus lost temporarily the influential position he had held over the throne. But Constantine died after only a few months, and the young Heracleonas, supported by his mother and the patriarch, became sole ruler.[62] The rule of Martina as regent, backed by Pyrrhus, did not last long. One of her first acts was to rescind an order of Constantine to drive out, or to convert, the monophysite refugees in Africa (although her order was never carried out – the exarch Gregory, realising the potential unrest this would cause among the orthodox Africans, declared the decree a falsification and ignored it).[63] Martina's lack of support in the senate and her unpopularity in the city, as well as the opposition of the commander of the troops in Anatolia, Valentinus, forced her and Pyrrhus to arrange for the crowning of the son of Heraclius Constantine, Constantine, or Constans, as he is normally known, as co-emperor. This compromise did not hold, however, and as rumours spread that Martina and Pyrrhus were plotting with the commander of one of the Anatolian field armies – possibly of the Armenian forces – to march against Valentinus and assist in the deposition of Constans, the senate ordered Martina and her offspring to be arrested, mutilated and banished. Pyrrhus managed to flee to Carthage, from where he was eventually recalled to office.[64]

After the turbulent events of 640–1 the young Constans II commenced sole rule on 9 November 641. Within a few months the patriarchal throne had been filled by the newly elected Paul II, who remained in office until 653. He was a monothelete and, although the young emperor and the senate accepted the letter of John IV to Heraclius Constantine and recog-

[61] See the text of Pope John VI's letter to Constantine, Mansi X, 682–6, and Van Dieten, *Geschichte der Patriarchen*, pp. 63–4 and note 22; and the strongly anti-monophysite order of the emperor to the bishops and exarch of Carthage in response to their request to deal with the refugee nuns spreading monophysite ideas in the exarchate. See Dölger, *Regesten*, no. 222; Bréhier and Aigrain, pp. 160ff.; Van Dieten, *Geschichte der Patriarchen*, pp. 67ff.; Stratos, *Byzantium in the Seventh Century*, vol. II, pp. 176–85; Ostrogorsky, *Geschichte*, p. 94.
[62] See Van Dieten, *Geschichte der Patriarchen*, pp. 63–8; Bréhier and Aigrain, pp. 143–4.
[63] Van Dieten, *Geschichte der Patriarchen*, pp. 68–9 and note 37; Stratos, *Byzantium in the Seventh Century*, vol. III, pp. 59ff.
[64] See Van Dieten, *Geschichte der Patriarchen*, pp. 70–5 for a summary; and chapter 2 above, pp. 49ff.

nised the Chalcedonian creed,[65] his appointment suggests the existence of powerful monothelete elements in the senate and at court, who were the effective government during the early years of Constans' minority. The general Valentinus, with a strong detachment of troops, had also established himself in Constantinople, however, and seems to have attempted to make himself officially regent or co-emperor. His attempt failed, chiefly as a result of the efforts of the patriarch Paul, and he was killed when the populace rioted against his use of soldiers brought into the city from the field army.

The rift between Rome and Constantinople was not overcome, however, by the imperial recognition of two natures and two wills, for the Pope Theodore insisted also on a formal and canonical deposition of the patriarch Pyrrhus[66] and on the removal of the Ekthesis from the narthex of Haghia Sophia. Initially, there was no response to these demands, perhaps a sign of uncertainty in the factions clustered around the young emperor. The debate did not rest, however. In 643 the archbishop Sergius of Cyprus wrote to Pope Theodore affirming his orthodoxy and that of the island; while in 645 the famous disputation between the monk Maximus and the ex-patriarch Pyrrhus took place – organised by the exarch Gregory himself in Carthage – in which Pyrrhus conceded the debate, travelled to Rome to confess his sins and received the pope's forgiveness and blessing. Maximus travelled with him.[67]

Maximus is perhaps one of the most important individuals about whom events revolve at this period. He was a confirmed Chalcedonian and anti-monothelete, a keen-witted theologian and a brilliant debater. Like his older contemporary Sophronius, also a fierce opponent of monotheletism from the Chalcedonian position, Maximus spent his early years as a monk in Palestine, where he came into contact with such men as John Moschus, compiler of one of the most important collections of edifying tales and extracts from the Lives of the desert holy men and monks, the so-called Spiritual Meadow. As refugees from Islam, both Maximus and Sophronius were active in the struggle against monophysitism and against the 'new' heresy, monotheletism. It was Maximus who wrote around to the orthodox communities of the Mediterranean world enlisting their support and promoting their opposition to the imperial policy; it was Maximus who became the effective leader of the African Church after his defeat of Pyrrhus

---

[65] Dölger, *Regesten*, no. 221; Bréhier and Aigrain, pp. 162f.; Van Dieten, *Geschichte der Patriarchen*, pp. 76f.
[66] Van Dieten, *Geschichte der Patriarchen*, pp. 80–2.
[67] *Ibid.*, pp. 82–7; Cameron, 'Byzantine Africa', 56ff.

The imperial Church and the politics of authority 307

in the debate of 645; and it was Maximus who was the guiding hand behind the convoking of the Lateran synod of 649.[68]

As a result of the defeat of Pyrrhus, the African Church held a number of local synods in the following year, all of which condemned monotheletism. The bishops of Byzacena, Numidia and Mauretania directed two letters, via Rome, to Constantinople, one to the patriarch and one to the emperor, appealing to the latter to invoke his imperial authority and to compel Paul to return to orthodoxy.[69] The degree of suspicion of the African Church in Constantinople – clearly expressed in letters of Victor, bishop of Carthage, and of other African bishops to Rome – was, of course, greatly exacerbated by the exarch Gregory's rebellion, which began soon after Maximus' victory over Pyrrhus.[70] The logic of Gregory's action is not entirely clear, but it is clearly connected with the results for the African Church and population of the defeat of Pyrrhus, the reaffirmation of orthodoxy, and the conflicting options open to him: either to follow his Constantinopolitan orders and enforce imperial policy – that would have entailed a massive persecution and political repression, which might well have seemed an impossible task – or to maintain his position and authority (and his popularity), throw in his lot with the orthodox sentiments of the greater part of the population and all the episcopate and, by refusing to follow orders, call down upon himself the wrath of the imperial government. Gregory decided evidently on the latter course, pre-empting the court's response by formally stating his rejection of the rule of the Emperor Constans.[71]

Gregory's death in battle with the Arabs in 647 brought a dramatic change in the situation. Pyrrhus – who had been anathematised by Paul following his rejection of monotheletism and who had perhaps hoped for a patriarchal throne in Carthage beside the pretender Gregory[72] – now changed his position once more, returned to monotheletism and claimed that his 'conversion' had been obtained under duress. Pope Theodore

[68] See Cameron, 'Byzantine Africa', 56f.; Haldon, 'Ideology and social change', 173 and note 85; Stratos, *Byzantium in the Seventh Century*, vol. III, pp. 60f. For the Lateran council, see the extensive works of R. Riedinger, listed in Winkelmann, *Die Quellen*, 538. On Maximus himself, see esp. J.M. Garrigues, *Maxime le confesseur. La charité, avenir divin de l'homme* (Paris 1976), esp. pp. 35–75 for a detailed biography; and the papers in F. Heinzer and Chr. Schönborn, *Maximus Confessor. Actes du Symposium sur Maxime le Confesseur. Fribourg 2–5 Sept. 1980* (Fribourg 1982).

[69] See *Vita Maximi Confessoris*, 84B; Theophanes, 337.8–10; Cameron, 'Byzantine Africa', 57; Stratos, *Byzantium in the Seventh Century*, vol. III, pp. 61–2.

[70] See the literature and discussion in Van Dieten, *Geschichte der Patriarchen*, pp. 85–7. It is uncertain whether the letters were sent, however, although the pope, Theodore, certainly used them in his own letter to the patriarch Paul in 647. See below.

[71] Cf. Cameron, 'Byzantine Africa', 57f.; Stratos, *Byzantium in the Seventh Century*, vol. III, pp. 62–7; Ostrogorsky, *Geschichte*, pp. 98f.

[72] Van Dieten, *Geschichte der Patriarchen*, pp. 87; 84–5.

immediately anathematised him and wrote a strongly worded letter to the patriarch Paul in which he intimated that the political loyalty of the West and Africa depended directly on the imperial government and the Constantinoplitan patriarchate returning to a dyothelete/dyophysite position. The consequence for the East of accepting this ultimatum, of course, would be – apart from the political defeat for the emperor – a *de facto* recognition of Rome's precedence in the ecclesiastical hierarchy and in matters of dogma. Paul replied in a gentler tone, affirming quite explicitly his and the imperial government's adherence to monotheletism and the formulation of the patriarch Sergius, invoking also the Pope Honorius' claimed adherence to this doctrine.[73] The pope answered quite simply by formally pronouncing the deposition of the patriarch Paul.[74]

This unilateral act immediately changed the tone of the disagreement. Up until this point, the debate had been restricted to matters of faith and confined to the Church. The imperial government had anyway been unable to respond effectively to Gregory's rebellion owing to its difficult situation in the East, and the problems of government by a council of advisers and the still minor Constans. Gregory's death had ended that particular threat, and the state seems to have been willing to remain silent while Paul carried on the debate – although the clear division within the Church, and especially the alienation of Africa, must have been very worrying. The pope's letter of 647 and his deposition of Paul changed all this. The first result was the issue in 648 of the Typos, clearly designed less to resolve the theological problem than to quell the uproar which this had effected and to restore order within the Christian community – for there were other, yet more pressing dangers to be faced.[75] Paul may well have been closely involved in its composition, but it was issued in the emperor's name and thereby took the debate on to a different level. Already in his letter of 647 the Pope had, by implication, threatened the state; his deposition of Paul was now a direct challenge to imperial authority. The emperor decreed that those who refused to comply with the demands of the Typos were to be severely punished: bishops would be removed from office, monks from their sanctuaries; civil and military personnel would lose their office and

---

[73] Paul's letter: *Lateran*, 196.16–204.4. Theodore's letter has not survived, but its tone and content can be re-established from Paul's reply. Note that Paul spent some time with the papal emissaries to Constantinople trying to reach some sort of compromise solution, without success, before making his position clear in his letter. See *Lateran*, 198.22sq.; *Liber Pontificalis* I, 333; cf. Grumel, *Regestes*, vol. I, no. 300.

[74] *Lateran*, 18.8–19 (Pope Martin's account at the Lateran council in 649).

[75] See Dölger, *Regesten*, no. 225; text: *Lateran*, 208.3–210.15; see Haldon, 'Ideology and social change', 173f., and Van Dieten, *Geschichte der Patriarchen*, pp. 92ff.; Ostrogorsky, *Geschichte*, p. 99; E. Caspar, 'Die Lateransynode von 649', *Zeitschrift für Kirchengeschichte* 51 (1932), 75–137; Herrin, *Formation of Christendom*, pp. 217–9 and 250–5. See also the references to the work of Riedinger in note 68, chapter 8, above.

The imperial Church and the politics of authority 309

their titles, senators and others would lose their lands, yet others would be chastised with corporal punishment and with imprisonment. And since the Typos forbade all debate, ordering simply that the orthodox should observe the canons of the first five ecumenical councils – thus leaving the question of the number of wills and energies open – the Ekthesis was also removed, thus complying with one of the earlier demands of the Roman primate.[76]

The Roman response, suggested and encouraged by Maximus, was not long in coming.[77] Pope Theodore commissioned the fiercely orthodox Stephen of Dor, spiritual comrade of Sophronius of Jerusalem, to extract a confession of faith from the clergy of Palestine. Those who refused to co-operate or remained monothelete were to be deposed. Such action was, of course, a direct interference in the affairs of the eastern patriarchates and a direct challenge to imperial policy, and resulted partly from the appeal of the monothelete Sergius of Joppa, who had succeeded Sophronius as patriarch of Jerusalem, together with the bishops whom he had appointed, to the patriarch Paul for confirmation of their appointments.[78] The imperial authorities responded by depriving the papal emissaries of their priestly titles and position, punishing them physically and exiling them from Constantinople.[79] The new Pope Martin – elected on 5 July 649, but without imperial confirmation – held a synod in the Lateran palace, a synod which was in fact organised by and dominated by Maximus and Stephen of Dor and their associates. The originators of monotheletism – Theodore of Pharan, Cyrus of Alexandria, the patriarchs Sergius, Pyrrhus and Paul, together with the Ekthesis of Heraclius and the Typos of Constans, were all anathematised. The acts of the council, again written up by Maximus and his associates, were then sent to Constans, together with a letter urging him once more to compel his patriarch to return to orthodoxy. The emperor himself, along with his grandfather Heraclius, was carefully excluded from the anathematisations and the condemnations, almost certainly a political gesture rather than a reflection of real sentiment.[80]

The events that followed are well known. The new exarch of Ravenna,

---

[76] See the summary of Van Dieten, *Geschichte der Patriarchen*, pp. 93–4; Stratos, *Byzantium in the Seventh Century*, vol. III, pp. 95ff.

[77] It is not clear from the sources whether Pope Theodore or his successor Martin received the Typos. Theodore died on 13 May 649, and since Martin's accession was never confirmed by the emperor, it is probable that the document arrived in time for Theodore to see it. See Van Dieten, *Geschichte der Patriarchen*, pp. 92–3 and note 73.

[78] *Lateran*, 46.1sq. For Sergius of Joppa, see Van Dieten, *Geschichte der Patriarchen*, p. 50.

[79] Cf. *Lateran*, 18.8–31; *Liber Pontificalis*, 336; *Hypomnesticum*, 70 (Greek version) and 196A (Latin version).

[80] For the text, see Riedinger, *Lateran*. See Van Dieten, *Geschichte der Patriarchen*, pp. 97ff.; Haldon, 'Ideology and social change', 174 and note 88; Stratos, *Byzantium in the Seventh Century*, vol. III, pp. 98–104; Ostrogorsky, *Geschichte*, p. 99.

Olympius, had already been ordered to arrest the pope, who had ascended the papal throne without imperial ratification, and to have the Typos read out in all the churches of Italy. Instead, Olympius came to an arrangement with Martin and ruled independently, ignoring his orders, just as Gregory had done in Africa. Only with the death of Olympius in 652 was the emperor able, through the new exarch, Theodore Calliopas, to rectify the situation.[81] Martin was arrested by Calliopas with contingents of the Ravenna army and taken to Constantinople where he was tried, initially condemned to death for high treason, then to exile. He died in Cherson on 16 September 655. Maximus was also arrested and taken to Constantinople. His trial, banishment, second trial or interrogation, followed by his mutilation and exile – he died eventually in Lazica in 662[82] – accurately reflects the anger at his obstinate and intellectually sharp defence of his position and also the main issue at stake: imperial authority. Indeed, it is interesting to observe how, throughout the debate, and from the earliest days of the conflict in 645/6 through to the final execution of Maximus' punishment, the government and Constans were eager to come to a peaceful compromise, an arrangement that would involve nothing more than the end of the debate, rather than any admission of fault on the part of either Pope Theodore or his successor Martin, or of Maximus. In the last resort, and with the secular demands of state politics firmly in view, the defeat of the anti-monotheletes was, perhaps, a foregone conclusion. The emperor had brutally reasserted imperial rights to be directly and centrally involved in both matters of faith, in the calling of synods and in the ratification of higher ecclesiastical appointments. This success, however, was bought at the cost of the alienation, even if only temporary, of Africa, which remained stubbornly anti-monothelete and, as its later history illustrates, unable or unwilling to offer any dynamic opposition – political or cultural – to the arrival of Islam.[83]

[81] Ostrogorsky, *Geschichte*, pp. 99–100; Haldon, 'Ideology and social change', 182 and note 123; Stratos, *Byzantium in the Seventh Century*, vol. III, pp. 105–11. There is some numismatic evidence to suggest that Martin did approve and bless Olympius' rebellion: a silver coin struck in the mint of Rome and dated to the years 651–2 by those who have examined it bears an effigy which is not that of Constans II and is probably to be identified with Olympius. See M.D. O'Hara, 'A find of Byzantine silver from the mint of Rome for the period A.D. 641–752', *Swiss Numismatic Review* 65 (1985), see no. 7, type 3, and 'Numismatic evidence for the treason of Pope Martin (A.D. 649–654)', in *Fourteenth Annual Byzantine Studies Conference, Abstracts of Papers* (Houston, Texas 1988), 53.

[82] See Van Dieten, *Geschichte der Patriarchen*, p. 101; Ostrogorsky, *Geschichte*, p. 100; Bréhier and Aigrain, pp. 170ff.; Stratos, *Byzantium in the Seventh Century*, vol. III, pp. 112–25.

[83] See Bréhier and Aigrain, *ibid.*; Van Dieten, *Geschichte der Patriarchen*, pp. 101f. and 107ff.; Haldon, 'Ideology and social change', 173–7; Cameron, 'Byzantine Africa', 57f.; on the question of synods and their legitimacy, see also, in addition to the literature cited by these authorities, V. Peri, 'I concili ecumenici come struttura portante della gerarchia ecclesiastica', in *17th International Byzantine Congress, Major Papers*, pp. 59–81. For a summary of

The imperial Church and the politics of authority 311

Before Maximus was exiled, however, the emperor had effectively won the battle. On 27 December 653, the patriarch Paul died and, after a lively debate as to his suitability, in which the emperor even called the captive Pope Martin as a character witness, Pyrrhus was elected for the second time to the patriarchal throne, although he died shortly after – in June of 654 – having achieved very little.[84] His successor, Peter, presided over the provisional reconciliation of Rome and Constantinople. Martin was in exile and, under pressure from the exarch, a new pope was elected in Rome, Eugenius I, whose position was confirmed in 655. The patriarch Peter presented the papal emissaries with a compromise formula, a formula which in essence resolved nothing, using an ambiguous terminology which left both the traditionalist and monothelete positions open. The apocrisiaries accepted it without demur.[85] The Typos remained in force, although its ban on discussion now became less significant; but in spite of these developments, Maximus still refused to admit that the emperor had any jurisdiction in the debate. Indeed, his disciples were able to inform the Roman Church of events in Constantinople, with the result that the patriarch Peter's *synodika* – his formal announcement of appointment and request for recognition – were rejected. Pope Eugenius was clearly under local pressure to conform with this turn of events.[86] On Eugenius' death, however, his successor Vitalian (657–72) recognised Peter and sent his own declaration of faith, in which he adopted as open and neutral a position as possible. Relations seemed to be restored, in spite of the ongoing difficulties with Maximus and his supporters.[87] And in 658, Constans formally renewed the privileges of the Roman Church in recognition of Vitalian's co-operative and reconciliatory stance.[88]

Maximus continued to maintain his position, however, in spite of these developments in the situation and, although from the emperor's point of view the situation was now under control, Maximus still constituted a vocal and dangerous source of opposition to imperial authority. In 662, finally, he and his disciples were brought back from exile in Thrace to the capital, where they were mutilated and exiled to distant Lazica. The great

---

the conflict between Rome and Constantinople, see Herrin, *Formation of Christendom*, pp. 255–9.

[84] See Theophanes, 351.23–4; Nicephorus, Chron., 118.17; Grumel, *Regestes*, vol. I, no. 194; Van Dieten, *Geschichte der Patriarchen*, pp. 104–5.

[85] Van Dieten, *Geschichte der Patriarchen*, pp. 106ff.

[86] Van Dieten, *Geschichte der Patriarchen*, pp. 107, note 6 and pp. 108–9; Stratos, *Byzantium in the Seventh Century*, vol. III, pp. 126–8. Cf. Grumel, *Regestes*, vol. I, no. 305; *Liber Pontificalis* I, 341.

[87] Stratos, *Byzantium in the Seventh Century*, vol. III, pp. 126–8; Van Dieten, *Geschichte der Patriarchen*, pp. 112–14; cf. Mansi XI, 200D, for Vitalian's name being added to the Diptychs at Constantinople.

[88] Dölger, *Regesten*, no. 229.

opponent of the emperor died in the same year.[89] His second 'trial' and exile, followed by his death, marked the end of the 'public' controversy over imperial and official Church monotheletism in the Eastern empire. The debate and its political ramifications illustrate the struggle conducted at an ideological level over the locus of authority – both in secular and theological respects. But, although this conflict took centre stage, it was by no means the only instance during the reign of Constans where the question of the nature and extent of imperial authority was raised.

Armenia, which had been predominantly monophysite since about 500, had been officially united with the imperial Church since an agreement of union made in 571; and in 591, as Maurice received further districts from the grateful Chosroes II, a Chalcedonian Catholicate was established in the Byzantine region of the country, paralleled on Persian territory by a monophysite Catholicate. In 633 at the synod of Theodosioupolis (Erzerum), Heraclius was able to win the Armenian Church over to his monenergite formula. But there was powerful opposition to this development. In 648/9, the patriarch Paul II and the emperor tried to reaffirm the union with the Armenian Church, partly inspired by the complaints of the non-Armenian soldiers in the Armenian districts of the empire that the local monophysite population and its leaders excluded them from communion and treated them as heretics. Constans and Paul ordered the formal union of the Churches, and the acceptance by the Armenians of both the Tome of Leo and the doctrine of Chalcedon.[90] In reply, the Armenian Church returned a clear statement of its monophysite faith at the synod of Dvin. Constans was only able to assert his authority by marching with a large army into Armenian territory and forcing acceptance of his policy, in 653. Needless to say, such an agreement remained superficial in the extreme, and monophysitism continued to be the creed of the Armenian Church.[91]

Constans' treatment of Maximus and his followers, however, had political repercussions for the emperor and his policies. It seems clear from the sources that he was not a popular ruler in Constantinople, especially after his brother Theodosius was compelled to enter the clergy; and it is not unlikely that his decision to transfer the seat of government to the West – Rome or Sicily – was at least in part stimulated by this atmosphere.[92] While in the West, the most important feature of his relations with the

---

[89] See Bréhier and Aigrain, pp. 173–5; Van Dieten, *Geschichte der Patriarchen*, p. 114.
[90] Dölger, *Regesten*, no. 227. For the background, see Frend, *The Rise of the Monophysite Movement*, pp. 308–15; R. Grousset, *Histoire de l'Arménie des origines à 1071* (Paris 1947), pp. 234ff. and 298–302; Bréhier and Aigrain, pp. 116f.
[91] See Sebeos, 112ff. and 134ff.; Van Dieten, *Geschichte der Patriarchen*, pp. 100f.; Bréhier and Aigrain, pp. 157–60.
[92] Bréhier and Aigrain, pp. 175 and 178f.; Van Dieten, *Geschichte der Patriarchen*, p. 115.

Church was his grant of autocephaly to the Church of Ravenna. This appears to have been primarily a result of the arguments and influence of the archbishop of Ravenna, Maurus, who will no doubt have pointed out the difficult and anomalous position of his Church, a suffragan of Rome and whose position in the hierarchy was obviously not commensurate with its much higher status in the civil and military establishment. The exarch Gregory supported Maurus' petition, possibly – as the document itself makes clear – because the Church of Ravenna had made payments in cash to the exarch – whether on a personal basis or officially for the support of the military-administrative needs of the exarchate remains unknown.[93] It is certainly clear that the imperial fisc benefited from the taxation raised from the Sicilian patrimony of Ravenna; and since it seems clear that from the sixth century the state had used the Church of Ravenna as its fiscal agent in its Italian territories, the reward of autocephaly was a measure of Constans' gratitude and the reliance of the state upon it.[94]

The sixth ecumenical council and the end of monotheletism

Constans' reign ended with his assassination in Sicily in 668. The abortive coup of the Armenian commander of the *Opsikion* forces, Mzez Gnouni (Mizizios in the Greek sources) was speedily followed by the establishment of a firm rule by Constantine IV, who also initiated the process of reconciliation with Rome. Constantine seems to have tried genuinely to adopt a neutral stance in the debate, concerned as he clearly was with the political, military and economic situation of the state. From his accession in 668, however, political and military problems had overshadowed such matters, and the great siege of Constantinople by the Arabs in the years 674–8 prevented any attempts to conduct a meaningful and consequential ecclesiastical policy. Only in respect of the Church of Ravenna does the emperor seem to have taken any decisions, and in two decrees of 671 and 677 the emperor regulated the rights of ordination of the archbishop of Ravenna and freed clerics from harbour- and customs-dues. He also limited the time that the archbishop of Ravenna should spend in Rome at his consecration – the latter already suggesting the first move in the subordination of Ravenna to Rome which was ordered in 682.[95]

Once the threat from the Arabs was past, however, and a truce had been

---

[93] See Dölger, *Regesten*, no. 233; and esp. T.S. Brown, 'The Church of Ravenna and the imperial administration in the seventh century', *EHR* 94 (1979), 1–28, see 12ff. and 16ff.; Guillou, *Régionalisme*, pp. 167ff. and 206–7.
[94] Brown, 'The Church of Ravenna', 17–20.
[95] Dölger, *Regesten*, nos. 237 and 238; Brown, 'The Church of Ravenna', 20ff.; Guillou, *Régionalisme*, pp. 177f.

arranged (in 678),[96] Constantine turned to the question of the relationship between Rome and Constantinople. Although the names of neither of the Popes Adeodatus (672–6) or Donus (676–8), the successors of Vitalian, had been entered in the Diptychs at Constantinople, relations seem nevertheless to have been less hostile than during the first half of Constans' reign. Hostility between Ravenna and Rome persisted until the deaths of the two main protagonists, Pope Vitalian himself (in 672) and archbishop Maurus (in 673), when the tension relaxed somewhat. The monothelete patriarch Theodore, however, who was elected in August 677, together with the patriarch of Antioch, Makarios (also a firm monothelete), requested that the emperor permit the erasure of the name of Pope Vitalian also from the Diptychs.[97] Constantine was not prepared to condone this step, however, the more so since, as he states in his letter to the pope, Vitalian had supported him against the usurper Mzez in 668. In this letter, addressed to Donus in 678, but delivered to the latter's successor Agathon, the emperor asked the pope to convene local councils to debate the key question of the relationship of the one or two wills and energies to the pronouncements of the Fathers of the Church and the five ecumenical councils. He represented the debate as one over terminological differences between two equally orthodox schools of thought. And while he intimated that an ecumenical council would be desirable, it was important first to debate the matter thoroughly, and he requested that the pope send representatives from Rome and the Western Churches to Constantinople to discuss the whole matter thoroughly.[98] Interestingly, Constantine admitted that an imperial edict would not itself resolve either the problem or end the debate, a marked change from the point of view of his predecessors, from Zeno on up to Constans II.[99]

The pope took some time to consider this approach; and in doing so he wrote to all the metropolitans of the Western Church, asking them to convoke local councils and transmit their conclusions to him. Some sent their responses directly to the emperor.[100] But by Easter of the year 680, the Western Church had sent its replies to Rome and, following a local meeting in Rome itself, the pope sent two letters to Constantinople, one to the emperor and another, shorter letter, containing a formal profession of

---

[96] Dölger, Regesten, no. 239.
[97] Bréhier and Aigrain, pp. 183f.; Van Dieten, Geschichte der Patriarchen, p. 126.
[98] Text of the letter: Mansi XI, 195–201; Riedinger, 2–10; Dölger, Regesten, no. 242; general background: Stratus, Byzantium in the Seventh Century, vol. IV, pp. 57ff. and 119ff.; and for background and summary of events leading up to the sixth ecumenical council, see Herrin, Formation of Christendom, pp. 274ff.
[99] Mansi, XI, 200C; Riedinger, 8.20–22.   [100] Bréhier and Aigrain, pp. 184f.

faith and a rejection of the heresy of monotheletism.[101] In the interim, the patriarch Theodore had managed to have Vitalian's name removed from the Diptychs, partly because the long delay in Rome's reply may have suggested to Constantine a rejection of his proposals. But in November 679 Constantine replaced Theodore, who was proving an embarrassment to his attempts at reconciliation, and enthroned the more amenable patriarch George, a Syrian by birth.[102]

In September of 680, therefore, the Western delegation arrived with the pope's letter in Constantinople; and on 10 December the emperor ordered the patriarch George to convoke a council and to invite also the patriarch of Antioch, Makarios, and his representatives, along with the representatives of the orthodox (Chalcedonian) patriarch of Alexandria.[103] The council met for its opening session in the imperial hall within the palace known as the Troullos, or cupola, on 7 November 680. The emperor himself opened the deliberations and personally presided over the first eleven and the last sessions of the eighteen which took place up to 16 September 681.[104] The results of the council were the abandonment of an imperial policy of monotheletism. Almost immediately, in the first session, the Roman delegation levelled accusations against the patriarchs Sergius, Pyrrhus, Paul and Peter, against Cyrus of Alexandria and Theodore of Pharan. Only Makarios of Antioch and his supporter, the monk Stephen, who seem to have genuinely represented the feelings of the neo-Chalcedonian communities of Syria and Palestine, defended their monothelete position, although with little success. In the ninth session, they were condemned also; and in the thirteenth session the supposed founders of the heresy were anathematised.[105]

In the final session, at which the emperor was once again present, the condemned patriarchs, along with Makarios of Antioch and Stephen, were formally condemned by name. Copies of the acts of the council were sent to all patriarchates, that to Rome accompanied by a letter in the name of the council and the emperor confirming the orthodoxy of the Roman see. But Agathon had died while the council was still meeting, and when news

---

[101] Mansi, XI, 234–86; Riedinger, 52–120 (to the emperor); and 286–315; Riedinger, 122–160. See Bréhier and Aigrain, p. 185; Van Dieten, *Geschichte der Patriarchen*, pp. 132–4.
[102] See Theophanes, 354.24; 355.1–4; and Bréhier and Aigrain, p. 185; Van Dieten, *Geschichte der Patriarchen*, p. 129.
[103] Dölger, *Regesten*, no. 244. The meeting was not originally understood as an ecumenical council, but adopted this title during its first session: see Bréhier and Aigrain, p. 186 and note 7.
[104] Bréhier and Aigrain, pp. 187–90; Van Dieten, *Geschichte der Patriarchen*, pp. 134–42; Stratos, *Byzantium in the Seventh Century*, vol. IV pp. 123ff.; Ostrogorsky, *Geschichte*, pp. 106f.
[105] Mansi, XI, 213A–B, 216C, 383C and 553D (Riedinger, 20.20–22.6; 24.7ff.; 270.4ff.; 578.12ff.). For the *confessio* of Makarios, see ibid., 349–59; Riedinger, 216.11–230.26.

316 *Byzantium in the seventh century*

arrived that Leo II had succeeded him, the letter was readdressed. Following tradition, an imperial edict was then drawn up and exhibited in the Hagia Sophia, in which the emperor confirmed the decisions reached during the council and threatened punishment on those who refused to conform.[106] Similarly, a *iussio* was issued to all the dioceses of the empire informing them in turn of the decisions of the council.

The sixth council thus sounded the death-knell for imperial monotheletism in the eastern empire, although it was to be briefly and unsuccessfully revived again under Philippicus Bardanes (711–13). It also marked the reconciliation of Eastern and Western Churches, although at the expense of Constantinopolitan claims to equality with Rome – the condemnation of the erring patriarchs by name meant as much. It signified in addition, however, the end of the unified Christian world, for the monophysite communities of the lost provinces were not even considered in the council's deliberations. This reflects primarily, of course, the fact that these monophysite communities were outside the empire. The questions which the sixth council was assembled to resolve were all questions which concerned the Christian communities still under Christian political authority. But the sixth council marks a break with the past, and at the same time the beginnings of a more emphatically introverted political-theological culture and ideological consensus. The East was no longer as important as it had been.[107] And the monophysites themselves regarded Constantine IV as having been bought by the papacy and as having abandoned his own convictions. Whether this later comment has any value is difficult to say, but there must be little doubt that the monophysite communities in the lost Eastern provinces can have had little sympathy with their Western brethren after this time.[108]

Constantine continued his policy of reconciliation with Rome at the expense of Ravenna, too. In 681 he ordered a reduction in the rate of assessment of the basic taxes on the papal patrimonial lands in both Sicily and Calabria;[109] and in 682/3 he placed the see of Ravenna once more

---

[106] Bréhier and Aigrain, pp. 189–90; Van Dieten, *Geschichte der Patriarchen*, pp. 141–3. For the letter to the pope, see Mansi XI, 683–8; Riedinger, 830.4–5 and the comments of Van Dieten, *Geschichte der Patriarchen*, p. 143 and note 53; see also Dölger, *Regesten*, no. 247; Grumel, *Regestes*. vol. I, no. 312. For the imperial edict, Dölger, *Regesten*, no. 245; and for the council and its significance, see Herrin, *The Formation of Christendom*, pp. 277–80, who stresses in particular the innovative procedures adopted to verify the texts read to the meetings, a major development in the intellectual and political history of the Church.

[107] See Winkelmann's comment, *Die östlichen Kirchen*, pp. 111–12.

[108] See Michael Syr., vol. II, 447–8 and 457. For the later history of these communities, see Bréhier and Aigrain, pp. 479ff.

[109] Dölger, *Regesten*, no. 250.

under papal jurisdiction.[110] On his death in 685 there was once again religious unity across the Christian world, although the continued existence of strong monophysite communities, as well as monothelete communities in the lands under Muslim political control, remained an important factor in the political and ecclesiastical make-up of the cultures of the east Mediterranean world.

The Quinisext council and the divergence of East from West

Constantine's son, Justinian II, clearly saw himself also as a true defender of orthodoxy. So much is clear in his letter to the pope of 687, in which he writes of his adherence to the decisions of the sixth council of 680/1, a letter drawn up after a general assembly of representatives of the pope, the patriarch, along with the metropolitans and bishops present in Constantinople, the demes, the palatine parade units and the provincial field-armies – *Opsikion, Anatolikōn, Armeniakōn, Thrakēsiōn*, Italy, Sicily, Africa and the imperial fleet – which was held to confirm the acts of the council.[111] He saw himself, too, as occupying the traditional position of the emperor in respect of the Church – it was his duty to convoke and organise general councils and to cater for the legislative activity of the Church; he was the defender of dogma and the faith; and he made this position clear by his actions in not inviting papal representatives, for example, to attend the Quinisext council of 692. They were present, but not by the emperor's invitation.[112]

The Quinisext council met primarily to impress upon the *oikoumenē* Justinian's own role, and to deal with a wide range of disciplinary and related matters. It did not concern itself directly with the major theological issues which had concerned the fifth and sixth general councils, the acts of which the council of 692 was called upon to confirm and to elaborate, hence its popular title, *penthektē*, or *quinisextum*. Instead, and as the emperor's opening statement makes clear, it was concerned with such matters as the evidence for paganism in the provincial communities. The canons of the council make this concern with Church discipline apparent. Opening with a general statement of orthodoxy and affirming the decisions of all six ecumenical councils, the first canon of the Quinisext repeats the anathemata pronounced in the sixth council – in particular that on Pope Honorius. The second canon recognises all the apostolic canons, but goes

---

[110] Dölger, *Regesten*, no. 251; Brown, 'The Church of Ravenna' above, 22f.; Guillou, *Régionalisme*, pp. 207–8; Herrin, *Formation of Christendom*, pp. 280–2.
[111] Text: Mansi XI, 737–8; Riedinger, 886f. See Dölger, *Regesten*, no. 254; Bréhier and Aigrain, pp. 192–3; Van Dieten, *Geschichte der Patriarchen*, pp. 146ff.
[112] Cf. *Liber Pontificalis*, I 372ff.; Stratos, *Byzantium in the Seventh Century*, vol. V, pp. 45ff.

on to regard the disciplinary canons of the ecumenical councils and the local synods of the Eastern Church only (with the exception of those of the council of Carthage) as valid. The remaining one hundred canons of the Quinisext deal exclusively with questions of clerical discipline and the regulation of the Christian communities, and they make clear the fact that, in spite of the numerous divergences between Eastern and Western Churches, this council assumed that it was acting for the whole Christian community – that it was ecumenical – and that it could, therefore, impose 'Byzantine' practice on the West, on the monophysite communities of the East and upon Armenia. Roman practice, indeed, was openly criticised in the acts and canons themselves.[113] Quite apart from this, canon 36 asserted the equivalence of Rome and Constantinople in the ecclesiastical hierarchy,[114] a ruling which demonstrates quite clearly the difference between the policies of Justinian II and those of his father. The latter worked for reconciliation and, as we have seen, was regarded in some circles as having betrayed the interests of the Eastern Church to Rome. Justinian, partly to reassert his authority on the Byzantine Church, partly, no doubt, out of a genuine conviction, defended the interests of Constantinople and thus, inevitably, came into conflict with Rome.[115]

The Roman response can hardly have come as a surprise. Pope Sergius, who succeeded in 687 after the death of Conon, repudiated the signatures of the papal legates, when he received his own copy of the canons, and refused to sign his own name. He protested that a number of the canons directly contradicted established Roman practice and traditions, in some cases even in the East. He refused likewise to recognise the claims of the Quinisext for the apostolicity of a number of canons from earlier synods; and he objected especially to canons 3 and 13 relative to the marriage of the clergy (which fixed less severe penalities for clerics involved in relationships within the prohibited degrees of affinity and which ordered clerics who were married to remain with their wives if they were of the rank of deacon or priest – conflicting with Roman practice, by which priests had to renounce their wives before entering the diaconate).

[113] For the canons of the Quinisext, see Mansi, XI, 921–1006. The acts of the council have not survived, only the concluding address to the emperor, the signatures of those present, and the canons themselves. For discussion, see Winkelmann, *Die östlichen Kirchen*, p. 113; Van Dieten, *Geschichte der Patriarchen*, pp. 153–4; Bréhier and Aigrain, pp. 195–6, 474f. and 485–8; and esp. V. Laurent, 'L'œuvre canonique du concile in Trullo (691–692), source primaire du droit de l'église orientale', *REB* 23 (1965), 7–41. For the most modern analysis, see Ohme, *Das Concilium Quinisextum und seine Bischofsliste*.
[114] Mansi, XI, 959.
[115] For a detailed treatment of subsequent events and Justinian's relationship with the papacy, see F. Görres, 'Justinian II. und das römische Papsttum', *BZ* 17 (1908), 440–50; also J.D. Breckenridge, 'Evidence for the nature of the relations between Pope John VII and the Byzantine emperor Justinian II', *BZ* 65 (1972), 364–74; Stratos, *Byzantium in*

Justinian responded in what was almost predictable fashion. The *magistros* Sergius was ordered to Italy, where he arrested immediately the bishop John of Porto and the clerk Boniface, two of the pope's close advisers, and had them sent off to Constantinople. Shortly thereafter, the *prōtospatharios* Zacharias was despatched with orders to arrest the pope himself.[116] But the situation was now very different from that of the 650s. Local sentiment and tradition, feelings of separateness and difference from the Eastern parts of the empire, together with a less pressing need for imperial military support (a peace had been concluded with the Lombards in about 680), meant that even the Ravenna troops were no longer willing to act unquestioningly on behalf of distant emperors. The Roman troops and those of Ravenna turned on Zacharias, and he escaped only with the aid of the pope.[117]

Justinian's deposition in 695 and his replacement by Leontius (695–8) and then Tiberius II Apsimar (698–705) do not seem appreciably to have altered this situation, and it was only during Justinian's second reign (705–11) that a reconciliation of sorts took place. In spite of his emphasis on the pre-eminence of Constantinople and his anti-Roman perspective in regard to Church discipline and practice, Justinian II seems also to have been fully aware of the wider context of his policies. In two *iussiones* of about 687, for example, that is at the outset of his reign, he ordered the repayment of monies extracted in lieu of unpaid tax from the Roman Church in Sicily and elsewhere, and the reduction of the tax-assessment on papal properties in Bruttium and Lucania, orders which follow on from the policies of his father's reign.[118] The papal response to the canons of the Quinisext changed this, of course, but the original direction of the first years of his reign are clear enough.

Justinian's second reign was marked by a distinct effort at reconciliation. In his first year he directed a request to the pope, that the latter might convene an apostolic Roman synod to discuss the decisions and canons of the Quinisext and decide which were acceptable and which not to the Roman Church.[119] The pope, John VII, died in 707 without taking advantage of this opportunity, and he was succeeded by Constantine, whom Justinian asked to pay a formal visit to Constantinople. In 710, the new pope, accompanied by a considerable retinue of clergy, set out, stopping *en*

---

the Seventh Century, vol. V, pp. 48–53; Ostrogorsky, *Geschichte*, p. 116; Herrin, *Formation of Christendom*, pp. 284–7; and see Grumel, *Regestes*, vol. I, no. 317.

[116] Dölger, *Regesten*, no. 259; Stratos, *Byzantium in the Seventh Century*, vol. V, pp. 53–6; Ostrogorsky, *Geschichte*, pp.116–17.

[117] Bréhier and Aigrain, p. 197; Brown, 'The Church of Ravenna' 25; Van Dieten, *Geschichte der Patriarchen*, pp. 153–5; Ostrogorsky, *Geschichte*, pp. 116–17; Guillou, *Régionalisme*, pp. 209–11.

[118] Dölger, *Regesten*, nos. 255 and 256. [119] Dölger, *Regesten*, no. 264.

route at Naples, Palermo, Reggio and Otranto (where the winter was spent), before proceeding to Chios and on to Constantinople. He met the emperor at Nicomedia in 711, and it seems that a compromise formula was worked out. Later evidence suggests that some fifty of the 102 canons of the Quinisext were formally accepted by the Western delegation. After state receptions and a mass, at which the pope celebrated the communion, he left in October 711 for Rome once more.[120] Shortly after, Justinian was deposed and killed by the rebels under Philippicus Bardanes.

While his second reign was marked by an eccentricity which has earned him a certain notoriety among historians,[121] the policies he pursued, especially in the period of his first reign from 685 to 695 demonstrate an emphasis on the assertion of his authority as emperor not over the details of dogma, but over the general welfare and direction of the Church, reinforced by the emphasis in the imperial ideology on his position as pious defender of the faith.[122] His relations with the Church, as far as the limited evidence suggests, were those of a protector and patron – the edict of 688 in favour of the church of St Demetrius in Thessaloniki is a good illustration.[123] His relations with the patriarch Callinicus, in contrast, were stormy, primarily on the grounds of Callinicus' efforts to hold the emperor back from his cruel persecutions of the last years of his first reign. But Justinian was to let nothing stand in his way, and when the patriarch attempted to change his mind with regard to the demolition of a church, which was to make way for a new, imperial construction, Justinian was unmoved.[124]

Justinian's deposition, and the short rule of the Armenian Philippicus Bardanes, brought with it a major shift, albeit of short duration, in imperial ecclesiastical policy. The new emperor announced his rejection of the acts of the sixth council even before entering the city and ordered both the removal of the image of that council from the palace precincts (before he would enter) and the restoration to the Diptychs of the patriarch Sergius and the other Churchmen condemned for their espousal and promotion of

---

[120] Bréhier and Aigrain, pp. 198–200; Van Dieten, *Geschichte der Patriarchen*, pp. 161ff. See Dölger, *Regesten*, nos. 266–9 (note 269, for October 711, by which the emperor renews all the privileges of the Roman Church). For the fifty acceptable canons, see the ninth-century account of Anastasius Bibliothecarius, in Mansi XII, 982; and for the background and sequence of events, Stratos, *Byzantium in the Seventh Century*, vol. V, pp. 131–5; Herrin, *Formation of Christendom*, pp. 287–9.

[121] Although attempts have been made to redeem his reputation: see C. Head, 'Towards a reinterpretation of the second reign of Justinian II: 705–711', B 40 (1970), 14–32.

[122] J.D. Breckenridge, *The Numismatic Iconography of Justinian II (A.D. 685–695, 705–711)* (New York 1959), esp. pp. 92f. For the general context, see Haldon, 'Ideology and social change', 189; also Van Dieten, *Geschichte der Patriarchen*, p. 146 and note 2.

[123] Dölger, *Regesten*, no. 258.

[124] Van Dieten, *Geschichte der Patriarchen*, pp. 157f.; see Theophanes, 367.22sq.

monotheletism. His actions are explained by the deacon Agathon, who later recopied the acts of the sixth council destroyed on Philippicus' orders, in terms of his probable monophysite background, but more especially in terms of his having been a pupil of the abbot Stephen of Antioch who, together with Makarios, had been the last defenders of monothelete doctrine at the sixth council.[125]

The patriarch Cyrus was deposed, probably because, like a number of others, he refused to sign Philippicus' *tomos* condemning the sixth council. He was replaced with a man more to Philippicus' liking, the deacon and chartulary John, who became John VI; although the orthodox establishment seems to have been able to have an original and much less acceptable imperial candidate dropped.[126] The new patriarch, along with other prominent Churchmen, including Andreas of Crete and Germanus of Cyzicus, later patriarch, faced with imperial pressure to conform, had little choice but to go along with the revived monothelete policy. The extent to which they may have seriously regarded it as a valid doctrine remains unknown;[127] but the context of the later seventh century provides a good reason for this last effort (as it turned out) to arrive at a compromise formula in the Christological debate.

In the first place, relations with Armenia were extremely difficult, due both to the constant strife within Armenia between different factions, pro-Byzantine and pro-Arab, and to the monophysite creed of the majority of the population. In addition, there was the frequent intervention of the Caliphate on one side or the other. The political and military importance of the country was recognised by both empire and caliphate, but religious differences meant that there existed a constant tension between the Byzantine and Armenian populations and their leaders. It is possible that Philippicus' monothelete policy reflects a desire to overcome these conflicts and represents a last effort at union. An edict of Justinian II for 711 ordered all Armenians within the empire to recognise the authority of the patriarch of Constantinople, partly a response to the recent desertion to the caliphate of the pro-Byzantine faction of the Armenian nobility: and the Caliphate took advantage of the situation by granting Armenia its autonomy and religious freedom, restoring the exiled nobles and placing Smbat Bagratuni, from a pro-Byzantine clan, at the head of the Armenian forces. Henceforth,

---

[125] See Mansi XII, 192C-E; Riedinger, 899.10ff.; and the account in Van Dieten, *Geschichte der Patriarchen*, pp. 163f.
[126] Van Dieten, *Geschichte der Patriarchen*, pp. 166f.
[127] Bréhier and Aigrain, pp. 206f.; Van Dieten, *Geschichte der Patriarchen*, pp. 167–71. See S. Vailhé, 'Saint André de Crète', EO 5 (1902), 378–87. Andreas seems later, like Germanus, to have repented of his decision: see PG LXXXXVII 1437–44, a short poem in which he suggests as much; and the discussion of this by H. Heisenberg, 'Ein jambisches Gedicht des Andreas von Kreta', BZ 10 (1901), 505–14.

Armenia remained under Arab suzerainty, and although contacts with the empire were never severed, the synod of Mantzikert of 719 – which ordered the expulsion of all Chalcedonians from Armenia – meant the end of any Byzantine pretensions in the region. Philippicus' monotheletism, given his Armenian, and possibly monophysite, background, seems to have been a forlorn attempt to bring the Armenians back into the political orbit of the empire.[128]

In the second place, Philippicus may have hoped that a return to the policies of Constans II would both enhance his own authority within the empire and regain divine support – the defeats of the previous years, the final loss of North Africa after 698, the increasing power of the Bulgars, all had a profound effect on contemporaries; and this policy may well have been seen as one potential way of reversing the process.[129] In the event, of course, it was a failure. The papacy predictably refused to condone the shift, rejecting both the imperial edict and Philippicus' portrait, and declaring him a heretic. At the news of the destruction of the icon of the sixth council, the clergy and population of Rome paraded all six conciliar images in affirmation of their orthodoxy.[130] The Bulgars, on the pretext of avenging their erstwhile ally Justinian, invaded Thrace and met with little or no opposition. Even within the army Philippicus seems to have had little real support, although whether as a result of his innovation in religious policy or his failures as emperor generally is unclear, and in 713 he was deposed by officers and soldiers of the *Opsikion* army based in Thrace.[131] His successor, the imperial secretary Artemius, took the imperial name Anastasius II and immediately reversed Philippicus' policies. The image of the sixth council was restored to its position; the pope was apprised of the new emperor's orthodoxy and his adherence to the sixth council's decisions; while the patriarch John VI now sent an explanatory letter to the pope, detailing his reasons for going along with the previous emperor's religious policies. John died in the summer of 715 and was succeeded by Germanus of Cyzicus who, having repudiated monotheletism, was supported by the papal legate in the election to the patriarchal throne.[132]

Anastasius himself did not survive John by more than a few weeks. Within a few months a mutiny of naval and land units compromised his

---

[128] Justinian's edict: Dölger, *Regesten*, no. 272 (wrongly ascribed to Philippicus); J. Laurent, *L'Arménie entre Byzance et l'Islam depuis la conquête arabe jusqu'en 886* (Paris 1919), pp. 202–6; Bréhier and Aigrain, pp. 203–4; Grousset, *Histoire de l'Arménie*, pp. 307–15.
[129] See Haldon, 'Ideology and social change', 186–9.
[130] Bréhier and Aigrain, p. 207; Ostrogorsky, *Geschichte*, pp. 127–8; Van Dieten, *Geschichte der Patriarchen*, pp. 170–1.
[131] See chapter 2, above.
[132] Bréhier and Aigrain, p. 208; Van Dieten, *Geschichte der Patriarchen*, pp. 172f.; Dölger, *Regesten*, no. 273.

The imperial Church and the politics of authority 323

position, and he was compelled to abdicate. Theodosius, his successor, was able to continue the preparations which had been set in motion by Anastasius for the imminent Arab siege of the city; but he, too, was soon compelled to vacate the throne for the general of the *Anatolikōn thema*, Leo. And it was Leo who opened the next chapter in Byzantine ecclesiastical and theological history. But the iconoclastic controversy is the subject of another book.[133]

As in the case of secular politics, the seventh century opened with a unity, a Christian Church which represented a unified *oikoumenē* – whatever the realities of the debate between Chalcedonian and monophysite communities, such differences were thought to be surmountable and subject to discussion and agreement. By the end of the seventh century, the Eastern monophysites were no longer part of the empire, and no longer merited much consideration, although the orthodox communities of Egypt and Syria continued to play a role in the affairs of the Church as a whole. More important, however, the split between Roman and Constantinopolitan politics and practice had finally come out into the open, and in a way which could no longer be papered over. The great split in the Christian world, which was to play such a crucial role in defining the cultural appearance of East and West, had taken place, and was to prove irrevocable.

[133] See chapter 2, above.

CHAPTER 9

Religion and belief

THE CHURCH AND CHRISTIANITY: NEO-CHALCEDONIAN UNIVERSALISM AND HETERODOX PLURALISM

Religion and belief are not, of course, synonymous. In this chapter, I want to look at the 'public' and the 'official' aspects of seventh-century religious and ideological history, rather than at the individual psychology of belief in the early medieval world of the Eastern Roman empire. But since the latter subject is, in several ways, the prerequisite for an understanding of the world as it was perceived and understood by people of this period, a few words on the assumptions which inform my approach are in order.

Although several scholars have approached this problem, of the Byzantine *mentalité*, at a general level, their work has on the whole been descriptive rather than analytic. That is to say, Byzantinists have generally tended towards a presentation of the data from the sources on the forms of belief and its appearance – the specific ideas which together form the imperial ideology, or orthodoxy, or attitudes to the everyday. In the process, the question of the actual generation and reproduction of ideas in their social-psychological context tends to be forgotten. More particularly, the question of the relationship between what people think (as this is presented at different levels in our sources, through histories, hagiographies, letters and so on), about both themselves and about their perceptions of the world and how they act upon that world, how those perceptions inform the possibilities open to them in respect of their social existence has been neglected. There is a dialectical relationship here, of course, between these two forms of human social praxis, and it is through the examination of that dialectical relationship – by relating contexts to effects – that the historian can best approach the whole problem of causal relationships.

The key question is, quite simply: what enabled Byzantines in the period with which we are concerned to think and act as they did? I have elaborated an approach to this problem elsewhere in terms of the interaction between a number of levels of cognition and practice which play a role in constituting both human beings as social beings and the world as perceived by them.

Briefly, these levels or 'moments' can be described as follows. First, the concept of symbolic universe, which refers to the totality of cultural knowledge and practice in a society, within which and through which everyday life is carried on. Within the symbolic universe and drawn from a number of its elements, specific ideological discourses are generated, chiefly a result of the contradictory nature of the social relations of production (that is to say, through the existence of antagonisms between different social groups in respect of their relationships to the means of production and distribution of wealth, to the sources of power and so on; antagonisms which need to be made sense of). Ideological discourses usually serve to mask such contradictions in social relations by first explaining and then legitimating them within a wider framework – that of the symbolic universe. Out of this ideological consciousness and practice specific discourses are then refined, from which they take their logic and vocabulary, and which legitimate through a series of symbolic statements the relationships between groups of individuals on one side, and between such groups and their world on the other. These are what are commonly termed political ideologies, and it is in this sense that the notion of an imperial ideology is employed.

As I have said, the relationship between consciousness and practice should be construed as dialectical and mutually constituting; an instrumental relationship through which individuals receive their sense of self and subjectivity, and which provides them with the conceptual apparatus with which they can express what they 'know' about the world, but that also limits what they can know, and how, to the culturally possible. Contingently, the symbolic universe, within which and through which this instrumental relationship works to constitute human individuals, is *itself* a product of, and is constantly reproduced by, social practice: by the activities of individuals in their social and physical context which serve to reproduce both themselves and the social relations of production, the roles and institutions of their society. It needs to be said that in reality, that is, in the expression of people's experience, consciousness and practice are hardly distinguishable; but an analytic distinction is necessary if this model of cognition and practice is to have any heuristic value.

A useful way into these relationships is to employ the concept of personal and group narrative as an element which generates the construction of social reality and a sense of self. I have argued elsewhere that narratives are important because they are crucial to the link between thinking and doing. For narratives are ways of organising experience in time, they reconstruct experience, whether first- or second-hand, and they therefore act as patterns for future action. But since they are reconstructions, they also necessarily involve evaluation and thus the potential for change. In particular, a change in the order or the relation of elements within a certain narrative involves a change in evaluation, and hence a change in perception of the relationship between self (or group) and the world. Narratives are the key structuring elements in ideology.

Now this is a useful approach to the question of the relationship between thinking and doing on the one hand, and to that of historical change on the other. For the latter is manifestly a result of human action (or reaction). Narratives serve as basic elements in describing and prescribing social practice. But if narratives, and the realities they purport to describe, no longer match the world as it is perceived or experienced, then changes in one or the other can follow: either the narratives are suitably altered in order to make them fit the new perceptions, or the world is acted upon in an effort to make it correspond more closely with the narratives. In the later sixth and seventh centuries it is precisely such efforts at both re-evaluation and the re-establishment of a desired world-order which our sources represent.[1]

---

[1] For useful descriptive surveys of the forms of orthodox Byzantine beliefs, see Beck, *Das byzantinische Jahrtausend*, pp. 257–89, 'Die Byzantiner und ihr Jenseits', SBB (Munich 1979), Heft 6, and 'Orthodoxie und Alltag', in Βυζάντιον. Ἀφιέρωμα στὸν Ἀνδρέα Ν. Στράτο (2 vols., Athens 1986), vol. II, pp. 329–46. See also A. Každan and G. Constable, *People and Power in Byzantium* (Washington D.C. 1982), esp. pp. 76ff.; and the useful general survey by P. Kawerau, *Das Christentum im oströmisch-byzantinischen Reich bis zur osmanisch-türkischen Eroberung Konstantinopels*, CSCO, vol. 441, Subsidia 64 (*Ostkirchengeschichte*, II) (Louvain 1982). See also C. Mango, *Byzantium: The Empire of New Rome*, esp. pp. 151–217.

I have outlined my own approach in greater detail in 'Ideology and social change', esp. 145–6 and 150–3, with literature. On the relationship between cognition and practice, see in particular R. Bhaskar, 'Emergence, explanation and emancipation', in *Explaining Human Behavior: Consciousness, Human Action and Social Structure*, ed. P.F. Secord (Beverly Hills, Calif. 1982), 275–310, esp. 278–88; D.-H. Ruben, *Marxism and Materialism: A Study in Marxist Theory of Knowledge* (Brighton 1979), pp. 95ff.; T.W. Goff, *Marx and Mead: Contribution to a Sociology of Knowledge* (London 1980). On the construction of roles and social realities, see A. Schütz, *Der sinnhafte Aufbau der sozialen Welt* (Vienna 1960); P. Berger and Th. Luckmann, *The Social Construction of Reality* (Harmondsworth 1967), pp. 65–70 and 110ff.; and on narrative, see esp. H. Garfinkel, *Studies in Ethnomethodology* (Englewood Cliffs, N.J. 1967) (together with the important critique of the work of Schütz and an appreciation of Garfinkel by J. Heritage, *Garfinkel and Ethnomethodology* (Cambridge and Oxford 1984)); D. Sperber, *Rethinking Symbolism* (Cambridge 1975), pp. 85–149; Goff, *Marx and Mead*, pp. 112ff.; and W. Labov and J. Waletzky, 'Narrative analysis: oral versions of personal experience', in *Essays on the Verbal and Visual Arts*, ed. J. Holm (Seattle 1967), pp. 12–44.

Pagan survivals?

The degree to which Christianity had been adopted by the populations of the territories remaining to the empire in the second half of the seventh century is still far from clear. While it had been the official religion of the Roman state since the time of Theodosius I, and while, by the end of the sixth century at least, non-Christians are treated by both Chalcedonian and monophysite writers alike as either marginal or backward, it is nevertheless clear that considerable numbers of people continued to observe traditional and pre-Christian cult practices, whether this occurred in a thinly disguised but nevertheless Christian form, in which non-Christian rituals and practices received a Christian veneer, or whether it occurred in an overtly pagan form. To some extent, the question is bound up with the survival of the native – non-Greek – languages of the East Roman world, particularly in Asia Minor, where it has sometimes been assumed that the survival of languages such as Phrygian or Galatian was accompanied also by the survival of pre-Christian cultural traditions and beliefs.[2] Now it is certainly true that non-Greek languages may have survived in Asia Minor well into the seventh century;[3] and they existed, of course, in the Middle Eastern provinces of Syria and Egypt, for example. But while linguistic differences certainly facilitated a degree of local particularism, and – in the cases of Syria, Egypt and North Africa – were on occasion combined with religious differences or disagreements to function as vehicles for sentiments and actions hostile to the state or to the Chalcedonian establishment, there is no reason for assuming automatically that the survival of pre-Hellenistic languages meant also the survival of pre-Christian religions.[4]

The universality of Christianity was the proclaimed reality of the seventh-century Byzantine world. It was necessarily accompanied, in theory at least, by the universality of a single orthodoxy, which from the council of Chalcedon of 451 was represented in the so-called Chalcedonian creed of the two natures – and from the middle of the reign of Justinian I by the neo-Chalcedonian theology based on this and the theological system of Cyril of Alexandria. The only serious challenge to this, within the frame-

---

[2] See especially K. Holl, 'Das Fortleben der Volkssprachen in Kleinasien in nachchristlicher Zeit', *Hermes* 43 (1908), 240–54; criticised by Sp. Vryonis, jr., *Decline of Medieval Hellenism*, pp. 45ff. and 59f.; and in *Βυζαντινά* 1 (1969), 214f.

[3] See esp. P. Charanis, 'Ethnic changes', 23ff., although vitiated by an acceptance of Holl's methodological assumptions. On the survival of Galatian in the first half of the seventh century, see Timotheus Constantinopolitanus, *De Receptione Hereticorum* (*PG* LXXXVI 11–68), 13B–16A; and note J. Gouillard, 'L'Hérésie dans l'empire byzantin des origines au XIIe siècle', *TM* 1 (1965), 299–324, see 304, on this text.

[4] So Charanis, 'Cultural diversity and the breakdown of Byzantine power in Asia Minor', *DOP* 29 (1975), 9–10.

work of Christianity, was monophysitism, which eventually lost the battle within the East Roman state when the provinces that professed it were lost to the Arabs. But while Christianity in its neo-Chalcedonian or its monophysite form was represented as universal, and was certainly taken by the establishment of Church and state to be so, non-Christian practices and traditions seem to have survived in a number of places. There is a difference, of course, between the subsumption of pagan traditions and practices, and sometimes cult observances, within a Christian framework and the survival of pagan cults as independent active forms of religious devotion and expression. The former represented a process which was, for the great mass of the population of the ancient and early medieval world, an inevitable feature of the transfer of devotion from one – syncretic and pluralistic – set of religious narratives and symbolic systems, to the explicitly anti-pluralistic soteriology of Christianity. In the West, the papacy explicitly permitted the incorporation of Christianised pagan practices or calendar events as a means of promoting the conversion of the barbarians.[5] In the East, such practices and traditions constituted an unacceptable challenge to Christian universality, and an intolerable threat to its claim to mediate between man and God. They had to be dealt with accordingly. In the context of the seventh century, the opposition between these two poles appeared even more starkly.

Pagan cults and practices were thus from the mid-fourth century proscribed. As the imperial Church evolved, along with the increasing identification of the state with the Christian *oikoumenē*, so the legal condemnation and persecution of heathens and 'pagans' increased in intensity, and those who did not openly proclaim their Christianity were progressively excluded from the apparatus of the state. The practice of 'magic', of taking *haruspices*, and related observances were strictly forbidden. Pagan temples and sites of worship were destroyed, sometimes being deliberately replaced with Christian buildings. Officials found guilty of participating in or condoning pagan rituals were dismissed, as were Christians who were found to have lapsed into heathen ways.[6] It was, of course, impossible to eradicate such ancient traditions in a matter of a few years or even over two centuries, forming as they did central elements in people's day-to-day experience and practice and in their narratives of that experience and of

---

[5] The policies of the early Church in Kent provide a good example: see Bréhier and Aigrain, p. 286.
[6] For a general survey of the state's response to the traditional religions and cults, see K.L. Noethlichs, *Die gesetzgeberischen Massnahmen der christlichen Kaiser des 4. Jahrhunderts gegen Häretiker, Heiden und Juden* (Cologne 1971). For the closing or destruction of temples, proscription of cult practices and 'magic', see *CTh*. XVI, 10.4 (a. 354) and XVI, 10.16 (a. 399), with IX, 16.1 and 2. For dismissal of officials and the formal declaration of Christianity, see *CTh*. XVI, 7.5 (a. 391).

their place in the world. On the other hand, Christianity was itself a dynamic social and ideological force, and the repressive measures of the state, while they certainly promoted the interests of the Church, were not themselves alone responsible for the long-term development and success of the new soteriology.

'Pagan' beliefs and practices did, therefore, continue to exist within the late Roman and Byzantine world well into the seventh century at least, and in certain more isolated areas probably longer. It is possible to distinguish two forms of 'survival', however. On the one hand, we have the conscious efforts of members of the social elite and the literate class of the state to maintain, somewhat self-consciously, an antique way of life and system of beliefs – these are chiefly members of the senatorial elite, of the academies with their ancient traditions, and of the educated urban bureaucracy. This form certainly disappears during the later sixth and early seventh centuries. On the other hand, there are the unreflective values and traditional practices of rural populations, particularly in the more remote areas of the empire, or in regions where local cults, for example, retained their social relevance and vigour. 'Pagan' is in this context a misnomer – indeed, the continued use of the term by historians today reflects a somewhat uncritical, and very unfortunate, because quite misleading adoption of a medieval term of reproach and condemnation.

In the former category belong the Academy of Athens, for example, closed by Justinian in 529, and the numerous members of the senatorial and governing elite, many of them purportedly Christians, indicted and tried for paganism during his reign.[7] Indeed, Justinian carried out a series of purges, re-enacting and reinforcing the anti-pagan legislation of his imperial predecessors.[8] Cult centres such as Baalbek/Hierapolis or

[7] See A. Cameron, 'The last days of the Academy of Athens', *Proc. Cambridge Philol. Soc.* 195 (1969), 7–29, and Malalas, 451. See also P. Lemerle, *Le premier humanisme byzantin. Notes et remarques sur enseignement et culture à Byzance des origines au Xe siècle* (Paris 1971), pp. 69f.; H. Blumenthal, '529 and after: what happened to the Academy?', *B* 41 (1978), 369–85; and for Justinian's persecution of senators and bureaucrats, see Jones, *LRE*, vol. I, pp. 285ff. In 529 he ordered the baptism of all pagans and non-Christians under threat of sequestration of property and dismissal from office: *CJ* I, 11.1–10. See also the survey of J. Irmscher, 'Heidnische Kontinuität im justinianischen Staat', in *Seventeenth International Byzantine Congress, Major Papers*, pp. 17–30.

[8] Jones, *LRE*, ibid.; Stein, *Bas-Empire*, vol. II, pp. 369ff.; note J. Constantelos, 'Paganism and the state in the age of Justinian', *Catholic History Review* 50 (1964), 372–80. This affected naturally enough many other aspects of traditional elite culture. Classical learning, inevitably associated in the Christian mind with the pagan past, tended to take an increasingly background role. Classical patterns of presentation and style retreat before the forms and modes of scriptural and patristic writing. While this does not necessarily mean that classical learning was driven out – as has sometimes been argued – it does suggest that it lost its formerly privileged position. Knowledge of the classics, of Attic style, and of classical mythology still retained a crucial significance and symbolised an important element in the self-image of the Byzantine ruling elite. But it had henceforth to be presented

Carrhae/Harran attracted a great deal of imperial attention, of course, and during the sixth century there were a total of seven purges there and in the surrounding districts.[9] But less well-known centres were also purged, and the legislation of the sixth century demonstrates clearly enough that 'paganism' was still regarded as a living force in many parts of the empire. The cult centres at Heliopolis and Harran were still active at the end of the reign of Maurice; the latter occurs in the early Islamic tradition as a well-known pagan centre which flourished well into the Islamic period. The tenacity of such ancient religions makes it clear that legislation and persecution alone were rarely enough to destroy such practices and the beliefs that promoted them.[10] On the other hand, it is clear from the response of the urban population of cities such as Antioch, who was outraged by the continued practice of pagan communities, that Christianity was the majority religion and that pagan centres were intensely localised phenomena.[11]

'Pagan' practices, as defined by contemporaries, existed on a more widespread – a more popular – basis in parts of Asia Minor, however. In 542 Justinian commissioned the monophysite John of Ephesus to carry out a large-scale missionary expedition in western Asia Minor, as a result of which tens of thousands, according to contemporary sources, were brought into the Church. His missionary activity continued throughout the reign of Justinian and into that of Justin II, chiefly in the provinces of Caria, Asia, Lydia and Phrygia.[12] Similar persecutions and missions took place in other parts of the empire, notably Syria and Egypt, although aimed usually at specific cult centres,[13] while in the Western provinces isolated elements of pagan cults continued to exist, although the evidence is sparse. According to a tenth-century source, the (non-Slav) inhabitants

within an entirely Christian and Christianised context. See Averil Cameron, *Agathias* (Oxford 1970), esp. pp. 89ff.; H.-G. Beck, 'Bildung und Theologie im frühmittelalterlichen Byzanz', in *Polychronion. Festschrift F. Dölger* (Heidelberg 1966), pp. 72–81; Lemerle, *Premier humanisme*, pp. 85–7; Cameron, 'Images of authority', 4 and 27f.; and 'New and old in Christian literature', in *Seventeenth International Byzantine Congress, Major Papers*, pp. 45–58.

[9] Jones, *LRE*, vol. II, p. 943; also Rochow, *Die Heidenprozesse unter den Kaisern Tiberius II Konstantinos und Maurikios*, pp. 120ff. See Evagrius, V, 18 (212–14); John of Ephesus, 114ff.

[10] See Rochow, *Die Heidenprozesse*, pp. 126ff.; and *Cambridge History of Islam*, vol. II: *The Further Islamic Lands. Islamic Society and Civilisation*, eds. P.M. Holt, A.K.S. Lambton and B. Lewis (Cambridge 1970), pp. 786–7, on the Sabians (Ṣābi'a) of Harran.

[11] Rochow, *Die Heidenprozesse*, pp. 128f. See also Herrin, *Formation of Christendom*, pp. 184f., for examples of high-ranking pagans in Edessa and Antioch including, according to John of Ephesus and Evagrius, the patriarch Gregory of Antioch. See in general F.R. Trombley, *Hellenic Religion and Christianization c. 370–529* (Religions in the Graeco-Roman World CXV. Leiden 1993).

[12] See Jones, *LRE*, vol. I, pp. 285f. and Rochow, *Die Heidenprozesse*, pp. 121ff. with sources and literature.

[13] See Jones, *LRE*, vol. II, pp. 942–3 (the centre at Philae on the Nile, and the centre and temple of Jupiter Ammon in the Augila oasis). See also Stein, *Bas-Empire*, vol. II, pp. 300–1 and 372.

of the Mani in the Peloponnese were Christianised only during the reign of Basil I,[14] while local cults in Thrace and Macedonia may also have persisted. Here, however, the arrival of Slav peoples may well have overwhelmed the old tradition, and it was the missionary activity of the eighth and, especially, the ninth centuries which reintroduced Christianity on a widespread basis. Paganism in Africa – excluding the case of Egypt – seems on the whole not to have been a significant problem, and to have been anyway confined to the Berber population of the hinterland.[15] But it is clear that, right to the end of the sixth century, pagan cults of one sort or another continued to exist in many parts of the empire and, in certain cases, to enjoy considerable local support; and that a wide range of pre-Christian practices continued to make up an important element of the day-to-day belief patterns of a great number of the ordinary population of the empire.[16]

It is not surprising, therefore, that evidence for pagan survivals, for 'magic' and 'superstition' is still to be found in seventh-century sources; and indeed, the conditions brought about by the Arab incursions and the consequent disruption of life in the provinces as well as in major urban centres – with the interruption in the activities of the local clergy and the episcopate – may have permitted many ancient traditions, which had survived in one form or another as long as this, to experience a revival of sorts.[17] The arrival of new populations – notably Slavs – either as immigrants into the Balkans or as the result of forced transfers to depopulated or underpopulated areas of Asia Minor, must also have affected the areas in which they were settled. Some older, non-Christian religious and linguistic

[14] *DAI* 50.71–6; see D.A. Zakythinos, *Le Despotat grec de Morée, vie et institutions*, revised edn Chr. Maltezou (London 1965), pp. 6–14 and 381f.
[15] See for a good general survey Rochow, 'Zu einigen oppositionellen religiösen Strömungen', 245–50. The slow assimilation and Christianising of the South Balkan Slavs had already begun in the middle of the seventh century. The leader of the Rouchinai in 674, Perbund, knew Greek, and this may reflect a Hellenisation of some leading elements among the immigrant clans. Whether this involved Christianisation is difficult to say. See Lemerle, *Les plus anciens recueils*, vol. II, pp. 113–14; P. Lemerle, 'La Chronique improprement dite de Monemvasie. Le contexte historique et légendaire', *REB* 21 (1963), 5–49, esp. 18ff. Note for the following period also F. Dvornik, *Les Slaves, Byzance et Rome au IXe siècle* (Paris 1926), pp. 235f. For Africa, see Jones, *LRE*, vol. II, p. 942; and see Cameron, *Byzantine Africa*, p. 40.
[16] See the apposite remarks of Jones, *LRE*, vol. II, p. 941.
[17] This is, at least, the implication of canons 8 and 18: the former attempts to re-establish the practice of calling yearly synods for each ecclesiastical province, abandoned due to enemy raids; the latter orders the clergy who had abandoned their flocks for the same reasons (or claimed to have done so) to return to their parishes. See H.J. Magoulias, 'The Lives of Byzantine saints as a source of data for the history of magic in the sixth and seventh centuries A.D.: sorcery, relics and icons', *B* 37 (1967), 228–69. More recently, F.R. Trombley, *The Survival of Paganism in the Byzantine Empire during the pre-Iconoclastic period (540–727)* (Ann Arbor 1981) is useful; but on the context and significance of these 'survivals', see below.

traditions may well have been dealt a fatal blow in this way; more importantly, the supposed universality of Christian belief within the empire must have been seriously jeopardised by these migrations, for such new arrivals can have been only superficially, if at all, Christianised. The regions in which John of Ephesus carried out his missions seem still in the later sixth century to have been populated by many non-Christians. During the trials of large numbers of 'pagans' under Tiberius Constantine in 579 and the following years, the province of Asia was picked out as a particular source of paganism.[18] It is highly likely that the traditional cult practices of such areas continued to receive popular support, in the countryside at least, and they may very well have been given a new lease of life by the destruction of urban centres – which had, on the whole, always been Christianised early and more completely than the surrounding country[19] – and by the consequent removal, or at least the weakening, of Christian supervision.

The probability is that both indigenous and imported non-Christian cults and beliefs proliferated in many regions of Asia Minor, and certainly in the Balkans, during the seventh century, especially in those regions which the clergy had abandoned.[20] But the evidence remains patchy. The canons of the Quinisext which, as we have seen, set out specifically to regulate the clergy and the behaviour and practices of the subjects of the empire, are directed at Christians and tell us little, and then only indirectly, about non-Christians. What they do illustrate, however, is the degree to which the population in different regions of the empire (although again, the canons rarely specify which regions) had subsumed many features of their traditional religious practices and beliefs into Christianity. As mentioned already, this was actually encouraged on occasion in the Western Church as a means of promoting conversion. It may well have been, implicitly, the case in the East, too, on occasion.

What the evidence does illustrate, importantly, is the difficulty faced by any commentator, modern or medieval, in disentangling the complex elements which go to make up any given set of beliefs. Christianity also had its demons and evil spirits, its exorcisms and its rites of purification or damnation, many of which were in effect no different from those of pagan belief, at least at the descriptive level. Members of late Roman and early Byzantine society, from the highest and most privileged to the lowest and

[18] See John of Ephesus III, 33sq.; and Rochow, *Die Heidenprozesse*, pp. 120ff.
[19] See Jones, *LRE*, vol. II, pp. 942f.
[20] The cult of Cybele, for example, which received great support from the local population of Caria and which was condemned by John of Ephesus in the sixth century, was still in existence in the mountains of the same region in the eighth century, as reported by Cosmas of Jerusalem – see Cosmas Hierosolymitanus, *Scholia in Gregorii Nazianzeni Carmina* (*PG* XXXVIII), 502. See also note 10, chapter 9 above.

most oppressed, accepted such ideas and practices as perfectly commonsensical, as part and parcel of day-to-day reality and practice. In Byzantine terms, the difference between magic and miracle is, quite simply, a functional one: the former serves, and is inspired by, the devil; the latter by God. The wondrous qualities of icons, relics, saints' tombs, pieces of the cross, talismans of various sorts, even the power of words recited or chanted at the correct moment in the appropriate form, this is the 'magic' of the Christian symbolic universe. The artifacts are different, but the principles, much older than the Church, are inscribed within the narratives of daily life for all the members of this early medieval world. And it is when these elements take on a broader and more public role – when they threaten the institutionalised and consecrated authority of the Church – that they also pose a threat to, and attract the (unfavourable) attention of the establishment.[21] What the canons of the Quinisext clearly reflect is a view among Churchmen that such practices were taking too significant a role within the otherwise generally Christian framework of life.[22]

The practices themselves reveal a great deal about rural belief and attitudes in the provinces; but what is important about them is that, while they were certainly condemned by the council as 'Hellenic' or pagan, they

[21] These points are made in greater detail and more graphically in the discussion of H.J. Magoulias, 'The Lives of Byzantine Saints'; see also the comments of Beck, *Das byzantinische Jahrtausend*, esp. pp. 264–9; A. Momigliano, 'Popular religious beliefs and the late Roman historians', Studies in Church History VIII (1971), 1–18; P.R.L. Brown, 'Sorcery, demons and the rise of Christianity: from late Antiquity into the Middle Ages', in *Witchcraft Confessions and Accusations* (Cambridge 1970), pp. 17–45; P.P. Joannou, *Démonologie populaire – démonologie critique au XIe siècle* (Wiesbaden 1971); C. Mango, 'Discontinuity with the classical past in Byzantium', in *Byzantium and the Classical Tradition*, eds. M. Mullett and R. Scott (Birmingham 1981) pp. 48–58 (repr. in *Byzantium and its Image: History and Culture of the Byzantine Empire and its Heritage* (London 1984 third essay), see pp. 55–7; and esp. Mango, 'Antique statuary and the Byzantine beholder', *DOP* 17 (1963), 55–75, see 59–64. For the excellent survey of the form and functions of talismans in this context see G. Vikan, 'Art, medicine and magic in early Byzantium', *DOP* 38 (1984), 65–84; and for the functions of icons in this context, C. Belting – Ihm, art. 'Heiligenbild', in *Reallexikon für Antike und Christentum*, fasc. 105 (Stuttgart 1987), 89–95. The debate impinges, of course, on the whole question of the nature of medieval religious culture, of the nature of different levels of practice and understanding, and of different discourses within a shared symbolic universe. See P.R.L. Brown, 'The saint as exemplar in late Antiquity', *Representations* 1 (1983), 1–25; and the survey article of J. Van Engen, 'The Christian Middle Ages as an historiographical problem', *American Historical Review* 91 (1986), 519–52. For the same problem in the context of a very different society, see I. Sorlin, 'Femmes et sorciers. Notes sur la permanence des rituels païens en Russie, XIe–XIVe siècle', *TM* 8 (1981), 459–75.

[22] Compare also the response of the state and the Church to the activities of a priest in the village of Triachia on Cyprus, whose trial is reported by Anastasius of Sinai to have taken place in 638: the priest had secretly led various magical rites and was accused also of corrupting the holy vessels of the Church liturgy. The prefect of the island himself presided over the trial, at which the accused was found guilty and condemned to death by burning. See Beck, *Kirche*, p. 464; for the text, see F. Nau, 'Le Texte grec des récits utiles à l'âme d'Anastase (le Sinaïte)', *OC* 3 (1903), 56–90, see 69f.

do not in fact represent pagan*ism*, that is, non-Christian religions or cults in operation. There is an important difference between the two – as I have already tried to stress – and it would, therefore, be a mistake to argue from the canons of the Quinisext that there was a 'revival of paganism' or anything of the sort at this time. The canons of the Quinisext represent the anxiety of Church and state, and their attitudes both to their own control over the patterns of belief of the populations of the provinces, and to the ways in which their authority was received among the ordinary people of the empire.

The practices which were condemned and forbidden had on the whole, then, nothing to do with paganism – they represented merely the deeply rooted and age-old traditions of local rural or urban culture, a way of life which, without being the least bit un-Christian, could hold on to those features of its pre-Christian traditions which helped it to regulate and understand the vagaries of daily existence, of the seasons and of natural and man-made disasters, or which helped protect against, or ward off, harmful events. The list is revealing. Canon 65 condemns the practice of building fires in front of houses and workshops at the time of the new moon, and of leaping over such fires 'according to the old tradition'; canon 61 condemns soothsayers and diviners, fortune-tellers and similar persons, including those who go about with trained animals such as bears and trick the simpler folk; canon 50 proscribes gaming with dice, and canon 62 forbade a whole series of 'hellenic' practices: celebrating the feast of the Brumalia, the Vota, the Calends, and the dances on the first day of March; it also forbade the invocation of the god Dionysus at the grape-crushing. Similarly, it proscribed the use of comic and satyric masks at such popular festivals, and in particular the practice of masquerading as members of the opposite sex. Canon 94 prohibits the use of 'Hellenic' oaths and curses, and so on.[23] All of these practices were clearly part of the traditional seasonal and yearly rituals of a predominantly Christian population; and while the Church may have had some successes in stamping them out, the survival of feasts such as the Brumalia – which was still celebrated at the imperial court in the mid-eighth century[24] – throws considerable doubt on the efficacy of the rulings. Indeed, the commentary to the canons of the twelfth-century canonist Balsamon shows quite clearly that very many of these practices continued unaffected well into the late Byzantine period, justified on the grounds of 'ancient tradition'.[25] The ninth-century Life of

[23] Canon 65: Mansi, XI, 973A–B; canon 61: 969E–972A; canon 50: 968A–B; canon 62: 972A–C; canon 94: 984B.
[24] See *Vita Stephani iun.*, 1169B–C.
[25] Rhalles-Potles, *Syntagma*, vol. II, see the commentary to canon 24 (p. 359); canon 51 (pp. 424f.); canon 60 (pp. 440f.); canon 61 (pp. 442–7); canon 62 (pp. 448–52). See also D. Simon, 'Balsamon zum Gewohnheitsrecht', in Σχόλια· *Studia ad Criticam Interpretatio-*

St Anthony the Younger records that the saint cured a woman's infertility by writing an incantation on a strip of parchment torn from a bible, a practice explicitly forbidden in canon 68 of the Quinisext;[26] in the early ninth century St Ioannicius was famed for his powers over wild animals – on one occasion at a feast he issued commands to a trained bear, again a practice expressly forbidden in canon 61.[27] The same canon is aware of the dangers of such practices for the ordinary population – as is Theodore of Studion over a century later;[28] yet only a few years later, the hagiographer of Michael of Synnada could write that his saint worked miracles in order to instil fear and respect into the uneducated.[29] The plain fact is that these practices were widespread, ancient and deep-rooted; legislation alone was unable to alter this; and they had been thoroughly integrated into the pattern of daily life.

Many other traditions, including the use of masks, the masquerading in the clothing of the opposite sex, the lighting of fires and so on, have remained part and parcel of peasant culture in the Balkans and Anatolia to the present day.[30] They have been thoroughly absorbed into a Christian framework of beliefs and a Christian calendar. Other practices reflect, similarly, folk-traditions which existed independent of any specific religion or cult, but which were clearly regarded for convenience as 'pagan' by the authorities. Canon 60 condemns the practice of imitating a trance-like state and imposes exorcism on the practitioners who thus permit evil spirits to take hold of them.[31] Mimes, popular theatre, pantomime and wild-animal hunts were similarly proscribed.[32] Yet the satirical theatre, certainly, continued throughout the Byzantine period, particularly in the cities, and dealt with popular and contemporary themes – political affairs, the character and mores of foreigners such as Armenians or Arabs, even aspects of New Testament history and, perhaps inevitably, the Church and its clergy.[33]

nemque Textuum Graecorum et ad Historiam Iuris Graeco-Romani Pertinentia Viro Doctissimo D. Holwerda Oblata, eds. W.J. Aerts, J.H.A. Lokin, S.L. Radt and N. van der Wal (Groningen 1985), pp. 119–33, for Balsamon's understanding of 'customary law' and its relationship to the civil law.

[26] F. Halkin, 'Saint Antoine le Jeune et Petronas le vainqueur des Arabes en 863', AB 62 (1944), 187–225, see 195; Mansi XI, 973C–D.
[27] Vita S. Ioannicii, in AS, Nov. II/1, Vita a Petro, 384–434; see 390B–C, 412C–413B.
[28] S. Theodori Studitae Epistolarum Lib., I (PG IC, 904–1116), ex. XIX (965D–968B).
[29] The Life is to be found in C. Doukakis, Μέγας συναξαριστὴς πάντων τῶν ἁγίων (12 vols., Athens 1889–96), Maii, 411–22, see 417; see BHG³, 2274x.
[30] See, for example, J. du Boulay, Portrait of a Greek Mountain Village (Oxford 1974), esp. pp. 60ff., and on local taboos and myths, such as fortune-telling, pp. 64ff. See also M.F. Herzfeld, The Poetics of Manhood. Contest and Identity in a Cretan Mountain Village (Princeton, N.J. 1985), esp. pp. 238ff.
[31] Mansi XI, 969D.   [32] Canon 51: Mansi XI, 968B.
[33] See F. Tinnefeld, 'Zum profanen Mimos in Byzanz nach dem Verdikt des Trullanums (691)', Βυζαντινά 6 (1974), 325ff.; and esp. Ja.N. Ljubarskij, 'Der Kaiser als Mime: zum Problem der Gestalt des byzantinischen Kaisers Michael III', JÖB 37 (1987), 39–50;

The effectiveness of the canons needs to be seen in this context, therefore; and it should be remembered that most of the prohibitions taken up by the Quinisext were, in fact, reiterations of earlier prohibitions going right back to the fourth century, measures which had clearly had only very limited success.[34]

The great majority of the practices condemned in the canons of the Quinisext, therefore, are 'pagan' primarily because the ecclesiastical establishment was bound to identify them as non-Christian and, on a variety of grounds, morally questionable, if not downright dangerous. But their existence both before and after the council need not in itself cause us to doubt that Christianity was by this time the dominant belief system in the early Byzantine world. Pockets of 'real' paganism – actual living cults, as opposed to occasional festivities and so on – undoubtedly did survive, even if we know next to nothing about them (the cult of Cybele in Caria was probably not an isolated phenomenon).[35] But the practices condemned by the Quinisext throw more light upon the traditional beliefs and superstitions of ordinary people who were also Christians, than upon paganism. And in this respect, it is perhaps time that historians abandoned the terminology of their medieval sources and viewed these practices for what they were (and are): essential elements of the social reproductive practice of the ordinary rural and urban populations of the empire. The anti-pagan legislation of the sixth century and before is not repeated in later codifications;[36] the Quinisext canons themselves make no mention of pagans as such, only 'Hellenic', which is to say, pagan, practices. Later Church legislation concentrates on the prevalent heresies of the time, but

---

see in particular 41ff. and 44–6. Note also the comments of Zonaras, the twelfth-century canonist and jurist, in Rhalles-Potles, *Syntagma*, vol. Ii, pp. 424ff. Those bishops who attended the Quinisext and who were familiar with life in the capital, will have been very well aware of the continued popularity of street theatres and related entertainments. If the fictional Life of Andrew the Fool is to be placed in the later seventh century, as Mango has reasonably argued (see introduction, above), there is plenty of evidence for this: see *Vita Andreae Sali* 648D, 652C and so on.

[34] Cf. Jones, *LRE*, vol. II, pp. 977f.

[35] The attitudes and fears of contemporaries and later commentators is well summed up in the gruesome story of the sacrifice of an unborn baby by the Byzantine population during the siege of Pergamon in 716. For, as has now been shown, the actual events were taken from an older apocalyptic tradition by an anonymous writer contemporary with the siege of Constantinople in 717–18, and later incorporated into the historiographical tradition of Theophanes and Nicephorus. They did not actually take place; but they symbolised the anxieties of the time both with regard to the ancient pagan rites and to the barbarians who threatened the empire. See W. Brandes, 'Apokalyptisches in Pergamon', *BS* 47 (1987), 1–11.

[36] Only one piece of Justinianic anti-pagan legislation was taken up in the later ninth-century *Basilika*, cf. *CJ* I, 11.9, a law forbidding the testamentary transmission of property to persons or institutions which support pagan cults and beliefs. Why this pronouncement alone was taken up is not immediately apparent. Cf. *Bas.*, I, 1.14 and II, 3.7.

paganism is not mentioned at all, except in the commentaries to the canons. Where pagan cults did survive, therefore, they must have done so in relative isolation; but it is unlikely that they survived long after the seventh century.

It seems quite reasonable to suppose that the conditions of the second half of the seventh century had exacerbated the problems of the Church in respect of the maintenance of Christian standards of morality and practice. The absence over several months or even years of the local clergy in areas most exposed to Arab or Slav activity can hardly have promoted a reinforcement of Christian mores.[37] On the other hand, the traditions, practices and beliefs which the canons of the Quinisext condemn are likely to have been an integral part of everyday life, in one form or another according to local cultural traditions, throughout much of the empire in normal times, and it was the conditions of the period in question which drew the attention of the Church to such matters, as much as the existence of the practices themselves. It is important to remember that there exists within any symbolic universe a whole series of registers of beliefs and practices, from the 'pure' and formalised theology and religious-philosophical logic of thinkers and intellectuals – theologians – right down to the day-to-day beliefs and attitudes of the uneducated and illiterate rural and urban populations. Such beliefs and ideas, and the practices which accompanied them, may well employ the vocabulary and the imagery of the formal system within which they are subsumed, but may themselves be both older, and fulfil a different functional role in the society as a whole, than the formal system. In the case of medieval Christianity, and in spite of the formal claims of Eastern orthodox political theology, there always existed a pluralism of beliefs, or registers of belief, of this sort. The continued existence of 'Hellenic' traditions is illustration enough. And it is at root not a question of the 'survival of paganism'.

Heretics and Jews

More important for the state, politically and also ideologically, were the various heretical groups which existed within the empire, important because they posed a more immediate and coherent challenge to neo-Chalcedonian orthodoxy, and thereby to the authority of the emperors.[38]

---

[37] See V. Laurent, 'L'Œuvre canonique du concile in Trullo (691–2), source primaire du droit de l'église orientale', REB 23 (1965), 10ff.; see also F. Trombley, 'The council in Trullo (691–2): a study of the canons relating to paganism, heresy and the invasions', Comitatus 9 (1978), 1–18, see 11–13.

[38] For a good discussion of the origins of the term 'heresy' in Christian thought, see F. Winkelmann, 'Einige Aspekte der Entwicklung der Begriffe Häresie und Schisma in der Spätantike', Κοινωνία 6 (1982), 89–109; and see the useful discussion of E. Patlagean,

But the most dangerous of these, monophysitism, became ever less relevant during the course of the seventh century. True, the imperial government and Church probably never wrote off entirely the possibility of reconquering the lost Eastern provinces in which monophysitism was the dominant creed. But by the 640s imperial attempts to find and impose a compromise – in the event, monotheletism – reflected rather the perceptions of those in power that the imperial authority was endangered, than the real desire to win over the populations of Syria and Egypt. Armenia remained a problem, of course, but again, a distant imperial power, even with the occasional use of force, could not seriously hope to compel a monophysite population to accept imperial and Chalcedonian authority.[39] And in the event, the alienation of the non-Byzantine Armenian nobility and the much cleverer politics of the caliphate lost this region, too. No doubt monophysitism remained among elements of the population of Asia Minor – according to John of Ephesus, Cilicia, Isauria, Asia and Cappadocia all possessed strong and flourishing monophysite communities. Other well-known monophysites, such as Jacob Baradaeus, had also been active in converting pagans to monophysitism in Asia Minor. Jacob travelled in Cappadocia, Cilicia, Isauria, Pamphylia, Lycaonia, Lycia, Phrygia, Caria, Asia, as well as on Chios, Rhodes and Lesbos. Monophysite bishops were consecrated for many of the cities of these regions.[40] And it is most unlikely that these communities did not survive well into the seventh century and beyond. But the effects of the Arab invasions and attacks and, in particular, the loss of the monophysite provinces, cut such communities off from the wider world which had nourished them hitherto. They can only have survived – where they were not destroyed or fragmented through hostile military activity – in relative isolation, and the pressing insistence of the state on orthodoxy within its own apparatus, at least for the vast mass of the bureaucracy, cannot have contributed to the maintenance of their ideological integrity. At any rate, while monophysite sentiment continued to exist within the empire, the canons of the Quinisext suggest that it played only a minor role. Only two canons, 81 and 82, reflect a clearly anti-monophysite tendency, the first

'Byzance, le barbare, l'hérétique et la loi universelle', in *Ni Juif ni Grec. Entretiens sur le racisme*, ed. L. Poliakov (Paris 1978), pp. 81–90 (= *Structure sociale, famille, chrétienté à Byzance* (XV London 1981)).

[39] Note canons 32, 33 and 99 of the Quinisext, which attempt to bring the Armenian Church into line in respect of certain matters of liturgical practice. See also the comments of Balsamon: Rhalles-Potles, *Syntagma*, vol. II, pp. 373–81 and 543–4.

[40] See Frend, *The Rise of the Monophysite Movement*, pp. 285ff.; and John of Ephesus I, 39, II, 4, III, 36f., IV, 19 and V, 6; and especially John of Ephesus, *Lives of the Eastern Saints* (PO XVIII), 535f.; (PO XIX), 154ff. Monophysite communities existed also in Constantinople and on Cyprus – see Van Dieten, *Geschichte der Patriarchen*, pp. 28–9; and John of Ephesus III, 15–16.

prohibiting the addition of the phrase 'who was crucified for us' to the creed, a theopaschite formulation which reflected a monophysite theology; the second prohibiting the depiction of Christ as a lamb, a practice which, it was argued, jeopardised the assumption of two natures, human and divine, of Christ.[41] Canon 95 also implies the continued existence of a variety of monophysite sects and tendencies, although the list must be treated with caution. In listing the process whereby heretics who wish to join or rejoin the true faith might be admitted to the Church, the canon notes that for certain groups, Severus of Antioch and the archimandrite Eutyches, two of the best-known monophysite polemicists, were to be first condemned (along with the patriarch Nestorius) before they could be accepted.[42] It is probable that various minor sects, which still held views that might be characterised as either monophysite or Nestorian, were intended here. On the whole, however, monophysites do not seem to be a serious concern, and indeed the fact that the canon stipulates the requirements for admission may well suggest that such monophysites as remained within the empire were being gradually assimilated into the Chalcedonian fold.

The hostile activity of the Arabs may well have played a central role here, for the devastation they brought about seems to have dislodged large numbers of the rural populace in many areas, forcing them to seek refuge in less exposed districts. Interestingly, canon 95 notes that numbers of heretics – including Eunomians, Sabellians and Montanists – had left the region of Galatia and sought baptism; and it is highly likely that this movement was a result of the economic and physical dislocation caused by raiding Muslim forces. More importantly, it forced hitherto isolated rural communities, who had probably been able to practise their form of Christianity with little interference, into the 'outside' world of neo-Chalcedonian orthodoxy, where the differences and divergences were more apparent, attracting the attention of the authorities. This general phenomenon must

---

[41] See Mansi XI, 977D–E and 977E–980B.
[42] Mansi XI, 984B–E. For Eutyches and Severus, see Winkelmann, *Die östlichen Kirchen*, pp. 44 and 81ff., and 50 and 54ff. For Nestorius, *ibid.*, pp. 36f. The text of canon 95 is itself taken mostly from earlier sources, chiefly the seventh canon of the council of 381 in Constantinople, together with other elements such as canon 19 of the council of Nicaea (325): see Hefele-Leclercq II, 1; Mansi II, 676f.; and Rochow, *Zu einigen oppositionellen religiösen Strömungen*, p. 266. Although monophysitism continued to be a target of theological polemic well into the seventh century (along with Arianism and other Christological heresies), as can be seen from a survey of the relevant literature in *CPG* III, this reflects the fact that it was seen as part of the monothelete debate, as well as the fact that the most important of these writings came from outside the empire, where the debate between Chalcedonian and monophysite Christians remained a live issue – the *Hodegos* of Anastasius of Sinai is perhaps the best example of this. See K.-H. Uthemann, *Anastasii Sinaitae Viae Dux* (Corpus Christianorum, series Graeca, vol. VIII) (Turnhout 1981); and see *CPG* III, nos. 7685 (Euboulus of Lystra), 7745, 7756–7, 7771 (?) (Anastasius of Sinai), 7798 (anon.).

surely have applied to other non-Chalcedonian or heretical groups. On at least one occasion, and possibly more often, we know that considerable numbers of refugees from a famine in Syria entered the empire (in 686, according to Theophanes), and this was yet another source of potential difference or disruption which the Church had to handle.[43]

It seems not unreasonable to suppose, therefore, that it was in fact the disruption of the seventh century which produced a greater uniformity of belief within Byzantine Asia Minor.

Other heresies and schismatic sects existed across the empire, of course. In North Africa, Donatism – which had come to represent local cultural-political feeling as well as religious dogmatic differences of opinion – seems to have experienced a very limited revival during the later years of the sixth century, if the letters of Pope Gregory are to be given credence; although their numbers seem to have been small, and their influence limited.[44] But whether the people in question are really Donatists, or whether the term is simply used of non-Chalcedonian heretics generally, is uncertain. Even so, a reference to Donatists in North Africa in a letter of Pope Gregory II for the year 722 suggests that it may have survived, albeit in isolation and on a very limited scale, throughout the period with which we are dealing.[45]

Arianism likewise survived on a limited scale, chiefly among Germanic mercenaries in the imperial armies in the later sixth and early seventh centuries. John of Ephesus reports the presence of an Arian church for the German community in Constantinople, and the popular hostility to it.[46] But this was an isolated incident; and while Arianism may have persisted in the West, particularly in North Africa after the defeat of the Vandals, and in Italy among the Lombards until 680,[47] it seems to have disappeared from

[43] Mansi ibid., repeated from the 7th canon of the council of 381: see Rhalles, Potles, Syntagma, II, 529–31f.; for the Syrians, see Theophanes, 364.3–4; and the seventh-century Syriac chronicle of Johannan bar Penkaye – see G.J. Reinink, 'Pseudo-Methodius und die Legende vom römischen Endkaiser', 95 and note 62.

[44] See W.H.C. Frend, The Donatist Church: A Movement of Protest in Roman North Africa (Oxford 1952), pp. 308–11; Diehl, L'Afrique byzantine, vol. II, pp. 508ff.; Bréhier and Aigrain, pp. 217–18; Goubert, Byzance avant l'Islam, vol. II, 2, pp. 229ff.; and B.H. Warmington, The North African Provinces from Diocletian to the Vandal Conquest (Cambridge 1954), pp. 76–102. R.A. Markus, 'The imperial administration and the Church in Byzantine Africa', Church History 36 (1967), 18 argues that Donatism in its proper sense no longer existed at this time.

[45] See PL LXXXIX, 502; and Frend, The Donatist Church, p. 313; Bréhier and Aigrain, p. 228, note 3. The debate is complex and depends also on the question of Gregory's use of the term for his own ecclesiastical-political ends. See esp. R.A. Markus, 'Christianity and dissent in Roman North Africa: changing perspectives in recent work', Studies in Church History IX (1972), 21–36; P.R.L. Brown, 'Religious dissent in the later Roman empire: the case of North Africa', History 46 (1961), 83–101; and the summary with literature in Averil Cameron, 'Byzantine Africa', 49f.

[46] John of Ephesus III, 13 and 26, and V, 16.

[47] See W.E. Kaegi, jr., 'Arianism and the Byzantine army in Africa, 533–546', Traditio 21 (1965), 23–53; and for Italy, K.D. Schmidt, Die Bekehrung der Ostgermanen zum Christen-

within the empire, including its Spanish territories (held until c. 625: the final conversion of the Visigothic Church to Chalcedonian orthodoxy took place at the council of Toledo in 589)[48] by the time of the accession of Heraclius.

The Montanist heresy, which had its centre in Phrygia, may have lingered on into the seventh and early eighth centuries, although the evidence is inconclusive: it is difficult to ascertain whether a source such as Theophanes means the real Montanists or merely uses the term as a convenient and well-known element in a list.[49] Later legislation – notably the condemnation of Montanists and Manichaeans in the Ecloga – seems to rely on the Justinianic codification for its inspiration, and the term is used once more as a convenient 'catch-all', as may also be the case with the 95th canon of the Quinisext. Montanism certainly seems to have existed into the late sixth century, however, as John of Ephesus, who led a major drive against their cult centres and converted many to orthodoxy (i.e. monophysitism), reports in detail. But his missionary activities, together with the fierce persecutions under Tiberius Constantine, may well have dealt the fatal blow to the Montanist communities.[50]

Similar considerations apply to the Messalians, sometimes called Marcianists, both terms used in the sixth and seventh centuries for defamatory purposes, rather than signifying actual practices or beliefs. Messalianism originated as an ascetic heresy in Syria during the fourth century; but by the later sixth century the term seems to have lost its real significance.[51] And the fact that it occurs in the *scholia* of Maximus Confessor to the

---

    tum (2 vols. Göttingen 1939), vol. I, pp. 387ff.; S.C. Fanning, 'Lombard Arianism reconsidered', *Speculum* 56 (1981), 241–58.

[48] See E.A. Thompson, *The Goths in Spain* (Oxford 1969), pp. 320ff.; P. Goubert, 'Influences byzantines sur l'Espagne wisigothique (554–711)', *REB* 2 (1944), 5–78, see 43–9; and the council of Toledo: Mansi IX, 985f.

[49] They were heavily persecuted by Justinian; see Stein, *Bas-Empire*, vol. II, pp. 374f.; P. de Labriolle, *La Crise montaniste* (Paris 1913), pp. 532ff. For their origins in the second century, see esp. S. Runciman, *The Medieval Manichee. A Study of the Christian Dualist Heresy* (Cambridge 1947), pp. 18ff.; F.E. Vokes, 'The opposition to Montanism from Church and state in the Christian empire', *Studia Patristica* IV, 2, ed. F.L. Cross (Berlin 1961), pp. 518–26; W. Schepelern, *Der Montanismus und die phrygischen Kulte* (Tübingen 1929). For the story of Theophanes (according to which an edict of Leo III in 722 ordered the forced baptism of all Montanists, and as a result of which the adherents to the heresy locked themselves in their churches and set them on fire, rather than be converted), see Theophanes, 401. But see also A. Sharf, 'The Jews, the Montanists and the emperor Leo III', *BZ* 59 (1966), 37–46, see 43; and Procopius, *Historia Arcana* XI, 23; Stein, *Bas-Empire*, vol. II, p. 375, which may be Theophanes' original source. Runciman, *The Medieval Manichee*, p. 18, accepts the story, as do Bréhier and Aigrain, p. 439.

[50] See *Ecloga* XVII, 52; and J. Gouillard, 'L'Hérésie', 308–9. For John of Ephesus, see Michael Syr., vol. II, 269ff.; John of Ephesus III, 13, 20, 21, 26 and 32. In general, see Sharf, 'The Jews, the Montanists and the emperor Leo III', esp. 38f.

[51] See the summary and the literature in Rochow, 'Zu einigen oppositionellen religiösen Strömungen', 274–8.

Pseudo-Dionysius Areopagite – 'Lampetianoi, that is, Messalianoi or Adelphianoi, which is to say, Markianistai' – is no evidence for the existence of Messalian heretics or communities.[52] Part of the difficulty in identifying such groups lies in the fact that orthodox critics of aberrant beliefs and heresies tended to use the descriptive terms of earlier writers and of an earlier period in their lists and classifications of heretics and heretical beliefs, and it is difficult to know to what extent these lists represent a contemporary situation, or merely reflect an antiquarian and condemnatory *topos*. Older terms were often applied, with little or no theological justification, to quite new groups of heretics. The term 'Messalian' was thus used also of Bogomils in the later period, while terms such as Montanist or Arian occur similarly alongside other names of actual, living, heresies from the seventh century on.[53] Thus references to the Meletians, Paulianists, Marcionists, Sabbatians, Novatians, Quartodecimans (Tessarakaidekatitai), Eunomians, Sabellians and many other sects must be treated cautiously.[54] In the early seventh-century handbook of the presbyter Timothy of Constantinople, *De receptione haereticorum*, and in the 95th canon of the Quinisext, such sects are mentioned without any real evidence that they actually survived. What both texts represent is a catalogue of traditional heresies, subdivided into three categories according to their degree of difference from orthodox Christianity and the mode in which their adherents are to be readmitted to the Church.[55] Similarly, in the anti-heretical compilation of Anastasius of Sinai and in a (probably) seventh-century text on the Messalians by the monk and presbyter George, lists of heretics also occur, and it is clear that in part, at least, the polemical tradition and the intention of the authors of such works have determined the composition of the lists themselves.[56]

[52] PG, IV, 169. Messalianism seems to have died out by the seventh century – see Rochow, 'Zu einigen oppositionellen religiösen Strömungen', 278 and note 1.
[53] D. Obolensky, *The Bogomils* (Cambridge 1948), pp. 240f.; Runciman, *The Medieval Manichee*, pp. 63ff.; M. Loos, *Dualist Heresy in the Middle Ages* (Prague 1974), pp. 72 and 330ff.; Rochow, 'Zu einigen oppositionellen religiösen Strömungen', 274 note 1.
[54] For the origins and history of these sects, see *Dictionnaire de théologie catholique*, eds. A. Vacant, E. Mangenot and E. Amann (Paris 1930), vol. IX, 2, 2009–32 (Marcionism); 1464–78 (Macedonianism); XIII, 2, 1445ff. (Quartodecimans); XIV, 1, 430–1 (Sabbatianism); T. Gregory, 'Novatianism. A rigorist sect in the Christian Roman empire', *Byzantine Studies* 2 (1975), 1–18; also *Lexikon für Theologie und Kirche*, eds. J. Höfer and K. Rahner, 2nd edn (Freiburg i. Br., 1957–68), vol. VI, 1313f. (Macedonianism); VII, 257f. (Meletians); IX, 192 (Sabbatianism); VIII, 213f. (Paulianism); see also *CMH*, vol. IV, part 2, pp. 190–2; Beck, *Kirche* pp. 349–50 (Messalianism); also Jones, *LRE*, vol. II, pp. 950–6.
[55] See PG LXXXVI, 11–68 and Beck, *Kirche*, pp. 401–2 (for Timothy of Constantinople); Mansi XI, 984B–E.
[56] See PG LXXXIX, 268, and Beck, *Kirche*, pp. 442f. and 446; and for George, see M. Richard, in *EEBΣ* 25 (1956), 350–62. See esp. Gouillard, 'L'Hérésie', 302 and 304 with note 37; Beck, *Kirche*, p. 447. Note the comments of Rochow, 'Zu einigen oppositionellen religiösen Strömungen', 277.

While it is quite probable that much of the rural population of Asia Minor – where these heresies had mainly had their roots in the period from the second to the fifth centuries[57] – did express their beliefs through ideas and liturgical practices which might have seemed heretical or aberrant to the strictly orthodox observer (and to the official Church position), and while such groups may even have referred to themselves by such sectarian names, it seems unlikely that any organised movements or sect Churches existed. Many may have seen their differences from the orthodox establishment as a symbol of their own cultural traditions – and even at times of their opposition to aspects of state rule as vehicles for the expression of their cultural and social solidarity.[58] The occurrence of these terms in later commentators, therefore, especially when used in connection with a known heretical movement or unorthodox activity, must be viewed with especial suspicion.[59] On the whole, with the exception of the Marcionist sect, which may have contributed to the development of the Paulician Church, the great majority of these sects seems to have vanished by the later sixth century.[60] The use of their names in later sources reflects either the age-old practice of using old names for new heresies where a connection, spurious or real, could be found; or their application to regional customary usages for which the observer may have felt little sympathy.[61]

If the great majority of the older heresies had disappeared in all but name by the later sixth or early seventh centuries, two groups seem to have their origins in this period. In the first, that of the Paulicians, the question of dualism in its Manichaean forms was encountered once more. The confrontation with dualism begins much earlier, of course, in the early Christian centuries: Manichaeism, with its systematised and sophisticated theology, gave dualism a new strength and provided later dualist heresies with a valuable arsenal of arguments.[62]

The beginnings of Paulicianism are shrouded in obscurity, and the question of when and where the sect was first established remains a subject

[57] See W.M. Calder, 'The epigraphy of the Anatolian heresies', *Anatolian Studies presented to Sir William Ramsay* (Manchester 1923), pp. 59–61; H. Ahrweiler, 'L'Asie mineure et les invasions arabes', 3–5; and for further literature, see Rochow, 'Zu einigen oppositionellen religiösen Strömungen', 278–82.
[58] See Ahrweiler, 'L'Asie mineure et les invasions arabes', 5; Köpstein, 'Zu den Agrarverhältnissen', pp. 33–4 on the bandit activities of the mountain population of Pisidia and Lycaonia in the sixth century.
[59] Thus the use of the term 'Nestorian' of the iconoclasts in the Life of Peter of Atroa, 22.9 probably has nothing to do with Nestorians as such, *pace* Vryonis, in Βυζαντινά 1 (1969), 215. See esp. Gouillard, 'L'Hérésie', 302ff.
[60] See P. Charanis, 'Cultural diversity and the breakdown of Byzantine power in Asia Minor', who revises his earlier arguments in this respect. See Gouillard, 'L'Hérésie', 304 and note 36.
[61] Gouillard, 'L'Hérésie', 307–12.
[62] For dualism, and more particularly Manichaeism, see the literature at Beck, *Kirche*, p. 335 and commentary and Loos, *Dualist Heresy*, pp. 21ff.

of debate. It was a dualist and egalitarian sect, which based its beliefs on an interpretation of the New Testament, regarding the Old Testament as irrelevant. Its rejection of baptism and of any formal ecclesiastical hierarchy brought it into conflict with the established Church and thus with the state; and in the second half of the seventh century it was heavily persecuted – the later evidence, at least, suggests that it already had at this time a considerable popular following in the still limited areas of the provinces Armenia I and II where it is first encountered. It was, of course, to become a major threat to imperial territorial and administrative integrity in the ninth century; but at this period although persecutions took place under Constantine IV and Justinian II, it remained a minor problem.[63]

The second heretical sect whose origins have been traced to the later seventh or early eighth centuries is that of the Athigganoi. They are first mentioned in the writings on heresy usually ascribed to the patriarch Germanus (715–30) between 727 and 733.[64] The nature of their beliefs is unclear, and they have been connected with both the Novatians, Montanists and Paulicians, and with the Jews. They were associated in Byzantine times with Phrygia and Lycaonia especially, and the Montanist connection is suggested by the fact that they were sometimes referred to as 'Phrygians', a term applied also to the older sect.[65] But they seem to have been few in number and relatively insignificant until the middle and later eighth century. From our point of view, their significance, as that of the Paulicians, lies in their

[63] The literature on the Paulician movement and its beliefs is vast. For the most recent survey, which includes also the older secondary literature, see P. Lemerle, 'L'Histoire des Pauliciens d'Asie Mineure d'après les sources grecques', TM 5 (1973), 1–144; N. Garsoian, 'Les Sources grecques pour l'histoire des Pauliciens d'Asie Mineure: texte critique et traduction', TM 4 (1970), 1–227; and M. Loos, 'Deux publications fondamentales sur le paulicianisme d'Asie Mineure', BS 35 (1974), 189–209, and Dualist Heresy, pp. 32–40; N.G. Garsoian, The Paulician Heresy. A Study of the Origins and Development of Paulicianism in Armenia and the Eastern Provinces of the Byzantine Empire (The Hague and Paris 1967); D. Obolensky, The Bogomils, pp. 28–58; Runciman, The Medieval Manichee, pp. 26ff. The major Greek source is the report of Peter of Sicily, compiled in the ninth century on the basis of his own observations, and accounts of their origins from the Paulicians themselves. See 'Pierre de Sicile, histoire des Pauliciens', ed. and trans. N. Garsoian, in Les Sources grecques, pp. 6–67, and esp. C. Ludwig, 'Wer hat was in welcher Absicht wie beschrieben?', in Varia II (Poikila Byzantina VI. Bonn 1987), pp. 149–227. Peter places the beginnings of Paulicianism in the middle years of the seventh century. Armenian sources in the last years of the seventh and first years of the eighth century. Some historians have argued for a mid-sixth-century origin; many have connected the heresy with the Marcionists. See Loos, Dualist Heresy, pp. 30–5; Obolensky, The Bogomils, pp. 45ff.: also Garsoian, The Paulician Heresy, pp. 131ff. (sixth-century origin). Against the Marcionist connection: H. Söderberg, La Religion des Cathares (Uppsala 1949), p. 120. See also Beck, Kirche, pp. 335–6 with literature.
[64] See Gouillard, 'L'Hérésie', 306–7 and 310; Stein, Bilderstreit, p. 262f.; the text, De Haeresibus et Synodis, is in PG XCVIII, 39–88; see 85.
[65] See especially J. Starr, 'An Eastern Christian sect: the Athinganoi', Harvard Theological Review 29 (1936), 93–106; Loos, Dualist Heresy, p. 61; Gouillard, 'L'Hérésie', 307–12.

possible connection with some of the earlier sects, which may have been reshaped during the seventh century, or may indeed have attracted new followers and adherents as the remnants of the majority of the older sects were dispersed or died out. It is at least likely, therefore, that while the Paulician and athigganoi movements developed their own independent and dynamic traditions, they were rooted in, and owed their beginnings to, the conditions which signalled the end of most of the other Christian sects of Anatolia.

The one group of believers who presented a real problem for both Christian theologians and the Christian state throughout the period dealt with here, and indeed throughout the history of the state itself, a group which, in spite of more or less constant persecution, occupying always a subordinate position within Eastern Christian society and culture, does survive and is able even to prosper, is represented, of course, by the Jews. Judaism presented a number of difficulties to Christian thinkers.

But it also presented difficulties for the state and for society at large, for the structure of Jewish beliefs and kinship gave Jewish communities a stubborn resilience which was able to weather the fiercest storms of persecution, forced baptism and so on. Up to the sixth century, the Jews had been tolerated, with only minor and occasional persecutions directed specifically against them. But they, along with certain other groups within Roman society, had fewer rights than orthodox subjects.[66] From Justinian's reign, however, begins a long period of persecution: Justinian himself deprived Jews, and Samaritans, of their few remaining rights within the state with regard to public office or state service in general. Under Justin they had already been deprived of the right to make wills and to receive inheritances, being also debarred from carrying out any legal act, such as being a witness in a law court. Justin and Justinian both began to apply the laws against heretics and pagans to Jews and Samaritans as well; and although forcible baptism had been applied to Jewish communities in the fifth century on occasion, such measures were enacted increasingly from Justinian's reign on in the East, and from the later sixth century

[66] The growing anti-Semitism of Christianity even produced imperial legislation to protect Jewish property; but during the later fourth and fifth centuries, increasingly, legislation to exclude them from state service was introduced. See Jones, *LRE*, vol. II, pp. 944–8. The best detailed analysis of the relationship between Jews and the rest of late Roman society and culture is the excellent article of L. Cracco Ruggini, 'Pagani, Ebrei e Cristiani: odio sociologico e odio teologico nel mondo antico', in *Gli Ebrei nell'alto Medioevo* (Settimane di Studio del Centro Italiano di Studi sull'alto Medioevo XXVI, Spoleto 1980), vol. I, pp. 13–101, esp. 90ff. For a survey of anti-Jewish polemic, see A.L. Williams, *Adversus Iudaeos. A Bird's-Eye View of Christian Apologiae until the Renaissance* (Cambridge 1935); and P. Browe, 'Die Judengesetzgebung Justinians', *Analecta Gregoriana* 8 (1935) 109–46; R.-M. Seyberlich, *Die Judenpolitik Kaiser Justinians I.* (Byzantinische Beiträge. Berlin 1964), pp. 73–80; S. Baron, *A Social and Religious History of the Jews* III (New York 1957), pp. 4–15.

in the West also. Under Tiberius Constantine, Maurice and Heraclius, similar persecutions took place, and the Jews were increasingly reduced to the position of a very marginalised social and cultural element within a predominantly Christian society.[67]

Under Heraclius, a series of forced baptisms of Jews culminated in 634 in the first general edict to compel all Jews within the empire to accept baptism.[68] While it seems to have met with very little success, and to have been only half-heartedly imposed, it is nevertheless symptomatic of a change in the situation of Jews. The days when Jews were accorded a privileged status, enshrined in the legal codifications of the emperors – including Justinian's – and based on both Roman legal theory and Christian notions of the Jews as a living testimony to the Christian interpretation of the Old and New Testaments, were gone. Even though Jews lost their 'civil rights' under Justin and Justinian, they were still, in general, set apart from pagans and heretics alike. Judaism was both permitted and protected. By the time of Heraclius, this situation had begun to change; and although there now existed a constant tension between the traditional approach on the one hand, enshrined in the *Codex Theodosianus* and the *Codex Iustinianus*, and on the other the exclusivism of emperors like Heraclius, or Leo III (who is reported to have issued a similar edict to that of Heraclius), the attempts to force the conversion of Jews to Christianity, repeated sporadically throughout Byzantine history, were on the whole a failure; the older Christian tradition, which set Jews apart from other marginal groups, retained its hold on Eastern Christian attitudes and beliefs.[69]

Accusations of Judaism began to be used increasingly from the later sixth century to denigrate heretical tendencies, or those suspected of deviating from the proper orthodox path – notably in the canons of the Quinisext, in the introductory declaration of which the assembly addressed the emperor and noted the survival of 'pagan and Jewish perversity'.[70] But already the increasing persecution of Jews within the empire in the sixth

---

[67] See Jones, *LRE*, vol. II, pp. 948–50; for the recent literature, J. Starr, *The Jews in the Byzantine Empire, 641–1204* (Athens 1939); A. Sharf, *Byzantine Jewry from Justinian to the Fourth Crusade* (New York 1971), esp. pp. 19ff.; Yannopoulos, *La Société profane*, pp. 243–51; Beck, *Kirche*, pp. 332–3 with further literature.

[68] See Dölger, *Regesten*, nos. 196, 197 and 206. The interesting contemporary *Doctrina Jacobi nuper Baptizati* records the events of the reigns of Phocas and Heraclius relevant to this policy, from the point of view of a supposedly genuine convert. See Beck, *Kirche*, p. 447; and R. Devreesse, 'La Fin inédite d'une lettre de S. Maxime: un baptême forcé de Juifs et de Samaritains à Carthage en 632', *Revue des sciences religieuses* 17 (1937), 25–35; see *CPG* III, 7699 (Epistula 8).

[69] See especially Sharf, *Byzantine Jewry*, pp. 19ff. and 53ff. On Leo's edict, *ibid.*, pp. 61ff.

[70] Mansi XI, 933E. Note also canon 11 (*ibid.*, 945E warning against the use of unleavened bread, mixing with Jews at the baths, dealing with Jewish doctors); canon 33 (957D) and canon 99 (985E) (against a variety of liturgical or related practices, especially in Armenia, which smacked of strong Jewish influence).

Religion and belief 347

century – possibly, if not probably, an imperial response to popular pressure – had encouraged Jews to re-examine their position and their role within the state. Their resentment expressed itself in terms of civil disturbances, and in particular in the collaboration of some Jewish communities with the Persians in the early seventh century.[71] The consequent Christian outrage merely exacerbated a vicious circle. By the time of the Quinisext, Jews were explicitly as bad as pagans and heretics in terms of the danger they posed to the state, and especially of the challenge they presented to the universalist claims of neo-Chalcedonian imperial orthodoxy. Anti-Jewish tracts now became a standard element of Christian polemic.[72] Regular persecution of Jews becomes a commonplace in Byzantine political history; and the regular use of the term 'Jew' to demean or insult becomes a topos of some genres of Byzantine literature.[73] Judaism itself becomes synonymous with a drift away from orthodoxy and with potential political-ideological subversion.[74] Whether there were, in fact, any substantial communities of Jews in the territories remaining to the empire after about 650 is

[71] Jewish and especially Samaritan revolts: see the summary in Köpstein, 'Zu den Agrarverhältnissen', pp. 36–7; S. Winkler, 'Die Samariter in den Jahren 529/30', Klio 43 (1965), 435–57. For the Jewish response to the Persians and Arabs, see Sharf, Byzantine Jewry, pp. 48–57 with literature, and analysis of the results for later Christian reprisals and state repression. On anti-Jewish polemic, see G. Dagron, V. Déroche, 'Juifs et Chrétiens dans l'Orient du VIIe siècle', TM 11 (1991), 17–273; V. Déroche, 'La polémique anti-Judaïque au VIe et au VIIe siècle. Un mémento inédit, les Kephalaia', TM 11 (1991), 275–311; G. Dagron, 'Judaïser', TM 11 (1991), 359–80.
[72] Of the surviving polemical literature usually ascribed to the sixth century, there is only one anti-Jewish tract, itself in the form of a dialogue between a Persian magus, Christians, pagans and Jews at the court of the Sassanid Great King. See Beck. Kirche, p. 381. Another 'Debate with the Jew Herban' dates also to the middle or later sixth century (Beck, Kirche, pp. 386 and 407); whereas from the seventh century there are, in contrast, at least three major polemical treatises: those of Stephen of Bostra (ed. G. Mercati, in Theologische Quartalschrift 77 (1895), 663–8; repr. in Opere minori I (Studi e Testi 76, Rome 1937), pp. 202–6); of Hieronymus of Jerusalem (cf. P. Batiffol, 'Jérôme de Jérusalem d'après un document inédit', Revue des questions historiques 39 (1886), 248–55; and PG XL, 845–66); and the so-called Τρόπαια κατὰ Ἰουδαίων ἐν Δαμάσκῳ (ed. G. Bardy, in PO XV (Paris 1927), pp. 189ff.), as well as a number of minor polemics, the Doctrina Iacobi nuper Baptizati, and hostile references in the hagiographical tradition. See Beck, Kirche, pp. 447ff. The contrast is very clear; and see the survey of M. Waegemann, 'Les Traités adversus Iudaeos: aspects des relations judéo-chrétiennes dans le monde grec', B 56 (1986), 295–313. See Averil Cameron, 'Byzantines and Jews: some recent work on early Byzantium', BMGS 20 (1996) 249–74.
[73] See Beck, Kirche, pp. 443 and 447–8. Note the use of the term to emphasise the superiority of Christian beliefs to Judaism (and implicitly to other doctrines) in a polemical context in the later seventh-century miracles of St Artemius (see 48.26sq., 63.13sq.); and note also the position of the Jew as instrument of the Devil typical in middle Byzantine literature, and exemplified in the later-seventh- or early-eighth-century story about the Church administrator in Adana (Cilicia II), who is deceived into making a pact with the Devil through a Jewish intermediary. See L. Radermacher, Griechische Quellen zur Faustsage (Vienna and Leipzig 1927) (= Sitzungsber. d. Akad. d. Wiss. in Wien, phil.-hist. Kl. CCVI, 4), pp. 164ff.
[74] See Sharf, Byzantine Jewry, passim, and 'Byzantine Jewry in the seventh century', BZ 48 (1955), 103–15.

difficult to say. Individuals and their families there must certainly have been; but (and ignoring the numerous literary topoi referred to) there is no evidence for organised communities of Jews in the empire until a much later date. Jews, nevertheless, became scapegoats for Christian apologists, as Byzantine society became more and more exclusivist and introverted. I will return to this below.

CHURCH, STATE AND SOCIETY: POLITICAL IDEOLOGY AND SYMBOLIC UNIVERSE

Introversion and the failure of mission

Byzantine society became during the later sixth and seventh centuries increasingly inward-looking and exclusivist. But this increasing uniformity of appearance and consensus, and the accompanying demand or expectation of conformity represented in many of the sources should not mislead us into thinking that the cultural practices and beliefs of the populations of the empire actually became uniform and less differentiated.

On the contrary, formal adherence to, and public recognition of, all the key elements of political and religious orthodoxy does not mean that in day-to-day terms observances, assumptions and explanations did not continue to vary very greatly from region to region and from community to community – geographical isolation and the strength or weakness of local cultural identities will have played an essential role.[75] But those who did not clearly commit themselves to the orthodox *oikoumenē*, which meant also the imperial state, were perceived as being against it. Persecutions of pagans and heretics, especially during the reign of Tiberius Constantine and those of his successors, became more severe as the Christian exclusiveness which promoted them became an ever more central element in Byzantine perceptions of their world and themselves as the Chosen People. The attitude is summed up by the question of the prefect of the city of Carthage to the Jewish community there in 632, two years before Heraclius' general edict: 'Are you all servants of the emperor? If you are, then you must accept baptism.'[76]

Hostility to non-conforming groups is apparent throughout the later sixth century, of course, and in many respects is merely a natural progression from the political theology of exclusiveness which becomes more obvious after the loss of the West and from the reign of Justinian in particular. But as the empire shrinks, and as East Roman orthodox culture

---

[75] I have described this phenomenon elsewhere as a form of 'ideological re-orientation'. See Haldon, 'Ideology and social change', 161ff.
[76] *Doctrina Iacobi nuper Baptizati*, 1.18sq.

begins to reassess the narratives of its place in the world, so this hostility becomes more pronounced. And it is not confined simply to elements of the social and economic elite. On the contrary, and for social reasons as well as for political-theological reasons, the popular hostility to the (mostly) upper-class persons accused, rightly or wrongly, of adherence to pagan beliefs and practices during the trials and persecutions of the years 579–82 and after, is an indicator of the direction of the feelings and the attitudes of ordinary people in cities such as Constantinople, Antioch, Edessa, Baalbek, Harran and others. What is important about the events is the fact that, whereas persecutions varying in intensity, imperial legislation and large-scale missionary activity – that of John of Ephesus is known best – had occurred before, they had been directed by the state and had rarely found more than a passive, if accepting, response among the ordinary orthodox populations.[77] Now popular riots ensued when the penalties imposed upon the accused were thought to be too lenient.[78] John of Ephesus and Evagrius ascribe this to the intense piety of the Christians in the empire; and while there is no reason to doubt the latter, it seems clear that this response is something quite new. Once again, the notions of exclusiveness and of religious solidarity, of marking off clear boundaries between true Christians and Romans, as opposed to pagans, heretics and 'outsiders' in general, is evident. The hostility of the population of Constantinople to the Arian church of the Germanic mercenary troops in the early seventh century is in the same mould.[79] And while it is no doubt possible to find or to assume more immediate reasons for these popular reactions, it was the changed ideological atmosphere which determined the particular form of the reaction, and not the immediate context.

This tendency to exclude those defined as marginal to the orthodox Christian community, which becomes increasingly evident in the actions and attitudes of ordinary people, and especially of the urban populations of the empire, is emphasised by the political shrinkage of the middle of the seventh century. Following the loss of Jerusalem, Antioch and Alexandria, only Constantinople remains to serve as the focus of Church and state hierarchies, as the source of power and authority, privilege and prestige. At the same time, there is a marked absence of any effort to continue the

[77] See I. Engelhardt, *Mission und Politik in Byzanz. Ein Beitrag zur Strukturanalyse byzantinischer Mission zur Zeit Justins und Justinians* (MBM XIX, Munich 1974), esp. pp. 12ff. for John of Ephesus; also pp. 128ff. and 178–86. For general remarks, H.-G. Beck, 'Christliche Mission und politische Propaganda im byzantinischen Reich', in Settimane di Studio del Centro Italiano di Studi sull'alto Medioevo XIV (Spoleto 1967), pp. 649–74 (repr. in *Ideen und Realitäten in Byzanz* IV (London 1972)).
[78] See the account in Rochow, *Die Heidenprozesse*, pp. 124ff. Sources: John of Ephesus III, 27–34; Evagrius V, 18.
[79] See Haldon, 'Ideology and social change', 162 and note 59.

policies of the reign of Justinian to proselytise among the pagans or the unorthodox. Instead, political fiat followed by repression seems to become the order of the day. The initial attempts of Sergius and Heraclius to win public support for their monenergite and monothelete doctrines through debate at local synods marks the only significant gesture towards reconciliation and persuasion. Once failed, the effort was not repeated; and as the seventh century wears on, even the monophysite communities come to be branded as a dangerous and subversive element, effectively ignored by the sixth council as irrelevant to the interests of Church, state and *oikoumenē*; and condemned in passing in the canons of the Quinisext as simply another subversive tendency.

It is difficult to know whether any missionary activity was carried on. There is virtually no evidence for it. It is often assumed, for example, that the Slav immigrants to Anatolia must have been converted before their settlement.[80] But the empire's immediate needs were for agricultural and military manpower; and in the two or three years over which the Justinianic transfer of 689 was organised and carried out, it seems unlikely that anything more than the most superficial proselytisation could have occurred. Once in Asia Minor, of course, it is probable that conformity with orthodox Christian practices became unavoidable, as the state and Church could hardly ignore the existence – and possible influence – of large numbers of non-Christians in the heart of the empire. Such groups, which, as we have seen, were under the general supervision of officials appointed from the capital, will undoubtedly have received ecclesiastical attention, and it is quite likely that new bishoprics were established specifically for them. The bishop of Gordoserbon in Bithynia (in the *Opsikion* district) was present at the Quinisext in 691/2 (although not at the sixth council in 680),[81] and the bishopric is referred to in the seventh-century Notitia of

---

[80] See Bréhier and Aigrain, pp. 200–1, where the Christianisation of the Slavs in the Balkans is assumed to have been under way by the time of the establishment of the Bulgars in the 680s.

[81] Mansi XI, 996E. See B. Grafenauer, *Die ethnische Gliederung und geschichtliche Rolle der westlichen Südslawen im Mittelalter* (Ljubljana 1966), p. 19. But doubts have been expressed as to the Slavic origin of the name – see P. Charanis, 'The Slavic element in Byzantine Asia Minor in the thirteenth century', B 18 (1946–48), 78 and note 1 (repr. in *Studies on the Demography of the Byzantine Empire* VII (London 1972)); but these are not very convincing: whether or not the name Serb has a Slavic root, the point is that the people in question used this name themselves, and Gordoserba may well reflect the establishment of an episcopal see for them in Bithynia. See Obolensky, *Byzantine Commonwealth*, pp. 59f.; and Lilie, 'Kaiser Herakleios und die Ansiedlung der Serben', 26ff. That such a procedure was not unusual at the time is clear from the canons of the Quinisext itself, where canon 38 (Mansi XI, 960E–961A) notes that newly founded or re-founded 'cities' should be subject to the traditional civil, fiscal and ecclesiastical authorities. Note also canon 39 (*ibid.*, 961A–C) on the establishment of the 'city' Nea Ioustinianopolis in Hellespontus for the refuge congregation of Constantia in Cyprus.

Pseudo-Epiphanius.[82] It is tempting to conclude that this reflects the activity of Church and state in the conversion and integration of the new settlers. The imposition of Christianity on such immigrant populations must anyway have been regarded as a duty of the emperor, and the fact that there is virtually no explicit evidence for this does not alter that. The exclusion of the monophysites from the Christian *oikoumenē*, implicit in the acts of the sixth council and in the canons of the Quinisext, demonstrates that the state can in no way have tolerated such overt heterodoxy. That the canons of the Quinisext wish to deal with pagan and Jewish tendencies, but make no reference to actual communities of pagans (for example), is surely suggestive of the fact that there were no such obvious targets to name – it is unlikely that all reference to such a dangerous element within the Christian community would have passed over in such silence, if it had actually existed.

We may reasonably conclude, therefore, that in name at least the population of the empire was by this time assumed to be entirely Christian, an assumption which certainly underlies the canons of the Quinisext; and that the chief problem was perceived to lie in the continued use of cult-practices, superstitions and so on, which for the contemporary Church were dangerous leftovers of pre-Christian tradition and had to be excised. The fact that the empire, nevertheless, retained its multiethnic and polyglot character – Greek-, Slav- and Armenian-speakers dominated, but other ethnic/linguistic groups counted themselves as 'Romans', too – gave Christianity and orthodoxy a particular importance, of course; and the relevance of notions of 'conformity' and 'belonging' at this time is particularly apparent, as we shall see.

If missionary activity continued at all in this period, it did so at a very low-key level. Specific groups – such as the Slav immigrants – may have been compelled by the power of the state to convert, even if at first only superficially. But massive undertakings of the sort carried out by John of Ephesus and others in the mid-sixth century do not appear in the sources at all, and it is tempting to conclude that they simply did not occur because it was felt that there was no need, or rather, no perceived need, for them.

For the cultural introversion which typifies Byzantine society from the later sixth to the middle of the eighth centuries (approximately) meant also a narrowing of horizons, cultural and ideological, as well as, more obviously, geopolitical. The shrinking of the empire to a rump of the Justinianic state brought with it, naturally enough, a loss of interest in what had now become very distant affairs – the question of the Christian communities in

---

[82] In Gelzer, *Ungedruckte und ungenügend veröffentlichte Texte der Notitiae Episcopatuum*, p. 538 number 187. In general, see also Ditten, 'Zur Bedeutung der Einwanderung der Slawen', pp. 153ff.

south Arabia or Ethiopia, for example, must have seemed very distant from the concerns of the government of the mid-seventh century. On the other hand, conversion for diplomatic-political reasons remained on the agenda; for Christianity marked out the Romans and their world empire clearly from their barbrian foes.[83]

Under Heraclius, attempts were made to Christianise the Serbs and the Croats 'invited' to settle in the western Balkans. While these efforts were not successful in the long term, short-term diplomatic success did follow.[84] The conversion of the Onogur ruler Organa with his son Kovrat and other followers at Constantinople in 619 similarly served diplomatic ends and belonged to a long and respected Roman political-diplomatic tradition. It was apparently – according to the limited and much later tradition incorporated into the History of the patriarch Nicephorus in the early ninth century – quite successful. But only the leadership of these Bulgaric clans seems to have accepted Christianity, so that their demise meant not only the end of their new religion, but also the hitherto friendly relations maintained with the Byzantine court.[85] In the same way, it has been argued that a serious plan to achieve the conversion to Christianity of Sassanid Persia was evolved and pursued during the 620s and 630s, a plan which was, in the event, brought to nothing by the Arab invasions.[86] Such missionary efforts may well have been stimulated by the eschatalogical attitudes which became apparent at the end of the sixth century and in the reign of Heraclius.[87]

Thereafter, and until the later eighth and early ninth centuries, neither state nor Church seems to have promoted or supported in any significant way – that is, which merited mention in the sources – a deliberate policy of missionary activity and proselytisation either within or without the empire. The conversion of the Chazar wife of Justinian II provides an example of one way in which non-Christians were converted; but it is an isolated and, in general terms, an insignificant example.[88] No doubt individuals did preach Christianity in neighbouring lands or along the

[83] Compare the speech attributed by Theophanes (307.3sq.) to Heraclius, delivered to the soldiers before battle: the Christian Romans are placed clearly on the side of God's struggle with evil, against the pagan and blasphemous barbarians.

[84] See the summary in Obolensky, *Byzantine Commonwealth*, pp. 59ff.; and Ditten, 'Zur Bedeutung der Einwanderung der Slawen', p..129 with literature; Lilie, 'Kaiser Herakleios und die Ansiedlung der Serben', 26ff. with sources and literature.

[85] Summarised in Obolensky, *Byzantine Commonwealth*, pp. 62–3.

[86] See C. Mango, 'Deux études sur Byzance et la Perse sassanide, II: Héraclius, Sahrvaraz et la vraie croix', *TM* 9 (1985), 105–18; note the earlier study by I. Shahid, 'The Iranian factor in Byzantium during the reign of Heraclius', *DOP* 26 (1972), 295–320.

[87] See Mango's final remark, *ibid.*, 117, with reference to the prophecy of Chosroes II reported in Theophylact Simocatta V, 15.1–11; and compare the argument in the text of the *Doctrina Iacobi nuper Baptizati*.

[88] Theophanes, 372.30sq.; Ostrogorsky, *Geschichte*, p. 119.

Religion and belief 353

border regions, when the opportunity presented itself; but these seem to have had little effect. As far as the sources reflect the actual situation in the Slav-occupied Balkans and the Peloponnese, in the early ninth century, for example, the population was still predominantly pagan.

Cultural introversion thus came to mean a preoccupation with the attempt to force the 'real' world of the time to fit the 'ideal' world or model of the political theology of state and Church. The only response the imperial government and the Church seemed able to offer to opposition within its frontiers, and within the Christian world at large, where straightforward argument or command proved insufficient, was military force and violence. And the imperial government – and Church – seem to have been far too involved with problems of internal political authority and the distribution of power, together with the determination to stamp out all heterodox belief and practice which accompanied this concern, to be able to commit the effort and the resources necessary to large-scale missionary activity. In ideological terms, such activity must have seemed simply ineffective, if it was considered seriously at all. Perhaps it was also the pressure placed on the Christian polity by the militant and aggressive force of Islam which emphasised this tendency – conversion by the sword seemed, at least according to this example, to be both quicker and more effective. The traditional missionary activity of the Church must have appeared in comparison simply not effective enough to make the effort worthwhile. For, more importantly, the military success of Islam was taken commonly by Byzantine society to be a sign of God's wrath against the Chosen People for the sins they had committed. It is not surprising, therefore, that the longer-term tendencies evident from the later sixth century were focused and intensified in the second half of the seventh century around a whole group of symbolic referents which bore directly or indirectly on this theme within the framework of the traditional imperial ideology: imperial authority, the universality of orthodoxy within the empire, imperial responsibility for both ensuring and maintaining orthodoxy, and for perceived failure to do so. In this context, the overriding concern was for internal order and correct belief – a prerequisite, after all, for any attempt to expand and recover the areas wrested from imperial control.[89] Only then could the question of the wider Christian world be considered – and this meant, first of all, relations with the West and in particular with the papacy. Only when all these problems had been resolved could the question of the conversion of the barbarians outside the empire seriously be considered.

Given these concerns and the different routes by which they could be

[89] See Haldon, 'Ideology and social change', esp. 165–7 and 175–7 with sources and literature for a summary of some aspects of this development.

achieved – represented by the state and its political ideology on the one hand and by elements within the Church, especially the traditional opposition to state intervention in (or attempts to direct) matters of theology and interpretation, on the other hand – it is not surprising that the conflicts which arose, over monenergism and monotheletism, over imperial authority and what amounted to the theory of imperial 'infallibility' and, later, over icons, did occur. Neither is it surprising that the intellectual – as opposed to the political-military – confrontation with Islam did not even begin until the middle of the eighth century. Islam, even according to John of Damascus still a Christian heresy, was not the cause of Byzantine defeats; it was the Christian community itself which had brought the forces of Islam down upon it, and the situation could be recovered, therefore, only by first putting the Christian house in order. The strengths or weaknesses of Islam, the existence of pagans in the Balkans – such questions were insignificant compared with the quest for orthodox purity, correct belief and the maintenance of the order and harmony derived from, and imitating, that reigning in heaven.[90]

These are some of the key motifs of seventh-century political-theological debate; and it is the attempts of different social/political groups within the empire to come to terms with the radically changed social, economic and political conditions of the *imperium Romanum* after the 640s which must figure at the centre of any modern attempts to understand and explain the political and ideological history of the Byzantine world in this period. For members of the Byzantine cultural-ideological world – the 'symbolic universe' of east Mediterranean imperial orthodox culture – the crux of the matter was the imbalance between the way the world was supposed to be and the perceived and experienced realities of the times. What the events of the seventh century actually present is the harsh juxtapositioning of realities against theoretical representations; or, put another way, it demonstrates the effects on people's understanding and explanation of the

---

[90] It was primarily the iconoclastic controversy, in particular the supposed Islamic influence on the first iconoclasts, especially Leo III, which stimulated this interest and the need to confront Islamic doctrine. The first informed treatise against Islam is by John of Damascus, being the second part of his Fount of Knowledge (Πηγὴ γνώσεως): see PG XCIV, 677–780 (*De Haeresibus*); see D. Sathas, *John of Damascus on Islam. The 'Heresy of the Ishmaelites'* (Leiden 1972). Later polemics – by Theodore Abu Qurra, for example, a pupil of John of Damascus – elaborate the basic argument which consists of a chapter-by-chapter refutation of the Koran, intended to demonstrate on the basis of patristic writings and of the scriptures the contradictions and inconsistencies of Islamic thought. See Beck, *Kirche*, pp. 337ff., 478 and 488f.; A.Th. Khoury, *Polémique byzantine contre l'Islam (VIIIe–XIIIe siècle)* (Leiden 1972); also E. Trapp, 'Manuel II. Palaiologos, Dialoge mit einem "Perser"', Wiener byzantinistische Studien II (Vienna 1966), see pp. 11–95 with literature and a general survey of the beginnings and development of Byzantine anti-Muslim polemic. Note also E.M. Jeffreys, 'The image of the Arabs in Byzantine literature', *Seventeenth International Byzantine Congress, Major Papers*, pp. 305–23, see pp. 316ff.

world and their own experience, both as individuals and as members of different social and institutional groupings, of the changes which occurred in their environment, which the traditional explanatory models available to them could not handle.[91]

Ideology vs. experience, or: old narratives for new

Already in the later sixth century the evident mismatch between the grandiloquent claims of the Justinianic world empire, and the fact of its actual structural weakness, had led to a reassessment of a number of key elements within the imperial ideology.

This does not mean to say that there had not been substantial criticisms of the emperor in, say, the time of Justinian I; nor that there had been no anxieties about the nature of imperial rule, the direction and effects of imperial policies and so on. Indeed, a number of writers voiced doubts, in different ways, about various facets of Justinian's rule. But such doubts were limited, on the whole (or so it would seem), to a relatively limited number of literati in Constantinople or other major cities. Opposition to Justinian's policies, and especially to the effects of his fiscal administration, high taxation, and the maladministration which led to hardship for the armies, were voiced in the Nika riot, for example, or in the various mutinies and rebellions which affected the army and some provinces. But such opposition was primarily concerned with immediate material conditions, as I have argued elsewhere, and was crushed quickly and effectively. The divisions it implied were papered over through the more obvious political and military successes of the reign, and the presentation – in an idealised and codified form (through the Code and the Novels) – of an orderly, imperially ruled and God-protected empire. The failure of the Justianianic reconquista, the collapse of Byzantine power in Italy with the arrival of the Lombards, the increasingly heavy raids from both Turkic and Germanic, as well as Slav, peoples in the Balkans, the costly warfare with the Sassanian state in the east – along with the consequent lack of resources, shortage of troops to defend the newly extended frontiers, increased oppression of the producing population by the state's fiscal apparatus – all these developments seem to have stimulated a move away from reliance upon, and trust in, the imperial cult and the symbols of imperial authority, and the hierarchy of the established imperial Church – features of late Roman society and its symbolic universe that evoked the relationships between God and mankind and provided a straightforward framework of authority within which the world could be understood.

[91] What follows has been argued at greater length and in more detail in Haldon, 'Ideology and social change'.

Instead, attention was drawn to less material and less fallible symbols of heavenly authority and, more importantly, of heavenly intercession. Local communities, in particular urban communities, overcame, at certain levels of social experience and group identity, the social and class differentiation within their society through appeal to a single divine intermediary and intercessor – a local saint or a figure from the divine hierarchy of angels, even (in the case of Constantinople) the Virgin herself. And this new emphasis was brought out and given expression in the cult of relics of many saints and in the icons through which the powerless human could approach directly – and not through the formal networks of the Church – a patron or protector.[92] At the same time, the peculiar holiness of the ascetic and hermit, who had confronted the devil and his hordes directly and not been overwhelmed, provided a similar attraction. A feature of both urban and rural society in the late Roman period, the significance of the 'holy man' lay in the function he came to fulfil as both social intermediary and intermediary between God and man. Importantly, however, neither icons nor holy men were part of any official framework of authority consecrated through the Church. On the contrary, they were implicitly blessed directly by God and the Holy Spirit, as the icons 'not made by human hand' demonstrate all too clearly. And as such they were both immensely attractive to people in search of answers and support, comfort and affirmation of their lives as they led them; and at the same time potentially subversive and anomic in respect of the 'establishment'.[93] They could undermine confidence in the Church, challenge its representatives in their interpretations and explanations, mislead or corrupt those who followed them. But this was not (yet) the issue at stake. Indeed, the popular shift of attention was quickly taken up

[92] Haldon, 'Ideology and social change', 161f.; and Cameron, 'Images of authority'; Nelson, 'Symbols in context'; E. Kitzinger, 'The cult of images in the age before iconoclasm', *DOP* 8 (1954), 85–150; Brown, 'Dark-age crisis'; for the cult of the Virgin, see Cameron, 'Theotokos'; and for the cult of relics, see Auzépy, 'L'évolution de l'attitude face au miracle à Byzance'. For the sixth-century situation and the latent contradictions, see Cameron, *Procopius*, esp. pp. 242–60 ('Procopius and sixth-century political thought').

[93] See Kitzinger, 'Images before iconoclasm'; and esp. Brown, 'Holy man'. For the icons 'not made by human hand' – *acheiropoiēta* – see Kitzinger, 'Images before iconoclasm', 112–15. Note also, however, the critical remarks of H.W. Drijvers, 'Hellenistic and oriental origins', in *The Byzantine Saint*, ed. S. Hackel (London 1981) (= Studies supplementary to *Sobornost*, V), pp. 25–33, who modifies Brown's original thesis in a number of aspects, noting that while the particular socio-ideological function of holy men evidenced in the Syrian tradition for that region was determined by local social and cultural structures, the holy man as such was not a purely Syrian phenomenon, having also a general relevance in late Antique society, the significance of which was structured and nuanced by local conditions. This comes out clearly in the miracle-collections, particularly those of St Artemius and St Therapon, and in the accounts of wonders worked by both holy men and monks, and icons or holy amulets – the stories attributed to Anastasius of Sinai, for example, or those in the Life of Andrew the Fool. See chapter 11 with notes 53 and 55.

Plate 9.1 Seventh-century icon (from a triptych) of St Theodore Tiro

Plate 9.2 Sixth- to seventh-century icon of St Peter

Plate 9.3 Seventh- to eighth-century icon of St Athanasius and St Basil

by the establishment of Church and state, and served to refocus the divergent tendencies within the symbolic universe of the late sixth-century Roman world around the Christ-loving emperors protected by God at Constantinople, and the ideological framework of Christian imperial theory.[94]

This displacement of ideological attention was, therefore, a result of the failure of the leading symbolic elements within the established political ideology of the state and the imperial Church to evoke adequately and to answer the challenge to Roman imperial universality and authority thrown down by the events of the post-Justinianic years. It had shaken and loosened the identity of Christians with their world order which was well structured and very much taken for granted. The clear divide between Roman and barbarian, Christian and non-Christian became less well defined;[95] and the response – diffused at first throughout the social formation, taken up and directed by the imperial authorities later – was the phenomena which I have described. The attempts, both deliberately fostered by the state and spontaneously generated within late Roman society, to reaffirm and restate the boundaries and structures which were thus shaken are clear enough in the formal ritualisation of imperial ceremonial, the distinction drawn between the sacred and the profane, holy and secular, and the emphasis placed upon exclusiveness, but – within the political bounds of the empire at least – universality of belief: the persecutions of the reigns of Tiberius and Maurice, and the popular echo they found, is one good illustration. Another, perhaps even more vivid, is

[94] See Cameron, 'Images of authority', and esp. P.J. Alexander, 'The strength of empire and capital as seen through Byzantine eyes', *Speculum* 37 (1962), 339–57, see 345. It must be emphasised that the Constantinopolitan element in the rhetoric of imperial ideology was itself nothing new. From the time of Constantine's transfer of the capital from Rome, efforts had been made to clothe imperial tradition in a new Christian garb, in terms of the 'new Rome' and the symbolism of renewal (see Alexander, 'The strength of empire and capital', 348ff.). But it was eminently suited to the ideological needs of the emperors of the later sixth century, who took it up and developed it in a much more explicit form – along with the symbolism of its divine protectress, the Virgin – and thereby determined the future course of a crucial component of Byzantine imperial ideology. See the literature and discussion in Cameron, 'Theotokos', *passim*, Alexander, 'The strength of empire and capital, 341ff., and esp. E. Fenster, *Laudes Constantinopolitanae* (Miscellanea Byzantina Monacensia IX, Munich 1968), pp. 20ff. See also the references in note 122, chapter 9, below.

[95] For the importance of such categories and the boundaries they represented, see esp. F. Dölger, 'Bulgarisches Cartum und byzantinisches Kaisertum', *Bull. de l'Institut archéologique Bulgare* 9 (1935), 57–68 (= *Byzanz und die europäische Staatenwelt. Ausgewählte Vorträge und Aufsätze* (Ettal 1953 and Darmstadt 1964), pp. 140–58), see 58f., and 'Rom in der Gedankenwelt der Byzantiner', *Zeitschrift für Kirchengeschichte* 56 (1937), 1–42 (= *Byzanz und die europäische Staatenwelt*, pp. 70–115); note also P. Brown, *Religion and Society in the Age of St Augustine*, pp. 46–73, see 55.

that expressed in the concern to draw the boundaries between 'real' and 'false' holy men – in the 'questions and answers' attributed to Anastasius of Sinai and, more dramatically, in the hagiographical tradition – in the Life of Andrew the Holy Fool and, thereafter, in the narrative literary tradition of the Byzantine world.[96]

The reaffirmation of the late sixth century, therefore, represents an attempt to explain change as perceived by members of the East Roman cultural world from their own particular position and sense of place within their society. It was thus a relatively diffuse set of developments. It is expressed most obviously in the focusing of attention on imperial ceremonial and, more specifically, in the centralising of a variety of elements within the framework of the imperial ideology around the figure of the emperor, the ruler appointed by God and the symbolism of the divinely bestowed imperial authority. An increase in the ceremonial and ritual aspect of court life – both public and private – had been an element of the imperial cult since the fourth century, of course; but the later sixth century saw a distinct quickening of pace.[97] But, crucially, this refocusing now also involved other elements which had hitherto been less central – heavenly guardians and guarantors of imperial authority, elements which had represented also the tendency to redirect attention away from God's agent on earth (and the vast established institutional framework through which imperial power was exercised) back to God Himself.[98] The saints and martyrs and other divine intercessors about whom civic and local saints' cults proliferated played a double role. While they publicly evoked the heavenly sources of imperial authority, they served at the same time to represent a more immediate and tangible source of divine authority and grace. Power in this respect, rather than being centralised, was in fact diffused and diversified at a multiplicity of local levels. Evidence for such cults and for the devotion they attracted increases dramatically at this time; so that while the central authority struggled at the formal, official and public level of Constantinopolitan and provincial ceremonial observance to centre attention on the emperor and his relation with God, it was this very emphasis on the divine source of the emperor's authority which contributed to and promoted the power of local saints and martyrs; for it

---

[96] See Anastasius of Sinai, *Quaestiones et Responsiones* (PG, LXXXIX, 329–824), qu. 62(648–52); *Vita Andreae Sali*, 776C–784A. See Brown, 'Sorcery, demons and the rise of Christianity', 17ff. On the 'Question and Answer' literature, see chapter 11.

[97] See A. Alföldi, 'Die Ausgestaltung des monarchischen Zeremoniells am römischen Kaiserhofe', *Mitteilungen des Deutschen Archäologischen Instituts*, römische Abt., 49 (1931), 1–118, see esp. 35ff., 63 and 100.

[98] See esp. Cameron, 'Images of Authority', 15–21; 'Theotokos', 120ff.

was the latter who represented a locally involved, committed and – crucially – an easily accessible source of mediation and intercession.[99]

The 'new' elements which appear within the imperial political ideology were new only in so far as they were brought to the fore to occupy a position that had hitherto been otherwise filled. Indeed, the response to the situation of the late sixth century in general was latent in the symbolic universe of the East Roman world, and more particularly within the framework of the imperial ideology itself, which was refined out of a complex of elements within that symbolic universe. The parallel between the Chosen People of the Old Testament and the Christian Romans, the notion of the emperor's position as divinely ordained, the notion of political and military success and social harmony being dependent upon right belief and practice, and the notion that God can – and does – punish the Chosen People when they stray from the path of righteousness; these and many other elements drawn from the traditional Roman imperial cult and from Hellenistic political theory, the Judaeo-Christian tradition as well, made up the complex whole of the Christian imperial ideology. They were articulated together in a unity, in which modern commentators have seen three main components: the religious-political rhetoric which tied the fate of Constantinople, the New Rome, to that of the Christian *oikoumenē* and to the future as foretold in the Old Testament; the theory of imperial rule based on the concept of renewal, that is, of the renewal of an original state of affairs; and the theory of the God-ordained nature of the Christian Roman empire.[100]

Now these varied elements were welded together both at the level of

[99] See Kitzinger, 'Images before iconoclasm', esp. 95ff. The realignment of imperial foreign policy under Justin II (an attempt to regain the prestige it was felt had been lost in the later years of Justinian's reign and to reaffirm strong imperial leadership) and the imperially sponsored persecutions under Justin, Tiberius II and Maurice illustrate the efforts of the emperors and the central government to put themselves back into the centre of the stage: see Haldon, 'Ideology and social change', 167 and note 73. Similarly, the Emperor Heraclius was placed even more prominently at the forefront and was presented as a parallel and indeed fulfilment of the Old Testament tradition, as divinely appointed ruler in the image of David. See Cameron, 'Images of authority', 21 and note 93; S. Spain Alexander, 'Heraclius, Byzantine imperial ideology and the David plates', *Speculum* 52 1977), 217–37, see 225 and 232–3.

[100] For the notion of the Chosen People, see F. Dvornik, *Early Christian and Byzantine Political Philosophy* (2 vols., Washington D.C. 1966), vol. II, pp. 797 and 823; Cameron, 'Images of authority', 21–2; Haldon, 'Ideology and social change', 166 and note 68. For the tripartite division of the imperial ideology, see esp. Alexander, 'The strength of empire and capital', 340ff. For some general discussion of key aspects of this ideological system, see Treitinger *Kaiser- und Reichsidee*, pp. 158ff. and 220ff.; Winkelmann, 'Zum byzantinischen Staat', pp. 171–4; H. Hunger, 'Ideologie und systemstabilisierung im byzantinischen Staat', *AHASH* 27 (1979), 263–72; and the literature cited in Haldon, 'Ideology and social change', 156 note 37. See, for the older literature, the essays collected in H. Hunger, ed., *Das byzantinische Herrscherbild* (Darmstadt 1975). All these elements were present in the sixth century, for example – see Cameron, *Procopius*, pp. 256–7.

Religion and belief 363

formally expressed statements of political-religious ideology – in the prooemia to imperial legislation, for example; or in secular or religious texts where the nature of the emperor's rule was set out for a wider readership or audience – where they were most coherently expressed; and at the level of ordinary, day-to-day rationalisations of personal and group experience.[101] And as far as possible, the leading elements represented and gave meaning to the perceived realities of that experience. Once circumstances had changed sufficiently for this no longer to be the case, that is, once contradictions between the world and man's place in it according to the generally accepted views held in society, and the world as it now came to be perceived, became apparent, then of course both individuals and groups within society would, sooner or later, have to confront the fact that the explanations available to them for what was happening to their world – however broadly or narrowly it was perceived – did not work. The result was, in the later sixth century, an attempt to rearrange the chief elements of the imperial ideology, bringing hitherto less central aspects or symbols to the fore; and an attempt on the part of the ordinary population of the empire – across all social classes, of course – to understand that experience of the world through different channels. The developments of the period, in particular the swing towards reliance upon sources of 'direct' and localised access to God, evident especially in seventh-century texts, represents this effort at reassessment.[102]

The reaffirmation of the traditional values and framework of the Christian Roman world, which took place through this reassessment of narrative elements both in people's day-to-day lives and in the formal political

---

[101] See, for example, H. Hunger, *Prooimion. Elemente der byzantinischen Kaiseridee in den Arengen der Urkunden* (Vienna 1964); and cf. an eighth-century view, in the romance of Barlaam and Joasaph, trans. in E. Barker, *Social and Political Thought in Byzantium* (Oxford 1957), esp. pp. 82f.; and see Beck, *Kirche*, pp. 482f. For this type of literature – the 'Fürstenspiegel' – see Hunger, *Profane Literatur*, vol. I, pp. 157ff.

[102] A useful way to look at such changes is through the medium of personal and group narrative, that is, accounts of events or situations in the sources which, whatever their conscious intention, contain implicit assumptions about the ways in which the world was perceived and how the individual perceived him or herself. It is through narrative – that is, through accounts of experience – that the construction of a personal social identity and a reality is made possible. I have discussed this approach at greater length in 'Ideology and social change', esp. 151ff., where further literature will be found. A further pointer to the direction of change can be seen in the hagiographical and other writings of the seventh century in particular, in which the direct personal relationship between God (or his representative, the saint, martyr or similar figure) and individual is both taken for granted and a *sine qua non* for the construction and understanding of the texts themselves. The accounts of the miracles of Artemius and of Therapon, for example, compiled during the later seventh and early eighth centuries, provide classic examples; and note the comments attributed to Anastasius of Sinai in Quaestio 55 (*PG* LXXXIX, 617A–620B) – but also in other questions – where this relationship and its mutual nature is discussed and stressed.

ideology of the state, seemed to be vindicated by the successes of the Emperor Heraclius in his wars with the Persians. It also explained the disasters of the reign of Phocas and of the early years of Heraclius himself.[103]

The rise of Islam, and the Arab conquests, marked a new, and in the event much more real, threat to imperial stability and to the very existence of the empire itself. It dislocated Byzantine society much more fundamentally and dramatically, and at all levels – political, economic, and in terms of beliefs and ideas about the world. Reasons for the onslaught, and for its successes, were not difficult to find within the existing framework of belief, in particular the assumption that the Chosen People had sinned in some way and were in consequence suffering their chastisement, a motif well established in Christian political theology.[104] Monotheletism, the last, unsuccessful attempt of the neo-Chalcedonian imperial establishment to win over the monophysite East – offered reason enough for many in both West and East for the continuing success of the Arabs, and of other barbarians in the Balkans. But the very fact of opposition to imperial policy – even though justified by Maximus Confessor on strictly theological grounds – was, in the context outlined above, in which imperial authority itself was at stake, a direct challenge that could not be ignored. Imperial insistence on acceptance of its policies, therefore, whether that involved accepting monotheletism itself, or merely agreeing not to discuss the nature of imperial authority, becomes quite understandable. All the emperor wanted was an acknowledgement – through acceptance of the Typos of 648 – that he remained the fount of all authority on earth, because he was God's direct choice for this role.[105] And the relevance of monotheletism to the question of reuniting the monophysites in the East in communion with the dyophysites in the West, whatever the hopes that may have been cherished about their political recovery, slips into the background.

The conscious and unconscious efforts to rethink the elements of the

---

[103] See especially P. Lemerle, 'Quelques remarques sur le règne d'Héraclius', *Studi Medievali* I (1960), 347ff. (repr. in *Le Monde de Byzance: histoire et institutions* III (London 1978)); S. Spain Alexander, 'Heraclius, Byzantine imperial ideology and the David plates'; Cameron, 'Images of authority', 21ff.; Shahid, 'The Iranian factor', 303f., and 'Heraclius, πιστὸς ἐν Χριστῷ βασιλεύς', *DOP* 34/5 (1980/1), 225–37.

[104] See S. Sophronii ... *Epistola Synodica ad Sergium Patr. CP* (PG LXXXVII, 3, 3148–200), 3197D; note also Anastasius of Sinai, Quaestio 17 (PG LXXXIX, 484A–500A), regarding the evils which befall the Romans; and cf. Quaestio 114 (765C–768A), on the reasons for pestilences and similar misfortunes. Note also *Lateran*, 40.28sqq.: Sophronius of Jerusalem's reason for not attending.

[105] For Maximus' position, see Ep. X (PG XCI, 449–53), 542D; and compare his other statements on his position during his various interrogations: PG XC, 116–17, 145C–D, 161D–164A and 164D–165A. See Haldon, 'Ideology and social change', 173–6 for a more detailed discussion.

imperial ideology and the traditional explanatory models of day-to-day realities thus received a further check. The framework which had been carefully constructed still depended for its cohesion and its explanatory power on the position of the emperor. Any dislocation of this structure would shake the whole system, and an imbalance between theory and 'reality', between divine and imperial authority, would once more appear. In the event, the disasters of the 630s, 640s and 650s, the massive restructuring of resource-allocation and distribution, and the damaging conflicts between the central government and some of its citizens on the issue of monotheletism, the Typos, and the unpopular trials and punishment of Maximus and Martin and their confederates, had precisely this effect. The tendency to reassess the relationship between the various elements which made up the social narratives of the subjects of the empire, represented as a transfer of spiritual and ideological allegiance away from the earth-bound to the less vulnerable heavenly sources of authority, picked up speed, facilitated by the fact that the heavenly intercessors had by now been thoroughly integrated into the fabric of the imperial ideology itself, and to a degree at the expense of the emperor's own position.[106]

The emperors found themselves in an even more difficult position. On the one hand, the cult which the court and Church maintained and fostered formally and explicitly recognised the centrality of heavenly authority and the emperor's absolute dependence upon it for his own authority; on the other hand, it was those very aspects of the imperial ideology which laid emphasis upon divine support and mediation which threatened and even bypassed imperial political power. While the Christian state, represented and symbolised by the emperor, attempted to reinforce its position by discrediting or damaging any claims to share or to circumvent the authority vested in it by God (illustrated, for example, by the fact that Constans II issued copper coins with the reverse inscription *ananeôsis* and *en toutô nika*),[107] other sections of Byzantine society likewise attempted to reinforce their own position and the framework of their beliefs (the order and structure of their narratives of the world), by clinging to those symbols which appeared to represent a less vulnerable and fallible source of authority; or, in the case of those who were able to do so, by opposing changes – and the imperial government – when such changes seemed to pose a threat to the traditional values, structures and framework of Christian society and the efficacy of its symbols.

Thus the state argued with the articulate and literate opposition pre-

---

[106] See especially Kitzinger, 'Images before iconoclasm', 126f.; Cameron, 'Images of authority', 6ff., and 'Theotokos', 100. Note also Haldon, 'Some remarks', 176f.

[107] Compare the nature of the charges levelled against Maximus and Martin, which make this concern absolutely clear: *PG* XC, 112A–D and 113C; Mansi X, 855D–E, 856A; and also 850D–E. See Haldon, 'Ideology and social change', 173ff. Constans' coins: Grierson, *DOC* II, pt 1, 101–2; pt. 2, 406, 408f.

sented by the Western and African clergy, and particularly those grouped around Pope Martin, Maximus Confessor and the organisers of the Lateran council of 649, and carried on a public debate over the source of authority within the empire, with all the public political implications this involved. But ordinary attitudes among the majority of the population – whether urban or rural, or members of the state apparatus or the army or whatever – had already shifted sufficiently to make the debate over the Typos or monotheletism itself irrelevant. In effect, the values represented by the more personal symbols of the icon, or the holy patron, in their roles as accessible mediators and intercessors, seem already to have superseded those vested explicitly in the figure of the emperor as the symbol of God's mediation between Himself and mankind. New narratives were already available, and the result was a parallelism or plurality of sources of authority on a scale not hitherto encountered.

Soldiers who visited Maximus during his imprisonment were more interested in ascertaining whether or not he had slandered the Virgin, than whether he rejected or challenged imperial authority. Indeed, the fact that the imperial government could find no better way of arousing hostility to Maximus than attributing this slur to his name is sufficient and revealing evidence of the direction in which private and public devotion was moving.[108]

In 692, the Quinisext had to confront one element of the problem when, in canons 41 and 42, it sought to regulate entry into the monastic life and, more especially, to control the movements and influence of itinerant holy men. It suggests that by the 690s, there had been a considerable increase both in the numbers and importance of such individuals, clearly not subject to any ecclesiastical discipline, a result, we may assume, of both the disruption of the Church administration in the provinces and the dislocation of provincial populations. Refugees, as we have seen, were clearly a problem for the ecclesiastical administration, and presumably for the civil administration, too.[109] In such conditions, the importance of these hermits and itinerant preachers must have risen considerably as the needs of the ordinary rural population for interpretation and explanation increased. Some of the questions supposedly addressed to Anastasius of Sinai reflect this preoccupation, concerned as they are with the existence of 'false prophets' and 'miracle workers', and with the question of whether or not it is possible to obtain the services of one holy man to undo the work of another. Similarly, a warning tale about a woman who took advice from a 'sorcerer' in the mistaken belief that he was a holy man, which occurs in

[108] See *PG*, XC, 168C–169B.
[109] See Mansi XI, 964A–C and 964D. A number of refugees from Syria who arrived in 686 (see Theophanes, 364.3–4) must have added to the confusion.

Religion and belief   367

the fictional Life of Andrew the Fool (later seventh century) deals with the same point. Such questions and stories illustrate the concerns of this time of uncertainty – as do queries such as why there were so many lepers, cripples, epileptics and others among the Romans, in contrast to other, non-Christian peoples; or whether prophesying and fortune-telling through *lachnistērion* (chance searching through pages of the Old and New Testaments) were permitted.[110]

The traditional ideological framework offered little comfort. But the apocalyptic prophecies, which represented a long popular tradition and responded most clearly to the needs felt by the uneducated mass of the population in the provinces especially, had become the bread-and-butter of such preachers and itinerant holy men.[111] And it is not surprising that it is at just this time that the greatest and most widely disseminated of the medieval compilatory apocalypses, that of Pseudo-Methodius of Patara, was produced.[112] What is particularly significant is that apocalyptic writings of this sort represented an alternative ideology of the future: the formal political ideology permitted an abstract and distanced statement of the relationship between empire and God; the eschatology of writings like the apocalypse of Pseudo-Methodius – which, following an increasingly important trend within the apocalyptic-eschatalogical tradition, identified the historical Christian Roman empire with the last of the four world empires of the vision of Daniel – in contrast, predicted an ultimate and

---

[110] See *Quaestiones* 20 (*PG*, LXXXIX, 517C–532B), 62 (648A–652D), 94 (732B–733C) and 108 (761A–B); and *Vita Andreae Sali*, 777C–781A. Compare canon 61 of the Quinisext (Mansi XI, 970E–972A), which condemns all forms of fortune-telling, palm-reading, prediction, as well as the use or sale of amulets and so on. These practices were certainly not peculiar to the seventh century; but the fact that the Quinisext felt obliged to deal with them, along with a wide range of problems of a similar nature, in such an explicit and directed manner, is eloquent in the context in question.

[111] See the comments of G. Podskalsky, *Byzantinische Reichseschatologie. Die Periodisierung der Weltgeschichte in den vier Grossreichen (Daniel 2 und 7) und dem tausendjährigen Friedensreiche (Apok. 20)* (Munich 1972), pp. 70–1, on the increasingly polemical and compilatory character of the apocalyptic tradition from the late fifth century on, and the gradual reduction of its original technical exegetical aspect. But it should be recalled that such writings were also part of a much older, and still very lively, Jewish tradition, which also experienced a revival at this time: see S.W. Baron, *A Social and Religious History of the Jews* V (8 vols.): *Religious Controls and Dissensions*, 2nd edn (New York 1957), pp. 138–50.

[112] See Podskalsky, *Byzantinische Reichseschatologie*, pp. 53ff.; Haldon, 'Ideology and social change', 168 and note 74; P.J. Alexander, 'Medieval apocalypses as historical sources', *American Historical Review* 73 (1968), 997–1018, see 998ff. (repr. in *Religious and Political History and Thought in the Byzantine Empire* XIII (London 1978); and especially G.J. Reinink, 'Pseudo-Methodius und die Legende von römischen Endkaiser', 82ff., who argues that it was originally intended as a sermon or homily: see also 'Ismael, der Wildesel in der Wüste. Zur Typologie der Apokalypse des Pseudo-Methodios', *BZ* 75 (1982), 336–44, esp. 338 and note 14.

assured victory over the enemy, in this case, the Arabs.[113] The Pseudo-Methodius apocalypse, originally written in Syriac, but very soon available in Greek and Latin, circulated probably in the 690s, and it was clearly intended to be directly relevant to the experiences of a confused and battered Byzantine population, as well as to the Christians outside the empire. The great popularity of the text bears out the observation that this type of literature flourished most at the times when people most needed it, that is, in times of social, political and economic upheaval. The apocalypse contained in the Life of Andrew the Fool, which dates to the same period, was likewise intended quite explicitly to generate hope and optimism about the future.[114] In the early part of the century, the Persian and early Arab attacks had similarly generated such apocalyptic compositions, notably the apocalypse of Pseudo-Ephraim and the Syrian Christian legend of Alexander.[115] Particularly telling is the short treatise composed by the monk Theophanius in about 710, which attempts to calculate the date of the end of the world using a cabbalistic process of attributing numerical values to the names of the key figures in the Old Testament. The work was compiled towards the end of the period with which we are concerned, at a time when popular fears about the end of the world, the threat from Islam and the problems of imperial authority were all central issues. It is an interesting reflection of the scepticism with which some popular

[113] Podskalsky, *Byzantinische Reichseschatologie*, pp. 54–5 and 72ff.
[114] Alexander, 'Medieval apocalypses as historical sources', 1005f. and 1002; J. Wortley, 'The literature of catastrophe', *Byzantine Studies* 4 (1977), 1–17. For the Life of Andrew the Fool, see C. Mango, 'The Life of St. Andrew the Fool reconsidered', *Rivista di Studi Bizantini e Slavi* 2 (= *Miscellanea A. Pertusi* II) (Bologna 1982), 297–313 (repr. in *Byzantium and its Image* VIII). The apocalypse known as the Exegesis of Ps-Daniel, dated to the years 716–17, is discussed in the same article (see 310–13) and fulfilled a similar function. On the Pseudo-Methodius Apocalypse in particular, see G. Reinink, 'Pseudo-Methodius: A Concept of History in Response to the Rise of Islam', in Averil Cameron and L.I. Conrad, eds., *The Early Medieval Near East: Problems in the Literary Source Material* (Princeton 1990), where its general ecumenical relevance is discussed. Note also, on another Syriac Apocalypse of the same period, H.J.W. Drijvers, 'The Gospel of the Twelve Apostles: A Syriac Apocalypse from the Early Islamic Period', *ibid*.
[115] See W. Brandes, 'Apokalyptisches in Pergamon', *BS* 47 (1987), 1–11, see 5–7 with literature, and 'Die apokalyptische Literatur', in *Quellen zur Geschichte des frühen Byzanz* (BBA, LV Berlin 1989). See also Th. Frenz, 'Textkritische Untersuchungen zu "Pseudo-Methodios": das Verhältnis der griechischen zur ältesten lateinischen Fassung', *BZ* 80 (1987), 50–8. Note also the interesting discussion of H. Suermann, *Die geschichtstheologische Reaktion auf die einfallenden Muslime in der edessenischen Apokalyptik des 7. Jahrhunderts* (Europäische Hochschulschriften, Reihe XXII: Theologie, 256. Frankfurt, a. M. Bonn and New York 1985); and G. Reinink, 'Die Entstehung der syrischen Alexanderlegende als politisch-religiöse Propagandaschrift für Herakleios' Kirchenpolitik', in *After Chalcedon. Studies in Theology and Church History Offered to Professor A. van Rooey* (Orientalia Lovanensia Analecta, 18. Leuven 1985), pp. 263–81. For a convenient survey of the effects of the Arab conquests on the Syrian monophysite Church and its later tradition, see S. Ashbrook-Harvey, 'Remembering pain: Syriac historiography and the separtion of the Churches', *B* 58 (1988), 295–308, esp. 304f.

mythology about the date of the last judgement, and the fate of the empire in the immediate future, may have been handled, that Theophanius produced the date of A.D. 880 (in our reckoning) for the end of the world.[116]

The activities of the itinerant holy men, the inability of the established Church to maintain ecclesiastical discipline and, in particular, the already established fact that the location of what was holy or sacred in Eastern Christian culture was both more widely dispersed and more ambiguous than in the West – and, therefore, more directly accessible, more open to immediate personal experience – all these elements contributed to a new atmosphere. Especially indicative is the proliferation of private chapels and, indeed, the fast-growing custom of celebrating the liturgy in private homes, something quite absent in the West, where the Church retained a much stricter control over such activities.[117] It was this new atmosphere which generated both an understanding of what was happening to the traditional framework of society, as well as the action which was felt to be necessary to preserve it intact, by allowing a more openly critical position with regard to imperial authority and the individual emperor's interpretation of that authority. It is worth adding, perhaps, that the attempts of the Church to control the hermits and preachers were, on the whole, unsuccessful: the itinerant, wonder-working holy man or monk remains a classic of Byzantine hagiography in the ninth and tenth centuries. The popularity and importance of such figures is borne out by the number of references to holy men competing for their audience and following – there must have been many more such figures than the hagiographical tradition alone would suggest. Just as significant is the effort of the Church to assert its authority over the scriptural and textual tradition upon which dogma and the canons were founded. Canon 9 of the Quinisext is particularly strongly worded: the clergy and bishops should interpret Scripture strictly in accordance with the Fathers of the Church, and not improvise – once more, the establishment of authority and the signalling of the existence of

---

[116] See Beck, *Kirche*, p. 473. The text is discussed by A. Dobschütz, 'Coislinianus 296', *BZ* 12 (1903), 534–67, see 549ff.

[117] See especially P.R.L. Brown, 'Eastern and Western Christendom in late Antiquity: a parting of the ways', Studies in Church History XIII (1976), 1–24, see 11f.; Nelson, 'Symbols in context, 111f. and 115f. For private chapels and the liturgy, see canons 31 and 59 of the Quinisext (Mansi XI, 956E and 969C); and the discussion of T. Mathews, '"Private" liturgy in Byzantine architecture', *Cahiers Archéologiques* 30 (1982), 125–38. Whether there was indeed a proliferation of 'domestic' icons during the seventh century, as has been maintained (e.g. J. Herrin, 'Women and the faith in icons in early Christianity', in *Culture, Ideology and Politics*, ed. R. Samuel and G. Stedman-Jones (London 1982), pp. 56–83, see 66ff.) has been seriously questioned by P. Speck, 'Wunderheilige und Bilder: Zur Frage des Beginns der Bilderverehrung', in *Varia* III (Poikila Byzantina XI. Bonn 1991) 163–247; idem, 'Das Teufelsschloß. Bilderverehrung bei Anastasios Sinaites?', in *Varia* V (Poikila Byzantina XIII. Bonn 1994) 295ff.

clear boundaries are the chief concerns. And these concerns are echoed also in the Questions and Answers of Anastasius of Sinai. Indeed, the effort made at this time to establish an authoritative set of texts from which dogma could be adduced, clear in the proceedings of the sixth ecumenical council and in the canons of the Quinisext, is an important affirmation of this preoccupation.[118]

The political and ideological history of the second half of the seventh century illustrates the extent of the changes. Political coups, military rebellions and attentats all had their immediate, conjunctural causes. But that they could occur, and that such actions could be envisaged as ideologically acceptable, shows that the ground rules within which individuals and groups situated themselves socially had been drastically revised. The later seventh century contrasts vividly with the sixth century, a period of relative internal stability, political expansion and ideological security, at least up to the 550s and 560s. In such a context, the imperial ideology left no room and made no provision for direct challenges to imperial authority. Conversely, however, the very different situation of the later seventh century and the realignment of elements within the symbolic universe and especially within the imperial ideology itself meant that such a challenge could appear both justifiable and worthwhile.

Justinian II's reformed coinage offers a clear example of the desperate efforts made by the emperors to keep up with these shifts in people's world view: the Quinisext had ordained that Christ should no longer be represented as a lamb, but in his human form, thereby the better to stress his incarnation (canon 82). Justinian's reformed coinage moved the emperor's bust from the obverse to the reverse of the gold coins, introducing a bust of Christ to the obverse. The intention must have been to emphasise the ordinance of the Quinisext; but it served also to stress the nature of Christ's role as mediator and intercessor between heaven and earth. And, given the ideological context we have described, it must also have served to emphasise the emperor's particular role in this relationship. The *Hodegos* of Anastasius of Sinai, written during the years from *c.* 640 to *c.* 680 and incorporating his own later additions, argues strongly for the value of certain representations from the life of Christ, in particular the crucifixion, as didactic means of refuting heresy. Together with canons 73, 82 and 100 of the Quinisext, which all deal with images, this may be evidence of a tendency at this time to recruit icons into the service of the Church as one more weapon in the battle against heterodoxy and the struggle to maintain the boundaries between orthodoxy and the 'outside' world. Once

---

[118] See the useful brief summary of K. Ringrose, *Saints, Holy Men and Byzantine Society, 726 to 843* (Ann Arbor 1976), pp. 83ff. For the Quinisext, see Mansi XI, 952; and for Anastasius, see qu. 117.

more, it would seem to represent an attempt on the part of the central authority to stress and reinforce the divine nature of their authority on earth. Justinian's successors, in reverting to the traditional type, seem to have sought to cement their authority by reversing the process and returning to the traditional, and legitimating, form.[119]

The search for order: the case of the soldiers

In this changed situation, and on the basis of this very different interpretation of the function and position of imperial authority, individuals and groups were able to take action directly and to intervene in imperial politics in order to protect what they perceived to be their interests, or the interests of the state; or indeed to re-establish a stability and security which had been lost.

One group in particular deserves our attention, since their activities at this time are highlighted in the sources, and hence serve to elucidate some of these developments, developments which were central to the contemporary perception of the world. For as the seventh century wore on, the provincial soldiery came increasingly to be drawn from, and to represent, at least implicitly and in a partially refracted form, the attitudes and sentiments of the provincial and rural populations. Their actions represent at the same time a generalised loss of faith in the traditional symbols of authority and the increasing ineffectiveness of traditional legitimating narratives; and, in however distorted a way, and in spite of the very different consequences which followed, they represent an attempt to restore an older, and irretrievably lost, pattern of relationships of authority. Officers and soldiers played the central role in all the political upheavals of the second half of the seventh century. Unlike the period up to, approximately, the last years of Heraclius, pay and conditions of service do not seem to have fired the discontent. On the contrary, ideological motives lie clearly at the root of a number of such demonstrations – the support for Constans II among the troops of Valentinus in 641–2, the rebellion of Gregory, the exarch of Africa, in 647 and of Olympius in Italy in 649–52, the demonstration of the *Anatolikōn* troops at Chrysoupolis in 681, the coups of 695, 698, 711 and of the years up to 717 – they all were

[119] See Haldon, 'Some remarks', 164–6; and for Justinian's coinage, see chapter 2, note 83 above; and A. Grabar, *L'Iconoclasme byzantin: dossier archéologique* (Paris 1967), esp. pp. 36ff. and 77–80 and plates. For Anastasius and the icons see Anna D. Kartsonis, *Anastasis: The Making of an Image* (Princeton 1986), pp. 59ff., and 'The *Hodegos* of Anastasius Sinaites and Seventh-century pictorial polemics', in XVI. *Internationaler Byzantinistenkongress. Résumés der Kurzbeiträge* (Vienna 1981), 10.3. For a general comment on the search for authoritative tradition, see C. Head, *Justinian II of Byzantium* (Madison, Wisconsin 1972), p. 61.

made possible by the ideological climate and assumptions of the times, as well as the fact of the political and military, and – indeed – the economic, instability of the times.[120]

Of course, soldiers may not always have been the direct instigators in these events; they may sometimes have been merely tools in the hands of politically more astute and self-interested officers; they may also have taken action for purely 'selfish' motives, having become aware of their political relevance and their strength. But in all these cases they were voicing more often than not the attitudes of the provinces and reflected in turn a genuine concern with the politics of the imperial government, given expression through the realignment of the key elements in the symbolic narratives through which the whole fabric of beliefs, intuitions and practices of Byzantine society was represented. The emperor and the imperial ideology stood at the centre of this complex, and it is not surprising, therefore, that they stood also at the centre of political conflict.

Soldiers became important in this period for a number of reasons. In the first place, the army represented a set of institutions which generated its own rules of conduct, identity, role-playing and its own language. It represented, in short, a specific set of practices, a discourse, within the larger framework of the social formation. It represented also one of the few organised contexts in which large numbers of individuals, especially those drawn from the dispersed rural communities of the provinces, came together. And in the context of the seventh century, this becomes especially significant. While the urban-centred society of the period up to the early seventh century was able to channel its social and cultural resources into and through the cities, the result of the long decline of corporate municipal life and of the economic-administrative independence of the cities, which had set in during the third century, meant that the cities lost this role.[121] They ceased to be self-governing administrative units responsible for both their own and the state's revenues. By the seventh century, the majority were rapidly becoming local centres of state provincial administration only, their single remaining function being as a collecting point for the extraction and forwarding of the state's taxes and other revenues. The cities themselves had no economic role in this process. As corporate bodies, they had lost effective control over their lands and rents, which now went to the state or to private landlords. The net result was the dissolution of the formal administrative and fiscal ties which had hitherto bound the city to its territorium; and the loss of the historic function of the cities within the

---

[120] See chapter 2, above; and Haldon, 'Ideology and social change', 177–89 with sources and literature.

[121] See chapter 3 above; and see also W. Goffart, 'Zosimus, the first historian of Rome's fall', *American Historical Review* 76 (1971), 412–41, see 425–6 and notes 63–6.

structure of the Roman state, as the basic and essential component of provincial fiscal administration. Cities may well have housed locally appointed fiscal and administrative officials, selected from the traditional sources; but it was centrally appointed, salaried bureaucrats who controlled and directed such appointments, supervised their activities and took charge of the revenue-collecting operations. In these circumstances, a transfer of the social and economic wealth previously invested in the provincial cities to the capital and the state apparatus is not surprising. The city had lost not only its economic and corporate personality, it had lost thereby its social and cultural relevance and attractiveness. Provincial notables and others whose family careers and importance had hitherto been firmly entrenched in provincial municipal culture now shifted their attention to Constantinople, where they vied for position, titles and honours within the ambit of the imperial court and the bureaucracy, and within the establishment of the Church.[122]

Given this development, cities could no longer function adequately as channels of acceses to authority at a local level, nor to the capital and the governing elite there. The corporate nature of provincial municipal life was replaced by a kin-based solidarity of family groupings, by the individualism of the competition for power and wealth within the imperial bureaucracy and the Church. And it was this 'blocking off' of routes of access to authority which disadvantaged the ordinary provincial, especially rural, populations. The wealthy could overcome the physical and cultural barriers; simple artisans and peasant cultivators could not.

The effect of this phenomenon was to push the provincial soldiery into the limelight. This group became, in practical terms, the only representatives of provincial opinion and attitudes which was in a position to make its views known; it had also the institutional organisation and hence the power to take action to make these views known. And while it is clear that such views must always, to some extent, have reflected the particular interests of a special – and in many ways privileged – group within society, they must also have represented the sentiments of their own social class and culture, their own loyalties and the loyalties of their region and so on, an association which can only have gained in strength as recruitment and

---

[122] See chapter 3 above; and note especially H. Hunger, *Reich der neuen Mitte*, on the process whereby Constantinople was transformed from the city of the imperial government, one among several equally important and prestigious cities in the sixth century, to *the city*, during the seventh century, a process completed by the loss of Alexandria, Antioch, Jerusalem and other large centres to the Arabs. But the process was initiated under Justinian, and taken up and promoted by his immediate successors. Cf. Cameron, 'Theotokos'; and H.-G. Beck, 'Konstantinopel, das neue Rom', *Gymnasium* 71 (1964), 166–74; W. Hammer, 'The concept of the new or second Rome in the Middle Ages', *Speculum* 19 (1944), 50–62.

service came to be identified with particular districts. Provincial fears and uncertainties, provincial attitudes to the government or the local administration, anxiety about and frustration at the failures of the government to deal effectively with the various barbarians besetting the empire and wrecking the rhythm of economic and social life; all of these feelings could now be expressed by the provincials through only one channel – the local army.

The attitudes and actions of soldiers thus take on a new significance. They serve to a degree, and however muted and refracted, as a barometer of the views and beliefs of provincial society. This explains also their 'incorporation' by the state into the framework of legitimacy, even if only nominally – both Constantine IV and Justinian II attempted to integrate the armies as an element of the state and its authority into some of their formal statements.[123] While military unrest or opposition to the government was obviously determined in its form and content by the specific context of the times, the public activities of soldiers can suggest a great deal about the responses of the ordinary people of the times, about whom we hear otherwise virtually nothing. It was because the existence of traditional society as it was understood seemed to be threatened and because the stable framework through which experience could be reconstructed via personal and social narrative was shaken, that soldiers could take the sorts of action that they did in the middle of the seventh century and afterwards. They were simply responding to their understanding of events, and their position both socially and institutionally gave them the power to intervene directly to restore the situation, as they perceived it, to a former state, a state of order, certainty and political and social harmony.

Taken as a whole, therefore, the period from the reign of Justin II up to that of Leo III presents a fascinating story, of a society and a culture in the process of redefining itself. 'Redefining' was, of course, not the conscious intention – reaffirmation of the traditional was what was intended – but this was nevertheless the end result, viewed from our vantage point. Every society or culture generates sets of legitimating ideas and theories, explanatory and descriptive mechanisms which are, in effect, the social-functional forms of personal and shared narrative reconstructions of experience, through which each group within the society is able to 'justify' or legitimate its practice and explain its position in terms of its physical and social environment. Such theories and explanations are themselves determined in their content by the subjective evaluation of the experiences of the institutional group or social class concerned, and, by the functions they fulfilled, given expression in the terms of what was culturally available, through the symbolic universe. They represent various aspects of the main ideological currents prevailing within a culture and, less immediately, the

[123] See Mansi, XI, 201C; Riedinger, 10.23f., and 737B–738A; Riedinger, 886.20–25.

material conditions of existence of the sections of society which maintain them; and they tend to be expressed through one set of terms or another within the dominant political ideology.

Now, when the stability of a social formation, or the position of one or more sections within it, is felt to be under threat, it becomes necessary to reaffirm the validity, the authority, and indeed the relevance of its own values and the narrative representation of those values. The history of Byzantine society in our period represents just such a situation. This is not to imply that Byzantine society – or indeed any socio-cultural formation – was a monolith. On the contrary, different sections reacted differently and at different times to their own subjective interpretations of what was going on, and how they should respond. The situation was stabilised at first through the development of social and political-ideological narratives which absorbed and tried to compensate for the effects of the apparent contradictions within the symbolic universe: an increased private and public, official reliance upon icons, for example, as more accessible mediators and intercessors between God and man; imperial ceremonial designed to augment and bolster the emperor's authority by emphasising its divine source, and stressing the emperor's piety and devoutness. This development was reinforced by Heraclius' successes against the Persians. But the successes of Islam introduced new strains upon the system, while the long-term structural changes in society – the fate of the cities, for example, with all that that entailed – increased those strains to breaking point. The attempts at religious unification made by Sergius and Heraclius, the attempt to impose absolute imperial authority under Constans II, these represent two approaches to the problems as they were perceived. The 'intervention' of soldiers and officers reflects the position of the provincial armies and the attitudes of the provincial populations themselves to these developments. It indicates also the growing inadequacy of the traditional legitimating narratives. Only with the iconoclastic controversy and its outcome would new sets of such legitimating theories be fully worked out. But it must also be emphasised that iconoclasm, as an imperial policy, was not simply a product of the 'crisis' generated by the advance of Islam in the East and the establishment of a new, threatening and rival cultural and political force, a point of view maintained by some historians.[124] It was much more complex than that. As we have seen, both long-term internal social and ideological tendencies, as well as the effects on Byzantine state and society of military, fiscal and political crises, were combined in an intricate pattern in the creation of the conditions which made imperial iconoclasm first of all thinkable and, secondly, practicable.'

---

[124] Most recently Herrin, *The Formation of Christendom*, p. 343.

CHAPTER 10

Forms of social and cultural organisation: infrastructures and hierarchies

As we have seen in the foregoing account, late Roman society was marked by a distinct introversion and introspectiveness from the late sixth century on. While this tendency is represented at the level of official, public consciousness – where it is most easily detected – as a form of ideological reorientation, as an attempt to reaffirm the traditions and values of the past, its roots lie in the material conditions of existence and the experiences and perceptions of people at all levels of society, from the lowliest tied peasant to the emperors themselves, and in the ways these people were able to give meaning to and come to terms with these experiences.

The interpretation placed upon these perceptions and experiences both promoted, and in its turn was promoted by, changes which also affected people's relationships to one another, and the concepts and vocabulary available to describe and explain these relationships. In terms of their response to the wider world, we have seen how some of these ideas were marked out. But they had effects upon what might be termed the social infrastructure, too, the relationships of individuals and groups through marriage and kinship, patronage and clientship and, most especially, in the context of seventh-century Byzantium, through and within the apparatuses and the hierarchy of the state.

INDIVIDUAL, FAMILY AND THE STATE

One of the most significant developments of the later Roman period was in the area of kinship structures,[1] and the ways in which Christian marriage, as a formal system of gift-exchange, property-transmission and social

[1] For some introductory comments on the problem, see J. Thirsk, 'The family', *Past and Present* 27 (1964), 116–22, the essays in S.C. Humphreys, *The Family, Women and Death: Comparative Studies* (London 1983), and in R.N. Anshen, ed., *The Family: Its Function and Destiny* (New York 1959), and esp. P. Laslett, 'Family and household as work group and kin group: areas of traditional Europe compared', in R. Wall et al., eds., *Family Forms in Historic Europe* (Cambridge 1983), along with the other essays in that volume.

alliances, came to play an increasingly central role in both the organisation of social relations and in the self-image of the society, as represented at least through the writings of Churchmen, hagiographers and jurists. The recognised forms of liaison which were inscribed in Roman law were modified in a number of ways. The possibility of divorce came to be increasingly restricted,[2] and by the eighth century the Church was developing a specific betrothal service.[3] While concubinage (the regular union between a free man and a slave or freedwoman) was tolerated by the Church (as was simple cohabitation if consented to by the parents), it was gradually assimilated to regular marriage, as the Church, during the sixth and seventh centuries, gained greater success in obtaining recognition from the state for its principles.[4] But even in the eleventh century, such relationships were still acceptable within the terms of the civil law; while the Ecloga clearly gives full recognition to a union which takes place by consent alone, made known either through a Church ceremony or through civil witnesses – this was especially so when poverty prevented the exchange of marriage gifts and the drawing up of a formal, written contract. Only in the reign of Leo VI (886–912) did the benediction of the Church become an absolute condition for the validity of a marriage.[5] The original distinction between the written and publicly witnessed marriage agreement of those belonging broadly to the estate of *honestiores*, and the non-binding arrangements (in terms of the law, of course, rather than in terms of the social bonds that followed) of the poorer in society, however, while it did not disappear, was gradually blurred over as both types of arrangement were brought within the supervision of the Church and the

---

[2] Divorce by mutual consent remained, however: *CJ* V, 17.8; 9; Justinian, *Nov.* 22 (a. 536). Justinian's novel 117 (a. 542) had stipulated a series of specific grounds, but Justin II withdrew these regulations in 566. Thereafter, novel 117 seems to have been in abeyance until the eighth century. See especially the survey of L. Bressau, *Il divorzio nelle chiese orientali* (Bologna 1976), pp. 21ff., esp. 22–3 and C.E. Zachariä von Lingenthal, *Geschichte des griechisch-römischen Rechts*, 3rd edn (Berlin 1892 and 1955), pp. 76–81.

[3] See *CTh.* III, 5.2 (a. 319), 6 (a. 336); *CJ* VI, 61.5 (a. 473); and especially E. Herman, 'Die Schliessung des Verlöbnisses im Recht Justinians und der späteren byzantinischen Gesetzgebung', *Analecta Gregoriana* 8 (1935), 79–107; K. Ritzer, *Formen, Riten und religiöses Brauchtum der Eheschliessung in den christlichen Kirchen des ersten Jahrtausends* (Munich 1961), pp. 77ff. and 143ff.

[4] See *Digesta* 25, 7.3 for the original Roman definition; and for the harsh measures of Constantine I against the institution, see *CTh.* IV, 6.2f.; *CJ* V, 26.1. Anastasius I and Justinian I both ameliorated these restrictive measures, on the grounds of the hardship caused to the offspring of such unions: Justinian, *Nov.* 89, see proem. Although permitted to unmarried, widowed and divorced men and women in the Ecloga, it was regarded effectively as an unwritten marriage contract, and treated thus. See *Ecloga* II, 6.

[5] See the cases in the *Peira*, for example, XLIX, 25 (*JGR* IV, 204–5); and see *Ecloga* II, 2 and 6. Note also the valuable discussion of A.E. Laiou, 'Consensus Facit Nuptias – et Non. Pope Nicholas I's Responsa to the Bulgarians as a source for Byzantine marriage customs', *Rechtshistorisches Journal* 4 (1985), 189–201. For the legislation of Leo VI, see esp. novel 89.

state; although again, the first clear evidence of this process is from the ninth century. Similarly, by the ninth century betrothal and marriage were seen, at least by the Church, as more or less equally binding: so much is implied in the replies of Pope Nicholas I to the questions on Christian practice addressed to him by the Bulgar Tsar Boris-Michael in 866; and this is the effect of novels 74 and 109 issued by Leo VI.[6] At the same time, the process of prohibiting marriage within an ever-widening range of cognates – beyond first, and later second, cousins – had been completed, in theory, by the later seventh century. Such prohibitions are embodied in the canons of the Quinisext council of 692 and are firmly laid down in the Ecloga – although it is probable that they finally obtained general and widespread acceptance and enforcement only in the eleventh century.[7] The Ecloga took up once more, although in a revised form, the heart of the Justinianic legislation on divorce, which had been abrogated by Justin II, and there is a very marked tendency to reinforce the permanence of the marital contract and to limit the possibilities for divorce. By the eighth century, divorce could only be obtained (again at least in theory) with some difficulty, after a hearing, a radical change from the traditional Roman practice. With its emphasis on family-law, especially the disappearance of the *patria potestas* of the family head over his offspring once they had attained the age of majority, the Ecloga marks an important stage in the consolidation of the orthodox nuclear family of the middle ages.[8]

The stimulus to this legislative activity on the part of both Church and state, it has been suggested, is to be located in the reaction to a very different tendency in many parts of the empire, namely the reassertion from the later third century of close ties of consanguinity in marriage arrangements, and in particular the emphasis on cross-cousin marriage (that is, between sons of sisters and daughters of brothers of the same

---

[6] See Justinian, *Nov.* 94 (a. 538), 4–5; and compare with *Ecloga* II, 6. See H.J. Wolff, 'The background of the post-classical legislation on illegitimacy', *Seminar* 3 (1945), 21–45 (repr. in *Opuscula Dispersa* (Amsterdam 1974), pp. 135–59). For the ninth-century evidence, see, for example, *Epanagōgē* XVI, 1.

[7] See the summary in Beck, *Kirche*, pp. 87ff. with literature.

[8] See canon 54 (Mansi XI, 968D-E); *Ecloga* II, 2. For some general comments, see Sp. Troianos, 'Ἡ μετάβαση ἀπὸ τὸ ρωμαϊκὸ στὸ Βυζαντινὸ δίκαιο', in *Seventeenth International Byzantine Congress, Major Papers*, pp. 211–35; and D. Simon, 'Zur Ehegesetzgebung der Isaurier', Fontes Minores I (1976), 16–43, see 30–42 (although the novel in question has now been shown to date from the reign of Leo V, the general argument made in this article remains valid). For the redating, see O. Kresten, 'Datierungsprobleme "Isaurischer" Eherechtsnovellen. I. Coll. I 26', Fontes Minores IV (1979), 37–106, see 49–53. For the Roman background, see the survey of Beryl Rawson, 'The Roman family', in *The Family in Ancient Rome: New Perspectives* (London and Sydney 1986), pp. 1–57; and esp. W.K. Lacey, 'Patria Potestas', *ibid.*, pp. 121–44. For a summary of the Byzantine developments, see A. Schminck, art. 'Ehebruch', in *Lexikon des Mittelalters* III (1986), 1660, and Zachariä, *Geschichte*, pp. 55–83.

parental group) and the consequent importance of uncle–nephew relationships. It has been argued that such consanguinous marriages, designed to maintain the continuity of lineage-property, were the norm in the period of the principate.[9] But, in fact, the elite strata of Roman society in the first three centuries A.D. and, as far as can be determined, much of provincial society, placed no more emphasis on this type of relationship than on the alternative exogamous forms.[10] A tendency to endogamy can be detected in the West, under the influence of Germanic settlers and their cultural traditions; while in parts of the East, especially Syria and Palestine, the revival of such endogamous structures has also been taken to mark the strengthening of village-based as opposed to urban-based forms of property acquisition and transmission. But whereas in the West, the establishment of the extended kinship-group or clan is firmly attested during the period from the sixth century and after, it is clear that in the East, this 'revival' (if the evidence for it has been correctly interpreted, a point about which there is still some debate) was strongly disapproved of by the state and frowned upon by the Church.[11] The reasons, I suggest, lie to a degree at least in the increasing cultural introversion within the Eastern Christian imperial lands from the sixth century, a phenomenon discussed at greater length in chapter 11, below; and in an increasing desecularisation of ideas about society and the relationship between God and man. In addition, the Constantinian legislation of the fourth century on sexual relations and marriage – even though later considerably revised and relaxed under Justinian – had condemned and proscribed many features of the traditional Roman marriage law and concubinage, effectively forcing changes in patterns of marriage behaviour among the social elite which, in spite of later ameliorations, had permanent results.[12]

All these pressures, together with the legal embodiment of the Church's assumption that parents were responsible for ensuring that their children

[9] See Patlagean, *Pauvreté économique*, pp. 118–28.
[10] See Brent D. Shaw and Richard P. Saller, 'Close-kin marriage in Roman society?' *Man*, new series 19 (1984), 432–44; note also K. Hopkins and G. Burton, 'Ambition and withdrawal: the senatorial aristocracy under the emperors', in *Death and Revewal. Social Studies in Roman History*, ed. K. Hopkins (2 vols., Cambridge 1983), vol. II, pp. 120–200.
[11] See, for example, Justinian, *Nov.* 22, the 48 paragraphs of which deal with a whole range of matters related to the question of marriage. See Patlagean, *Pauvreté économique*, pp. 118ff. For the West, compare the comments of D. Bullough, 'Early medieval social groupings: the terminology of kinship', *Past and Present* 45 (1969), 9–18. See also K. Schmid, 'Über das Verhältnis von Person und Gemeinschaft im früheren Mittelalter', *Frühmittelalterliche Studien* 1 (1967), 225–49, the contributions in T. Reuter, ed., *The Medieval Nobility* (Amsterdam 1979), and C.J. Wickham, *Early Medieval Italy* (London 1981), pp. 115ff.
[12] See *CTh.* VIII, 16.1 (a. 321); and the commentary of H.J. Wolff, 'Doctrinal trends in post-classical Roman marriage law', *Zeitschrift der Savigny-Stiftung*, romanist. Abt., 67 (1950), 261–319.

were betrothed and married, strengthened the nuclear family unit at the expense of both older, more diffused forms of kinship group, and of simple concubinage and cohabitation. In effect, the Church tried to extend its supervision over all areas of sexual relations by confining and limiting them to a specific form of marital relationship, accompanied by a series of concomitant parental rights and duties, property-regulating stipulations and associated institutions such as God-parenthood. Another result was the legal and the moral privileging of legitimate as opposed to illegitimate children in respect of inheritance.

Parallel to these developments there evolved also the institution of spiritual parenthood, between godparents and godchildren. Even these relationships were assimilated within the general system of prohibited degrees of affinity, so that the two systems constituted a mutually reinforcing whole. Indeed, in Christian thought the spiritual relationship was regarded as much superior to the merely fleshly kinship bond itself.[13]

These changes did not occur evenly or all at once. Their evolution begins already in the later third and early fourth centuries, if not before, in Roman civil law; and still in the seventh century the stable system of later centuries had not been attained. In the later ninth century, Leo VI had still to legislate on relationships of spiritual and adoptive parenthood in order to deal with continued failures to observe the relevant canons of the Quinisext council, a point which demonstrates nicely the often considerable gap between legislative theory and social practice. A similar divide no doubt existed in respect of many other of the developments outlined above. But the popular response to Heraclius' marriage to his niece Martina shows that by this time at least the idea of conjugal and sexual ties between such close kin was regarded with considerable distaste. One must recall, of course, that figures greatly in the public eye attract more attention, and are often expected to behave more closely in accordance with the codes stipulated by the moral universe, than the rest of society. But the story is at least indicative.[14]

[13] See *Ecloga* II, 2, and XVII, 25 and 26; cf. canon 53 of the Quinisext (Mansi XI, 968C). For the Justinianic legislation (less restrictive) see *CJ* V, 4.26/2 (a. 530); and compare with the ultimate results of these developments in terms of the attitudes to marriage, kinship, and 'blood' relationships in modern Greek rural society, as surveyed in J. Du Boulay, 'The blood: symbolic relationships between descent, marriage, incest prohibitions and spiritual kinship in Greece', *Man*, new series, 19 (1984), 533–56, with literature. In general on godparenthood, see E. Patlagean, 'Christianisation et parentés rituelles: le domaine de Byzance', *Annales E.S.C.*, 33 (1978), 625–36 (repr. in *Structure sociale*, no. XII); and, for a recent survey of later developments, Ruth Macrides, 'The Byzantine godfather', *BMGS* 11 (1987), 139–62. See also the essay by A.A. Čekalova, in Udal'cova, ed., *Kul'tura Vizantii*.

[14] See chapter 8 above, p. 304; and see Leo VI, *Nov.* 24 (in P. Noailles and A. Dain, *Les Novelles de Léon VI le sage: texte et traduction* (Paris 1944), pp. 92–5). Note also the comments of the twelfth-century canonist Balsamon on the relevant canon, 53, of the Quinisext (Rhalles-Potles, *Syntagma*, vol. II, pp. 430f.). Whether the patriarch Sergius was

In addition, a very important change in attitudes towards the family seems to have taken place during the fourth century, most clearly represented in the startling expansion of monasticism and the evolution of the concept of an alternative, celibate life devoted to God. The specifically Christian tendency to reject marriage and the reproduction of the family became significant enough to make celibacy a reasonable social alternative for many, although the motivation for such a choice varied greatly from individual to individual – poverty, tax-burdens and debts, the onerous duties of the curial class, or at least the poorer members thereof, as well as less concrete religious grounds – all played a role. By the sixth century, the choice was clear and open to all, and it retains henceforth a central position in late Roman and Byzantine thinking about the family, sexuality and 'society': marriage, family and the reproduction of the social ties and the economic relationships which accompanied them on the one hand; rejection of these relationships, with a clear choice of celibacy in contrast, on the other. The stark opposition between the two modes of living reinforced the identity and the perceived role of the family unit.[15]

The Christianisation of the institution of marriage and the system of kinship-relations revolving around the family was thus a gradual and many-sided process. A crucial impetus was lent to the development by Justinian's order that the canons of the Church should henceforth have the validity of state law – although there still remained substantial areas of disagreement and even conflict between the secular and the ecclesiastical legislation. The process was further consolidated by the appearance of the first collection of *nomocanones* in the later sixth century, in which both secular and ecclesiastical regulations were assimilated in a common corpus. The Ecloga of the early eighth century is based in these respects even more clearly on the canon law of the Church and is usually taken to mark an important moment in the process of change.[16]

None of this is to suggest that the nuclear family unit had not always been at the basis of most kinship structures which existed in the east Mediterranean world. Indeed, there is a problem in reconciling the gen-

---

also involved in this is unclear: see P. Speck, 'Die Interpretation des Bellum Avaricum und der Kater Μεχλεμπέ', in Poikila Byzantina VI: *Varia* II (Bonn and Berlin 1987), pp. 374–5.

[15] See Patlagean, *Pauvreté économique*, pp. 128–45; and note the review by L. Couloubaritsis, in *Revue belge de philosophie et d'histoire* 60 (1982), 374–82, esp. 379f.

[16] See Justinian, *Nov.* VI, 1.8 (a. 535); for the nomocanons, see Beck, *Kirche*, pp. 145ff.; and see A. Schminck, art. 'Ehe', in *Lexikon des Mittelalters* III (1986), 1641–4.

For the different trajectories of Eastern and Western Christianity in these respects, see J. Goody, *The Development of the Family and Marriage in Europe* (Cambridge 1983), pp. 103ff.; but note the critique of C.J. Wickham, in *Journal of Peasant Studies* 14 (1986), 129–34; and D. Herlihy, *Medieval Households* (Cambridge, Mass. and London 1985), pp. 10ff.; cf. also A. Esmein, *Le Mariage en droit canonique* (Paris 1929–35).

eralised use of the term *familia* in the sources, to refer to the wider 'extended' family network, with that for the actual practical, functioning family unit, which was clearly the 'nuclear' unit. For the latter group no real equivalent term existed; and it has been convincingly shown that, until the wider network began to lose its more extended and ramified elements, this remained the case. This evolution was part and parcel of the social and cultural changes of the period from the third century on, of course, and it is only when they are well under way that *familia* comes actually to represent the reality of the elementary family group. The practical disappearance after the fifth century of clan names, and the reappearance of *nomina gentilia* only during the ninth century on any substantial scale in the Byzantine world – a development which corresponds more or less exactly with the rise of the new aristocracy of the middle Byzantine period – is significant. The intervening centuries were marked by the radical loosening of such wider ties and the absence of any integrative kinship structure higher than the elementary family. The almost complete lack of family names on seals or in the literary sources – excluding nicknames or ethnonyms – during the later sixth, seventh and earlier eighth centuries is in this respect particularly relevant.[17]

By the end of the seventh century, therefore, Christian marriage seems to have become, in legislative terms at least, the preferred form of social-sexual organisation; while the elementary, or nuclear, family was rapidly becoming the only significant unit of any social relevance. The legislation itself marks only specific moments in the evolution and generalisation of the social institutions themselves, of course, and its clear-cut formulations can by no means be taken to mean that other forms of familial structure did not continue to exist for some considerable time. There remained still substantial areas of conflict between Church and state – over the question of divorce, for example, and especially of remarriage, and over the question of whether civil or ecclesiastical courts should have the final competence over matters pertaining to marriage and divorce; but the attention paid to, and emphasis placed upon, the elementary family unit, with its limited lateral extensions, and the parallel institutions of spiritual parenthood, demonstrates that by the later seventh and early eighth centuries these were well on the way to becoming the key terms within which the social relationships of Byzantine society were understood.

[17] See the excellent analysis of Brent D. Shaw, 'The family in late Antiquity: the experience of Augustine', *Past and Present* 115 (May 1987), 3–51, with extensive literature; and the comments of B. Rawson, *The Roman Family*, pp. 7ff. For the Byzantine period, see F. Winkelmann, 'Probleme der gesellschaftlichen Entwicklung im 8./9. Jahrhundert', in *Seventeenth International Byzantine Congress, Major Papers*, pp. 577–90, see 581ff., and *Quellenstudien*, pp. 143ff.

These changes have been examined at length elsewhere,[18] and we need not dwell on them further here. What has, on the whole, not received adequate attention is their long-term role within the structure of late Roman and early Byzantine society. For the substitution of the limited nuclear family unit for the extended kinship group from the fourth to the seventh century meant in the first instance a potential fragmentation of kinship solidarity and property transmission. While in the latter case this will hardly have affected the greater part of the peasant population, it certainly affected the property-owning elite throughout the empire. And kin-groups must have been affected by this compartmentalisation. The Church now replaced the extended kinship-community. Indeed, it can be plausibly argued that the institution of godparenthood was an effective social-communal substitute for wider kinship ties, if not in respect of property, then certainly in respect of social and family solidarity.[19]

The close-knit, autonomous elementary family unit was the result of all these changes – already in the ninth century it contrasted with the basic family unit in the West[20] – but it seems unlikely that Christian ideology alone, even in conjunction with the various late Roman factors referred to, brought about the qualitative transformation which has been described. In the West, the Church was engaged for a far longer period in trying to enforce canon law evenly and throughout the area under the jurisdiction of Rome.[21] Likewise, the legislation itself reflects the theoretical demands of

[18] On all these developments, see Jones, *LRE*, vol. II, pp. 972ff.; and esp. B. Cohen, 'Betrothal in Jewish and Roman Law', *Proceedings of the American Association for Jewish Research* 18 (1949), 67–135; J. Gaudemet, 'Les Transformations de la vie familiale au Bas-Empire et l'influence du Christianisme', *Romanitas* 4/5 (1962), 58–85, and *L'Eglise dans l'empire romain (IVe-Ve siècles)* (Paris 1957), pp. 515ff.; E. Herman, 'Die Schliessung des Verlöbnisses' (see note 3, chapter 10, above), and 'De Benedictione Nuptiali quid Statuerit Ius Byzantinum sive Ecclesiasticum sive Civile', *OCP* 4 (1938), 189–234; H. Hunger, 'Christliches und Nichtchristliches im byzantinischen Eherecht', *Österr. Archiv für Kirchenrecht* 18 (1967), 305–25 (repr. in *Byzantinische Grundlagenforschung* XI (London 1973)); J. Gaudemet, *La Formation du droit séculier et du droit de l'église aux IVe et Ve siècles* (Paris 1957); A. Hage, *Les Empêchements de mariage en droit canonique oriental* (Beirut 1954); E.F. Bruck, 'Kirchlich-soziales Erbrecht in Byzanz. Johannes Chrysostomus und die mazedonischen Kaiser', *Studi in onore di S. Riccobono* (3 vols., Rome and Palermo 1933), vol. III, pp. 377–423; A. Christophilopoulos, *Σχέσεις γονέων καὶ τέκνων κατὰ τὸ Βυζαντινὸν δίκαιον* (Athens 1946); Patlagean, *Pauvreté économique*, esp. pp. 114–28, and 'Christianisation et parentés rituelles' (see note 13, chapter 10, above). Note also the remarks of Každan and Constable, *People and Power in Byzantium*, pp. 32ff., and the old, but still valuable general survey of Zachariä, *Geschichte*, pp. 71–6.
[19] See Macrides, 'The Byzantine Godfather' (see note 13, chapter 10, above), esp. 155ff.
[20] See K. Ritzer, *Formen, Riten und religiöses Brauchtum der Eheschliessung in den christlichen Kirchen des ersten Jahrtausends* (Münster 1961), p. 104.
[21] See Goody, *The Development of the Family and Marriage in Europe*, passim; and see also D. Herlihy, 'Family solidarity in Medieval Italian history', in *Economy, Society and Government in Medieval Italy: Essays in Honour of Robert C. Reynolds* (Kent, Ohio 1970), pp. 177–84. For the results of these developments, see the comments of A.P. Každan, 'Small social groupings (microstructures) in Byzantine society', *Akten des XVI. Int. Byzanti-*

the Church or the state, as is clear from the canons of the Quinisextum, for example, where canons 53 and 54 assume a continuing gulf between theory and practice. Traditional relationships between cousins, for example, seem to have survived.[22] What other factors, therefore, contributed to the transformation?

In the first instance, we may recall the general situation of early Byzantine culture. The introversion described in an earlier chapter affected the whole of society, albeit in different ways in different contexts.[23] It is surely no accident that the dominance of the elementary family unit offers parallels to this development. It represents a turning-away from the wider context of the kinship group, a system of social relations in which the units that make up the group exchange property – including wives – on the basis of a self-reproducing, horizontal reciprocity. Instead, the isolated nuclear unit, which depends absolutely on the wider institutions of society for its legitimation and its perpetuation (and less as a group than as a community of individuals) takes its place. Under the powerful influence of the Church, which stressed the reliance of human beings upon heavenly authority, rather than upon the community and its ties, the tendency can only have been encouraged. The imperial ideology itself reflected this emphasis on heavenly authority, of course; the harsh penalties imposed in the Ecloga serve to underline this, the stress on conformity and orthodoxy across the whole society, unity of belief and culture, and the determination to eradicate any form of oppositional thinking or practice, are significant features.[24] The extent to which formal statements in legal and canonical writings reflect, or fail to reflect, the wide diversity of local and regional practice, of course, cannot be gauged. But the ideological message and intention is clear enough.[25] It is perhaps also useful to remember that the

---

nisten-Kongresses, II/2, pp. 3–11 (= JÖB 32, 2 (1982)); but with the reservations expressed by Laiou, (see note 5, chapter 10, above), 198–9 and note 32.

[22] Mansi XI, 968C.   [23] See chapter 9, pp. 348ff.

[24] Cf. Ecloga XVII, esp. 23–7 and 30ff. It should be remembered that the various punishments involving corporal mutilation listed in the Ecloga and embodied in the Farmers' Law, for example, were not new: from late Roman times (and indeed earlier) physical mutilation had been practised, intended as a physical demonstration of the authority vested in the state and its institutions, and the marginalisation and exclusion, both literally and metaphorically, of offenders. On the 'philanthropic' element behind the nature of punishment in the Ecloga, see T.E. Gregory, 'The Ecloga of Leo III and the concept of Philanthropia', Βυζαντινά 7 (1975), 267–87, with the remarks of D. Simon, in BZ 69 (1976), 665. For a differently nuanced view, see E. Patlagean, 'Byzance et le blason pénal du corps', in Du châtiment dans la cité: supplices corporels et peine de mort dans le monde antique (Rome 1984), pp. 405–26, who – in my view quite rightly – attempts to relate the types of punishment to a symbolic system in which the body and its parts were related through metaphor to both power and sexuality. A more traditional approach is that of Sp. Troianos, 'Bemerkungen zum Strafrecht der Ecloga', in Ἀφιέρωμα στὸν Νίκο Σβορώνο (2 vols., Rethymnon 1986), vol. I, pp. 97–112.

[25] See Hunger, 'Christliches und Nichtchristliches', 305f. and 324f. (cited note 18, chapter 10, above).

concept of apartness and privacy seems to have received a considerable stimulus at just this time. A number of historians have noted in particular the great contrast between the open, public lifestyle of the classical *polis*, with its style of domestic architecture, which seems to last until the sixth century, and the closed, private, almost secretive lifestyle of the Byzantine town-dweller from the seventh century on. This aspect of Byzantine life is especially evident in Byzantine literature of the period, which speaks of, and often emphasises, the importance of privacy, and the closed-off, compartmentalised organisation of domestic architecture.[26]

In the second place, the physical and cultural disruption which the Byzantine world experienced from the middle of the seventh century, and earlier in the West, must also have had effects on the population in respect of its social-institutional organisation and coherence. Many communities were dislodged or destroyed, as we have seen.[27] The traditional ties of dependence will in many regions have suffered, and – given the circumstances – have become irrelevant to the immediate demands of individual families or communities. In such conditions, reliance upon the state and the Church, both materially as well as spiritually, for leadership and defence, and upon heavenly intercessors, or earthly mediators with access to the heavenly realm, for explanations and reassurance, must have increased; and indeed, we know that in the latter case this did occur.

In the third place, the presence of large numbers of soldiers in the Anatolian provinces, mostly for the first time, must have been significant. The permanent garrisoning of substantial forces in provinces which had hitherto had – with some exceptions – little or no military presence, and the logistical problems alone that this brought with it, must have affected local society in many ways.[28] The increasing emphasis on localised recruitment, for example, and the status and privileges which soldiers brought with them, made them as individuals an attractive proposition to a family with daughters of marriageable age or younger. The socio-sexual intervention of the first and second generations of these newcomers will have affected the demography of the provinces where they were stationed from the 640s and 650s, and consequently the traditional bonds between and within communities in respect of patterns of marriage and kinship. We have already seen that soldiers appear to identify themselves with provincial and local issues in the later years of the seventh century; and there is no reason to doubt that this local identity is rooted in their incorporation or absorption into local society. Given this influx of alien groups into the

---

[26] See Každan and Constable, *People and Power in Byzantium*, p. 50 and Mango, *Byzantium: the Empire of New Rome*, p. 83. Note also P. Brown, *The Body and Society. Men, Women and Sexual Renunciation in Early Christianity* (London and Boston 1988), pp. 320–1.
[27] See chapter 3 above.   [28] See chapter 6, pp. 220ff.

social and demographic structures of the different regions of Asia Minor, and given the fact that the armies were clearly billeted or quartered on a relatively widespread basis, the effect must have been to introduce a whole new set of variables into the social make-up of the districts concerned. And this will undoubtedly have affected patterns of marriage within local communities, along with the patterns of distribution of wealth both in land and in movable property.

The reinforcement of local populations from outside in this way – even though the numbers in absolute terms may have been relatively limited – must, therefore, have affected the demographic balance in many villages, modifying the customary patterns of conjugal selection. It will have also directly affected the structure of kinship relations and contributed thereby to further strengthening the nuclear family unit and to breaking down endogamous marriage practices. Soldiers' status and privileges, both juridically and fiscally, will have been a major factor.

The last point must remain, of course, to a large degree, hypothetical. But it is an hypothesis based firmly in the actual context, and in respect of the known developments of the period it possesses a coherency and a logic that cannot be denied. There is some evidence to support it, of course; for the lateral fragmentation of lineage and the centrality of the nuclear family have been emphasised also in respect of the village community. The so-called Farmers' Law exemplifies the point, for it deals very clearly with a community of separate, independent households, each with (or without) its own property in land and livestock, each carefully guarding its rights *vis à vis* its neighbours, and each physically marking itself off from its neighbours with fences, walls, ditches or other forms of boundary.[29] The key feature of Byzantine rural society from the time of the Farmers' Law and after was the possession by each family unit – each head of household, in effect – of its own holding, whether owned or leased on a long-term basis.[30] Common rights took the form of collective interests in specific and often seasonal activities, such as the pasturing of animals on uncultivated fields, or making hay; or in village land held to belong to the community;[31] or in respect of the fisc, as the common liability for fiscal assessments, especially on abandoned or uncultivated land.[32] Village solidarity appears as a function of specific activities and fiscal obligations, therefore, as the totality of socially distinct yet interconnected family units; and as the public expression – religious festivals and activities, for example, or on the

[29] See *Farmers' Law*, articles 50, 51, 58 and 66.
[30] See Každan, 'Small social groupings' (cited note 21, chapter 10, above), pp. 4–5 and A.E. Laiou-Thomadakis, *Peasant Society in the Late Byzantine Empire: A Social and Demographic Study* (Princeton 1977), esp. pp. 72ff.
[31] See *Farmers' Law*, articles 23ff., 30ff. and 81–82.
[32] *Farmers' Law*, articles 18 and 19.

occasion of marriages or funerals – of a common identity of interests in respect of the outside world.[33] But the economic independence of the households, and the structured competition within the village, the possibility of both the fragmentation of property and the amassing of wealth, illustrate the separateness and the potential internal structural oppositions latent within the community.[34] The medieval village society depicted in the Farmers' Law, with its constant emphasis on neighbours' rights, or in the lives of saints such as Theodore of Sykeon or Philaretus the Merciful (set in the early seventh and later eighth centuries respectively) was a community of independent and often competing economic units. Village solidarity through kinship – even where marriage was not unusual within a single community – was not a significant structuring element, at least in respect of enhancing mutual solidarities and promoting interdependencies. In these respects, of course, medieval village society was not dissimilar to that of contemporary or recent Greek and Aegean rural culture.[35]

These considerations bring us to a fourth, and much wider, point: namely, the centrality of the state as a source of power and authority, a determinant of social status, and a route to personal advancement.

HIERARCHIES, SOLIDARITY AND STRATIFICATION

As we have seen, the political and economic irrelevance and, in many cases, the virtual physical disappearance, of a great number of provincial cities within the area still under effective imperial control after the 650s, left a vacuum in provincial society, a vacuum that was partially filled, in terms of local modes of access to the capital, by soldiers. In particular, the army represented a vocal source of provincial opinion – refracted though it may have been through the localised and self-interested concerns of the soldiery and their leaders – and in many ways, given the disappearance of the independent municipalities of the previous era, the only source which had any authority. The army was, of course, only one aspect of the institutions of the state. But there were other aspects which were equally important. The demise of the corporate municipal culture which had survived – albeit in a much debased form – into the early seventh century, buttressed, it is true, by the state itself, meant not only the end of local representation through the medium of the cities, in the structure of state and administration at large; it meant the transfer of provincial interest to

---

[33] Compare the common front presented by the inhabitants of Amnia to the imperial visit to Philaretus' house: *Vita Philareti*, 137.23–6.

[34] The varied forms of independent exploitation of resources mentioned in the Farmers' Law (e.g. art. 81) and the social differences noted in, for example, the Life of Philaretus, testify to this. See Köpstein, 'Zu den Agrarverhältnissen', pp. 50–3.

[35] See J. Du Boulay, *Portrait of a Greek Mountain Village* (London 1974), for example.

the centre of power, wealth, authority and status, to Constantinople. Only state and Church now offered any prospect of advancement, of social improvement, and yet at the same time held out the promise of stability; and the state, with its complex system of ranks and titles, represented in addition an alternative social structure, a bureaucratic, hierarchical society dependent upon the emperor – God's appointee – with its own rewards and its own values. Even as a simple soldier, one received an enhanced social status, with tangible benefits in respect of fiscal exemptions, and with the possibility of promotion, or attachment to the personal retinue or guard of an officer, as powerful inducements offering potentially greater rewards. Various classes of clerk and bureaucrat received similar benefits. It is reasonable to suppose, therefore, that in a society where lateral solidarity through kinship had begun to fragment, and where access to power at the local, provincial level through the municipalities had been blocked, horizontal and intra-provincial social mobility and stability was replaced by the competitive, vertical mobility of individuals operating within the apparatuses of state and Church.

That the enhanced development and prominence of the elementary family unit during the later seventh century is not merely hypothetical is borne out by other forms of evidence: in the first instance, the effective disappearance of the old senatorial-municipal elite, and its subsumption within and replacement by a new, meritocratic elite of provincials of widely varied social and cultural backgrounds. Armenians in particular have been singled out, but other ethnic groups are also represented. The crucial point is that there are a great number of individuals of high rank who are clearly 'new men'. Their presence is itself suggestive of the open, competitive and individualistic nature of the upper levels of Byzantine society.[36]

In the second place, the dominant position of the system of titles and precedence dependent upon the emperor and court during the seventh and eighth centuries and after is crucial. Social and economic status in the sixth century and before had been marked out by a variety of attributes: family name, although less important than during the principate, was an element; occupation of an imperial position and the possession of an appropriate title, active or honorific, another; origin, and position in the local community – the municipality – constituted a third element; and wealth, together with membership of the senate and the possession of the appropriate cultural capital, a fourth. These could be, and were, combined in a variety of ways. But they constituted together a rather loose, open and pluralistic system – wealth and family background, along with the appro-

[36] The classic survey of Charanis, 'Ethnic changes', illustrates the point well.

priate classical education were as relevant as the office or title held by an individual, and the two were not always or necessarily interdependent.[37]

Membership of the wider senatorial order, one's role in the local community, an imperial sinecure or title, they all bestowed status and social respect – although from the fourth century the imperial bureaucracy and its system of precedence had become increasingly important. The relative social and economic stability of the late Roman, east Mediterranean world, however, along with its social and political institutions, in particular the city and the ideology of municipal civilisation and local patriotism – however weakened they may have become – still contributed to the pluralism of status which is reflected in the sources until the early seventh century.[38] By the fifth century, of course, the senate, and membership of the senatorial order, represented the ultimate source of status, and escape from curial burdens by the acquisition of senatorial rank pointed to a dangerous drain of wealth and manpower from the curial order. But the senatorial order was itself broad and even in the later sixth century represented only superficially a unified social elite: its members were still drawn from a wide variety of social backgrounds and attained senatorial rank by a multiplicity of routes.

With the upheavals and the territorial losses of the Persian and then the Arab attacks, however, and the concomitant shifts in ideological perspectives which had slowly taken form during the later sixth century, late Roman and early Byzantine society came to adopt a much more defensive posture. While the senate itself, sitting in Constantinople, retained its importance until the middle of the seventh century – until at least the later years of the reign of Constans II – representing as it did an assembly of the leading officers of the court, the senatorial order in the wider sense seemed to lose in status and eventually to disappear during the seventh and eighth centuries. Of course, by the middle of the sixth century, if not before, the role of the emperor and of the court had become crucial in the selection of the leading officials and title-holders in the state establishment, and therefore of the senate.[39] But given the educationally and economically privileged position of the landowning social elite of the empire, the majority of such appointees tended in any case to be drawn from their ranks, and this

---

[37] For later Roman systems of status-recognition, see Jones, LRE, vol. II, pp. 543ff.; K.M. Hopkins, 'Elite mobility in the Roman empire', Past and Present 32 (1965), 12–26, and 'Social mobility in the later Roman empire: the evidence of Ausonius', Classical Quarterly, new series, 11 (1961), 29–48; R. MacMullen, 'Social mobility and the Theodosian Code', JRS 54 (1964), 49–53.

[38] See Jones, LRE, vol. II, pp. 546ff. and 737–57; and chapter 4 above.

[39] Jones, LRE, vol. I, pp. 387–90, and vol. II, pp. 551ff.; note also Cameron, 'Images of authority', 27f.

has often given a false sense of the political hegemony of the senatorial elite and those aspiring to membership of it.

In fact, the crucial position of the emperor in the whole edifice becomes really clear only during the seventh century, for it is then that the economic and cultural dominance of the old broad senatorial establishment, with its roots ultimately in the landowning, but still municipal, elite of the provinces, finally crumbles under the various internal and external pressures that have been discussed already. Its survival into the middle decades of the seventh century is suggested by what little prosopographical evidence there is; beyond the 650s and 660s, however, it seems clearly to have been unable to provide the staff and the leaders of the state's apparatus that it had done hitherto. Increasingly, 'outsiders' of all kinds, linguistically, ethnically and culturally, appear in important positions in the administrative apparatus of the state, military and civil.[40] This phenomenon is accompanied by a marked increase in the prominence and relative value of what are in later sources referred to as 'imperial' as opposed to 'senatorial' titles of rank, a distinction found in treatises on titulature and precedence from the ninth century on, but which has its roots in the late Roman period, more particularly in the developments of the seventh century.

The original distinction is clear enough in the sixth century. As we have seen, those who belonged hereditarily to the senatorial order bore the title of *clarissimus*, and this is what was passed on by higher-ranking persons – of *illustris* rank, for example – to their sons. By Justinian's reign, only those who also held the titles of *patricius*, ex-consul, *illustris* and *illustris inter agentes* could sit on the senate proper; and of these, it was mostly the active *illustres*, who bore the epithet *gloriosus* or *gloriosissimus* (Gr. *endoxotatos*) who represented the real power and who also occupied the higher posts, civil and military, in the state.

These epithets all signified membership of the wider senatorial order. They were not equated with specific positions or functions, referred to as dignities, *dignitates*. Apart from titles awarded by the emperors in exceptional circumstances, such as *nobilissimus*, *curopalates*, *Caesar* (the latter regularly employed during the sixth century to signify the emperor's intended successor) and more commonly *patricius*, dignities were in the first instance derived from offices, which could be bestowed on an active basis, a titular basis (including the *cingulum*, or mark of office) or on an honorary basis (involving the title only). It is likely that initially at least a titular office was bestowed on persons who had actually held the office in question. But by the sixth century the titles of consul, prefect and *magister*

[40] See chapter 4, p. 153–72.

militum were conferred regularly on persons who held or had held no related office. At the same time, the highest offices were automatically associated with senatorial status.[41]

The lower palatine titles represented a different route of access to privilege and – potentially – senatorial status. They were drawn from active, titular and honorary office-holders, at court or *in absentia*, of posts in the various palatine *scholae*: the *spatharii, candidati, scribones, stratores, silentiarii, cubicularii*, even the imperial bath-attendants, *balnitores*, and palatine doctors, *archiatroi*.

The hallmark of the late Roman system, therefore, was the fixed association of titles – dignities – with offices. The few exceptions have already been mentioned. During the seventh century, however, this relationship was severed. The original association of the later Byzantine dignities was still recalled, so that the *Kletorologion* of Philotheus, for example, along with many other sources, notes the division of titles into senatorial and imperial.[42] But the senatorial order itself ceased to exist, as the disappearance of the epithets which denoted it illustrates – *endoxotatos, gloriosus, illustris, clarissimus* and related grades do not survive into the second half of the eighth century.[43] At the same time, a distinction

---

[41] See chapter 4.   [42] See *Klet.Phil.*, 87.32–3; Oikonomidès, *Préséance*, pp. 295–6.
[43] The last datable reference to *gloriosissimus*/ἐνδοξότατος I can find: *Ecloga*, pr. 40–1 and 103; see P. Koch, *Die byzantinischen Beamtentitel* (Jena 1903), pp. 69ff. The title *clarissimus* had become more or less meaningless by the seventh century, although it continued to have some application and value in the exarchate of Ravenna: see Brown, *Gentlemen and Officers*, p. 133 with note 11. *Illustris* disappears from use during the seventh century. For examples, see Maximus Confessor, *Ep.* XIII (*PG* XCI, 509B) and *Ep.* XLIV (644D) – note that in the latter case Maximus uses the appropriate epithet for an *illustris* – μεγαλοπρεπέστατος – which suggests that the illustrate still retained a degree of social relevance and status; see also Martini Papae, *Ep.* II (Mansi X, 825A), probably to the same Peter as in letter XIII of Maximus. The letter is datable to 646. See also *Miraculi S. Demetrii*, 161.7 (Lemerle); *Miracula S. Artemii*, 42.7 – where again the *illoustrioi* are taken for granted as an *ordo* distinguished by their clothing, signifying in the last example the members of the Constantinopolitan senate. For seals, see Schlumberger, *Sigillographie*, pp. 518–19; cf. Zacos and Veglery, index V, p. 1884, s.t. ἰλλούστριος. Some 35 persons are listed bearing this title, some with administrative functions, such as *trakteutēs* of the islands (914A, cf. 909A) or *dioikētēs* (131), all dating to the sixth and seventh centuries. See also Laurent, *Orghidan*, 273, and *Vatican*, 52; and note Schlumberger, *Sig.*, p. 518, no. 4, for a seventh-century seal of an *illoustrios* and *hypatos*, possibly implying that *illoustrios* was still associated with senatorial rank; and Konstantopoulos, *Molybdoboulla*, no. 295, for a seal of John, *illoustrios* and *anthypatos* (seventh to eighth century). But by the later seventh century a seal of Theodore, *illoustrios* and *basilikos chartoularios* (Laurent, *Orghidan*, 273) suggests a relatively low value for the title. After this time, the title disappears. The epithets *endoxotatos* and *peribleptos* are revived in the later ninth century and applied to *magistroi* and *patrikioi*, but bear no relation to a senatorial *ordo*. See, for example, Laurent, *Orghidan*, 186 and 187 (tenth century), and *Vatican* 51 (eleventh century), and p. 37 with notes 2 and 3 for commentary. Many other epithets used in the later Roman period for senators occur also in middle Byzantine texts; but these appear to have been used with little or no technical precision. See the list in Yannopoulos, *La société profane*, p. 75 note 458.

between active posts and the older order of dignities appears, so that the posts known in the later period as ἀξίαι διὰ λόγου (meaning that they were awarded by the emperor's word), actual functional positions, while they could be held on a titular basis (ἀπρατῶς), were held in addition to a title from the older order of dignities; the latter represent positions in the hierarchy only. The development reflects a major change from and elaboration upon the late Roman system, according to which any office among higher grades could be awarded as a dignity of one sort or another and was recognised as such even when it was at the same time an active appointment.[44] The reasons for the change are not difficult to see. The great government departments of the late Roman state were for the most part fragmented during the seventh century, and a whole new range of leading posts came to the fore. The majority of the older functional posts became obsolete and disappeared entirely; only those dignities which were already forming a distinctive order of titles and honorific ranks, alongside the newly created or newly prominent functional posts of the seventh century Byzantine state, survived.

The textual and sigillographic material for the period illustrates the development. In the first place, a reference in the Typos of Constans II of 648, followed by an edict of Constantine IV in 680, orders the punishment of laypersons who do not conform to the imperial order by depriving them of their *axiai*, *zōnē* or *strateia*.[45] Here are the three Latin terms of *dignitas*, *cingulum* and *militia*, and it seems reasonable to assume that they represent the traditional late Roman distinction between, respectively, the possession of an honorary or actual *dignitas*; the conferment of an office (whether *in actu* or *in vacante*) and straightforward service in a branch of the imperial civil or military establishment.[46] The distinction between *axia* and *strateia* is more clearly expressed in the Ecloga, where a difference between dignity and function is clear; although the former may well signify also the assumption of an accompanying high post.[47] But the Byzantines themselves used the terms interchangeably, which leaves the modern commentator, unsure of the exact context or the intentions of the writer, with a number of difficulties.[48]

What is clear, however, is the formation and existence by the later

---

[44] See chapter 4. For the later system, see the discussion of Oikonomidès, *Préséance*, pp. 281ff. and Bury, *Administrative System*, pp. 21f. The difference was expressed in the ways the dignities were awarded: known as ἀξίαι διὰ βραβείων, they were bestowed through insignia. The sixty or so functioning offices were awarded directly by the emperor, hence their being referred to as ἀξίαι διὰ λόγου. See Oikonomidès, *Préséance*, pp. 281–2, and Bury, *Administrative System*, pp. 20ff. and 36ff.

[45] Mansi X, 1032D and XI, 712D.   [46] See *CJ* XII, 8.2 (a. 440–1).

[47] *Ecloga* XIV, 1 (Burgmann, 214.636).

[48] Oikonomidès, *Préséance*, pp. 281–3; Yannopoulos, *La Société profane*, pp. 30ff.

seventh century of a definite number of imperially awarded titles whose origins lie in the dignities of the late Roman period and in the granting of titular membership of various late Roman palatine *ordines*. The seals of the seventh and early eighth centuries suggest the following titles or combinations of titles, in a roughly descending order of value: (1) *hypatos*, (2) *apo hypatōn patrikios*, (3) *apo hypatōn*, (4) *patrikios*, (5) *prōtospatharios*, (6) *spatharios*, (7) *stratēlatēs*, (8) *skribōn*, (9) *balnitor*, (10) *apo eparchōn*, (11) *kandidatos* and (12) *silentiarios*. Other titles, such as those of *vestitor* or *mandator*, were also awarded. Of those listed here, (1)–(4) represent consular and senatorial dignities or combinations thereof, of the highest order in late Roman times, and all accompanied by the senatorial epithet *gloriosissimus*; while (7), (10) and (12) represent titular senatorial dignities of the late Roman period. The rest represent titular membership of the appropriate palatine *ordo*. All these titles are found in combination with a variety of functional posts; although the first four seem to represent the leading group and are generally attached to functions of importance.[49] The title of *prōtospatharios* appears late in the seventh century and represents in the first instance a post, becoming by the early eighth century a title as well.[50] Similarly, the title of *spatharokandidatos* represents the combination of two titles and appears in the later eighth century, although officers bearing both titles – one probably representing a function – appear in the early seventh century.[51]

The hallmark of the Byzantine system, therefore, was the clear distinction between the chief palatine offices on the one hand and the orders of dignities on the other. But the majority of dignities were themselves drawn from what continued to be active palatine *scholae* – such as those of the *spatharii* and *mandatores*, for example – so that the title *spatharios* in a text or on a seal by itself might signify either a dignity or membership of the actual palatine *schola* of the same name. Similarly, active posts could be held *in vacante*, but did not represent stages in the order of dignities itself.

Careful analysis of the ways in which these titles are combined, either together or with functional posts, has shown that the traditional notion of a clear vertical hierarchy, based on assumptions taken from much later

---

[49] Winkelmann, *Rang- und Ämterstruktur*, pp. 31–7. For the senatorial titles and their origins, see esp. Bury, *Administrative System*, pp. 23ff., and Stein, *Bas-Empire*, vol. II, p. 430 and note 3. The establishment of a privileged group of *silentiarii* with senatorial dignity, and the consequent association of the *schola silentiariorum* with the senatorial privileges lies in the time of Theodosius II. See *CTh*. VI, 23.4. *Vestitor* was likewise a senatorial rank, whose origins lie in similar circumstances.

[50] See Haldon, *Byzantine Praetorians*, p. 184 and note 394; Winkelmann, *Rang- und Ämterstruktur*, pp. 46f.

[51] Haldon, *Byzantine Praetorians*, pp. 156 and 188, and note 417 with literature; but see also Winkelmann, *Rang- und Ämterstruktur*, p. 39, who argues for the appearance of the rank *spatharokandidatos* in the early eighth century.

documents which attempt formally to set out the whole system (such as the *Kletorologion* of Philotheus of the year 899), simply does not work at this period, or indeed through much of the eighth century.[52] There does appear to be an association between the titles of *hypatos, apo hypatōn* and *patricius* with the higher posts. But equally, persons with quite low-ranking titles occupy powerful functional posts. At the same time, the order of precedence among the different groups of titles seems to vary: it is unclear, for example, whether *hypatos* or *patrikios* had precedence in the second half of the seventh century; although *patrikios* seems to rise at the expense of *hypatos*, which during the eighth century could also be combined with the ranks or titles of *spatharios, silentiarios* and *vestitor*.[53] Indeed, the multiplicity of combinations of lower titles suggests a roughly horizontal system of alternative titles, awarded according to very approximate spheres of competence. Even here, however, no exact relationship between a given title and, say, military or civil posts seems to hold: and it has been pointed out that in the eighth and early ninth centuries at least both posts and titles must have been awarded on the basis of individual competence or patronage, rather than according to any formalised systematisation of functions actually exercised. The same will undoubtedly have applied during the seventh century.[54] One or two examples serve to illustrate the point. The deacon of the Hagia Sophia, one John, a confidant of the Emperor Anastasius II, was made *genikos logothetēs* and was also given command of an expedition to intercept an Arab fleet in 715. In a similar fashion the Abbot Theodotus, a confidant of Justinian II, was made *genikos logothetēs*. There are many other examples of the practice.[55]

There appears, however, at least initially, to have been an attempt to differentiate between those who held a title only and those who held a title which signified an actual function (such as *spatharios*, for example) through the addition of the epithet 'imperial' to the title of certain officials, presumably those in active service and *in praesenti*. It is noticeable that this relates always to the titles of persons who are associated with a palatine *ordo* or *schola* (and hence originally signifying also presence at court): *spatharioi, kandidatoi, mandatores* and so forth; but never to titles awarded on an individual basis: *magistros, patrikios, hypatos, stratēlatēs* and so on, a difference which seems to confirm the point.[56]

---

[52] See the important comments of Winkelmann, *Rang- und Ämterstruktur*, pp. 19–28.
[53] *Ibid.*, p. 41.
[54] *Ibid.*, pp. 45–61 and 138.
[55] See Zacos and Veglery, no. 2007; Laurent, *Corpus*, vol. II, no. 278 with sources; and Theophanes, 367.22sq.
[56] See Haldon, *Byzantine Praetorians*, pp. 183–4, and Haldon's review of Winkelmann, *Rang- und Ämterstruktur*, in *BS* 47 (1986), 229–32, see 232.

THE NEW POWER ELITE

But what is particularly important is that the titles – including those which ought properly to be classed as 'senatorial': *hypatos, apo hypatōn, apo eparchōn, stratēlatēs, silentiarios* and *vestitor* – now seem to be part of a single system dependent upon the emperor's pleasure, which can be combined with other titles according to the appointments currently or formerly held.[57] Indeed, the titles listed above seem now to be the only marks of membership of the senatorial 'order' itself, since the generic epithets of *illustris* and *magnificus* seem to drop out of using during the first part of the seventh century. *Gloriosissimus* is retained, as we have seen, in its Greek form of *endoxotatos*, but only until the 740s. The fact that the first two – *hypatos, apo hypatōn* – were, at least until the eighth century, of high status supports the contention that the senate as a body in Constantinople retained a degree of prestige; but equally, the titles of *eparchon* and *stratēlatēs* both lose in value. The titles of *apo hypatōn* and *hypatos* had rated the epithet *gloriosus* and ranked at the top of the scale according to novel 62 of the Emperor Justinian; the titular ranks of *apo eparchōn* and *magister militum* were classed among the second grade of *illustres*, as *magnifici*.[58] The devaluation of the latter titles during the second half of the seventh century and the first part of the eighth is important, because it reflects the firm establishment of the title *stratēlatēs*, for example, as a titular dignity; its replacement in functional and practical respects by the office and title of *stratēgos*; and its concomitant loss of status and value as it becomes progressively divorced from the active, functional establishment of the state.[59] Similarly, *apo eparchōn* loses in value over the same period; and both titles disappear after 899. The loss of status in the case of the title ex-prefect may reflect the demise of the praetorian prefecture and the splitting up of its civil-administrative functions, a development outlined in chapter 5. The sigillographic evidence makes it clear that the 'senatorial' titles were now part of a single system of hierarchy and were awarded on just the same basis as the palatine or 'imperial' titles. Senatorial rank no longer existed, for no senatorial order existed. Instead, a number of senatorial titles survived, titles which presumably also conferred membership of the ceremonial body of the senate which played such an important part in imperial and state ritual.[60]

[57] Winkelmann, *Rang- und Ämterstruktur*, pp. 45ff.
[58] Justinian, *Nov.* 62, 2 (a. 537); for the equivalence of *magister militum* and prefect see Justinian, *Nov.* 70 (a. 538).
[59] By the middle of the ninth century, it had come to occupy the lowest place in the hierarchy: see Winkelmann, *Rang- und Ämterstruktur*, p. 39.
[60] See Oikonomidès, *Préséance*, p. 295 and references. The history of these titles in the exarchate of Ravenna is, as might be expected, very similar. See the analysis of Brown,

What this implies, of course, is that the older senatorial order had withered away.[61] All 'senators' were henceforth imperially sponsored, as the incorporation of 'senatorial' titles into an imperial system of precedence demonstrates. And this implies that the economic power and cultural authority of the socio-economic groups from which the *illustres* had been drawn had been fragmented or destroyed. In effect, while the senate may still have had some authority in state affairs, by nature of its physical context – in the capital city of the empire – and its traditions, it no longer represented any sort of economic interest, a class of landowners whose existence, however broadly defined and loosely composed in the late Roman period, nevertheless reflected the dominance of a landowning aristocracy of privilege, sharing in a common cultural heritage. Additionally, the older senatorial elite had also based its position on the tenure of high civil office, the provincial magistracies and governorships, and so forth, and the majority of these seem either to have disappeared as they became irrelevant to the changed situation or were very greatly reduced in status, from about the middle of the seventh century.[62] From this time, the senate was increasingly an assembly of imperially sponsored title-holders, whose only real functions were to act on ceremonial occasions as a symbol of Roman imperial tradition. Obviously, the senate could still serve as a focus of opposition to, or a source of counsel and support for, an emperor, simply because it included many of the leading officers of the court – all those with the ranks of *hypatos, apo hypatōn* and *patrikios*, for example. This can clearly be seen at the beginning of the reign of Constans II, at the beginning of this evolution, and in the last years of the seventh century.[63]

At first, as we have seen, the highest senatorial titles, those of *hypatos* and *apo hypatōn*, retained their status. But even they begin during the eighth century to lose ground to 'imperial' titles, and the reasons for this must surely be sought in the development sketched out above. As the

---

Gentlemen and Officers, pp. 136ff., with a critique of E. Stein, 'La Disparition du Sénat de Rome à la fin du VIe siècle', *Bull. de la Classe des Lettres de l'Acad. de Belgique* 23 (1937), 365–90 (repr. in *Opera minora selecta* (Amsterdam 1968), pp. 359–84).

[61] While the situation in Italy was by no means the same, the process of the withering-away of the older senatorial elite offers a number of important parallels: see Brown, *Gentlemen and Officers*, pp. 21–37. Continuity, on the other hand, can be much more clearly observed in the early medieval West, as shown in the analysis of A. Demandt, 'Der spätrömische Militäradel', *Chiron* 10 (1980), 601–36.

[62] See Arnheim, *Senatorial Aristocracy*, esp. pp. 155–71 for the senate as a social-economic elite in the later Roman period.

[63] See Beck, *Senat und Volk*, pp. 31f., 42ff. and 49, and the remarks at 57f. Since the leading state offices were usually accompanied by the rank of *patrikios, apo hypatōn, hypatos* and so on, all such officials, whether active or titular, will have been of senatorial status. Even in the later period this was the assumption: see, for example, *De Cer.*, 15.6–7; 174.11–12; 290.16sq.

senate came increasingly to represent an assembly of title-holders appointed at the emperor's pleasure, and especially as the hereditary element – the clarissimate – lost its social relevance during the seventh century, so its institutional significance and its social-political attractiveness must have dwindled. Those anxious for advancement may no longer have sought senatorial titles, of course; while the emperors themselves may have increasingly disregarded these titles, preferring instead to promote their favourites or others who had been brought to their attention by appointing them to titular membership of the palatine ordines or by granting them the highest imperial titles, such as that of *patrikios*. This does not seem to have been a particularly long drawn out process. The lesser senatorial ranks lost ground before the middle of the eighth century; *apo hypatōn* disappears during the second half of the eighth century;[64] the title of *hypatos* itself is widely held during the eighth century, and the tendency to award it to an ever-widening range of officials and others might again reflect the process of devaluation in operation.[65] The devaluation of the senatorial titles also suggests the increasing dominance of the military administrative element within the state, as has been suggested elsewhere.[66] At any rate, the incorporation of senatorial titles into a single hierarchy of status, whatever the actual complexities of its operation and in spite of the survival of the different traditions, precedents and privileges associated with them, parallels and reflects the disappearance of the late Roman senatorial establishment and the hereditary clarissimate, and the concomitant rise of a purely imperially sponsored 'meritocratic' elite whose status and authority were secured, initially at least, only through imperial patronage. The relative pluralism of the late Roman period disappears, to be replaced by an authoritarian system of precedence and advancement rooted in state service alone. The contradiction inherent in the whole lies in the fact that this rather more rigid and conformist system seems to have made social mobility no less common or difficult; it merely channelled it through different routes of access, and demanded different abilities and social qualifications from those aspiring to advancement.

The effects of this centralisation of access to authority, status and precedence around the emperor and the court, in a more radical and more pronounced way than had ever been the case in the later Roman period, is clear by the later seventh century. The titles and dignities held by those selected to carry out diplomatic or other imperial missions reflect this imperial monopoly. Without exception, these persons bear titles such as

---

[64] See Winkelmann, *Rang- und Ämterstruktur*, pp. 32f., 34f. and 36–7.
[65] *Ibid.*, p. 41 and the list at pp. 48ff. Note that the *Liber Pontificalis* (I, 351) associates those of consular rank (*ypati*) with the senate and *patricii* in 681, but not in 710 (I, 390).
[66] Winkelmann, *Rang- und Ämterstruktur*, p. 51.

spatharios, *silentiarios* and *koubikoularios*, or higher grades still, or they occupy posts which will have merited such titles.[67] Whether these titles signified membership of an active corps based at court, or the honorary title alone, is in this context not important. The point is that all forms of social and political advancement now depended on association with the imperial court and its system of precedence. It might be objected, of course, that this was also the case in the fourth, fifth and sixth centuries. But in practice, there existed always a greater openness of opportunity, a greater pluralism and less rigorously centralised system of advancement in the earlier period. The attention and favour of the emperors had always been crucial. But the traditional senatorial elite establishment of landed wealth and state office had been able to maintain itself by the assimilation of new elements into its culture and traditions, and thereby retain its position as the social and economic elite, the 'ruling class' of the later Roman period. Nobility of birth and ancestry was as relevant in the late Roman world as any other qualification for membership of the senatorial order.[68] The changed economic and political circumstances of the years after the middle of the seventh century especially destroyed this capacity for social and political renewal. The senate as an institution and as a social elite suffered as it became entirely dependent upon the emperors – the court – for its personnel and for the status thereby attached to membership of it. Over the same period, local centres of wealth and power lost in prestige and in relevance to Constantinople and the court, which thus came to represent the only source of access to social advancement. Notions of lineage and nobility of ancestry became, for a while at least, secondary issues; where the social origins of an individual from a well-to-do background are described in the contemporary or near-contemporary sources, then terms such as 'well-born', 'of noble/ancient lineage', 'of high rank' or 'high-born' seem to denote the wealth and status of a family at the time, rather than its real or supposed lineage. And the fact that a very wide range of terms is used, in both hagiographical and in other sources, demonstrates that no single and uniformly accepted formula for 'noble' or 'aristocratic' lineage was actually in common use. The use of the description 'son of' on seals and in the literary sources reflects most probably the assertion of a new-found status rather than any long-term continuity of lineage.[69] The

[67] See, for example, Haldon, *Byzantine Praetorians*, pp. 185ff. (*spatharioi*); Guilland, *Recherches*, vol. I, pp. 277–9; Diehl, *L'Exarchat de Ravenne*, p. 173 note 2 (*koubikoularioi*); see Laurent, *Corpus*, vol. II, s.t. *koubikoularios*, *silentiarios*, *chartoularios*, *sakellarios*; and Haldon, *Byzantine Praetorians*, p. 188 note 415; Brown, *Gentlemen and Officers*, pp. 134–5.

[68] See Jones, *LRE*, vol. II, pp. 523ff.; Arnheim, *Senatorial Aristocracy*, pp. 103ff.

[69] See the useful list of Yannopoulos, *La Société profane*, pp. 14ff. In general, see the articles of R. Guilland, 'La Noblesse de race à Byzance', *BS* 9 (1948), 307–14 (repr. in *Recherches*,

popular idea of noble ancestry persisted, of course, and appears frequently in hagiographical literature, for example, as a means of expressing approval of the character of the individual in question, especially in the period up to the middle of the seventh century and from the later eighth century onwards. A very similar development has been noted for Italy and especially the exarchate in the same period.[70] But it was only through association with the state and its apparatuses, or the Church, that social advancement and preferment could be assured, the more so since the state now intervened more directly than ever before in the affairs of the provinces. And it is worth noting that it is in the period from the 640s to the middle of the eighth century that this association predominates, after which – as concepts of nobility and lineage begin to become relevant once more to the state and begin to be applied with more precision and care – both associations coexist.[71]

While it would be wrong to take either of the two developments outlined above as alone responsible for the change in the character of late Roman society which we have observed, together they do add up to a very real transformation of the ways in which that society perceived itself (as seen, for example, through the canons of the Quinisext or through the Ecloga) and the ways in which it functioned. Under the all-pervasive influence of Christian ideas, reinforced by imperial legislation and stimulated by the radicalising effects on social practice of the social and economic changes of the seventh century, the late Roman or early Byzantine idea of the family and its practical relationship in the world underwent a major revision. Society was perceived as an agglomeration of individual primary family units occupying a definite space with regard to one another and to God, rather than as a corporate body of individuals united within, first, the

---

vol. I, pp. 15–22); 'La Noblesse byzantine à la haute époque', Ἑλληνικά, παράρτημα 4: Προσφορὰ εἰς Στίλπωνα Π. Κυριακίδην (Thessaloniki 1953), pp. 255–66 (repr. in Recherches, vol. I, pp. 23–31). For the epithet 'son of' in its various forms, see Nesbitt, 'Double names on early Byzantine lead seals', 109ff.

[70] E.g. Vita Theod. Stud., 116B (ἐν γένει ... λαμπρῶν); Vita Blasii Amor., 659E (τῶν ἐπισήμων); Vita Evaristi, 300.20-1 (ἐπιφανέστατοι καὶ περίδοξοι); Vita Nicephori Medic., 405, cap. 5.9 (γένους περιβλέπτου); Vita Euthymii Iun., 16.21 (εὐπατρίδαι); Vita Ioannis Psichaitae, 18.22 (ἐπιφανεῖς); Vita Alypii styl., 161.11 (περιφανεῖς); and so on. For the exarchate of Ravenna, see Brown, Gentlemen and Officers, pp. 166ff.

[71] For example, Anastasius of Sinai, Quaestiones, 504A; Vita Ioannis Eleemosyn., 77.18; Miracula S. Artemii, 14.22; Vita Greg. Agrigent., 633B; Vita Antonii Iun., 197.28 (ἄρχοντες); Miracula S. Artemii, 11.21–2; 44.22 (ἔνδοξοι τοῦ παλατίου); and the list at Yannopoulos, La Société profane, p. 15 notes 32–50. For the reassertion of these concepts in the ninth century, see E. Patlagean, 'Les Débuts d'une aristocratie byzantine et le témoignage de l'historiographie: système des noms et liens de parenté aux IXᵉ-Xᵉ siècles', in The Byzantine Aristocracy, IX to XIII centuries (BAR, Int. Ser., 221, Oxford 1984), pp. 23–43. See also Winkelmann, Quellenstudien, pp. 143ff.

municipality, and second, the wider polity. Personal loyalty to God and to one's family eventually came to be expressed as priorities at the very least equivalent to, when not actually superior to, loyalty to the state or to a notion of 'society'. The development is clearly expressed at a later date – in the vernacular tradition of the akritic cycle, for example, or in the eleventh-century Strategikon of Kekaumenos[72] – but its origins lie in the transformations of the later sixth and seventh centuries.

Individuals were now perceived of as the responsible – culpable – elements in God's universe and in society, in a way which had not been the case before. The new emphasis, as has been pointed out, is most apparent in the way in which the body and the individual become the centre of attention in the penal law of the later seventh century and the eighth century, especially and most explicitly in the Ecloga.[73] Indeed, by a series of metaphors drawn from the Christian and the Judaic traditions, a body-symbolism was evolved which, while it had come into being already in the Roman period, was first formally elaborated in the Ecloga. Nasal mutilation was thus associated with sexual offences, while the putting out of eyes was related to crimes of sacrilege and, by extension, to treason. The two were, of course, associated, for power and sexuality, and the metaphors by which these were represented in symbolic discourse, are universally related.[74]

Emphasis on the body as the individual, and on public and dramatically obvious physical punishment as retribution, as evidence of the nature of the crime and as a demonstration of imperial authority, is only one side of the coin, however. For at the same time, the linking of notions of corporal mutilation with both Christian morality and imperial philanthropy and the very concept of the individual's direct responsibility to God for his or her sins[75] flew in the face of the traditional Roman ideal of the family headed and guided by the just paterfamilias. It was a set of attitudes which could have flourished only at the cost of both the concept and the structure of the traditional family, however these may have been shaped; and, as we have seen, one of the key developments over this period was the reduction in the authority of the head of the family and a strengthening of the moral

[72] For some valuable comments on the representation of relationships of honour, shame and patronage in these texts, see P. Magdalino, 'Honour among Romaioi: the framework of social values in the world of Digenes Akrites and Kekaumenos', BMGS 13 (1989) 183–218. On the developments outlined here, see Haldon, 'The miracles of Artemios and contemporary attitudes'.
[73] See E. Patlagean, *Byzance et le blason pénal du corps*, 405ff. (cited note 24, chapter 10, above).
[74] See *ibid.*, 407.
[75] These elements are all fundamental to the narrative in the miracles of Artemius and Therapon, and many others; and they are echoed in many other texts with increasing emphasis from the seventh century on. See, for example, Anastasius of Sinai, *Quaestiones*, 55 (617A–620B, esp. 617B–C).

personality and therefore individual responsibility of the separate members of the family.

The traditional Roman notion of the state as an enlarged or 'super *familia*' was given a Christian guise and fitted without difficulty into this new framework. The emperor was still the paterfamilias of his family, but now with the clearly delineated, but less absolute, authority of the Christian head of the household as set out in the canons of the Quinisext or in the provisions of the Ecloga.[76] The subjects of the emperors remained their 'children'.[77] But whereas late Roman society had provided a series of intermediate levels of social and community organisation, within each of which the individual could find an identity, the society which had evolved by the later seventh and early eighth centuries was a society of individuals deemed directly responsible for their actions before God. The Church proclaimed (and legislated for) the elementary nuclear family; and the collapse of the older order under the strain imposed by the change in its circumstances brought on by the events of the seventh century could only have promoted its rapid evolution and consolidation. The individual, and the concomitant open and competitive social individualism, the career-building on a necessarily 'meritocratic' basis in response to the urgent needs of the state and its apparatus, were the result. The symbolism embodied in mutilation, the firm establishment of the nuclear family unit, and the foregrounding of the relationship between individual and God as both a private and public one, are thus all closely interconnected, albeit in ways which may not at first be apparent.

None of this is to say, of course, that the nuclear or elementary family was itself a novelty or that loyalty to one's kin and family was something new in late Roman times. As we have said, the former had been a feature of Mediterranean culture for centuries, although its extent and its importance varied from region to region and from culture to culture. What I am suggesting here is that the imposition of uniformity and consensus from above – by state and by Church – and the striving for a common identity, along with both social and political survival which was a feature of daily existence in the lands which remained 'Roman', took its toll on the traditions and the practices necessary at a structural level for the social reproduction of late Roman culture, a culture which still remained, even in the later sixth century, relatively open, both in its attitude to the outside world and in its attitudes to physical space and to institutions. Certainly, signs of considerable change were already apparent from the end of the reign of Justinian and during the reigns of his immediate successors. But the physical shrinking of the Roman world promoted the changes already

---

[76] On the *patria potestas*, see the literature in note 8, chapter 10, above.
[77] See the evidence assembled in Hunger, *Prooimion, passim*.

implicit in the structure of late Roman social organisation and culture, and also emphasised the isolation of the East Roman world and the imperial Church. It is hardly surprising that the motif of the Chosen People found a particular echo in the surviving literature of the time.[78]

[78] The concomitant representation of the emperor as a new David illustrates and emphasises the attitudes of the times: see Cameron, 'Images of authority', 21–2; see also S. MacCormack, in *B* 52 (1982), 287–309, see 295ff.; Dvornik, *Early Christian and Byzantine Political Philosophy*, vol. II, pp. 797 and 823.

CHAPTER 11

Forms of representation: language, literature and the icon

The literature and the art of the period we are concerned with represents one aspect of the social and cultural whole of the late antique and early medieval east Mediterranean civilisation which is the object of our enquiry. In itself it is, of course, a vast field which has been studied under a number of subcategories, and I shall not attempt a descriptive account of them all here.

My concern is rather with the ways in which these forms of representation functioned during the course of the seventh century in a way which has rendered them peculiarly difficult of access to later commentators. They were vehicles for the self-representation of the culture which produced them. They symbolised and transmitted, for different elements of the population, according to their means of access to them, fragments of an ideological system and a cultural universe. And at the same time, they constituted the shape of that cultural and symbolic universe, which we can observe both through these forms and through other sources.

These are normal and fundamental functions of artistic and literary production. But in the east Mediterranean world of the later sixth century and after, symbols that were culturally available evoked and were focused around specific aspects of that symbolic universe in a way which contrasts with that of the preceding years, a focusing which is part and parcel of the attempts at re-evaluation and reaffirmation discussed already in chapter 9. This is not to suggest that this process, at least in its main elements, was in any way one which was consciously undertaken or executed. In one of its most obvious – and fundamental – features, it clearly was not: by the later sixth century, the linguistic Hellenisation of the state and its administrative apparatuses, and all that depended upon or was associated with the state (the senatorial elite or the Church, for example), was well advanced, a process that was effectively completed during the years of the early Arab conquests.[1] The old world of Latin West and Greek East, sharing a unified political culture, was a thing of the past, in spite of the continued existence of Byzantine possessions in North Africa until the late seventh century and in Italy until after the middle of the eighth century.[2]

Latin left its mark, of course, most clearly in legal terminology and literature, where it remained the basis of the technical jurisprudential vocabulary; and also in the field of mechanics and especially military equipment and organisation, as well as in numerous words and terms for items of everyday use, both in domestic and agricultural terms. But the language of state and diplomacy was Greek, and already by the middle of the century letters and other documents to and from Constantinople to the West were accompanied by translations.[3]

By the end of the reign of Phocas, the Slav occupation of much of the Balkans, and the existence of the Avar dominion, had severed any regular and direct land link between the Greek-speaking southern Balkans and the Latin-speaking provinces around the Danube. Most importantly, the lan-

---

[1] For general surveys, see H. Zilliacus, *Zum Kampf der Weltsprachen im oströmischen Reich* (Helsingfors 1935); L. Hahn, 'Zum Sprachenkampf im römischen Reich bis auf die Zeit Justinians', *Philologus*, Suppl. 10 (1907), 675–798, and 'Zum Gebrauch der lateinischen Sprache in Konstantinopel', in *Festgabe für Martin von Schanz* (Würzburg 1912), pp. 173–83; note also the review by F. Dölger of Zilliacus, *Zum Kampf der Weltsprachen*, in *BZ* 36 (1936), 108–17. More recently, H. Mihăescu has studied the relationship between Greek, Latin and Daco-Roman or Slav cultural-linguistic zones in the late Roman and early Byzantine world. See especially the summary article, with more up-to-date literature, in 'Die Lage der zwei Weltsprachen (Griechisch und Latein) im byzantinischen Reich des 7. Jahrhunderts als Merkmal einer Zeitwende', in *Studien zum 7. Jahrhundert*, pp. 95–100. On the background to the changes of this period, see G. Dagron, 'Aux origines de la civilisation byzantine: langue de culture et langue d'état', *RH* 241 (1969), 23–56; see esp. 36ff.

[2] For North Africa, see Cameron, 'Byzantine Africa', and for Italy, Brown, *Gentlemen and Officers*, pp. 65ff. and esp. H. Steinacker, 'Die römische Kirche und die griechischen Sprachkenntnisse des Frühmittelalters', *Mitteilungen des Instituts für österreichische Geschichtsforschung* 62 (1954), 28–66. Southern Italy and Sicily had since the sixth century B.C. had notable Greek elements, of course, and this seems to have been strengthened during the seventh century A.D., at least in the far south and in Sicily, by refugees from the Peloponnese. See A. Guillou, 'Italie méridionale byzantine ou Byzantins en Italie méridionale', *B* 44 (1974), 152–90 (repr. in *Culture et société en Italie byzantine* XV (London 1978); C. Mango, 'La Culture grecque et l'Occident au VIIIe siècle', in *Settimane di Studio del Centro Italiano di Studi sull' alto Medioevo* XX, 2 (Spoleto 1973), pp. 683–719; P. Charanis, 'On the question of the Hellenization of Sicily and southern Italy in the Middle Ages', *American Historical Review* 52 (1946/7), 74–87.

[3] Note the comments of Pope Gregory I (*Gregorii I Papae Registrum Epistolarum*, eds. P. Ewald and L.M. Hartmann, in *MGH*, Epp. 1 and 2 VII, 27 (2nd edn, Berlin 1957), p. 474: 'hodie in Constantinopolitana civitate, qui de latino in graeco dictata bene transferant non sunt.' For Latin in military language, see Mihăescu, *Die Lage der zwei Weltsprachen*, 99 and note 24, and 'Les Termes de commandement latins dans le Strategicon de Maurice', *Revue de Linguistique* 14 (1969), 261–72. In the field of law, Latin clearly had a considerable influence; but already by the later sixth century the greater part of imperial legislation promulgated from Constantinople was in Greek. See L. Wenger, *Die Quellen des römischen Rechts* (Vienna 1953), esp. p. 660.

guage of the orthodox Church in the East was always firmly Greek, and it had indeed been predominantly Greek-speaking thinkers and theologians who had been pre-eminent in the religious controversies and who had set the pace in theological debate in the centuries since the peace of the Church. It is perhaps symptomatic that the great leaders of the religious opposition to monotheletism in North Africa and Italy were – with the exception of Pope Martin – Greek-speakers and that the key debates in the controversy were carried out in Greek, even in North Africa – the famous debate between Maximus and Pyrrhus, for example, in Carthage in the year 645.[4] It is this accelerating process of linguistic Hellenisation which provides the backdrop to the developments described in what follows.

Two phenomena in particular deserve our attention; and although neither is limited exclusively to the seventh century, it is then that the context described in the foregoing chapters of this book gives them a particular weight and significance. It should be made clear from the outset that these elements played themselves an equal part in painting the picture of the seventh century that we can construct from our sources, they were integral aspects of a continuing dialectical process. The two phenomena in question are: the increased centrality in both ideological and artistic-representational terms of icons and the decline and near disappearance of secular literature. They are not linked directly, but they are part of the same pattern of cultural changes which I have attempted to describe. And they constitute a crucial pointer to the character of seventh-century culture and belief.

ICONS, EVOCATIONS AND EXPECTATIONS

The increasing importance of relics and icons, as both channels of access to their archetypes and as sources of miracles and divinely inspired power in their own right has been discussed and analysed in detail by several scholars.[5] All have noted that it is particularly from the later sixth century – the immediately post-Justinianic period – that the sources begin to mention the existence, the use of and the power of icons more and more frequently. As we have seen in chapter 9, this was associated causally with an attempt

[4] See *PG* XCI, 287–354. See Van Dieten, *Geschichte der Patriarchen*, pp. 57ff., and Guarrigues, *Maxime le confesseur*, pp. 51f. Of course, North Africa remains in some respects a special case, upon which a great deal of work remains to be done; but the example is illustrative of the developments described.

[5] See esp. Kitzinger, 'Images before iconoclasm', 95–128; A. Grabar, *L'Iconoclasme byzantin* (Paris 1957), pp. 21ff.; Brown, 'A Dark-age crisis'; Cameron, 'Images of authority', 18ff.; Haldon, 'Ideology and social change', 161ff.; G. Dagron, 'Le Culte des images dans le monde byzantin', in *Histoire vécu du peuple chrétien*, ed. T. Delumeau, vol. I (Toulouse 1979), pp. 133–60 (repr. in *La Romanité chrétien en Orient. Héritages et mutations* XI (London 1984)); Herrin, *Formation of Christendom*, pp. 307ff.

within the culture of the East Mediterranean in general to reaffirm the narratives of social practice by seeking a more immediate mode of access to God and the heavenly realm, and by the imperial power in particular to reassert its paramount position by stressing the divine origins of its authority. But as first relics, and then icons became part and parcel of daily life, so the context within which they originally became so important became irrelevant, and their centrality to the experience of the everyday unquestioned. It was, of course, this very situation and the narratives that derived from it which made the imperial iconoclasm of the eighth century possible.[6] But it was also the all-present icon – whether static or portative, large or small, public or private – which lends Byzantine Christianity from the seventh century on one of its most prominent and enduring characteristics. It was icons which focused people's attention on local saints, and on local traditions and observances, beliefs and practices. Icons reminded the congregations of churches of their history, and with it the traditions of Christianity and – if distantly – of empire and imperial rule, of identity with a wider Christian community and so on. Icons worked didactically and performed functions similar to those of the holy man or hermit familiar from the late Roman period.[7] There was one crucial difference, of course: icons outnumbered holy men by far. Icons became a commonplace in a way that the holy man – at least in the normal run of events – never could. Icons were available to all – whether in monumental form in churches or in the humbler context of the household. Pope Gregory the Great justified their use in a much-quoted passage from a letter to the bishop of Marseille: 'For what writing presents to readers, the picture presents to the unlearned, who behold; for in it even those who are ignorant see what they should follow; in it, the unlettered read. Thus is a picture, especially to the barbarians, instead of reading.'[8] Thus, icons were attributed with a functional ideological aspect, they could be seen as the literature of the illiterate in early Byzantine society; and although this argument for their role – while it was revived and elaborated during iconoclasm – had become a less significant justification by the later sixth century, as we shall see, pictorial representation was clearly regarded by the later seventh century as an important alter-

---

[6] See my comments in 'Some remarks', esp. 176ff.
[7] See the comments of R. Cormack, *Writing in Gold* (London 1985), pp. 75ff.; and H.-G. Beck, 'Von der Fragwürdigkeit der Ikone', SBB 7 (1975), pp. 1–44; and G. Lange, *Bild und Wort. Die katechetischen Funktionen der Bilder in der griechischen Theologie des sechsten bis neunten Jahrhunderts* (Würzburg 1969); J. Gouillard, 'Contemplation et imagerie sacrée dans le christianisme byzantin', *Annuaire de la Ve section de l'Ecole Pratique des Hautes Etudes* 86 (1977–8), 29–50, see esp. 37ff. (repr. in *La Vie religieuse à Byzance* II (London 1981)). Note also the useful discussion of L. Rydén, 'The role of the icon in Byzantine piety', in *Religious Symbols and their Functions*, ed. A. Biezais (Uppsala 1979), pp. 41–52.
[8] PL LXXVII, 1128C.

native element to texts in the elaboration of Christian dogma – Anastasius of Sinai, for example, argues strongly in its favour.[9]

The seventh century marks an important stage in the evolution of the icon, and in particular of the modes of representation which came to be associated with it. It has been suggested that of the modes available to artists in the later sixth century, the dominant tradition (which Kitzinger terms 'Hellenistic', but which others prefer to call 'illusionist')[10] seems increasingly at this time to give way to an alternative tradition, referred to as the 'abstract' style. The latter is characterised by a linear, two-dimensional mode of representation, with passive, motionless figures, contrasting with the naturalistic, three-dimensional representation of the 'Hellenistic' or 'illusionist' style.[11] Both systems continue to exist side by side throughout the period with which we are concerned and through the iconoclastic era; and their employment was by no means even and regular in all areas of the empire at the same time.[12] A clear-cut distinction between separate examples of both styles is sometimes difficult to detect, indeed, since many works contain elements from both. For example, formal portraits of Justinian and Theodora in the church of San Vitale in Ravenna are set in a clearly three-dimensional physical context within a building, perhaps a part of the palace. Yet the figures themselves, represented as approaching the observer, are portrayed in a way that suggests

[9] See Kitzinger, 'Images before iconoclasm', 136ff. The argument was given new strength in the context of iconoclasm by John of Damascus. See *Contra imaginum calumniatores orationes tres*, in B. Kotter, ed., *Die Schriften des Johannes von Damaskos* III (Berlin 1975), I, 17. But the 'educational' element was never forgotten: the canons of the Quinisext include an ordinance ordering the destruction of corrupting or misleading pictures. See Mansi XI, 985D; in his *Hodegos*, Anastasius of Sinai recommends pictorial representations for didactic purposes to refute heresy. See especially Anna D. Kartsonis, *Anastasis: The Making of an Image* (Princeton 1986), especially pp. 40–67, for a detailed analysis.

[10] E. Kitzinger, 'Byzantine art in the period between Justinian and iconoclasm', in *Berichte zum XI. Internationalen Byzantinisten-Kongress* IV 1 (Munich 1958), pp. 1–50. For the use of 'illusionist', see R. Cormack, 'The arts during the age of iconoclasm', in *Iconoclasm*, eds. Bryer and Herrin, pp. 35–44, see pp. 41f.; D.H. Wright, 'The shape of the seventh century in Byzantine art', in *First Annual Byzantine Studies Conference, Abstracts of Papers* (Cleveland, Ohio 1975), pp. 9–28; and esp. J. Onians, 'Abstraction and imagination in late Antiquity', *Art History* 3 (1980), 1–23. 'Illusionist' is also used, along with 'Hellenistic', by D. Talbot Rice, *The Appreciation of Byzantine Art* (Oxford 1972); and G. Mathew, *Byzantine Aesthetics* (London 1963).

[11] The 'abstract' style had evolved gradually from a variety of elements, as Kitzinger has suggested, 'Byzantine art in the period between Justinian and iconoclasm', 16ff., esp. 28, a function of both traditional Hellenistic and oriental modes of figural representation. The roots of the Hellenistic style lie, as the name suggests, in the development of classical Hellenistic styles of the period from the second century B.C. to the second century A.D. The shift applies to all figural and representational art, of course, whether three- or two-dimensional.

[12] See the valuable and detailed survey by Kitzinger, *Byzantine Art in the Making*, pp. 99–126; and 'Byzantine art in the period between Justinian and iconoclasm', 30ff.; and Cormack, 'The arts during the age of iconoclasm,' 42–3.

Plate 11.1 The Empress Theodora and attendants, San Vitale, Ravenna

to a modern western eye a lack of motion, and great gravity. Dynamism is present in the composition as a whole, but it is not located in the actual figures. (See plate 11.1) This combination of modes does not mean an artistic eclecticism, and certainly not an unconscious application of such elements by the artists who produced the works – icons, frescoes, mosaics – in question. Rather, and as Kitzinger has suggested, the artists applied different modes with the deliberate intention of thus signifying or suggesting different levels of symbolic reference.[13] So, in the case of the Ravenna mosaics, the imperial figures can be understood to gain in stature, both physically and symbolically, from their mode of portrayal. In icons of saints and holy figures, the dominant trend is to represent in abstract, linear form, the key figures, and this does seem in part to be a reflection of the way in which the icons were meant to be conceived of and employed.

To illustrate this point we must, of course, refer to the compositions themselves. Perhaps the clearest contrast between the two traditions in a single context comes from the church of St Demetrius in Thessaloniki, where the 'Hellenistic' or 'illusionist' style of the later sixth and early seventh centuries is represented by a number of mosaics of the period before the fire of the 620s which led to its refurbishing and redecoration shortly thereafter;[14] and where the 'abstract' style of the phase of rebuilding, dated to about the middle of the century, can be compared directly. (See plates 11.2(a) and (b).) Elsewhere, and within a single composition, the use of these two modes, along with other elements to emphasise different degrees of symbolic evocation and the different roles of the figures portrayed with regard to the beholder can be found in some of the well-known icons in the monastery of St Catherine on Mt. Sinai. The icon of the Virgin and child, for example, who are flanked on both sides by two saints, and with two angels behind, provides a good example of the use of space, movement (or lack of it) and frontality within a single composition. The saints look sternly and protectively out at the onlooker, the angels are portrayed in a quite different, illusionist and naturalistic style, gazing up at the hand of God and heaven. (See plate 11.3)

These shifts in 'style' and in the choice of representational technique is significant. It has been suggested on the one hand that the popularity of icons was in part stimulated in the sixth century by their illusionist style

[13] Kitzinger, 'Byzantine art in the period between Justinian and iconoclasm', 47–8, although he sees a more explicit evocation of levels of spiritual being. See also J. Trilling, 'Late antique and sub-antique, or the "decline of form" reconsidered', *DOP* 41 (1987), 469–76.

[14] For the date of the fire and the mosaics, see Lemerle, 'La Composition et la chronologie des deux premiers livres des Miracula S. Demetrii', *BZ* 46 (1953), 349–61, see 356; Kitzinger, 'Byzantine art in the period between Justinian and iconoclasm', 26 and notes 100 and 101; and see Cormack, *Writing in Gold*, p. 83, and 'The mosaic decoration of St Demetrios, Thessaloniki: a re-examination in the light of the drawings of W.S. George', *Annual of the British School at Athens* 64 (1969), 17–52.

Plate 11.2(a) Late sixth- to seventh-century mosaic decoration from St Demetrius, Thessaloniki (water-colour W.S. George)

Plate 11.2(b) St Demetrius with patrons and benefactors. Mosaic of post-
reconstruction period, second quarter of seventh century

and their lifelike and almost humanly accessible quality. This may have been the case; although it assumes without argument a questionable essentialism of perception – that what we might today feel to be 'more approachable' held the same symbolic and emotive values for a medieval observer. I will return to this problem shortly. For it is clear, on the other hand, that accessibility and receptiveness could equally well be expressed in the 'abstract' form. It is less the style itself which promotes or inhibits accessibility than the context in which the figures are represented, and in which 'style' and 'form' are attributed with specific meaning, and symbolic-evocational functions. As we will see, it is important to remember that different cultures also perceive differently – from each other as well as from us. And it seems a reasonable surmise that it was the linear, hieratic and abstract mode of representation which came to meet best the demands of the producer and the beholder. It seems to have responded to and reflected the attitudes of the late sixth and seventh centuries, which sought an affirmation of the heavenly, and therefore unsullied, unassailable, status and authority of the prototypes which the icon encapsulated. Imperial parallels, on coins of the later seventh century, for example, would appear to bear this out, given the need to express and reinforce imperial authority at this time. We may reasonably conclude that authority and status were represented iconographically by an abstract, hieratic style, more effectively than by the alternatives.[15]

Both in theological argument (elaborated during the sixth and seventh centuries)[16] and in the common perception, icons came to be understood as being transcendentally related to their prototypes; they were sources, therefore, of the holy and the sacred. Icons seem to have responded, both in their physical dissemination and their easy availability, on the one hand, and in the style in which they were executed, on the other hand, to the need for a more immediate mode of access to God or his representatives. At first, the 'illusionist' or 'Hellenistic' mode dominated. But I would argue that the adoption of an abstract mode – a style in which, as we have said,

[15] For a detailed description and analysis of this icon, see K. Weitzmann, *The Monastery of St. Catherine at Mt. Sinai, the Icons*, I: *From the sixth to the tenth century* (Princeton 1976), pp. 19–21. For the notion that icons were rendered more approachable through the use of an illusionist mode of representation, see J. Herrin, 'Women and the faith in icons in early Christianity', in *Culture, Ideology, Politics: Essays for Eric Hobsbawm*, eds. R. Samuel and G. Stedman-Jones (London 1982), pp. 56–83; and for imperial models of solemnity, authority and power, and the ways in which these were thought to be best represented, see the detailed fourth-century description of the Emperor Constantius by Julian: Oratio I (in *Julian, Letters and Works*, ed. and trans. W.C. Wright (London and Canmbridge, Mass. 1954), p. 96); and see note 19, chapter 11 below

[16] Kitzinger, 'Images before iconoclasm', 139–46. Note in particular qu. 39 of the Ps.-Athanasius *Quaestiones ad Antiochum ducem* (PG XXVIII, 597–708) datable possibly to the 630s, which is a brief justification of the use of holy images, and in which their miraculous attributes are taken quite for granted – see 621A–D.

Plate 11.3 Icon of the Virgin and child (detail) between St Theodore and St George, with flanking angels, monastery of St Catherine, Sinai

Plate 11.4(a) *Solidus* of Justinian I (obverse and reverse)

Plate 11.4(b) *Solidus* of Constans II with Constantine, his son (obverse and reverse)

the key figures were represented as passive and motionless, attentive and ready to be approached by the supplicant – must have been also a functional response to a qualitative change in the nature of this demand; more particularly, to the need for both accessibility, differentiation from the earthly world, *and* undeniable spiritual authority – something which the naturalistic portraits of the Hellenistic tradition were perhaps less able to communicate. For the 'illusionist' mode, at least when individual or small groups of figures were concerned, was less approachable, if only because it depended upon a dynamism and narrative involvement within the composition itself, which necessarily restricted the observer to that role alone, excluding him or her from actually approaching and being received by the object of devotion.[17]

The process by which painters of icons and mosaicists arrived at this particular mode of expression is a more difficult problem of course, and one which I cannot do justice to here. What is clear is that, by the later sixth

[17] See E. Kitzinger, 'On some icons of the seventh century', in *Late Classical and Medieval Studies in Honor of Albert Mathias Friend, jr.* (Princeton 1955), pp. 132ff. For the lack of personal accessibility and involvement inherent in the three-dimensional, dynamic art of the classical period, see T.J. Boatswain, 'Images of uncertainty: some thoughts on the meaning of form in the art of late Antiquity', *BMGS* 12 (1988). Note also the comments of J.-M. Spieser, 'Image et culture: de l'iconoclasme à la renaissance macédonienne', in G. Siebert, ed., *Méthodologie iconographique* (Strasbourg 1981), 96f. and esp. Onians (see note 10 chapter 11 above).

century, Constantinople had become the chief centre of artistic inspiration in the eastern Mediterranean basin, exercising an influence over artistic production in both Italy, for example, and in the Eastern provinces. The building activities of the reign of Justinian alone seem to have contributed a great deal to the spread of a broadly Constantinopolitan style and provided a further unifying element in the developing art of late antique Christianity. The common symbolic and representational elements in mosaics, frescoes, sculpture and metalwork, for example, which had developed from the fourth century, are apparent in the Christian art of the sixth century. The shared artistic heritage is expressed in both the production of clay *ampullae* from the holy places, for example, brought back by pilgrims, and in the commissioning by the wealthy of silverware in the style of Constantinople. As the sixth century drew on, so this Constantinopolitan influence became more and more important – not to the exclusion of purely provincial styles, but nevertheless as a leader in style and form. The presence of the court was, of course, the crucial factor in this.[18]

It is not impossible that a preference for a more abstract style for devotional and authoritative figures, such as the Virgin and the saints, for example, was given added stimulus by the adoption of such a style for imperial figures – it has been argued that, as a general rule (although there are exceptions) the imperial coinage up to Justin II exemplifies a broadly Hellenistic or illusionist style for the figures of the emperor, but that thereafter a more distinctly linear, two-dimensional style dominates. Religious icons clearly did owe a great deal to the portrayals of secular figures of authority such as emperors, as has been pointed out by several art historians. And although there are specific exceptions to this general tendency, as we have noted – notably the coinage of Constantine IV, for example, which seems to reflect a 'Justinianic revival' based on the styles of the mid-sixth century[19] – there is no doubt that it was in the end just this

[18] Kitzinger, 'Byzantine art in the period between Justinian and iconoclasm', 33ff., esp. 39, and *Byzantine Art in the Making*, esp. pp. 113ff.; J. Hubert, J. Porcher and W.F. Volbach, *Europe in the Dark Ages* (London 1969), pp. 245f.; K. Weitzmann, '"Loca sancta" and the representational art of Palestine', *DOP* 28 (1974), 31–55; A.P. Každan and A. Cutler, 'Continuity and discontinuity in Byzantine history', B 52 (1982), 429–78.

[19] For the connection between imperial and religious iconography, see K. Weitzmann, with M. Chatzidakis, S. Radojčić and K. Miatev, *Icons from South Eastern Europe and Sinai* (London 1968), p. x; Kitzinger, 'Images before iconoclasm', 121ff.; 'Byzantine art in the period between Justinian and iconoclasm', 20; and esp. Graber, *L'Empereur*, in particular pp. 189ff., with pp. 196–243. For abstraction and linearism on the coin-portraits of emperors in the period after Justinian and up to Constantine IV, see esp. M. Restle, *Kunst und byzantinische Münzprägung von Justinian I. bis zum Bilderstreit* (Athens 1964), esp. pp. 65ff.; and Kitzinger, *Byzantine Art in the Making*, pp. 102ff., and 'Byzantine art in the period between Justinian and iconoclasm', 120 (with fig. 20); P.D. Whitting, *Byzantine Coins* (London 1973), pp. 106–60, esp. p. 150. For the 'Justinianic' revival under Constantine IV, see Kitzinger, *Byzantine Art in the Making*, pp. 121f.

Plate 11.5(a) *Solidus* of Justin II (obverse and reverse)

Plate 11.5(b) *Solidus* of Maurice (obverse)

Plate 11.5(c) *Solidus* of Phocas (obverse)

Plate 11.5(d) *Solidus* of Heraclius and Heraclius Constantine (obverse)

Plate 11.5(e) *Solidus* of Constantine IV (obverse and reverse)

Plate 11.5(f) *Solidus* of Justinian II (obverse)

Plate 11.5(g) *Solidus* of Anastasius II (obverse)

Plate 11.5(h) *Solidus* of Philippicus Bardanes (obverse and reverse)

abstract and hieratic style, even if tempered by many illusionist elements, which was adopted by the artists of the post-iconoclastic era for devotional portraits.[20] (See plates 11.5(a)–(h).)

Of course, there are difficulties in assessing the aesthetic significance of a particular style or mode of execution of a work of art for contemporary beholders, both in respect of the possible variety of different situation-bound perceptions (social class and status, for example, may play a role in the evocational process which a specific image sets in train) and in terms of the function of a representational or figural aesthetic as understood by contemporaries. The effect a particular iconographic style has on the modern interpreter, and the language we might use to describe those effects, might be quite inappropriate when applied to the culture which produced the artifact. And we are confronted here, of course, with the old problem of whether or not we can posit some universal aesthetic principle; or at least the possibility of long-term cultural-aesthetic continuities within a specific cultural-ideological continuum, in terms of both geography and space. In this particular case, the assumption of a common Greco-Roman and Christian 'heritage' plays a significant role.

There are a number of arguments here, of course, not the least of which is the practical and functional difference in respect of the production of works of art: modern, individualist art-production (and consumption) operates in a very different context from that of the medieval religious art, whatever the individual elements contributed by the actual artist or craftsman. The question of intentionality and the ambiguity of aesthetic codes – and, therefore, the number of potential interpretations – in modern cultures makes the notion that meaning is immanent, rather than constructed in the process of consumption, dubious. There may be a (culturally or individually) 'preferred' understanding on the part of the artist or onlooker, but this cannot be exclusive.[21] In medieval religious art, on the other hand, painters or craftsmen clearly worked within a specific and sometimes very tightly controlled framework or set of instructions, both as far as the demands of the patron of the work and the inherited modes of representation available were concerned. Individual interpretation was not thereby excluded, but it was very limited. And within this limited interpretational field, it is clear that certain meanings or readings were both intended and

---

[20] See, for example, K. Weitzmann, 'The study of Byzantine book illumination, past and present', in *The Place of Book Illumination in Byzantine Art*, ed. G. Vikan (Princeton 1975), p. 160, see 3–4.

[21] For a general survey of the concept of 'art' in modern culture, see Janet Wolff, *Aesthetics and the Sociology of Art* (London 1983), and *The Social Production of Art* (London 1981); and for the question of aesthetic value-attribution, R. Ingarden, 'Artistic and aesthetic values', in H. Osborne, ed., *Aesthetics* (Oxford 1972), pp. 39–54. See also R. Wollheim, *Art and its Objects* (Harmondsworth 1968).

understood. The crucial problem for the modern interpreter is to grasp the modalities of style which represent shifts in the interpretational patterns, first of all; and then – much more difficult – to relate these changes in style to the functional demands placed upon artistic representation (whether those demands were explicit or – as is more usual – implicit). This assumes, of course, that shifts in modes of representation also tie in with, affect and reflect, shifts in the perceived or the required significance of a representation. The real problem is to see to what emotional and psychological needs a change in aesthetic actually responds, or may itself stimulate. And it is at just this point that the question of universals must be addressed.

Now, it seems to be a reasonable assumption that certain elements of our aesthetic responses are universal – if only because all human creative and artistic activity is carried on by the same biological being. Just as there appear to be phylogenetically determined capacities to generate linguistic structures or to employ different modes of cognition – symbolic, semantic and so on – so the probability of some phylogenetically determined faculty to respond to certain types of form – size, depth and so on – and colour, which structures the possibilities of production and interpretation, seems unavoidable. Sentiments or moments in human experience which remain universal and constant – such as love, hate, fear, death, birth, ageing and so on – whatever the cultural variation in their mode of expression and representation, are common to all. And, if – using socially inflected conventions – an artist, or a whole style of representation, is able to evoke such basic elements of experience, this serves at least as part of the explanation for the ability of some works to transcend cultural barriers.[22] The problem remains to recognise exactly what each different culture understands by a specific style and how its effects were given expression.

If we accept the possibility of both a deep structure of aesthetic responses and a given cultural-aesthetic continuum, then we can justifiably apply some of our criteria to artifacts not directly of our own culture, but of cultures which have a specific and determinate historical affinity with ours. If we reject these premises, of course, then we must seek some direct statement from the culture itself on the aesthetic qualities concerned, and the role they were held to play.[23]

In the case of the orthodox, Byzantine world we are fortunate to have some comments from members of the culture itself; and so, while I would certainly argue for both a historical-cultural affinity as well as a generative

---

[22] See in particular the work of Sebastian Timpanaro, *On Materialism* (London 1975); and Raymond Williams, 'Problems of materialism', *New Left Review* 109 (May–June, 1978), 3–17, see 10.
[23] See in this respect R. Wollheim, 'Aesthetics, anthropology and style', in M. Greenhalgh and V. Megaw, eds., *Art in Society* (Ithaca and London 1978), esp. pp. 5ff.

and phylogenetically determined aesthetic faculty, this need not be the only basis for any assumptions we might make. Such statements confirm the validity of our interpretation of the different modes of representation; in particular, the difference between, and different aesthetic-psychological functions of, the 'illusionist' and the 'abstract' styles described.[24] Later Byzantine writers stress particularly the centrality of 'order' and motionlessness, both in invoking the accessibility of the figures portrayed and in emphasising their other-worldliness and authority, themes which have been discussed and stressed by other scholars.[25] Of course, such conscious formulations were also subject to long-term historical evolution and represent possibly only a certain stage in the development of Byzantine understanding and explanations of their figurative art. But it is at least clear that such art was always open to interpretation and explanation and that there existed at different times differently nuanced but generally available sets of notions about the function of images.[26] In the sixth century, Nilus Scolasticus remarked that the image of an angel immediately evoked the heavenly sphere; Agathias comments that the image imprints itself within the beholder.[27] What these, and many other comments, suggest is the evocational, which is to say the symbolic, power of images.

Some scholars have argued that there is no (conscious) symbolism in Byzantine art, and that, on the contrary, it was intended to be explicit and realistic. But this seems to miss the point at issue. The problem revolves not around whether or not Byzantine commentators or theologians imbued religious art with a conscious symbolism, but rather whether the notion of 'reality' in figural art was broadened or redefined and whether it became more nuanced, according to the nature and explicit function of the work in question.[28] In other words, and as I have argued above, the shifts in mode, and the choice of a particular mode, may well represent explicit decisions and intentions on the part of the craftsman or the patron; but this in itself reflects the availability to the culture of a choice in mode of representation at a tacit or subconscious level, that is, at a level at which emotional and evocational stimuli operate, and as a function of iconographic intention.[29]

---

[24] See especially Henry Maguire, 'Truth and convention in Byzantine descriptions of works of art', *DOP* 28 (1974), 113–40; and the essays of Byčkov, Popova and Komec (chapters 15, 16 and 17) in Udal'cova, ed., *Kul'tura Vizantii*.

[25] For example, Každan and Constable, *People and Power in Byzantium*, pp. 104f.

[26] See Mathews, *Byzantine Aesthetics*, for example, whose survey of the literary sources makes this abundantly clear, whether one accepts his conclusions or not.

[27] *Anthologia Palatina* I, 33 and 34.

[28] Mango, *Byzantium: the Empire of New Rome*, p. 264, for example, argues against any symbolism. But see H. Maguire, *Earth and Ocean: The Terrestrial World in Early Byzantine Art* (London, Pa. 1987), pp. 5–15, 81–4.

[29] See, for example, the comments of Th. Adorno, *Aesthetic Theory*, eds. G. Adorno and R. Tiedemann, Engl. trans. C. Lenhardt (London and New York 1984), esp. pp. 8–9.

Representation changes, therefore, in response to a need to fulfil the functional requirements placed upon it.

What we are talking about, of course, is symbolism as a mechanism of evocation and metaphor. Whatever theologians and Churchmen may have claimed, all works of art are endowed with a latent or potential symbolic value, whether this is understood, made explicit, desired or not. For this is the way in which the human cognitive system functions.[30] The symbolic value in question may or may not be part of a conscious theological or other intellectual system, of course – symbols operate at a variety of levels, from the most personal and individual experience to the most general social level. The crucial point is that a particular mode of representation will have on each beholder both a personal specific and a general social, evocational effect. A gradual shift in the particular mode, therefore, or the use of a combination of modes in a particular way, whatever the intentions of the artist might be, cannot but evoke a shift in response of some sort from the onlooker. Since systems of figural representation do not develop by chance or in an anarchic manner – in a social vacuum, as it were – the gradual dominance of a particular style or combination of styles, in a particular context, must also reflect in some way the expectations of the onlooker. It operates at both an explicit and a symbolic level.[31]

Symbolic systems, and the narratives with which they are bound up, depend, of course, on the experience of individuals and groups within the culture for their effectiveness and the specificity of the evocations they generate. Whether Byzantines endowed their icons with explicit symbolic values is, therefore, not such an important question.[32] What is important is to understand that a figural representation inevitably 'evoked' in the mind of the onlooker, just as it also portrayed in a more or less explicit manner, a particular individual or event or whatever; and that changes in style reflect

---

[30] See esp. R. Bhaskar, 'Emergence, explanation, emancipation', in P.F. Secord, ed., *Explaining Human Behaviour: Consciousness, Human Action and Social Structure* (Beverly Hills, Ca. 1982), pp. 275–310; T.W. Goff, *Marx and Mead, Contribution to a Sociology of Knowledge* (London 1980), pp. 86ff. See Haldon, 'Ideology and social change', 150ff.

[31] The best demonstration of how symbolic systems operate, and also the best challenge in this context to a semiological approach to symbolism, is D. Sperber, *Rethinking Symbolism* (Cambridge 1975). On the dialectic between perception and representation, see the comments of V. Burgin, 'Diderot, Barthes, *Vertigo*', in *The End of Art Theory. Criticism and Post-Modernity* (London 1986), pp. 112–39; and 'Seeing sense', *ibid.*, pp. 51–70.

[32] In fact, of course, Byzantine Churchmen did endow them with express symbolic functions: canon 82 of the Quinisext makes this quite clear when it orders the representation of Christ in human form, rather than in that of a lamb, in order to proclaim and emphasise the incarnation of the word in Christ and to evoke the doctrine of salvation. See Mansi XI, 977E–980B. This is, precisely, a conscious symbolism, in the sense used here. The fact that the medieval Church abandoned the totemic symbolism of lamb and fish, for example, has nothing to do with a relinquishing of symbolic functions inevitably bound up with the production and use of visual representations such as icons or frescoes in churches.

deeper social-psychological trends. Such trends must, therefore, be one element in the wider set of social and cultural transformations which late Roman and early Byzantine society underwent at this time.

The modal changes which I have described seem to fit in also with (and presumably are causally linked with) a change in the perception of the effects of an icon or similar figural portrayal, which can be shown to have occurred over the period from the later sixth century, approximately, to the ninth century. The central element in this change involves the transfer of emotional weight from the representation itself to the onlooker. This impression is gained from examining the composition and form of figural representations, the Hellenistic or illusionist mode depending upon an inwardly directed and narrativistic involvement within the frame of the composition; the abstract mode invoking attentiveness, accessibility, the direct involvement of the onlooker with the main subject of the composition, and, potentially, the intervention of the portrayed figure into the world of the onlooker. In the former, the figures inhabit their own world; in the latter, they look out and touch the world of the onlooker.

Later Byzantine writers lay greater stress on the physical pain endured in scenes of martyrdom, for example, than do earlier writers, and they emphasise the emotion and pathos expected from the onlooker.[33] Tears and grief – greatly in contrast to the earlier period – were assumed, if not demanded, from a true Christian. The ninth-century account of Ignatius the Deacon, in the Life of patriarch Tarasius, of a martyrdom cycle, assumes just this response;[34] the council of 787 clearly accepted as fundamental the principle that the sanctity of an icon was guaranteed if it moved the onlooker to tears;[35] and, perhaps most significantly – since it clearly relates to a general attitude to, and set of assumptions about, representative art, whether two- or three-dimensional – the anonymous writers of the eighth-century Brief Historical Notes (*Parastaseis syntomoi chronikai*) are clearly interested in the effects antique monuments and statuary have on the onlooker, paying little or no attention to their actual

---

[33] See, for example, C. Mango, *The Art of the Byzantine Empire. Sources and Documents* (Englewood Cliffs, N.J. 1972), p. 38 (description of the martyrdom of St Euphemia, late fourth century); and esp. H. Maguire, *Art and Eloquence in Byzantium* (Princeton 1981), pp. 34ff., and 'Truth and Convention' (cited, note 24, chapter 11, above), 22f. The development has been discussed at length, for the ninth century, by Leslie Brubaker, 'Byzantine art in the ninth century: theory, practice and culture', *BMGS* 13 (1989), 23–94 and 'Perception and conception: art, theory and culture in ninth-century Byzantium', *Word and Image* 5 (1989), 19–32. The importance of tears as a purifying and cleansing element is made apparent in the writings of Anastasius of Sinai. In qu. 105 (*PG* LXXXIX, 757C4–760A8) and at several points in his *Oratio de Sacra Synaxi* (*PG* LXXXIX, 832D–833A, 837A) their importance for true repentance and understanding is made very clear.

[34] See *Vita Tarasii*, 414.18sq.   [35] Mansi XIII, 9, 11 and 32.

appearance.[36] For the twelfth-century Nikolaos Mesarites, describing the Church of the Holy Apostles in Constantinople, the figures represented for him and for fellow onlookers the reality of their prototypes; they could be smelled and seen to move, they evoked an instant emotional response.[37]

These descriptions of the effects a work of art had on an onlooker tell us little or nothing about the mode of representation of course. And one must be careful not to assume that the response expected from an onlooker was constant from the fourth or fifth centuries through to the twelfth: this was clearly not the case. But that a change in the perception of effects did take place, and began at about the same time as the increasing importance of an abstract figural mode becomes apparent, and that this change was well developed by the middle of the eighth century, does seem significant.

The change is implicit in the enormous increase in the use of icons, particularly the intensely personal and private nature of their use, which can be dated from the later sixth century. The argument has returned to its starting-point.[38] The change is quite clear from the expectations which people clearly came to have of icons and the powers which were ascribed to them. Images intervened directly in the day-to-day lives of ordinary people. According to a (possibly interpolated) passage in the Spiritual Meadow of John Moschus, an image of Jesus appeared before a crowd at Antioch dressed in clothes previously given to a beggar, thus acting out a story from the New Testament.[39] The pilgrim Arculf, who visited the Holy Land in the 670s, relates a number of tales he heard about an image of St George at Lydda – it made promises to those who prayed before it, was immune to attack, worked miracles;[40] other icons bled when attacked or even fought back at their opponents. The famous image of Christ at Edessa was later credited with beginning a fire which destroyed the siege-ramps of the Persians in 544. In the Life of Theodore of Sykeon, images are able directly to effect cures, while in the miracles of Artemius, a collection of which was put together in Constantinople in the 660s, wax taken from a holy icon is an effective cure.[41] Images gave aid in battles and sieges; they provided assistance in other contexts as well; and they were clearly venerated and

---

[36] See edition by Cameron and Herrin, introduction, p. 53.
[37] G. Downey, ed., 'Nicholas Mesarites, Description of the Church of the Holy Apostles at Constantinople', in *Trans. American Philos. Society* 47 (1957), see ch. 26, 6
[38] See the texts for this period collected in Mango, *The Art of the Byzantine Empire*, pp. 133–9; and Kitzinger, 'Images before iconoclasm', 95ff.
[39] See Th. Nissen, 'Unbekannte Erzählungen aus dem Pratum Spirituale', *BZ* 38 (1938), 351ff., see 367 no. 12.
[40] Arculf, *Relatio de Locis Sanctis* III, 4 (ed. T. Tobler, *Itinera et Descriptiones Terrae Sanctae* I (Geneva 1877), 195ff.)
[41] See the long list of such wonders, all dating to the later sixth and seventh centuries, given by Kitzinger, 'Images before iconoclasm', 101–9; and excerpts in Mango, *The Art of the Byzantine Empire*, pp. 133–9; and see *Miracula S. Artemii*, 16–17; *Vita Theod. Syk.*, 8.5–10.

respected, both in public and in private. Supplicants placed candles before them, lamps were lit and maintained before them, curtains or hangings were placed before or around them, to the extent that the latter, too, gained a certain power through association; and incense was burned in their presence.[42] In short, there takes place a marked intensification of interest in the role and effectivity attributed to icons by the sources of the later sixth and seventh centuries, in comparison with the preceding period. Again, this development parallels the changes in the modes of representation which were employed for images at the same period. The most likely explanation for this shift in mode is, quite simply, therefore, that it represented in ways which can no longer be entirely accessible to us the evocational and interventionist power of images, conjuring up through the frontal, unavoidable gaze of the figure or figures represented in the image an immediacy, authority and, above all, an externality which an illusionist mode – a mode which, as we have seen, evoked rather an internalised narrative – could not attain so effectively. It did not exclude or inhibit the use of the illusionist mode, of course, both in images and in other contexts; and we should take into account the fact that frontality and directness of gaze might be represented in a more naturalistic or Hellenistic mode, and still achieve the desired result. But the abstract mode does seem to indicate what we can associate most clearly both visually (aesthetically) and through the textual evidence of the period in question with the intensification and elaboration of the use of icons, and the enormous emotional power vested in them.[43] By the end of the seventh century, the evidence suggests that icons had begun to be an absolutely unremarkable feature of Byzantine piety and of daily life, both public and private. As we have seen, canon 82 of the Quinisext specifically ordained the representation of Christ in human form, rather than as a lamb, for didactic purposes – to make clear the incarnation of the word in Christ, to affirm the dogma of Chalcedonian Christology; canon 100 ordained that art which might corrupt or confuse be destroyed, again stressing the key role it was seen to play both as an educational and as a spiritual mediator. Such texts confirm the suggestion that there existed a general tendency in this period to enlist images formally in the service of the Church – more particularly, the imperial Church.[44] The icon was, in several ways, a true 'sign of the times'.

---

[42] Kitzinger, 'Images before iconoclasm', 96–100; and see V. Nunn, 'The encheirion as adjunct to the icon in the middle Byzantine period', *BMGS* 10 (1986), 73–102.
[43] For a similar point, although from a different standpoint, J. Onians, 'Abstraction and imagination in late Antiquity', *Art History* 3 (1980), 1–23.
[44] Mansi XI, 977E–980B and 985D; see Kitzinger, 'Images before Iconoclasm', 120f.; Anna Kartsonis, *Anastasis: The Making of an Image* (Princeton 1986), p. 59.

LITERATURE, PIETY AND THE END OF ANTIQUITY

The second of the two phenomena noted above, namely the more or less complete disappearance after the first quarter of the seventh century of a secular literature, has invoked much comment and discussion. The obvious explanation – that the conditions of that century, and indeed of much of the following century, did not provide an environment at all conducive to such activity – is clearly correct. But how does this very general explanation relate to the specific developments in question? After the late-sixth- or early-seventh-century works of Theophylact Simocatta, for example, or the anonymous Paschal Chronicle, or that of John of Antioch, there is a lacuna of almost two centuries until the next surviving historical work. Similarly, the seventh and much of the eighth century provide no examples of geographical, philosophical or philological literature; there is no historical poetry after George of Pisidia, and only a trickle of legal literature and secular rhetoric. Apart from supposed lost histories of a certain Trajan *patrikios* of the seventh century and of the so-called *megas chronographos*, or 'great chronographer', of the eighth century, the letters of a few Churchmen and the powerful, the very small amount of legal literature mentioned already and the surviving documents of state and Church as institutions, the literary output of the seventh century appears to have been almost entirely theological in nature, or at the least concerned with matters of dogma, devotion, various aspects of liturgical practice, problems of day-to-day piety and observance, and so on.[45]

Now the fact that theological and related literary genres maintain a written existence, whereas the forms of secular literary activity suffer a dramatic decline, is clearly a reflection of the difficulties of the seventh century and must in the first instance be a reflection of a change in the

---

[45] The relevant data with detailed surveys can be found in Hunger, *Profane Literatur*, vols. I and II. See, too, the chapter of A.A. Averincev on late Roman literature in Udal'cova, ed., *Kul'tura Vizantii*, who remarks also on the break in genre and continuity which sets in with the work of George of Pisidia and John Moschus. For Trajan *patrikios* see Hunger, *Profane Literatur*, vol. I, pp. 337 and 345; D. Serruys, 'Recherches sur l'epitomé', BZ 16 (1907), 1–52; A. Markopoulos, 'A la recherche des textes perdus. L'historiographie byzantine de la haute époque jusqu'au VIIIᵉ siècle. Etude préliminaire', in *From Late Antiquity to Early Byzantium*, ed. V. Vavřínek (Prague 1985), pp. 203–7. The cultural break which the seventh century represents affected secular letter-writing also. See M. Mullett, 'The classical tradition in the Byzantine letter', in *Byzantium and the Classical Tradition*, pp. 75–93, see p. 86. Note also the survey of E. Jeffreys, 'The image of the Arabs in Byzantine literature', *Seventeenth International Byzantine Congress, Major papers* (New York 1986), pp. 305–23, see pp. 312–14. For a good survey of the nature of late Roman historical writing and the problem of the break in the tradition, see L.M. Whitby, 'Greek historical writing after Procopius: variety and vitality', in Averil Cameron, and L. Conrad, eds., *The Early Medieval Near East: Problems in the Literacy Source Material* (Princeton 1990); also J.D.C. Frendo, 'History and Panegyric in the Age of Heraclius: the Literary Background to the Compositon of the *Histories* of Theophylact Simocatta', DOP 42 (1988), 143–56.

conditions within which the literary culture associated with late Roman society had existed and flourished. Two elements in particular seem to be relevant: the decline during the later sixth, but especially during the seventh, century of traditional municipal society and culture; and the qualitative change in the nature and constitution of the ruling elite. The two are intimately bound up together, as I have tried to show in chapters 3 and 4 above. And it is clear that the demise of the urban civilisation within which late Roman literary culture had flourished had a dramatic effect. A real shift took place in the relationships between social class and literacy, and more especially between the traditional sources of late Roman culture and education, and the developing imperial elite of the court and the state bureaucracy. The latter – for which there is evidence from the middle of the seventh century – while it will certainly have incorporated established families and representatives of the old senatorial elite, was recruited more directly through imperial service and received its rewards through a more centralised and autocratic system of precedence and hierarchy. It was drawn from a variety of ethnic and cultural sources, and selection was based more than previously, it would appear, upon practical administrative, political and military ability, along with the patronage and influence of those already 'in place'. It was this new, meritocratic elite which began to dominate both provincial and central administrative apparatuses, along with the sources of wealth and the means of controlling its distribution. The older, leisured cultural elite quite simply lost its social prestige and its economic standing. There is no reason to assume, of course, that the new elite did not acknowledge the value of the old culture and its traditions, nor indeed that it did not itself aspire to participate in that culture – so much is clear from the later revival of interest in 'classical' learning and models of literacy, and the enormous power of the notion of 'the past' in Byzantine thinking. But the dominant tendency does seem to have been at least apathetic in our period with regard to these traditions.

The lack of literature in the fields mentioned above – which cannot possibly be a reflection of some supposed (and mysteriously selective) failure of the literary output of the seventh and early eighth centuries to survive – confirms the hypothesis; the fact that theological literature does survive, and in considerable volume, makes it certain. For the Church maintained its traditional administrative organisation and, to a great extent, within the empire, its sources of revenue. It needed to be able to educate its clergy, and it needed literate and cultured men for its highest offices.[46] But even here, it was topical questions of the day, the study of the writings of the Church fathers and of the general councils, along with

[46] Beck, *Kirche*, pp. 67–74 and 79ff.

Language, literature and the icon 427

scripture and exegesis that provided the main fields of concern. Interest in the pre-Constantinian, much less the pre-Christian, culture of the past was a rarity.[47]

The nature of hagiographical writing from the eighth century underlines the character of the shift. Not only does the hagiography of the later eighth century and after deal with a very different type of saint or holy man from that familiar from the period up to the Arab conquests (as we might expect, given the nature of the social and cultural changes already discussed); it represents a different style of hagiographical narrative, in which the connection with the forms of late antique literary types has been severed. The seventh century did not by any means see the end of hagiography, but it did witness a major qualitative change in its composition and presentation.[48] Just as significantly, the ethos which underlay the collection and preservation through recopying of classical, patristic and historical texts in the ninth and tenth centuries especially reinforces the nature of the break. For the fear of losing forever the literature of the past (meaning, in effect, of the period up to the mid-seventh century) seems to be a central motif.[49]

By the same token, it is illustrative that the traditional secular system of education seems to have disappeared almost entirely – with one or two individual exceptions – and even in Constantinople was reduced to insignificance. Whatever the value of the remark of the ninth-century chroniclers that after 726 learning in the Roman world was extinguished, their comments certainly reflect a general situation.[50] Only an elementary form of primary schooling seems to have carried on, if we exclude the private tuition that must have been available to the wealthier; and it is interesting that the regular use of the Psalter as the basic reading primer in both Constantinople and the provinces probably begins in the years about the middle of the seventh century.[51] As we have seen, there does seem to

[47] Beck, *Kirche*, esp. pp. 430–73 on the period of the monenergite and monothelete debates, for a representative survey.

[48] See the discussion of L. Rydén, 'New forms of hagiography: saints and heroes', *Seventeenth International Byzantine Congress, Major Papers*, pp. 537–54; and note W. Lackner, 'Die Gestalt des Heiligen in der byzantinischen Hagiographie des 9. und 10. Jahrhunderts', *ibid.*, pp. 523–36.

[49] As has been emphasised by H. Hunger, 'The reconstruction and perception of the past in literature', *Seventeenth International Byzantine Congress, Major Papers*, pp. 507–22, esp. 519.

[50] Theophanes, 405.10sq., and especially the story recorded in *Georg. Monachi Chronicon*, 742.2–22.

[51] See Mango, *Byzantium: The Empire of New Rome*, pp. 136f., for a brief survey of the evidence; and for a more detailed picture, Anne Moffatt, 'Schooling in the iconoclast centuries', in *Iconoclasm*, eds. Bryer and Herrin, pp. 85–92. See also Lemerle, *Le premier humanisme byzantin*, pp. 98–103. See, for example, Vita Andreae Cretensis, ch. 3, where Andreas receives an education in *ta peza grammata*, and later in *ta hypsēlōtera mathēmata*. That a traditional education of sorts continued to be available, to some, however, albeit subordinated to the demands of theology and 'orthodoxy' (whether from a Chalcedonian

have been a limited legal training available at Constantinople in the last years of the seventh century, as canon 71 of the Quinisext suggests. But there is no evidence for any other form of higher education. The use of the Psalter reinforces the impression gained from the types of literary activity that did flourish at this time that the Church and clergy came to play a much more central role in basic and more advanced education than hitherto, as well as in the transmission of literacy and a literary culture in general, especially in respect of what was read. In effect, a cycle of developments was set in train that could have had only one result: a decline, even if temporary, of interest in, and transmission of, the secular literature of the sixth century and before, contrasting with the emphasis that fell upon the reading and production of theological literature. The more pivotal position of the clergy in the maintenance of literacy and the selection of reading matter was to have important consequences for a later period. And it marks also a decisive break with the literary and cultural pluralism of the late antique world.

What I am suggesting, therefore, is quite straightforward. The old culture had been maintained within a specific ideological and social-economic framework, that of the municipal economies and society of the late Roman world and the senatorial elite which dominated central and provincial culture and politics. During the seventh century this economic and ideological framework was shattered. In its place there developed gradually from the second half of the seventh century a new, and quite different, social and political elite drawn from a wider variety of social and cultural backgrounds, and founded within a centralised imperial establishment which came to be the sole effective source of wealth, power and privilege. This new elite had very much less interest in and commitment to the traditional literary culture and its values, concerning itself more immediately with cementing its own power and position by and through the imperial administrative apparatus which it served. Needless to say, this tendency represents the sum of a host of individual aspirations and careers – a conscious set of discourses and narratives which provided a common political ideology for this group had hardly begun to develop at this stage.

Slowly, as this new elite became entrenched and as the structures of the medieval Byzantine state began to emerge from the difficulties of the seventh and eighth centuries, it began once more to cultivate its interest in a supposedly classical past that was, as several historians have shown, more late Roman than pre-Christian. Both the very limited degree of literacy in the Byzantine world (in contrast with popular views on the

or a monophysite point of view) is clear from the case of the Armenian Ananias of Sirak, whose 'biography' illustrates the point well. See J.-P. Mahé, 'Quadrivium et cursus d'études au VIIe siècle en Arménie et dans le monde Byzantin', TM 10 (1987), 159–206.

subject), and the methods and subject-matter of Byzantine literati in the ninth century and after – in other words, the very nature of the break in the secular literary culture at this time – testify clearly to this aspect, a point borne out by the motivations underlying the so-called renaissance of the later ninth and tenth centuries.[52]

These two developments, in the use of icons on the one hand and in the nature of literary activity on the other, can now be considered together. For in reflecting on the forms of supposedly 'popular' literary activity – hagiography and miracle-collections especially – and the expansion of icon-use over the same period, the real nature of the changes in late Roman and early Byzantine culture can be most clearly seen. The crucial importance for the inhabitants of this threatened world of belonging, and being seen to belong, to the Chosen People, of being a meaningful part of God's plan, is the message constantly reiterated in the public and private culture of the second half of the seventh century: the icon, whether of Christ, the Virgin, a saint or an archangel, reminds of and invokes a Christian orthodox and local tradition.[53] The church sermon, and more especially the hagiography, the collection of *apophthegmata*, or sayings of the Church Fathers, the accounts of the doings of holy men and monks, or the collection of miracles, read out in a church or in some other community gathering (and it must not be forgotten that a parallel oral tradition which has not always left clear traces had as great an influence), fulfilled the same function. The very process of teaching to read and write were now almost entirely under the guidance of the clergy. And these forms were, in a sense, classless. They were not directed at any specific social group, but at all the faithful; and the sources make it clear that their effectiveness was indeed universal.[54] The popularity of hagiographical and miracle literature, of the

[52] See esp. R.D. Scott, 'The classical tradition in Byzantine historiography', in *Byzantium and the Classical Tradition*, pp. 61–74; and C. Mango, 'Discontinuity with the classical past in Byzantium', *ibid.*, pp. 48–57, see 52ff.; see also the literature in notes 48 and 49; and note the discussion of P. Lemerle, 'Elèves et professeurs: Constantinople au Xe siècle', *CRAI* (1976), 576–87.

[53] Dagron, *Le Culte des images dans le monde byzantin*, esp. pp. 138ff. and 152ff. with literature; Ryden, *The role of the icon* (cited note 7, chapter 11 above), esp. 45ff. and 51. The importance of icons to the ordinary household, as well as their vulnerability to the agents of the devil, can be seen in the story of the woman who unwittingly goes to a magician or false holy man for help, recounted in the Life of Andrew the Fool (see *PG* CXI, 776C–784A). The magician is able to drive out the grace of God through magical spells uttered before a lighted oil lamp, which results eventually in the icon being defiled and covered in excrement. Only through the 'white magic' of the holy fool are the icons purified. Compare these stories with the context discussed by G. Vikan, 'Art, medicine and magic in early Byzantium', *DOP* 38 (1984), 65–86; and C. Belting-Ihm, art. 'Heiligenbild', in *Reallexikon für Antike und Christentum*, fasc. 105 (Stuttgart 1987), 66–96, especially 89–95 on icons as media of healing and miraculous intervention.

[54] See Beck's remark in *Das byzantinische Jahrtausend*, pp. 147–52 and *Kirche*, pp. 267–75 (on hagiography); also H. Delehaye, *Les Recueils antiques des miracles des saints* (Brussels

erōtapokriseis, or collections of 'questions and answers', selected from the sayings of famous hermits, holy men and monks, the icons in churches and in homes, all expressed a common cultural focus and a unity of belief, a common fund of narrative accounts about the nature of the world.[55] More importantly, perhaps, it demonstrated the quest for common motifs, common interests, shared explanations of the world and what was happening, a quest which reached its goal first in local solidarities and identities, but which evoked and symbolised also a wider Christian polity and ideological community. The cultural pluralism and relative openness of literary forms, which still typified the period before the Persian and especially the Arab invasions (and in spite of the increasingly successful screening out of classical motifs which became a feature of post-Justinianic culture), was past. Religious writings which had been tolerated, but which had come to be regarded by the later seventh century as dangerous or

---

1925) (originally in *AB* 43 (1925), 5–85 and 303–25); note esp. E. Patlagean, 'Ancienne hagiographie byzantine et histoire sociale', *Annales ESC* 1 (1968), 106–26 (repr. in *Structure sociale* V) who stresses precisely this point in relation to hagiography, collections of miracles, and so forth. See also Patiagean, 'Discours écrit, discours parlé. Niveaux de culture à Byzance aux VIIIe–IXe siècles', *Annales ESC* 2 (1969), 264–78 (repr. in *Structure sociale* VI).

[55] See Beck, *Kirche*, pp. 430ff., esp. 437 and 444; G. Dagron, 'Le Saint, le savant, l'astrologue. Etude de thèmes hagiographiques à travers quelques recueils de "Questions et réponses" des Ve–VIIe siècles', in *Hagiographie, cultures et société (IVe–VIIe siècles). Etudes Augustiniennes* (Paris 1981), pp. 143–55 (repr. in *La Romanité chrétienne* IV); A. Garzya, 'Visages de l'hellénisme dans le monde byzantin (IVe–XIIe siècles)', *B* 55 (1985), 463–82. Cf. H. Dörries, art. 'Erotapokriseis', in *Reallexikon für Antike und Christentum* 6, pp. 347–70. See also G. Bardy, 'La Littérature patristique des Quaestiones et Responsiones sur l'Ecriture sainte', *Revue Biblique* 41 (1932), 210–36, 341–69 and 515–37; ibid., 42 (1933), 328–52. Two collections of 'Questions and Answers' in particular deserve our attention: the *Quaestiones ad Antiochum ducem* of Ps.-Athanasius (in *PG* XXVIII, 597–708) and those attributed to Anastasius of Sinai (in *PG* LXXXIX, 312–824; see *CPG* III, 7746). The former collection, compiled in the eighth or ninth century, clearly draws on the latter, itself a product of the last years of the seventh century. The Ps.-Athanasius incorporates what may be an earlier text, compiled at about the time of the forced baptisms of Jews (632–4) undertaken by Heraclius, as the presence of a long argument clearly designed to persuade Jews of the justice of the Christian case might suggest (*PG* XXVIII, 684C–700C; see *CPG* III, 7795). See in particular the literature cited at *CPG* III, 7746; and J.F. Haldon, 'The works of Anastasius of Sinai: a key source for the history of seventh-century east Mediterranean society and belief', in Averil Cameron and L. Conrad, eds., *The Early Medieval Near East: Problems in the Literary Source Material* (Princeton 1990).

Just as important a source, both for the attitudes and beliefs of ordinary people, as well as for the cultural and social history of the period, are the collections of *narrationes* or stories about the doings and sayings of holy men and monks of the time. Perhaps the best known are those contained in the *Spiritual Meadow* of John Moschus, a collection of the early seventh century, including both earlier and contemporary eye-witness reports (*CPG* III, 7367 for editions and literature). But those attributed to the monk or abbot Anastasius, who may be Anastasius of Sinai, are equally important for the seventh century, shedding light in particular on the Christian populations of the areas conquered by Islam. See *CPG* III, 7758; and Haldon, 'The works of Anastasius of Sinai'.

subversive, were banned. Canon 63 of the Quinisext council, for example, ordered the destruction of the apocryphal Acts of the Apostles.[56]

The disappearance of secular literature and the concentration of both rural and especially urban culture (for it is from the latter context that the greater part of the evidence comes) on these devotional forms of a consciously collective identity, an awareness made all the more powerful through the emphasis on the individual's relationship and responsibilities within the wider society to the Almighty, marks a qualitative cultural transformation. Late antique civilisation had given way to that of the early medieval world.

The focusing on a (broadly defined) theological and religious literary production marks also a change in the centre of attention of literate Byzantine society. For the most popular forms – in particular the hagiographical genre and the 'questions and answers' – are at the same time representatives of differing and sometimes contradictory positions, deeply concerned with the immediate, the 'here and now', everyday world and the place of the individual within that world. The hagiographical tradition and the collection of miracles associated with relics, icons and saints stresses direct divine intervention in the affairs of humankind. But an alternative tradition, represented, for example, by some late seventh-century 'questions and answers' among those attributed to Anastasius of Sinai, stresses the role of physiological and natural elements in the history and environment of human society. It avoids the determinism of ancient astrology, relating the natural world and the human (social) world to God's plan. It thus attempts to reconcile both the contemporary Christian world view with an older, secular (and pre-Christian) tradition.

This alternative can be traced back into the literature of the sixth century, for example. John Lydus, John Philoponus and Procopius, in their very different works, present versions of both Aristotelian material causal explanation (for earthquakes, for example) and of a purely scriptural explanation, related to the sins of mankind and the will of God. But the latter tradition is clearly the more widespread, especially among the illiterate mass of the population (or so we may, I think justifiably, surmise), and dominates, certainly by the later seventh century.[57]

[56] For canon 63 of the Quinisext, see Mansi XI, 972D. For comments on the literary production and the variety of genres of the sixth century see Cameron, 'Images of authority', 4; and esp. Averil and Alan Cameron, 'Christianity and tradition in the historiography of the late empire', *Classical Quarterly* 14 (1964), 316–28; Averil Cameron, 'The scepticism of Procopius', *Historia* 15 (1966), 466–82; S.S. Averincev, in Udal'cova, ed., *Kul'tura Vizantii* (ch.6) and Garzya, *Visages de l'hellénisme*. Both of the last two detect a qualitative shift in the writings of Moschus and George of Pisidia, as noted above, chapter 11 note 45.

[57] The nature of the debate has been summarised and analysed by Dagron, 'Le Saint, le savant, l'astrologue' (cited note 55, chapter 11, above), esp. 144–6. For the sixth century,

The extent of the debate between these two opposing interpretational poles, and its effect upon its audience or readership, remains unclear. But that it took place at all is important, for it demonstrates the liveliness of these forms of literature and consequently – since both are known from their wide dissemination in manuscript form to have been listened to or read by a large circle – the centrality of this sort of discussion to the understanding, the piety and the interest and concern of ordinary people of all social groups. Questions on the nature of earthly rulers, the satisfactory identity of a true holy man or saint, the nature and origins of miracles, the cause of the different states of public health between the Christians and their barbarian and pagan neighbours, the origins, power and value of wise men and 'magicians', talismans and incantations, and many other topics – they all reflect the common concerns and anxieties of this genre and of hagiography.[58] Particularly to the point are questions on how to differentiate between Satan's trials and God's just punishments, why sinners appear often to be spared the wrath of God (a poignant query in such a bureaucratic and socially stratified culture), whether or not the incursions of the barbarians represent God's punishment, or why Satan has caused more schisms and heresies among the Christians than among other peoples.[59]

This material reinforces once more the impression of a society passionately interested in reassuring itself about the nature of its relationship with the divine world, an interest that was of as much relevance to the cultural and spiritual survival of individuals, as was that of the physical defence of the empire to the career interests of members of the political-administrative elite. The answer to the question of how one differentiates between true and false holy men – an old question, of course, and not

see Cameron, *Procopius*, pp. 257–9. The alternatives are represented equally, although less self-consciously, in the later Ps.-Athanasian *Quaestiones ad Antiochum Ducem*; and it appears most clearly in relation to medical matters. For Christianity, which saw itself as a healing faith in particular, inevitably had difficulty in reconciling the Hellenistic and Roman medical tradition with its own principles and dogmas. Evidence of a rather loose compromise is clear in both the Ps.-Athanasian and the earlier Anastasian collections. For a survey, from the medical perspective, see V. Nutton, 'From Galen to Alexander: Aspects of medicine and medical practice in late antiquity', *DOP* 38 (1984), 1–14, see 5–9; and especially O. Temkin, 'Byzantine medicine: tradition and empiricism', *DOP* 16 (1962), 97–115 (repr. in O. Temkin, *The Double Face of Janus and Other Essays on the History of Medicine* (Baltimore 1977, pp. 202–22)); D.W. Amundsen, 'Medicine and faith in early Christianity', *Bulletin of the History of Medicine* 56 (1982), 326–50. On the 'Question and Answer' literature, see J.F. Haldon, 'The Works of Anastasius of Sinai', cited at note 55, chapter 11 above.

[58] On all these questions, see Haldon, 'The works of Anastasios of Sinai', esp. 129–47; *idem*, 'The miracles of Artemios and contemporary attitudes'; and Auzépy, 'L'évolution de l'attitude face au miracle à Byzance'. For literary and archaeological evidence for these concerns, see G. Vikan, 'Art, medicine and magic in early Byzantium', *DOP* 38 (1984), 65–86.

[59] *Quaestiones* 9 (PG LXXXIX, 409–32), 10 (432–6), 17 (484–500) and 118 (769–72).

Language, literature and the icon 433

confined just to the seventh century – takes on a new importance in this period, illustrating the nature of ordinary hopes and fears.[60]

The questions in the collection of 'questions and answers' ascribed to Anastasius of Sinai, the popularity of apocalyptic literature,[61] the collections of miracles and hagiographies, which increasingly through the seventh century elaborate on the theme of the relationship between God and man, the divine realm and the earthly empire, all point to a greater intensity in the search for security, for clear-cut and solid answers and explanations to the questions which most reflected the concerns of day-to-day existence in this changing and hence – in many ways – threatening world. As we have seen, the process of change is reflected also in the mode of figural representation on icons. The increasingly hieratic, distanced and spiritualised figures of this period represent a world above which is orderly, dignified and holy, presenting implicitly a stark contrast to the drama-laden and disorderly chaos of the earthly world. And all the shifts and tendencies I have noted so far seem to aim to defeat this disorderliness, and lack of harmony: the developments in imperial ceremonial, in popular literary forms and in the interests and priorities they reflect, even in attitudes towards the legal inheritance of the Justinianic 'golden age', people's activities seem directed towards limiting the damage, as it were, wrought by the sins of the Chosen People on the one hand, and by the satanic hordes who had invaded the empire, on the other.[62]

The results of this brief survey can be summarised as follows. The period from the middle decades of the seventh century demonstrates the rapid collapse of the traditional forms of secular literary culture, a phenomenon which accompanied the disappearance of the old educated social elite and the conditions which maintained it. Municipal culture died with the cities. In its place occurred a levelling out of cultural niveaux, in which a new ruling elite of administrative officialdom, many of whom can have been only marginally acquainted with the older literary culture, comes to share a set of common cultural beliefs and values with the greater part of the

---

[60] See Dagron, 'Le Saint, le savant, l'astrologue', 146ff. and chapter 9, above, pp. 364ff. Compare the story of the magician and the icon recorded in the Life of Andrew the Fool (note 53, chapter 11, above); Vikan, 'Art, medicine and magic', 68–70.

[61] The so-called Apocalypse of pseudo-Methodius seems to have had a very wide audience; that appended to the Life of Andrew the Fool occupied a similar place in the tradition. Both represented and stressed the powerful (and predestined) bond between the Chosen People and the divine plan, and placed much emphasis on the temporary nature of the set-backs suffered by the empire in the second half of the seventh century. See the discussion in chapter 9 above, pp. 367ff.; and Mango, 'The Life of Andrew the Fool reconsidered', 305–8.

[62] See E. Kitzinger, *The Art of Byzantium and the Medieval West* (Bloomington and London 1976), pp. 200ff.; and the remarks of N. Baynes, 'The Hellenistic civilisation and East Rome', in *Byzantine Studies and Other Essays* (Oxford 1960), pp. 5f.

rural and urban population of the empire, cultural patterns determined by the stubborn anti-pluralism of the Church and the increasingly dominant role played by the clergy – and by religious literature – in the maintenance of literacy.

Of course, this is a generalised picture: individuals at court and in the provinces still continued to be acquainted with and to foster the literature of the past; and there can be no doubt that the average state official or member of the imperial senate was different in his cultural horizons and aspirations from the average peasant – even though these aspirations operated within the shared general framework just described. Further differentiation between the populations of the now limited number of real urban centres and that of the rural hinterland of the empire was inevitable. Indeed, the population of Constantinople as a whole will have had a very different view of things – bearing in mind the fact that the perspectives expressed through hagiography, apocalyptic writings, collections of 'questions and answers' of miracles and so on, while shared by the whole culture at a general level, differed in respect of local and regional outlook and interests. The maintenance of a literary tradition, with its classical pretensions, rhetorical artifice and stylistic conservatism is not to be doubted. The theological, homiletic and hagiographical traditions testify to this, quite apart from the surviving secular texts.[63] In addition, it must be remembered that the functional importance of style in different contexts was crucial – the level of style, as has been shown, was associated with specific genres,[64] and this certainly ensured a crucial functional framework and stimulus for the continued cultivation of the literary, especially the rhetorical, registers. Exegesis demanded very different stylistic techniques from, for example, panegyric, and these different styles were already firmly embedded in the literary tradition, religious and secular, by the fifth century.[65]

[63] Compare, for example, the style of the encomium on the miracles of the martyr Therapon, compiled in the late seventh or early eighth century (ed. L. Deubner, *De Incubatione Capita Quattuor* (Leipzig 1900), 120ff.) with that of the miracles of Artemius; or the classical allusions and references in the homilies of Andreas of Crete – compiled in a more accessible style to reach a wider audience, but nevertheless full of traditional rhetorical motifs. See Th. Nissen, 'Diatribe und consolatio in einer christlichen Predigt des achten Jahrhunderts', *Philologus* 92 (1937), 177–98 and 382–5. On the importance of rhetoric, see esp. H. Hunger, 'The classical tradition in Byzantine literature: the importance of rhetoric', in *Byzantium and the Classical Tradition*, pp. 35–47; and for the rhetorical link between art and literature, Maguire, *Art and Eloquence*, esp. pp. 22–52.

[64] See I. Ševčenko, 'Levels of style in Byzantine prose', *Akten des XVI. Internationalen Byzantinisten-Kongresses*, I, 1 (Vienna 1981) (= *JÖB* 31, 1). For a valuable comparative analysis of these stylistic trends, see M.B. Cunningham, 'Andreas of Crete's Homilies on Lazarus and Palm Sunday: a critical edition and commentary' (Unpubl. PhD., Univ. of Birmingham, Centre for Byzantine Studies and Modern Greek, 1983).

[65] See in particular T.E. Ameringer, *The Stylistic Influence of the Second Sophistic on the Panegyrical Sermons of St. John Chrysostom: A Study in Greek Rhetoric* (Washington D.C. 1921); R.R. Ruether, *Gregory of Nazianzus, Rhetor and Philosopher* (Oxford 1969); Šev-

But the elite literary culture of late antique municipal society had passed away for ever, and with it the pluralistic and multi-faceted world which it represented. The icon and the Psalter are the hallmarks of the later seventh-century world, a world which, while now more compact and tightly controlled than before, was inhabited by individuals searching for unity and a common identity through the symbols available to them – the orthodox faith, the icon and the emperor.

čenko, 'Additional remarks to the report on levels of style', *Akten des XVI. Internationalen Byzantinisten-Kongresses* II, 1 (Vienna 1982), 220–38 (= *JÖB* 32, 1), with examples.

CHAPTER 12

Conclusion: the transformation of a culture

PIETY AND SECURITY: THE POLES OF AUTHORITY

The history of East Roman or Byzantine culture in the later sixth and seventh centuries can be most easily represented in terms of two dominant motifs: the increasing introversion of orthodox culture and the quest for security. By the former, I mean the generalised concentration in the thinking of the society as a whole on the personal relationship of individuals to God, the identity of orthodox thinking with the survival of the Roman *oikoumenē*, and the exclusion of all marginal or heterodox groups from consideration, in a much more emphatic way than had been the case before the last years of Justinian. By the latter, I mean the manifest collapse of confidence in the traditional symbols of earthly supremacy, in particular the institutions of the imperial establishment, and the search for ways in which an imagined older order – of stability and confidence – could be recovered, which would fulfil the desire both to conform to the spirit and the letter of Chalcedonian orthodoxy, and at the same time to reassert the political dominance of East Rome and the symbolic universe it represented. The first is evident in the literary texts of the period; the second is implicit in the assumptions, actions and responses of individuals and groups within Byzantine society in the period from the 640s and beyond.

These two motifs were, of course, inseparable, since the maintenance of orthodoxy and the exclusion of heterodoxy automatically – it was believed – brought with it, ultimately, political supremacy, at least until the events immediately preceding the Last Judgement. In this respect, it seems to me that some of the apocalyptic literature of the times conceals also – sometimes rather obviously – elements of optimism which belie the belief in a supposedly imminent Day of Judgement. The Apocalypse of Pseudo-Methodius especially – understandably extremely popular and widely disseminated throughout the orthodox world in the Middle Ages – looks forward to the defeat of the Muslims and the reconquest of all the lost lands of the empire before the Second Coming, and thus – given the bleak outlook in the second half of the seventh century – implicitly provides what must have been a rather lengthy breathing-space before the end of the world could be expected.[1]

It is in this context that we must try to interpret and understand the evolution of seventh-century social, political and cultural history, and not just within the empire. Similar concerns and anxieties affected also the monophysite and neo-Chalcedonian communities in the Near and Middle East, too. It is a world in which the public pluralism of the late antique past had been eradicated, because it no longer represented a comfortable mode of understanding and acting within (and upon) the world as it was perceived. Security, and the assurance of doing the 'right thing', could be found in a uniformity of belief, both imposed from above and at the same time desired by the 'ordinary' people. Yet the contradictions between the theory of the world represented by Church and state at the public level, and the rapidly changing circumstances in which people found themselves, at different times and in different places, could not be papered over so easily by the imposition of a rationale from above. Individuals continued to ask questions and to seek answers, whatever their social and cultural position. Men such as Maximus Confessor represented the anxieties and uncertainties of many less literate and articulate than themselves. A common motif remained 'orthodoxy' – but how to attain it, how even to understand it? These were questions to which neither the official Church nor the Byzantine state were able always to find answers that could be translated immediately into action, although not for want of trying. And even Maximus' theology remains just that: a theology, intellectually rigorous, but politically no more nor less valid than the theories of imperial absolutism against which he pitted his talents.

Within the framework of orthodox piety, therefore, and the exclusivist, anti-pluralistic political ideology of the imperial state, recourse to the resolution of problems through an intensely individualistic or personalised devotion was predictable; for the umbrella of official belief could not handle the multiplicity and variety of personal needs, nor could it provide more than the most generalised response to the detailed questions of people anxious about the very foundations of their day-to-day lives.[2] The daily worries which afflicted everyone were ever-present, of course; and it was

---

[1] Ps.-Methodius, *Apokalypse* XIII, 7ff. Even more optimistic is the short chronological treatise of the monk Theophanius, compiled in about 710, in which the calculation of the end of the world, based on a cabbalistic-numerical equation, falls in the year 880. See E. Dobschütz, 'Coislinianus 296', *BZ* 12 (1903), 534–67, see 549ff., and Beck, *Kirche*, p. 473. See chapter 9 and note 116 above.

[2] Some of these aspects are described by N.H. Baynes, in *Byzantine Studies and Other Essays* (Oxford 1960), p. 5.

partly as a result of their effectiveness in providing answers and advice, as well as alternative models for repentance and the absolution of sins, that the hermits and holy men of the later Roman world had become so numerous and popular. And in the shrinking world of the second half of the seventh century, such issues took on a greater significance: not only did they affect one's personal life and salvation; but individuals were regarded as being jointly responsible for the salvation and maintenance of orthodoxy, the safety of the Chosen People and the restoration of the Christian *oikoumenē*. The sorts of questions which occur in the 'questions and answers' attributed to Anastasius of Sinai, and in particular the tension which they express between divine will and foresight, on the one hand, and human self-determination and responsibility on the other (although understood within a divine plan in which this limited freedom was inscribed), bears a new significance in this context.

It would be quite misleading, of course, to suggest that the sorts of conditions which I have described above and the attitudes, beliefs and practices which seem to me typical of late sixth- and seventh-century society, in both Constantinople and the provinces, came into being overnight or developed uniformly across the empire in clearly detectable 'acts' on the historical stage. On the contrary, the evidence is relatively sparse and relates to only limited areas of the empire, or to a limited context at a specific moment. It represents a brief glimpse into the lives of individuals or anonymous groups of people for which we have to provide both the interpretational framework and the specific rationale or logic. In this respect, any conclusions we may draw are bound to be incomplete, flawed and, in some cases, still quite hypothetical or tendentious. On the other hand, the evidence from all the different sources – literary, archaeological, sigillographic and so on – when considered as a whole and within a single cultural context, does bear out the interpretation offered here. It is important to remember that we are dealing with several generations of lives – a short period for the historian, perhaps, but each life represents the growth of an individual personality and psychology constituted within the cultural context into which it is born, with all the aspirations, desires and relationships of a social being. The changes which we observe, detected through different forms of evidence in different ways, affected people differentially and qualitatively over a longer or shorter period in all these respects. We observe what we take to be the results of change, but it is not always easy to discern the causal relationships which generate change in the first place, nor to determine the point at which quantitative evolves into qualitative transformation.

It is useful to bear these points in mind when looking at a period of such complexity as the seventh century. For there is no doubt that many of the practices which we can detect or observe – for example, in the accounts of miraculous cures and the wonder-working power of icons, or implicit in the questions and answers which we have referred to – are, individually, not new, nor are they surprising in the cultural milieu of early medieval Christianity in the east Mediterranean basin. And it also seems to be clear that we are dealing with a period which represents only the resolution of many much more long-term developments; indeed, it is perhaps only the later eighth century which sees the completion of these processes of transformation. But the specific context of the seventh century, in which the cultural traditions we have mentioned were carried on, does give them a particular significance and importance, both in respect of their motivation and in respect of the results which they were intended or thought to have, on the one hand, and which they may actually have had, on the other.

It is, therefore, precisely this 'whole', this context, which makes it possible to understand individuals and their actions, whether singly or in groups, consciously or unconsciously, in the historical past. The seventh century is clearly a qualitatively very different era from the sixth, or it becomes so as it progresses; and the beginnings of this cumulative qualitative evolution, which affected different aspects of different elements of East Roman culture and perceptions at different times, can be situated, as we have seen, already in the last years of Justinian. What the evidence represents, therefore, are the efforts of different elements and groups within Byzantine culture to come to terms with what was perceived as a changing situation over several generations. The central concern was the reaffirmation of the validity and relevance of the values and perceptions of the world which had been affected by the dislocations we have described – in other words, the reassertion of the narrative representations of the society as a whole and in terms of the various social groupings which made it up.

The growth of social and political explanations of the world which seemed to make sense of the changes of the later sixth and early seventh centuries is evidence of their initial success. Increased public and private reliance upon icons, for example, as more direct channels of mediation and access between God and man, imperial ceremonial emphasis upon the emperor as devout servant of God and the conjunctural effects of Heraclius' successful 'crusade' against the Persians, they all served to stabilise the situation, to reaffirm an interpretation of the world in which the imperial state and the Chosen People would ultimately triumph. But shifts in perception, leading in turn themselves to shifts in social praxis, are themselves constitutive of change. And the new situation thus attained was very different from that of the sixth century, both as regards the position of the empire militarily and politically with respect to neighbouring powers (especially in the West), and in terms of the ideological issues taken for granted which now dominated.

The trauma of the Arab attacks and victories, the loss of the East, the devastation of much of Anatolia and the great siege of the years 674–8, as well as the loss of effective imperial control in the greater part of the Balkans – together with the cumulative results of the withering away of urban centres as meaningful social, economic and political elements within both state and society – all had a drastic effect, throwing once more the legitimating theories of the imperial political ideology into question, opening up a gulf between the 'reality' of actual events and the traditional narrative representation of the world. The emperors (rather than the imperial position as such) were now also to feel the effects of the consequent search for a reordering of the elements of the available legitimating theories, and their response was predictable. The monenergite and monothelete policies of Heraclius and Sergius, but especially of Constans II, signalled one attempt to redress the balance and to try to regain the stability which had been regained for a short time by the 630s. And while the attempt failed, the question of the maintenance of (imperial) authority became increasingly crucial in the ever-more uncertain situation which developed during the 650s and beyond, as is clear from the ways in which the imperial government handled the cases of Pope Martin and Maximus Confessor and their adherents.

As we have seen, one of the most significant aspects of later seventh-century history is the increasing 'interference' of officers and soldiers from the provincial armies in the internal politics of the state. This activity – less 'interference' than 'participation', for soldiers had traditionally long had a role in certain aspects of the imperial succession, for example – reflects the position of the soldiers in provincial society, and given the increasingly localised recruitment-patterns which take hold from the 650s, the attitudes also, however refracted, of the provincial populations. The actions of soldiers at this time can be shown to represent a general loss of faith in the efficacy of the traditional symbols of authority, and hence the growing ineffectiveness of traditional legitimating narratives. Military unrest was obviously determined in form and content by its specific context.[3] It expressed itself in terms of the situation as it existed, and it was precisely because the traditional, stable framework through which the world could be made sense of began to break down, and was perceived to be under threat, that soldiers took the sorts of action which are described in the sources.

The activities of soldiers, which constituted a direct threat to imperial

---

[3] Haldon, 'Ideology and social change', 178ff.

authority, and the activities of the emperors themselves, seem to confirm this interpretation. Whether usurpers or not, emperors struggled through various means to reinforce and to assert their authority, both through the traditional ideology and by emphasising all those aspects of the systems of legitimation which were central to Byzantine ideas about the world – the role of the emperor as God's vicegerent on earth, servant and implementer of his will, guardian of orthodoxy and so on. Constans II's reign is particularly striking in this respect. But equally, Constantine IV did not hesitate to deal in an exemplary manner with the soldiers who wished him to crown his two brothers as co-emperors in 681,[4] at the same time attempting clearly to integrate the armies into the framework of his authority, just as Justinian II did a few years later.[5] Constantine's convening of the sixth ecumenical council and the confirmation of the doctrine of Chalcedon similarly served to reassert imperial authority and prestige; Justinian II, with the Quinisext, reasserted even more forcefully the position of the Eastern emperor, both with regard to the Byzantine Church and more especially the papacy.[6] His coinage stresses both his role as victorious emperor over his enemies and the enemies of orthodoxy, as well as his position as the defender of orthodoxy and the humble servant of God. The failed attempt of Philippicus Bardanes to re-establish a monothelete policy on a permanent basis likewise represented an attempt to reassert imperial authority and the search for a set of narrative evaluations of the past which would provide explanations and solutions to the problems of the earthly rulers and provide a practice acceptable to God which would bring an end to the chastisement of the Chosen People at the hands of their enemies.

The activities of soldiers, when seen in this context, become also much easier to understand. Their intervention seems to have very little to do with grievances over matters such as pay, equipment or service conditions (although these undoubtedly existed), in clear contrast with the years up to the middle of the reign of Heraclius, all the more surprising in view of the desperate situation of the state at this time.[7] From the early 640s there are some eleven recorded instances of successful military rebellion – excluding the deposition of Justinian II in 695 – up to and including the accession of Leo III.[8] All these examples demonstrate either an immediate political

---

[4] J.B. Bury, *The Later Roman Empire, from Arcadius to Irene (395–800)* (2 vols., London and New York 1889), vol. 2, pp. 308–9; Winkelmann, 'Zum byzantinischen Staat', p. 217; Stratos, *Byzantium in the Seventh Century*, vol. IV, pp. 135–40.

[5] Mansi XI, 201C; Riedinger, 10.21ff. and 737 (Riedinger, 10.21ff. and 886.2–24).

[6] See Mansi XI, 201C-D for Constantine IV's opening remarks in the *sacra* to the patriarch George; and for the Quinisext, see Winkelmann, *Die östlichen Kirchen*. In general, see chapters 2 and 8 above.

[7] See Haldon, 'Ideology and social change', 178f.; Kaegi, *Military Unrest*, pp. 110ff.

[8] See the summary in Haldon, 'Ideology and social change', 182ff. with literature.

objective or commitment of the soldiers or officers or a general attitude of hostility to the Constantinopolitan government or the emperor himself, which could be exploited for or against a particular party. The accession of Leo III, generally looked at by modern historians as a watershed in these trends, did not in fact end this activity. Indeed, the rebellion of Sergius, the commander in Sicily, in 718, and the plot of Anastasius II, exiled in Thessaloniki, in the same year, emphasise the fact that Leo's position was no more secure at this stage than that of any other usurper.

What is clear is that officers and soldiers were central players in all the coups and attempted coups of this period. It would be an oversimplification, of course, to suggest that the same motives, nuanced in the same ways, were present in every case. Soldiers may well have been the tools of more particularly aware and/or self-interested officers at times (although the latter must have been able to exploit an already given frame of mind which did not prohibit such actions); while on at least one occasion – the overthrow of Anastasius II in 715 – the troops of the *Opsikion* seem to have acted quite arbitrarily. But this in itself seems to indicate both the soldiers' awareness of their central position and the power they could consequently invoke, as well as a possible provincial hostility to Constantinople and its privileges (as perceived, perhaps, from the provinces).[9] Soldiers and officers were involved in the politics of government at this time because they were directly committed to reasserting a stable framework within which the world could be understood.

The quest for security referred to at the beginning of this chapter, therefore, was carried on at several levels and produced a range of conflicts between the representatives of different interpretations of how the 'problem' – likewise, perceived differently from each of several perspectives – should be tackled. We are confronted in the seventh-century Byzantine world with a society and culture full of contradictions. On the one hand, the theoretical (but in many ways also quite real) unity of an orthodox culture in which individuals sought to maintain a common front against outsiders and heresy, through the attainment of piety and the observance of the commands of the Church. The degree of actual uniformity between regions, and within them, whatever the exhortations or formal demands of the Church and canon law, was probably minimal, given both the physical disruption of the times, the degree of awareness of the problems and the degree of literacy of the priesthood. But a consensual uniformity – a desire to conform – did exist.

On the other hand, the conflicts which took place, as those with the power to pursue a particular solution took up their case, show how fragile

[9] See my comments in chapter 9: The search for order: the case of the soldiers, above.

this consensus might be and how variously the perspectives of different social and economic groups affected their interpretation. It is no accident that provincial soldiers concentrate their hostility, and their interest, on the capital and on the emperor, for this was ideologically the only sensible way of approaching the problem as it was perceived. While orthodox piety and conformity to the canons of the Church represented the values in accordance with which the Chosen People could recover their sense of direction and destroy their enemies, as well as marking out the role of emperor and Church in society at large, it also provided the justification for alternative interpretations of the world, interpretations which were informed by and generated within a very different context from that of the imperial court.

CONTRADICTION AND REGENERATION: THE DYNAMIC OF THE BYZANTINE SOCIAL FORMATION

Why did the Byzantine empire not succumb to the various forces, internal and external, which during the seventh century threatened to destroy it? The question has often exercised the minds of historians. Some have seen its survival as mere accident, the failure of its foes adequately to organise their efforts at conquest or the result of unavoidable internal divisions within the caliphate. Others have seen the impregnable position of Constantinople, the queen of cities, as the key; yet others have regarded the strength of orthodox Christianity and the cultural bonds it forged as a crucial factor; while some historians have seen the well-structured and flexible administrative, fiscal and military apparatuses of the state as the foundation of its survival.[10] All of these – although I should wish to modify each statement in different ways – played a role, of that there can be little doubt. But to look for single causes, or indeed prime movers, is to misunderstand the very nature of historical change. For in many ways the late Roman state did not survive, at least not in the sense that protagonists of a 'continuity' approach to the problem would have us believe. The physical space – albeit much reduced – the geography and climate (with natural and usually very gradual shifts) remain much the same. But late Roman urban culture vanishes entirely, along with much of the cultural baggage it carried with it. Instead, new systems of thought develop, new

---

[10] For the most recent attempt, see G. Huxley, *Why Did the Byzantine Empire not Fall to the Arabs?* (Athens, Gennadius Library, 1986), pp. 1–14; and the resumé of the argument in *BS* 68 (1987), 267; and see the article of G. Weiss, 'Antike und Byzanz: die Kontinuität der Gesellschaftsstruktur', *Historische Zeitschrift* 224 (1977), 529–60. For a useful survey of the literature on the question of continuity and discontinuity, see the discussion of V. Vavřínek, 'The Eastern Roman empire or early Byzantium? A society in transition', in *From Late Antiquity to Early Byzantium*, ed. V. Vavřínek (Prague 1985), pp. 9–20.

approaches to art and representation are refined, new administrative structures are evolved. Power relationships within the ruling elite also change – the old senatorial establishment, with much of the literary culture associated with it, disappears, to be replaced by a very different elite, of different social, cultural and often ethnic origins. Those aspects of the traditional elite culture that did survive came to play a different role in the ideological world of this new class, although there is no reason to doubt that this new medieval elite included elements of the older establishment. Continuity of language, at least as regards Greek and Armenian, is clear; while the native languages of Asia Minor were by the early seventh century mostly extinct. Continuity of tradition, in terms of economic organisation at community level, of the rituals accompanying birth, marriage, death, of popular forms of music and song, these can all be found, or assumed, to a degree. But even here, the developments of the seventh century brought about considerable changes, both in respect of the organisation of property and property relations (and hence the exploitation of arable and pastoral land) and in the Christianisation of the rituals and meaning of social and biological relationships.

Whatever continuities and survivals one might point to, therefore, a very different culture emerges on the surviving remains of late Antiquity. Of course, it is not hard to find a vast array of single elements which continued to exist, whether in terms of social and cultural praxis, administrative organisation, titles and ideas about order and hierarchy, literary motifs and stylistic systems, and so on. But this is hardly surprising, given the fact that the entire population of the late Roman world, along with its culture, was neither wiped out nor enslaved and transported far away. No one would seriously claim that eighteenth-century English culture and society were the same as that of the fourteenth century, in spite of the obvious elements of continuity. The point is that continuity in some form can always be discovered where one social and cultural formation develops qualitatively enough to be transformed into something which is clearly different. But when the basic structures which determine how that social formation works and reproduces itself can be seen to have been fundamentally changed, then we can hardly talk of a real continuity, but only, at the most, of the survival of traditions and forms – survivals which may often be determined by the levels of technology available, for example, rather than by any preference for doing things in a particular way; or by ideological 'hangovers' from earlier times, self-conscious notions about how things 'ought' to be done, none of which affect the structural dynamics of the society.

An East Roman or Byzantine state 'survived' the seventh century, therefore, for all the reasons listed at the beginning of this section. But it was, as I hope I have been able to show in this book, a very different state in its workings from that of the late Roman period. The question now arises, how we set about characterising the society and state formation which developed, and within what sort of explanatory framework we can clarify the nature of the transformations which took place in order to understand how that society functioned at a structural level.

The first, and probably the most obvious point, concerns the fate of the late Roman cities.[11] The evidence which we have reviewed suggests quite clearly that the urban centres of the late ancient world were almost totally eclipsed during the period with which we are concerned. The classical city had come during the Roman period to occupy a central role both in the social and economic structure of Mediterranean society and in the administrative machinery of the Roman state, as focus of market-exchange activity, of regional agricultural activity and, especially, as tax-collectors. Where cities in the Mediterranean sense did not exist, the Roman state created them, either establishing entirely new foundations, or amalgamating earlier settlements and providing them with the corporate identity and legal personality of a *civitas* or *polis*. These are terms which, we must remember, bore a specific administrative and fiscal significance in the late Roman world and did not necessarily imply a major urban centre. The long-drawn-out shift in the economic and social function of these cities from the third century on, the final suppression of their economic independence during the later fifth and early sixth centuries, and their physical and social devastation during the seventh century, had consequently very considerable implications for the fiscal and civil administrative structure of the late Roman state. Equally, it marked the end of classical city life and culture, with its urbanocentric economy. One way of looking at these changes is to see in them a decline in urban civilisation. A more productive approach is to see them as a gradual change in the function and relevance of cities to the needs of the late Roman state and the society which supported it. However we approach the problem, of course, the results were the same for late Roman culture and, in particular, for the state. Centralisation of tax-collection and the replacement of local centres of power by Constantinople, with the resultant attraction of social and cultural life to the capital, were part of the history of the late Roman world which the events of the seventh century brought to completion. The Byzantine state which emerged into the eighth century was effectively an empire of one major urban centre, together with a few fortunate provincial urban centres which were able to survive as emporia and ports.

This development had several implications. In the first place, it meant

---

[11] For a fuller survey of the points made here, see Haldon, 'Some considerations', 78ff.

that the state on the one hand, and large landowners (private and institutional) on the other, inherited the wealth, or at least the territories, which had previously been exploited by the municipalities. But it also meant that, on the whole, the wealth extracted from such regions (chiefly in the form of surplus agricultural and pastoral produce) tended to flow towards Constantinople, for this was where power was increasingly concentrated. It was to Constantinople that the provincial wealthy would send their sons to be educated or to gain an entrée to Church or state service; it was there that the emperor and court were resident, from where titles and privileges, offices and emoluments were bestowed, and from where the imperial administrative machinery, as well as that of the Church, was directed. The state centred at Constantinople inherited the social role of the cities, in so far as the absence of cities meant that, with the exception of one (state) institution, the armies, there was no longer a formal and institutional intermediary between the mass of the provincial population and the imperial government. It is this lack which goes part of the way to explaining the significance of the armies and their leaders – a point we have already examined.

The second point relates to the economic structure of late Roman and early Byzantine society. The city had never been a centre of industrial production. Commercial and industrial centres existed, of course, but they were relatively few in number and were in any case more or less entirely dependent upon their hinterland for basic supplies of foodstuffs, means of transport and, more often than not, for the extra labour needed for major building programmes. The cost of overland transport was, for most cities, prohibitive, which meant that those situated away from the coast or from easy access to a port were unable to exist on a non-agricultural basis. Ports were in a different position, of course, and the major cities of the late Roman world were almost all on navigable rivers or had good coastal harbours. The exceptions can generally be explained in terms of state intervention – the state was the only agency which could maintain the resources sufficient for this activity – or local and usually short-lived economic booms. The greater part of the state's income came from taxes on land and property of one sort or another. Commerce brought in a very limited income, although it was probably greater in the eastern part of the empire than in the western. Until the middle of the seventh century the empire was made up, in effect, of an agglomeration of city-states and subsistence economies; with the final demise of the cities, this essential local subsistence character did not change, although the local centres were eradicated. The agricultural population of the empire, whatever the different social and juridical categories into which it was divided, had to rely upon its own resources, depending upon local market-exchange through the medium of the lower-denomination bronze currency or, in the absence of the latter, upon direct exchange between producers, for those items which they could not produce themselves. Since overland transport was so expensive and slow, the provinces of the empire had of necessity to be economically self-supporting. While wealthier landowners could invest surpluses from their estates in luxuries, the extent of this investment was limited again by their proximity to trade routes or large entrepôts, and by the state of market-exchange and the availability of cash with which to buy. Since it was the local wealthy – both *curiales* and independent landowners, members of the senatorial elite – who provided much of the wealth to invest in their municipalities, the shift in their attention away to the capital must have clearly had drastic implications for the physical maintenance and the social and cultural life of their cities. Of course, in times of relative political stability, market-exchange was able to flourish in the most remote regions of the empire, too; and even after the cities had lost their fiscal-administrative functions, the larger ports and administrative-economic centres continued to flourish under state patronage. But such activity generated only a very small proportion of the surplus wealth expropriated by the state as tax or by landowners as rent. What was the role of the state in this wider structure of economic relationships?

The only institution capable of maintaining large-scale overland transport activities was, of course, the imperial government, whose complex system of posting- and baggage-stations was intended to further the movement of supplies and other necessary requirements for the army – by far the single most expensive item in the imperial 'budget' – the civil administration and related institutions. The transport system was itself supported through extraordinary levies and impositions in services and in kind, placed upon the agricultural population of the empire.

Just as this transport system was evolved to serve the needs of the state, so the imperial coinage fulfilled a similar function, and the role of the gold coinage is the linchpin of the system. Coin was issued in the first instance to serve the requirements of the administration and the army. Naturally enough, it also gravitated towards commercial centres, but this was not a deliberate policy in its issue. It was a tool and a symbol of the state and, more specifically, of the emperor, and it was also expected that gold coins issued for the state's purposes would eventually be returned through the medium of tax. In the period before a stable relationship between gold and bronze currencies, in the late fifth century, the lack of an adequate medium had forced the state – during the fourth and first part of the fifth century especially – to fall back upon taxation and the maintenance of its own apparatus, in kind, for which a vast and complex system of tariff equivalents had been set up. The establishment of a reliable gold currency and a related bronze coinage made much of this redundant, and it also made easier market-exchange on a much more widespread basis. The fact that the state demanded the payment of taxes in gold implies the existence of some sort of market sphere in which the agricultural produce of either peasant smallholders or large estates could be exchanged for gold coin. But this market was itself stimulated to a large extent by state demands, since it was chiefly the army and the state administration who consumed agricultural surpluses on a grand scale, and they received their salaries – usually – in gold. Limited amounts of gold might be absorbed through commercial activity in larger cities or taken out by elite trade or hoarding. But it was intended that, through taxation, as much as possible would be recovered. To what extent gold actually changed hands, for example, between peasants, or even big landowners, and the tax-collectors, is very difficult to establish. Much of the agricultural produce may have been collected directly from individual farmers or the storehouses of larger landowners by the prefectural officials responsible for supplying the army. Receipts against their tax-assessment will have been issued in return. Likewise, the payments for the military supplies may have been taken out of the soldiers' salaries before these were issued, being then handed over directly by the military paymasters or *optiones* to the prefecture, the cost of *annonae* and *capitus* having been established in advance. These procedures are known to have applied quite normally under certain conditions, and there is no reason to suppose that they did not apply in these circumstances, too. Such a process permitted the state to maximise the extraction of surpluses for its apparatus, while at the same time ensuring that as great a proportion as possible of its gold issue was returned directly as tax. At the same time, the tax-officials practised a system of unequal exchange, in which taxes demanded in gold were rounded up for convenience and change given in the bronze currency. Large-scale tax-farming – either to wealthy landowners or to other private contractors – also encouraged the maximisation of the return of gold, although it undoubtedly meant in addition the existence of widespread profiteering.

The gold and bronze currencies served different functions. Gold was intended to promote the operations of the state and the extraction of surpluses in the form of tax. The bronze and occasional silver issues (after the reign of Anastasius) were intended for local exchange activities and day-to-day commerce. The bronze coinage in particular was a nominal money of account used at a relatively low level of transaction and was dependent for its acceptability as a means of exchange on the stability of the gold, to which it was tied. As we have seen, the lack of any evidence in the period from *c*. 660 to *c*. 800 for issues of bronze on any substantial scale and its use in market contexts strongly suggests that no such activity took place, except in the highly localised context of major centres such as Constantinople – by its very nature an exception. In contrast, the continued issue of a stable gold coinage demonstrates the role of the state in regulating the distribution of surplus wealth according to its own requirements. Of course, in certain circumstances the issue of gold coin may not have been sufficient to meet the exigencies of the moment, and so state officials may have had to accept bronze coins as payment – such was the case in the reign of Heraclius, for example, and under Constans II in Italy, where the scarcity of resources reached crisis proportions.[12]

These considerations are valid both for the later Roman period and for that from the ninth century on. What evidence there is makes it clear that they apply equally to the seventh and eighth centuries. While the municipalities of the late Roman world vanish, the essential relationship between state and resources continued to be mediated on the same principles. The disappearance of the cities, the centralisation of fiscal control, the shift in production relations which followed the expansion of emphyteutic leasing and the demise of the senatorial landowning elite, all these factors, together with the dramatic loss of revenue which resulted from the Islamic conquests of the second half of the seventh century, meant that the structural details of the state's extraction and redistribution of resources were changed, sometimes rapidly, sometimes more gradually. The slow dissolution of the prefectural instance of fiscal and civil administration provides a good example of the latter; the rapid transformation of the central *officia* in the 620s and 630s one of the former. In terms of continuity, therefore, the principles of the state's mode of surplus appropriation remain much the same: a surplus redistribution system based on a subsistence peasant economy, a system facilitated by a gold coinage which served both to promote the extraction of tax and the maximisation of the state's returns. On the other hand, the structures which evolved to fulfil these functions changed very considerably after the later sixth century, and there is no doubt that the seventh century marks a major break with the late Roman system.

More than anything, however, the seventh century marks in many respects the reassertion of imperial authority and the power of the state over its resources. All the factors we have examined in the course of this book point to this conclusion. The decline of the senatorial elite, the shrinkage of the empire territorially, the centralisation of fiscal administration, the disappearance of the cities as intermediate levels of government, the rise of a new military and administrative bureaucracy dependent much more directly upon the emperor than hitherto – all are crucial to this shift.

---

[12] See the comments of Hendy, *Studies*, pp. 228ff. and 415–16.

Along with the developments in ideology in the period after Justinian I and the urgent need for the state to intervene much more directly in provincial administrative matters in order adequately to respond to the political and financial demands of the period after about 640, these factors resulted in a much stronger and more centralised state apparatus and a society ideologically much more homogeneous, and in some respects more dependent on the emperor, than hitherto. The contrast between the loose hegemony of the sixth century and the authoritarian centralisation of the later seventh century is clear. Of course, government control was considerably tempered by the difficulties of communications and transport, and so we should not assume a great deal of 'efficiency' in the contemporary sense of the term, for either period. But the dominant and leading element in seventh- and eighth-century society was the imperial court, which had no longer to compete for wealth or authority with a large and wealthy, and potentially – economically and in many respects culturally – independent ruling class, nor with centres of urban civilisation outside Constantinople itself.

All these changes, both in structure and in emphasis, within late Roman social relations and ideology, are part of a process through which Byzantine society – that is, the medieval, orthodox culture of the east Mediterranean – comes into being. In many ways, the seventh century is the end, rather than the beginning, of many of the qualitative transformations I have described.[13] But, in a wider context, how are we to define this social formation?

Here, inevitably, we must address the question of concepts and theories – often dismissed by historians as an irrelevant exercise involving the setting-up of descriptive boxes which serve no functionally relevant purpose to the real task of research and analysis. Sometimes, it is true, historians and social scientists have tended to use general theories as a substitute for real explanation, fitting in the evidence and their description of it to pre-ordained explanatory models which are often in themselves inadequately thought through or far too general to be of any value in understanding the causal relationships which bring about historical change. I have touched upon this subject in the introduction, where I have also suggested the importance and heuristic value of such theories. For

[13] Here I would part company with Patlagean, *Pauvreté économique*, who regards the seventh century as only one stage in a longer process, culminating in the eleventh century; and I would argue a radically different historical development from that set out by Weiss (see note 10, chapter 12, above). Of recent commentators, both Mango, *Byzantium: The Empire of New Rome*, and D. Zakythinos, 'La grande brèche dans la tradition historique de l'Hellénisme du septième au neuvième siècle', in *Charistērion eis Anastasion K. Orlandon*, 3 vols. (Athens 1966), vol. III, pp. 300–27, argue for a transformation in, or completed by, the seventh century. My own view is that the seventh century marks a crucial turning point in an evolution that was completed by the early ninth century.

Marxist historians, the problem of the adequacy of the analytical categories at their disposal is particularly pressing, since historical materialism claims above all to be able to provide both a general theory of social and historical change and the heuristic categories which facilitate a detailed analysis of historical phenomena within a social formation. And for any historian, adequate categories are essential if we are to be able to focus on real causal relationships.[14]

The two fundamental categories for a historical materialist analysis are those of mode of production and social formation or, more generally, 'society'. In the Byzantine and late Roman case, therefore, we are faced with the specific problem of whether or not a transition took place over the period from the later third century to the later eighth and ninth centuries, and at what level: from one mode of production to another – from the 'ancient' to what is traditionally referred to as the 'feudal' mode but which I prefer to call the 'tributary' mode? – or from one social formation to another: what elements within the social formation were representative of these modes, which of them dominated, and how were they articulated to produce a specific and recognisable late Roman or Byzantine society?

Let us review, briefly, the two categories mentioned above, since these provide the framework within which any discussion of the generative structures which causally explain qualitative change must take place. A mode of production consists in 'the relations of production in their totality', that is to say, the forces of production (land, water-power, draught animals and so on) and the relations of production (chiefly between those who operate the forces of production, and those who effectively control those forces, the produce which results from their exploitation and the distribution of that produce). This totality constitutes in the widest sense the economic structure of society, the framework within which political, cultural and ideological structures are embedded and with which they 'correspond', that is, within which their fields of effect and potential paths of development are delineated. A mode of production is thus an abstraction, a purely theoretical and heuristic construct designed to provide a model of how certain types of economic and social organisation of human beings actually work. And within this construct, what is known as the mode of surplus appropriation (that is to say, the mechanisms by which one social class is able to exploit the labour of another in order to extract surplus wealth for its own consumption or some other purpose) which dominates is a crucial feature in differentiating between modes of pro-

---

[14] See J.F. Haldon, '"Jargon" vs. "the facts"? Byzantine history-writing and contemporary debates', BMGS 9 (1984–5), 95–132; F. Favory, 'Validité des concepts marxistes pour une théorie des sociétés de l'antiquité. Le modèle impérial romain', Klio 63 (1981), 313–30; and the remarks in Haldon, 'Some considerations', 99ff.

duction. It is this, above all, which enables a distinction to be made between the relations of production in so-called feudal, or ancient, or capitalist societies.[15]

A social formation, in contrast, is a particular historical articulation of these relationships under specific conditions, an articulation which determines the effectivity of the different elements; that is to say, the dialectical relationship between these elements and the sort of result this might produce – in a structural, rather than a particular, sense.[16]

Now it has usually been argued that the Roman state consisted of a number of locally distinct social formations in which one variant or another of the ancient mode of production dominated. The ancient mode is characterised, in its initial form, as an economic and social system in which a (city-based) citizen body controlled a surrounding agricultural hinterland as private persons, but with collective rights in their ownership of public land and co-operating together in their economic and political activities as a community. The state represents this body politic, 'exploiting' the citizens only in so far as it is responsible for the collection of taxes and other customary obligations. Taxation represents, in the first instance, merely that part of the surplus contributed by the producer-citizen body on a contractual basis towards the maintenance and reinforcement of the political and legal apparatus which secures them in the possession of their means of production and social reproduction.

Of course, in historical terms, such 'abstract' systems were greatly coloured by older tribal and clan divisions and organisation, the sexual division of labour and so on. And as the division of labour increased (that is, as an increasing differentiation of economic and craft, as well as intellectual, activities evolved – a process usually accompanying improvements in the mode of exploitation of the means of production, either qualitatively or quantitatively), so the 'community' of citizens becomes more and more fragmented. Conquest and expansion might then bring in supplies of cheap slave labour, so that the egalitarian, peasant-agriculturalist citizens are displaced both economically and socially, resulting in limited areas in a 'slave mode of production', in which large estates or plantations dominate the productive sector, replacing small-scale freehold-

---

[15] See K. Marx, *Pre-Capitalist Economic Formations*, ed. Eric Hobsbawm (London 1964), intro., pp. 38ff.; and text, pp. 67ff.

[16] See K. Marx, *A Contribution to the Critique of Political Economy*, ed. M. Dobb (Moscow 1970), pp. 20ff. (Dobb's introduction); and for modern discussions of the concepts and their relevance, see G. Cohen, *Karl Marx's Theory of History: A Defence* (Oxford 1978), pp. 28ff.; and more especially the much-criticised B. Hindess and P.Q. Hirst, *Pre-Capitalist Modes of Production* (London 1975), esp. pp. 1–20; P.Q. Hirst, 'The uniqueness of the West', *Economy and Society* 4 (1975), 446–75 (review of P. Anderson, *Passages from Antiquity to Feudalism* (London 1974)); A. Foster-Carter, 'The modes of production controversy', *New Left Review* 107 (Jan.-Feb., 1978), 47–77.

ers or tenant-farmers entirely. At the same time, the subordination of citizen to citizen and the generation of objective antagonisms between different groups in respect of their relationships to the means of production and distribution of wealth means that the state becomes the legislative and executive organ of the ruling class of citizens, which can henceforth use it to maintain and promote the extraction of tax and their own social-economic position. The early history of the city of Rome and the republic provide a good illustration of such an evolution. In the case of Rome, of course, its dramatic expansion and the gradual imposition of its own administrative-institutional and tax-raising traditions (much influenced, naturally, by the methods of the conquered states or peoples) resulted in the qualitative assimilation of a number of different social formations within this ancient mode to the Roman model – although, inevitably, a wide range of regional particularities and idiosyncrasies survived.[17] As I will suggest below, there are problems with this way of understanding the ancient mode.

The tributary mode of production operates on different principles, and it is important to us because, in the effort to understand how and why the change from ancient to medieval social, cultural and economic forms took place in the Roman and Byzantine world, it has been held by some historians that Byzantine society was, in contrast to Roman society, feudal (in the wider usage described above) – although the date from which this can be said to be the case is also debated: the seventh, eleventh and the twelfth or thirteenth centuries have all been put forward on different grounds.[18]

Tributary relations of production are characterised by a mode of surplus appropriation dependent upon the exercise of non-economic coercion over producers in possession of their own means of production; in other words,

[17] See S. Cook, 'Beyond the Formen: towards a revised Marxist theory of pre-capitalist formations and the transition to capitalism', *Journal of Peasant Studies* 4 (1976–7), 360–89; and see also Hindess and Hirst, *Pre-Capitalist Modes of Production*, pp. 18f. and 79ff. For the debate on slavery and the 'slave mode of production', see O. Patterson, 'On slavery and slave formations', *New Left Review* 117 (Sept.–Oct., 1979), 31–67; E. Wood, 'Marxism and Ancient Greece', *History Workshop Journal* 11 (Spring 1981), 3–22; and J.-P. Vernant, 'La Lutte des classes', in *Mythe et société en Grèce ancienne* (Paris 1974), pp. 11–29.

[18] The debate has taken place for the most part in the Soviet and Eastern European literature. For representative works see V. Hrochová, 'La Place de Byzance dans la typologie du féodalisme Européen', in V. Vavřinek, ed., *Beiträge zur byzantinischen Geschichte im 9.–11. Jahrhundert* (Prague 1978), pp. 31–45; G.G. Litavrin, *Vizantiiskoe obščestvo i gosudarstvo v X–XI vv.* (Moscow 1977); Z.V. Udal'cova and K.A. Osipova, 'Tipologičeskie osobennosti feodalisma v Vizantii', in *Problemy social'noi struktury i ideologii srednevekovogo obščestva* I (Leningrad 1974), pp. 4–28. For a Western comment, see Anderson, *Passages from Antiquity to Feudalism*, pp. 190ff., and Haldon, 'Some considerations', 99ff. with literature. For some theoretical observations in respect of the current debate within Western Marxism, see the brief comments of G. McLennan, 'Marxist theory and historical research: between the hard and soft options', *Science and Society* 50 (1986), 85–95.

the payment of rent or tax by peasant producers on the basis of customary or other obligations or rights, backed up ultimately by the exercise of physical force. This emphasis on non-economic pressure is to contrast with capitalist relations of production, which are economic in so far as the labourer is free, but possesses in effect only his labour-power, not his means of production and subsistence – the need to work, to earn a living by selling that labour-power as a commodity on the labour market is a result of purely economic pressures.

'Feudalism' is often summarised in terms of the dominance of landlord–tenant relations, in which the economic and social position of the landlord depends upon rent appropriated from the productive labour of tenants and upon the landlord's ability effectively to control the means of economic and social reproduction of those tenants. But the extraction of tribute or taxes by a state power is, at the level of the mode of surplus appropriation, no different; and in respect of this, crucial, differentiating factor, most pre-capitalist social formations not dominated by either slave-exploitation or by the communal or kinship mode can be said to be dominated by 'feudal' relations of production, in this very general sense. But since this usage has frequently led to misunderstanding, I prefer to use the term 'tributary' to define the general category, and to restrict 'feudal' to those social formations which were dominant in the medieval West from the ninth to the fifteenth centuries. It can be objected, of course, that such a broad application of the term deprives it of any specific analytical and descriptive value. But this is easily countered when it is remembered that tributary relations of production describe a general mode of surplus appropriation – the specific forms that general mode takes in different historical contexts is for the historian to ascertain. The general category helps in establishing certain criteria for that analysis. And, anyway, the alternative is to abandon all forms of general theory of pre-capitalist economic systems or to provide a specific mode to match every particular historical articulation – every different society – of the forces and relations of production. The latter really does take us in to the realm of category-collecting for its own sake!

The maintenance of a particular form of exploitative relations of production, of course, depends itself upon features which are in themselves not strictly part of the economic equation – the legal, juridical and political conditions necessary to the reproduction of a particular social-political formation. Serfdom alone, for example, if it coexists with other forms of exploitation, may not be enough to justify categorising a society as 'feudal' – a social formation is dominated by one mode of production or another according to whichever mode of surplus appropriation is dominant and determines the main features of the society as a whole. But this dominance does not need to be exclusive – elements from other modes of production may also be present, and it is quite usual for societies to contain elements from at least two modes, often mutually antagonistic, the possibilities being determined by conjunctural as well as technical and environmental factors. Importantly, too, the dominant mode will be reflected also in the institutional and economic machinery of the state, for example. Where different relations of production are gaining ascendancy, the state – which is a product of an older order – will generally adopt an oppositional stance as the representative of an established set of power relations; but, where the old order is unable to resist the new, it will be undermined or radically transformed.[19] This process, of course, involves also a process of class struggle, since every change in the relations of production is precisely a change in the relationship of one socio-economic class to another.[20]

Looked at from this point of view, it must be clear that the ancient mode as traditionally understood is by no means dominant in the Mediterranean world after the end of the fifth century B.C. For already, class antagonisms and the evolution of clear levels of social and economic subordination within the city-states of Greater Greece and Italy signify a shift in the relations of production. While the dominance of slavery at times and in limited areas varies the pattern (in the Greek city-states of the fifth century B.C., for example, or in Roman Italy during the period from the second century B.C. to the second century A.D.), it seems to me that the dominant mode of production in the ancient world was, in the strictly political-

[19] Discussion of the elements of the feudal mode are, as might be expected, numerous: see Marx, *Pre-Capitalist Economic Formations*, ed. Hobsbawm, pp. 125ff. For some useful surveys, see Anderson, *Passages from Antiquity to Feudalism*; Hindess and Hirst, *Pre-Capitalist Modes of Production*; and G. Bois, *Crise du féodalisme* (Paris 1976), pp. 351ff.

[20] Class is used by Marxist historians as more than just a description of the status of a given social group. Class refers to the relations pertaining between those who own or control the means of production and distribution of social wealth, and those who do not – usually the producers themselves. It is in this sense that the term 'class struggle' is to be understood – not to signify constant, or even occasional, open conflict between social groups occupying antagonistic positions in respect of the means of production; but rather the fact of the very existence of such a structural antagonism between social groups. This may express itself in terms of violence, but this then depends on the context and the conjuncture – it may equally express itself within the framework of a legal system. It is the actual relationships of a social class to the means of production which determines its objective economic interests, interests which may in themselves not necessarily be apparent to the members of that class, but represented instead in different forms through ideology. By the same token, we cannot expect to find 'class consciousness' in the modern sense of the term, that is, an awareness of the economic position of a social group in relation to other social groups. But this does not affect the validity of the concept of class as both a heuristic device and as a real description of embedded economic relationships. Awareness of social position, of course, does occur – represented in terms of status groups, wealth, power, birth and ancestry, and so on. See my comments in 'A touch of class', *Rechtshistorisches Journal* 7 (1988), 37–50.

economy sense defined above, that of the tributary mode.[21]

What has confused the issue for medievalists and historians of the late ancient world has been the nature and structure of the late Roman state. For it is also apparent that, in the light of the evidence which we have now reviewed, the dominance of the state and taxation, the imposition by the state of its surplus-extracting machinery and the employment of those surpluses in the maintenance and extension of state supervision of the surplus wealth produced within its lands (however inefficient this may appear to modern eyes) are key elements – both in the idea we have of the nature of East Roman society and in the reasons for its survival.

Unlike the situation prevailing in the late Roman West, the contradiction between the state and its interests, on the one hand, and the wealthy senatorial elite who dominated its civil apparatus, on the other, never reached crisis proportions. In the West, the growth of senatorial landed property stimulated a polarisation of economic and ideological interests. Increased wealth meant a quest for the avoidance of tax-liability, so that eventually the interests of the ruling elite as landowners outweighed their public interests and duties as tax-payers and supporters of the state. For a variety of reasons, partly connected with the force and effect of the Germanic invasions, partly with the greater sparsity of large cities and the more central position of large-scale estate exploitation in the relations of production, partly also with the extension of relations of patronage and subordination between landlords and tenants on a widespread basis, the extraction of rent by private landlords as opposed to that of tax by the state came to dominate production-relations – and therefore surplus appropriation – as a whole. The result was that taxation and the hegemony of the state were weakened to the point where they were no longer able to maintain themselves against the interests of the powerful private landlord or magnate class.[22]

The East presents a vivid contrast to this picture. There, during the fourth, fifth and sixth centuries, and as a result of a much more diversified set of production-relations, a far greater proportion of independent smallholders and tenants, a less dominant senatorial elite and a much greater number of towns and commercial centres, the state was able to keep the contradiction between its own interests and those of the ruling class in check, although it was certainly present. But during the sixth and seventh centuries, as we have seen, the dominance of this class of landowners is

---

[21] See J.F. Haldon, 'The feudalism debate once more: the case of Byzantium', *Journal of Peasant Studies* 17/1 (1989), 5–39; and especially the detailed discussion in my *The State and the Tributary Mode of Production* (London 1993).

[22] For a more detailed analysis, see C.J. Wickham, 'The other transition: from the ancient world to feudalism', *Past and Present* 103 (May 1984), 3–36.

broken. The state remains as the sole focus of economic and political power, and although the Church, as the major single landowner after the state, must be seen as a potential rival, the interests of Church and state were ideologically so closely bound together (in the long term: ruptures of the sort typified by the monothelete controversy, for example, did not affect the institutional, property-owning Church in its economic relations with the state) that this was not an important source of conflict at this period.

Landlord–tenant relations and the privatised extraction of surpluses – as rent – on a widespread basis represented the major element in the relations of production, of course. The state was itself a major landowner, along with the Church. But the evidence suggests that the proportion of wealth extracted by the state through tax was at least as structurally significant as that collected as rent; and the continued existence of a powerful, centralised state, with an elaborate bureaucracy and professional (or at least permanent) army, maintained by the extraction of tax, necessarily limited the degree to which private rent could be extended. It certainly made any challenge to the dominance of the state at this period impossible.

The taxation policy of the state dominated the economy of the empire, promoting some developments, while hindering or preventing others. In particular, it meant the constant involvement in and attention of the state upon rural relations of production and the possibilities for surplus extraction. So much is clear from the incidence of state legislation concerned with safeguarding the sources of its revenue: it is surely no accident that the major collections of state legislation dealing with land and the production of wealth which control of land brought with it come from the sixth and tenth centuries, two periods when major shifts in rural relations of production were taking place (excluding, of course, the difficulties associated with the lack of legislation in the later seventh century on these matters, discussed in chapter 7 above) and when a potential or actual threat to the tax-base was perceived.

Only when the state began to lose control over the means of production and the rate of surplus appropriation (that is to say, when private rent began to outstrip tax) and hence to obtain the income necessary to its existence – in other words, only when the exaction of tribute or private rent by the landowning class rather than by the state becomes dominant – can we speak of a real shift within the balance of the tributary relations of production in Byzantine society.[23] But even at this stage, the entrenched ideology of

[23] See Litavrin, *Vizantiiskoe obščestvo i gosudarstvo*, pp. 289f.; A.P. Každan, *Social'nii sostav*, pp. 253ff. Note also G. Ostrogorsky, 'Observations on the aristocracy in Byzantium', *DOP* 25 (1971), 12ff. The first clear, albeit tentative, institutional steps towards this process can be seen in the eleventh century, with the development of the system of *pronoia* grants and the temporary award of fiscal revenues by the state to private persons in return for (military) service. But again, this is only one element in a complex picture. For the classic

the state, which found expression in the role of the emperor and the existence of a centralised state bureaucracy, held the continued expansion of privatised tributary relations – feudal relations in a sense akin to those pertaining in the medieval West – back. For the Byzantine aristocracy was committed to this ideology and political theory even after they had ceased to represent their objective economic class interests. Like the state which it represented, and yet for whose resources it competed, the aristocracy was ideologically divided between serving the state and thus not promoting (or actually damaging) its own interests as a group of independent landowners and landlords, on the one hand, and opposing the state – the emperor – in order to protect and enhance its privileges and its power-base. This compromise existed in its clearest form after the eleventh century. But while the economic contradictions were gradually resolved in favour of the magnates, the political contradiction was less apparent, a result of the close ties between imperial political ideology, orthodoxy and the Church, and the fact that this political system was focused upon the emperor, not on a concept of 'the state' as such. The political and ideological support of the elite, and the residual political authority of the emperors (and therefore of the state) made possible the survival of the state as a parasitic political form doomed to economic and therefore military and political extinction.

The seventh century thus saw the establishment of conditions which made possible the survival of one form of the ancient state. For the senatorial elite had been weakened sufficiently for the state to ignore it as a class, while the new service elite (from which the middle Byzantine aristocracy develops by the ninth century) was still in its infancy, dependent entirely upon the state for its existence. Until the eleventh century at least, the transformed structures of the ancient state provided the dominant structures of the Byzantine social formation. It is clear from our survey that a fundamental transformation took place in the late Roman world, a transformation that made possible, and prolonged, the survival of the Roman state in the East.

<small>study of this development, see G. Ostrogorsky, *Pour l'histoire de la féodalité byzantine* (Brussels 1954). The question has been extensively discussed in the Soviet literature: see the references in chapter 1, note 36.</small>

Addendum: Further observations on the question of the late ancient city (see Chapter 3)

This issue continues to receive substantial attention, but many problems remain to be resolved or even addressed. Further archaeological work has produced results which confirm the general pattern outlined here, but with more differentiation between settlement types and functions. It has recently, and quite correctly, been stressed that the evolution of the types of settlement most commonly associated with the term *kastron* is in fact rather more complex than has often been assumed. Indeed, the evidence suggests that one should avoid overemphasising the contrast between the late ancient *polis* and the middle Byzantine *kastron*: rather, of the large number of settled sites which are differentiated from undefended rural settlements in form, function and situation, only a small proportion bore the official or unofficial characteristics of a *polis*; whereas a large number were characterised already in the fourth and fifth centuries, and especially in the sixth century, by features normally associated archaeologically and topographically with the later Byzantine *kastron*. The examples upon which this conclusion is based come from the Balkan context; but they are as valid, from the sixth and seventh centuries, for Asia Minor. See A. Dunn, 'The transformation from *polis* to *kastron* in the Balkans (III–VII cc.): general and regional perspectives', *Byzantine and Modern Greek Studies* 18 (1994), pp. 60–80; J.F. Haldon, 'Quelques remarques sur l'économie byzantine de 600 à 1100. Esquisse comparative', in R. Francovich, G. Noyé, *La Storia dell'Alto Medioevo Italiano (VI–X secolo) alla Luce dell'Archaeologia* (Rome 1994) 71–84, esp. 75–6; and T.E. Gregory, 'Kastro and diateichisma as responses to early Byzantine frontier collapse', *B* 62 (1992) 235–53. In particular, it should be clear that the transformations which occurred did not, except in a relatively small number of cases, involve a universal abandonment of formerly urban sites (*poleis*) in favour of hilltop fortified sites (*kastra*). Rather, it involved a change in the way populations were distributed between such sites, and how they were occupied. At the same time, it is possible to argue that many cities did indeed continue until well into the first half of the seventh century to flourish as centres of local provincial society, but that the mode of socio-cultural investment had changed. Churches rather than civic, secular public buildings seem to have attracted investment, for example: see J.-M. Spieser, 'Les villes en Grèce du IIIe au VIIe siècle', in *Villes et peuplement dans l'Illyricum protobyzantin* (Rome 1984) pp. 315–38. While certain major cities did decline – as a result both of warfare and natural calamities (Antioch, for example, or Apamaea: see J.C. Balty, 'Apamée au VIe siècle. Témoignages archéologiques de la richesse d'une ville', in *Hommes et richesses* I, pp. 79–96) – there is plenty of incidental evidence for the continuity of provincial urban life (see M. Whittow, 'Ruling the Late Roman and early Byzantine City: a Continuous History', *Past and Present* 129 (Nov. 1990), pp. 3–29). What changed was the emphasis on civic and corporate 'monumentality', a point well illustrated in the work of Spieser. The important question of the extent to which cities may have continued to exercise control over their *territoria* is taken up in F.R. Trombley, 'Byzantine "Dark Ages" cities in comparative context', in *To Ελληνικον. Studies in Honor of Speros Vryonis, jr.* I: *Hellenic Antiquity and Byzantium*, eds. J.S. Langdon et al. (New York 1993) 429–49. But the possibilities for clarifying the situation in the sixth and seventh centuries are still severely restricted by the patchy and limited archaeological data, in particular the still very partial and fragmentary ceramic record.

The archaeological material, albeit sparse, can nevertheless be used to suggest a resolution to one aspect of the problem. In some Byzantine texts, mostly hagiographical, there occur descriptions of 'cities' which can be interpreted to mean that there remained a population inhabiting the 'lower' town. As we have seen, it has been argued that either this means that the whole ancient city area continued to be occupied; or that the text(s) in question consists of *topoi* and that only a citadel is actually meant (see p. 109 above, and note 40). The preliminary results of excavations at Amorion and several other sites show that while the very small fortress-citadel continued to be defended and occupied, discreet areas within the late Roman walls also continued to be inhabited, often centred around a church. In Amorion there were at least two and probably three such areas (C. Lightfoot, in *Anatolian Studies* 44 (1994) 105ff.). It seems probable that what these findings represent are small but distinct communities whose inhabitants regarded themselves (in one sense, that of domicile, quite legitimately) as 'citizens' of the city within whose walls their settlement was located, and that the *kastron*, which retained the name of the ancient *polis*, provided a refuge in case of attack (whether or not it was permanently occupied, still less permanently garrisoned). Many of the *poleis* of the seventh to ninth centuries thus may have survived as such because their inhabitants, living effectively in distinct 'villages' within the area delineated by the walls, saw themselves as belonging to the *polis* itself, rather than to a village, which may well have been referred to by the name of its church or its older suburban quarter. Cf. the example of Ephesos, which served as a refuge for the local rural population, as a fortress and military administrative centre, but also retained its role as a market town. Survey and excavation suggest that it was divided into three small, distinct and separate occupied areas, including the citadel (Foss, *Ephesus After Antiquity*, pp. 106–13); Sardis similarly shrank to a small fortified acropolis, and one or more separate occupied areas within the circumference of the original late ancient walls (Foss, *Byzantine and Turkish Sardis*, pp. 55–61); Miletos was reduced to some 25 per cent of its original area, and divided into two defended complexes (W. Müller-Wiener, 'Das Theaterkastell von Milet', *Istanbuler Mitteilungen* 17 (1967), pp. 279–90; C. Foss, 'Archaeology and the "Twenty Cities" of Byzantine Asia', 469–86, at 477f.); Didyma, close by Miletos, was reduced to a small defended structure based around a converted pagan temple and an associated but unfortified settlement nearby (Foss, 'Archaeology and the "Twenty Cities" of Byzantine Asia', 479 with literature). Examples can be multiplied. See the survey of Brandes, *Städte*, pp. 82–111, 132ff. with further literature and sources.

For the wider perspective, see the essays in J. Rich, ed., *The City in Late Antiquity* (London 1992) and in N. Christie, S.T. Loseby, eds., *Towns in Transition. Urban Evolution in Late Antiquity and the Early Middle Ages* (Aldershot 1996); and in *Trade and Exchange in the Late Antique and Early Islamic Near East* (Studies in Late Antiquity and Early Islam 1, V), eds. L.A. Conrad, G.R.D. King (Princeton forthcoming).

Bibliography

Primary sources

Agathias   ed. R. Keydell, *Agathiae Myrinaei Historiarum Libri V* (CFHB 2, Berlin 1967)
Agathon diaconus (account of events in 713), in Mansi XII, 189–96
Ambrosius (of Milan), *Sermo de Basilicis Tradendis vel contra Auxentium*, in PL XVI, 875–1286
Anastasius Monachus   ed. F. Nau, 'Le texte grec des récits utiles à l'âme d'Anastase (le Sinaïte)', *OC* 3 (1903), 56–90; see also *OC* 2 (1902), 58–89
Anastasius of Sinai   *Interrogationes et Responsiones*, in PG LXXXIX, 311–824
   Sermo adversus Monotheletas, in PG LXXXIX, 1152–80; new edn by K.-H. Uthemann, *Anastasii Sinaitae Opera. Sermones duo in Constitutionem Hominis secundum Imaginem Dei necnon Opuscula adversus Monotheletas (Corpus Christianorum Series Graeca* XII. Brepols and Turnhout, 1985), pp. 55–83
Anonymi Chronicon ad Annum Domini 1234 Pertines, trans J.-B. Chabot (part 1), in *CSCO* scriptores Syri, 56; trans. A. Abouna (part 2), in *CSCO* scriptores Syri, 154
Anonymi Peri stratēgias, ed. and trans. G.T. Dennis, in *Three Byzantine Military Treatises* (CFHB XXV. Washington, D.C., 1985), pp. 1–135
Anonymus Vári   Incerti Scriptoris Byzantini saec. X. Liber de re Militari, ed. R. Vári (Leipzig, 1901); new edn and trans. G.T. Dennis, *Three Byzantine Military Treatises* (CFHB XXV. Washington, D.C. 1985), pp 247–327
Anthologia Palatina   Anthologia Graeca, I–IV, ed. and trans. H. Beckby (Munich 1957–8, second edn 1970)
Appendix Eclogae   eds. L. Burgmann and Sp. Troianos, 'Appendix Eclogae,' FM III (1979), 24–125
Arculf, *Relatio de locis sanctis*, ed. T. Tobler, in *Itinera et Descriptiones Terrae Sanctae* I (Geneva 1877), pp. 195ff.
Balādhurī   *Al-Balādhurī, Kitāb futūh al-Buldān. The Origins of the Islamic State*, trans. P.K. Hitti (London 1916 and Beirut 1966)
Basilica   eds. H.-J. Scheltema, N. Van Der Wal and D. Holwerda, *Basilicorum Libri LX*. A I–VII (Textus librorum I–LIX); B I–VIII (Scholia in libros I–LX, 16) (Groningen, Jakarta and The Hague 1953–83)
Beševliev, V.   *Spätgriechische und spätlateinische Inschriften aus Bulgarien* (Berlin 1964)
Cedrenus   *Georgii Cedreni Compendium Historiarum*, ed. I. Bekker 2 vols. (CSHB, Bonn 1838–9)

Chronicon Anonymi ad Annum Domini 813 Pertinens, ed. and trans. E.W. Brooks, in CSCO scriptores Syri, ser. 3., vol. IV: *Chronica Minora*, 3, 1, 185–96

Chronicon Maroniticum, ed. E.W. Brooks, trans. J.-B. Chabot, in CSCO scriptores Syri, ser. 3, vol. IV: *Chronica Minora*, 2, 3, 35–57

Chronicon Miscellaneum ad Annum Domini 724 Pertinens, ed. E.W. Brooks, trans. J.-B. Chabot, in CSCO scriptores Syri, ser. 3, vol. IV: *Chronica Minora*, 2, 4, 63–119

Chronicon Miscellaneum ad Annum Domini 846 Pertinens, ed. E.W. Brooks, trans. J.-B. Chabot, in CSCO scriptores Syri, ser. 3, vol. IV: *Chronica Minora*, 2, 5, 123–80

Chronicon Paschale, ed. L. Dindorf (*CSHB*, Bonn 1832)

Codex Iustinianus in *CIC* II

Codex Theodosianus Theodosiani Libri XVI cum Constitutionibus Sirmondianis, eds. Th. Mommsen, P. Meyer et al. (Berlin 1905)

Concilium universale Constantinopolitanum tertium, ed. R. Riedinger, 2 vols. (Acta Conciliorum Oecumenicorum II/2.1–2. Berlin 1990/1992)

Constans II, *Typos* in *Lateran* 208. 15–210. 15; Mansi X, 1029C–1032D

Constantine IV, *Edict* in Mansi XI, 697A–712D

Corpus Inscriptionum Graecarum, ed. A. Böckh (vols. I and II) and I. Franz (vols. III–ff.) (Berlin 1828–77).

Corpus Iuris Civilis I, *Institutiones*, ed. P. Krüger; *Digesta*, ed. Th. Mommsen; II, *Codex Iustianianus*, ed. P. Krüger; III, *Novellae*, eds. R. Schöll and W. Kroll (Berlin 1892–5; repr. Berlin 1945–63)

Corpus Scriptorum Ecclesiasticorum Latinorum (Vienna 1866–)

Cosmas Hierosolymitanus, *Scholia in Gregorii Nazianzeni Carmina*, in *PG* XXXVIII, 341–679

Cumont, F. 'Les Inscriptions chrétiennes d'Asie Mineure', in *Mélanges d'archéologie et d'histoire* 15 (1895)

De Administrando Imperio Constantine Porphyrogenitus, De Administrando Imperio I: Greek Text, ed. Gy. Moravcsik, Engl. trans. R.J.H. Jenkins. New revised edn (*CFHB* I = Dumbarton Oaks Texts I, Washington, D.C. 1967); II, *Commentary*, ed. R.J.H. Jenkins (London 1962)

De Cerimoniis Constantini Porphyrogeniti De Cerimoniis Aulae Byzantinae Libri Duo, ed. J.J. Reiske (*CSHB*, Bonn 1829–30)

De Thematibus Costantino Porfirogenito, De Thematibus, ed. A. Pertusi (Studi e Testi 160, Città del Vaticano 1952)

Devreesse, *Hypomnesticum* R. Devreese, 'Le Texte grec de l'hypomnesticum de Théodore Spoudée', *AB* 53 (1935), 66–80 (BHG³2261)

DOC, vol. II Ph. Grierson, *Catalogue of the Byzantine Coins in the Dumbarton Oaks Collection and in the Whittemore Collection*, vol. II: *Phocas to Theodosius III, 602–717* (Washington D.C. 1968)

Doctrina Iacobi nuper Baptizati, ed. N. Bonwetsch, Abhandlungen der königlichen Gesellschaft der Wissenschaften zu Göttingen, phil.-hist. Klasse, XII, 3 (Berlin 1910)

Ecloga Ecloga. Das Gesetzbuch Leons III. und Konstantinos' V., ed. L. Burgmann (Forschungen zur byzantinischen Rechtsgeschichte X, Frankfurt am Main 1983)

Epanagoge ed. C.E. Zachariä von Lingenthal, in *Collectio Librorum Iuris Graeco-Romani Eclogam Leonis et Constantini, Epanagogen Basilii, Leonis et Alexandri Continens* (Leipzig 1852), 53–217; repr. in *JGR* II, 229–368

Eparchikon Biblion   I. Dujčev, Τὸ Ἐπαρχικὸν Βιβλίον – *The Book of the Prefect – Le Livre du préfet*. Text, translation and commentary (London 1970)
Exc. de Insid.   *Excerpta Historica Iussu Imp. Constantini Porphyrogeniti Confecta* III: *Excerpta de Insidiis*, ed. C. de Boor (Berlin 1905)
Exc. de Leg.   *Excerpta Historica Iussu Imp. Constantini Porphyrogeniti Confecta* I: *Excerpta de Legationibus*, 2 parts, ed. C. de Boor (Berlin 1903)
Farmers' Law   W. Ashburner, 'The Farmers' Law', *JHS* 30 (1910), 85–108; *JHS* 32 (1912), 68–95.
Fiscal Treatise ed. F. Dölger, in *Beiträge zur Geschichte der byzantinischen Finanzverwaltung besonders des 10. und 11. Jahrhunderts* (Byzantinisches Archiv IX Munich 1927 and Hildesheim 1960)
Georgii Monachi Chronicon, 2. vols., ed. C. de Boor (Leipzig 1904)
George of Pisidia   A. Pertusi, ed., *Georgio di Pisidia, Poemi 1. Panegirici Epici* (Studia Patristica et Byzantina 7, Ettal 1959): *Expeditio Persica*, pp. 84–136; *In Bonum Patricium*, pp. 163–70; *Bellum Avaricum*, pp. 176–200; *Heraclias*, pp. 240–61
Ghevond   G. Chahnazarian, *Ghévond: histoire des guerres et des conquêtes des Arabes en Arménie* (Paris 1856)
Grégoire, H., *Recueils des inscriptions grecques chrétiennes d'Asie Mineure* (Paris 1922)
Gregorii I Papae Registrum Epistolarum, eds. P. Ewald and L.M. Hartmann, in *MGH*, Ep. 1 and 2 (second edn, Berlin 1957)
Grumel, V., *Les Regestes des actes du patriarcat de Constantinople*; I: *Les Actes des patriarches* (Paris 1972); II (Chalcedon 1936); III (Chalcedon and Bucharest 1947)
Heraclius, *Ekthesis*   in Mansi X, 991B–997A; Lateran 156, 20–162.13
Hierocles   E. Honigmann, ed., *Le Synekdémos d'Hiéroklès et l'opuscule géographique de Georges de Chypre* (Corpus Bruxellense Historiae Byzantinae I, Brussels 1939)
Hudūd al-ᶜĀlam, The Regions of the World, trans. V. Minorsky (Oxford 1937)
Ibn Hawqal, *Kitāb Surat al-ard, Configuration de la terre*, trans. J.H. Kramer, G. Wiet (Beirut and Paris 1964) (text, ed. J. Kramer, (Leiden 1938))
Inscriptions grecques et latines de la Syrie, eds. L. Jalabert, R. Mouterde et al. (Paris 1929–70)
Inscriptions grecques et latines de la Syrie, ed. W.H. Waddington (Paris 1870 and Rome 1969) (= *Inscriptions grecques et latines recueillies en Grèce et en Asie Mineure*, III, 1/2 (Paris 1870 and 1876))
Isidore of Seville   *Chronicon Isidori Iunioris*, in *MGH (AA)* XI, 2, 424–81
Isidori Iunioris Episcopi Hispalensis Historia Gothorum Wandalorum Sueborum ad an. DCXXIV, in *MGH (AA)* XI, 2, 267–303
Continuationes Isidorianae Byzantina Arabica et Hispana, in *MGH (AA)* XI, 2, 334–68
Ius Graeco-romanum, eds. J. and P. Zepos, 8 vols. (Athens 1931 and Aalen 1962)
John of Antioch   *Ioannis Antiocheni Fragmenta*, in *FHG* V, 27–38; *Exc. de Insid.*, 58–150
John of Biclar   *Ioannis Abbatis Monasterii Biclarensis Chronicon*, in *MGH (AA)* XI, 2, 211–20
John of Damascus   *Contra Imaginum Calumniatores Orationes tres*, in B. Kotter, ed., *Die Schriften des Johannes von Damaskos* III (Berlin 1975)
Fount of Knowledge Πηγὴ Γνώσεως, part 2: *De Haeresibus*, in *PG* XCIV, 677–780

John of Ephesus   *The Third Part of the Ecclesiastical History of John of Ephesus*, ed. and trans. R. Payne-Smith (Oxford 1860)
   Lives of the Eastern Saints, ed. and trans. E.W. Brooks, in *PO* 17–19 (Paris 1923–5)
John of Nikiu   *The Chronicle of John, Bishop of Nikiu*, ed. and trans. R.H. Charles (London 1916)
Julian, *Oratio I*   in *Julian, Letters and Works*, ed. and trans. W.C. Wright (London and Cambridge, Mass. 1954)
Justinian, *Digesta*   in *CIC* I
Justinian, *Edict.   Edicta*, in *CIC* III, 759–95
Justinian, *Nov.   Novellae*, in *CIC* III
Kekaumenos   *Soveti i rasskazi Kekavmena: socinenie vizantijskogo polkovodtsa XI veka*, ed., trans. and comm. G.G. Litavrin (Moscow 1972); older edn B. Wassiliewsky and V. Jernstedt, *Cecaumeni Strategicon et incerti scriptoris de officiis regiis libellus* (St Petersburg 1896 and Amsterdam 1965)
Klet. Phil.   Kletorologion of Philotheos, in Oikonomidès, *Préséance*, pp. 81–235
Konidares, J., 'Die Novellen des Kaisers Herakleios', *FM* V (1980), 33–106 (text 62–95)
Konstantopoulos, K., Βυζαντιακὰ μολυβδόβουλλα τοῦ ἐν Ἀθηναῖς Ἐθνικοῦ Νομισματικοῦ Μουσείου (Athens, 1917) (= *JIAN* 5 (1902), 149–64, 189–228; 6 (1903), 49–88, 333–64; 7 (1904), 161–76, 255–310; 8 (1905), 53–102, 195–222; 9 (1906), 61–146; 10 (1907), 47–112
John Mauropous   P. de Lagarde and J. Böhlig, eds, *Johannis Euchaitarum Metropolitae quae Supersunt in Cod. Vaticano Graeco 676* (Abhandlungen der Göttinger Gesellschaft der Wissenschaften 28, Berlin 1882)
Lateran   *Concilium Lateranense a. 649 Celebratum*, ed. R. Riedinger (Acta conciliorum oecumenicorum, ser. 2, vol. I, Berlin 1984)
Laurent, V., 'Bulletin de sigillographie byzantine I', *B* 5 (1929–30), 571–654
   Le Corpus des sceaux de l'empire byzantin, vol. II: *L'Administration centrale* (Paris 1981)
   Documents de sigillographie. La collection C. Orghidan (Bibliothèque byzantine. Documents, I, Paris 1952)
   Les Sceaux byzantins du médailler vatican (Medagliere della Biblioteca Vaticana I, Città del Vaticano 1962)
Leges Militares   ed. W. Ashburner, 'The Byzantine mutiny act', *JHS* 46 (1926), 80–109 (repr. in *JGR* (Zepos) II, 75–9) (earlier redaction); ed. E. Koržensky, 'Leges poenales militares e codice Laurentiano LXXV', *Egypetemes Philologiae Közlöny* (Budapest 1930), 155–63, 215–18 (repr. in *JGR* (Zepos) II, 80–9) (later redaction)
Leo VI, *Nov.*   P. Noailles and A. Dain, *Les Novelles de Léon VI le sage: texte et traduction* (Paris 1944)
Leo, *Tactica   Leonis imperatoris tactica*, in *PG* CVII 672–1120; ed. R. Vári, *Leonis Imperatoris Tactica* I (proem., const. I-XI); II (const. XII-XIII, XIV, 1–38) (*Sylloge Tacticorum Graecorum* III, Budapest 1917–22)
Liber Pontificalis, ed. L. Duchesne, 2 vols. (Paris 1884–92)
Lydus   *Ioannis Lydi De Magistratibus Populi Romani Libri Tres*, ed. R. Wünsch (Leipzig 1903)
Malalas   ed. L. Dindorf, *Ioannis Malalae Chronographia* (CSHB, Bonn 1831); Engl. translation: *The Chronicle of John Malalas. A Translation*, by E. Jeffreys, M. Jeffreys, R. Scott et al. (Byzantina Australiensia IV, Melbourne 1986)

Mansi J.D. Mansi, ed., *Sacrorum Conciliorum Nova et Amplissima Collectio* (Florence, 1759–1927).

Martin, Pope S. *Martini Papae Commemoratio*, in Mansi X, 853–61; and *PL* 129, 591–600
Epistolae, in Mansi X, 682–853
Encyclical letter, in Mansi X, 1169–84

Maurice, *Strategikon* *Das Strategikon des Maurikios*, ed. G.T. Dennis, trans. E. Gamillscheg (*CFHB* XVII, Vienna 1981)

Maximus Confessor *Maximi Confessoris Relatio Motionis*, in *PG* XC, 109–29
Gesta in Primo Eius Exsilio, in *PG* XC, 135–72
Disputatio S. Maximi cum Pyrrho, in Mansi X, 709–60
Maximi Confessoris Epistolae, in *PG* XCI, 364–649

Menander Protector *Menandri Protectoris Fragmenta*, in *Exc. de Leg.* I, 170–221; II, 442–77

Michael Syr. *La Chronique de Michel le Syrien, Patriarche Jacobite d'Antioche* (4 vols., Paris 1899, 1901, 1905, 1924)

Miklosich, F. and Müller, J., *Acta et Diplomata Graeca Medii Aevi Sacra et Profana* I, II (Acta Patriarchatus Constantinopolitani) (Vienna 1860–2)

Miracula S. Artemii, in A. Papadopoulos-Kerameus, *Varia Graeca Sacra* (St Petersburg 1909), 1–75 (*BHG*³173)

Miracula S. Demetrii P. Lemerle, ed., *Les plus anciens recueils des miracles de S. Demetrius* I: *Le Texte* (Paris 1979); II: *Commentaire* (Paris 1981)

Miracula Therapontis in L. Deubner, *De Incubatione Capita Quattuor* (Leipzig 1900)

Monumenta Asiae Minoris Antiqua, eds. W.M. Calder, J. Keil et al. (Manchester 1928–62)

Nicephorus *Breviarium*, in *Nicephori Archiepiscopi Constantinopolitani Opuscula Historica*, ed. C. de Boor (Leipzig 1880), 1–77

Nicephorus, *Chron.* *Chronographikon syntomon*, in *Nicephori Archiepiscopi Constantinopolitani Opuscula Historica*, ed. C. de Boor (Leipzig 1880), 79–135

Nicephorus, Patriarch of Constantinople. Short History, ed. and trans. C. Mango (Washington D.C., 1990)

Notitia Dignitatuum Utriusque Imperii, ed. O. Seeck (Leipzig 1876)

Notitiae Episcopatuum Ecclesiae Constantinopolitanae, ed. J. Darrouzès (Paris 1981)

Notitia Ps.-Epiphanii ed. H. Gelzer, *Ungedruckte und ungenügend veröffentlichte Texte der Notitiae Episcopatuum. Ein Beitrag zur byzantinischen Kirchen- und Verwaltungs-geschichte* (Abhandlungen der bayerischen Akademie der Wissenschaften, phil.-hist. Klasse, XXI 3, Munich 1900)

Optatus Milevitanus, *Contra Parmenianum Donatistam*, in *CSEL* XXVI (1893)

Parastaseis syntomoi chronikai, ed. Th. Preger, in *Scriptores Originum Constantinopolitanarum* (2 vols., Leipzig 1901, 1907; repr. New York 1975), vol. I, pp. 19–73
see Averil Cameron and Judith Herrin, *Constantinople in the Eighth Century* (Leiden 1984)

Paul the Deacon *Pauli Diaconi Historia Langobardorum*, ed. G. Waitz, in *MGH* (Scriptores Rerum Langobard. et Ital. Saec. VI-IX), 45–187

Peira Πεῖρα sive *Practica ex Actis Eustathii Romani*, in *JGR* IV, 1–260

Pelagius II Papa *Epistolae et Decreta*, in *PL* LXXII, 703–60

Peter of Atroa, *Life* *La Vie merveilleuse de S. Pierre d'Atroa*, ed. V. Laurent (*Subsidia Hagiographica* 29, Brussels 1956) (*BHG*³2364)

Popescu, E., *Inscriptiile Grecești și Latine din Secolele IV-XIII descoperite în România* (Bucharest 1976)

Priscus of Panium, *Fragmenta* in *FHG* IV, 71–110
Procheiros Nomos Ὁ Πρόχειρος Νόμος. Imperatorum Basilii, Constantini et Leonis Prochiron, ed. C.E. Zachariä von Lingenthal (Heidelberg 1837) (partially repr. in *JGR* II, 107–228)
Procopius *Procopii Caesariensis Opera Omnia*, ed. J. Haury (3 vols., Leipzig 1905–13; revised edn with corrections and additions by G. Wirth, 4 vols., Leipzig 1962–4)
Procopius, *De Bello Gothico*, in *Procopii Caesariensis Opera Omnia* II
De Bello Persico, in *Procopii Caesariensis Opera Omnia* I
De Bello Vandalico, in *Procopii Caesariensis Opera Omnia* I
Historia Arcana (Secret History), in *Procopii Caesariensis Opera Omnia* III
Ps.-Athanasius, Quaestiones ad Antiochum ducem, in *PG* XXVIII, 597–708
Pseudo-Denys de Tell-Mahré, Chronique, ed. J.B. Chabot (Paris 1895)
Ps.-Methodius, *Apokalypse* A. Lolos, ed., *Die Apokalypse des Ps.-Methodios* (Beiträge zur klassischen Philologie LXXXIII, Meisenheim am Glan 1976)
Radermacher, L. *Griechische Quellen zur Faustsage* (Sitzungsberichte der Akademie der Wissenschaften in Wien, phil.-hist. Klasse CCVI, 4, Vienna and Leipzig 1927)
Regesta Pontificum Romanorum ab Condita Ecclesia ad Annum MCXCVIII, eds. P. Jaffé, revised by P. Ewald, F. Kaltenbrunner, S. Löwenfeld et al. (2 vols., Leipzig 1885 and 1888)
Rhalles, K. and Potles, M. *Syntagma* (Σύνταγμα τῶν θείων καὶ ἱερῶν κανόνων) (4 vols., Athens 1852–9)
Rhodian Sea Law ed. W. Ashburner, Νόμος Ῥοδίων Ναυτικός. *The Rhodian Sea-Law* (Oxford 1909 and Aalen 1976) (repr. in *JGR* II, 91–103)
Schreiner, P., ed., *Die byzantinischen Kleinchroniken* (2 vols., *CFHB* XII, 1 and 2, Vienna, 1975 and 1977)
Scylitzes *Ioannis Scylitzae Synopsis Historiarum*, ed. J. Thurn (*CFHB* V, Berlin and New York 1973)
Sebeos F. Macler, trans., *Sébéos, Histoire d'Héraclius* (Paris 1904)
Seibt, W., *Die byzantinischen Bleisiegel in Österreich I: Kaiserhof* (Vienna 1978)
Strabo, *Geographica*, ed. H.L. Jones (8 vols., London and New York 1917–32)
Supplementum Epigraphicum Graecum, eds. J.J.E. Hondius and A.G. Woodhead (Leiden 1927–71, 1976–7)
Taktikon Uspenskij ed. N. Oikonomidès, in *Préséance*, pp. 47–63
Tabari ed. M.J. De Goeje, *Annales quos Scripsit Abu Djafar Mohammed Ibn Djarir al Tabari cum Aliis* (3 vols., Leiden 1879)
Themistius *Orationes*, ed. W. Dindorf (Leipzig 1832)
Theodore of Studion *S. Theodori Studitae Epistolarum Lib. I*, in *PG* XCIX, 904–1116
Theodori Studitae Epistulae, ed. G. Fatouros (*CFHB* XXXI 1/2. Berlin 1992)
Theodore Sygkellos, Περὶ τῆς τῶν ἀθέων Βαρβάρων καὶ Περσῶν ... κινήσεως καὶ ἀναχωρήσεως, ed. L. Sternbach, in *Analecta Avarica* (Rozprawy Akademii Umiejetnosci Wydzial Filologisczny, ser. 2, vol. XV, Cracow 1900), pp. 2–24 (= L. Sternbach, *Studia Philologica in Georgium Pisidam* (Cracow, 1900), pp. 297–334)
Theophanes *Theophanis Chronographia*, ed. C. de Boor (2 vols., Leipzig 1883–5)
Theophanes cont. Theophanes continuatus, Ioannes Caminiata, Symeon Magister, Georgius Monachus continuatus, ed. I. Bekker (*CSHB*, Bonn 1825), pp. 1–481.

Theophylact Simocatta *Theophylacti Simocattae Historia*, ed. C. de Boor (Leipzig 1887; ed. and corr. P. Wirth, Stuttgart 1972)
Timotheus Constantinopolitanus, *De Receptione Haereticorum*, in *PG* LXXXVI, 11–68
Taktikon Uspenskij in Oikonomidès, *Préséance*, pp. 43–63
Vie de S. Michel Maleinos, ed. L. Petit, in *ROC* VII (1902), 543–603   (*BHG*³1295)
Vita Alypii Stylita ed. H. Delehaye, in *Les Saints stylites* (Subsidia Hagiographica, XIV, Brussels, 1923), 170–87   (*BHG*³1295)
Vita Andreae Cretensis ed. A. Papadopoulos-Kerameus, in Ἀνάλεκτα Ἱεροσολυμιτικῆς Σταχυλογίας, V (St Petersburg 1891), 169–80, 422–4   (*BHG*³113)
Vita Andreae Sali in *PG* CXI, 621–888   (*BHG*³117)
Vita Antonii Iunioris ed. A. Papadopoulos-Kerameus, in *Pravoslav. Palestinskij Sbornik*, 19/3 (57) (St Petersburg 1907), 186–216; suppl. F. Halkin, in *AB* 62 (1944), 187–225   (*BHG*³142)
Vita Blasii Amoriensis in *AS* Nov. IV, 657–69   (*BHG*³278)
Vita Danielis Stylitae ed. H. Delehaye, in *AB* 32 (1913), 121–214; repr. in H. Delehaye, *Les Saints stylites* (Subsidia Hagiographica XIV, Brussels 1923), 1–94
Vita Eustratii ed. A. Papadopoulos-Kerameus, in Ἀνάλεκτα Ἱεροσολυμιτικῆς Σταχυλογίας, IV (St Petersburg 1891–8), 367–400   (*BHG*³645)
Vita Euthymii Iunioris ed. L. Petit, 'Vie et office de S. Euthyme le jeune', *ROC* VIII (1903), 155–205; 503–6 (repr. L. Clugnet in *Bibl. Hag. Or.*, 5 (1904), 14–51)   (*BHG*³655)
Vita Eutychii Archiepiscopi Constantinopolitani, in *PG* LXXXVI/2, 2273–390   (*BHG*³657)
Vita Evaresti ed. Ch. van de Vorst, 'La Vie de S. Evariste, higoumène à Constantinople', *AB* 41 (1923), 288–325   (*BHG*³2153)
Vita Gregorii Agrigentini in *PG*, XCII, 549–716 (*BHG*³707; see Beck, *Kirche*, pp. 466f.)
Vita S. Ioannicii (a Petro) in *AS* Nov. II/1, 384–434   (*BHG*³936)
Vita Johannis Eleemosyn. ed. H. Gelzer, *Leontios' von Neapolis Leben des heiligen Johannes des barmherzigen Erzbischofs von Alexandrien* (Sammlung ausgewählter kirchen- und dogmengeschichtlicher Quellenschriften V Freiburg and Leipzig 1893), 1–103   (*BHG*³886)
Vita Ioannis Psichaita ed. P. Van den Ven, in *Le Muséon*, new series 3 (1902), 103–25   (*BHG*³896)
Vita Maximi Confessoris in *PG* XC, 68–109 (*BHG*³1234); Syriac *Life*, ed. S. Brock, 'An early Syriac Life of Maximus the Confessor', *AB* 91 (1973), 299–346
Vita Michaelis Synnadensis, ed. C. Doukakis, in Μέγας συναξαριστὴς πάντων τῶν ἁγίων (12 vols., Athens, 1889–96), Maii, 411–22   (*BHG*³2274x)
Vita Nicephori Medicii ed. F. Halkin, 'La Vie de S. Nicéphore, fondateur du Médicion en Bithynie (mourut 813)', *AB* 78 (1960), 396–430   (*BHG*³2297)
Vita Philareti eds. M.H. Fourmy and M. Leroy, 'La Vie de S. Philarète', *B* 9 (1934), 85–170   (*BHG*³1511z)
Vita Stephani Iunioris in *PG* C, 1069–186   (*BHG*³1666)
Vita Tarasii ed. J.A. Heikel, 'Ignatii Diaconi Vita Tarasii Archiepiscopi Constantinopolitani', *Acta Societatis Scientiarum Fennicae* 17 (1889), 395–423   (*BHG*³1698)

Vita Theodori Syceotis   ed. A. Festugière, *Vie de Théodore de Sykéon* (2 vols., Subsidia Hagiographica III., Brussels 1970)   (BHG³1748)
Vita S. Theodori Studitae ed. A. Mai, in *NPB* VI, 291–363   (BHG³1754)
Vita et Miracula Theodori (tironis)   ed. H. Delehaye, in *Les Légendes grecques des saints militaires* (Paris 1909), 183–201   (BHG³1764)
Zacos, G. and Veglery, A., *Byzantine Lead Seals*, vol. I, parts 1–3 (Basel 1972)
Zonaras   *Ioannis Zonarae Epitomae Historiarum Libri XIII usque ad XVIII*, ed. Th. Büttner-Wobst (*CSHB*, Bonn 1897)
Zos. (Zosimus)   *Zosimi Comitis et Exadvocati Fisci Historia Nova*, ed. L. Mendelssohn (Leipzig 1887 and Hildesheim 1963)

(B) SELECTED SECONDARY LITERATURE

Abrahamse, D. de F. *Hagiographic Sources for Byzantine Cities* (Ann Arbor, Michigan 1967)
Ahrweiler, H. 'L'Asie mineure et les invasions arabes', *RH* 227 (1962), 1–32
   'Recherches sur l'administration de l'empire byzantin aux IXe–XIe siècles', *BCH* 84 (1960), 1–109
Alexander, P.J. 'Medieval apocalypses as historical sources', *American Historical Review* 23 (1968), 997–1018 (repr. in P.J. Alexander, *Religious and Political History and Thought in the Byzantine Empire* XIII (London 1978))
   'The strength of empire and capital as seen through Byzantine eyes', *Speculum* 37 (1962), 339–57
Anderson, P. *Passages from Antiquity to Feudalism* (London 1974)
Antoniadis-Bibicou, H. *Etudes d'histoire maritime à Byzance, à propos du Thème des Caravisiens* (Paris 1966)
   Recherches sur les douanes à Byzance, l' 'octava', le 'kommerkion' et les commerciaires (Paris 1963)
Arnheim, M.T.W. *The Senatorial Aristocracy in the Later Roman Empire* (Oxford 1972)
Auzépy, M.-F. 'L'évolution de l'attitude face au miracle à Byzance (VIIe–IXe siècle)', in *Miracles, prodiges et merveilles au Moyen Age* (Paris 1995), pp. 31–46
Avenarius, A. *Die Awaren in Europa* (Bratislava 1974)
Balty, J.C. 'Apamée au VIe siècle. Témoignages archéologiques de la richesse d'une ville', in *Hommes et richesses* I, pp. 79–96
Barker, E. *Social and Political Thought in Byzantium* (Oxford 1957)
Beck, H.-G. *Kirche und theologische Literatur im byzantinischen Reich* (*Handbuch der Altertumswissenschaft* XII, 2.1 = *Byzantinisches Handbuch* 2.1, Munich 1959)
   Senat und Volk von Konstantinopel. Probleme der byzantinischen Verfassungsgeschichte (Sitzungsberichte der bayerischen Akad. d. Wissenschaften, phil.-hist. Kl. (1966), Heft 6, 1–75). Repr. in H.-G. Beck, *Ideen und Realitäten in Byzanz* XII (London 1972)
Bertolini, O. 'Riflessi politici dell'controversie religiose con Bisanzio nelle vicende del sec. VIII in Italia', in *Caraterri del secolo VIII in Occidente* (Settimane di Studio del Centro Italiano di Studi sull'alto Medioevo V, Spoleto 1958), pp. 733–89
Boak, A.E.R. *The Master of Offices in the Later Roman and Byzantine Empire* (New York 1919), in A.E.R. Boak and J.E. Dunlop, *Two Studies in Late Roman and Byzantine Administration* (New York 1924)

Brandes, W. 'Die byzantinische Stadt Kleinasiens im 7. und 8. Jahrhundert – ein Forschungsbericht', *Klio* 70 (1988), 176–208
Die Städte Kleinasiens im 7. und 8. Jahrhundert (BBA LVI Berlin 1989)
Brandes, W., Winkelmann, F., eds., *Quellen zur Geschichte des frühen Byzanz* (BBA LV. Berlin, 1990).
Brett, M. 'The Arab conquest and the rise of Islam', in *The Cambridge History of Africa*, vol. II (Cambridge 1978), pp. 490–555
Breckenridge, J.D. *The Numismatic Iconography of Justinian II (A.D. 685–95 and 705–711)* (New York 1959)
Bréhier, L. in A. Fliche and V. Martin, eds., *Histoire de l'église depuis les origines jusqu'à nos jours V: Grégoire le grand, les états barbares et la conquête arabe (590–757)* (Paris 1938)
Brooks, E.W. 'Byzantines and Arabs in the times of the early Abbasids', *EHR* 15 (1900), 728–47
'The Arabs in Asia Minor (641–750) from Arabic sources', *JHS* 18 (1898), 182–208
Brown, P. *The Body and Society. Men, Women and Sexual Renunciation in Early Christianity* (London and Boston 1988)
'A Dark-Age crisis: aspects of the iconoclastic controversy', *EHR* 88 (1973), 1–34
Religion and Society in the Age of St Augustine (London 1972)
'Sorcery, demons and the rise of Christianity: from late Antiquity into the Middle Ages', in *Witchcraft Confessions and Accusations* (Cambridge 1970), pp. 17–45
'The rise and function of the holy man in late Antiquity', *JRS* 61 (1971), 80–101
The World of Late Antiquity (London 1971)
Brown, T.S. *Gentlemen and Officers. Imperial Administration and Aristocratic Power in Byzantine Italy, A.D. 554–800* (Rome 1984)
'The Church of Ravenna and the imperial administration in the seventh century', *EHR* 94 (1979), 1–28
'The interplay between Roman and Byzantine traditions and local sentiment in the Exarchate of Ravenna', in *Bisanzio, Roma e l'Italia nell'alto Medioevo* (Settimane di Studio del Centro Italiano di Studi sull'alto Medioevo XXIV, Spoleto 1988), pp. 127–60
Bury, J.B. *A History of the Eastern Roman Empire from the Fall of Irene to the Accession of Basil I (802–67)* London 1912)
The Imperial Administrative System in the Ninth Century, with a revised text of the Kletorologion of Philotheos (British Academy Suppl. Papers, I, London 1911)
Byzanz im 7. Jahrhundert: see Winkelmann et al.
Cambridge Medieval history, vol. IV, parts 1 and 2, ed. J. Hussey (Cambridge 1966–7)
Cameron, Averil 'Byzantine Africa – the literary evidence', in University of Michigan Excavations at Carthage VII (1982), pp. 29–62
'Images of authority: elites and icons in late sixth-century Byzantium', *PP* 84 (1979), 3–35
Procopius and the Sixth Century (London 1985)
'The Theotokos in sixth-century Constantinople: a city finds its symbol', *JThS* 29 (1978), 79–108
'Byzantines and Jews: some recent work on early Byzantium', *BMGS* 20 (1996) 249–74
The Mediterranean World in Late Antiquity AD 395–600 (London 1993)
Changing Cultures in Early Byzantium (Aldershot 1996)

Cameron, Averil, Conrad, L., eds., *The Byzantine and Early Islamic Near East* I: *Problems in the Literary Source Material* (Studies in Late Antiquity and Early Islam 1, I. Princeton 1992)
Charanis, P. 'Ethnic changes in the Byzantine Empire in the seventh century', *DOP* 13 (1959), 23–44
'Observations on the demography of the Byzantine empire', in *XIII International Congress of Byzantine Studies, Main Papers* XIV (Oxford 1966), pp. 1–19
Studies on the Demography of the Byzantine Empire (London 1972)
'The monk as an element of Byzantine society', *DOP* 25 (1971), 61–84
'The transfer of population as a policy in the Byzantine Empire', *Comparative Studies in Society and History* 3 (The Hague 1961), 140–54
Christie, N., Loseby, S.T., eds., *Towns in Transition. Urban Evolution in Late Antiquity and the Early Middle Ages* (Aldershot 1996)
Claude, D. *Die byzantinische Stadt im 6. Jahrhundert* (Byzantinisches Archiv, XIII, Munich 1969)
Conrad, L.I. 'Theophanes and the Arabic Historical Tradition: Some Indications of Intercultural Transmission', *BF* 15 (1990), 1–44
'Epidemic disease in central Syria in the late sixth century. Some new insights from the verse of Hassân ibn Thâbit', *BMGS* 18 (1994) 12–58
Cormack, R. 'The arts during the age of iconoclasm', in *Iconoclasm*, eds. A.A.M. Bryer and J. Herrin (Birmingham 1977), pp. 35–44
Writing in Gold (London 1985)
Cruikshank-Dodd, E. *Byzantine Silver Stamps* (Dumbarton Oaks Studies VII, Washington D.C. 1961)
Dagron, G. 'Entre village et cité: la bourgade rurale des IVe–VIIe siècles en Orient', *Koinonia* 3 (1979), 29–52 (repr. in G. Dagron, *La Romanité chrétienne en Orient* III)
La Romanité Chrétienne en Orient. Héritages et mutations (London 1984)
'Le Saint, le savant, l'astrologue. Etude de thèmes hagiographiques à travers quelques recueils de "Questions et réponses" des Ve–VIIe siècles', in *Hagiographie, cultures et société (IVe–VIIe siècles). Etudes Augustiniennes* (Paris 1981), pp. 143–55 (repr. in G. Dagron, *La Romanité chrétienne en Orient* IV)
Dagron, G. 'Judaïser', *TM* 11 (1991) 359–380
Dagron, G, Déroche, V. 'Juifs et Chrétiens dans l'Orient du VIIe siècle', *TM* 11 (1991) 17–273
Déroche, V. 'La polémique anti-Judaïque au VIe et au VIIe siècle. Un mémento inédit, les *Kephalaia*', *TM* 11 (1991) 275–311
Diehl, Ch. *L'Afrique byzantine: histoire de la domination byzantine en Afrique (533–709)* (2 vols., Paris 1896)
Etudes byzantines (Paris 1905)
'Le Sénat et le peuple byzantin aux VIIe et VIIIe siècles', *B* 1 (1924), 201–13
Ditten, H. *Ethnische Verschiebungen zwischen der Balkanhalbinsel und Kleinasien vom Ende des 6. bis zur zweiten Hälfte des 9. Jahrhunderts* (BBA LIX. Berlin 1993)
Ditten, H. 'Zur Bedeutung der Einwanderung der Slawen', in *Byzanz im 7. Jahrhundert*, eds. F. Winkelmann et al., pp. 73–160
Dölger, F. *Beiträge zur Geschichte der byzantinischen Finanzverwaltung bes. des 10. und 11. Jahrhunderts* (Byzantinisches Archiv IX, Munich 1927 and Hildesheim 1960)
Regesten der Kaiserurkunden des oströmischen Reiches von 565–1025, parts 1–3 (Munich and Berlin 1924, 1925 and 1932)
Duncan-Jones, R. *Structure and Scale in the Roman Economy* (Cambridge 1990)

Dunn, A. 'The transformation from *polis* to *kastron* in the Balkans (III–VII cc.): general and regional perspectives', *BMGS* 18 (1994) 60–80
'The *Kommerkiarios*, the *Apotheke*, the *Dromos*, the *Vardarios*, and *The West*', *BMGS* 17 (1993) 3–24
Durliat, J. *Les Dédicaces d'ouvrages de défense dans l'Afrique byzantine* (Collection de l'école française de Rome, Rome 1981)
'Les Finances municipales africaines de Constantin aux Aghlabides', in *Bulletin archéologique du comité des travaux historiques et scientifiques*, new series, 19 (1983), 377–86
'Les Grands propriétaires africains et l'état byzantin', Cahiers de Tunisie XXIX (1981), 517–31
De la ville antique à la ville byzantine. Le problème des subsistances (Collection de l'école française de Rome 136. Rome 1990)
Dvornik, F. *Early Christian and Byzantine Political Philosophy*, 2 vols. (Washington D.C. 1966)
Ebersolt, J. *Musées impériaux ottomans. Catalogues des sceaux byzantins* (Paris 1922)
'Sceaux byzantins du Musée de Constantinople', *RN*, 4ᵉ sér., 18 (1914), 207–43, 377–409
Fögen, M.-Th. 'Gesetz und Gesetzgebung in Byzanz. Versuch einer Strukturanalyse', in *Ius Commune. Zeitschrift für europäische Rechtsgeschichte* 14 (1987), 137–58
Foss, C. 'Archaeology and the "Twenty Cities" of Byzantine Asia', *American Journal of Archaeology* 81 (1977), 469–86
Byzantine and Turkish Sardis (Cambridge, Mass. and London 1976)
Ephesus after Antiquity: A Late Antique, Byzantine and Turkish City (Cambridge 1979)
'Late antique and Byzantine Ankara', *DOP* 31 (1977), 29–87
'The Persians in Asia Minor and the end of antiquity', *EHR* 90 (1975), 721–43
Frend, W.H.C. *The Donatist Church: A Movement of Protest in Roman North Africa* (Oxford 1952)
The Rise of the Monophysite Movement (Cambridge 1972)
Gabrieli, F. *Muhammad and the Conquests of Islam* (London 1968)
Garsoian, N. 'Les Sources grecques pour l'histoire des Pauliciens d'Asie Mineure: texte critique et traduction', *TM* 4 (1970), 1–227
Gelzer, H. *Die Genesis der byzantinischen Themenverfassung* (Abhandlungen der königlichen sächsischen Gesellschaft der Wissenschaften, phil.-hist. Klasse, Leipzig 1897 and Amsterdam 1966)
Goffart, W. *'Caput' and Colonate: Towards a History of Late Roman Taxation* (*Phoenix* suppl. vols., 12, Toronto, 1974)
Goodchild, R. 'Byzantines, Berbers and Arabs in seventh-century Libya', *Antiquity* 41 (1967), 114–24
Goubert, P. *Byzance avant l'Islam. Byzance et l'Orient sous les successeurs de Justinien* I: *L'Empereur Maurice*; II: *Byzance et les Francs*; II 2: *Rome, Byzance et Carthage* (Paris 1951, 1956 and 1965)
Gouillard, J. 'L'Hérésie dans l'empire byzantin des origines au XIIᵉ siècle', *TM* 1 (1965), 299–324
Grabar, A. *L'Empereur dans l'art byzantin. Recherches sur l'art officiel de l'empire d'Orient* (Paris 1936 and London 1971)
Gray Birch, W. de. *Catalogue of Seals in the Department of Manuscripts in the British Museum* V: *Byzantine Empire* (London 1898)

Great Britain, *Naval Intelligence Division, Geographical Handbook series. Greece,* 3 vols. (London 1944–5)
Naval Intelligence Division, Geographical Handbook series. Turkey, 2 vols. (London 1942–3)
Gregory, T.E. 'Kastro and diateichisma as responses to early Byzantine frontier collapse', *B* 62 (1992) 235–53
Grousset, R. *Histoire de l'Arménie des origines à 1071* (Paris 1947)
Grumel, V. 'Recherches sur l'histoire du Monothélisme', *EO* 27 (1928), 6–16, 257–77; 28 (1929), 272–83; 29 (1930), 16–28
Guilland, R. 'Les Patrices byzantins de la première moitié du VIIe siècle', Τόμος εἰς μνήμην Κ.Ι. Ἀμάντου (Athens 1960), pp. 11–24 (repr. in R. Guilland, *Recherches sur les institutions byzantins,* pp. 162–9)
'Patrices de Constantin IV à Théodose III', Ἑλληνικά 23 (1970), 287–98 (repr. in R. Guilland, *Titres et fonctions* VIII)
Recherches sur les institutions byzantins, 2 vols. (Berlin and Amsterdam 1967)
Titres et fonctions de l'empire byzantin (London 1976)
Guillou, A. *La Civilisation byzantine* (Paris 1974)
Régionalisme et indépendance dans l'empire byzantin au VIIe siècle: l'exemple de l'exarchat et de la pentapole d'Italie (Istituto Storico Italiano per il Medio Evo, Studi Storici, LXXV–LXXVI, Rome 1969)
'Transformation des structures socio-économiques dans le monde byzantin du VIe au VIIIe siècle', *ZRVI* 19 (1980), 71–8
Haldon, J.F. *Byzantine Praetorians: An Administrative, Institutional and Social Survey of the Opsikion and Tagmata, c. 580–900* (Poikila Byzantina III, Bonn and Berlin 1984)
'Comes horreorum – Komes tes Lamias?', *BMGS* 10 (1986), 203–9
'Ideology and social change in the seventh century: military discontent as a barometer', *Klio* 68 (1986), 139–90
'"Jargon" vs. "the Facts"? Byzantine history-writing and contemporary debates', *BMGS* 9 (1984–5), 95–132
Recruitment and Conscription in the Byzantine Army c. 550–950: A Study of the Origins of the Stratiotika Ktemata (Sitzungberichte der österreichischen Akademie der Wissenshaften, phil.-hist. Klasse CCCLVII, Vienna 1979)
'Some considerations on Byzantine society and economy in the seventh century', *BF* 10 (1985), 75–112
'Some Remarks on the background to the iconoclast controversy', *BS* 38 (1977), 161–84
'The Writings of Anastasius of Sinai: a key source for seventh-century East Mediterranean history', in: Cameron, Conrad, eds., *The Byzantine and Early Islamic Near East* I, pp. 107–47
The State and the Tributary Mode of Production (London 1993)
'Quelques remarques sur l'économie byzantine de 600 à 1100. Esquisse comparative', in: R. Francovich, G. Noyé, *La Storia dell'Alto Medioevo Italiano (VI–X secolo) alla Luce dell'Archaeologia* (Rome 1994) 71–84
'Synônê: Re-Considering a Problematic Term of Middle Byzantine Fiscal Administration', *Byzantine and Modern Greek Studies* 18 (1994) 116–53 (repr. in *State, Army and Society in Byzantium* VIII)
State, Army and Society in Byzantium (Aldershot 1995)
'The Miracles of Artemios and Contemporary Attitudes: Context and Significance',

in *The Miracles of Saint Artemios: Translation, Commentary and Analysis*, by J. Nesbitt, V. Crysafulli (Leiden–New York–Köln 1997), 33–73.

'Administrative continuities and structural transformations in East Roman military organisation c. 580–640', in *L'Armée romaine et les barbares du 4e au 7e siècle*, eds. F. Vallet, M. Kazanski (Paris 1993) 45–51 (repr. in *State, Army and Society in Byzantium* V)

'Seventh-century continuities: the *Ajnâd* and the "Thematic Myth"', in *The Byzantine and Early Islamic Near East* III: *States, Resources and Armies*, ed. Averil Cameron (Studies in Late Antiquity and Early Islam 1. III. Princeton 1995), 379–423

'Military service, military lands, and the status of soldiers: current problems and interpretations', *DOP* 47 (1993) 1–67 (repr. in *State, Army and Society in Byzantium* VII)

Haldon, J.F. and H. Kennedy, 'The Arab-Byzantine frontier in the eighth and ninth centuries: military organisation and society in the borderlands', *ZRVI* (1980), 79–116

Hayes, J.W. *Excavations at Saraçhane in Istanbul*, vol. 2: *The Pottery* (Princeton 1992)

Hendy, M.F. 'On the administrative basis of the Byzantine coinage, c. 400–900, and the reforms of Heraclius', *Birmingham University Historical Journal* 12/2 (1970), 129–54

Studies in the Byzantine Monetary Economy, 300–1450 (Cambridge 1985)

Hermann, E. 'Die Schliessung des Verlöbnisses im Recht Justinians und der späteren Gesetzgebung', *Analecta Gregoriana* 8 (1935), 79–107

Herrin, J. *The Formation of Christendom* (Princeton 1987)

Hild, F. *Das Byzantinische Strassensystem in Kappadokien* (Denkschriften der österreichischen Akademie der Wissenschaften CXXXI, Vienna 1977)

Hindess B. and P.Q. Hirst, *Pre-Capitalist Modes of Production* (London 1975)

Hoffmann, D. *Das spätrömische Bewegungsheer und die Notitia Dignitatum* (Epigraphische Studien, VII/1, Düsseldorf and Cologne 1969)

Hommes et richesses dans l'Empire byzantin 1: *IVᵉ–VIIᵉ siècle* (Paris 1989)

Hunger, H. 'Christliches und Nichtchristliches im byzantinischen Eherecht', *Österreichisches Archiv für Kirchenrecht* XVIII (1967), 305–25 (repr. in H. Hunger, *Byzantinische Grundlagenforschung* XI (London 1973))

Hunger, H. ed., *Das byzantinische Herrscherbild* (Wege der Forschung CCCXXXXI, Darmstadt 1975)

Die hochsprachliche profane Literatur der Byzantiner (2 vols., Handbuch der Altertumswissenschaft, XII, 5.1 and 2 = *Byzantinisches Handbuch*, 5.1 and 2, Munich 1978)

Reich der neuen Mitte. Der christliche Geist der byantinischen Kultur (Vienna, Graz and Cologne 1965)

Jones, A.H.M. '*Capitatio* and *iugatio*', *JRS* 47 (1957), 88–94 (repr. in A.H.M. Jones, *The Roman Economy*, pp. 280–92)

The Greek City from Alexander to Justinian (Oxford 1940)

The Later Roman Empire 284–602: A Social, Economic and Administrative Survey (3 vols., Oxford 1964)

'The Roman Colonate', *PP* 13 (1958), 1–13 (repr. in A.H.M. Jones, *The Roman Economy*, pp. 293–307)

The Roman Economy: Studies in Ancient Economic and Administrative History, ed. P.A. Brunt (Oxford 1974)

Kaegi, W.E. jr., *Byzantine Military Unrest 471–843: An Interpretation* (Amsterdam 1981)

'Two studies in the continuity of late Roman and early Byzantine military institutions', *BF* 8 (1982), 87–113

Kaplan, M. 'L'Economie paysanne dans l'empire byzantin du Ve au Xe siècle', *Klio* 68 (1986), 198–232

'Les grands propriétaires de Cappadoce (VIe–XIe siècles)', in *Le aree omogeneee della Civiltà Rupestre nell'ambito dell'impero Bizantino: la Cappadocia* (Galatina 1981)

Les hommes et la terre à Byzance du VIe au XIe siècle (Byzantina Sorbonensia 10. Paris 1992)

Les Propriétés de la couronne et de l'église dans l'empire byzantin (V^e–VIe siècles) (Paris 1976)

'Les Villageois aux premiers siècles byzantins (VIe–Xe siècles): une société homogène?' *BS* 43 (1982), 202–17

'Quelques aspects des maisons divines du VIe au IXe siècle', Ἀφιέρωμα στὸν Νίκο Σβορώνο, vol. I (Rethymnon 1986), pp. 70–96

'Remarques sur la place de l'exploitation paysanne dans l'économie rurale', in *Akten des XVI. Internat. Byzantinisten Kongresses*, II/2 (Vienna 1982), pp. 105–14 (= *JÖB* 32/2)

Karayannopoulos, J. *Das Finanzwesen des frühbyzantinischen Staates* (Südosteuropäische Arbeiten, Munich 1958)

Die Entstehung der byzantinischen Themenordnung (Byzantinisches Archiv X, Munich 1959)

'Fragmente aus dem Vademecum eines byzantinischen Finanzbeamten', in *Polychronion. Festschrift Franz Dölger zum 75. Geburtstag* (Heidelberg 1966), pp. 317–33

Πηγαὶ τῆς Βυζαντινῆς Ἱστορίας (Thessaloniki 1978)

Karayannopoulos, J. and G. Weiss, *Quellenkunde zur Geschichte von Byzanz (324–1453)* (2 vols., Wiesbaden 1982)

Kartsonis, A. *Anastasis: The Making of an Image* (Princeton 1986)

Každan, A. 'Vizantijskie goroda v VII–IX vv.', *Sovietskaya Arkheologija* 21 (1954), 164–88

Každan, A. and G. Constable, *People and Power in Byzantium: An Introduction to Modern Byzantine Studies* (Washington D.C. 1982)

Kirsten, E. 'Die byzantinische Stadt', in *Berichte zum XI. Internationalen Byzantinisten-Kongress* (Munich 1958), V, 3, pp. 1–48

Kitzinger, E. *Byzantine Art in the Making. Main Lines of Stylistic Development in Mediterranean Art, 3rd–7th Century* (London 1977)

'Byzantine art in the period between Justinian and iconoclasm', in *Berichte zum XI. Internationalen Byzantinisten-Kongress* (Munich 1958), IV, 1, pp. 1–50

'The cult of images in the age before iconoclasm', *DOP* 8 (1954), 85–150

Koder, J. *Der Lebensraum der Byzantiner* (Vienna, Graz and Cologne 1984)

'Zur Bedeutungsentwicklung des byzantinischen Terminus *Thema*', *JÖB* 40 (1990) 155–65

Köpstein, H., ed. *Besonderheiten der byzantinischen Feudalentwicklung* (BBA L, Berlin 1983)

'Zu den Agrarverhältnissen', in *Byzanz im 7. Jahrhundert*, eds. F. Winkelmann et al., pp. 1–72

Konstantopoulos, K. Βυζαντιακὰ μολυβδόβουλλα τοῦ ἐν Ἀθηναῖς Ἐθνικοῦ Νομισματικοῦ Μουσείου (Athens 1917)

Kresten, O. 'Datierungsprobleme "Isaurischer" Eherechtsnovellen. I. Coll. I 26', *FM* IV (1979), 37–106

Kulakovskij, J. *Istoria Vizantii*, vol. III (Kiev 1915 and London 1973)

Kurbatov, G.L. *Osnovnje problemy vnutrennego razvitija vizantijskogo goroda v IV–VII vv.* (Leningrad 1971)

Laurent, V. 'L'Œuvre canonique du concile in Trullo (691–2), source primaire du droit de l'église orientale', *REB* 23 (1965), 7–41

Lemerle, P. 'Esquisse pour une histoire agraire de Byzance: les sources et les problèmes', *RH* 219 (1958), 32–74, 254–84; *RH* 220 (1958), 42–94. (See now the revised version in English, published as *The Agrarian History of Byzantium from the Origins to the Twelfth Century: The Sources and the Problems* (Galway 1979).)

'Invasions et migrations dans les Balkans depuis la fin de l'époque romaine jusqu'au VIIIe siècle', *RH* 211 (1954), 265–308

Le Premier humanisme byzantin. Notes et remarques sur enseignement et culture à Byzance des origines au Xe siècle (Paris 1971)

Les Plus anciens recueils (See *Miracula S. Demetrii* in the bibliography of primary sources.)

Lilie, R.-J. *Die byzantinische Reaktion auf die Ausbreitung der Araber* (Miscellanea Byzantina Monacensia XXII, Munich 1976)

'Die zweihundertjährige Reform: zu den Anfängen der Themenorganisation im 7. und 8. Jahrhundert', *BS* 45 (1984), 27–39, 190–201

'Kaiser Herakleios und die Andiedlung der Serben', *Südost-Forschungen* 44 (1985), 17–43

'"Thrakien" und "Thrakesion". Zur byzantinischen Provinzorganisation am Ende des 7. Jhdts.', *JÖB* 26 (1977), 7–47

Litavrin, G.G. *Vizantijskoe obščestva i gosudarstvo v X-XI veka* (Moscow 1977)

Loos, M. *Dualist Heresy in the Middle Ages* (Prague 1974)

'Quelques remarques sur les communautés rurales et la grande propriété terrienne à Byzance, VIIe–XIe siècles', *BS* 39 (1978), 3–18

Louggis, T.K. *Δοκίμιο για την κοινωνική εξέλιξη στη διάρκεια των λεγομένων σκοτεινών αιώνων* (Athens 1985)

Ludwig, C. 'Wer hat was in welcher Absicht wie beschrieben?' in *Varia II* (Poikila Byzantina VI. Bonn 1987), pp. 149–227

'Kaiser Herakleios, Georgios Pisides und die Perserkriege', in *Varia III* (Poikila Byzantina XI. Bonn 1991), pp. 73–128

Maas, M. *John Lydus and the Roman Past* (London 1992)

Macrides, R. 'The Byzantine godfather', *BMGS* 11 (1987), 139–62

Magie, D. *Roman Rule in Asia Minor* (Princeton 1950)

Magoulias, H.J. 'The lives of Byzantine saints as a source of data for the history of magic in the sixth and seventh centuries A.D.: sourcery, relics and icons', *B* 37 (1967), 228–69

Maguire, H. 'Truth and convention in Byzantine descriptions of works of art', *DOP* 28 (1974), 113–40

Earth and Ocean: The Terrestrial World in Early Byzantine Art (London, Pa. 1987)

Malingoudis, Ph. *Oi Slaboi sti Mesaioniki Ellada* (Athens 1988)

Mango, C. 'Antique statuary and the Byzantine beholder', *DOP* 17 (1963), 53–75 (repr. in C. Mango, *Byzantium and its Image* V)

'The *Breviarium* of the Patriarch Nicephorus', in *Byzantion: Tribute to Andreas N. Stratos* (Athens 1986), II, pp. 545–8

Byzantium: The Empire of New Rome (London 1980)

Byzantium and its Image (London 1984)

Le Développement urbain de Constantinople (IVe–VIIe siècles) (Paris 1985)

The Art of the Byzantine Empire. Sources and Documents (Englewood Cliffs, N.J. 1972)

'The Life of St Andrew the Fool reconsidered', *Rivista di Studi Bizantini e Slavi* II (= *Miscellanea A. Pertusi* II, Bologna 1982), pp. 297–313 (repr. in C. Mango, *Byzantium and its Image* VIII)
'Who wrote the Chronicle of Theophanes?', *ZRVI* 18 (1978), 576–87 (repr. in C. Mango, *Byzantium and its Image* XI)
Martin-Hisard, B. 'La domination byzantine sur le littoral oriental du Pont Euxin (milieu du VIIe–VIIIe siècles)', *Byzantinobulgarica* 7 (1981) 141–54
Marx, K. *Pre-Capitalist Economic Formations*, ed. E. Hobsbawm (London 1964)
Mathew, G. *Byzantine Aesthetics* (London 1963)
Momigliano, A. ed. *The Conflict between Paganism and Christianity in the Fourth Century* (Oxford 1963)
Moravcsik, Gy. *Byzantinoturcica*, vol. I (third edn, Berlin 1983)
Morrisson, C. 'Byzance au VIIe siècle: le témoignage de la numismatique', in *Byzantion: Tribute to Andreas N. Stratos* (Athens 1986), I, pp. 149–63
Müller-Wiener, W. 'Von der Polis zum Kastron', *Gymnasium* 93 (1986), 435–75
Murphy, F.X. and P. Sherwood, *Constantinople II et Constantinople III* (Paris 1974)
Nelson, J. 'Symbols in context: rulers' inauguration rituals in Byzantium and the West in the early Middle Ages', *Studies in Church History* XIII (1976), 97–119
Nesbitt, J.W. 'Double names on early Byzantine lead seals', *DOP* 31 (1977), 111–21
Noth, A. (with Lawrence Conrad), *The Early Arabic Historical Tradition. A Source-Critical Study* (Studies in Late Antiquity and Early Islam 3. Princeton 1994)
Obolensky, D. *The Byzantine Commonwealth. Eastern Europe 500–1453* (London 1971)
Ohme, H. *Das Concilium Qunisextum und seine Bischofsliste. Studien zum Konstantinopeler Konzil von 692* (Arbeiten zur Kirchengeschichte LIV. Berlin-New York 1990)
Oikonomidès, N. *Les Listes de préséance byzantines des IXe–Xe siècles* (Paris 1972)
'De l'impôt de distribution à l'impôt de quotité à propos du premier cadastre byzantin (7e–9e siècles)', *ZRVI* 26 (1987), 9–19
'Les Premiers mentions des thèmes dans le chronique de Théophane', *ZRVI* 16 (1975), 1–8
'Middle Byzantine provincial recruits: salary and armament' in *Gonimos, Neoplatonic and Byzantine Studies presented to Leendert G. Westerink at 75*, eds. J. Duffy and J. Peradotto (Buffalo, N.Y. 1988)
'Silk trade and production in Byzantium from the sixth to the ninth century: the seals of kommerkiarioi', *DOP* 40 (1986), 33–53
Olster, D. *The Politics of Usurpation in the Seventh century: rhetoric and revolution in Byzantium* (Amsterdam 1993)
Onians, J. 'Abstraction and imagination in late Antiquity', *Art History* 3 (1980), 1–23
Ostrogorsky, G. 'Byzantine cities in the early middle ages', *DOP* 13 (1959), 47–66
'Das Steuersystem im byzantinischen Altertum und Mittelalter', *B* 6 (1931), 229–40
'Die Chronologie des Theophanes im 7. und 8. Jahrhundert', *BNJ* 7 (1930), 1–56
'Die ländliche Steuergemeinde des byzantinischen Reiches im X. Jahrhundert', *VSW* 20 (1927), 1–108
Geschichte des byzantinischen Staates (Handbuch der Altertumswissenschaft, XII, 1.2 = Byzantinisches Handbuch, 1, 2, Munich 1963)
Patlagean, E. 'Byzance et le blason pénal du corps', in *Du châtiment dans la cité: supplices corporels et peine de mort dans le monde antique* (Rome 1984), pp. 405–26

'Christianisation et parentés rituelles: le domaine de Byzance', *Annales E.S.C.* 33 (1978), 625–36 (repr. in E. Patlagean, *Structure sociale* XII)
Pauvreté économique et pauvreté sociale à Byzance, 4e–7e siècles (Paris 1977)
Structure sociale, famille, chrétienté à Byzance (London 1981)
Pernice, A. *L'imperatore Eraclio* (Florence 1905)
Pieler, P.E. 'Byzantinische Rechtsliteratur', in Hunger, *Profane Literatur*, vol. II, pp. 343–480
Piganiol, A. *L'Empire Chrétien, I (325–93). Histoire romaine*, vol. IV, part 2 (Paris 1947)
Podskalsky, G. *Byzantinische Reichseschatologie. Die Periodisierung der Weltgeschichte in den vier Grossreichen (Daniel 2 u. 7) und dem tausendjährigen Friedensreiche (Apok. 20)* (Munich 1972)
Pringle, D. *The Defence of Byzantine North Africa from Justinian to the Arab Conquest* (British Archaeological Reports, Int. Series 99, Oxford 1981)
Rawson, B. 'The Roman family', in *The Family in Ancient Rome: New Perspectives* (London and Sydney 1986), pp. 1–57
Reinink, G.J. 'Pseudo-Methodius und die Legende vom römischen Endkaiser', in *The Use and Abuse of Eschatology in the Middle Ages*, eds. W. Verbeke, D. Verhelst and A. Welkenhuysen (Leuven 1988), pp. 82–111
Rich, J., ed., *The City in Late Antiquity* (London 1992)
Riedinger, R. 'Die Lateransynode von 649 und Maximos der Bekenner', in *Maximus Confessor. Actes du Symposium pour Maxime le confesseur (Fribourg, 2–5 Sept. 1980)*, eds. F. Heinzer and Chr. Schönborn (Fribourg 1982), pp. 111–21 (= *Paradosis* 27)
Rochow, I. 'Die Heidenprozesse unter den Kaisern Tiberius I. Konstantinos und Maurikios', in *Studien zum 7. Jhdt.*, eds. F. Winkelmann et al., pp. 120–30
Byzanz im 8. Jahrhundertt in der Sicht des Theophanes (BBA LVII. Berlin 1991)
'Die monenergetischen und monotheletischen Streitigkeiten in der Sicht des Chronisten Theophanes', *Klio* 63 (1981), 669–81
'Zu einigen oppositionellen religiösen Strömungen', in *Byzanz im 7. Jahrhundert*, eds. F. Winkelmann et al., pp. 225–88.
Ruhrbach, G. ed. *Die Kirche angesichts der konstantinischen Wende* (Darmstadt 1976)
Runciman, S. *The Medieval Manichee. A Study of the Christian Dualist Heresy* (Cambridge 1947)
Rydén, L. 'The *Life* of St Basil the Younger and the *Life* of St. Andreas Salos', in *Okeanos. Essays Presented to Ihor Ševčenko on his Sixtieth Birthday by his Colleagues and Students* (= *Harvard Ukrainian Studies*, 7 1983 (Cambridge, Mass. 1983) pp. 568–86
Sathas, D. *John of Damascus on Islam. The 'Heresy' of the Ishmaelites* (Leiden 1972)
Schlumberger, G. *Sigillographie de l'empire byzantin* (Paris 1884 and Turin 1963)
Schminck, A. art. 'Ehebruch', in *Lexikon des Mittelalters* III (1986), 1660
art. 'Ehe' in *Lexikon des Mittelalters* III (1986), 1641–4
Schreiner, P. 'Der byzantinische Bilderstreit: kritische Analyse der zeitgenössischen Meinungen und das Urteil der Nachwelt bis heute', in *Bisanzio, Roma e l'Italia nell'Alto Medioevo* (Settimane di Studio del Centro Italiano di Studi sull'Alto Medioevo XXXIV. Spoleto 1988) 319–427
Seibt, W. *Die byzantinischen Bleisiegel in Österreich I: Kaiserhof* (Vienna 1978)
Ševčenko, I. 'Hagiography of the iconoclast period, in *Iconoclasm. Papers of the ninth Spring Symposium of Byzantine Studies*, University of Birmingham (March 1975), eds. A.A.M. Bryer and J. Herrin (Birmingham 1977), pp. 113–31

Sharf, A. *Byzantine Jewry from Justinian to the Fourth Crusade* (New York 1971)
'The Jews, the Montanists and the Emperor Leo III', *BZ* 59 (1966), 37–46
Studien zum 7. Jahrhundert: see Winkelmann et al.
Simon, D. 'Byzantinische Hausgemeinschaftsverträge', in *Beiträge zur europäischen Rechtsgeschichte und zum geltenden Zivilrecht. Festgabe für J. Sontis* (Munich 1977), pp. 91–128
'Provinzialrecht und Volksrecht', *FM* I (1976), 102–116
Rechtsfindung am byzantinischen Reichsgericht (Frankfurt a. M. 1973)
'Zur Ehegesetzgebung der Isaurier', *FM* I (1976), 16–43
Spain Alexander, S. 'Heraclius, Byzantine imperial ideology and the David plates', *Speculum* 52 (1977), 217–37
Speck, P. 'Wunderheilige und Bilder: Zur Frage des Beginns der Bilderverehrung', in *Varia* III (Poikila Byzantina XI. Bonn 1991) 163–247
'Das Teufelsschloß. Bilderverehrung bei Anastasios Sinaites?', in *Varia* V (Poikila Byzantina XIII, Bonn 1994) 295–309
'Die Interpretation des *Bellum Avaricum* und der Kater Μεχλεμπε', in *Varia* II (Poikila Byzantina VI. Bonn 1987), pp. 371–402
Das geteilte Dossier. Beobachtungen zu den Nachrichten über die Regierung des Kaisers Herakleios und die seiner Söhne bei Theophanes und Nikephoros (Poikila Byzantina IX. Bonn 1988)
Ich bin's nicht, Kaiser Konstantin ist es gewesen. Die Legenden vom Einfluß des Teufels, des Juden und des Moslem auf den Ikonoklasmus (Poikila Byzantina X. Bonn 1990)
'Der "zweite" Theophanes. Eine These zur Chronographie des Theophanes', in *Varia* V (Poikila Byzantina XIII. Bonn 1994), pp. 433–83
Spieser, J.-M. 'Les villes en Grèce du IIIe au VIIe siècle', in *Villes et peuplement dans l'Illyricum protobyzantin* (Rome 1984), pp. 315–38
Starr, J. *The Jews in the Byzantine Empire, 641–1204* (Athens 1939)
Ste Croix, G.E.M. de. *The Class Struggle in the Ancient Greek World* (Oxford 1981)
Stein, E. 'Ein Kapitel vom persischen und vom byzantinischen Staate', *BNJ* 1 (1920), 50–89
Histoire du Bas-Empire, 2 vols. (I: Paris and Bruges 1939 and Amsterdam 1968; II: Paris and Bruges 1949 and Amsterdam 1968)
Studien zur Geschichte des byzantinischen Reiches vornehmlich unter den Kaisern Justinus II und Tiberius Konstantinus (Stuttgart 1919)
Stratos, A.N. *Byzantium in the Seventh Century* (Eng. trans.), I: 602–34 (Amsterdam 1968); II: 634–41 (Amsterdam 1972); III: 642–68 (Amsterdam 1975); IV: 668–85 (Amsterdam 1978); V: 686–711 (Amsterdam 1980)
Svoronos, N. 'Notes sur l'origine et la date du Code Rural', *TM* 8 (1982), 487–500
'Recherches sur le cadastre byzantin et la fiscalité aux XIe–XIIe siècles: le cadastre de Thèbes', *BCH* 83 (1959), 1–166 (repr. in N. Svoronos, *Etudes sur l'organisation intérieure, la société et l'économie de l'empire byzantin* III (London 1973)
Teall, J. 'The Byzantine agricultural tradition', *DOP* 25 (1971), 34–59
'The grain-supply of the Byzantine empire', *DOP* 13 (1959), 87–139
TIB Tabula Imperii Byzantini: vol. I, J. Koder, F. Hild, *Hellas und Thessalia* (Vienna 1976); vol. II, F. Hild, M. Restle, *Kappadokien (Kappadokia, Charsianon, Sebastia und Lykandos)* (Vienna 1981); vol. III, P. Soustal (with J. Koder), *Nikopolis und Kephallenia* (Vienna 1981); vol. IV, K. Belke with M. Restle, *Galatia und Lykaonien* (Vienna 1984) (= Denkschriften der österr. Akad. der Wissenschaften CXXV, CIL, CL, CLXXII)

Tinnefeld, F.H. *Die frühbyzantinische Gesellschaft. Struktur – Gegensätze – Spannungen* (Munich 1977)
Toynbee, A. *Constantine Porphyrogenitus and his World* (London 1973)
Treadgold, W.T. 'The military lands and the imperial estates in the Middle Byzantine Empire', in *Okeanos. Essays Presented to Ihor Sevcenko on his Sixtieth Birthday by his Colleagues and Students* (= Harvard Ukrainian Studies VII (1983)) (Cambridge, Mass. 1983), pp. 619–31
Treitinger, O. *Die oströmische Kaiser- und Reichsidee nach ihrer Gestaltung im höfischen Zeremoniell* (Jena 1938)
Trombley, F. 'The decline of the seventh-century town: the exception of Euchaita', in *Byzantine Studies in Honor of Milton V. Anastos*, ed. Sp. Vryonis, jr. (Malibu 1985), pp. 65–90
Trombley, F.R. *Hellenic Religion and Christianization c. 370–529* (Religions in the Graeco-Roman World CXV. Leiden 1993)
Udal'cova, Z.V. ed., *Kultura Vizantii, IV – pervaja VII v.* (Moscow 1984)
Udal'cova Z.V. and K.A. Osipova, 'Tipologičeskie osobennosti feodalizma v Vizantii', in *Problemy social'noj struktury i ideologii srednevekovogo obščestva* I (Leningrad 1974), pp. 4–28
Van Dieten, J.-L. *Geschichte der Patriarchen von Sergios I. bis Johannes VI. (610–715)* (Amsterdam 1972)
Vryonis, Sp., jr., *The Decline of Medieval Hellenism in Asia Minor and the Process of Islamization from the Eleventh through the Fifteenth Century* (Berkeley, Los Angeles and London 1971)
Weber, Max 'Die Stadt. Begriff und Kategorien', in *Die Stadt des Mittelalters* I: *Begriff, Entstehung und Ausbreitung*, ed. C. Haase (Darmstadt 1969)
Wenger, L. *Die Quellen des römischen Rechts* (Vienna 1953)
Whitby, L.M. 'The Great Chronographer and Theophanes', *BMGS* 8 (1982–83) 1–20
Whittow, M. 'Ruling the Late Roman and early Byzantine City: a Continuous History', *PP* 129 (Nov. 1990) 3–29
The Making of Orthodox Byzantium, 600–1025 (Basingstoke–London 1996)
Wickham, C.J. *Early Medieval Italy. Central Government and Local Society, 400–1000* (London 1981)
'The other transition: from the ancient world to feudalism', *PP* 103 (1984), 3–36
Winkelmann, F. 'Ägypten und Byzanz vor der arabischen Eroberung', *BS* 40 (1979), 161–82
Byzantinische Rang- und Ämterstruktur im 8. und 9. Jahrhundert (BBA LIII, Berlin 1985)
Die östlichen Kirchen in der Epoche der christologischen Auseinandersetzung (5.–7. Jahrhundert) (Kirchengeschichte in Einzeldarstellungen I/6, Berlin 1980)
'Die Quellen zur Erforschung des monenergetisch- monotheletischen Streites', *Klio* 69 (1987), 515–59
ed., *Quellen zur Geschichte des frühen Byzanz* (BBA LV Berlin 1989)
Quellenstudien zur herrschenden Klasse von Byzanz im 8. und 9. Jahrhundert (BBA LIV, Berlin, 1987)
'Zum byzantinischen Staat (Kaiser, Aristokratie, Heer)' in *Byzanz im 7. Jahrhundert*, eds. F. Winkelmann et al., pp. 161–288
Winkelmann, F., and H. Köpstein, eds., *Studien zum 7. Jahrhundert in Byzanz. Probleme der Herausbildung des Feudalismus* (BBA XLVII, Berlin 1976)

Winkelmann, F. H. Köpstein, H. Ditten and I. Rochow, *Byzanz im 7. Jahrhundert. Untersuchungen zur Herausbildung des Feudalismus* (BBA XLVIII, Berlin 1978)
Yannopoulos, P. *La Société profane de l'empire byzantin des VIIe, VIIIe et IXe siècles* (Université de Louvain, Recueil de Travaux d'Histoire et Philologie, 6e sér., fasc.6) (Louvain 1975)
Zachariä von Lingenthal, C.E. *Geschichte des griechisch–römischen Rechts* (third edn, Berlin 1892 and 1955)
Zepos, P.I. 'Die byzantinische Jurisprudenz zwischen Justinian und den Basiliken', in *Berichte zum XI. Internationalen Byzantinisten-Kongress* (Munich 1958), V, 1, pp. 1–27

Index

Abbasid rule, 84
ᶜAbd al-Malik, 69f., 72, 193
Abydus, 83, 107
Academy (of Athens), 329
Achaemenids, 20
acheiropoiēta, 356
Acroinum, 84, 107, 109
Acts of the Apostles, 431
actuarius, 221
Adelphianoi, 342
adiectio sterilium (*see also epibolē*), 29, 142
adiutor, 178
adnoumia, 241, 243
Adrianople, 82, 239
Adriatic, 21, 120
Aegean, 10, 12, 116, 120, 156, 210, 217, 294, 387
Africa, 4f., 10f., 15, 20, 34, 36, 41, 57, 60, 69f., 74, 76, 177, 209f., 235, 239, 249, 252, 282, 305, 307f., 310, 366
Agathias, 420
Agathon (deacon), 78, 321
Agnellus, 78
Alexander (the Great), 20, 368
Alexandretta, 224
Alexandria, 38f., 48, 54, 287f., 291, 302, 315, 327
Alexios Mousele, 204
ᶜAli, 55
Amaseia, 80, 107
Amastris, 107
Ambrosius of Milan, 282
Amisus, 107
Amorium, 55, 83, 107, 113, 216
ampullae, 415
ᶜAmr, 54f.
Anastasian walls, 120
Anastasioupolis, 134, 218
Anastasius (ex-consul), 192

Anastasius of Sinai, xxvff., 342, 371, 431ff., 438
Anastasius (Sygkellos), 88, 90
Anatolikōn (district, *thema*), 69ff., 197ff., 212ff.
Anchialus, 67
Ancyra, 103, 107, 108, 113, 118, 218, 226
Andreas (son of Troilus), 168
Andreas of Crete, 79, 321, 434
Anemurium, 109, 111, 118, 226
annona(e), 28, 177, 224–6, 229, 238, 242, 245, 448
Antakya, 236
antecessores, 260, 265, 266
anthypatoi, 195, 202–6, 275f., 391
antigrapheis, 193, 267, 274
Antioch, xxiii
Antioch (Isauria), 107
Antioch (Pisidia), 80, 107
Antiochene tradition, 289
Anthony IV (Patriarch 1389–90), 297
Apamea, 34, 102f.
Aphrodisias, 108, 111, 118, 226
apo eparchōn, 393, 395
apo hypatōn, 165, 193ff., 199, 393–7
Apocalypse (of Ps.-Methodius), 144, 433, 436
apocalyptic literature, 367ff., 433, 436f.
Apollonia, 108
apophthegmata, 429
Apostles of Christ, 283
apothēkai, 188ff.
Appendix Eclogae, 265
Apsimar (Tiberius, *drouggarios*), 75
Arabic chronicles, xxiiif.
arcae/arklai, 177, 189, 196, 251
archiatroi, 391
archon (tes), 272, 275
Arculf (pilgrim), 423

482

Areopagite (Ps.-Dionysius), 342
Arian(s), and Arianism, 339f., 342, 349
armamenta, 240
Armenia, and Armenians, 62f., 76, 209, 213f., 216, 219f., 252, 286, 300, 305, 312, 321f., 338, 351
Armeniakōn (district, *thema*), 78ff., 197ff., 212ff.
army: late Roman, 208–11; Byzantine, 211ff.; equipment, 224, 232ff., 238ff.; pay/remuneration, 223ff.; provisions/supplies, 220ff., 227f., 229–32; in politics, 371ff.
Artavasdus, 82, 90
Artemius (*prōtoasēktrētis*), 80
Asia (province), 13, 39, 234, 236, 330, 332, 338
Asiana, 187, 218
Asparuch (Khan of Bulgars), 47, 67
Assus, 108, 118
Athens, 118, 250
Athigganoi, 344f.
Attalia, 110
Attic (style), 329
Augila (oasis), 330
Aurelioupolis/Tmolus, 109
Avars, xxv, 32, 37, 44–8
Aya Solük, 104
axiai, 392

Baalbek/Hierapolis, 329, 349
Bacaudae, 31
Baghdad, 84, 112
Balādhurī, xxiv
balnitores, 391, 393
Balsamon (canonist), 334
banda/bandon, 212
Bar Hebraeus, xxiii
Basil I of Moscow, 297
basilikoi, 391
Belisarius, 16, 21, 165, 252
Benevento, 60
Benjamin (monophysite patriarch), 54
Berber tribes, 21, 34, 36, 69f., 210, 331
Bessarabia, 67
Bithynia, 11ff., 197, 219
Blachernai, 303
Black Death, 146
Black Sea, 10, 20f., 210
blattion, 237
Blues (deme), 74f.
Bogomils, 342
Bononia, 114
Boniface (papal clerk), 319
Book of Ceremonies, 195, 203, 240
Book of the Eparch, 273

Boris-Michael (Tsar), 378
Bosphorus, 43
Boukellariōn, 155f.
Bouraphos, 169
Brief History (of Patriarch Nicephorus), xxi–xxii, 116, 352
brigandage, 31
Britannia, 39
Brumalia, 334
bucellarii, 211
Bulgaria, 156
Bulgaro-Slav state, 67
Bursa, 236
Byzacena, 70, 307
Byzacium, 210

Caesar, 51, 54, 77, 390
Caesarea, 42, 55, 102f., 107, 239
Cain, 59
Calabria, 90, 148, 316
Calends, 334
Callinicus (Patriarch), 77, 320
Callinicus (mechanic), 64
Camuliana, 107
candidati, 391
canon law, 304, 318, 334ff., 378ff.
canonicum, 294
capita/capitus, 148f., 224–6, 229, 448
capitatio/iugatio, 28f., 133, 141–3, 178
Cappadocia, 13, 42, 55, 71, 83, 144f., 174, 219, 229, 236, 239, 249
caput, 28f.
Caravisiani (Karabisianoi), 214, 217
Caria, 110, 219, 229
Carrhae/Harran, 330
Carthage, 5, 35, 42, 56, 75, 210f., 234, 306f.
Carthagena, 176
castrensis, 186
Catania, 176, 186, 211
Catholicate, 312
Caucasus (Albania), 71
Caucasus (region), 13, 20, 46, 58, 103, 156, 169, 215
Cephallenia, 71
Chalcedon, 52, 69, 73, 103, 107, 286f., 293, 298
Chalkē gate, 88
Charsianon, 155–7
chartoularios/chartularius, 84, 178, 180–2, 188, 192, 194, 196, 200, 212
Chazars, 67, 76ff., 84, 352
Chazaria, 77
Cherson, 58, 74, 76, 78, 168, 176, 310
Chersonnesos (Aegean), 234
Chios, 320, 338

484 Index

Chonae, 109
chōrion, 137ff.
Chosroes I, 20, 46
Chosroes II, 35, 312, 352
Chronica maiora, xxiii
Chronicle of George the Sygkellos, xxi
Chronicle of John of Nikiu, xxiii
Chronicle of Michael the Syrian, xxiif.
Chronicle of Monemvasia, 44
Chronography of Theophanes the Confessor, xxif., 214
Chrysoupolis, 107, 370
Church, xxff.; in Armenia, 312, 321f.; imperial, 281ff.; relations with state, 281–6; and wealth, 289f.; administration, 291–3; and monasteries, 293f.; schisms, 301f., 306ff., 318f.; of Ravenna, 78, 313, 316f.
Church buildings, xxvi
Church of the Holy Apostles, 61, 304, 423
Church of the Holy Sepulchre, 43
Church of the Holy Wisdom, 16
Church of St Peter, 42
Cilicia, 39, 43, 69, 80, 83, 109, 220, 234, 338, 348
cingulum, 390, 392
cities: evolution, function, decline of, 445f.; definition of, 99ff.; fate in seventh century, 102–17; and market exchange, 104f., 117ff., 445ff.; and plagues/earthquakes, 111f.
civitas, 96, 100, 176, 266, 445
clarissimus, 161ff., 165, 390f.
climate (of imperial lands), 10ff.
Cnidas, 110
Codex Iustinianus, 25, 97, 103, 135, 255, 268, 292, 346
Codex Theodosianus, 346
coemptio (see also synōnē), 147f., 179, 231f.
coinage: function of, 117–20, 447ff.; reform, 370
collatio lustralis, 177
collegia, 28
Colonae, 109
Colossus (of Rhodes), 55
Comana, 102
comes, 54ff.
comitatenses, 28, 208f., 211
comitatus, 176
comitiva, 173, 186, 193
commemoratio, 273
commentariensis, 273
commercia/commerciarius, 189, 251
compulsores (expelleutai), 178
consiliarius, 272

Constantia (Cyprus), 55, 224, 350
Constantine (son of Heraclius), 46
Constantine (bishop), 87f.
Constantine (ex-consul), 192
Constantine Lardys, 187f.
Constantinople (sieges of), 45f., 63f., 82ff.
consularis, 203
conventus, 271
Copts, xxiif., 43, 54, 287f.
Corinth, 60, 118
cornicularius, 273
Corpus Iuris Civilis, 16, 19, 25, 268
Corsica, 209
Corycus, 220
Cos, 55, 63
Cotyaeum, 218
councils (of Church, lists of signatories), 121ff.
courts: ecclesiastical, 303; secular, 269ff., 292, 303
Crete, 55, 75, 90, 234, 240
Crimea, 10
Croats, 47, 352
Ctesiphon, 43
cubicularius/koubikoularios, 60, 185, 191
cubiculum, 194
curator, 96, 127
curiales, 96ff., 162f., 447
curopalates, 390
Cybele, 336
Cyclades, 234
Cyprus, 55ff.
Cyril of Alexandria, 289, 300, 327
Cyrus (Patriarch of Alexandria), 48f., 54f., 300ff., 309, 315
Cyrus (Patriarch of Constantinople, 705–11), 78, 296, 321
Cyzicus, 63f., 71, 76, 107, 176, 186, 218, 239

Dacia, 209
Dalmatia, 66
Damascus, 1, 42, 112, 216, 239
Damian (Patriarch of Alexandria), 287
Damietta, 80
Daniel (vision of), 367
Danube, 1, 21, 32, 43
Danubian forces, 12, 41
Dardanelles, 83
'Dark Ages', 1
David Tiberius, 51f.
Day of Judgement, 436
defensores civitatis, 97, 269, 275
delegatoriae, 221
dēmosia, 182
Denis of Tell-Mahré, xxiii

De Thematibus, 219
diagrafa, 148
Dniester, 67
Digest, 25, 255, 260, 265, 268
dignitas, 390, 392
dikastai, 275
dioceses (boundaries), 218
dioikētai, 182, 196–201, 212, 221, 391
Dionysus, 334
diptychs, 314, 320
Dobrudja, 67
domesticus, 186, 193, 202, 216f.
domus divinae, 125, 174, 192
Donatists/Donatism, 282, 340
donativa, 247
Dorylaeum, 107, 218
drouggoi, 212
ducatus, 215
duces, 209ff., 251
Duke of Istria, 247
Durostorum, 114
Dvin (synod of), 312
dyophysite (Chalcedonian), 286f., 308
dyothelete, 308

earthquakes, 111
Ecloga, 85ff., 254ff.
Edessa, 59, 239, 349, 423
edicta, 22
Edict (of 681), 255, 261
Edict on Faith (of 610), 300
education, 427ff.; legal, 265, 268f., 271f., 274, 428f.
Egypt, 1, 10f., 31, 35, 41, 46, 50, 55, 70, 177, 209f., 216, 229, 249, 286f., 301
eidikon/eidikos, 180, 182, 189, 204, 206, 212, 233, 238, 240, 243
Ekthesis (of 638), 49, 56f., 255, 261, 301f., 306, 309
Emesa, 216
emperors: Alexius I, 292; Anastasius I, 96ff.; Anastasius II, 80, 82–5, 168, 322f., 394, 442; Arcadius, 269; Basil I, 72, 331; Constans II, xxif., 52ff., 67, 113, 119, 168, 226f., 255f., 273, 304ff., 371, 389, 392; Constantine I, 96, 160, 176f., 211, 270, 283, 289; Constantine IV, 63–70, 313ff., 374, 392; Constantine V, 72, 84f., 90f., 116, 134, 192, 202, 242, 255; Constantine VII, 47, 159, 195, 219, 225, 240, 246; Constantius, 96, 412; Diocletian, 22, 160f., 176f., 211; Hadrian, 25; Heracleonas, 51, 53f., 167, 225, 304f.; Heraclius, xxv, 37, 41ff., 75, 118, 166f., 186, 188, 190f., 194f., 196, 199f., 206f., 217, 219, 224, 250, 254, 256, 262, 272f., 287, 300ff., 346, 348, 352, 371, 375, 380, 440, 449; Heraclius Constantine, 51–3, 165, 167, 184, 304f.; Honorius, 269; Julian, 96; Justin I, 17, 31, 35, 345; Justin II, 31f., 127, 255, 261, 330, 362, 374, 378, 415; Justinian I, 15ff., 35f., 177, 179, 185, 187, 209f., 254, 265, 283f., 289ff., 327, 329f., 345, 377f., 395, 407, 439; Justinian II, 56ff., 71–4, 76–80, 83, 168, 193, 213, 250, 263, 317–22, 370, 374, 394, 441; Leo I, 210, 289; Leo III, 1f., 18, 82, 84–91, 168, 242, 277, 323, 346, 374, 441f.; Leo IV, 250; Leo V, 256, 264; Leo VI, 258, 292, 377f., 380; Leontius, 74f., 77, 168, 319; Marcian, 162; Maurice, 31, 35ff., 39, 211, 224, 268, 298f., 330, 346, 360; Nicephorus I, 142, 149, 154, 243, 262; Nicephorus II, 295; Philippicus Bardanes, 78f.; Phocas, 31, 35f., 41ff., 167, 185, 265, 268, 299, 404; Romanus I, 246; Romanus II, 159; Theodosius II, 163, 289; Theodosius III, 80–3, 168; Theophilus, 204, 279; Tiberius Apsimar, 75–7, 319; Tiberius (usurper), 84; Tiberius Constantine, 1, 31, 36, 211, 255, 298, 332, 341, 346, 348, 360, 362; Tiberius (son of Justinian II), 77f.; Valens, 96, 176; Valentinian, 96, 161, 176; Valentinian III, 282; Zeno, 97, 183, 270, 314
empresses: Eirene, 149f., 155, 202, 204, 256; Eudocia, 304; Martina, 51f., 54, 167, 304f., 380; Sophia, 297; Theodora, 16f., 31, 297, 407
emphyteusis, 135
endoxotatos, 165, 391
endoxotatoi patrikioi, 164
England, 146
epanō tōn deēseōn, 194
eparchiai, 197ff., 202, 206, 276, 395
Ephesus, 82, 98, 104, 107f., 111, 117f., 226
epibolē, 137, 142, 151
Epiphanius, 168
Epirus, 71
epistolarum (*scrinium*), 193, 271
epi tēs trapezēs, 186
epoptai, 182, 200, 212
ergodosia, 238
Erzerum (*see* Theodosioupolis)
eschatology/eschatological literature, 367f.
Ethiopia, 352
Euboea, 197
Euchaita, 95, 107, 109, 117, 120
Eunomians, 339, 342

Euphratensis, 209
Euphrates, 1, 10, 25
Euprepius, 274
Eustathius Maleinus, 156
Eutyches (archimandrite), 339
Eutychius (exarch), 89
Evagrius, 349
exarchates, 35–6
excubitores, 54, 192, 210
exisōtai, 182, 212
extraordina/extraordinaria, 147

fabricae, 77, 233, 239
familia, 382, 401
family: structure and evolution, 376ff.; legal status – betrothal, marriage, divorce, 377f.
Farmers' Law, 132ff., 254, 386f.
Faustinoupolis, 109
Felix (Bishop of Ravenna), 77
feudalism/feudal mode of production, 451ff.
Fiscal Treatise, 144
foederati, 211, 247, 250
follis, 119
Francia, 39
fundi (patrimoniales), 125, 138

Galatia, 107ff.
Gangra, 107
genikon, 180ff.
genikos logothetēs, 193f., 200, 394
genikos nomos, 303
geography (of the empire), 9ff.
George (*apo hypatōn*), 197, 234
George (*kommerkiarios*), 235
George I (Patriarch), 68, 315
George (presbyter), 342
George (of Pisidia), xxv, 425, 431
George (*Sygkellos*), xxi
geōrgos, 135
Gepids, 32
German/Germanic, 17, 32, 166, 211, 349, 355, 379, 456
Germanus (*magister militum*), 210
Germanus (of Cyzicus, Patriarch of Constantinople), 79, 82, 88, 168, 321f., 344
Ghassanids, 20
Ghevond, xxiii
Gibraltar, 15
gloriosus/gloriosissimus, 162–5, 169, 188, 390, 391, 393, 395
Golden Horn, 75
Gordoserbon, 124, 350
Gothograeci, 80
Goths, xix, 21, 72, 102, 211

Great Bulgaria, 66
Great Church (*see also* Church of the Holy Wisdom/Hagia Sophia), 56
Greek fire, 64, 83
Green deme, 75
Gregory (exarch), 57f., 60f., 305–8, 310, 313, 369
Gregory Mousoulakios, 204
Gulf of Attalia, 220
Gulf of Burgas, 82

Hagia Sophia (*see also* Great Church/Church of the Holy Wisdom), 49, 52, 57, 82, 284, 301, 306, 316, 394
hagiography, xxi, 427, 429ff.
Harran, 349
haruspices, 328
Helenopontus, 107, 157, 220, 234
Heliopolis, 330
Hellas, 39, 74, 197
Hellespontus, 218f., 239, 350
Henotikon, 298
Heraclea, 45, 107f., 239
Heraclea (Pontica), 108
Heraclius (the elder), 41
Heraclius (brother of Tiberius Apsimar), 76
Heraclius (son of Constans II), 59, 68
heresies/heretics, 337ff.
Hierapolis, 108, 287
Hiereia, 46
Hikanatoi, 202
Hispania, 39
historiography, 425
Hodegos (of Anastasius of Sinai), 370
Holy Land, 423
holy men, 356ff., 369
honestiores, 377
honorarii, 162
Honorias, 196, 219
Hormisdas, 187, 192
Horreum Margi, 239
humiliores, 27
Hungary (plain of), 64
Huns, 103
hypatos, 165, 192, 199, 205, 391, 393–7
Hypomnestikon, 273

Iberia, 70f.
Ibn az-Zubair, 71
Ibn Hawkal, 112
Iconium, 107
iconoclasm, 84, 87, 323
icons: role and function of, 356ff., 366, 405ff., 423f.; style and mode of expression, 407ff.

ideology: imperial, 19f., 37–9, 348; and symbolic universe, 324ff., 348ff.
idikē trapeza, 182
idikon, 180, 182, 233
Ignatius the Deacon, 422
illustris/illoustrios, 161ff.
Illyricum, 12, 21, 90, 151, 177, 187, 195, 209, 252
imperium Romanum, 354
indictio, 177
Institutiones, 25, 255
Ionian Sea, 10
Iraq, 172
Irenopolis, 239
Isauria, 43, 103, 107, 176, 209f., 219, 224, 338
Isidore of Seville, xxiii
Islam: rise and conquests of, 49ff.; invasions and economic effects, 143ff.;
iudices pedanei, 271
iuga, 28f., 149
iussio, 148, 213ff., 261f., 316, 319

Jacob Baradaeus, 286, 298, 338
Jacob (Jew of Palestine), 39
Jacob ('recently baptised'), 304
Jacobite(s), 287, 298
Jerusalem, 38ff.
Jews/Judaism, 87ff., 345ff.
John of Antioch, 425
John Athalarich, 51
John of Biclar, xxiii
John the Cappadocian, 16
John II (Chalcedonian Patriarch of Alexandria), 287
John III (Chalcedonian Patriarch of Alexandria), 288, 291
John VI (Patriarch of Constantinople), 77, 321f.
John (ex-consul), 192
John of Damascus, 354
John (deacon of Hagia Sophia), 394
John of Ephesus, 330, 332, 338, 341, 349, 351
John Lydus, 15, 24, 431
John Mauropous, 117
John Moschus, 306, 423, 430f.
John (*patrikios*), 75
John of Porto (bishop), 319
John Philoponus, 431
Julian (ex-consul), 192
Jupiter Ammon (temple of), 330
justice (administration of), 264ff.
Justinian (*patricius*), 168

Kallinikon, 298

Kamacha, 107
kandidatoi, 170, 205, 393f.
kapnikon, 142, 149f., 182, 231
Kappadokia, 155ff.
Karabisianoi, 212
kastron, 102, 459–61
Kavadh/Siroes, 46
keleuseis, 261f.
Kibyra/Cibyra, 220
Kibyrrhaiotai, 74f., 220
kinship, 376ff.
kleisoura, 212, 220
Kletorologion (of Philotheos), 180, 190, 194, 273, 391, 394
koitōn, 183, 192
koitōnion, 197
Koloneia, 107
komē, 137f., 204
kommerkia/kommerkiarioi, 196ff.
komēs, 213f., 216
koubikoularioi, 186, 398
Kovrat, 47, 67, 352
kritai, 181, 275f.
Kuban, 47

lachnistērion, 367
laeti, 247, 250
Lampetianoi, 342
Laodicea, 108, 111
largitiones, 182, 188–91, 196, 218, 270
Last Judgement, 436
Lateran (council), xxiv, 57, 285, 307, 309, 366
latifundia, 132
Latin, xxii, 368, 404
law: function and symbolism of, 258ff., 276ff.; legal texts, 254ff.
Lebanon, 66, 71
legislation (imperial), 254–64
Leontius (general), 71
Leontius (*domestikos tēs vasilikēs trapezēs*), 186
Leontius (ex-consul), 192
Leontius (*dioikētēs* of the *eparchiai*), 197
Lesbos, 338
libellorum (*scrinium*), 271
Liber Pontificalis, xxiii
Libya, 70, 209
Life of Andrew the Fool, xxvii, 116, 336, 356, 361, 367f., 429, 433
Life of Anthony the Younger, 335
Life of the Patriarch Tarasius, 422
Life of Philaretos the Merciful, 131, 141, 155, 160, 243, 245, 387
Life of Theodore of Sykeon, 134, 137, 141, 387, 423

Liguria, 34
limes, 210
limitanei, 28, 208f., 211, 216f.
literature (theological and secular), 425ff.
Liutprand (Lombard king), 89
locator, 134f.
logothesion, 180, 188f., 191, 195, 200
logothetēs, 181, 183, 185, 187f., 190, 192f., 206, 274
long walls (of Constantinople), 45, 209
Loulon, 109
Lucania, 148, 319
Lycaonia, 31, 107, 157, 209f., 219, 236, 338, 344
Lycia, 219, 234, 338
Lydda, 423
Lydia, 13, 107, 109, 145, 197, 219, 330

Macedonia, 71, 156, 256, 331
Macedonius (Patriarch of Antioch), 302
Maeander, 108, 159
magic (and superstition), 331, 333
magister memoriae, 194
magister militum, 43, 165, 209ff., 215ff., 227, 252, 390f.
magister officiorum, 181, 194, 201, 233
magistri (of palatine *scrinia*), 271
magistros, 84, 195
Magnesia, 108, 158
magnificus, 162f., 395
Makarios (Patriarch of Antioch), 56, 302, 314f., 321
manceps, 226
mandator, 393f.
Mani, 331
Manichaeans, 341, 343
Mantzikert (synod), 322
Marcionists, 342f.
Marcianoupolis, 239
Mardaites, 66, 71
Marinus (son of Martina), 52
Marinus (*apo eparchōn*), 197, 201
Maritsa, 82
Markianistai, 342
Marseille, 406
Maslama, 83
Mauretania, 210, 307
Maurus (Archbishop of Ravenna), 313f.
Maximus Confessor, xxv, 56ff., 285, 306f., 309ff., 365f.
Medina, 55
megaloprepestatos, 196
Megas chronographos, 425
megas kouratōr, 183, 192f.
Meletians, 342
Melitene, 80, 103, 107

Melkite (Church,) 287f.
mentalité (Byzantine), 324ff.
Mesopotamia, 50, 209, 219
Messalians, 341f.
mētrokomia, 136
Michael (*hypatos*), 194
Michael of Synnada, 335
Miletus, 108, 111
miliarēsia, 149
Milion gate, 79
military lands, 244–50
militia, 163, 392
missionary activity, 350ff.
Misthia, 80, 107
mode of production, 451ff.
moderator, 203, 206
Moesia, 67, 209f., 269
monasteries, 293–6
monenergism, 300f.
monophysites, 24, 31f., 286ff., 305f., 321, 328f., 364, 440
monotheletes, 56ff., 67f., 86f., 297ff., 314ff., 321f., 364f., 440
Montanists, 339, 341f., 344
Moorish troops, 41
Mopsuestia, 107
mortē, 135
Mount Sinai (icons), xxvii, 409
Mousoulios, 243, 245
Muᶜawiya, 55, 63, 64
Muhammad, 55
Mulberry (*morus alba*), 236
munera, 127, 178, 240
Myakios, 169
Myra, 107f.
Mzez Gnouni (Mizizios), 61, 213, 313f.

Nacolea, 87
Naissus, 239
Naples, 60, 77, 320
Narses, 16, 184
navicularii, 176
Nea Justinianopolis, 350
Neocaesarea, 107
Nestorian (theology), 339
Nestorius, 339
'new Marcian', 'new Justinian' (of Constantine IV), 68
New Testament, 335, 344, 346, 367, 423
Nicaea, 82, 102, 107, 110, 158
Nicetas (cousin of Heraclius), 41, 43
Nicetas (ex-consul), 192
Nicetas Xylinites, 84
Nicomedia, 82, 102, 107, 176, 186, 218, 239, 320
Nicopolis, 71, 103, 107f., 111

Nika riot, 15, 17, 22, 167, 171, 354
Nikiu, xxiii
Nikolaos Mesarites, 423
Nile, 330
Nilus Scholasticus, 420
Nineveh, 46
nobilissimus, 390
nomikoi/tabellarioi, 274
nomina gentilia, 155, 170, 382
nomismata, 69
nomocanones, 381
Notitia of Ps.-Epiphanius, 351
Notitia Dignitatum, 251
Novatians 342, 344
novels (*novellae*), xxiv, 22, 25, 255ff., 261ff.
numerarii, 178, 188f.
Numidia, 210, 307

Odessus, 114
officiales, 275
officium, 174f., 180, 193, 200, 273, 449
oikeiakon (*vasilikon vestiarion*), 183
oikonomoi, 292
oikoumenē, 258ff.
old Great Bulgaria, 47
Old Testament, 85, 344, 346, 362, 367f.
Olympius (Exarch of Ravenna), 57f., 61, 310, 370
Onogur Huns/Bulgars, 47, 66, 352
Opsikion, 54, 212ff., 218f., 225, 234
Optatus of Milevis, 282
optimates, 80, 211
optiones, 448
ordinarii iudices, 269
ordines, 165, 393
Organa, 47, 352
Oriens, 103, 157, 170, 187f., 218, 220, 252
Orontes, 237
Osrhoene, 209
Ostrogoths, 15, 19, 21f., 174
ᶜOthman, 55
Otranto, 60, 320
Ottoman Sultan, 282

paganism (survivals), 327ff.
Palermo, 320
Palestine, 39ff.
Pamphylia, 102, 109, 209, 219, 338
Pannonia Secunda, 32, 209
Paphlagonia, 11, 107, 131, 155ff., 220
parakoimōmenos, 183, 193
paroikos, 136, 154
Paschal Chronicle, xviii, 425
Patara, 108

pater civitatis, 96
Patras, 60
patria potestas, 378
patricius/patrikios, 47, 75, 161f., 168ff., 192, 390f., 393f., 396f.
patrimonium, 174, 186, 192
patrocinium, 128, 130
Paul (*apo hypatōn*), 193
Paul (*endoxotatos apo hypatōn*), 196, 198
Paul (ex-consul), 192
Paul (*chartoularios*), 84
Paul (exarch), 89
Paul (*genikos logothetēs*), 194
Paul (*hypatos*), 197f.
Paul (Patriarch of Constantinople), 57, 68, 305-9, 311f., 315
Paulianists, 342
Paulician Church, 343f.
peculium, 127
Peloponnese, 44f., 48, 66, 71, 331, 353
Pentapolis, 54, 70, 209
penthektē (*quinisextum*), 317
Perbund, 331
Pergamum, 83, 102, 107f., 226, 336
Perge, 109
periblebtos, 391
Persians (*see also* Sassanid), xxv, 32, 34f.
Persian war (of Heraclius), 42f., 45f.
Pessinus, 107
Petasius, 89
Peter (ex-consul), 192
Peter (Exarch), 311
Peter (Patriarch of Constantinople), 315
Peter IV (monophysite Patriarch of Alexandria), 287
Philae, 330
Philagrius, 184
Philippoupolis, 82
Philon, 23
Phoenice, 209
Phoenicia, 36, 239
Phrygia, 13, 217ff., 229, 330, 338
Pisidia, 31, 107, 157, 209f., 219
Pitzigaudes, 169
plague (effects of), 111, 144
Platon (*patricius*), 168
Pliska, 67
Plotinus, 23
Podandus, 107
Poinalion, 266
polis (*see also* cities), 100ff., 113, 116, 120, 385, 445, 459-61
Polyeuctes (ex-consul), 192
Pontic, 102, 110, 187, 218
Pontus, 11, 13, 31, 59, 131, 209f., 224, 294

popes: Adeodatus, 314; Agathon, 314f.;
  Conon, 148, 318; Constantine, 77, 79,
  319; Donus, 314; Eugenius, 311;
  Gregory I, 42, 406; Gregory II, 89, 340;
  Gregory III, 90; Honorius, 49, 68, 301f.,
  308, 317; John IV, 302, 305; John VII,
  319; Leo II, 316; Martin, xxv, 57f., 305,
  309ff., 365f.; Nicholas I, 378; Sergius,
  318; Severinus, 302; Theodore, 306f.,
  309f.; Vitalian, 60, 311, 314
population transfers, 63, 71f., 145
possessor, 134, 141
potentiores, 27
power élite, 395ff.
Praefectus Augustalis, 177, 210
praepositus, 174, 181, 183, 189, 192
praescriptio fori, 270
praeses, 203
praetorian prefects, 195–207, 223
praitores, 276
precedence (system of), 388ff.
Priene, 108, 118, 226
primiscrinius, 273f.
princeps, 273f.
principales, 97
Priscus, 167
Priscus of Panium, 279
proceres sacri palatii, 166
Procopius, 15, 21, 29, 217, 252, 431
procuratores/epimelētai, 175, 178
prooemium (of Ecloga), 266–9, 272, 274
proskynēsis, 88
prostagmata, 261
protectores et domestici, 210
prōtokagkellarios, 274
prōtonotarioi, 181ff.
protosecretarius, 273
prōtospatharioas, 74, 319, 393
prōtovestiarios, 183, 193
provinces (late Roman), 217ff., 227ff.
Prusa, 102, 218
Prymnessus, 109
Psalter, 427, 435
Psamathion (monastery), 75
Pseudo-Dionysius (Areopagite), 23, 342
Pseudo-Ephraim, 368
Pseudo-Methodius of Patara, 367f.
Pyrrhus (Patriarch of Constantinople), 49, 57, 305ff., 315

quaestor, 185, 211, 213, 269, 271, 274
quaestura exercitus, 12, 177, 210, 217, 251, 269
Quartodecimans/Tessarakaidekatitai, 342
Questions and Answers, 370, 431ff., 438

Quinisext council, 73, 317f., 332ff., 338, 351, 366, 384, 421, 431

Ratiaria, 239
Ravenna, 35, 58, 74, 77, 309, 313f., 316, 319
Reggio, 320
renovatio imperii, 17, 19, 26
reconquests (of Justinian I), 16ff., 20f.
relics, cult of, 86, 405f.
res privata, 96ff.
res publica, 127
resources (agricultural and mineral), 10–13
Rhodes, 52, 55, 63, 80, 234, 269, 338
Rhodian Sea Law, 254
rhogai, 223, 225, 242, 245
Rizokopos, 169
Romanitas, 279
Rome, 17, 49, 56, 176, 286, 314
Rouchinai, 331
Rūm, 64
Russian steppes, 45
Rusticus (*sacellarius*), 184

Sabbatians, 342
Sabellians, 339, 342
sacellarius/sakellarios/sakellion, 74, 180ff., 192ff., 296f.
Sahara, 15
Šahin, 46
Šahrbaraz, 46
saints: Artemius, 116, 273, 347, 356, 363, 400, 423, 434; Catherine, 409;
  Demetrius, 39, 45, 214, 320, 409;
  George, 423; Ioannicius, 335; John the Theologian, 117; Philaretus, 132, 138, 154; Stephen (chapel of), 41, 284;
  Theodore (Tiro), 95, 117; Therapon, 356, 363, 400
Salona, 176
Samaritans, 345
Samo, 46
Samos, 217
San Vitale (Ravenna), 407
Saracens, 248
Sardinia, 148, 209f.
Sardis, 83, 103, 107f., 118, 226, 239
Sassanid(s) (*see also* Persians), 20, 45, 50, 102, 347, 352, 355
Satala, 102f., 107
Scamares, 31
Schemarion, 58
scholai, 202, 210, 217f., 226, 391, 393
scholastikoi, 260, 265, 268, 274
Scotia (i.e. Ireland), 39
Scotland, 15

scribones, 190, 391, 393
scrinia, 174, 177f., 180, 188, 193, 196, 200, 270
Scripture, 369
Scythians, 71, 209f., 269
Scythopolis, 239
Sea of Azov, 47
Sebaste, 107
Sebastea, 102, 107
Sebastopolis, 234
Sebeos, xxiii, 167
Second Coming, 437
secretarius, 273f.
Secret History, 16
sekreta, 180, 182, 193, 202, 204, 206, 212
Seleucia, 176, 197, 224
senatorial 'class', 129f., 160–72, 389ff., 395ff., 444
Serbs, 47, 350, 352
Sergius (Archbishop of Cyprus), 306
Sergius (*epi tēs trapezēs*), 168
Sergius (*magistros*), 319
Sergius (son of Mansur), 193
Sergius of Joppa, 302, 309
Sergius (Patriarch of Constantinople), 41f., 48f., 57, 300ff., 309, 315, 320
Sergius (*stratēgos*), 84f., 442
Sergius (ex-consul), 192
servus Christi, 72
Severi, 67
Severus of Antioch, 297, 339
Short Chronicle (of the Patriarch Nicephorus), xxii
Sicily, 21, 59f., 142, 148, 211, 229, 313
Side, 108
silentiarii, 391, 393ff., 398
silentium, 271
silk production, 235–8
Sinope, 98, 107
Sirmium, 32, 44
Siroes (*see* Kavadh)
Sisium, 80, 107, 109
Sklaviniai, 44, 56
Slavs, 21, 32, 35, 37, 42ff., 52, 56, 66f., 144f., 234ff., 247f.
Smbat Bagratuni, 321
Smyrna, 63, 107, 110
social formation (and mode of production), 451ff.
society (chief characteristics and structure of), 13ff., 26–31, 125ff., 153–60
soldiers (in political context), 371ff., 441ff.
Solomon (*magister militum*), 210
Sophronius (Patriarch of Jerusalem), 49f., 295f., 301, 306, 309

Soviet historians, 27
spatharius/spatharocandidatus, 83, 185, 202, 205, 391, 393f., 398
Spain, xxiii, 21, 34, 209
spectabilis, 161ff., 165, 169, 206, 269
Spiritual Meadow (of John Moschus), 306, 423, 430
state: structure and form of, 14f., 22–4; fiscal apparatus, 125, 173–201; ideology and authority, 449ff.; and taxation, 452ff.; in the west, 456; in the east, 456ff.
Stephanus (*antecessor*), 265
Stephen (*sacellarius*), 74
Stephen of Antioch (abbot), 321
Stephen of Dor, 309, 315
Strategikon (of Kekaumenos), 400
Strategikon (of Maurice), 222, 241, 252, 268
stratēgos, 62, 72, 82f., 88, 202, 204, 212
strateia, 392
stratēlates, 165, 195, 393ff.
stratiōtikon, 180ff., 204, 206, 212, 241
stratores, 391
Strymon region, 71
Suania, 20
subadiuva, 273
Suevi, xxiii
Sufetula, 57
Suleyman (Caliph), 83
Suleyman (commander), 83
superindictiones, 178
susceptores/hypodektai, 178f.
Sykai, 75
Syllaeum, 109
symbolic universe, 24f., 325f., 348, 403
symbolism/symbolic systems, 420f.
Synnada, 107
synodika, 311
synōnē, 142, 147–50, 231
Syracuse, 60
Syria, 1, 20, 28, 31, 35f., 42f., 46, 49f., 56, 69, 209, 249, 286f., 301, 303f., 379
Syriac (Life of Maximus Confessor), 303

Tabarī, xxiv, 112f.
tabellarioi (*see nomikoi*)
tagma, 202
Taktikon Uspenskij, 190, 194, 202–6, 223, 276
Tarenta, 107
Tarsus, 43, 103, 107
Taurus, 13, 220
taxes/taxation (*see also capitatio/iugatio, coemptio, synōnē*), 28ff. 36, 141–52

Index

territoria (municipal), 100ff., 141
Tervel (Khan of Bulgars), 76f., 80, 84f.
Thebaid, 209f.
thelēma, 49
themata/theme system, 35, 202ff., 208f., 212ff.
Theodore (*apo hypatōn*), 197, 199
Theodore (*illoustrios*), 196
Theodore (ex-consul), 192
Theodore (commander), 46
Theodore (Bishop of Pharan), 300, 309, 315
Theodore Calliopas (exarch), 310
Theodore (anti-Patriarch of Alexandria), 287
Theodore Spoudaios, 273
Theodore (son of John the *candidatus*), 168
Theodore the Studite, 149f., 335
Theodore Trithyrius, 184
Theodore (the Sygkellos), xxv
Theodore (Patriarch of Constantinople), 68, 314f.
Theodosian walls, 115
Theodosiani, 49, 301
Theodosius (brother of Constans II), 59, 69, 312
Theodotus (general, logothete and abbot), 74, 193, 394
Theodosioupolis/Erzerum, 103, 312
Theophanes Confessor, xxif., 56, 69, 122, 214, 243, 340
Theophanius (monk), 368f., 437
Theophilus (*antecessor*), 265
Theophylact Simocatta, 425
Theophylactus (*hypatos*), 198
Thera/Therasia, 88
Thessaloniki, 21, 35, 45, 60, 66, 71, 176f., 214, 442
Thomas (ex-consul), 192
Thrace, 10f., 21, 48, 71, 124, 209, 213ff., 218, 220, 229, 234
Thracianus (*exercitus*)/*Thrakēsianoi*/*Thrakēsiōn*, 159, 212, 214, 220, 225, 317
Three Chapters controversy, 24, 289, 298
Tiberias, 303
Tiberius (son of Constans II), 59, 68
Timothy of Constantinople, 342
titles (senatorial/imperial *see* precedence)
Tius, 108
Tmolus (*see* Aurelioupolis)
Toledo, 341
Tome of Leo, 312
tomos (of Philippicus), 321
topoi (legal/legislative), 267, 278
topotērēsia, 212
tourmai, 212
trade, 11f.
Tralles, 159
Trajan (*patrikios*), 425
tractores/*trakteutai*, 178, 196, 200, 391
Triachia (Cyprus), 333
Tribonian, 16
tributary mode of production, 451, 453f., 456–58
Trinity, 69
Tripolis/Tripolitania, 54, 70, 210
Troilus (*sacellarius*), 168
Troullos (imperial palace), 73, 315
True Cross, 43, 46, 304
Turkey, 236
Turkic peoples/Turks, 21, 158, 355
Türkmen, 107, 121
Tyana, 80, 107, 109
Tyre, 10, 239
Typos (of Constans II), 57f., 67, 255, 261, 309f., 311, 364f.

ʿUmar II (Caliph), 83, 87
ʿUqba (general), 69

Valentinus, 54, 61, 305f., 370
Vandals, xxiii, 15, 19–21, 72, 340
Venetia, 32
vestiarion, 180, 182f., 186, 190, 193f., 206
vestitor, 393ff.
vicarii, 178, 207, 209, 269
Victor (Bishop of Carthage), 307
vigla, 202
village, 132ff.
vindices, 96f., 178f.
Virgin (Theotokos), 38, 356f., 409, 415, 429
Visigoths, 15, 21, 34, 341
Vota, 334

Wallachia, 67

Xerolophus (in Constantinople), 75

Yarmuk (battle), 50, 216, 219
Yazid I (Caliph), 64
Yazid II (Caliph), 87

Zacharias (*prōtospatharios*), 74, 319
zōnē (*cingulum*), 392
Zwangswirtschaft, 28
zygostatēs, 190